Christianity in
Late Antiquity
300–450 C.E.

Christianity in Late Antiquity

300–450 C.E.

A READER

Bart D. Ehrman

Andrew S. Jacobs

New York   Oxford
Oxford University Press
2004

Oxford University Press

Oxford   New York
Auckland   Bangkok   Buenos Aires   Cape Town   Chennai
Dar es Salaam   Delhi   Hong Kong   Istanbul   Karachi   Kolkata
Kuala Lumpur   Madrid   Melbourne   Mexico City   Mumbai
Nairobi   São Paulo   Shanghai   Taipei   Tokyo   Toronto

Published by Oxford University Press, Inc.
198 Madison Avenue, New York, New York, 10016
http://www.oup-usa.org

Oxford is a registered trademark of Oxford University Press

Illustration Credits
All images in Chapter 13: 1. Timothy McCarthy / Art Resource, NY. 2. Scala / Art
Resource, NY. 3. Werner Forman / Art Resource, NY. 4. Scala / Art Resource, NY. 5.
Scala / Art Resource, NY. 6. Scala / Art Resource, NY. 7. Scala / Art Resource, NY. 8.
Scala / Art Resource, NY. 9. Scala / Art Resource, NY. 10. Scala / Art Resource, NY. 11.
Erich Lessing / Art Resource, NY. 12. Erich Lessing / Art Resource, NY. 13. Giraudon /
Art Resource, NY. 14. Scala / Art Resource, NY.

Library of Congress Cataloging-in-Publication Data
Christianity in late antiquity, 300–450 C.E. : a reader / [compiled by] Bart D. Ehrman,
   Andrew S. Jacobs.
      p. cm.
      Includes bibliographical references.
      ISBN 0-19-515460-6 (alk. paper)—ISBN 0-19-515461-4 (pbk. : alk. paper)
      1. Christian literature, Early. I. Ehrman, Bart D. II. Jacobs, Andrew S., 1973–
BR63.C47 2004
270.2—dc21

                                                                    2003042905

Printing number: 9   8   7   6   5   4   3   2   1

Printed in the United States of America
on acid-free paper

for Liz

Contents

Preface

This book originated as an attempt to supplement the early Christian texts collected in *The New Testament and Other Early Christian Writings: A Reader* and *After the New Testament: A Reader in Early Christianity*. The goal has been to extend into the fourth and fifth centuries of the Christian era these earlier volumes' focus on the rich primary literature that can help students of early Christianity understand this complex and diverse religious history. Our reasons for choosing these specific texts, from among the welter of early Christian writings, are explained further in Chapter 1. Briefly, we have chosen texts that are representative of the ideas and cultures of early Christianity, without narrowly confining the possibilities for interpretation and analysis. Most of the texts exist in current, readable translations and are reproduced here with the permission of authors and publishers. Other texts have been translated for this edition by Andrew Jacobs. Language usage—spelling, punctuation, and so forth—has been made consistent throughout. Short introductions have been provided for the chapters and the texts.

The intended audience is the student of early Christianity, in the broadest possible sense: the reader in the undergraduate classroom, graduate seminar, public or private university, or seminary or the inquisitive reader who wants to know more about this significant period of religious history. Much of what we think of as "natural" about politics, religion, and culture and the intersections between them emerged from this period of Mediterranean and Near Eastern history. To understand more fully why we think the way we do about church and state, body and soul, the mundane and the celestial, it is necessary, we believe, to look to this formative period.

The idea for this volume arose at an academic conference, a place where the concerns of scholars, teachers, and students should intersect and become productive. The editors would like to thank Andrew McGowan and Stephen Shoemaker, who were present at the genesis of this project and have continued to provide advice along the way. In addition, we would like to thank our research assistants: Carl Cosaert at the University of North Carolina, Chapel Hill, who tirelessly sought out the copyrights and permissions that make such a volume possible, and Megin Freaney at the University of California, Riverside, who diligently tracked down the texts from libraries far and near and provided clean copies to work with. In addition, we would like to thank scholars from across the world of early Christian studies who provided comments and suggestions on issues large and small: Caroline T. Schroeder, Rebecca Krawiec, Susan Ashbrook Harvey, H. A. Drake, and Birgitta Wohl. Special thanks also to our editor at Oxford University Press, Robert Miller, for his guidance and foresight. This volume is dedicated to Elizabeth A. Clark, teacher, mentor, and good friend.

Time Line

Authors and texts included in the volume are in capital letters.

301	King of Armenia converts to Christianity
303	"Great Persecution" begins under Diocletian and his co-emperors
305	COUNCIL OF ELVIRA
306	Constantine is proclaimed Augustus (emperor) by the imperial troops in York
310s	Donatist schism begins in North Africa
312	Constantine defeats Maxentius and marches into Rome; Constantine's conversion
313	EDICT OF MILAN
314/15	LACTANTIUS, *Death of the Persecutors*
320s	ARIUS defrocked by ALEXANDER OF ALEXANDRIA; PACHOMIUS founds monasteries
325	COUNCIL OF NICAEA
337	Death of Constantine
339	EUSEBIUS of Caesarea, *Life of Constantine;* death of EUSEBIUS of Caesarea
340s	APHRAHAT writing in Persia; Shapur II begins persecution of Persian Christians
ca. 356	ANTONY the monk dies
361/63	JULIAN ("The Apostate"), emperor
367	ATHANASIUS, *Easter Letter 39*

370s	EPIPHANIUS of Salamis, *Medicine Chest Against Heresies*
372	Martin made bishop of Tours
373	Death of EPHRAIM, the Syrian; death of ATHANASIUS of Alexandria
374	AMBROSE made bishop of Milan
378	DIODORE made bishop of Tarsus
ca. 380	TYCONIUS, *Book of Rules;* EGERIA sets out for the holy land
381	COUNCIL OF CONSTANTINOPLE
ca. 386	Execution of PRISCILLIAN of Avila; JEROME, Paula, and Eustochium settle in Bethlehem
387	AUGUSTINE baptized
before 395	GREGORY OF NYSSA, *Homilies on the Song of Songs*
395	PAULINUS settles in Nola; death of Theodosius I
396	AUGUSTINE made bishop of Hippo Regius; VICTRICIUS OF ROUEN, *In Praise of the Saints;* SULPICIUS SEVERUS, *Life of Martin of Tours*
before 400	*HISTORY OF THE MONKS OF EGYPT*
404	JOHN CHRYSOSTOM forced out of Constantinople
410s	AUGUSTINE forces the integration of Donatist schismatics
410	Sack of Rome
414	Relics of Saint Stephen discovered; conversion of Jews of Minorca
418	AUGUSTINE secures the condemnation of Pelagius
431	COUNCIL OF EPHESUS; NESTORIUS goes into exile
438	Publication of the THEODOSIAN CODE
440s	THEODORET of Cyrrhus, *Religious History;* SOZOMEN, *Church History*
450s	First written collections of the *SAYINGS OF THE DESERT FATHERS* circulating
451	COUNCIL OF CHALCEDON

York

Rhine

Rouen

Moselle

GAUL

Tours

Nantes

Lyons

Milan

Aquileia

DALMATIA

Ravenna

Danube

Rhone

Arles

Rome

Nola

Avila

Minorca

Hippo Regius

Carthage

Elvira

Thagaste

NUMIDIA

AFRICA

MEDITERRANEAN
SEA

Christianity in Late Antiquity

Dnieper

CASPIAN
SEA

BLACK SEA

ARMENIA

PONTUS

Constantinople
Chalcedon
Nicomedia
Nicaea

Ancyra

Nyssa

Nisibis

MESOPOTAMIA

Edessa

Caesarea

Nazianzus

Cyrrhus

CAPPADOCIA

Tigris

Iconium

Tarsus

ASIA

CILICIA

Antioch

Ctesiphon

Aegean
Sea

Dura-Europos

Ephesus

Euphrates

Salamis

Damascus

CYPRUS

Tyre

CRETE

Caesarea

Jerusalem

Bethlehem

Dead Sea

Alexandria

Nitria

SINAI

Kellia

Scetis

Tabennisi/
Phbow

Atripe

RED
SEA

Nag-Hammadi

THEBAID

Christianity in
Late Antiquity

300–450 C.E.

CHAPTER 1

General Introduction

Christianity in Late Antiquity is a relatively new concept in the academic world. Until about forty years ago, historians and theologians were more likely to talk about the "Early Church." By this they meant a single organism that evolved from the simple ministry of Jesus and the apostles into the institutionally and theologically complex system of clergy, canons, and creeds that became the dominant religion of the Mediterranean world. According to this older view, this evolving organism was plagued with challenges: persecution from pagans and Jews, internal attacks from theological deviants (heretics), and the general cultural and political malaise that characterized the "decline and fall of the Roman Empire." Eventually (according to this older account) the Early Church overcame these challenges and emerged in the sixth century as the new stabilizing force of the medieval West and the Byzantine East.

The intellectual shift from the Early Church to Christianity in Late Antiquity has usefully complicated this evolutionary narrative. We no longer envision Christians as set apart from or in constant conflict with their wider Greco-Roman social context, and we no longer view the fourth and fifth centuries merely as a period of precipitous decline. Christianity in Late Antiquity was very much a part of the political, cultural, and intellectual intricacies of its time. Christians did not arrive from a distant planet, conspire in their remote cells, and bide their time until the world around them fell apart, allowing them to step into the mainstream and "take over." Christians were deeply embedded in their cultural landscape. We also no longer view this historical period primarily as the "beginning of the end" for the Roman Empire. Christians in Late Antiquity lived through a vibrant period of Mediterranean and Near Eastern history, as new cultural and social forms emerged from old ones and new modes of thinking and living took hold in a world that managed to merge innovation and tradition at all levels of life. If the study of the Early Church was the study of religious evolution—organic, holistic, and self-contained—then the study of Christianity in Late Antiquity has become the study of religious revolution: unpredictable, multifaceted, and diverse.

This collection of Christian primary sources from Late Antiquity is designed to facilitate understanding and study of this unpredictability and diversity. The texts (with two exceptions) were all written by Christians in the fourth and fifth centuries, the period during which Christianity underwent a dramatic transformation following the conversion of the Roman

Emperor Constantine in 312. Also included are images of Christian art and architecture from the period to give a sense of how Christian identity was embedded in the physical and aesthetic worlds of Late Antiquity. Certainly, the selection of texts and images cannot claim to be exhaustive; indeed, it would be paradoxical to demonstrate the diversity and multiplicity of ancient Christianity through a definitive and closed collection of sources. The thought worlds of the early Christians might defy any attempt at historical canonization. Nonetheless, the sources presented here are meant to be representative of the intellectual, cultural, and social diversity of Christianity in Late Antiquity and the particular issues faced by Christians who were seeking self-understanding in this period. Some texts are "classics" (such as Augustine's *Confessions*), others are less well known (such as Priscillian's *On Faith and Apocrypha*); they all give insight into significant aspects of ancient Christianity. The geographic scope of the collection is meant to be equally representative of the vast diversity of Christians' local contexts: from western Europe to north Africa to Mesopotamia. The map at the beginning of this volume is provided to give a sense of this geographic diversity.

We have limited the chronological range of our sources to the fourth and fifth centuries. Since the 1970s, Late Antiquity has had rather flexible chronological boundaries. For some historians, it begins as early as the first Roman emperor, Augustus; for others, it begins with the political reconstruction of the third-century Emperor Diocletian. Some historians see Late Antiquity ending with the deposition of the last Roman emperor in the West in 476; other historians see Late Antiquity continuing until the fall of the Roman Empire in the East at the capture of Constantinople in 1453. Periodization is always an exercise in academic construction after the fact and therefore is always somewhat artificial. For the purposes of this collection, we have chosen the rough dates 300–450 C.E., choosing as our beginning and end points the onset of the Great (and last) Persecution of Christians under the Emperor Diocletian and the convocation of the Fourth Ecumenical Council at Chalcedon under the Emperor Marcian and Empress Pulcheria. These moments of Christian history vividly illustrate the ways in which Christianity in Late Antiquity was marked by intersections of politics, culture, and religion; they also show the ways in which shifts in religious identity existed alongside attempts to maintain forms of social continuity. Of course, these end dates are no less artificial than are any other attempts to demarcate a chronological period. We believe, however, that this period witnessed some of the most crucial changes in the way Christians viewed their place in the world. After 450, the options of living a Christian life were profoundly different from what they were before 300. The sources we have collected outline the contours of these changes and differences. Given the specific chronological boundaries of this collection, it is useful to provide the reader with some context: both the background and trajectories that flow into and out of this delimited period. This context is necessarily somewhat abbreviated and focused, but should nonetheless provide the novice student of early Christianity with important points of contrast, continuity, and change.

Christianity began as a religious revival movement among Jews of Galilee and Jerusalem in the first century. Debate continues as to the particular nature of this movement's goals and aspirations, as well as the highly fraught and ongoing "Quest(s) for the Historical Jesus." It seems likely that the "Jesus movement" among first-century Jews constituted a familiar pattern of ritual atonement, moral preaching, and expectation of an imminent, cosmic cataclysm to restore divine order (apocalypse), ushered in by a divine figure (a Messiah). This Jewish, apocalyptic revival movement moved out from Galilee and Judea through the efforts of

Jesus' earliest followers (apostles) to spread the message of atonement, repentance, and messianism. The movement began accepting non-Jewish (gentile) adherents and soon faced important decisions concerning the particularity and universality of salvation through faith in Jesus. Although fierce controversy on this point is evident from the writings of the New Testament, the push toward universality—that is, salvation for all peoples, Jews and Gentiles, on equal terms—prevailed. As the movement spread across the Roman Empire in the first centuries, it acquired a distinctive religious character: the new religion of Christianity.

By the third century C.E., Christianity had become a widespread religious movement that crossed ethnic, class, and gender lines throughout the Roman Empire. While population numbers for the ancient world are notoriously elusive, conservative estimates suggest that by the year 300, Christians may have numbered in the several millions (out of a population of about 60 million). Despite the highly rhetorical presentation of Christian apologists and historians from these early centuries, however, this rapid growth was neither uniform nor coherent. In its first centuries, Christianity was characterized by diversity and marginalization. From its origins, different groups understood the significance of "faith in Christ" in radically different ways and expressed their belief in different forms.

In addition to this internal diversity, various forms of antagonism from the dominant culture around them meant that Christians were often viewed with suspicion and mistrust. After all, they met in private homes, performed secretive rituals of initiation and communion, and stayed away from the public religious festivals of their friends and neighbors. Organized, government-sponsored persecution was rare in the first two hundred years of Christianity (although no less painful for being rare), but localized and sporadic attempts to root out religious subversives resulted in violence against some Christian communities. Our earliest account of martyrs (witnesses) who died rather than renounce Christianity appear in the mid-second century, and the circulation of martyr texts provided a theological and political framework within which Christian resistance and opposition to "the world" crystallized. This sense of marginalization cut across the diversity of Christian beliefs and practices: the perceived Christian conflict with the "powers of this world" perhaps predominated for a time over the internal pressures and contradictions of diversity within the movement.

The late third and early fourth centuries brought sweeping changes to the Roman Empire and to Christianity. In 284 a successful general named Diocles assumed the imperial throne under the name Diocletian and set out to enact military, political, and economic reorganizations. He instituted fixed prices, new provincial boundaries, and a system of shared governance between two senior emperors (called *Augustuses*) and two junior emperors (called *Caesars*). Diocletian also instituted reform that was designed to ensure religious unity in the Roman Empire, including confiscation of Christian churches and property and punishment of Christian leaders. Diocletian retired in 305, and the Augustuses and Caesars continued his policy of enforcing uniformity around the Empire, including the legal proscription of Christianity.

In 306, Constantine, the son of one of Diocletian's imperial colleagues, was proclaimed Augustus by the imperial troops stationed in York. Constantine cemented his place in the imperial structure through a strategic marriage and military prowess. Conflicts with his brother-in-law and rival co-emperor, Maxentius, led to military confrontation in 312: after a decisive victory over Maxentius, Constantine was the sole emperor of the western half of the Roman Empire. It was at this point that Christianity emerged from the margins of Roman history:

along with his eastern co-emperor, Licinius, Constantine passed an edict of religious tolera-tion in 313 that recognized Christianity as a legal religion in the Roman Empire. The last "Great Persecution" initiated by Diocletian came to an end. (The persecuting Emperor Ga-lerius, just before his death in 311, issued an edict of toleration as well, but Constantine's and Licinius's edict was remembered by Christians as the turning point.) Constantine began to lavish his patronage on Christian churches, building basilicas and enacting legislation that fa-vored Christian clergy. Although he continued to employ non-Christian imagery and deferred baptism until he lay dying, Constantine seems to have undergone some sort of conversion and is rightly recognized as the first Christian Roman emperor.

It is difficult to overestimate the significance of Constantine's conversion and patronage of Christianity, both for the history of the Roman Empire and for the history of Christianity in Late Antiquity. The end of persecution and the beginning of imperial patronage of Chris-tianity (and the subsequent proscription of traditional Roman religious practices in the 390s) forever altered Christian conceptions of religious, cultural, and political identity. In some ways, Christianity followed many of the trajectories on which it had been set before Con-stantine's conversion, but the increasing intertwining of Roman imperial and Christian reli-gious identity throughout the fourth and fifth centuries also enabled entirely new forms of re-ligious identity and community.

Some of the basic tensions that existed in Christianity before Constantine's conversion still remained, now recast into new contexts. Issues of cultural marginalization and internal division persisted as Christians came to terms with their increasingly prominent place in so-ciety. Whereas Christians of the second and third century had struggled to achieve intellec-tual and social legitimacy in the face of their non-Christian neighbors, they now strove to de-lineate with more care the precise boundaries between Christian and "pagan" culture. The incorporation of classical literatures and philosophies into the elaboration of Christian the-ology and interpretation caused, for some, a crisis of cultural identity. When was ancient Greek philosophy "pagan," and when could it be appropriately Christianized? When were classical ideals of family, society, and politics to be rejected as suspect, irreligious remnants of a bygone era, and when might they be fruitfully employed to articulate a new vision of im-perial Christianity? The conceptual transition from "Church of the Martyrs" to "Church Tri-umphant" required reimagining historical and social categories from new vantage points. Cultural and political distinction was increasingly expressed along religious lines. Although the fourth-century non-Christian Roman politician Symmachus tried to argue for religious plurality, famously remarking that "we cannot arrive at so great a mystery by only one road," Christians in Late Antiquity insisted more and more on creating and policing sharp external boundaries.

Likewise, the manner in which internal religious difference was theorized continued to trouble many Christians as the perils of deviance were projected onto a wider, imperial stage. Christians in the second and third century had already introduced the categories of orthodoxy ("right thinking") and heresy ("deviance") in ways that drew absolute boundaries among var-ious Christian communities. But as Christian networks of community now overlapped di-rectly with the political concerns of Roman emperors, these intolerant discourses of ortho-doxy and heresy took on a new absolutist character. Debates over correct belief and practice were now always intertwined with questions of political loyalty and social deviance. Pre-Constantinian concerns for uniformity within the Roman Empire and within Christian communities now dovetailed, producing new forms of authority and new anxieties about difference. Bishops, charged with enforcing orthodoxy, now operated with the backing of Roman law and imperial troops, and theological debates could now erupt into wide-scale violence.

While older patterns of Christian self-definition adapted to imperial forms, entirely new modes of religious expression emerged as well. As Christianity became more and more mainstream in Roman society, a small minority of Christian faithful sought new ways to express the depths of their religious devotion. Asceticism, extreme forms of physical renunciation in the name of spiritual devotion, came to define a new echelon of religious elites in the fourth and fifth centuries. Monks and other ascetic virtuosi practiced extraordinary feats of physical self-discipline and were venerated as holy men and women operating (often) outside the bounds of clerical and imperial control. Although the number of ascetics was always a small percentage of all Christians, asceticism came to dominate the language of religious purity and devotion from Late Antiquity throughout the Middle Ages. Alongside the martyrs of the previous Christian era, the superstars of ascetic practice were venerated as arbiters of divinity and humanity, as Christian saints. Even the "everyday" Christian who could not hope to aspire to such heights of personal devotion was affected by new understandings of piety, family, sexuality, and society that were emerging from an ascetizing Christian elite.

The legalization of Christianity also permitted the religion to take on a more public face, to inscribe religious practices and beliefs more immediately into the physical world. Enormous churches rose in the urban landscape, and particular sites were believed to be imbued with special sanctity that could more immediately connect the human and divine worlds. The veneration of saints' relics and the cult of visiting and venerating holy places (particularly the holy land) became common ways of expressing piety in Late Antiquity and would structure the entire landscape of the medieval and Byzantine worlds.

As this overview suggests, many of the transformations, adaptations, and innovations that we find in Christianity in Late Antiquity continued well beyond the fifth century. Politics, culture, and religion continued to overlap in troubling and productive ways. Difference and deviance continued to be theorized and enforced, often with violent consequences. The practice of Christianity, as a lived experience, as well as a doctrinal mind-set, continued to flourish in diverse and influential patterns. The political infrastructure of the Roman Empire grew strained and overburdened in the fifth century and slowly crumbled. The eastern half of the Roman Empire, centered on Constantinople, continued as a vital force for centuries (although drastically reduced by the rise of Islam in the seventh century). The western half of the Roman Empire succumbed to the superior military forces of non-Roman groups (called collectively, and inaccurately, "barbarians"). The European Middle Ages was characterized by the demarcation of several small, loosely affiliated kingdoms that often had little in common apart from their Christian religious profession. For this reason, the developments of Christian culture and belief in Late Antiquity had a profound impact on medieval European modes of identity. Although the selections in this reader gesture toward these future developments and hearken back to the historical and religious background of the second and third centuries, they focus squarely on the period of religious transformation that we call Christianity in Late Antiquity.

Since this reader is designed to function as a representative account of this period of religious transformation through a collection of primary texts, a few words about the selection and organization of these texts is in order. Whenever possible, we have reproduced whole texts, or significant portions of texts. As we mentioned earlier, all but two of the selections (Texts 5 and 6) were written by Christians. Of course, this does not mean that important and helpful writings that might illuminate the developments of Christianity in Late Antiquity were not produced by non-Christians, but we decided to collect and analyze Christian voices, which are often dissonant and as revealing of diversity as of development and uniformity.

We have arranged the readings thematically, beginning in Chapter 2 with texts that treat the end of the last persecution of Christianity and its legalization by Constantine and his co-Emperor Licinius. The intervention of Roman emperors both to persecute and legitimate Christianity leads to the subject of Chapter 3, the relations between Christianity and the imperial house. The Roman emperor had, for centuries, been the guardian of traditional religion, serving as the *pontifex maximus,* or "high priest," of Roman religion. The conversion of Christian emperors forced rulers and subjects to negotiate much more delicately the conceptual relation between religious and political authority. Chapter 4 continues to explore the ways in which religion and public discourse intertwined through imperial legislation on religion, exploring one facet by which Christianity achieved normative status in the empire.

The process of becoming a member of the Christian community is the subject of Chapter 5, which explores both ideals of conversion and methods of Christian initiation and education. The exploration of the inner workings of Christian ecclesiastical communities continues in Chapter 6, an examination of the roles and ideals of Christian leaders and the shape and significance of liturgical drama. Chapter 7 enters into the complex ways in which debates over orthodoxy and heresy served to construct both positive and negative positions of Christian theology and practices, looking at ways in which descriptions of God, Christ, human salvation, the church, and the relation between Judaism and Christianity became flashpoints for the articulation of Christian identity and difference. The formal inscription of religious identity on the wider stage of Christian politics is addressed in Chapter 8, containing the creeds and canons of the first four ecumenical ("universal") councils of Christian bishops invoked by Roman emperors.

In Chapter 9 we explore some of the particular developments of Christianity in Late Antiquity, beginning with the rise of asceticism and monastic movements. Chapter 10 examines the ways in which the veneration of physical space and objects became an integral part of Christian piety through the veneration of relics and pilgrimage. Chapter 11 deals with a new literary form, the saint's life, or hagiography, that served to shape (in often surprising fashion) ideals of Christian perfection in Late Antiquity. The cultural and ecclesiastical dimensions of biblical canon and interpretation are explored in Chapter 12, while Chapter 13 turns to material expressions of Christian identity through art, architecture, and aesthetics. Finally, in Chapter 14, we look at the expansion of Christianity outside the boundaries of the Roman Empire as the politics of religious difference and identity expanded into northern Europe, Africa, and central Asia.

In organizing this collection of late ancient Christian texts, we have avoided using categories that might constrain a reader's analysis. For instance, we have not separated "theology" from "social history," since religious doctrine, practice, and controversy were not so neatly divided for the early Christians themselves. We have also made a point not to separate groups that have traditionally been marginalized in scholarship of the history of Christianity. We found no need to put together a separate chapter on "women" or "Jews," figures who were fully integrated into the discourses of early Christian identity in all its complexity and multiplicity. Likewise we did not deem it necessary to separate "the easterners" (Syriac authors, such as Aphrahat or Ephraim), whose views on Christianity were no less bizarre or incomprehensible than those of their Greek- or Latin-speaking counterparts and need not be conceptually ghettoized.

Texts are reproduced here from recent, reliable translations. A few texts, in the interests of clarity or accessibility, have been translated anew. Citations from the Bible follow modern numbering of chapters and verse. Biblical citations that reflect ancient versions that disagree with standard modern translations are marked as coming either from the Greek Septuagint (LXX) or the Latin Vulgate (Vulg.). Among these texts, the student of early Christianity may find many familiar names: Athanasius, Chrysostom, Jerome, Augustine. Figures such as Aphrahat, Priscillian, and Optatus may be less familiar, but they are no less significant for the light they shed on ancient Christianity. A time line and a map are provided to help contextualize all of the included readings. We have included short introductions for each chapter and each text, in order to provide sufficient context and background for the beginning student of early Christianity; in addition, each chapter includes suggestions for further reading.

As Christianity grew into, and beyond, the limits of the Roman Empire, the canons of Christian literature grew exponentially. The writings from the so-called Fathers of the Early Church fill hundreds of volumes in libraries, and this selection can only hope to be representative. It is our hope, however, that these representative views of Christianity in Late Antiquity will provide a meaningful glimpse into a world of political, cultural, and religious transformation and that the reader inspired by them will be able to pursue the study of this period in more depth.

FOR FURTHER READING

Bowersock, G. W., Brown, Peter, and Grabar, Oleg, eds. *Late Antiquity: A Guide to the Postclassical World*. Cambridge, Mass.: Belknap Press of Harvard University, 1999.

Brown, Peter. *The World of Late Antiquity*. New York: Norton, 1986.

Chadwick, Henry. *The Church in Ancient Society: From Galilee to Gregory the Great*. Oxford History of the Christian Church. Oxford, England: Oxford University Press, 2001.

———. *The Early Church*. London: Penguin, 1967.

Dopp, Siegmar, and Geerlings, Wilhelm. *Dictionary of Early Christian Literature*. New York: Herder and Herder, 2000.

Ferguson, Everett, ed. *Encyclopedia of Early Christianity*, 2 vols. New York: Garland, 1997.

Frend, W. H. C. *The Early Church: From the Beginnings to 461*, 3rd ed. London: SCM Press, 1991.

Rousseau, Philip. *The Early Christian Centuries*. New York: Longman, 2002.

CHAPTER 2

The End of Persecution

In the third century, local, sporadic, and occasional hostility against Christians combined with the pervasive anxiety about divine protection of the empire to produce the first widespread and systematic legal proscription of Christianity: the Emperor Decius, in 250 C.E., declared the religion illegal and demanded proof of loyalty to the official gods of Rome. For sacrificing at a public altar, a Roman citizen would receive a certificate of proof (a *libellus*). Those who refused to sacrifice (including Christians) were subject to punishment, including execution. After Decius died in 251, there was a swift parade of emperors; some favored Christianity, some ignored Christianity, some sought to reinstitute local, sporadic persecution of the Christians.

When Diocletian became emperor, in 284, he set out to restructure the Roman Empire politically, economically, and militarily. In addition, he instituted an empirewide attempt to root out nontraditional religious practices, which Christians came to call the "Great Persecution." Diocletian most likely viewed this action along the lines of his other social reforms: the re-institution of religious unity among an increasingly fragmented Roman population. Toward this end, he attempted to close churches, confiscate books of Scripture, and coerce the public renunciation of Christian leaders. The persecution lasted approximately ten years but was unevenly enforced because of a shared form of imperial governance that Diocletian had instituted (he shared power with a senior co-emperor and two junior emperors).

The Great Persecution came to a sudden and unpredictable end with the rise to power of Constantine, who was declared emperor by his troops in York in 306 C.E. Over the course of the next ten years, Constantine pursued an aggressive reunification of the empire under shared rule with his colleague Licinius. When the two achieved victory over the other emperors in 313, they reversed many of the policies of their predecessors, including religious persecution. Their joint resolution granting official toleration to Christians became known as the "Edict of Milan." The legalization of Christianity and its eventual ascendance to quasi-official status in the Roman Empire over the course of the fourth century marks a turning point not just for Christianity, but for the Roman Empire and Mediterranean history in general.

FOR FURTHER READING

Barnes, Timothy D. *The New Empire of Diocletian and Constantine.* Cambridge, Mass.: Harvard University Press, 1982.

Bowersock, Glen. *Martyrdom and Rome.* New York: Cambridge University Press, 1995.

Boyarin, Daniel. *Dying for God: Martyrdom and the Making of Christianity and Judaism.* Stanford, Calif.: Stanford University Press, 1999.

Digeser, Elizabeth DePalma. *The Making of a Christian Empire: Lactantius and Rome.* Ithaca, N.Y.: Cornell University Press, 2000.

Droge, Arthur, and Tabor, James D. *A Noble Death: Suicide and Martyrdom Among Jews and Christians in Antiquity.* San Francisco: HarperSanFrancisco, 1991.

Frend, W. H. C. *Martyrdom and Persecution in the Early Church: A Study of a Conflict from the Maccabees to Donatus.* Garden City, N.Y.: Anchor Books, 1967.

The Texts

1. The Acts of Saint Felix

This account of the martyrdom of a bishop named Felix in North Africa during the Great Persecution (304 C.E.) contains many of the standard scenes of early Christian martyrology: the judicial scene before the Roman official who attempts to persuade the Christian to renounce his faith (here replicated up through the chain of Roman administrators in North Africa), the refusal of the martyr to place the commands of the emperor before the will of the Lord, and the confession of faith before execution. Other elements, however, give a sense of the particular issues and concerns at stake during this last Great Persecution. Martyrs of the second and third centuries usually refused to offer sacrifices to the *genius* of the emperor; here, Felix refuses to turn over the Christian Scriptures to the Roman officials, a demand made exclusively during the persecution under Diocletian. In addition, we find an extended confession on Felix's part, in which he notes not only his age and service, but the fact that he has "guarded [his] virginity." The refusal to hand over Scriptures and the rigorous ascetic practices of North African Christians became hallmarks of the later Christian movement called Donatism (see Chapter 7).

(1) Under the Augusti Diocletian (consul for the eighth time) and Maximian (consul for the seventh time), an edict of the emperors and caesars went out over the whole face of the earth. It was promulgated in the towns and cities by the officials and magistrates, each in his own area. They were to wrest by force the sacred books from the hands of bishops and presbyters.

On the Nones of June[1] the edict was posted in the city of Thibiuca. At that time Magnilianus the curator ordered the *seniores* of the people to be brought to him. (On that same day Felix the bishop [of Thibiuca] left for Carthage.) Magnilianus ordered Aper the

presbyter and Cyril and Vitalis the lectors to be brought to him.

(2) Magnilianus the curator said to them, "Do you have the sacred books?"

Aper said, "We do."

Magnilianus the curator said, "Turn them over to be burnt in the fire."

Then Aper said, "Our bishop has them with him."

Magnilianus the curator said, "Where is he?"

Aper said, "I don't know."

Magnilianus the curator said, "Then you will remain in custody until you render an account to Anulinus the proconsul."

(3) The next day, however, Felix the bishop arrived at Thibiuca from Carthage and Magnilianus the

---

[1] June 5.

From *Donatist Martyr Stories: The Church in Conflict in Roman North Africa,* trans. Maureen A. Tilley. Liverpool, England: Liverpool University Press, 1996. Used with permission.

curator ordered him to be brought in by an officer. Magnilianus said to him, "Are you Felix the bishop?"

Felix answered, "I am."

Magnilianus the curator said, "Turn over whatever books or parchments you have."

Felix the bishop said, "I have them but I won't turn them over."

Magnilianus the curator said, "Turn over the books so they can be burned."

Felix the bishop said, "It is better for me to be burned in the fire than the sacred Scriptures, because it is better to obey God than any human authority (Acts 5:29)."

Magnilianus the curator said, "What the emperor ordered takes priority over what you say."

Felix the bishop said, "The Lord's command takes priority over human authority."

Magnilianus the curator said, "Think it over for three days, because if you fail to obey what was commanded in this city, you will go before the proconsul and you will continue this conversation in his court."

(4) Then, after three days, the curator ordered Felix the bishop to be brought to him and he said to him, "Have you thought it over?"

Felix the bishop said, "What I said before I am saying now and I will say before the proconsul."

Magnilianus the curator said, "Then you will go to the proconsul and you will render an account there." Then Vincentius Celsinus, a decurion of the city of Thibiuca, was assigned to him as an escort.

(5) So Felix the bishop set out from Thibiuca to Carthage on the eighteenth day before the Kalends of July. When he had arrived, he was presented to the legate who ordered him to be thrown into prison. The next day, however, Felix the bishop was brought out before dawn. The legate said to him, "Why don't you hand over your useless Scriptures?"

Felix the bishop said, "I have them but I will not turn them over." So the legate ordered him to be sent into the lowest reaches of the prison.

After sixteen days Felix the bishop was brought out in chains to Anulinus the proconsul at the fourth hour of the night. Anulinus the proconsul said to him, "Why don't you give up your useless Scriptures?"

Felix the bishop responded, "I cannot give them up." At that point Anulinus the proconsul ordered him to be executed by the sword on the Ides of July.[2]

Felix the bishop, raising his eyes to heaven, said with a loud voice, "Thank you, God. I have been in this world for fifty-six years. I have guarded my virginity, I have served the gospel, and I have preached the truth. Lord God of heaven and earth, Jesus Christ, I bend my neck to you as a sacrificial victim, you who remain forever."

When he finished speaking, he was led off by soldiers and beheaded. He was buried in [the Basilica] Fausti on the road called Scillitan.

---

[2] July 15.

2. Lactantius: The Deaths of the Persecutors

Lactantius (full name: Lucius Caelius Firmianus Lactantius; ca. 260–340 C.E.) served as a professor of rhetoric in Diocletian's imperial capital of Nicomedia (mentioned in the text) and later as private tutor to the Emperor Constantine's son Crispus. Lactantius is best known for his apologetic work *Divine Institutes,* in which he defended the intellectual and philosophical foundations of Christianity. *The Deaths of the Persecutors* recounts the horrible and

From *Lactantius: Minor Works,* trans. Sr. Mary Francis McDonald. Washington, D.C.: Catholic University of America Press, 1965. Used with permission.

divinely administered ends met by the imperial persecutors of the Christian church. After brief chapters concerning Nero, Domitian, Decius, Valerian, and Aurelian, Lactantius spends most of the work describing the ten-year period (303–313 C.E.) between the onset of the Great Persecution and the triumph of Constantine over the persecutors (Diocletian, Galerius, Maximian, and Maximin Daia). The entire work is structured like many non-Christian imperial histories (see Chapter 3), in which the author evaluates the merits and failures of the emperors of Rome from political, economic, social, and cultural perspectives. In the *Deaths of the Persecutors,* all these views are ultimately subordinated to the perspective of Christian suffering and triumph.

Two selections from this work are included here. First are the chapters describing the instigation of persecution of the Christians under Diocletian and Galerius. Lactantius combines classically structured evaluations of these men as poor leaders (greedy, ignorant, and immoral) with their particularly evil persecution of Christians. Also presented is Lactantius's version of the so-called Edict of Milan (313 C.E.). Celebrated by Christian historians as the "legalization of Christianity," this was actually a joint resolution by the co-emperors Licinius and Constantine granting official toleration to Christians in both the eastern and western halves of the Roman Empire.

CHAPTER 7

Diocletian, who was an inventor of crimes and a manufacturer of evils, although he destroyed everything else, could not refrain from laying hands even on God. He subverted the world at the same time by both avarice and timidity. He made three men sharers in his power, dividing the world into four parts and multiplying armies, for each one of them strove to have a greater number by far than earlier princes had had when they were sole rulers of the state. The number of receivers had begun to be so much greater than that of givers, the strength of the colonists being sapped by the enormity of impost duties, that fields were deserted and cultivated areas were turned into forests. And in order that all things might be filled with terrors, the provinces, too, were cut up into sections. Many officials and many bureaus were set up in the individual regions, and they burdened almost each city. Likewise, there were many financial officers and magistrates and vicars of prefects. The civil acts of these were very rare; only condemnations and proscriptions were frequent; their exactions of innumerable taxes were, I will not say frequent, but perpetual; and the injuries in these exactions were such as were beyond endurance.

Matters which were concerned with the employing of soldiers were also not to be tolerated. In his insatiable avarice, he wished the treasury to be never diminished, but he was always laying up extraordinary funds and resources in order to keep those funds which he had accumulated preserved intact. When, because of his iniquities, he made things extremely high-priced, he attempted to fix by law the price of saleable goods. Then, on account of scarcity and the low grade of articles, much blood was spilled, and because of fear nothing purchaseable appeared. Therefore, expensiveness raged much worse, until, after the death of many, the law was dissolved by sheer necessity.

To this there was added a certain limitless desire of building, and for supplying all the workers, craftsmen, carts, and whatever was necessary for constructing the works, there was an additional taxing (no less than the others had done) of the provinces. Here, there were basilicas; here, a circus; here, a mint; here, an armory; here, a house for his wife; here, one for his daughter.

All of a sudden, a great part of the city [of Nicomedia] was razed to the ground. All left with their wives and children as though the city were captured by the enemy. And when these works had been completed at the price of the ruin of provinces, he said: "They were not done properly; let them be done another way." Again, it was necessary for tearing down and changing and, perhaps, it would fall again. Thus, he kept on going mad, desiring to equal Nicomedia with Rome.

I pass by the fact that many perished for the sake of their having possessions or fortunes. This was usual and generally permitted because of the customariness of evils. That was an outstanding quality in this ruler because wherever he had seen a more cultivated field or more ornate building, then, a charge of calumny and capital punishment was prepared for the owner, as though he could not plunder and steal without bloodshed.

CHAPTER 8

What shall we say of his brother Maximian who was called Herculius? He was not unlike him, for they could not have stuck together in such a faithful friendship unless there were one mind in the two, the same thought, a like will, and equal judgment. They differed in this respect alone, that there was greater avarice in one but more timidity, and in the other less avarice but more spirit, not for the doing of good, but of evil. For although he held Italy, the very seat of empire, and had the richest provinces subject to him, Africa and Spain, he was not so careful in guarding the riches, the supply of which lay at hand. And since there was need, very wealthy senators were not lacking who were said to have affected the imperial power by providing witnesses in such a way that the eyes of the senate members were constantly being torn out. Its very bloody treasury was getting packed with ill-gained wealth.

Now the passion in this libidinous man was directed, not only to the corruption of young men, an odious and detestable thing, but also to the violation of the daughters of the first citizens. For wherever he went, young girls would be torn from the embrace of their parents immediately and at his whim. He judged himself happy because of these things; he considered the felicity of his power to rest upon them, so long as nothing was denied his passion and evil desire.

I pass by Constantius because he was different from the rest, and he was worthy to hold command of the world alone.

CHAPTER 9

But the other Maximian [Galerius], whom Diocletian attached to himself as son-in-law, was worse, not only than those other two whom our own times knew, but also worse than all the evil rulers there have ever been. A natural barbarism was inherent in this beast, a savagery alien to Roman blood. Nor was this strange, since his mother, a woman from the other side of the Danube, had fled into new Dacia by crossing the river when the Carpians were infesting the land. His bodily appearance was in keeping with his character: towering in stature and massive in corpulence, he was swollen and spread to a horrible magnitude. With voice and action and appearance, he struck fear and terror into all.

Even his father-in-law had a very great fear of him. This was its cause. Narses, king of the Persians, under the inspiration of the example of his grandfather and ancestors, was eager to seize upon the Orient with great forces. Then Diocletian, as he was fearful and cast down in spirit at every upset and fearing, at the same time, the lot of Valerian[1] did not dare to stand in his way, but he sent this man (his son-in-law) to Armenia, himself remaining in the Orient to observe the turn of events. The son-in-law, using the tricks which it is the custom for barbarians to use in conducting war with all their own peoples, attacked the enemy, impeded because of their number and burdened with packs, without difficulty. When King Narses had been put to flight, he returned with booty and huge spoils, adding haughtiness to himself and fear to Diocletian. After this victory, he was exalted to such heights that he was now taking honor from the name of Caesar. When he had learned this from letters brought to him, he shouted in a terrible voice and with a violent expression: "How long will it be

---

[1] The Emperor Valerian (d. 260) was captured and executed by the Persian King Shapur I.

'Caesar'?" Then he began to rant most insolently that he wished to be seen and spoken of as sprung from Mars and that he preferred to be as another Romulus and to soil the reputation of his mother, Romula, with disgrace, in order that he himself might seem sprung from the gods.

But I am postponing a discussion of his deeds so as not to confuse the time order. For after he had accepted the title of emperor, his father-in-law despoiled and out of the way, then he began to rage wildly at last and to despoil all things.

Diocles—for thus he was called before his reign—although he subverted the state with such plans and such accomplices, and although for his crimes he did not gain anything like what he merited, reigned, however, a long time and with great felicity, for as long as he did not defile his hands with the blood of the just.

Now I will reveal the cause which finally led him to instigate a persecution.

CHAPTER 10

Once, while he was conducting affairs in parts of the Orient, as he was from fear a searcher into the future, he was offering a sacrifice of cattle and was seeking from their entrails what things were to happen. Then, certain of his ministers who had knowledge of the Lord, while they stood near him as he sacrificed, made the immortal sign on their foreheads.[2] When this was done, the demons took to flight and the sacred rites were disturbed. The augurs trembled; they did not perceive the customary signs in the entrails, and, as though the offerings had not already been made, they began to perform the rites again and again. But each time the slain victims showed nothing, until the master-augur, a Tages, either because he suspected something or had seen the action, said that the sacred signs were not making any response for this reason, that some profane men were present at the divine rites. Then, in a rage, Diocletian ordered, not only those who were ministers of the sacred rites, but all who were in the palace to make sacrifice. He

---

[2] That is, the cross.

gave orders that any who might refuse were to be punished with clubbings. By means of these orders, which were delivered through officers, he charged even the soldiers to be forced to the nefarious sacrifices. Those who would not obey were withdrawn from service. His raging fury went so far that it could not do anything more against the law and religion of God.

Then, after some time had passed, he came to Bithynia to spend the winter, and to the same place there came Maximian Caesar [Galerius] also inflamed with crime, so that he instigated the doting old man to conduct a persecution of the Christians because he had already made a start.

I have found out that the account which follows was a cause of that one's (i.e., Galerius's) fury.

CHAPTER 11

The mother of Galerius was a worshiper of the gods of the mountains. Since she was a very superstitious woman, she offered sacrificial repasts almost every day and made donations of the meals to her countrymen. Christians kept away, and while she would be dining with her fellow-pagans, they would redouble fasts and prayers. Therefore, she conceived a hatred for them and, with womanly complaints, she prevailed upon her son, no less superstitious, to get rid of these men.

Therefore, secret councils were held during a whole winter, when no one was admitted, and all thought that the greatest affairs of state were being treated. For a long time, the old man, the Augustus, resisted his fury, showing how dangerous it was to have the whole world disturbed and the blood of many shed, that they were accustomed to die willingly, and that it would be enough if he would keep only those of the palace household and his soldiers from the practice of that religion. However, he was not able to influence the wildness of the impetuous man. He decided, then, to get the opinion of his friends. This was Diocletian's type of malice. When he had determined what was a good thing to do, he did it without counsel so that he himself might get the praise; when there was something evil, since he knew it would be criticized, he called many into his counsel so that whatever he himself should be found wanting in would be ascribed to the fault of others.

A few judges, therefore, and some military leaders who held superior rank were called in and questioned. Certain ones among them, from a personal hatred of Christians, believed that these were enemies of the gods and of state religion and, therefore, ought to be done away with. Those who thought differently, either fearing the man or wishing to gratify his wishes because they knew what he wanted, voiced a pretended agreement with that same opinion. Not even in this way was the emperor swayed to give his assent, but he thought it best to consult the gods and sent an augur to Milesian Apollo. The response came that the God of the Christians was an enemy of the divine religion. Thus he was led away from his own decision, and although he was not able to resist his friends, his Caesar, and Apollo, he did attempt to hold this moderation, that he ordered the affair to be conducted without bloodshed, although the Caesar wanted those who refused to sacrifice to be burned alive.

CHAPTER 12

A favorable and propitious day was sought for carrying out the affair and the Terminalia feast days, which occur seven days before the Kalends of March,[3] were selected especially, so that a terminus, as it were, should be placed on this religion. "That day was the first of death and it was first the cause of evils,"[4] those which befell themselves and the world.

When this day dawned—one of the old men being consul for the eighth time, the other for the seventh—suddenly, while it was still not full daylight, the prefect came to the church with leaders and tribunes and officers of the treasury. They tore down the door and searched for a picture or image of God. When the Scriptures were found, they were burned. The chance

---

[3] February 23.
[4] Vergil, *Aeneid* 4.169–70.

for booty was given to all. There was pillaging, trepidation, running about all around.

The rulers themselves in their observatory-site (because the appointed church was visible as they looked up from the palace because of its high position) for a long time argued together whether it would be necessary for fire to be applied. Diocletian won, having a cautious attitude, lest part of the city be destroyed when a great conflagration (such as the persecution would warrant) should be set. For many great houses encircled the church on all sides.

So the praetorians came in a drawn up battle line with axes and other implements, and throwing these from all sides, they leveled that most outstanding temple to the ground in a few hours.

CHAPTER 13

The next day the edict was published in which it was ordered that men of that religion should be deprived of all honor and dignity and be subjected to torments, and no matter from what rank or grade they came every action against them would hold weight, and they themselves would not be able to plead in a court against a charge of injury or adultery or theft; in short, they would not have freedom of speech. Although it was not right, still it was with great courage that a certain man pulled down and tore up this edict, as he said deridingly that victories of the Goths and Sarmatians were proposed in it. Immediately, he was taken, and he was not only tortured, but he was actually cooked, according to the directions of a particular recipe, and then finally burned up, having suffered with admirable patience.

CHAPTER 14

But the Caesar was not content with the laws of the edict. He prepared to set Diocletian off on another score. In order to drive him to the determination of the most cruel persecution, he set fire to the palace through the aid of secret agents. And when part had been burned, the Christians were charged with being public enemies and, because ill-will was so high, the name of the Christians was being burned along with the palace. They were charged with having plotted with the eunuchs for the death of the princes, the two emperors having been almost burned alive in their own palaces.

Diocletian, however, who always wished to appear clever and intelligent, was able to discover nothing, but, inflamed with wrath, he began at once to put all his domestics to torture. He himself sat and had the innocent roasted at the fire. Likewise, all the judges and all those, in short, who were officials in the palace received the faculties and put them to torture. They vied with each other so as to be first to find out something.

Nothing was ever discovered though, for, of course, no one tortured the household of the Caesar. That one was present and kept pressing the matter, nor did he allow the anger of the ill-advised old man to settle. After fifteen days, he again contrived another fire. This one was discovered more quickly, but it did not become apparent who caused it. Then the Caesar, whose departure had been in readiness since the middle of winter, rushed out that very same day, claiming that he was taking flight so as not to be burned alive.

CHAPTER 15

Then the emperor raged, not only against those of his own household, but against all. In the first place, he compelled his daughter, Valeria, and her husband, and Prisca to be defiled by pagan sacrifice. When those who had been the most powerful eunuchs were killed, those on whom the palace and he himself depended, the priests and deacons were seized and condemned without any proof or confession. They were led away with all their families. There was no respect for sex or age. Men were seized and burned, not individually, because there was such a great number, but they were herded into devouring fires. The domestic servants of the palace were plunged into the sea, millstones tied to their necks.

The persecution was no less intense against the rest of the people. The judges went about through all the temples and forced everybody to sacrifice. The prisons were full. Unheard of kinds of torment were conceived. In order that justice might not be rashly applied in favor of anyone, altars were set up in secretarial rooms and before the tribunal so that those coming to court should sacrifice first and then plead their cases, and, therefore, the approach to the judge was as though an entrance hall to the gods.

Letters had found their way even to Maximian and Constantius so that they would do the same things. Their opinion had not been looked for in such great matters. And, indeed, the old Maximian willingly carried out the instructions throughout all of Italy for he was not a very clement man. Constantius, so as not to seem to disapprove of the precepts of the previous rulers, allowed the church buildings, the meeting places, that is, the wall which could be restored, to be torn down, but the temple of God, which is in men, he left untouched.

CHAPTER 16

So the whole world was upset, and outside of the Gauls, from the East even to the West, the three wildest beasts were raging. "Not if I had a hundred tongues and a hundred mouths and a voice of iron, could I comprehend all the forms of their crimes, could I get through all the names of the punishments,"[5] which the judges throughout the provinces inflicted upon the just and the innocent. Anyway, why is there any need of relating those things, especially to you, very dear Donatus, who have experienced more than the rest the storm of raging persecution?

For, although you had fallen into the hands of Flaccinus the prefect, a violent murderer, and then when you had come before Hierocles, the governor who had been a vicar, who was an author and councilor for the carrying out of the persecution, you fi-

---

[5] Vergil, *Aeneid* 6.625–27.

nally furnished to all an example of unconquered fortitude before Priscillian, his successor. Nine times subject to torments and various sufferings, you nine times overcame your adversary with your glorious confession; in nine battles, you unwarred the devil with his satellites; by nine victories, you triumphed over the world with its terrors. How pleasing was that spectacle to God when he beheld you as victor, not bringing under subjection to your chariot white horses or huge elephants, but, best of all, the very triumphant ones themselves!

This is true triumph, when the masters (of the world) are mastered. For they were conquered and subjected by your virtue, inasmuch as by despising their abominable order you spurned with stable faith and strength of mind all their trappings and the slight terrors of tyrannical power. The beatings accomplished nothing against you; the hooks availed nothing; the fire nothing; the sword nothing; the various kinds of torments did nothing. No power could wrest faith and devotion from you. This is being a disciple of God. This is what it means to be a soldier of Christ, one whom no enemy may attack, no wolf drive from the heavenly fold, no snare induce, no pain overcome, no suffering afflict. Finally, after those nine most glorious combats in which the devil was vanquished by you, he did not dare to engage with you any further, whom he tested in so many conflicts and found not able to be overcome. And although the victor's crown has been prepared for you, he has ceased to demand anything further of you, lest you should take it now. Though you may not receive this at present, however, it is being preserved for you completely in the kingdom of God because of your virtues and merits.

But let us get back to the outline of our discussion.

CHAPTER 17

After this crime had been perpetrated, Diocletian, although his good luck had already left him, set out at once for Rome to celebrate there the day of the *vicennalia,* which was to be on the twelfth day before the Kalends of December.[6] When the solemn rites were celebrated, because he could not bear the freedom of the Roman people, impatient and sick in soul, he left the city as the first of January was drawing near, when the consulship was being conferred on him for the ninth time. He could not endure the thirteen days of waiting so that he might begin this consulship at Rome, rather than at Ravenna, but setting out in the dead of winter and struck by cold and storms, he contracted a sickness, slight but chronic, and being disturbed and bothered throughout the journey, he had to be carried most of the way on a litter.

And so, when summer had gone, through a circuitous route along the bank of the Hister, he reached Nicomedia, but the sickness had now become severe. Although he saw that he was oppressed with it, he was carried on, nevertheless, in order to dedicate a circus which he had built. It was now a full year after the *vicennalia.*

Then he was so overcome with weakness that the sparing of his life was asked from all the gods. Finally, on December 13, grief suddenly appeared in the palace; there was sadness and weeping on the part of the judges, trepidation and silence in the whole city. Now they were saying that he was not only dead, but buried as well, when suddenly, in the morning of the next day, the report was spread that he was living, and the expressions of the domestics and the judges changed with alacrity. Nor were there lacking those who suspected that his death was being concealed until the Caesar should come, lest some revolution be instigated, perhaps, by the soldiers. This suspicion had such weight that no one would have believed that he was alive, except that on March 1 he appeared, scarcely recognizable, of course, since he had suffered under sickness for almost an entire year. He who had slept in death on the Ides of December had recovered life. But it was not an entire recovery,

---

6 The *vicennalia,* celebrated on November 20, 303, commemorated the twentieth anniversary of Diocletian's ascension to the imperial throne.

however, for he became demented, so that at certain times he would be insane and at others would seem clear.

CHAPTER 18

Not many days later the Caesar arrived, not to congratulate his (adoptive) father, but to force him to yield his power. He had now but recently been in conflict with the old Maximian, and he had alarmed him by injecting the fear of civil war.

So, at first, he met Diocletian gently and in a friendly manner, telling him that he was old now, and not strong, and not capable of the management of the affairs of state, that he ought to rest after his labors. At the same time, he suggested to him the example of Nerva who had handed over the empire to Trajan. Diocletian, however, said that it was not fitting if he should fall back into the shadows of a lowly life after having reached such great brilliance in his peak position. He said also that it was not at all safe because during such a long rule he had gained the hatred of many people. He showed that Nerva, reigning only a year, had abdicated from the control of the state and returned to private life, in which he had grown old, because he was not able to bear the burden and care of such great concerns, either on account of his age or his lack of experience. But, he went on to say that if Galerius wished to have the name of emperor, it would not bother him if they were all called Augusti.

That one, however, who had already in hope seized upon the whole world, since he saw that nothing, or not much more, besides the name was coming to him, answered that the original arrangement of Diocletian himself ought to be held to, so that there might be two greater ones in the state who would exercise supreme control, and then two lesser ones to be assistants. He argued that between the two concord could easily be preserved, but that it could be kept in no way among four equals. And if Diocletian should not want to yield to him, he would take matters into his own hands and see to it that he would no longer be a lesser ruler and the last of them all. Already fifteen years had passed since he had been relegated to

Illyricum, that is, to the banks of the Danube, to struggle with the barbarian peoples, while the others were ruling in more relaxed and quieter lands in a luxurious manner.

Upon hearing this, the sick old man, who had already received the letters of old Maximian (who had written all that that one would say) and who had learned that an army was being raised by him, said to him in a voice full of tears, "Let it be, if this is what you want."

It remained for Caesars to be chosen by the common deliberation of them all.

"What is the point of deliberation, since it must be necessary for those other two to agree to what we will have done?"

"Clearly it is so, for their sons must be the ones named."

Now, Maximian had a son, Maxentius, son-in-law of this Maximian [Galerius], a man of perverse and evil mind, so proud and stubborn that he was wont to give deference to neither his father nor his father-in-law, and for this reason, he was hateful to both of them.

Constantius also had a son, Constantine, a most upright young man and very worthy of that high rank. He was loved by the soldiers and wanted by private citizens as well because of his distinguished and fine appearance, his military accomplishments, the probity of his morals, and his exceptional congeniality. He was then present at Diocletian's court, having been long since made a tribune of the first rank by him.

"What shall be done, then?" asked Galerius. "The former," he said, "is not worthy. He who has despised us when he was but a private citizen, what will he do when he gains power?"

"But the latter is quite pleasing, and he will rule in such a way that he will be judged better and more clement than his father," said Diocletian.

"Then it will come to be that I am not able to do what I wish. Men should be named," added Galerius, "who are to be at my disposal, those who fear me, who will do nothing except at my order."

"Whom shall we appoint, then?"

"Severus," he said.

"What! That excitable dancer, that drunkard, to whom night is as day and day as night?"

"He is worthy," he answered, "because he faithfully exercised his command of the soldiers, and I have already sent him to Maximian to be invested by him."

"All right. But whom will you make the other Caesar?"

"This man," he said, indicating a certain young Daia, a semibarbarian, whom he had recently ordered to be called Maximin after his own name. For Diocletian, too, had formerly changed his name for him in part, on account of an omen, because Maximian [Galerius] displayed loyalty most scrupulously.

"Who is this whom you present to me?" asked Diocletian.

"A relative of mine," he said.

Then the other groaned and said: "You do not give me capable men to whom the guardianship of the state can be entrusted."

"I have approved of them," he retorted.

"You seem to be on the verge of taking control of the empire," capitulated Diocletian. "I have labored enough, and I have seen to it that under my command the state should stay unharmed. If any harm comes to it, it will not be my fault."

CHAPTER 19

When these matters had been determined, action was taken on the first of May. All eyes were fixed upon Constantine. There was no doubt in anyone's mind. The soldiers who were present and the officers who had been chosen and summoned from the legions were rejoicing, intent upon this one man; they were desiring him and they were making known their wishes.

There was a lofty place about three miles outside the city. On its height, Maximian himself had assumed the purple, and there a column with an image of Jupiter had been erected. Everybody went there. An assembly of the soldiers was convoked. The old prince addressed them in tears, saying that he was old, that he was seeking rest after labors, that he was turning the power over to stronger rulers, and that he was

replacing them with other Caesars. The expectation of everyone as to what appointments he would make was very high. Then suddenly, he named Severus and Maximinus the Caesars. All were struck dumb. Constantine was standing on the platform head held high. There was some general hesitation as to whether the name of Constantine had been changed. Suddenly, however, in the sight of all, Maximian made a gesture of turning away from Constantine and brought Daia forth from behind and placed him in a central position, having removed from him the garment of private citizen. Everyone wondered who this man was and where he came from. No one, however, dared to cry out against it, though all were disturbed by the unexpected strangeness of the situation.

Diocletian put on him his own purple, which he removed from himself, and Diocletian became Diocles again. Thereupon, he stepped down from the platform. Then, the old king was conducted through the city and carried outside it in a carriage and sent back to his native place.

Daia, however, recently raised from the cattle and the forests, became at once a soldier of the guard, then a protector, and soon a tribune. The following day, as Caesar, he received the Orient to beat it down and trample underfoot, for he who knew neither military service nor state affairs was now a shepherd, not of sheep, but of soldiers.

CHAPTER 20

Maximian [Galerius], after he accomplished what he wished, the expulsion of the old Augusti, was now conducting himself as the sole lord of the whole world. He despised Constantius, even though it was necessary for him to be named first, because he was of a gentle nature and was impeded by poor health. He was hoping that Constantius, his co-Augustus, would die shortly, but if he did not, it seemed that he would divest the hated one easily. What would happen if he were forced by the other three incumbents to lay down his command?

Galerius himself had a friend, an old tent-mate and associate of early service, Licinius, whose suggestions he followed in all his acts of ruling. He did not wish to make him a Caesar, so as not to thus name him an adoptive son, in order that later on he might put him into the place of Constantius and call him Augustus and brother. Then, in truth, he himself would hold the principate and, reveling wildly throughout the world according to his own caprice, he would celebrate the twentieth-anniversary affair and would himself put his enemy out of the way, substituting for the Caesar his own son who was then nine years old. Thus, when Licinius and Severus would hold the supreme command and when Maximin Daia and Candidianus would have the second name of Caesar, surrounded by an unattackable wall, he would spend a secure and tranquil old age. His plans were tending in this direction. But God, whom he made his enemy, shattered all his contrivings.

CHAPTER 21

When he had secured the greatest power, therefore, he directed his mind toward the disruption of the world which he had opened out before himself. For after the defeat of the Persians (whose rite and practice it is to devote themselves as slaves to their kings and whose kings use their people as a slave-household), that nefarious man wished to introduce their custom into the Roman world. From the time of his victory, he praised it shamelessly. Because he could not practice it openly, he acted in such a way that he himself would take liberty away from men. First of all, he took the honors of public office. Not only decurions were tortured by him, but also the first men of cities, distinguished and very perfect men, and, indeed, for quite unimportant and purely civil cases. If they seemed deserving of death, crosses were ready for them; if not, shackles were prepared. Mothers of families, freeborn and even noble girls, were seized for the *gynecaeum*.[7] If someone were to be beaten, four stakes were fixed in an enclosure upon which no slave even was ever stretched.

---

[7] Imperially run weaving factories.

Why should I relate his sport or his distractions? He had bears, very much like himself in fierceness and size, which he had selected throughout the whole time of his reign. As often as he wanted to be amused, he ordered each one of these, selected by name, to be brought forward. Men were thrown to them, not to be eaten, but to be swallowed down. When their limbs were strewn about, he laughed quite delightedly, nor did he ever dine except in the presence of human blood.

Fire was the punishment of those who did not have dignity. This is the type of death which he had at first directed against the Christians, when the laws were made, so that, after torture, the condemned might be burned with slow fires. After they had been bound, a light flame was applied first to the feet for so long a time until the flesh of the soles, contracted by the heat, would be pulled away from the bones. Then torches, lighted and immediately extinguished, were applied to the individual members of the body, so that no part of it was left untouched. During all of this, the face was sprinkled with cold water and the mouth was washed with a liquid, lest, the jaws becoming stiff with dryness, the breath would leave too quickly. This would take place finally, only after all the skin had been roasted away throughout a long day, when the force of the fire had penetrated to the inner organs. Then they made a pyre, and the already charred bodies were cremated. The bones, ground and reduced to powder, were tossed into the rivers and the sea.

CHAPTER 22

Those practices, therefore, which he had learned in torturing the Christians, from very habit he applied to all. With him no punishment was slight. There were no islands, no prisons, no metal mines, but fire, the cross, wild beasts were daily and ordinary occurrences. His domestic slaves and functionaries were punished by the lance. In the case of the death penalty, punishment by the sword was for very few cases, and this type was conferred as though a benefit upon those who, because of services or merits, had been granted this "favorable" death.

But now those previous penalties were light in comparison with these: eloquence was extinguished; advocates were put out of the way; lawyers were exiled or killed; literature was regarded as a wicked profession, and those who were skilled in it were proscribed and execrated as enemies and an opposition party; license for everything was assumed because laws were disregarded; and military judges, devoid of all culture and humanity, were sent into the provinces without assessors.

CHAPTER 23

However, that was public calamity and the common grief of all once the census was taken up in the provinces and cities. Because census agents were spread everywhere exacting everything, there was hostile disturbance and the likeness of horrible captivity. Fields were measured out piece by piece; vines and trees were counted; animals of every kind were marked down; men were counted individually; in the cities, urban and rustic population were united; all the marketplaces were packed with families; each one was present with his children and his slaves. Torturings and beatings resounded; sons were held up against their parents; the most faithful slaves were questioned and harassed against their masters, and even wives against husbands. If all things else failed, men were tortured to self-accusation, and when pain had overcome them, crimes which were not their own they had ascribed to them. No excuse was made for age or health. The sick and weak were brought out; the ages of individuals were reckoned, years being added to the young and taken away from the old. Everything was full of grief and sadness.

The things which those of old had done against conquered peoples by right of war, he dared to do against Romans and those subject to Romans because his forefathers had been subjected to a census which Trajan victoriously imposed upon the constantly rebelling Dacians as a punishment. After this, men put down a price for their heads, gave a fee for life. And faith was not put in the same census takers, but others were sent in their wake to find out more in-

formation, and the process was ever repeated. Though these did not find out anything, they added what they pleased, so that they might not seem to have been sent in vain. Meanwhile, the animals diminished in number and men died; nevertheless, taxes were exacted for the dead, so that it was not free of charge either to live or to die.

There remained only the beggars from whom nothing could be exacted as a fee. Misery and hard luck had made them safe from every kind of injury. But, indeed, that "reverent" man pitied them so that they should not want! He ordered them all to be collected, carried off on ships, and dumped into the sea. Such a merciful man, to see to it that there would be no one in wretched circumstances under his rule! Thus, while he takes care that no one avoids the census through pretense of destitution, he kills a multitude of the truly destitute contrary to all human principles.

CHAPTER 24

Now, there drew near to him the judgment of God, and a period followed in which his affairs began to waver and fall to ruin. He had not yet directed his attention to the overthrow and expulsion of Constantius, while he was engaged in those affairs which I described above. And he was waiting for that one's death, though he did not think that he would die so quickly.

When Constantius was suffering under serious illness, he had issued instructions that his son, Constantine, be sent back to him. He had now pleaded for him for long, but in vain. That one (i.e., Galerius), however, wished nothing less than this. He had often striven after the youth in insidious ways, for he dared nothing openly, lest he stir up against himself civil war and, what he feared especially, the hatred of the soldiers. Under pretense of exercise and games, he had put him in the way of wild beasts, but it was to no avail because the hand of God was protecting the man. God liberated him from the hands of that Galerius at the very turning point. After the request had been asked of him very often, Galerius, since he could no longer refuse, gave the sign at the end of the day, but ordered that he was not to set out until the next day when he would receive the orders. This was because either he himself was going to retain him on some pretext, or he was going to send letters so that he would be held by Severus.

Since Constantine suspected this, after supper when the emperor was at rest, he hastened to set out, and taking all the state horses from the many stopping places, he rode away quickly. The following day, after he had slept until midday according to his purpose, the emperor (Galerius) ordered Constantine to be summoned. He was told that Constantine had set out immediately after supper. He began to rage furiously. He called for the state horses so that he could have him brought back. He was told that the relay stations were robbed of their mounts. He held back his tears only with difficulty.

But Constantine, using incredible speed, had reached his father, now failing rapidly, who gave the command into his hands with the approval of his soldiers. And thus he received the repose of his days at his bed, as he had wished.

When he took control, Constantine Augustus did nothing until he returned the Christians to their religion and their God. This was his first sanction of the restoration of the holy religion. . . .

CHAPTER 48

Licinius, however, after he had taken and distributed part of that army, led his army across into Bithynia a few days after the battle. Entering Nicomedia, he rendered thanks to God by whose help he had conquered, and on the thirteenth day of June, Constantine and himself being consuls for the third time, he ordered a letter published about the "restoration of the Church." The letter was to be put before the *praeses* and was of this nature:

When I, Constantine Augustus, and I also, Licinius Augustus, had met together under happy circumstances at Milan, and were giving consideration to all matters which pertained to the public good and security, we decided that these things, among others, which we saw would be for the advantage of many men, should be ordained first of all, namely, by which means reverence of the divinity was held. We believed that we should give both to Christians and to all men the freedom to follow religion, whichever one each one chose, so that whatever sort of divinity there is in heavenly regions may be gracious and propitious to us and to all who live under our government.

And, therefore, we have determined that this purpose should be undertaken with sound and most upright reason, that we think the opportunity should be denied to no one whatsoever who has given his attention to the observance of the Christians or to that religion which he feels to be most suited to himself, so that the highest deity, whose religion we foster with free minds, may be able to show to us in all affairs his customary favor and benevolence. Wherefore, it was fitting that your devotedness know that this was our pleasure, that all those conditions with reference to the Christians, which were contained in our former letters and sent to your office, now being completely removed, everything which seemed severe and opposed to our clemency may be annulled, and now all who have the wish to observe the religion of the Christians may hasten to do so without any worry or molestation. We believed that these things should be most fully made known to Your Solicitude, so that you might know that we had given to those same Christians free and untrammeled opportunity to practice their religion. Since you see that this has been granted by us to these same Christians, your devotedness understands also that to others as well the freedom and full liberty has been granted, in accordance with the peace of our times, to exercise free choice in worshipping as each one has seen fit. This has been done by us so that nothing may seem to be taken away from anyone's honor or from any religion whatsoever. And in addition we have decreed that this should be decided concerning the Christians. If those same places, in which they had been formerly accustomed to assemble, and about which in the letters formerly sent to your devotedness a different order had been given; if some are seen to have purchased them before this, either from the treasury or from some other person, they shall restore the same to the Christians without money payment or any seeking of a price, all frustration and ambiguity being put away. Those who have received them as a gift shall likewise restore them to these same Christians as quickly as possible. Also, if those who have bought these places or those who have received them as a gift seek anything of our benevolence, let them apply to the vicar so that provision may be made for them through our clemency. All these things are to be taken care of for the body of the Christians by your direction and without delay.

And since those same Christians are known to have possessed not only those places in which they were accustomed to assemble, but also others which belonged not to individual men but to the corporate society, that is, their churches, you will order that all these, according to the law which we have stated above, should be restored to these same Christians, that is, to their society and congregation, without any hesitation or quarrel, the above mentioned reasonableness being preserved, that those who restore them without price shall, as we said, look for indemnity from our bounty. In all these provisions for the benefit of the aforementioned body of Christians, you will apply your most efficacious concern, so that our command may be very quickly fulfilled, and that in this also provision may be made through our bounty for the public peace.

To this extent it will happen, therefore, that the divine favor toward us, as has been stated above, which we have experienced in such great matters, will continue through all time, that our successive acts will prosper with public blessings. And that the formula of our graciousness and of this sanction may reach the attention of all, it will be expected that this be written and proclaimed by you and that you publish it and bring it to the knowledge of all, so that it may not be possible that this provision of our generosity be hidden from anyone.

He urged by this written proclamation and also by the spoken word that the meeting places be returned to their early status. Thus, from the overthrow of the Church until its restoration, there was a period of ten years and four months, more or less.[8]

---

[8] From February 303 to June 313.

CHAPTER 3

Christianity and the Imperial House

We may never know the real reasons for Constantine's conversion, although many have been proposed; it is likewise impossible to gauge the depth of Constantine's dedication to Christian doctrine. Many scholars ascribe sincere religious motives to him, while others see him as an opportunist currying favor with a vocal minority. We do know that Constantine's contemporaries and successors viewed his patronage of Christianity as a watershed: for pagans, such as Zosimus, it was the beginning of the end of a proud empire; for Christians, such as Eusebius, it was the dawning of a bright new day of Christian triumph. Constantine put a great deal of financial and political support behind Christianity, beyond the simple legalization of the movement in 313 C.E. (see the so-called Edict of Milan in Text 2). He built churches in the major cities of the empire, gave Christian clergy tax incentives and other perquisites, and intervened to settle intra-Christian disputes. For centuries, Christians had imagined the Roman Empire as their persecuting enemy; now they had an involved patron at the highest level of society. Over the course of the fourth and fifth centuries, Christian leaders and emperors both sought to articulate this new relationship.

Constantine's sons and successors (Constans, Constantius, and Constantine II) were as involved as their father in matters of ecclesiastical patronage and debate. Quickly, Christians came to see the role of the emperor in religious matters as natural and inevitable. This intertwining of imperial and Christian ideals was disrupted by the reign of Constantine's nephew, Julian. Soon after his ascension to the imperial throne in 361, Julian publicly renounced his Christian upbringing and set out to revitalize the traditional "Hellenic" (i.e., Greco-Roman or pagan) religious practices throughout the empire. Julian's reign was short (he died during a failed military campaign against the Persians in 363), but the effects were long lasting. Every emperor after Julian was pressed to prove his Christian loyalty. Gratian (reign 367–83) officially renounced the title of Pontifex Maximus, the imperial guardianship of pagan priesthoods. The Theodosian dynasty (beginning with the ascent of Theodosius I in 378 and ending with the death of his grandson Theodosius II in 450) further united imperial and Christian religious concerns. Under the Theodosians, Christianity became, for all intents and purposes, the official religion of the empire; pagan sacrifice and worship were outlawed, and heretics were subject to civil liabilities (see Chapter 4). The welfare of the empire was increasingly a matter of Christian fidelity as much as military or economic success.

In this chapter are diverse literary portraits of Roman emperors. Constantine, the first Christian emperor, is presented from three perspectives: religiously neutral ("The Origin of Constantine"), pro-Christian (Eusebius), and anti-Christian (Zosimus). Julian's attempts to de-Christianize the Roman Empire are presented in his own terms through his letters on religion and from the perspective of the Christian hymnographer Ephraim. Finally, a funeral oration for Theodosius I by Bishop Ambrose of Milan gives a sense of how Christianity not only became intertwined with the imperial house, but sought to exert religious authority over the person of the emperor. All of these writings give a sense of the urgency with which emperors and bishops, Christians and pagans, viewed the growing link between "church" and "state" in the later Roman Empire.

FOR FURTHER READING

Barnes, Timothy D. *Constantine and Eusebius.* Cambridge, Mass.: Harvard University Press, 1981.

Bowersock, Glen W. *Julian the Apostate.* London: Duckworth, 1978.

Drake, H. A. *Constantine and the Bishops: The Politics of Intolerance.* Baltimore: Johns Hopkins University Press, 2000.

Holum, Kenneth. *Theodosian Empresses: Women and Imperial Dominion in Late Antiquity.* Berkeley: University of California Press, 1982.

Lieu, Samuel N. C., and Monsterrat, Dominic. *Constantine: History, Historiography, and Legend.* New York: Routledge, 1998.

Williams, Stephen, and Friell, Gerard. *Theodosius: The Empire at Bay.* New Haven, Conn.: Yale University Press, 1994.

The Texts

3. The Origin of Constantine

Although this brief life of Constantine survives only as incorporated into a later (sixth-century) text, it may, in fact, be the earliest biographical record of the first Christian emperor. References to Constantine's Christian enthusiasm were inserted by a later Christian editor, taken mainly from the early fifth-century *History against the Pagans* by Orosius, a disciple of Augustine. The original text probably ended with the defeat of Constantine's co-emperor Licinius and the founding of Constantinople and may have been written before or soon after Constantine's death in 337. Particulars that were later expunged from Constantine's more favorable biographies still appear without apology, such as the prominent role of Constantine's eldest son Crispus (later executed by his father) and Constantine's own modest origins as the "scantily instructed" son of Constantius's first wife (or concubine), Helena. The author seems more interested in narrating Constantine's political and military legitimacy apart from religious considerations, so he highlights Constantine's (perhaps bogus) relation to the third-century Emperor Claudius Gothicus (reign ca. 268–70 C.E.); he recounts the political career of Constantine's father, Constantius; and he places great emphasis on Constantine's military hardiness and sobriety. "The Origin of Constantine" presents a favorable, but not overly tendentious, narrative of the rise of Constantine to sole rule over the Roman Empire, without the later veneer of Christian adoration or the backlash of anti-Christian resentment.

1 (1) Diocletian ruled for twenty years with Herculius Maximianus. Constantius, a grand-nephew of the divine Claudius (Gothicus), best of princes, through his brother, first became protector, then tribune, and afterward governor of the Dalmatias. Then he was made Caesar by Diocletian, along with Galerius. Having left Helena, his previous wife, he took to wife Theodora, daughter of Maximianus, by whom he subsequently had six children, the brothers of Constantine. But by Helena, his previous wife, he already had a son, Constantine, who later became the most mighty of princes.

2 (2) This Constantine, therefore, was born of a very humble mother, Helena, in the town of Naissus and brought up there (he later adorned this town most splendidly). Having been scantily instructed in letters, he became a hostage with Diocletian and Galerius and fought bravely under them in Asia. After Diocletian and Herculius had laid down their power, Constantius asked for Constantine back from Galerius, but Galerius threw him into the path of many dangers. (3) For when he was a young man fighting in the cavalry against the Sarmatians, having seized a fierce barbarian by his hair, he captured him and brought him to the

From *Constantine to Julian: Pagan and Byzantine Views: A Source History,* trans. Jane Stevenson, ed. S. N. C. Lieu and Dominic Montserrat. London: Routledge, 1996. Used with permission.

feet of the emperor Galerius. Then, having been sent by Galerius into a swamp, he entered it on horseback and made a way for the rest of the army to the Sarmatians and brought victory to Galerius, having killed many of them. (4) Then Galerius sent him back to his father. And Constantine, so that he might avoid Severus as he was passing through Italy, crossed the Alps with the greatest possible speed, having killed the post horses behind him, and came to his father at Bononia, which the Gauls previously called Gesoriacum. After his victory over the Picts, his father Constantius died at York and Constantine, by the will of all the soldiers, was made Caesar.

3 (5) Meanwhile, two Caesars had been created, Severus and Maximinus [i.e., Maximinus Daia]. Maximinus was given rule over Oriens, and Galerius kept for himself Illyricum, Thrace, and Bithynia. Severus took Italy and whatever Herculius [i.e., Maximianus] had previously gained. (6) After Constantius had died in Britain and Constantine his son had succeeded him, suddenly the Praetorian Guard in the city of Rome created Maxentius, the son of Herculius, emperor. But at the order of Galerius, Severus took an army against Maxentius, but he was suddenly deserted by all his men and fled to Ravenna. After that, Galerius went to Rome with a vast force, threatening the destruction of the city, and encamped at the fort Interamna on the Tiber. (7) Then he sent Licinius and Probus to the city as ambassadors, asking, in negotiation, that the son-in-law [Maxentius] should seek to obtain what he wanted from his father-in-law Galerius by requesting it, rather than by making war. This was spurned, and he learned that on account of Maxentius's promises, [many] men had deserted his side. Disturbed by this, he turned back, and so that he could give his army some kind of booty, he told them to steal things along the Via Flaminia. (8) Maximinus himself fled to Constantine. Then Galerius made Licinius Caesar in Illyricum. Next, leaving him behind in Pannonia, he himself retired to Serdica, having been attacked by a fearsome disease, and he so melted away that he died with his entrails exposed and rotting, in punishment for the most dreadful persecution, a most just penalty returning on the author of a wicked edict. He had ruled for eighteen years.

4 (9) Severus Caesar was ignoble, both in his way of life and his birth, and an alcoholic and thus a friend of Galerius. It was for this reason that Galerius made him and Maximinus Caesars, with Constantine knowing nothing of the matter. To this Severus were given cities in Pannonia, Italy, and Africa. It is for this reason that Maxentius was made emperor: because Severus, having been abandoned, fled from his own men to Ravenna. (10) Herculius came there on behalf of his son after being summoned, and having deceived Severus with false promises, took him into custody and brought him into the city in the guise of a captive and had him kept in a house belonging to the state thirty [Roman] miles down the Via Appia from Rome. Afterward, when Galerius sought Italy, he was murdered and then brought to a place eight miles from Rome and put in the monument of Gallienus.

(11) Galerius was such an alcoholic that when he was drunk, he would issue orders which ought not to be obeyed, and on the warning of his prefect, he directed that none of his orders issued after dinner should be implemented.

(12) Meanwhile Constantine, having defeated the generals of the tyrant [Maxentius] at Verona, sought out Rome. When Constantine was coming to the city, Maxentius, coming out of the city, chose a plain above the Tiber as the place where they would fight. There he was defeated and, fleeing with all his men, perished, trapped in the crowd of people and thrown down by his horse into the river. On the following day, his body was taken up from the river, and his head was cut off and brought into the city. His mother, when she was questioned about his origins, confessed that he had been begotten by a certain Syrian. He ruled for six years.

5 (13) Licinius too was a man of humble birth from New Dacia, who had been made emperor by Galerius so that he would fight against Maxentius. But after Maxentius had been suppressed, and Constantine had retaken Italy, he bound Licinius into alliance with him, provided that Licinius would take his sister Constantia as his wife in Milan. Once the marriage had been celebrated, Constantine went to Gaul, and Licinius returned to Illyricum. (14) Some time later, Constantine sent Constantius to Licinius, suggesting that he should make Bassianus (who had married Constantine's other sister Anastasia) a Caesar, so that Bassianus could hold Italy as a buffer between Constantine and Licinius, following the example set by Diocletian and Maximianus. (15) But Licinius spoiled this arrangement, and through the influence of Senicio, Bassianus's brother, who was loyal to Licinius, Bassianus took up arms against Constantine. He was seized while still preparing himself, and at Constantine's order, was convicted and executed. When Senicio, as the person responsible for the plot, was demanded for punishment, Licinius refused to hand him over, and the peace between them was broken. There was an additional reason besides because Licinius had destroyed images and statues of Constantine at Emona. Open war was declared between the two of them.

(16) Both their armies were taken to the plain of Cibalae. Licinius had 35,000 men, infantry and cavalry; Constantine commanded 20,000 infantry and cavalry. After an indecisive battle, in which 20,000 of Licinius's infantry and part of his armored cavalry were killed, Licinius escaped to Sirmium with the greater part of his horse-troops under cover of night. (17) From there, having picked up his wife and son and treasure, he went to Dacia. He made Valens, commander of the frontier, a Caesar. Then, a huge force having been assembled by means of Valens at Hadrianopolis (a city in Thrace), he sent ambassadors to Constantine, who had settled himself at Philippopolis, to talk of peace. The ambassadors returned, baffled, and having taken to war again, they fought together on the plain of Ardia. After a lengthy and indecisive battle, Licinius's men gave way and fled under cover of night. (18) Licinius and Valens turned away and went into the region of Beroea, believing (which was actually true) that Constantine in order to pursue them would be heading further toward Byzantium. Then as Constantine was eagerly hurrying ahead, he learned that Licinius remained at his back. Just then, when his soldiers were weary with battle and route marching, Mestrianus was sent to him as an ambassador to ask for peace, at the re-

quest of Licinius, who promised that he would henceforth do as he was told. Valens was commanded to return to his private rank as he had been before, and, when this was done, peace was confirmed between the two emperors, and Licinius held Oriens, Asia, Thrace, Lesser Moesia, and Scythia.

(19) Then, returning to Serdica, Constantine decided in Licinius's absence that Constantine's sons Crispus and Constantine and Licinius's son Licinius should be made Caesars, and thus rule should be carried on harmoniously, as from both of them. Therefore, Constantine and Licinius were made consuls simultaneously. (20) In the region of Oriens, during Licinius's and Constantine's consulship, Licinius, seized by sudden insanity, ordered that all the Christians should be expelled from the palace. Soon after that, war broke out again between Licinius and Constantine.

(21) Again, while Constantine was at Thessalonica, the Goths broke through the neglected frontiers, devastated Thrace and Moesia, and began to take spoils. Then, in fear of Constantine, after their onset had been checked, they returned prisoners to him and peace was granted them. But Licinius complained that this was a breach of trust, since an area belonging to him had been relieved by someone else. (22) Then, since he alternated between wheedling and haughty orders, he justifiably roused the wrath of Constantine. During the time when civil war was not yet actually being waged but was being prepared for, Licinius wallowed in the crimes of avarice, cruelty, and lust, murdering many wealthy men and seducing their wives.

(23) Then the peace was broken with the consent of both sides. Constantine sent the Caesar Crispus with a huge fleet to take Asia, and Amandus, acting for Licinius, opposed him with a similarly large naval force. (24) Licinius himself filled the slopes of a high mountain near Hadrianopolis with a great army. Constantine turned thither, with his entire force. While the war was going on by both land and sea, Constantine was victorious, due to his troops' discipline in battle (though they had difficulty with the heights), and his luck, and the army of Licinius was thrown

into confusion and disorganized while Constantine was slightly wounded in the thigh. (25) Licinius, fleeing from there, sought Byzantium; and while his scattered forces tried to reach him, Licinius, having closed Byzantium, prepared for a siege on the landward side, feeling secure to seaward. But Constantine put together a fleet out of Thrace. Then, with his usual foolishness, Licinius made Martinianus Caesar. (26) But Crispus, with Constantine's fleet, reached Callipolis, and there he conquered Amandus in a sea battle so comprehensively that the latter was scarcely able to escape alive with the help of those who had stayed on shore. Licinius's fleet was either destroyed or captured. (27) Licinius, abandoning hope of the sea, by which he saw that he would be blockaded, fled to Chalcedon with his treasure. Constantine, having met up with Crispus and heard of his sea victory, invaded Byzantium. Then Licinius staged a battle at Chrysopolis, greatly aided by the Goths whom their ruler Alica had brought: Constantine's force was victorious and destroyed 25,000 armed men of the other side, while the rest took to flight. (28) Then, when they saw Constantine's legions coming in troopships, they threw down their weapons and gave themselves up. On the following day, Constantia, sister of Constantine and wife of Licinius, came to her brother's camp and begged for her husband's life, which he granted. Then Licinius was made a private citizen and entertained at a feast by Constantine, and Martinianus's life was conceded to him.

(29) Licinius was sent to Thessalonica, but Constantine was influenced by the example of his father-in-law Herculius Maximianus, and lest he should assume again the purple he had laid down, to the danger of the state, he ordered Licinius to be killed, as the soldiers of Thessalonica hotly demanded, and likewise Martinianus in Cappadocia. Licinius had ruled for nineteen years and left a wife and son behind him. Although all the participants in the dreadful persecution were already dead, this man was also clearly asking for punishment, who had been a persecutor as far as he was able to.

6 (30) Constantine, in memory of his famous victory, called Byzantium Constantinople, after himself.

As if it were his native city, he enriched it with great assiduity and wanted it to become the equal of Rome. He sought out citizens for it from everywhere and lavished so much wealth on it that he almost exhausted the resources of the imperial treasury. There he founded a Senate of the second rank; the members were called *clari.*

(31) Then he took up arms against the Goths and gave assistance to the Sarmatians, who had begged for it. Thus, through Constantine Caesar, nearly 100,000 died of starvation and cold. Then he accepted hostages, among whom was Ariaric, son of the king. (32) Thus, when peace had been confirmed, he turned against the Sarmatians, who had proved to be of doubtful loyalty. But all the slaves of the Sarmatians rebelled against their masters, and when the latter had been expelled, Constantine willingly accepted them and distributed more than 300,000 people of all ages and both sexes throughout Thrace, Scythia, Macedonia, and Italy.

(33) This Constantine was the first Christian emperor except for Philip (the Arab) who, as it seems to me, became Christian simply in order that the thousandth year of Rome might be said to belong to Christ rather than to idols. From Constantine up to the present day, all the emperors have been Christians, with the exception of Julian, whose impious life left him in the middle of what he is said to have been plotting.

(34) Constantine made the change with due order and care. He issued an edict that the temples of the pagans should be closed without any loss of life.

Soon after, he destroyed that most powerful and numerous race, the Goths, in the very bosom of barbarian territory—that is, in the land of the Sarmatians.

(35) He destroyed a certain Calocaerus, who aspired to a revolution in Cyprus.

He made Dalmatius, son of his brother Dalmatius, a Caesar. He gave Dalmatius's brother Hannibalianus to his daughter Constantia and made him King of Kings and ruler of the peoples of Pontica. Then he ordained that Constantine the younger should rule the Gauls, Constantius Caesar the Oriens, Constans should rule Illyricum and Italy, and Dalmatius should protect the Gothic shore.

While Constantine was preparing to make war on Persia, he ended his days in an imperial villa on the outskirts of Constantinople, near Nicomedia, handing on a well-organized state to his sons. He had ruled for thirty-one years and was buried in Constantinople.

4. Eusebius: The Life of Constantine

Eusebius (ca. 260–ca. 339), bishop of Caesarea in Palestine, is best known as the "father of Christian history" because of his highly influential *Church History* (see an excerpt in Text 50). He portrayed himself as an ecclesiastical spokesperson for Constantine's house, although it is unclear how well he knew the first Christian emperor personally. He wrote the laudatory *Life of Constantine* shortly after Constantine's death. The work contains elements of a typical imperial biography: the relation between Constantine's upright character and the economic, military, and political revitalization of the empire (cf. Text 3, "The Origin of Constantine"). It is also a religious history; the triumph of Christianity is part of Constantine's own religious awakening (cf. Text 2, Lactantius's "The Deaths of the Persecutors"). This text also hints at a Christian genre that had not yet taken shape in Eusebius's day: hagiography (see Chapter 11). Constantine the holy man is, like Moses, the prophets, and the apostles, a divinely guided figure.

The following selections from the *Life of Constantine* show how Eusebius blends imperial biography with sacred history. Constantine's imperial election in the West is confirmed and enabled by God's direct assistance (including the famous vision of the cross-shaped *labarum,* or "Chi-Rho," with the words: "By this conquer"). As sole emperor, Constantine actively constructs a Christian empire, building the holy land through magnificent churches. Eusebius portrays Constantine as a legislator Christianizing the empire, as well as uniting the church under imperial control. This image of Constantine as paradigmatic Christian emperor would remain influential in both the eastern and western empires, emerging in models of "sacred kingship" in the West and in the tight link between Byzantine emperors and Orthodox bishops in the East.

BOOK ONE

22 (1) The empire, however, was not left ungoverned. Arrayed in his father's own purple robe, Constantine emerged from his father's halls, showing to one and all that, as though revived, his father reigned through him. Then he led the cortège, and with his father's friends about him, he formed the escort for his father. Enormous crowds of people and military guards, some before and some following behind, attended the Godbeloved in full state. All of them honored the Thriceblessed with acclamations and laudations and, with unanimous consent, praised the accession of the son as a new life for the dead; and immediately from the first word in their cries of acclamation they proclaimed the new Emperor Imperator and Venerable

From *Eusebius' Life of Constantine: Introduction, Translation, and Commentary,* trans. and ed. Averil Cameron and Stuart G. Hall. Oxford, England: Clarendon Press, 1999. Used with permission.

Augustus. (2) They lauded the deceased with their acclamations for the son, and they blessed the son as appointed to succeed such a father; all the provinces under his rule were full of happiness and unutterable joy because not even for the briefest moment had they been deprived of orderly imperial rule. This was the end of a pious and devout life that God displayed to our generation in the case of the Emperor Constantius.

23 As to the others who used the methods of war to persecute the churches of God, I have decided that it is not proper to report the way their lives ended in the present account or to stain the record of good deeds by presenting their contrary. Experience of the events is sober warning enough to those whose own eyes and ears have known the story of what happened to each one.

24 In such a way, then, did God, the President of the whole world, of his own will select Constantine, sprung from such a father, as universal ruler and governor, that no man could claim the precedence that he alone possessed, since the rest owed the rank they held to election by others.

25 (1) Once he was established in imperial power, he first attended to the needs of his father's portion, supervising with loving care all the provinces that had previously been allotted to his father's government; if any barbarian tribes living beside the River Rhine and the Western Ocean dared to rebel, he subdued them all and turned their savagery to gentleness, while others he repulsed and chased off his territory like wild beasts, when he saw that they were incurably resistant to change to a gentle life.

(2) When these things were settled to his satisfaction, he turned his attention to the other parts of the inhabited world and first crossed to the British nations, which lie enclosed by the edge of Ocean; he brought them to terms and then surveyed the other parts of the world, so that he might bring healing where help was needed. **26** When he then perceived that the whole earthly element was like a great body and next became aware that the head of the whole, the imperial city of the Roman Empire, lay oppressed by bondage to a tyrant, he first gave opportunity for those who governed the other parts to rescue it, inas-

much as they were senior in years, but when none of these was able to give aid and even those who did make the attempt had met a shameful end, he declared that his life was not worth living if he were to allow the imperial city to remain in such a plight and began preparations to overthrow the tyranny.

27 (1) Knowing well that he would need more powerful aid than an army can supply because of the mischievous magical devices practiced by the tyrant, he sought a god to aid him. He regarded the resources of soldiers and military numbers as secondary, for he thought that without the aid of a god, these could achieve nothing, and he said that what comes from a god's assistance is irresistible and invincible. (2) He therefore considered what kind of god he should adopt to aid him, and while he thought, a clear impression came to him, that of the many who had in the past aspired to government, those who had attached their personal hopes to many gods, and had cultivated them with drink offerings, sacrifices, and dedications, had first been deceived by favorable predictions and oracles that promised welcome things, but then met an unwelcome end, nor did any god stand at their side to protect them from divinely directed disaster; only his own father had taken the opposite course to theirs by condemning their error, while he himself had throughout his life honored the God who transcends the universe and had found him a savior and guardian of his Empire and a provider of everything good. (3) He judiciously considered these things for himself and weighed well how those who had confided in a multitude of gods had run into multiple destruction, so that neither offspring nor shoot was left in them, no root, neither name nor memorial among mankind, whereas his father's God had bestowed on his father manifest and numerous tokens of his power. He also pondered carefully those who had already campaigned against the tyrant. They had assembled their forces with a multitude of gods and had come to a dismal end: one of them had retreated in disgrace without striking a blow, while the other had met a casual death by assassination in his own camp. He marshaled these arguments in his mind and concluded that it was folly to go on with the vanity of the gods that do not exist and to persist in error in the face of so much evidence, and he decided he should venerate his father's God alone.

28 (1) This God he began to invoke in prayer, beseeching and imploring him to show him who he was and to stretch out his right hand to assist him in his plans. As he made these prayers and earnest supplications, there appeared to the emperor a most remarkable divine sign. If someone else had reported it, it would perhaps not be easy to accept, but since the victorious emperor himself told the story to the present writer a long while after, when I was privileged with his acquaintance and company, and confirmed it with oaths, who could hesitate to believe the account, especially when the time that followed provided evidence for the truth of what he said? (2) About the time of the midday sun, when day was just turning, he said he saw with his own eyes, up in the sky and resting over the sun, a cross-shaped trophy formed from light and a text attached to it that said, "By this conquer." Amazement at the spectacle seized both him and the whole company of soldiers, which was then accompanying him on a campaign he was conducting somewhere, and witnessed the miracle.

29 He was, he said, wondering to himself what the manifestation might mean; then, while he meditated, and thought long and hard, night overtook him. Thereupon, as he slept, the Christ of God appeared to him with the sign that had appeared in the sky and urged him to make himself a copy of the sign that had appeared in the sky and to use this as protection against the attacks of the enemy. **30** When day came, he arose and recounted the mysterious communication to his friends. Then he summoned goldsmiths and jewelers, sat down among them, and explained the shape of the sign and gave them instructions about copying it in gold and precious stones.

This was something that the emperor himself once saw fit to let me also set eyes on, God vouchsafing even this. **31** (1) It was constructed to the following design. A tall pole plated with gold had a transverse bar forming the shape of a cross. Up at the extreme top, a wreath woven of precious stones and gold had been fastened. On it two letters, intimating by its first characters the name "Christ," formed the monogram of the Savior's title, *rho* being intersected in the middle by *chi*. These letters the emperor also used to wear upon his helmet in later times. (2) From the transverse bar, which was bisected by the pole, hung suspended a cloth, an imperial tapestry covered with a pattern of precious stones fastened together, which glittered with shafts of light, and interwoven with much gold, producing an impression of indescribable beauty on those who saw it. This banner, then, attached to the bar, was given equal dimensions of length and breadth. But the upright pole, which extended upward a long way from its lower end, below the trophy of the cross and near the top of the tapestry delineated, carried the golden head-and-shoulders portrait of the Godbeloved emperor and likewise of his sons. (3) This saving sign was always used by the emperor for protection against every opposing and hostile force, and he commanded replicas of it to lead all his armies.

32 (1) That was, however, somewhat later. At the time in question, stunned by the amazing vision and determined to worship no other god than the one who had appeared, he summoned those expert in his words and inquired who this god was and what was the explanation of the vision that had appeared of the sign. (2) They said that the god was the Onlybegotten Son of the one and only God and that the sign that appeared was a token of immortality and was an abiding trophy of the victory over death, which he had once won when he was present on earth. They began to teach him the reasons for his coming, explaining to him in detail the story of his self-accommodation to human conditions. (3) He listened attentively to these accounts, too, while he marveled at the divine manifestation that had been granted to his eyes; comparing the heavenly vision with the meaning of what was being said, he made up his mind, convinced that it was as God's own teaching that the knowledge of these things had come to him. He now decided personally to apply himself to the divinely inspired writings. Taking the priests of God as his advisers, he also deemed it right to honor the God who had appeared to him with all due rites. Thereafter, fortified by good hopes in him, he finally set about extinguishing the menacing flames of tyranny.

33 (1) Indeed, the one who had thus previously seized the imperial city was busily engaged in abominable and sacrilegious activities, so that he left no outrage undone in his foul and filthy behavior. He parted lawful wives from husbands, and after misusing them quite disgracefully, returned them to their husbands. He did this not to obscure or insignificant persons, but insolently to those who held the highest positions in the Roman Senate. So he misused disgracefully innumerable freeborn women, yet found no way to satisfy his unrestrained and insatiable appetite. (2) But when he turned his hand also to Christian women, he was no longer able to devise convenient means for his adulteries. They would sooner yield their life to him for execution than their body for immoral use. **34** One woman, the wife of one of the senators with the office of prefect, when she learned that those who procured such things for the tyrant had arrived—she was a Christian—and knew that her own husband out of fear had ordered them to seize her and take her away, having requested a little time to put on her customary attire, went into her room and once alone plunged a dagger into her breast. Dying at once, she left her body to the procurers, but by her actions, which spoke louder than any words, she showed to all mankind, both present and future, that the only thing that is invincible and indestructible is the chastity acclaimed among Christians. Such then did she prove to be.

35 (1) Before the one who committed such outrages all men cowered, peoples and princes, high and low, and were worn down by savage tyranny. Even if they kept quiet and endured the harsh servitude, there was still no respite from the tyrant's murderous cruelty. On one occasion on a slight pretext he gave the people over to slaughter by his escorting guards, and there were killed countless multitudes of the people of Rome right in the middle of the city, by the weapons and arms, not of Goths or barbarians, but of their own countrymen. (2) The number of senators whose murder was encompassed as a means to acquire each one's property it would not be possible to calculate, since thousands were put to death, sometimes on one fictitious charge, sometimes on another. **36** (1) At their peak the tyrant's crimes extended to witchcraft, as for magical purposes he split open pregnant women, sometimes searched the entrails of

newborn babies, slaughtered lions, and composed secret spells to conjure demons and to ward off hostilities. By these means he hoped he would gain the victory. (2) Ruling by these dictatorial methods in Rome, he imposed on his subjects unspeakable oppression, so that he brought them finally to the utmost scarcity and want of necessary food, such as our generation never remembers happening in Rome at any other time.

37 (1) Constantine meanwhile was moved to pity by all these things and began making every armed preparation against the tyranny. So taking as his patron God who is over all, and invoking his Christ as savior and succor, and having set the victorious trophy, the truly salutary sign, at the head of his escorting soldiers and guards, he led them in full force, claiming for the Romans their ancestral liberties. (2) Maxentius put his confidence more in the devices of sorcery than in the loyalty of his subjects and did not even dare to go beyond the gates of the city, but fortified every place and territory and city that was under his dominion with an immense number of soldiers and countless military units. But the emperor who relied upon the support of God attacked the first, second, and third formations of the tyrant, overcame them all quite easily at the very first onslaught, and advanced to occupy most of the land of Italy.

38 (1) He was now very near to Rome itself. Then, so that he should not be forced because of the tyrant to fight against the people of Rome, God himself drew the tyrant out, as if with chains, far away from the gates, and those ancient words against the wicked, widely disbelieved as mere legend, though in sacred books believably recorded for believers, by his divine actions he proved to be true for every single eye that saw his marvels, believing and unbelieving alike. (2) Accordingly, just as once in the time of Moses and the devout Hebrew tribe "Pharaoh's chariots and his force he cast into the sea, and picked rider-captains he overwhelmed in the Red Sea" (Exod 15:4), in the very same way Maxentius and the armed men and guards about him "sank to the bottom like a stone" (Exod 15:5), when, fleeing before the force that came from God with Constantine, he went to cross the river lying in his path. When he himself joined its banks with boats and bridged it perfectly well, he had built an engine of destruction for himself, intending thus to catch the friend of God. (3) But the latter had his God present at his right hand, while Maxentius constructed in his cowardice the secret engines of his own destruction. Of him it could also be said that "he dug a hole and excavated it, and will fall into the pit he made. His labor will return on his head, and on his pate will his wickedness fall" (Ps 7:15–16). (4) Thus then by God's will the mechanism in the link and the device concealed in it gave way at a time that was not intended, the crossing parted, and the boats sank at once to the bottom with all their men, the coward himself first of all, and then the infantry and guards about him, just as the divine oracles had previously proclaimed: "They sank like lead in much water" (Exod 15:10). (5) So even if not in words, yet surely in deeds, in the same way as those who accompanied the great Servant Moses, these who won this victory from God might be thought thus to have raised the same hymn against the ancient wicked tyrant and said: "Let us sing to the Lord, for he is gloriously glorified; horse and rider he threw into the sea; he became a succor and shelter for my salvation" (Exod 15:1–2); and, "Who is like you among the gods, Lord, who is like you? Glorified among the saints, wonderful, gloriously doing miracles" (Exod 15:11).

39 (1) These and other praises akin to them Constantine expressed in deeds to the universal Captain, the timely Giver of his victory, in the same way as the great Servant, and then rode in triumph into the imperial city. (2) Immediately all the members of the Senate and the other persons there of fame and distinction, as if released from a cage, and all the people of Rome, gave him a bright-eyed welcome with spontaneous acclamations and unbounded joy. Men with their wives and children and countless numbers of slaves with unrestrained cheers pronounced him their redeemer, savior, and benefactor. (3) He, however, being possessed of inward fear of God, was not inflated by their cries nor overexuberant at their praises, but was conscious of the help of God; so he immediately offered up a prayer of thanksgiving to the Giver of his victory. **40** (1) He announced to all people in large lettering and inscriptions the sign of the Savior,

setting this up in the middle of the imperial city as a great trophy of victory over his enemies, explicitly inscribing this in indelible letters as the salvific sign of the authority of Rome and the protection of the whole empire. (2) He therefore immediately ordered a tall pole to be erected in the shape of a cross in the hand of a statue made to represent-himself, and this text to be inscribed upon it word for word in Latin: "By this salutary sign, the true proof of valor, I liberated your city, saved from the tyrant's yoke; moreover the Senate and People of Rome I liberated and restored to their ancient splendor and brilliance."

41 (1) The Godbeloved emperor, proudly confessing in this way the victory-bringing cross, was entirely open in making the Son of God known to the Romans. (2) All the city's population together, including the Senate and all the people, as they recovered from bitter tyrannical repression, seemed to be enjoying beams of purer light and to be participating in rebirth to a fresh new life. All the nations that bordered on the Ocean where the sun sets, set free from the evils that formerly oppressed them, kept rejoicing in happy gatherings as they hymned the mighty Victor, the Godfearing, the general Benefactor, and with one single voice they all acknowledged the common good of mankind, which by God's grace had dawned in Constantine.

(3) An imperial letter was also published everywhere, granting the enjoyment of their goods to those whose property had been confiscated and recalling to their own homes those who had suffered unjust exile. It also released from imprisonment and every kind of liability or threat at law those subjected to them by the tyrant's savagery.

42 (1) The emperor personally called together the ministers of God, regarding them honorably and cherishing them with highest consideration, since he favored those men by deed and word as consecrated to his God. Thus he had as his table companions men whose appearance was modest as to style of dress, but by no means modest in the consideration he gave them, because he thought he should have regard not to the man as most people see him but to the God honored in each. He took them with him also wherever he set out on campaign, trusting that in this, too, the one they worshipped would be present at his right hand. (2) Indeed he also supplied rich help from his own resources to the churches of God, enlarging and elevating the places of worship, while beautifying the grander ecclesiastical sacred buildings with many dedications.

43 (1) He made all sorts of distributions to the poor, and apart from them showed himself compassionate and beneficent to those outside who approached him. For some poor desperate wretches who publicly solicited alms he would provide not only money or necessary food, but decent clothing for the body. For those who were originally of higher birth but had run on hard times, he made more generous provision, with imperial magnanimity providing munificent benefactions to such persons: to some he made grants of land, others he promoted to various offices. (2) Those unfortunate enough to be orphaned he cared for in the father's stead and repaired the vulnerability of widowhood for women by personal concern, so far as to find them husbands from his acquaintance, and rich men for orphaned girls deprived of parents. He managed this by supplementing the dowry needed for the brides to bring to those who were receiving them in the bond of marriage. (3) Just as the sun rises and spreads the beams of its light over all, so also Constantine shone forth with the rising sun from the imperial palace, as though ascending with the heavenly luminary, and shed upon all who came before his face the sunbeams of his own generous goodness. It was not possible to come near him without receiving some benefit, nor would the good hopes of those who looked to him for support ever be disappointed.

44 (1) Toward all people in general he was such a man. But to the Church of God he paid particular personal attention. When some were at variance with each other in various places, like a universal bishop appointed by God he convoked councils of the ministers of God. (2) He did not disdain to be present and attend during their proceedings, and he participated in the subjects reviewed, by arbitration promoting the peace of God among all, and he took his seat among them as if he were one voice among many, dismissing his praetorians and soldiers and bodyguards of every kind, clad only in the fear of God and sur-

rounded by the most loyal of his faithful companions. (3) Then such as he saw able to be prevailed upon by argument and adopting a calm and conciliatory attitude, he commended most warmly, showing how he favored general unanimity, but the obstinate he rejected. **45** (1) There were even some who spoke harshly against him, and he tolerated them without resentment, with a gentle voice bidding them to behave reasonably and not be contentious. Some of them respected his rebukes and desisted, while those who were past curing and could not be brought to a sound mind he left in the hands of God, being unwilling himself to devise anything whatever to any person's hurt.

(2) For this reason it came about that those in Africa reached such a pitch of dissension that crimes were committed, some evil demon apparently resenting the unstinted present prosperity and driving those men on to criminal actions, in order to provoke the emperor's fury against them. (3) His envy however did not prosper: the emperor treated what was being done as ridiculous and said he understood the provocation of the Evil One; the crimes were not done by sane men, but by those either out of their minds or goaded to frenzy by the evil demon; they ought to be pitied rather than punished; he was in no way harmed by their lunatic folly, except in so far as he felt pain for them out of extreme kindness of heart.

46 Thus then the emperor, serving God the overseer of all with his every action, took untiring care of his churches. God repaid him by putting all the barbarian nations beneath his feet, so that always and everywhere he raised trophies over his foes, and by proclaiming him Victor among them all and making him a terror to foes and enemies, though he was not naturally such, but the gentlest, mildest, and kindest man there ever was.

47 (1) While he was thus engaged, the second of those who had retired from power was caught organizing an assassination plot and met a shameful death. He was the first whose honorific inscriptions and statues and whatever else of the kind had been accorded him anywhere in the world to acknowledge his rank were removed because of his profane impiety. (2) After him others of the same family were caught organizing secret conspiracies against him, God miraculously disclosing the plots of all these to his servant by supernatural signs. (3) Indeed, he often vouchsafed him manifestations of deity, when divine visions were miraculously displayed to him and provided him with all sorts of foreknowledge of future events. It is not possible to describe in words those unspeakable marvels from God's grace that God himself saw fit to bestow on his servant. (4) By these he was safely hedged about to the end as he lived his life, pleased at the loyalty of his subjects, and pleased also that he saw all those under him passing their lives in contentment and utterly overjoyed at the happiness of the churches of God.

48 Such was he until the tenth anniversary of his accession was reached. For that he celebrated popular festivals everywhere and offered up prayers of thanksgiving to God the King of all like sacrifices without fire and smoke. . . .

BOOK THREE

25 Such was the situation when another memorable work of great importance was done in the province of Palestine by the Godbeloved. It was this. He decided that he ought to make universally famous and revered the most blessed site in Jerusalem of the Savior's resurrection. So at once he gave orders for a place of worship to be constructed, conceiving this idea not without God, but with his spirit moved by the Savior himself.

26 (1) Once upon a time wicked men—or rather the whole tribe of demons through them—had striven to consign to darkness and oblivion that divine monument to immortality, at which, brilliant with light, the angel who had descended from heaven had rolled away the stone of those whose minds were set like stone in their assumption that the Living One was still with the dead, when he announced the good news to the women and removed the stone of disbelief from their minds by the information that the one they sought was alive. (2) It was this very cave of the Savior that some godless and wicked people had planned to make invisible to mankind, thinking in

their stupidity that they could in this way hide the truth. Indeed with a great expenditure of effort they brought earth from somewhere outside and covered up the whole place, then leveled it, paved it, and so hid the divine cave somewhere down beneath a great quantity of soil. (3) Then as though they had everything finished, above the ground they constructed a terrible and truly genuine tomb, one for souls, for dead idols, and built a gloomy sanctuary to the impure demon of Aphrodite; then they offered foul sacrifices there upon defiled and polluted altars. They reckoned there was one way alone and no other to bring their desires to realization, and that was to bury the Savior's cave under such foul pollutions. (4) The wretches could not understand that it would be against nature for the one who had crowned his brow with the conquest of death to leave his accomplishment hidden. No more could the sun remain unnoticed by the whole world inhabited by man, as it shines after rising above the earth and drives its proper chariot course across the sky; but brighter than this the Savior's power as it illuminates the souls, though not the bodies, of men was filling the entire world with his own beams of light.

(5) Nevertheless the devices of these godless and wicked men against truth lasted for long ages, and no one was ever found—no governor, no commander, no emperor even—competent to clear away what had been perpetrated but one alone, the friend of God the universal King. (6) Possessed therefore by the divine Spirit, he did not negligently allow that place that has been described to remain smothered by all sorts of filthy rubbish through the machination of enemies consigned to oblivion and ignorance, nor did he yield to the malice of the guilty; but calling upon God to be his collaborator, he ordered it to be cleared, thinking that the very space that enemies had sullied should especially benefit from the great work being done through him by the All-good. (7) At a word of command those contrivances of fraud were demolished from top to bottom, and the houses of error were dismantled and destroyed along with their idols and demons.

27 His efforts however did not stop there, but the emperor gave further orders that all the rubble of stones and timbers from the demolitions should be taken and dumped a long way from the site. This command also was soon effected. But not even this progress was by itself enough, but under divine inspiration once more the emperor gave instructions that the site should be excavated to a great depth and the pavement should be carried away with the rubble a long distance outside because it was stained with demonic bloodshed. **28** This also was completed straightaway. As stage by stage the underground site was exposed, at last against all expectation the revered and all-hallowed Testimony (*martyrion*) of the Savior's resurrection was itself revealed, and the cave, the holy of holies, took on the appearance of a representation of the Savior's return to life. Thus after its descent into darkness, it came forth again to the light, and it enabled those who came as visitors to see plainly the story of the wonders wrought there, testifying by facts louder than any voice to the resurrection of the Savior.

29 (1) With these things thus completed, the emperor next gave orders by the stipulations of pious laws and by generous grants for a place of worship worthy of God to be built with rich and imperial munificence around the Savior's cave, as if he had intended this for a long time and had looked into the future with superior foreknowledge. (2) He instructed those who governed the eastern provinces by generous and lavish grants to make the building out of the ordinary, huge, and rich, and to the bishop of the church who then presided in Jerusalem, he sent the following document. By it he displayed in clear terms the love for God in his own soul and the purity of his faith in the Savior's Word, writing in this fashion:

30 (1) *Victor Constantinus Maximus Augustus to Macarius.*

So great is our Savior's grace, that no words seem enough to match the present miracle. For the evidence of his most sacred passion, long since hidden under the ground, to have remained unknown for such a long period of years, until through the removal of the enemy of the whole republic it was ready to be revealed, once they were set free, to his servants, truly surpasses all marvels. (2) *If all those from every part of the world with a reputation for wisdom were*

to gather together in one place and ⸍ thing worthy of the event, they wou⸍ compete with the least part of it. The evide⸍. miracle surpasses every natural capacity of hu⸍. thought in the same degree that heavenly things are by common consent mightier than human. (3) *That is why it is always my first and only goal, that, just as the evidence for the truth manifests itself with newer wonders every day, so all our souls may by utter seriousness and unanimous endeavor also become more earnest about the holy law.* (4) *The thing therefore which I consider clear to everybody is what I want you in particular to believe, namely, that above all else my concern is that that sacred place, which at God's command I have now relieved of the hideous burden of an idol that lay on it like a weight, hallowed from the start by God's decree, and now proved yet holier since it brought to light the pledge of the Savior's passion, should be adorned by us with beautiful buildings.*

31 (1) *It is thus for your own Good Sense to make such order and provision of what is needed that not only a basilica superior to those in all other places, but the other arrangements also, may be such that all the excellences of every city are surpassed by this foundation.* (2) *As to the building and decoration of the walls, be advised that our friend Dracillianus, who exercises his office among the* praefecti illustrissimi, *and he who is governor of the province have been entrusted by us with its care. For my Religious Care has ordered that craftsmen and laborers and everything they may learn from your Good Sense to be needed for the building work should forthwith be supplied by their provision.* (3) *As to the columns or marble, you should after a survey yourself write promptly to us about what you may consider to be of most value and use, so that whatever quantity and kind of materials we may learn from your letter to be needful may be competently supplied from all sources. It is right that the world's most miraculous place should be worthily embellished.* **32** (1) *As to the vault of the basilica, whether you decide that it be coffered or in another style of construction I would wish to learn from you. If it were to be coffered, it might also be decorated with gold.* (2) *In short, in* *order that your Holiness may make known with all speed to the aforementioned magistrates how many laborers and craftsmen and what other expenditures are required, take care to refer immediately also to me not only the matters of the marble and pillars, but also the lacunary panels, should you judge that best.*

God preserve you, dear Brother.

33 (1) Thus did the emperor write. No sooner had he written than the commands were put into effect. New Jerusalem was built at the very Testimony to the Savior, facing the famous Jerusalem of old, which after the bloody murder of the Lord had been overthrown in utter devastation, and paid the penalty of its wicked inhabitants. (2) Opposite this then the emperor erected the victory of the Savior over death with rich and abundant munificence, this being perhaps that fresh new Jerusalem proclaimed in prophetic oracles, about which long speeches recite innumerable praises as they utter words of divine inspiration.

(3) As the principal item he first of all decked out the sacred cave. It was a tomb full of agelong memory, comprising the trophies of the great Savior's defeat of death, a tomb of divine presence, where once an angel, radiant with light, proclaimed to all the good news of the rebirth demonstrated by the Savior. **34** This then was the first thing, like a head of the whole, which the emperor's munificence decorated with superb columns and full ornamentation, brightening the solemn cave with all kinds of artwork. **35** He then went on to a very large space wide open to the fresh air, which was decorated with a pavement of light-colored stone on the ground, and enclosed on three sides by long surrounding colonnades.

36 (1) On the side opposite the cave, which looked toward the rising sun, was connected the royal temple, an extraordinary structure raised to an immense height and very extensive in length and breadth. Its interior was covered with slabs of varied marble, and the external aspect of the walls, gleaming with hewn stone fitted closely together at each joint, produced a supreme object of beauty by no means inferior to marble. (2) Right up at the top the material that encased the outside of the roofs was lead, a sure protection against stormy rain, while the interior of the

structure was fitted with carved coffers and like a vast sea spread out by a series of joints binding to each other through the whole royal house, and being beautified throughout with brilliant gold made the whole shrine glitter with beams of light. **37** Round each of the sides extended twin ranges of double colonnades, in upper and lower stories, their tops also decorated with gold. Those at the front of the house rested upon huge pillars, while those inside the front were raised under blocks plentifully decorated all round their surfaces. Three doors well placed to face the sunrise received the crowds flowing in. **38** Facing these as the chief point of the whole was the hemisphere attached to the highest part of the royal house, ringed with twelve columns to match the number of the Apostles of the Savior, their tops decorated with great bowls made of silver, which the emperor himself had presented to his God as a superb offering.

39 For those going on from there to the entrances situated at the front of the shrine, another open space awaited them. Arcades stood there on either hand, a first court and colonnades beyond, and finally the gates of the court. Beyond these, right in the middle of the open square, the porticoes forming the entrance to the whole, beautifully wrought, offered to those passing outside a striking view of what was to be seen within.

40 This, then, was the shrine that the emperor raised as a manifest testimony of the Savior's resurrection, embellishing the whole with rich imperial decoration. He adorned it with untold beauties in innumerable dedications of gold and silver and precious stones set in various materials. In view of their size, number, and variety, to describe in detail the skilled craftsmanship that went into their manufacture would be beyond the scope of the present work.

41 (1) He took in hand here other sites venerated for their two mystic caves, and he adorned these also with rich artwork. On the cave of the first divine manifestation of the Savior, where he submitted to the experience of birth in the flesh, he bestowed appropriate honors, while at the other he dignified the monument on the mountaintop to his ascension into heaven. (2) These also he artistically honored, perpetuating the memory of his own mother, who had bestowed so much good on human life. **42** (1) This lady, when she made it her business to pay what piety owed to the all-sovereign God and considered that she ought to complete in prayers her thank-offerings for her son, so great an emperor, and his sons the most Godbeloved Caesars her grandchildren, came, though old, with the eagerness of youth to apply her outstanding intellect to enquiring about the wondrous land and to inspect with imperial concern the eastern provinces with their communities and peoples. (2) As she accorded suitable adoration to the footsteps of the Savior, following the prophetic word that says, "Let us adore in the place where his feet have stood" (Ps 132:7), she forthwith bequeathed to her successors also the fruit of her personal piety.

43 (1) She immediately consecrated to the God she adored two shrines, one by the cave of his birth, the other on the mountain of the ascension. For the God with us allowed himself to suffer even birth for our sake, and the place of his birth in the flesh was announced among the Hebrews by the name of Bethlehem. (2) Thus then the most devout empress beautified the Godbearer's pregnancy with wonderful monuments, in various ways embellishing the sacred cave there. The emperor himself shortly afterward honored this, too, with imperial dedications, supplementing his mother's works of art with treasures of silver and gold and embroidered curtains. (3) Again the emperor's mother erected on the Mount of Olives the monument to the journey into heaven of the Savior of the Universe in lofty buildings; up by the ridges at the peak of the whole mountain she raised the sacred house of the church and constructed just there a shrine for prayer to the Savior who chose to spend his time on that spot, since just there a true report maintains that in that cave the Savior of the Universe initiated the members of his guild in ineffable mysteries. (4) There also the emperor bestowed all kinds of offerings and ornaments on the great King.

These then were the two everlastingly memorable, noble, and utterly beautiful dedications to her Savior at two mystic caves, which Helena Augusta, the Godbeloved mother of the Godbeloved emperor, founded as tokens of her pious intent, her son providing her with the right arm of imperial authority. (5) But the

lady not long after reaped the due reward. She had traversed a whole lifespan amid everything good to the very portal of old age; by words and deeds she had produced luxurious growth from the Savior's commandments; and then she had completed in full vigor of mind a life so orderly and calm in both body and soul, that as a result she also met an end worthy of her religion and a good reward from God even in this present life.

44 As she visited the whole East in the magnificence of imperial authority, she showered countless gifts upon the citizen bodies of every city and privately to each of those who approached her, and she made countless distributions also to the ranks of the soldiery with magnificent hand. She made innumerable gifts to the unclothed and unsupported poor, to some making gifts of money, to others abundantly supplying what was needed to cover the body. Others she set free from prison and from mines where they labored in harsh conditions, she released the victims of fraud, and yet others she recalled from exile. **45** Brilliantly though she shone in such things, she did not despise the other aspects of devotion to God. She allowed herself to be seen continually making personal visits to the church of God. She adorned the places of worship with shining treasures, not neglecting the shrines in even the smallest of towns. One might see the wonderful woman in dignified and modest attire joining the throng and manifesting reverence toward the divinity by every kind of practice dear to God.

46 (1) When she had finally completed the course of a long-enough life and was called to the higher sphere, having lived to something like 80 years of age, when she was very near the end she made arrangements and dispositions, drawing up her last will in favor of her only son the emperor, the monarch and world-ruler, and his sons the Caesars, her own grandchildren, bequeathing to each of her issue part of her estate, everything she possessed in the whole world. (2) Having settled her affairs in this way, she finally came to the end of her life. So great a son was present and stood by her, ministering and holding her hands, so as to make it seem likely to right-thinking people that the thrice-blessed one was not dead, but had in reality undergone a transformation and removal from earthly life to heavenly. Her very soul was thus reconstituted into an incorruptible and angelic essence as she was taken up to her Savior. **47** (1) Even the temporal dwelling of the blessed one deserved no ordinary care, so with a great guard of honor she was carried up to the imperial city, and there laid in the imperial tombs.

Thus passed away the emperor's mother, one worthy of unfading memory both for her own Godloving deeds and for those of the extraordinary and astonishing offspring that arose from her. (2) He deserves to be blessed, all else apart, for his piety to the one who bore him. So far had he made her Godfearing, though she had not been such before, that she seemed to him to have been a disciple of the common Savior from the first, and so far had he honored her with imperial rank that she was acclaimed in all nations and by the military ranks as *Augusta Imperatrix,* and her portrait was stamped on gold coinage. (3) He even remitted to her authority over imperial treasuries, to use them at will and to manage them at her discretion, in whatever way she might wish and however she might judge best in each case, her son having accorded her distinction and eminence in these matters, too. It was therefore right that while recording his memory, we should also record those things wherein, by honoring his mother for her supreme piety, he satisfied the divine principles that impose the duty of honoring parents. . . .

BOOK FOUR

14 (1) Thus finally, all nations of the world being steered by a single pilot and welcoming government by the Servant of God, with none any longer obstructing Roman rule, all men passed their life in undisturbed tranquillity.

(2) The emperor judged that the prayers of the godly made a great contribution to his aim of protecting the general good, so he made the necessary provision for these, becoming himself a suppliant of God and bidding the leaders of the churches make intercessions for him. **15** (1) The great strength of the divinely inspired faith fixed in his soul might be deduced by considering also the fact that he had his own portrait so depicted on the gold coinage that he appeared to look upward in the manner of one reaching out to God in prayer. (2) Impressions of this type were circulated throughout the entire Roman world. In the imperial quarters of various cities, in the images erected above the entrances, he was portrayed standing up, looking up to heaven, his hands extended in a posture of prayer. **16** Such was the way he would have himself depicted praying in works of graphic art. But by law he forbade images of himself to be set up in idol-shrines, so that he might not be contaminated by the error of forbidden things even in replica.

17 One might observe the more solemn aspects of these things by noting how he conducted matters even in the imperial quarters in the manner of a church of God, being himself the leader in earnestness of those constituting the church there. He would take the books in his hands and apply his mind to the meaning of the divinely inspired oracles and would then render up lawful prayers with the members of the imperial household. **18** (1) He also decreed that the truly sovereign and really first day, the day of the Lord and Savior, should be considered a regular day of prayer. Servants and ministers consecrated to God, men whose well-ordered life was marked by reverent conduct and every virtue, were put in charge of the whole household, and faithful praetorians, bodyguards armed with the practice of faithful loyalty, adopted the emperor as their tutor in religious conduct, themselves paying no less honor to the Lord's saving day and on it joining in the prayers the emperor loved.

(2) The Blessed One urged all men also to do the same, as if by encouraging this he might gently bring all men to piety. He therefore decreed that all those under Roman government should rest on the days named after the Savior, and similarly that they should honor the days of the Sabbath, in memory, I suppose, of the things recorded as done by the universal Savior on those days.

(3) The Day of Salvation, then, which also bears the names of Light Day and Sun Day, he taught all

the military to revere devoutly. To those who shared the divinely given faith he allowed free time to attend unhindered the church of God, on the assumption that with all impediment removed, they would join in the prayers. **19** To those who did not yet share in the divine Word, he gave order in a second decree that every Lord's Day they should march out to an open space just outside the city, and that there at a signal they should all together offer up to God a form of prayer learned by heart; they ought not to rest their hopes on spears or armor or physical strength, but acknowledge the God over all, the giver of all good and indeed of victory itself, to whom it was right to offer the lawful prayers, lifting up their hands high toward heaven, extending their mental vision yet higher to the heavenly King, and calling on him in their prayers as the Giver of victory and Savior, as their Guardian and Helper. He was himself the instructor in prayer to all the soldiery, bidding them all to say these words in Latin:

20 (1)

"You alone we know as God,
You are the King we acknowledge,
You are the Help we summon.
By you we have won our victories,
Through you we have overcome our enemies.
To you we render thanks for the good things past,
You also we hope for as giver of those to come.
To you we all come to supplicate for our Emperor
    Constantine and for his Godbeloved Sons:
That he may be kept safe and victorious for us in long,
    long life, we plead."

(2) Such were the things he decreed should be done by the military regiments every Sunday, and such were the words he taught them to recite in their prayers to God. **21** Furthermore, he caused the sign of the saving trophy to be marked on their shields and had the army led on parade, not by any of the golden images, as had been their past practice, but by the saving trophy alone.

22 (1) He himself, like someone participating in sacred mysteries, would shut himself at fixed times each day in secret places within his royal palace chambers and would converse with his God alone, and kneeling in suppliant petition would plead for the objects of his prayers. On days of the Feast of the Savior, intensifying the rigor, he would perform the divine mysteries with his whole strength of soul and body, on the one hand wholly dedicated to purity of life, and on the other initiating the festival for all. (2) He transformed the sacred vigil into daylight, as those appointed to the task lit huge wax tapers throughout the whole city; there were fiery torches that lit up every place, so as to make the mystic vigil more radiant than bright day. When dawn interposed, in imitation of the beneficence of the Savior, he opened his beneficent hand to all provinces, peoples, and cities, making rich gifts of every kind to them all. (3) Such then was his religious practice toward his own God.

23 For all those under Roman rule, both civilian and military, access was universally blocked to every form of idolatry, and every form of sacrifice banned. A decree went also to the governors of each province directing that they should similarly reverence the Lord's Day. These same persons at the emperor's behest honored the days of martyrs as well, and adorned the times of festival with public gatherings. Such things were all carried out as the emperor desired. **24** Hence it is not surprising that on one occasion, when entertaining bishops to dinner, he let slip the remark that he was perhaps himself a bishop, too, using some such words as these in our hearing: "You are bishops of those within the Church, but I am perhaps a bishop appointed by God over those outside." In accordance with this saying, he exercised a bishop's supervision over all his subjects and pressed them all, as far as lay in his power, to lead the godly life.

25 (1) Hence it is not surprising that in successive laws and ordinances he prohibited everyone from sacrificing to idols, from practicing divination, from having cult figures erected, from performing secret rites, and from defiling the cities by the carnage of gladiatorial combat. (2) To those in Egypt and especially Alexandria, who had a custom of worshipping their river through the offices of effeminate men, another law was sent out, declaring that the whole class of homosexuals should be abolished as a thing depraved, and that it was unlawful for those infected with this gross indecency to be seen anywhere.

(3) Whereas the superstitious supposed that the river would no longer flow for them in its customary way, God cooperated with the emperor's law by achieving quite the opposite of what they expected. For although those who defiled the cities by their abominable practice were no more, the river, as though the land had been cleared for it, flowed as never before and rose in abundant flood to overflow all the arable land, by its action teaching the senseless that one should reject polluted men and attribute the cause of prosperity to the sole giver of all good.

26 (1) Indeed, with countless such measures taken by the emperor in every province, there would be plenty of scope for those eager to record them. The same applies to the laws that he renewed by transforming them from their primitive state to a more hallowed one. It will be easier to explain briefly the nature of these reforms also.

(2) Ancient laws had punished those without children by stopping them inheriting from their kinsmen. This was a harsh law against the childless, since it punished them as criminals. By repealing this, he permitted the proper persons to inherit. The emperor made this change toward sacred justice, saying that it was those who offended deliberately who ought to be corrected with fitting punishment. (3) Nature has made many childless, when they have prayed to be blessed with large families, but have been disappointed through bodily infirmity. Others have become childless, not through rejecting the natural succession of children, but through abstaining from intercourse with women, an abstinence that they chose through a passion for philosophy, and women consecrated to the sacred service of God have practised a chaste and absolute virginity, consecrating themselves by a pure and all-holy life of soul and body. (4) Ought this then to be thought to deserve punishment, and not admiration and approval? Their zeal is highly deserving, their achievement surpasses nature. Those therefore who are disappointed in their desire for children by bodily infirmity should be pitied rather than penalized, and the lover of the Supreme deserves the highest admiration and not punishment. Thus the emperor with sound reasoning remodeled the law.

(5) Furthermore for those near death ancient laws prescribed that even with their last breath the wills they made must be expressed in precise verbal formulas, and that certain phrases and terminology must be used to state them. This led to much malicious manipulation to circumvent the intentions of the deceased. (6) The emperor noted this and changed this law, too, saying that the dying person should express what he had in mind in plain simple words and everyday speech and compose his will in an ordinary document or even unwritten if he wished, provided he did this in the presence of trustworthy witnesses, able to preserve accurately what is entrusted to them.

27 (1) He also made a law that no Christian was to be a slave to Jews, on the ground that it was not right that those redeemed by the Savior should be subjected by the yoke of bondage to the slayers of the prophets and the murderers of the Lord. If any were found in this condition, the one was to be set free, the other punished with a fine.

(2) He also put his seal on the decrees of bishops made at synods, so that it would not be lawful for the rulers of provinces to annul what they had approved, since the priests of God were superior to any magistrate.

(3) He made countless decrees like these for those under his rule. It would need leisure to commit them to a separate work for the precise analysis of the emperor's policies in those also. What need is there now to set out in detail how, having attached himself to the God over all, he pondered from dawn to dusk on which of mankind to benefit or how he was fair to all and impartial in his benefits?

28 But to the churches of God in particular he was exceptionally generous in his provision, in one place bestowing estates, and elsewhere grain allowances to feed poor men, orphan children, and women in distress. Then with great concern he also provided huge quantities of clothing for the naked and unclad. He singled out as worthy of special honor those who had dedicated their lives to godly philosophy. He would all but worship God's choir of those sanctified in perpetual virginity, believing that in the souls of such as these dwelt the God to whom they had consecrated themselves.

29 (1) Indeed in order to enlarge his understanding with the help of the divinely inspired words, he would spend the hours of the night awake, and repeatedly made public appearances without calling upon speechwriters; he thought that he ought to rule his subjects with instructive argument and establish his whole imperial rule as rational. (2) Consequently when he gave the invitation, countless multitudes rushed to join the audience to hear the emperor's philosophy. If while speaking he had occasion to mention God, standing quite straight with intense face and subdued voice, he would seem to be initiating the audience with deep awe in the inspired doctrine, and then when the hearers let out favorable exclamations, he would indicate that they should look to heaven and save the adulation and honor of their reverent praises for the King over all.

(3) In planning his addresses, he would at one point set out refutations of polytheistic error, showing that the religion of the heathen is a deception and a façade for atheism; at another point he would recommend that the sole Godhead should be acknowledged and would systematically expound providence both in general and in particular cases. From there he would proceed to the Savior's dispensation, demonstrating the necessity for it to happen in terms of what is appropriate. He would then go on to deal with the doctrine of divine judgment. (4) Next he would touch on things that struck the audience most forcefully, rebuking thieves and frauds and those who committed themselves to greedy profiteering. Striking them, and as if actually flogging them, with his argument, he made some of his courtiers bow their heads as their conscience was smitten. Testifying in plain words, he announced to them that he would give an account to God of their activities, for the God over all had given him sovereignty over things on earth, and he in imitation of the Supreme had committed particular administrative regions of the empire to them; all however would in due course be subject to scrutiny of their actions by the Great King. (5) Such were the constant themes of his affirmation, his admonition, his teaching.

With the assurance of the authentic faith he held and expressed such views, but they were slow to learn and deaf to what is good; they would cheer his words with cries and acclamations of approval, but in practice they ignored them through greed. **30** (1) So in the end he tackled one of those round him and said, "How far, my man, do we make greed stretch?" Then on the ground he drew with the staff that he had in his hand the measure of the height of a man and said, "If all the wealth in the world and all the land there is becomes yours, you will still not possess more than this plot here marked out—assuming you even get that." (2) But in spite of what he said and did, not one was restrained by the blessed one; yet events have manifestly convinced them that the pronouncements of the emperor were like divine oracles and not mere words. **31** But since the fear of death failed to deter the wicked from their evil ways, the emperor being wholly given to clemency, and none of those who governed the various provinces took any steps anywhere at all against the offenders, this certainly brought no small reproach upon the whole regime. Whether that was fair or not is for each to judge as he sees fit, and I content myself with recording the truth.

32 However that may be, Latin was the language in which the emperor used to produce the text of his speeches. They were translated into Greek by professional interpreters. By way of example of his translated works, I shall append immediately after this present book the speech that he entitled, "To the assembly of the saints," dedicating the work to the Church of God, so that none may think our assertions about his speeches to be mere rhetoric.

33 (1) One other thing seems to me to be unforgettable, a deed that the marvelous man did in our own presence. On one occasion, emboldened by his devotion to divine things, we asked permission to deliver an address about the Savior's tomb for him to hear. He listened with rapt attention, and where a large audience was standing round right inside the palace he stood up and listened with the others. When we begged him to rest on the imperial throne that was nearby, he would not do so, but made a shrewdly considered critique of the speech and affirmed the truth of its doctrinal theology. (2) Since it took a long time and the speech still continued, we suggested breaking off; he however would not allow it, but urged us to go on to the end. When we asked him to sit, he kept refusing, saying at one time that when the doctrine of God was being discussed, it was wrong for him to relax while he listened, and at another that it was good and beneficial for him to stand: it was a holy thing to listen to divinity standing up. When this, too, came to an end, we returned home and took up our regular business.

5. Zosimus: The New History

The adamantly anti-Christian historian Zosimus composed his history of the "corruption" of the Roman Empire some time around the year 500. His vitriolic account of Constantine, reproduced, in part, here, relies on an earlier account by the equally ardent non-Christian Eunapius (writing around 400). It is, in some respects, an accurate historical account; we read about Constantine's reorganization of the political, military, and economic structures of the empire following his rise to sole rule. We read about his foundation of New Rome, the eponymous city of Constantinople, on top of the old city of Byzantium. We read about episodes that are usually absent from Christian accounts like Eusebius's, such as the mysterious execution of Constantine's wife Fausta and eldest son Crispus. All these events are framed by Zosimus (and his source Eunapius), however, as the result of Constantine's defective character and his self-serving adherence to Christianity, described here as the last religious resort of a blood-stained killer. Constantine's conversion, for Zosimus, is merely one more sign of the man's outrageous impiety and one more factor that would lead to the corruption and deterioration of a proud, pious empire. As Zosimus plainly states: "Constantine was the origin and beginning of the present destruction of the empire" (*New History* 2.34).

29 (1) The whole empire now devolved on Constantine alone. At last he no longer needed to conceal his natural malignity but acted in accordance with his unlimited power. He still practiced the ancestral religion, although not so much out of honor as necessity, and he believed the seers, since he had learned by experience that they prophesied the truth in all his successes. But when he came to Rome, he was filled with arrogance, and thought fit to begin his impiety at home. (2) Without any consideration for natural law, he killed his son, Crispus (who, as I related before, had been considered worthy of the rank of Caesar) on suspicion of having had intercourse with his stepmother Fausta. And when Constantine's mother, Helena, was saddened by this atrocity and was inconsolable at the young man's death, Constantine, as if to comfort her, applied a remedy worse than the disease: he ordered a bath to be overheated and shut Fausta up in it until she was dead. (3) Since he was himself aware of his guilt and of his disregard for oaths as well, he approached the priests seeking absolution, but they said that there was no kind of purge known that could absolve him of such impieties. A certain Egyptian, who had come from Spain to Rome and was intimate with the ladies of the court, met Constantine and assured him that the Christian religion was able to absolve him from guilt and that it promised every wicked man who was converted to it immediate release from all sin. (4) Constantine readily believed what he was told and, abandoning his an-

From *Zosimus: A New History*, trans. Ronald T. Ridley. Canberra: Australian Association for Byzantine Studies, 1982. Used with permission of Australian Catholic University.

cestral religion, embraced the one that the Egyptian offered him. He began his impiety by doubting divination, for since many of its predictions about his successes had been fulfilled, he was afraid that people inquiring about the future might hear prophecies about his misfortunes. For this reason, he applied himself to the abolition of divination. (5) When an ancient festival fell due and it was necessary for the army to go up to the Capitol to carry out the rites, for fear of the soldiers he took part in the festival, but when the Egyptian sent him an apparition that unrestrainedly abused the rite of ascending to the Capitol, he stood aloof from the holy worship and thus incurred the hatred of the Senate and people.

30 (1) Unable to endure the curses of almost everyone, he sought out a city as a counterbalance to Rome, where he had to build a palace. When he found a place in the Troad between Sigeum and old Ilium suitable for constructing a city, he laid foundations and built part of the wall, which can still be seen to this day as you sail toward the Hellespont. But he changed his mind and, leaving the work unfinished, went to Byzantium. (2) The site of the city pleased him, and he resolved to enlarge it as much as possible to make it a home fit for an emperor, for the city stands on a hill that is part of that isthmus formed by the so-called Horn and the Propontis. Formerly it had a gate at the end of the portico built by the Emperor Severus (this was when he was reconciled to the Byzantines after being angry with them for harboring his enemy Niger) (3) and the wall used to run down from the western side of the hill to the temple of Aphrodite and the sea opposite Chrysopolis. On the northern side of the hill, the wall ran down to the harbor called Neorion (the Docks) and thence to the sea that lies opposite the channel through which one enters the Black Sea. The length of this narrow channel leading into the sea is about three hundred stades. (4) This, then, was the extent of the old city.

Constantine built a circular forum where the gate used to be and surrounded it with double-roofed porticoes. He set two huge arches of Proconnesian marble opposite each other, through which one could enter the portico of Severus or go out of the old city.

To make the city much larger, he surrounded it with a wall fifteen stades beyond the old one, cutting off the whole isthmus from sea to sea.

31 (1) When he had thus enlarged the original city, he built a palace scarcely inferior to the one in Rome. He decorated the hippodrome most beautifully, incorporating the temple of the Dioscuri in it; their statues are still to be seen standing in the porticoes of the hippodrome. He even placed somewhere in the hippodrome the tripod of Delphic Apollo, which had on it the very image of Apollo. (2) There was in Byzantium a huge forum consisting of four porticoes, and at the end of one of them, which has numerous steps leading up to it, he built two temples. Statues were set up in them, in one Rhea, mother of the gods. This statue the Argonauts had set up on mount Dindymus overlooking the city of Cyzicus, but they say Constantine damaged it through his disregard for religion, by taking away the lions on each side and changing the arrangement of the hands; (3) for whereas previously she was apparently restraining lions, now she seemed to be praying and looking to the city as if guarding it. And in the other temple he set up the statue of *Fortuna Romae*. Houses were then built for the senators who accompanied him.

Constantine fought no more successful battles; when the Thaiphallians, a Scythian people, attacked him with five hundred horses, not only did he not oppose them, but when he had lost most of his army and saw them plundering as far as his fortified camp, he was glad to save himself by flight.

32 (1) Being thus at peace, he devoted his life to pleasure. He distributed a daily grain ration to the people of Byzantium, which they continue to receive to this day. Public money was spent on structures that were mostly useless, while some he built were shortly after pulled down, being unsafe owing to their hasty construction. He also thoroughly confused the ancient and established magistracies. (2) Previously there were two praetorian prefects who administered the office together, and not only the court soldiers were under their care and command, but also those entrusted with the protection of the city and those on the frontier. For the prefecture was considered second only to the emperor, and it was in charge of the corn dole and corrected military crimes with proper punishments.

33 (1) Constantine upset this sound organization and divided the one office into four. He assigned to one prefect all Egypt, in addition to the Pentapolis in Africa; the East as far as Mesopotamia; Cilicia, Cappadocia, and Armenia; the whole coast from Pamphylia to Trapezus and on to the forts near Phasis; Thrace and the neighboring provinces of Moesia (which extends to the river Asamus) and Rhodope (to the city of Topirus); Cyprus; and the Cyclades save Lemnos, Imbros, and Samothrace. (2) To the second he gave Macedonia, Thessaly, Crete, Greece and the islands around her, the two Epiruses, Illyricum, Dacia, the Triballi, Pannonia, as well as Valeria and upper Moesia. To the third went all Italy and Sicily; the adjacent islands, Sardinia and Corsica; and Africa from the Syrtes to Mauretania Caesariensis. To the fourth he gave the Gaul beyond the Alps, Spain, and also the island of Britain. (3) After thus dividing the office of the prefects, he was anxious to reduce their influence still further, for whereas the commanders of the soldiers everywhere used to be centurions and tribunes and *duces* who held the rank of generals in each place, Constantine set up Magistri Militum, one of horse, the other of infantry, and to these he transferred power to command the troops and to punish those guilty of crimes, depriving the prefects of this authority. (4) That this was damaging both in peace and war I shall immediately show. Since the prefects had collected taxes everywhere by means of their subordinates to cover military expenses, and since the soldiers were subject to their discretion in penalties for crimes, the troops naturally realized that the person who supplied them with provisions also punished those who made a mistake, and so did not dare do anything contrary to duty through fear both of losing their allowance and of immediate punishment. (5) Now, however, since one person is paymaster and another is in charge of discipline, the soldiers do what they like and, furthermore, the greater part of the provisions goes into the pockets of the magister and his subordinates.

34 (1) And Constantine did something else that gave the barbarians unhindered access to the Roman Empire. By the forethought of Diocletian, the frontiers of the empire everywhere were covered, as I have stated, with cities, garrisons, and fortifications that housed the whole army. Consequently it was impossible for the barbarians to cross the frontier because they were confronted at every point by forces capable of resisting their attacks. (2) Constantine destroyed this security by removing most of the troops from the frontiers and stationing them in cities that did not need assistance, thus both stripping of protection those being molested by the barbarians and subjecting the cities left alone by them to the outrages of the soldiers, so that henceforth most have become deserted. Moreover he enervated the troops by allowing them to devote themselves to shows and luxuries. In plain terms, Constantine was the origin and beginning of the present destruction of the empire.

35 (1) He proclaimed his son, Constantine, Caesar, and later appointed his other sons, Constantius and Constans, the same rank. The size of Constantinople was increased until it was by far the greatest city, with the result that many of the succeeding emperors chose to live there and attracted an unnecessarily large population that came from all over the world—soldiers and officials, traders and other professions. (2) Therefore, they have surrounded it with new walls much more extensive than those of Constantine and allowed the buildings to be so close to each other that the inhabitants, whether at home or in the streets, are crowded for room and it is dangerous to walk about because of the great number of men and beasts. And a lot of the sea round about has been turned into land by sinking piles and building houses on them, which by themselves are enough to fill a large city.

36 (1) I have often wondered why, since the city of Byzantium has grown so great that no other surpasses it in prosperity or size, no divine prophecy was given to our predecessors concerning its progress and destiny. (2) After thinking about this for a long time and reading through many historical works and collections of oracles and spending time puzzling over them, I finally came across an oracle said to be of the Sibyl of Erythrae or Phaennis in Epirus (who is said to have been inspired and given out some oracles).

Nicomedes, son of Prusias, believed this oracle and, interpreting it to what seemed his own advantage, made war on his father at Attalus's instigation. The oracle runs thus:

37 (1)

O king of Thrace, you will leave your city. Among the
 sheep you will rear a great lion, crooked-clawed and
 terrible,
Who will plunder the treasures of your country
And take the land without toil. I say to you, not long
Will you enjoy your royal honors (5)
But will fall from your throne which is surrounded by
 columns.
You will disturb a sleeping wolf, crooked-clawed and
 terrible,
Who will put the yoke on your unwilling neck.
Wolves will then make their lair in the land of
 Bithynia
By Zeus' decree. But power will soon pass to (10)
The men who dwell in Byzas' seat.
Thrice-blessed Hellespont, walls built for men by the
 gods
At the gods' behest,
Before whom the terrible wolf must submit, compelled
 by necessity.
O inhabitants of Megara's city, my holy place, (15)
I will no longer keep silent about my father's
 intentions but reveal
The divine oracles' message clearly to mortals.
Thrace will bring forth a great woe, and the birth is
 imminent,
A serpent child bringing evil to the land sometime.
A savage ulcer will grow on the side of the land (20)
Which will swell and swell until, suddenly bursting,
It will pour blood.

(2) This oracle tells, although ambiguously and in riddles, virtually all the evils that were to befall the Bithynians because of the burdens that later fell upon them, and how power was swiftly "to pass to the men who dwell in Byzas' seat." The fact that the predictions did not eventuate for a long time should not induce anyone to think that the prophecy refers to another place, for all time is short to the god who is and always will be. These are my conclusions from the words of the oracle and from subsequent events, but if anyone thinks it ought to be interpreted differently, he may do so.

38 (1) After this, Constantine continued wasting revenue by unnecessary gifts to unworthy and useless people and oppressed those who paid taxes while enriching those who were useless to the state, for he thought that prodigality was liberality. (2) He also laid a gold and silver tax on all merchants throughout the empire, including the poorest urban shopkeepers; he did not allow even unfortunate prostitutes to escape. The result was that as each fourth year came round when this tax had to be paid, weeping and wailing were heard throughout the city because beatings and tortures were in store for those who could not pay owing to extreme poverty. (3) Indeed, mothers sold their children and fathers prostituted their daughters under compulsion to pay the exactors of the *chrysargyron*. Anxious also to contrive some harm for the more affluent, Constantine appointed each of them to the rank of praetor and used this honor as a pretext for demanding a large sum of money. So when those appointed to arrange this came to the various cities, everyone could be seen fleeing and going abroad, for fear of gaining this honor and losing all their property. He also made a list of the property of the richest people, on which he imposed a tax called a *follis*. By such exactions the cities were exhausted, for as these demands persisted long after Constantine, they were soon drained of wealth and most became deserted.

39 (1) After oppressing the state in all these ways, Constantine died from a disease. His three sons (born not from Fausta, the daughter of Herculius Maximianus, but from another woman whom he killed on a charge of adultery) succeeded him, but abstained from administration and devoted themselves to the inclinations of youth, rather than to the service of the state. (2) First of all, then, they divided the empire, and Constantine, the eldest, and Constans, the youngest, obtained everything beyond the Alps, Italy, and Illyricum, as well as the countries around the Black Sea and Carthaginian Africa, while to Constantius were entrusted Asia, the East, and Egypt. And in a sense Delmatius, his brother Constantius, and Hannibalianus acted as their colleagues: they all wore purple robes adorned with gold and out of respect for their relationship to himself had been appointed to the rank of the so-called *nobilissimate* by Constantine.

6. Julian: Letters on Religion

Flavius Claudius Julianus (ca. 331–363) reigned as emperor for only nineteen months (361–363), but left a lasting impact on subsequent Christian conceptions of the imperial house. Although raised a Christian, Julian took the opportunity of his ascension to power to renounce his Christian upbringing and publicly declare himself a worshipper of the traditional gods of Greece and Rome. He called himself a "Hellene," emphasizing the link between traditional culture and cult; later Christians called him the "Apostate." Julian recounted his early attraction to non-Christian philosophy and religion; Maximus, to whom Julian writes plaintively in Letter 8, was an early charismatic influence in this respect. Julian supposedly pursued this religious vocation secretly until his rise to power (see his description in Letter 19, "To a Priest").

Once empowered, Julian's Hellenism comprised a rigorous program of religious restoration: the revival of defunct priesthoods; the funding of festivals and temple renovations; and the creation of a network of Hellene priesthoods that, perhaps ironically, mimicked the ecclesiastical structure of Christianity (see Letter 20, "To the High-Priest Theodore"). His zeal for religious revivalism was so great that even his fellow non-Christians, such as the favorable historian Ammianus Marcellinus, complained of (literal) overkill: "He has thoroughly soaked through the altars with an abundance of sacrificial blood, over and over again to the point of excess."

Julian's Hellenic revival was also distinctly anti-Christian: he wrote a lengthy treatise "Against the Galileans" (his preferred term for "Christians," emphasizing their backwater origins and lack of cultural tradition) and passed legislation barring Christians from teaching the "classics" of Greek literature (see Letter 36, one reconstruction of this edict). Julian also showed marked favor to the Jews, as a people with an impressive religious and cultural tradition. He allegedly permitted the Jews to rebuild their Temple in Jerusalem, so they, too, could resume sacrifice, and requested their prayers on behalf of his imperial person (see Letter 51). Although there is no particular reason to suspect Julian's sincerity in his respect for the Jews, there can also be little doubt that his brief favoritism toward the Jews was simultaneously a way of striking back at and weakening Christian claims of triumphalism.

8. TO MAXIMUS, THE PHILOSOPHER

Everything crowds into my mind at once and chokes my utterance, as one thought refuses to let another precede it, whether you please to class such symptoms among psychic troubles or to give them some other name. But let me arrange what I have to tell in chronological order, though not until I have first offered thanks to the all-merciful gods, who at this present have permitted me to write and will also perhaps permit us to see one another. Directly after I had been made emperor—against my will, as the gods know, and this I made evident then and there in every way possible—I led the army against the barbarians. That expedition lasted for three months, and when I returned to the shores of Gaul, I was ever on the

From *The Works of the Emperor Julian*, trans. Wilmer Cave Wright. New York: G. P. Putnam's Sons, 1923. Used with permission of Harvard University Press.

watch and kept inquiring from all who came from that quarter whether any philosopher or any scholar wearing a philosopher's cloak or a soldier's tunic had arrived there. Then I approached Besontio. It is a little town that has lately been restored, but in ancient times it was a large city adorned with costly temples and was fortified by a strong wall and further by the nature of the place, for it is encircled by the river Doubis. It rises up like a rocky cliff in the sea, inaccessible, I might almost say, to the very birds, except in those places where the river as it flows round it throws out what one may call beaches that lie in front of it. Near this city there came to meet me a certain man who looked like a Cynic with his long cloak and staff. When I first caught sight of him in the distance, I imagined that he was none other than yourself. And when I came nearer to him, I thought that he had surely come from you. The man was in fact a friend of mine, though he fell short of what I hoped and expected. This then was one vain dream I had! And afterward I thought that because you were busied with my affairs, I should certainly find you nowhere outside Greece. Zeus be my witness and great Helios, mighty Athene, and all the gods and goddesses, how on my way down to Illyricum from Gaul I trembled for your safety! Also I kept inquiring of the gods— not that I ventured to do this myself, for I could not endure to see or hear anything so terrible as one might have supposed would be happening to you at that time, but I entrusted the task to others, and the gods did indeed show clearly that certain troubles would befall you, nothing terrible however, nor to indicate that impious counsels would be carried out.

But you see that I have passed over many important events. Above all, it is right that you should learn how I became all at once conscious of the very presence of the gods and in what manner I escaped the multitude of those who plotted against me, though I put no man to death, deprived no man of his property, and only imprisoned those whom I caught redhanded. All this, however, I ought perhaps to tell you rather than write it, but I think you will be very glad to be informed of it. I worship the gods openly, and the whole mass of the troops who are returning with me worship the gods. I sacrifice oxen in public. I have

offered to the gods many hecatombs as thank-offerings. The gods command me to restore their worship in its utmost purity, and I obey them, yes, and with a good will. For they promise me great rewards for my labors, if only I am not remiss. Evagrius has joined me. . . . of the god whom we honor. . . .

Many things occur to my mind, besides what I have written, but I must store up certain matters to tell you when you are with me. Come here, then, in the name of the gods, as quickly as you can and use two or more public carriages. Moreover, I have sent two of my most trusted servants, one of whom will escort you as far as my headquarters; the other will inform me that you have set out and will forthwith arrive. Do you yourself tell the youths which of them you wish to undertake which of these tasks.

19. TO A PRIEST

I should never have favored Pegasius unhesitatingly if I had not had clear proofs that, even in former days, when he had the title of Bishop of the Galilaeans, he was wise enough to revere and honor the gods. This I do not report to you on hearsay from men whose words are always adapted to their personal dislikes and friendships, for much current gossip of this sort about him has reached me, and the gods know that I once thought I ought to detest him above all other depraved persons. But when I was summoned to his headquarters by Constantius of blessed memory I was traveling by this route, and after rising at early dawn, I came from Troas to Ilios about the middle of the morning. Pegasius came to meet me, as I wished to explore the city—this was my excuse for visiting the temples—and he was my guide and showed me all the sights. So now let me tell you what he did and said, and from it one may guess that he was not lacking in right sentiments toward the gods.

Hector has a hero's shrine there, and his bronze statue stands in a tiny little temple. Opposite this they have set up a figure of the great Achilles in the unroofed court. If you have seen the spot, you will certainly recognize my description of it. You can learn from the guides the story that accounts for the fact that great Achilles was set up opposite to him and takes up the whole of the unroofed court. Now I found that the altars were still alight, I might almost say still blazing, and that the statue of Hector had been anointed until it shone. So I looked at Pegasius and said: "What does this mean? Do the people of Ilios offer sacrifices?" This was to test him cautiously to find out his own views. He replied: "Is it not natural that they should worship a brave man who was their own citizen, just as we worship the martyrs?" Now the analogy was far from sound, but his point of view and intentions were those of a man of culture, if you consider the times in which we then lived. Observe what followed. "Let us go," said he, "to the shrine of Athene of Ilios." Thereupon with the greatest eagerness he led me there and opened the temple, and as though he were producing evidence, he showed me all the statues in perfect preservation, nor did he behave at all as those impious men do usually, I mean, when they make the sign on their impious foreheads, nor did he hiss to himself as they do. For these two things are the quintessence of their theology, to hiss at demons and make the sign of the cross on their foreheads.

These are the two things that I promised to tell you. But a third occurs to me that I think I must not fail to mention. This same Pegasius went with me to the temple of Achilles as well and showed me the tomb in good repair, yet I had been informed that this also had been pulled to pieces by him. But he approached it with great reverence; I saw this with my own eyes. And I have heard from those who are now his enemies that he also used to offer prayers to Helios and worship him in secret. Would you not have accepted me as a witness even if I had been merely a private citizen? Of each man's attitude toward the gods, who could be more trustworthy witnesses than the gods themselves? Should I have appointed Pegasius a priest if I had any evidence of impiety toward the gods on his part? And if in those past days, whether because he was ambitious for power, or, as he has often asserted to me, he clad himself in those rags in order to save the temples of the gods, and only pretended to be irreligious so far as the name of the thing went—indeed it is clear that he never injured

any temple anywhere except for what amounted to a few stones, and that was as a blind, that he might be able to save the rest—well then we are taking this into account and are we not ashamed to behave to him as Aphobius did and as the Galilaeans all pray to see him treated? If you care at all for my wishes, you will honor not him only but any others who are converted, in order that they may the more readily heed me when I summon them to good works, and those others may have less cause to rejoice. But if we drive away those who come to us of their own free will, no one will be ready to heed when we summon.

20. TO THE HIGH-PRIEST THEODORUS

I have written you a more familiar sort of letter than to the others because you, I believe, have more friendly feelings than others toward me. For it means much that we had the same guide, and I am sure you remember him. A long time ago, when I was still living in the West, I learned that he had the highest regard for you, and for that reason I counted you my friend, and yet because of their excessive caution, I have usually thought these words well said, "For I never met or saw him";[1] and well said is "Before we love we must know, and before we can know we must test by experience." But it seems that after all a certain other saying has most weight with me, namely, "The Master has spoken." That is why I thought even then that I ought to count you among my friends, and now I entrust to you a task that is dear to my heart, while to all men everywhere it is of the greatest benefit. And if, as I have the right to expect, you administer the office well, be assured that you will rejoice me greatly now and give me still greater good hope for the future life. For I certainly am not one of those who believe that the soul perishes before the body or along with it, nor do I believe any human being but only the gods; since it is likely that they alone have the most perfect knowledge of these matters, if indeed we ought to use the word "likely" of what is in-

---

[1] *Iliad* 4.374, *Odyssey* 4.200.

evitably true; since it is fitting for men to conjecture about such matters, but the gods must have complete knowledge.

What, then, is this office which I say I now entrust to you? It is the government of all the temples in Asia, with power to appoint the priests in every city and to assign to each what is fitting. Now the qualities that befit one in this high office are, in the first place, fairness, and next, goodness and benevolence toward those who deserve to be treated thus. For any priest who behaves unjustly to his fellow men and impiously toward the gods or is overbearing to all, must either be admonished with plain speaking or chastised with great severity. As for the regulations that I must make more complete for the guidance of priests in general, you as well as the others will soon learn them from me, but meanwhile I wish to make a few suggestions to you. You have good reason to obey me in such matters. Indeed in such a case I very seldom act offhand, as all the gods know, and no one could be more circumspect, and I avoid innovations in all things, so to speak, but more peculiarly in what concerns the gods. For I hold that we ought to observe the laws that we have inherited from our forefathers, since it is evident that the gods gave them to us. For they would not be as perfect as they are if they had been derived from mere men. Now since it has come to pass that they have been neglected and corrupted and wealth and luxury have become supreme, I think that I ought to consider them carefully as though from their cradle. Therefore, when I saw that there is among us great indifference about the gods and that all reverence for the heavenly powers has been driven out by impure and vulgar luxury, I always secretly lamented this state of things. For I saw that those whose minds were turned to the doctrines of the Jewish religion are so ardent in their belief that they would choose to die for it and to endure utter want and starvation rather than taste pork or any animal that has been strangled or had the life squeezed out of it, whereas we are in such a state of apathy about religious matters that we have forgotten the customs of our forefathers, and therefore we actually do not know whether any such rule has ever been prescribed. But these Jews are in part god-fearing, seeing that they revere a god who is truly most powerful and most good and governs this world of sense and, as I well know, is worshipped by us also under other names. They act as is right and seemly, in my opinion, if they do not transgress the laws, but in this one thing they err in that, while reserving their deepest devotion for their own god, they do not conciliate the other gods also; but the other gods they think have been allotted to us Gentiles only, to such a pitch of folly have they been brought by their barbaric conceit. But those who belong to the impious sect of the Galilaeans, as if some disease. . . .

36. RESCRIPT ON CHRISTIAN TEACHERS

I hold that a proper education results, not in laboriously acquired symmetry of phrases and language, but in a healthy condition of mind, I mean a mind that has understanding and true opinions about things good and evil, honorable and base. Therefore, when a man thinks one thing and teaches his pupils another, in my opinion he fails to educate exactly in proportion as he fails to be an honest man. And if the divergence between a man's convictions and his utterances is merely in trivial matters, that can be tolerated somehow, though it is wrong. But if in matters of the greatest importance a man has certain opinions and teaches the contrary, what is that but the conduct of hucksters, and not honest but thoroughly dissolute men in that they praise most highly the things that they believe to be most worthless, thus cheating and enticing by their praises those to whom they desire to transfer their worthless wares. Now all who profess to teach anything whatever ought to be men of upright character and ought not to harbor in their souls opinions irreconcilable with what they publicly profess; and, above all, I believe it is necessary that those who associate with the young and teach them rhetoric should be of that upright character, for they expound the writings of the ancients, whether they be rhetoricians or grammarians, and still more if they are sophists. For these claim to teach, in addition to other things, not only the use of words, but morals also, and they assert that political philosophy is their peculiar field. Let us leave aside, for the moment, the question whether this is true or not. But while I applaud them for aspiring to such high pretensions, I should applaud them still more if they did not utter falsehoods and convict themselves of thinking one thing and teaching their pupils another. What! Was it not the gods who revealed all their learning to Homer, Hesiod, Demosthenes, Herodotus, Thucydides, Isocrates, and Lysias? Did not these men think that they were consecrated, some to Hermes, others to the Muses? I think it is absurd that men who expound the works of these writers should dishonor the gods whom they used to honor. Yet, though I think this absurd, I do not say that they ought to change their opinions and then instruct the young. But I give them this choice: either not to teach what they do not think admirable, or, if they wish to teach, let them first really persuade their pupils that neither Homer nor Hesiod nor any of these writers whom they expound and have declared to be guilty of impiety, folly, and error in regard to the gods is such as they declare. For since they make a livelihood and receive pay from the works of those writers, they thereby confess that they are most shamefully greedy of gain and that, for the sake of a few drachmae, they would put up with anything. It is true that, until now, there were many excuses for not attending the temples, and the terror that threatened on all sides absolved men for concealing the truest beliefs about the gods. But since the gods have granted us liberty, it seems to me absurd that men should teach what they do not believe to be sound. But if they believe that those whose interpreters they are and for whom they sit, so to speak, in the seat of the prophets, were wise men, let them be the first to emulate their piety toward the gods. If, however, they think that those writers were in error with respect to the most honored gods, then let them betake themselves to the churches of the Galilaeans to expound Matthew and Luke, since you Galilaeans are obeying them when you ordain that men shall refrain from temple worship. For my part, I wish that your ears and your tongues might be "born again," as you would say (John 3:7), as regards these things in which may I ever have part, and all who think and act as is pleasing to me.

For religious and secular teachers let there be a general ordinance to this effect: Any youth who wishes to attend the schools is not excluded, nor indeed would it be reasonable to shut out from the best way boys who are still too ignorant to know which way to turn and to overawe them into being led against their will to the beliefs of their ancestors. Though indeed it might be proper to cure these, even against their will, as one cures the insane, except that we concede indulgence to all for this sort of disease. For we ought, I think, to teach, but not punish, the demented.

51. TO THE COMMUNITY OF THE JEWS

In times past, by far the most burdensome thing in the yoke of your slavery has been the fact that you were subjected to unauthorized ordinances and had to contribute an untold amount of money to the accounts of the treasury. Of this I used to see many instances with my own eyes, and I have learned of more, by finding the records that are preserved against you. Moreover, when a tax was about to be levied on you again, I prevented it and compelled the impiety of such obloquy to cease here; and I threw into the fire the records against you that were stored in my desks, so that it is no longer possible for anyone to aim at you such a reproach of impiety. My brother Constantius of honored memory was not so much responsible for these wrongs of yours as were the men who used to frequent his table, barbarians in mind, godless in soul. These I seized with my own hands and put them to death by thrusting them into the pit, that not even any memory of their destruction might still linger among us. And since I wish that you should prosper yet more, I have admonished my brother Iulus, your most venerable patriarch, that the levy that is said to exist among you should be prohibited and that no one is any longer to have the power to oppress the masses of your people by such exactions, so that everywhere, during my reign, you may have security of mind, and in the enjoyment of peace may offer more fervid prayers for my reign to the Most High God, the Creator, who has deigned to crown me with his own immaculate right hand. For it is natural that men who are distracted by any anxiety should be hampered in spirit and should not have so much confidence in raising their hands to pray, but that those who are in all respects free from care should rejoice with their whole hearts and offer their suppliant prayers on behalf of my imperial office to Mighty God, even to him who is able to direct my reign to the noblest ends, according to my purpose. This you ought to do, in order that, when I have successfully concluded the war with Persia, I may rebuild by my own efforts the sacred city of Jerusalem, which for so many years you have longed to see inhabited, and may bring settlers there and, together with you, may glorify the Most High God therein.

7. Ephraim: Hymns Against Julian

Ephraim (ca. 306–73) lived in the far eastern reaches of the Roman Empire, where the language of daily life was Syriac (a dialect of Aramaic, related to Hebrew). Until 363, Ephraim was a teacher and hymnographer for the church in Nisibis; following Julian's disastrous campaign against the Persians and the surrender of Julian's successor Jovian (in 363), Nisibis was ceded to the Persian Empire. Ephraim, along with other Christian refugees, found himself transplanted to the city of Edessa. There Ephraim served as a deacon and directed choirs that chanted his compositions. Although Ephraim's many hymns and prose compositions are often used to show the particularities of Syriac Christianity, Ephraim was also, in many ways, a typical Christian author of the Roman Empire. He was a voracious defender of Nicene orthodoxy against the Arians (see Chapter 7). His *Hymns Against Julian* (the first and third of which are reproduced here) also show an affinity to other Christian attempts to come to terms with Julian's non-Christian imperial rule.

Hymn 1 describes Julian's ascent to the imperial throne as the coming of the "bad shepherd": apostates and Jews (the "People") helped Julian usher in a season of demonic confusion. Hymn 2 describes Julian's attempts to revive "paganism" in the empire, drawing on familiar biblical parallels between idolatry and sexual license. Hymn 3 describes the death of Julian in particularly gruesome and joyful terms, as one pagan king fell to another while Christ triumphed over both. Hymn 4 continues the mocking description of Julian's failed pagan campaign against the Persians and discusses Julian's abortive attempt to allow the Jews to rebuild their Temple in Jerusalem.

Ephraim seems familiar with Julian's religious agenda: he calls Julian the "Hellenic" king (Julian's own preferred term for his religious system was "Hellenism"). He makes fun of Julian, who wrote a long treatise in praise of the Greek god of the sun (a "Hymn to Helios") for setting out to attack his fellow sun worshippers, the Persians. He refers to Julian's famous long, philosopher's beard, which was apparently the butt of jokes during Julian's life. Ephraim's tone throughout is triumphant (the "Galilean" has definitively conquered "the Hellenic king"), but also mournful: the price of Julian's brief, demonic rampage has been the loss of Nisibis and the transplantation of Ephraim and his fellow Nisibene Christians.

HYMN 1

On the melody: Rely on the truth

1   The sceptre of kingship shepherds humankind,
cares for cities, drives away wild animals.
The opposite was the sceptre of the king who
    apostatized.
The wild animals saw it and exulted:
the wolves were his partisans; the leopard and the lion
    raged;
even the foxes raised their voices.

2   The wolves saw the clouds, rain, and whirlwind.
Calling to one another, they attacked. Ravenous, they
    rampaged.
Utterly hemmed in, they were all furious.
They surrounded the blessed flock.
But the sceptre that had gladdened them was broken
    and moved them to regret.
A crushed reed (Isa 36:6) was the support of the left
    hand.

3   They fled back into their caverns, dark and primeval.
The fear they had stripped off, they put on again in
    their dens.
The creation that had been gloomy, brightened and
    exulted,
but the rebels were trampled.
The heads of leviathan were smashed in the midst of
    the sea (cf. Ps 74:13–14),
and his crawling tail was shattered in the midst of the
    dry land.

4   The living dead awoke and were resuscitated.
Thinking themselves revived, they were rebuked—
    how they were disgraced!
Being resuscitated, they revived graven images.
The idols confuted the apostates.
One is the death of pagans and tares,
all of whom took refuge at once in the same one.

5   At that time, then, the mud seethed and spewed out
vermin of all sizes and worms of every sort.
They bred, and the earth was full of them in the
    middle of winter.
The breath of the dragon made the earth seethe,
but the One equipped with the sandal of truth
despised the poison of the stings of the sons of error.

6   Those who stood with the overthrown fell with the
    fallen.
They persevered, thinking even they could stand firm.
The fools clung to one another, but as it transpired
    they all fell.

Their fall attested their impediment:
although divided, they agreed on the stumbling block.
In the love of one king they were joined.
When demons rejoiced, they suddenly revived with   7
    them.
When the Evil One was jubilant, they exulted with
    him.
As if by a mystery, time arranged
for all of them at once to be dependent on one.
They made themselves brothers and members of one
    another,
for they all depended on the head of the left hand.
For while the right hand was grieved over sinners,   8
the children of the left hand rejoiced greatly.
In the season of the penitents, angels alone rejoice.
Without realizing it, fools behave in the opposite way.
Only the church agrees with the Watchers in both:
she suffers over the sinners but rejoices over penitents.
The Evil One saw that he had intoxicated and   9
    confused people.
He rejoiced and mocked freedom all the more
that people have so thoroughly enslaved themselves to
    him.
The Evil One was astounded how much he tore us to
    pieces,
but the fools, torn to pieces, did not feel their pains.
Although the Physician was near, they despised the
    cure.
The ugly, dark, all-gloomy winter   10
robbed the beauty of the all-rejoicing spring.
Thornbushes and tares were disgorged and sprang up.
The dry frost moistened
brambles in the inner rooms and thistles in the courts.
In this time the naked and the barefoot shivered.
How the late seeding was afraid and terrified!   11
For without effort it was sown and took root.
Uprooted were the aftergrowth, the self-sown growth
    sprouting throughout the world,
and that which had quickly risen to the surface,
but the seed of effort that struck root profusely—
its fruit came a hundredfold, sixty and thirtyfold.
The truth-loving kings in the symbol of two bulls   12
yoked together equally the two Testaments.
With the yoke of harmony they worked and adorned
    the earth.
But the thorns clothed themselves in the beauty of the
    wheat,
and the seed spread its appearance even upon the tares.
Those who stripped away beauty did so in freedom.

13 Some of them were brambles, and some were wheat.
Some were gold, and some were dust.
The tyrant became a crucible for the beauty of the true
ones.
Who has ever seen such a glorious sight?
For Truth entered and was tested in the crucible of the
False One.
Unwittingly, Error has glorified the true ones.

14 All who were apostates rejoiced in the apostate—
the sons of the left hand in the head of the left hand.
In him they could see who they themselves were,
since he became a mirror for all of them.
Those who rejoiced over his victory shared his lot,
inasmuch as disgrace befell them from his death.

15 For it was the church alone that opposed him utterly,
and they and he together opposed her utterly.
Without dispute this is sufficient to teach
that they were on one side and she on the other.
The furtive ones, who were believed not to belong to
them,
hastily associated themselves with them.

16 The People raged and raved and blared the trumpet.
They rejoiced that he [was] a soothsayer and were
jubilant that he was a Chaldean.
The circumcised saw the image that suddenly was a
bull.
On his coins they saw the shameful bull,
and they began to keep its feast with cymbals and
trumpets,
for they recognized in that bull their ancient calf.

17 The bull of paganism engraved on his heart
[Julian] imprinted on that image for the People who
love it.
Perhaps the Jews cried out to that bull,
"Behold the gods who will lead
your captives up from Babylon into the land they
devastated,
as the molten calf led you out of Egypt (Exod 32:8)!"

18 A king, the Babylonian king, suddenly became a wild
ass,
but he learned to be subjugated; he who used to kick,
kicked no more.
A king, the Hellenic king, suddenly became a bull
and gored the churches, but he was dragged away.
The circumcised saw the bull imprinted on the staters,
and they rejoiced that the calves of Jereboam were
revived (cf. 1 Kings 12:25–33).

19 Perhaps because of that silver coin on which the bull
was portrayed,

the Jews were overjoyed that [Julian] carried it in his
heart
and also in his purse and in his hand
as a type of that calf of the wilderness
that was before his eye and heart and mind;
and probably in his dreams he used to see the calf.

20 A king, the Babylonian king, went mad and went out
into the countryside.
He was made to wander in order to be gathered in; he
was maddened in order to come to his senses (cf.
Dan 4:31–37).
He made God rejoice and made Daniel exult.
A king, the Hellenic king, has been rebuked,
for he angered God and denied Daniel,
and there near Babylon he was judged and
condemned.

HYMN 3

1 A wonder! By chance the corpse of that accursed one,
crossing over toward the rampart met me near the city!
And the Magus took and fastened on a tower
the standard sent from the east,
so that this standard-bearer would declare to the
onlookers
that the city was slave to the lords of that standard.

*Refrain: Glory to the One Who wrapped the corpse in
shame!*

2 I wondered, "Who indeed set a time for meeting
when corpse and standard-bearer both at one moment
were present?"
I knew it was a prearrangement, a miracle of justice
that when the corpse of the fallen one crossed over,
the fearful standard went up and was put in place to
proclaim
that the evil of his conjurers had surrendered that city.

3 For thirty years Persia had made battle in every way
but was unable to cross over the boundary of that city;
even when it had been broken and collapsed, the cross
came down and saved it.
There I saw a disgraceful sight:
the standard of the captor set up on the tower,
the corpse of the persecutor laid in a coffin.

4 Believe in "yes" and "no," the word of a trustworthy
man (cf. Matt 5:37),
that I went right up, my brothers, to the coffin of the
filthy one,

and I stood over him and derided his paganism
and said, "Is this indeed he who exalted himself
against the Living Name and forgot that he is dust?"
[God] turned him back into his dust to let him know he
    was of dust.

5   I stood and wondered at him whose downfall I had so
    fully seen.
"This is his majesty and this is his pomp!
This is his kingship and this is his chariot!
This is a clump of earth that has disintegrated!"
I argued with myself, "Why in [the time of] his
    power
did I not foresee this would be his end?"

6   I wondered about the many who, in seeking to please
the diadem of mortality, denied the universal Life-
    giver.
I looked above and below and was amazed, my
    brothers,
that our Lord [is] His height, the Glorious One,
and the accursed one in [his] downfall, and I said,
"Who will fear this corpse and deny the True One?"

7   He prevented the cross that came down from gaining
    victory,
not because the victorious [cross] was unable to gain
    victory,
but so that a pit might be dug for the evildoer
who came down with his conjurers to the east.
But since he came down and was struck, the
    discerning saw
that the battle in which he would be put to shame had
    been lying in wait for him.

8   Know that because of this the time was long and
    delayed
so that the pure one might complete the years of his
    kingship
and the accursed one might also complete the measure
    of his paganism.
But when he had completed his story, he came to ruin.
So both sides rejoiced, and so there was peace
through the believing king, companion of the glorious
    [kings].

9   The Just One by all [manner] of deaths was capable of
    destroying him,
but he kept [for him] a downfall fearful and bitter,
so that on the day of his death all things should be
    drawn up before his eyes:
Where is that oracle that reassured him?
and the goddess of weapons that she did not come to
    his aid?

and the companies of his gods that they did not come
    to save him?
The cross of the All-knowing marched before the   10
    army.
It endured being mocked: "It cannot save them!"
It kept the king in safety; it gave the army to
    destruction,
for it knew that paganism [was] among them.
Let the cross of Him Who searches all, therefore, be
    praised—
[the cross] that fools without discernment reviled at
    that time.
For they did not persevere with the standard of the   11
    Savior of all.
Indeed that paganism that they showed in the end
was manifest to our Lord from the beginning.
Yet although He knew well that they were pagans,
His cross saved them, but when they apostatized from
    Him,
they ate corpses there; they became a parable there.
When the People was defeated at Ai of the weak,   12
Joshua tore his garments before the Ark [of the
    covenant]
and spoke fearful [words] before the Most High.
A curse [was] among the People, without his knowing.
Just so paganism was hidden in the army,
but instead of the Ark they were carrying the cross.
But Justice summoned him with wisdom,   13
for not by force did she govern his freedom.
By an enticement he marched out to the lance that
    struck:
he saw that he subdued citadels, and he became proud.
For adversity did not cry out to him to turn back
until he marched out and fell into the midst of the
    vortex.
The lance of Justice passed through the belly of him   14
who despised Him Who made the lance of paradise
    pass away.
The divination of the conjurers tore open a pregnant
    [animal].
[Julian] groaned at length to recall
what he had written and published that he would do to
    the churches.
The finger of Justice blotted out his memory.
The king saw that Easterners came and deceived him.   15
Simple men [deceived] the wise man; common men
    [deceived] the diviner.
Those whom he, wrapped up in his vestment,
    summoned,

confined his wisdom by ignorant men,
and he gave orders to set fire to his victorious ships,
and his idols and diviners were entangled in a trap.

16 But when he saw that his gods were confuted and
    exposed
and that he could neither gain victory nor flee,
[that] between fear and disgrace he was prostrate and
    beaten,
he chose death to escape into Sheol.
Cunningly he stripped off his armor in order to be
    wounded,

in order to die so that the Galileans would not see his
    shame.
For he had mockingly named the brothers Galileans. 17
Behold in the air the wheels of the Galilean king!
He thunders in His Chariot; the Cherubim bear
    Him.
The Galilean revealed [the chariot] and handed over
the flock of the soothsayer to the wolves in the
    wilderness,
but the Galilean herd increased and filled the whole
    earth.

8. Ambrose: On the Death of Theodosius

Before he became bishop of Milan (from 374 to 397), Ambrose was a politician, serving as provincial governor before being abruptly drafted (according to his biographer) into episcopal service. Ambrose's political savoir-faire may explain his success in crafting a particular relationship between the ecclesiastical and political hierarchies. As bishop, he triumphed in several notorious confrontations with Roman officials: the prominent pagan prefect Symmachus, who unsuccessfully sought to have a pagan altar restored in Rome; emperors and empresses labeled heretical, such as the "Arians" Valentinian II and his mother Justina; and even good orthodox emperors, whom Ambrose nonetheless felt empowered to challenge, such as Theodosius (in incidents Ambrose alludes to here). His funeral oration at the death of Theodosius I (in 395) does not just eulogize an emperor, but subordinates imperial power to Christian authority. Ambrose advises Theodosius's sons and heirs, Arcadius and Honorius, above all to be "humble" and obedient to their mother Church (and, presumably, her bishops) as their father had been. He concludes by emphasizing the debt owed by imperial power to the holiness of Christ and the church through an account of Helena's discovery of the True Cross (see Chapter 10).

(1) Severe earthquakes, continual rains, and darkness denser than usual gave notice of this, that our most merciful Emperor Theodosius was about to leave the earth. The very elements, then, were mourning his death. The heavens were veiled in obscurity, the air was shuddering in unbroken gloom, the earth was shaken by tremors and filled with floods of waters. Why should not the universe itself bemoan the fact that this prince was presently to be snatched away, for was he not accustomed to alleviate the hardships of this world when by forgiveness he forestalled the punishment of crime?

(2) And he has indeed departed to receive his kingdom, which he did not lay aside, but, admitted by right of piety into the tabernacles of Christ, he has exchanged it for the heavenly Jerusalem. Having taken his place there, he says: "As we have heard, so have we seen in the city of the Lord of hosts, in the city of our God," which "God has founded forever" (Ps 48:8). But he has left behind many deprived of a

From *Funeral Orations,* trans. Leo McCauley. New York: Fathers of the Church, Inc., 1953. Used with permission.

father's protection, as it were, and, above all, his sons. But they are not destitute whom he left as the heirs of his piety; they are not destitute for whom he gained the grace of Christ and the loyalty of the army, to which he was a proof that God cherishes devotion and is the avenger of treachery.

(3) Recently, then, we lamented the death of this prince, and now we are celebrating the fortieth day, with the prince Honorius assisting at the holy altar. For as holy Joseph performed the burial rites for his father Jacob during forty days, so this son also renders his just due to his father Theodosius. And because some are accustomed to observe the third and the thirtieth day, others the seventh and the fortieth, let us consider what the scriptural text tells us. When Jacob died, it says, "Joseph commanded the servant undertakers to bury him, and the undertakers buried Israel, and forty days were completed for him; for thus the days of the funeral rites are reckoned. And Egypt mourned for him seventy days" (Gen 50:2–3). Accordingly, the observance that Scripture prescribes is to be followed. In Deuteronomy, also, it is written that "the children of Israel mourned for Moses thirty days, and the days of mourning were finished" (Deut 34:8). Both observances, then, have authority because the necessary duty of filial piety is fulfilled.

(4) And so Joseph was good, who furnished the model for filial devotion, whom his father loved, and to whom his father said: "May my God aid you, and may he bless you with the blessing of the earth holding all things because of the blessing of the breasts and of the womb, blessings of your mother, and because of the blessings of your father" (Gen 49:25–26). Joseph was the good offspring of a devoted father. So he, too, celebrates the fortieth day of his father, Jacob, that great supplanter, and we celebrate the fortieth day of Theodosius, who, after the example of Jacob, supplanted the perfidy of tyrants, who put away the idols of the Gentiles. For his faith removed all worship of images and stamped out all their ceremonies. He grieved, too, that the remission of punishment that he had granted to those who had transgressed against him had come to naught, the opportunity for pardon had been denied him. But his

sons will not refuse what their father granted, nor will they refuse, even though anyone should attempt to confuse or disturb them. Those who honor his grants to individuals will not be able to refuse what he granted for all.

(5) The death of so great a prince had in it nothing more glorious, who had already consigned all to his sons: his empire, his power, and the title Augustus. Nothing, I say, more splendid was reserved for him in death than the fact that while the promised mitigation of the necessary payment of the grain tax in some cases was delayed, his successor has become the heir of these indulgences, and the one who wished to prevent this has created ill will for himself. Nevertheless, the crown of so great a favor has not been taken away from Theodosius. And not undeservedly, for if the last wishes of private citizens and the testaments of the dying have permanent validity, how can the testament of so great a prince be considered void? Theodosius is also glorious in this, that he did not make his will in the ordinary manner, for he had no further provision to make for his sons, to whom he had given everything, except to commend them to a relative who was present. He was obliged to provide by will for all who were subject to him or committed to his care, so that he might discharge legacies and designate trusts. He ordered that a law of indulgence that he left in writing be published. What is more worthy than that this law be the last will of the emperor?

(6) Thus the great emperor has withdrawn from us, but he has not wholly withdrawn, for he has left us his children in whom we should recognize him, and in whom we behold and possess him. Let not their age disquiet you. The loyalty of his soldiers is the perfect age of an emperor, for age is perfect where strength is perfect. These characteristics are reciprocal, for the faith of an emperor also is the strength of his soldiers.

(7) You recall, I am sure, what triumphs the faith of Theodosius acquired for you. When, because of the difficulties of the terrain and the hindrance of camp followers, the army was deploying too slowly into combat position and through delay in offering battle the enemy seemed to be charging, the emperor

leaped down from his horse and, advancing alone before the line, he cried out: "Where is the God of Theodosius?" He spoke thus when already close to Christ, for who could have said this except one who knew that he was attaching himself to Christ? By this cry he aroused all, and by his example he armed all. He was already indeed somewhat advanced in years, but robust in faith.

(8) The faith of Theodosius, then, was your victory: let your faith be the strength of his sons. Faith, therefore, adds to age. Hence, even Abraham did not consider age when in old age he begot a son, nor Sarah, when she gave birth. And it is not astonishing if faith adds to age, since it anticipates the future. For what is faith except the substance of those things for which we hope (cf. Heb 11:1)? So the Scriptures teach us. Therefore, if faith is the substance of those things for which we hope, how much the more of those that we see? Good is the faith of which it is written: "But the just man lives by faith. But if he draws back, he will not please my soul" (Heb 10:38).

(9) Now, let us not draw back at the expense of our souls, but let us cling to faith for our soul's gain; for in this warfare of faith our elders, Abraham, Isaac, and Jacob, obtained proof, and thus they left us a heritage of faith. Abraham was faithful, who was justified not by works but by faith, since he believed in God. Isaac was faithful, who through faith did not fear the sword of his father as he was about to strike him. Jacob was faithful, who followed in the footprints of his father's faith and, while he was journeying, saw an army of angels and called it the council of God.

(10) Elsewhere, also, that is, in the Books of Kings we read that Elisha was in Samaria, and suddenly an army of Syrians surrounded and set upon him. Giezi saw them and said to his master: "O Master, what shall we do?" And Elisha the Prophet said: "Fear not, for there are more with us than with them." And he prayed that the Lord would open the eyes of Giezi. And his eyes were opened, and he saw the mountain full of horses and chariots around Elisha. And Elisha prayed that God would strike them with blindness. And they were struck, and they entered into the city where they were going, seeing not at all (2 Kings 6). Surely, you soldiers who have been surrounded have heard that where there is perfidy there is blindness. Rightly, therefore, was the army of the unbeliever blind. But where there is faith there is an army of angels. Good, then, is faith, which often exercises its power among the dead. Hence, our Adversary and his legions are daily hurled back by the virtue of the martyrs. So I think that the strings of the cithern are called *fides*[1] because, although dead, they give forth sound.

(11) Wherefore, we must strive more and more, lest while engaged in the tasks of life we be ungrateful, and let us bestow constant and paternal affection on the children of the pious prince. Pay to his sons what you owe to their father. You owe more to him now that he is dead than you owed to him while he was living. For, if among the children of private citizens the rights of minors are not violated without grave crime, how much more is this true in the case of the children of an emperor!

(12) It may be added: "Of what an emperor!" Of a pious emperor, of a merciful emperor, of a faithful emperor, concerning whom the Scripture has spoken in no ordinary manner, saying, "Great and in honor is the merciful man; but to find a faithful man is difficult" (Prov 20:6 [LXX]). If it is a great thing to find anyone who is merciful or faithful, how much more so an emperor whom power impels toward vengeance, but whom, nevertheless, compassion recalls from taking vengeance? What is more illustrious than the faith of an emperor whom power does not exalt, pride does not elevate, but piety bows down? Of him Solomon admirably says: "The threatening of an unjust king is like the roaring of a lion, but as dew upon the grass, so also is his cheerfulness" (Prov 19:12). Therefore, what a great thing it is to lay aside the terror of power and to prefer the sweetness of granting pardon!

(13) Theodosius of august memory thought he had received a kindness whenever he was asked to pardon, and he was more disposed to forgiveness at the

---

[1] Ambrose is making a Latin pun between a musical instrument, the cithern (*fides*), and Christian faith (*fides*).

time when the emotion of his wrath had been greatest. A token of forgiveness was that he had been angry, and what was feared in others was desired in him, that he be moved to wrath. It was the relief of the accused that, although he had power over all, he preferred to expostulate as a father rather than to punish as a judge. Often we have seen men whom he was rebuking tremble when convicted of crime, and then, when they had despaired, we have seen them freed from the charge. For he wished to win them as a fair judge, not to crush them as a dispenser of punishment, for he never denied pardon to one confessing guilt. If there was anything that the secret conscience concealed, he reserved that for God. Men feared that voice of his more than punishment because the emperor acted with such modesty as to prefer to attach men to himself by reverence rather than by fear.

(14) It is said that the greatest of the philosophers granted immunity from punishment to those crimes that had been committed through anger, but the divine Scripture says better: "Be angry and sin not" (Ps 4:4). It preferred rather to cut off sin than to excuse it. It is better to find praise for mercy in an occasion for indignation than to be incited by wrath toward vengeance.

(15) Who, then, will doubt that he will be a powerful protector for his sons in the house of God? By the favor of the Lord, the Emperor Arcadius is already a robust youth; Honorius now knocks on the door of manhood, a little older than Josiah. For the latter, having lost his father, assumed the government and reigned continuously for thirty-one years. He pleased the Lord because, better than the other kings of Israel, he celebrated the Pasch of the Lord and abolished false religious practices. Asa, likewise, though still of immature age when he succeeded to the throne, reigned in Jerusalem forty years. When he was hard pressed by an infinite and innumerable multitude of Ethiopians, he had trust in the Lord that he could be among the few saved. Would that he had been as faithful during his course as he was devout at its beginning! For, one of the few saved and a victor, he afterward abandoned the Lord and asked aid from the Syrians and summoned physicians to cure a disease of the feet. Since he had received such great in-

dications of divine favor, he ought not to have abandoned his Helper but to have retained him. Therefore, the physicians did not benefit him, and as an unbeliever he paid the penalty of death.

(16) But their fathers, Abiam and Amon, were both unbelievers. Theodosius, however, was filled with the fear of God, was filled with mercy, and we hope that he stands before Christ as a protector of his children, if the Lord be propitious to human affairs. The merciful man is a blessing. While he assists others, he is mindful of himself, and by applying remedies to others he cures his own wounds. For he who knows how to forgive realizes that he is human, and he follows the way of Christ who, by assuming flesh, chose to come into this world as a Redeemer rather than as a Judge.

(17) Hence the Psalmist has said beautifully: "I have loved, because the Lord will hear the voice of my prayer" (Ps 116:1). While this psalm was being read, we heard, as it were, Theodosius himself speaking. "I have loved," he says. I recognize his pious voice, and I recognize also his testimonies. And truly has he loved who fulfilled his duty diligently, who spared his enemies, who loved his foes, who pardoned those by whom he was entreated, who did not even allow those who strove to usurp his power to perish. That voice is of one not partially, but fully perfected in the Law, saying: "I have loved. For love is the fulfillment of the law" (Rom 13:10). But let us hear what he has loved. When the kind of love is not mentioned, surely the grace of divine charity is signified, whereby we love what is to be desired above all desirable things. Of this it is written: "You shall love the Lord your God" (Matt 22:37).

(18) Thus the good soul, on departing from earth and filled with the Holy Spirit, when questioned, as it were, by those who hastened to meet it as it rose to the high and lofty regions above, kept saying: "I have loved." Nothing is fuller than this, nothing is clearer. Angels and archangels asked repeatedly: "What have you done on earth?" For God alone is the witness of secret things. The soul kept saying, "I have loved," that is, "I have fulfilled the Law, I have not neglected the Gospel"; that is, "I have offered myself to death, and all the day long I am regarded as a sheep for the

slaughter. For I am sure that neither death, nor life, nor angels, nor powers, nor height, nor depth, nor any other creature will be able to separate us from the love of God that is in Christ Jesus our Lord" (Rom 8:38–39).

(19) The Lord Jesus also teaches in the Gospel that this commandment of the Law must be observed, when he says to Peter: "Simon, son of John, do you love me?" And he answered: "You know, Lord, that I love you." And he said a second time: "Simon, son of John, do you love me?" And again he answered: "Yea, Lord, you know that I love you." And when asked a third time, said: "Lord, you know all things, you know that I love you" (John 21:15–17). And so his threefold answer confirmed his love and effaced the fault of his threefold denial. And here, if we seek, we find the threefold answer: "I have loved, because the Lord will hear the voice of my prayer. I have loved since he has inclined his ear to me, that in my day I might call upon him. I have loved because I have found tribulation and sorrow, and for the sake of my God I have not fled the dangers of hell but have waited that they might seize and find me."

(20) And beautifully does he say: "I have loved," because now he had completed the course of this life. Wherefore, the Apostle also says in the midst of his suffering: "I have fought the good fight, I have finished the course, I have kept the faith. For the rest, there is laid up for me a crown of justice" (2 Tim 4:7–8). Great is the Lord who has given us the struggle, whereby he who has conquered merits to be crowned. "I have loved," he says trustingly, "because the Lord will hear the voice of my prayer" (Ps 116:1).

(21) "I have loved" and therefore "he has inclined his ear to me" (Ps 116:2), to raise up the fallen, to quicken the dead. For God does not incline his ear so as to hear corporally but to condescend to us. He deigns thus to hear us and to lift up the substance of our weakness. He inclines himself toward us that our prayer may ascend to him. He who offers mercy does not need a voice. He did not need a voice who heard Moses, though silent, and he said that Moses cried out to him, although he did not speak, but was pleading with unutterable groanings. God also knows how to hear blood, for which no voice exists nor tongue is

present, but it received a voice by virtue of the sacred Passion. It cried out in martyrdom, it cried out in the parricide that it suffered as a sacrifice.

(22) "I have loved," he said, and therefore, "with love I have done the will of the Lord, and I have called upon him not on a few, but on all the days of my life." For to call upon him on certain days and not on all is the mark of one who is proved, not of one who hopes. It is to return the debt of gratitude after the manner of those who abound in wealth and not from a spirit of devotion. And so Paul said: "Give thanks for all things" (1 Thess 5:18). For when do you not have something which you owe to God? Or when are you without a gift of God, since your daily enjoyment of living is from God? "For what do you have, that you have not received?" (1 Cor 4:7). Therefore, because you always receive, always call upon God, and since what you have is from God, always acknowledge that you are his debtor. I prefer that you pay your debts rather through love than as one forced to do so.

(23) Do you hear him saying: "The sorrows of death have encompassed me" (Ps 116:3)? "Still, I have loved the Lord even in the sorrows of death. The perils of hell have found me, not fearing indeed, but loving, but hoping, because no distress, no persecution, no dangers, no sword shall separate me from Christ." Therefore, he found tribulation and sorrow willingly, knowing that "tribulation works out endurance, and endurance tried virtue, and tried virtue hope" (Rom 5:3–4). As a good athlete, he sought the contest that he might gain the crown, but he knew that this was given to him not through his own strength but by the aid of God. He could not have been victorious had he not called upon him who helps contenders.

(24) Miserable man enters the contest to be victorious, and he rushes headlong into danger unless the name of the Lord be present with him, unless, when he fears, he prays, saying: "O Lord deliver my soul" (Ps 116:4). Hence we have these words of the Apostle: "But I see a law of my flesh warring against the law of my mind and making me prisoner to the law of sin, that is in my members. Unhappy man that I am! Who will deliver me from the body of this death?

The grace of God, by Jesus Christ our Lord" (Rom 7: 23–25).

(25) He is victorious who hopes for the grace of God, not he who presumes upon his own strength. For why do you not rely upon grace, since you have a merciful Judge in the contest. "For the Lord is merciful and just, and our God shows mercy" (Ps 116:5). Mercy is mentioned twice, but justice once. Justice is in the middle, enclosed by a double wall of mercy. Sins superabound. Therefore, let mercy superabound. With the Lord there is an abundance of all powers, for he is the Lord of hosts. Yet there is neither justice without mercy, nor without the exercise of mercy is there justice, for it is written: "Be not overjust" (Eccl 7:16). What is above measure, you cannot endure, even if it is good. Preserve measure that you may receive according to the measure.

(26) Yet mercy has not impeded justice because mercy is itself justice. "He has distributed, he has given to the poor, his justice remains forever" (Ps 112:9). For the just man knows that he ought to succor the weak and the needy. Wherefore, the Lord, coming to baptism in order to forgive us our sins because we are weak, said to John: "Let it be so now, for so it becomes us to fulfill all justice" (Matt 3:15). Thus, it is clear that justice is mercy, and mercy is justice. For if the mercy of God did not sustain us, how would we survive as infants in the very beginning when, issuing from the womb, from warmth into cold, from moisture into dryness, we are cast forth like fishes that a flood of nature, as it were, has cast shipwrecked into this life? Reason is lacking, but divine grace does not fail. Therefore, he himself guards the little ones or, at least, those who humbly confess that they are as little ones.

(27) Good, therefore, is humility. It delivers those who are in danger and raises those who have fallen. This humility was known to him who said: "Behold it is I that have sinned, and I the shepherd have done wickedly; and these in this flock, what have they done? Let your hand be against me" (2 Sam 24:17). Well does he say this who made his kingdom subject to God and did penance and, having confessed his sin, asked pardon. He attained salvation through humility. Christ humbled himself to raise up all, and whoever follows the humility of Christ attains the rest of Christ.

(28) And so because Theodosius, the emperor, showed himself humble and, when sin had stolen upon him, asked for pardon, his soul has turned to its rest, as Scripture has it, saying: "Turn my soul unto your rest, for the Lord has been bountiful to you" (Ps 116:7). Beautifully is it said to the soul: "Turn," that the soul, tired out, as it were, with the daily sweat of its toil, may turn from labor to rest. The horse is turned toward the stable when it has finished its course; the ship to the port, where it is given safe anchorage protected from the violence of the waves. But what is the meaning of the phrase, "to your rest," unless you understand it according to the words of the Lord Jesus: "Come, blessed of my Father, take possession of the kingdom prepared for you as an inheritance from the foundation of the world" (Matt 25:34)? For we receive, as it were, an inherited possession, the things that have been promised to us, for God is trustworthy and does not withdraw what he has once prepared for his servants. If our faith endures, his promise likewise endures.

(29) See, O man, the grace of Christ about you. Even while you are harassed on earth, you have possessions in heaven. There, then, let your heart be where your possession is. This is the rest that is due the just and is denied the unworthy. So says the Lord: "As I swore in my wrath, that they shall not enter into my rest" (Ps 95:11). For they who have not known the ways of the Lord shall not enter into the rest of the Lord, but to him who has fought the good fight and has finished his course it is said: "Turn to your rest." It is a blessed rest to pass by the things of the world and to find repose in the celestial fellowship of the mysteries that are above the world. This is the rest toward which the Prophet hastened, saying: "Who will give me wings like a dove and I will fly and be at rest?" (Ps 55:6). The holy man knows this as his rest, and to this rest he says his soul must turn. Therefore was his soul in its rest, to which he says it must return. This is the rest of the great Sabbath, in which each of the saints is above the sensible things of the world, devoting

himself entirely to deep and invisible mystery and cleaving to God. This is that rest of the Sabbath on which God rested from all the works of this world.

(30) Theodosius, now at peace, rejoices that he has been snatched away from the cares of this world, and he lifts up his soul and directs it to that great and eternal rest. He declares that he has been admirably cared for, since God has snatched his soul from death, the death that he frequently withstood in the treacherous conditions of this world, when he was disturbed by the waves of sin. And God has snatched his eyes from tears, for sorrow and sadness and mourning shall flee away. And elsewhere we have: "He shall wipe away every tear from their eyes, and death shall be no more; neither shall there be mourning, nor crying, nor pain" (Rev 21:4). If, then, death will be no more, he cannot suffer a fall when he is in that rest, but he will please God in the land of the living. For while man is here enveloped in a mortal body subject to falls and transgressions, that will not be so there. Therefore, that is the land of the living where the soul is, for the soul has been made to the image and likeness of God; it is not flesh fashioned from earth. Hence, flesh returns to earth, but the soul hastens to celestial rest, and to it is said: "Turn, my soul, to your rest."

(31) Theodosius hastened to enter upon this rest and to go into the city of Jerusalem, of which it is said: "And the kings of the earth shall bring their glory into it" (Rev 21:24). That is true glory that is assumed there, and that is a most blessed kingdom that is possessed there. To this the Apostle was hastening when he said: "We have the courage, then, and we prefer to be exiled from the body and to be at home with the Lord, and therefore we strive, whether in the body or out of it, to please him" (2 Cor 5:8–9).

(32) Thus freed from an uncertain struggle, Theodosius of august memory now enjoys perpetual light and lasting tranquility, and in return for what he did in this body, he rejoices in the fruits of a divine reward. Therefore, because Theodosius of august memory loved the Lord his God, he has merited the companionship of the saints.

(33) And to conclude my discourse by a kind of peroration, I have loved a merciful man, humble in power, endowed with a pure heart and a gentle disposition, a man such as God is accustomed to love, saying: "Upon whom shall I rest, unless upon the humble and gentle?" (Isa 66:2).

(34) I have loved a man who esteemed a reprover more than a flatterer. He threw on the ground all the royal attire that he was wearing. He wept publicly in church for his sin, which had stolen upon him through the deceit of others. He prayed for pardon with groans and with tears. What private citizens are ashamed to do, the emperor was not ashamed to do, namely, to perform penance publicly, nor did a day pass thereafter on which he did not bemoan that fault of his. Need I mention also that when he had gained an illustrious victory, yet because the enemy lay fallen in battle he abstained from participation in the sacraments until he recognized the grace of God toward him in the arrival of his children?

(35) I have loved a man who in his dying hour kept asking for me with his last breath. I have loved a man who, when he was already being released from the body, was more concerned about the condition of the Church than about his own trials. I have loved him, therefore, I confess, and for that reason I have suffered my sorrow in the depths of my heart and thought to be consoled by the delivery of a lengthy discourse. I have loved, and I presume upon the Lord that he will receive the voice of my prayer, with which I accompany this pious soul.

(36) "The sorrows of death have encompassed me, the perils of hell have found me" (Ps 116:3). For perils affect many, but remedies are found for few. A bishop participates in the perils of all, and he suffers anguish in all sinners. What others suffer he himself endures; in turn, he is freed when others who are beset with dangers are freed from them. I am crushed in heart because a man has been taken from us whom it is almost impossible to replace. Yet, O Lord, you alone should be called upon, you should be implored to replace him in his sons. You, Lord, the keeper also of little ones in this lowliness, save those hoping in you. Give perfect rest to your servant Theodosius, that rest that you have prepared for your saints. Let his soul turn from where it descended, where he can-

not feel the sting of death, where he knows that this death is not the end of nature but of guilt. "For the death that he dies, he died to sin" (Rom 6:10), so that there can no longer be a place for sin. And he will rise again, that his life may be restored more perfectly by a renewed gift.

(37) I have loved, and so I accompany him to the land of the living, and I will not abandon him until, by my tears and prayers, I shall lead the man to where his merits summon, unto the holy mountain of God, where there is eternal life, where there is no corruption, no sickness, no mourning, no sorrow, no companionship with the dead. It is the true land of the living where "this mortal body shall put on immortality and this corruptible body shall put on incorruption" (1 Cor 15:53). It is the great repose which fulfills the prayer of the living, a most glorious promise. Therefore, Psalm 116 bears the title "Alleluia." And, accordingly, above in Psalm 15 we have learned the perfection of man. But while the man represented there may be perfect, he still is subject to sin because he is living in this world. There above is true perfection, where sin has ceased and the beauty of perpetual rest has shone forth.

(38) We have Psalm 116 because it is the recompense of love. From this the Pasch of the Lord received its law of celebration at the fourteenth moon, since he who celebrates the Pasch ought to be perfect.[2] He should love the Lord Jesus who, cherishing his people with perfect love, offered himself in his Passion. And let us so love that if there should be need, we shall not avoid death for the name of the Lord, we shall not have thought for my suffering, and we shall fear nothing, "for perfect love casts out fear" (1 John 4:18). Sublime mystery of number, since the Father delivered his only Son for us all when the moon shone with the full orb of its light! For so is the Church, which devoutly celebrates the Pasch of our Lord Jesus Christ. As the perfect moon, she abides forever. Whoever during life fittingly celebrates the Pasch of the Lord shall be in perpetual light. Who celebrated it

more gloriously than he who removed sacrilegious errors, closed temples, destroyed idols? For in this was King Josiah preferred to his predecessors.

(39) Theodosius, then, abides in the light and glories in the assembly of the saints. There he now embraces Gratian, who no longer grieves for his wounds, for he has found an avenger. Although he was snatched away prematurely by an unworthy death, he possesses rest for his soul. There those two good and generous exponents of devotion rejoice in the common reward for their mercy. Of them it is well said: "Day to day utters speech." On the other hand, Maximus and Eugenius are in hell, as "night to night shows knowledge" (Ps 19:2). They teach by their wretched example how wicked it is for men to take up arms against their princes.[3] And of them it is admirably said: "I have seen the wicked highly exalted and lifted up like the cedars of Lebanon, and I passed by and lo, he was not!" (Ps 37:35–36). The pious man passed over from the darkness of the world to eternal day, and the wicked man was no more, for through his wickedness he ceased to be.

(40) Now, Theodosius of august memory knows that he reigns, since he is in the kingdom of our Lord Jesus Christ and contemplates his temple. Now, indeed, he is conscious of his kingship when he receives Gratian and Pulcheria, his sweetest children, whom he had lost here; when his Flacilla, a soul faithful to God, embraces him; when he rejoices that his father has been restored to him; and when he embraces Constantine. Although Constantine was in his last hours when he was freed by the grace of baptism from all sins, yet, since he was the first of the emperors to believe and left after him a heritage of faith to princes, he has found a place of great merit. Of his times the following prophecy has been fulfilled: "In that day that which is upon the bridle of the horse shall be holy to the Lord Almighty" (Zech 14:20). This was revealed by the great Helena of holy memory, who was inspired by the Spirit of God.

(41) Blessed was Constantine with such a mother! At her son's command she sought the aid of divine

---

[2] The "14" refers to the late antique numbering of the Psalms, in which Ps 116 was Ps 114.

[3] Maximus and Eugenius were usurpers.

favor in order that he might take part safely even in battles and not fear danger. Noble woman, who found much more to confer upon an emperor than she might receive from an emperor! The mother, solicitous for her son to whom the sovereignty of the Roman world had fallen, hastened to Jerusalem and explored the scene of the Lord's Passion.

(42) It is claimed that she originally was hostess of an inn, and thus became acquainted with the elder Constantine, who afterward obtained the imperial office. Good hostess, who so diligently searched for the manger of the Lord! Good hostess, who did not ignore that host who cared for the wounds of the man wounded by robbers! Good hostess, who preferred to be considered dung, to gain Christ! For that reason Christ raised her from dung to a kingdom, for it is written that "he raised up the needy from the earth and lifted up the poor out of the dunghill" (Ps 113:7).

(43) Helena, then, came and began to visit the holy places. The Spirit inspired her to search for the wood of the Cross. She drew near to Golgotha and said: "Behold the place of combat: where is your victory? I seek the banner of salvation and I do not find it. Shall I," she said, "be among kings, and the cross of the Lord lie in the dust? Shall I be covered by golden ornaments, and the triumph of Christ by ruins? Is this still hidden, and is the palm of eternal life hidden? How can I believe that I have been redeemed if the redemption itself is not seen?

(44) "I see what you did, O Devil, that the sword by which you were destroyed might be obstructed. But Isaac cleared out the wells stopped up by foreigners and did not permit the water to lie concealed. So let the ruins be removed that life may appear; let the sword by which the head of the real Goliath was cut off be drawn forth; let the earth be opened that salvation may shine out. Why did you labor to hide the wood, O Devil, except to be vanquished a second time? You were vanquished by Mary, who gave the Conqueror birth. Without any impairment of her virginity, she brought him forth to conquer you by his crucifixion and to subjugate you by his death. Today, also, you shall be vanquished when a woman discovers your snares. That holy woman bore the Lord; I shall search for his cross. She gave proof that he was born; I shall give proof that he rose from the dead. She caused God to be seen among men; I shall raise from ruins the divine banner that shall be a remedy for our sins."

(45) And so she opened the ground and cleared away the dust. She found three fork-shaped gibbets thrown together, covered by debris and hidden by the Enemy. But the triumph of Christ could not be wiped out. She hesitated in her uncertainty. She hesitated, as a woman, but the Holy Spirit inspired her to investigate carefully because two robbers had been crucified with the Lord. Therefore, she sought the middle-beam, but it could have happened that the debris had mixed the crosses one with another and that chance had interchanged them. She went back to the text of the Gospel and found that on the middle gibbet a title had been displayed, "Jesus of Nazareth, King of the Jews." Hence, a sequence of sound reasoning was established, and the Cross of salvation was revealed by its title. This is what Pilate answered to the Jews who petitioned him: "What I have written, I have written," that is: "I have not written these things to please you, but that future ages may know them. I have not written for you, but for posterity," saying, as it were: "Let Helena have something to read whereby she may recognize the cross of the Lord."

(46) She discovered, then, the title. She adored the King, not the wood, indeed, because this is an error of the Gentiles and a vanity of the wicked. But she adored him who hung on the tree, whose name was inscribed in the title; him, I say, who, as a scarab, cried out to his Father to forgive the sins of his persecutors. The woman eagerly hastened to touch the remedy of immortality, but she feared to trample under foot the mystery of salvation. Joyful at heart, yet with anxious step, she knew not what she should do. She proceeded, however, to the resting place of Truth. The wood shone and grace flashed forth. And, as before, Christ had visited a woman in Mary, so the Spirit visited a woman in Helena. He taught her what as a woman she did not know and led her upon a way that no mortal could know.

(47) She sought the nails with which the Lord was crucified and found them. From one nail she ordered a bridle to be made, from the other she wove a dia-

dem. She turned the one to an ornamental, the other to a devotional, use. Mary was visited to liberate Eve; Helena was visited that emperors might be redeemed. So she sent to her son Constantine a diadem adorned with jewels which were interwoven with the iron of the Cross and enclosed the more precious jewel of divine redemption. She sent the bridle also. Constantine used both and transmitted his faith to later kings. And so the beginning of the faith of the emperors is the holy relic that is upon the bridle. From that came the faith whereby persecution ended and devotion to God took its place.

(48) Wisely did Helena act who placed the cross on the head of sovereigns, that the Cross of Christ might be adored among kings. That was not presumption but piety, since honor was given to our holy redemption. Good, therefore, is the nail of the Roman Empire. It rules the whole world and adorns the brow of princes, that they may be preachers who were accustomed to be persecutors. Rightly is the nail on the head, so that where the intelligence is, there may be protection also. On the head, a crown; in the hands, reins. A crown made from the Cross, that faith might shine forth; reins likewise from the Cross, that authority might govern and that there might be just rule, not unjust legislation. May the princes also consider that this has been granted to them by Christ's generosity, that in imitation of the Lord it may be said of the Roman emperor: "You have set on his head a crown of precious stones" (Ps 21:3).

(49) On that account the Church manifests joy, the Jew blushes. Not only does he blush, but he is tormented also because he himself is the author of his own confusion. While he insulted Christ, he confessed that he was King; when he called him king of the Jews, he who did not believe confessed his sacrilege. "Behold," they say, "we have crucified Jesus, that Christians after death may rise again and, having died, may reign! We have crucified him whom kings adore; him whom we do not adore they do adore! Behold, even the nail is held in honor, and he whom we crucified to death is the remedy of salvation and by an invisible power torments demons! We thought that we had conquered, but we confess that we ourselves are conquered! Christ has risen again, and princes ac-

knowledge that he has risen. He who is not seen lives again." Now we have a greater struggle; now the battle against him becomes more furious. We have despised him whom kingdoms attend, whom power serves. How shall we resist kings? Kings are bowed under the iron of his feet! Kings adore him, and Photinians deny his divinity! Emperors prefer the nail of his Cross to their own diadem, and Arians violate his power!

(50) But I ask: Why was the holy relic upon the bridle if not to curb the insolence of emperors, to check the wantonness of tyrants, who as horses neigh after lust that they may be allowed to commit adultery unpunished? What infamies do we not find in the Neros, the Caligulas, and the rest, for whom there was nothing holy upon the bridle?

(51) What else, then, did Helena accomplish by her desire to guide the reins than to seem to say to all emperors through the Holy Spirit: "Do not become like the horse and mule" (Ps 32:9), and with the bridle and bit to restrain the jaws of those who did not realize that they were kings to rule those subject to them? For power easily led them into vice, and like cattle they defiled themselves in promiscuous lust. They knew not God. The Cross of the Lord restrained them and recalled them from their fall into wickedness. It raised their eyes that they might look toward heaven and seek Christ. They threw off the bit of unbelief. They took the bridle of devotion and faith, following him who said: "Take my yoke upon you, for my yoke is easy and my burden light" (Matt 11:29–30). Thereafter, the succeeding emperors were Christians, except Julian alone, who abandoned the Author of his salvation when he gave himself over to philosophic error. After him came Gratian and Theodosius.

(52) Prophecy did not lie, then, when it said: "Kings shall walk in your light" (Isa 60:3[LXX]). They shall walk openly, and especially Gratian and Theodosius before other princes, no longer protected by the weapons of their soldiers, but by their own merits; clothed not in purple garments, but in the mantle of glory. In this world they took delight in pardoning many. How much the more are they consoled in the other life by the remembrance of their goodness, recalling that they had spared many? They now

enjoy radiant light, and, possessing far nobler dwellings there than they enjoyed here, they say: "O Israel, how great is the house of the Lord, and how vast is the place of his possession! It is great and has no end" (Bar 3:24–25). And they who have endured the greatest hardships converse with each other, saying: "It is good for a man when he has borne the heavy yoke from his youth. He shall not sit solitary, and shall hold his peace because he has borne a heavy yoke" (Lam 3:27–28). For he who has borne the heavy yoke from youth rests afterward. Removed from the throng, he possesses a distinguished place for his rest, saying: "For you, O Lord, singularly have settled me in hope" (Ps 4:8).

(53) Lazarus, the poor man, bore the heavy yoke from his youth, and so he rests apart in Abraham's bosom, according to the testimony of the sacred text (Luke 16:20). Theodosius bore the heavy yoke from youth, since those who had killed his victorious father were plotting against his safety. He bore the heavy yoke, since he endured exile because of filial devotion and since he assumed the imperial power when the Roman Empire was overrun by barbarians. He bore the heavy yoke that he might remove tyrants from the Roman Empire. But, because he labored here, he rests there.

(54) But now let us come to the transportation of the illustrious body. You weep, Honorius, illustrious scion, and give testimony of your filial love by your tears. You are sending the body of your father on a long and distant journey, for it still lacks the honor of a tomb. But the patriarch Jacob, because of the necessity of liberating his people who were being oppressed by the dangers of a great and bitter famine, also left his home, though an old man, and hastened to a foreign land. When he had died, his body, escorted by his son, was brought in the course of some days to the sepulcher of his fathers. And nothing was taken away from his merits; rather, it redounded to his praise that having suffered the loss of his rightful home for the sake of his family, he traveled like an exile even after his death.

(55) You weep, also, august emperor, because you yourself will not escort the honored remains to Constantinople. We are both in the same situation. We all shall accompany them with due sorrow. We should all like, if it were possible, to go with you as an escort for the body. But Joseph went into a neighboring province. Here, many different regions intervene; here, seas must be crossed. Even this would not be laborious to you, did not the public welfare restrain you, which good emperors place before parents and children. Therefore, your father made you emperor, and God has confirmed this, so that you might not serve under your father only, but that you might have command over all.

(56) Do not fear lest the triumphant remains may seem to be unhonored wherever they go. This is not the feeling of Italy, which witnessed his magnificent triumphs, which, freed for a second time from tyrants, acclaims the author of her liberty. This is not the feeling of Constantinople, which for a second time has sent a prince to victory. Although she wished to retain him, she could not. She was indeed awaiting triumphal celebrations at his return and the tokens of victories. She was awaiting the emperor of the whole world, surrounded by the army from Gaul and supported by the might of the whole world. But now Theodosius returns there, more powerful, more glorious. Choirs of angels escort him, and a multitude of saints accompanies him. Surely, blessed are you, Constantinople, for you are receiving a citizen of paradise, and you will possess in the august hospice of his buried body a dweller of the celestial city.

CHAPTER **4**

Christianity and Roman Law

Law in the Roman Empire was something of a jumble. Legal arbitration was not a full-time profession, but rather the job of political appointees who held local administrative office for a limited time. These administrator-judges acted on common sense, some legal precedent, and the advice of professional experts. Often regional law in the provinces contradicted laws emanating from the Senate or imperial courts, as documentary evidence from Egypt has shown. There was no standing police force: both civil and criminal legal actions were initiated by private parties (often paid snitches) or, occasionally, intervening agents of the state.

The first great systematization of Roman law executed under imperial auspices came when the eastern Emperor Theodosius II (408–50) put together a panel of legal experts to sift through more than a century of opinions, rulings, and rescripts. The final product, the Theodosian Code, was presented to the Senates in Rome and Constantinople in 438. On the surface, this was not an overtly Christian project: the Code's sixteen books treat topics such as taxation, inheritance and family law, slavery, politics, the military, and public works. Only the final book explicitly treats religion. But this omnibus attempt to systematize Roman law is, nonetheless, shot through with Christian significance. Theodosius's commission did not include laws dating prior to 312, the date of Constantine's conversion to Christianity; that is, no laws promulgated by a non-Christian emperor are included (the one exception is Julian). In addition, the project itself, initiated by the superpious Theodosius, hints at a new imperial concern for totality and uniformity: an orthodoxy of law to match the new orthodoxy of the spirit. It is significant, in this respect, that previous, more limited attempts to systematize Roman law came under Diocletian, who also sought religious uniformity through the Great Persecution. An additional impetus for creating a new law code for a Christian empire may have come from the rise of a new site of legal arbitration: episcopal courts, where Christian parties sought satisfaction for claims from a local bishop without recourse to Roman authorities. Historians still debate, however, whether Christianity had any real impact on the already morally and socially conservative legal stance of Roman emperors.

The scattershot execution of Roman jurisprudence makes historical evaluation of the social significance of the Code difficult. At a minimum, we may assume that laws would not forbid something if people were not actually doing it (although even this legal truism must be weighed against the highly rhetorical nature of ancient laws, which were prone to exaggerated outrage). In addition, financial and family laws give a sense principally of the concerns of the moneyed elites. Moreover, we may perhaps never know the extent to which these laws were enforced or even the degree to which citizens were aware of them. We can, however, gain a sense of how Roman emperors deployed the rhetoric of legal and moral correctness as they set out to fashion a comprehensive and uniform Christian empire in Late Antiquity.

FOR FURTHER READING

Arjava, Antti. *Women and Law in Late Antiquity.* Oxford, England: Clarendon Press, 1996.

Evans Grubbs, Judith. *Law and Family in Late Antiquity: The Emperor Constantine's Marriage Legislation.* Oxford, England: Clarendron Press, 1995.

Harries, Jill. *Law and Empire in Late Antiquity.* Cambridge, England: Cambridge University Press, 1999.

Harries, Jill, and Wood, Ian, eds. *The Theodosian Code.* Ithaca, N.Y.: Cornell University Press, 1993.

Honoré, Tony. *Law in the Crisis of Empire, 379–455 AD: The Theodosian Dynasty and Its Quaestors.* Oxford, England: Clarendon Press, 1998.

Lamoreaux, John. "Episcopal Courts in Late Antiquity." *Journal of Early Christian Studies* 3 (1995): 143–67.

Matthews, John. *Laying Down the Law: A Study of the Theodosian Code.* New Haven, Conn.: Yale University Press, 2000.

The Texts

9. Theodosian Code: On Religion

Book 16, the final book of the Theodosian Code, treats religion. The tenor and contents of this book give us a sense of how the imperial court refashioned its own religious authority in the centuries following the legalization of Christianity. Although bishops might attempt to subordinate the imperial house to episcopal authority (see Text 8), the emperors still maintained their role as guardians of religious equilibrium. So emperors convoked Christian councils (see Chapter 8) and legislated on religion.

Such legislation might be broad and sweeping, such as the famous 16.1.2, making "Catholic" Christianity the official Christianity (although not quite the official religion) of the empire. This law was later deemed to be so significant that it was promoted to the head of the massive law code commissioned by the sixth-century Emperor Justinian. The concern not only to recognize and proscribe, but to catalog and delimit, Christian heresies with a proliferation of labels has been adopted for legal purposes from the writings of heresiologists (see Chapter 7). But the laws do not merely codify religious biases. We see emperors attempting to balance the good of the state with their blazing zeal for Christian orthodoxy as they debate clerical exemption from costly public service and rein in exuberant monastics (male and female). The status of non-Christians in imperial law is also notable: at times, emperors legislate against non-Christian religious practices (animal sacrifice, public Jewish festivals) in the name of Christian loyalty, but they are also careful to protect non-Christian persons against religious violence (see 16.10.24). Imperial legislation on religion—Christian and non-Christian—thus provides an ambivalent window into the overlap and conjunction of law and faith.

Note: The year each law was issued is noted in parentheses at the end of that law's text.

1 (2) Emperors Gratian, Valentinian, and Theodosius Augustuses: An Edict to the People of the City of Constantinople.

It is Our will that all the peoples who are ruled by the administration of Our Clemency shall practice that religion that the divine Peter the Apostle transmitted to the Romans, as the religion that he introduced makes clear even unto this day. It is evident that this is the religion that is followed by the Pontiff Damasus and by Peter, bishop of Alexandria, a man of apostolic sanctity; that is, according to the apostolic discipline and the evangelic doctrine, we shall believe in the single Deity of the Father, the Son, and the Holy Spirit, under the concept of equal majesty and of the Holy Trinity.

We command that those persons who follow this rule shall embrace the name of Catholic Christians. The rest, however, whom We adjudge demented and insane, shall sustain the infamy of heretical dogmas, their meeting places shall not receive the name of churches, and they shall be smitten first by divine vengeance and second by the retribution of Our own initiative, which We shall assume in accordance with the divine judgment (380).

2 (2) The same Augustus [Constantine] to Octavianus, Governor of Lucania and of Bruttium.

Those persons who devote the services of religion to divine worship, that is, those who are called clerics, shall be exempt from all compulsory public services whatever, lest, through the sacrilegious malice of certain persons, they should be called away from divine services (313).

2 (3) The same Augustus [Constantine] to Bassus, Praetorian Prefect.

A constitution was issued that directs that thenceforth no decurion or descendant of a decurion or even any person provided with adequate resources and suitable to undertake compulsory public services shall take refuge in the name and the service of the clergy, but that in the place of deceased clerics thereafter only those persons shall be chosen as substitutes who have slender fortunes and who are not held bound to such compulsory municipal services. But We have learned that those persons also are being disturbed who became associated with the clergy before the promulgation of the aforesaid law. We command, therefore, that the latter shall be freed from all annoyance and that the former, who in evasion of public duties have taken refuge in the number of the clergy after the issuance of the law, shall be completely separated from that body, shall be restored to their orders and to the municipal councils, and shall perform their municipal duties (329).

2 (27) Emperors Valentinian, Theodosius, and Arcadius Augustuses to Tatianus, Praetorian Prefect.

According to the precept of the Apostle, no woman shall be transferred to the society of deaconesses unless she is sixty years of age and has the desired offspring at home (cf. 1 Tim 5:9). Then, after she has sought a curator for her children if their age should so require, she shall entrust her goods to suitable persons, to be managed diligently and conscientiously. She herself shall receive only the income from her landed estates, which she shall have full power to keep, to alienate, to give, to sell, or to bequeath, as long as she lives or when she is departing to her fate, and her will is unrestricted. She shall expend none of her jewels and ornaments, none of her gold and silver and other embellishments of a sumptuous home, under the pretext of religion. Rather, she shall transfer in writing all her property intact to her children or next of kin or to any other persons whatsoever, according to the judgment of her own free will. However, when she dies, she shall designate as heirs no church, no cleric, or no pauper. For her will shall necessarily lack all force if it should be composed by the decedent contrary to the prohibition concerning the persons specifically mentioned above. Furthermore, if anything should be extorted from the decedent by the aforesaid persons, nothing shall be bestowed on clerics, to the fraud of Our venerable sanction, by secret trust, through cunning artifice or the disgraceful connivance of any person. Rather, they shall be deprived of all the goods which they had coveted. Moreover, if anything is revealed to have been transferred in writing through a letter, codicil, gift, or testament, or finally, in any way whatsoever, to those persons whom We have excluded by this sanction, such deed of transfer shall not be cited in court. On the contrary, according to the limitation prescribed by this statute, that person shall succeed as heir through intestacy who understands that he is entitled to the goods, provided that he acknowledges that he is a child or proves that he is a near kinsman; or finally, if either by chance or by will he is found to be an heir, a legatee, or a beneficiary of a trust for all or for a portion of the goods, by an open codicil; he shall enjoy the gift of his fortune, the reward of his knowledge, and after the above-mentioned persons have been disqualified and rejected, he shall assume the authority of an heir over the hereditary substance.

Women who cut off their hair, contrary to divine and human laws, at the instigation and persuasion of some professed belief, shall be kept away from the doors of the churches. It shall be unlawful for them to approach the consecrated mysteries, nor shall they be granted, through any supplications, the privilege of frequenting the altars that must be venerated by all. Moreover, if a bishop should permit a woman with shorn head to enter a church, even the bishop himself shall be expelled from his position and kept away, along with such comrades. Not only if he should recommend that this be done, but even if he should learn that it is being accomplished by any persons, or, finally, that it has been done in any way whatsoever, he shall understand that nothing will exonerate him. This shall indisputably serve as a law for those who deserve correction and as a customary practice for those who have already received correction, so that the latter may have a witness, and the former may begin to fear judgment (390).

3 (1) Emperors Valentinian, Theodosius, and Arcadius Augustuses to Tatianus, Praetorian Prefect.

If any persons should be found in the profession of monks, they shall be ordered to seek out and to inhabit desert places and desolate solitudes (390).

3 (2) The same Augustuses to Tatianus, Praetorian Prefect.

We direct that the monks to whom the municipalities had been forbidden, since they are strengthened by judicial injustices, shall be restored to their original status, and the aforesaid law (i.e., **3** (1) above) shall be repealed. Thus indeed, We revoke such a decree of Our Clemency, and We grant them free ingress into the towns (392).

5 (65) Emperors Theodosius and Valentinian Augustuses to Florentius, Praetorian Prefect.

The madness of the heretics must be so suppressed that they shall know beyond doubt, before all else, that the churches that they have taken from the orthodox, wherever they are held, shall immediately be surrendered to the Catholic Church, since it cannot be tolerated that those who ought not to have churches of their own should continue to detain those possessed or founded by the orthodox and invaded by such rash lawlessness.

Next, if they should join to themselves other clerics or priests, as they consider them, a fine of ten pounds of gold for each person shall be paid into Our treasury, both by him who created such cleric and by him who allowed himself to be so created, or if they should pretend poverty, such fine shall be exacted from the common body of clerics of the aforesaid superstition or even from their offertories.

Furthermore, since not all should be punished with the same severity, the Arians, indeed, the Macedonians, and the Apollinarians, whose crime it is to be deceived by harmful meditation and to believe lies about the Fountain of Truth, shall not be permitted to have a church within any municipality. Moreover, the Novatians and Sabbatians shall be deprived of the privilege of any innovation, if perchance they should so attempt. The Eunomians, indeed, the Valentinians, the Montanists or Priscillianists, the Phrygians, the Marcianists, the Borborians, the Messalians, the Euchites or Enthusiasts, the Donatists, the Audians, the Hydroparastatae, the Tascodrogitae, the Photinians, the Paulians, the Marcellians, and those who have arrived at the lowest depth of wickedness, namely, the Manicheans, shall nowhere on Roman soil have the right to assemble and pray. The Manicheans, moreover, shall be expelled from the municipalities, since no opportunity must be left to any of them whereby an injury may be wrought upon the elements themselves. No employment at all in the imperial service shall be permitted them except on gubernatorial office staffs in the provinces and as soldiers in the camp. They shall be conceded no right at all to make reciprocal gifts, no right to make a testament or last will. All the laws that were formerly issued and promulgated at various times against such persons and against all others who oppose our faith shall remain in force forever, by vigorous observance, whether concerning gifts made to the churches of the heretics or property left in any manner by last will, whether concerning private buildings in which they have assembled with the permission or connivance of the owner and that shall be vindicated to the Catholic Church, which must be venerated by us, or concerning a procurator who has permitted such assembly without the knowledge of the owner and who shall be subject of a fine of ten pounds of gold or to exile if he is freeborn, or, if he is of servile condition, he shall be flogged and sent to the mines. Moreover, such heretics shall not be able to assemble in any public place or to build churches for themselves or to devise any scheme for the circumvention of the laws. They shall be prevented therefrom by all civil and military power and also by the power of the municipal councils and defenders and the judges, under threat of a fine of twenty pounds of gold. Furthermore, all those laws that were promulgated concerning the imperial service and concerning the right to make gifts or with reference to testamentary capacity, a capacity that must either be denied altogether or one that was barely conceded to certain persons, and those laws concerning various penalties against the different heretics, shall remain in full force, and not even a special grant of imperial favor impetrated contrary to the laws shall avail.

None of the heretics shall be given permission to lead again to their own baptism either freeborn persons or their own slaves who have been initiated into the mysteries of the orthodox Church, nor indeed shall they be allowed to prevent from following the religion of the Catholic Church those persons whom they have bought or have possessed in any way and who are not yet adherents of their superstition. If any person should administer such baptism or should permit it to be administered to him and should not report the fact, if he is freeborn, he shall be condemned to exile and a fine of ten pounds of gold, and to both offenders shall be denied the right to make a testament or a gift.

We decree that all the foregoing provisions shall be so enforced that no judge may order a minor punishment or no punishment at all for such a crime when it is reported to him, unless he himself is willing to suffer the penalty that through connivance he has remitted for others (428).

8 (18) Emperors Honorius and Theodosius Augustuses to Anthemius, Praetorian Prefect.

The governors of the provinces shall prohibit the Jews, in a certain ceremony of their festival[1] Haman

in commemoration of some former punishment, from setting fire to and burning a simulated appearance of the holy cross, in contempt of the Christian faith and with sacrilegious mind, lest they associate the sign of Our faith with their places. They shall maintain their own rites without contempt of the Christian law, and they shall unquestionably lose all privileges that have been permitted them heretofore unless they refrain from unlawful acts (408).

10 (10) The same Augustuses [Valentinian, Theodosius, and Arcadius] to Albinus, Praetorian Prefect.

No person shall pollute himself with sacrificial animals; no person shall slaughter an innocent victim; no person shall approach the shrines, shall wander through the temples, or revere the images formed by mortal labor, lest he become guilty by divine and human laws. Judges also shall be bound by the general rule that if any of them should be devoted to profane rites and should enter a temple for the purpose of worship anywhere, either on a journey or in the city, he shall immediately be compelled to pay fifteen pounds of gold, and his office staff shall pay a like sum with similar haste unless they resist the judge and immediately report him by a public attestation. Governors with the rank of consular shall pay six pounds of gold each, their office staffs a like amount; those with the rank of corrector or of praeses shall pay four pounds each, and their apparitors, by equal lot, a like amount (391).

10 (24) The same Augustuses [Honorius and Theodosius] to Asclepiodotus, Praetorian Prefect.

(After other matters.) We punish with proscription of their goods and exile, Manicheans and those persons who are called Pepyzites. Likewise, those persons who are worse than all other heretics in this one belief, namely, that they disagree with all others as to the venerable day of Easter, shall be punished with the same penalty if they persist in the aforesaid madness.

But We especially command those persons who are truly Christians or who are said to be, that they shall not abuse the authority of religion and dare to lay violent hands on Jews and pagans who are living quietly and attempting nothing disorderly or contrary to law. For if such Christians should be violent

---

[1] That is, the Jewish festival of Purim.

against persons living in security or should plunder their goods, they shall be compelled to restore not only that property that they took away, but after suit they shall also be compelled to restore triple or quadruple that amount that they robbed. Also the governors of the provinces and their office staffs and the provincials shall know that if they permit such a crime to be committed, they, too, will be punished in the same way as the perpetrators of the crime (423).

10. The Novellas

The promulgation of the Theodosian Code did not close the door on Roman law and did not give the final word on imperial intervention into religious matters. The emperors of the fifth and sixth centuries (up to the publication of a new Code by Emperor Justinian in 529) continued to issue supplemental laws, "novellas." The following are two such novellas, from the Emperors Theodosius II and Valentinian III, that return to themes of religious significance addresssed in the Theodosian Code: the ambivalent place of non-Christians in a legally Christian empire and the increasing demonization and legal penalization of heretics (here the Manicheans, who, as the novella points out, were, in fact, outlawed even by the pagan Emperor Diocletian and who would be deemed the "archheretics" of the Middle Ages). Law was perceived, even after the publication of the Code, as an evolving, creative effort, constantly amended to enforce better the unwavering truth of Christian, and now imperial, orthodoxy.

THEODOSIUS'S NOVELLA 3

ON JEWS, SAMARITANS, HERETICS, AND PAGANS

Emperors Theodosius and Valentinian Augustuses to Florentius, Praetorian Prefect

Among the other anxieties that Our love for the State has imposed upon Us for Our ever watchful consideration, We perceive that an especial responsibility of Our Imperial Majesty is the pursuit of the true religion. If We shall be able to hold fast to the worship of this true religion, We shall open the way to prosperity in human undertakings. This We have learned by the experience of Our long life and by the decision of Our pious mind We decree that the ceremonies of sanctity shall be established by a law of perpetual duration, even to posterity.

(1) For who is so demented, so damned by the enormity of strange savagery, that when he sees the heavens with incredible swiftness define the measures of time within their spaces under the sway of the divine guidance, when he sees the movements of the stars that control the benefits of life, the earth richly endowed with the harvests, the waters of the sea, and the vastness of this immense achievement confined within the boundaries of the natural world, he does not seek the author of so great a mystery, of so mighty a handiwork? We learn that the Jews, with blinded senses, the Samaritans, the pagans, and the other breeds of heretical monsters dare to do this. If We should attempt by a remedial law to recall them to the sanity of an excellent mind, they themselves will be blameworthy for Our severity, since they leave no place for pardon by the obstinate wickedness of their unyielding arrogance.

(2) Wherefore, since according to the ancient

From *The Theodosian Code and the Sirmondian Constitutions,* ed. Clyde Pharr et al. Copyright © 1952 by Clyde Pharr, renewed 1980 by Roy Pharr. Reprinted by permission of Princeton University Press.

maxim,[1] no cure must be employed for hopeless diseases, in order that these deadly sects, oblivious of Our age, may not spread too wantonly into the life of Our people like an indistinguishable confusion, We finally sanction by this law, destined to live in all ages, that no Jew, no Samaritan, who does not rely on either law shall enter upon any honors or dignities; to none of them shall the administration of a civil duty be available, nor shall they perform even the duties of a defender. Indeed, We believe that it is wrong that persons hostile to the Supernal Majesty and to the Roman laws should be considered the avengers of Our laws under the protection of a surreptitious jurisdiction; that they should be protected by the authority of a dignity thus acquired; that they should have the power to judge or to pronounce whatever sentence they may wish against the Christians and very often against the bishops themselves of the holy religion, as if they were insulting Our faith.

(3) With an equally reasonable consideration also, We prohibit any synagogue to arise as a new building, but license is granted to strengthen the ancient synagogues that threaten immediately to fall in ruin.

(4) To these regulations We add the provision that if any person should seduce a slave or a freeborn person, against his will or by punishable persuasion, from the worship of the Christian religion to an impious sect or ritual, he shall suffer capital punishment, together with the forfeiture of his fortune.

(5) If any person of these sects, therefore, has assumed the insignia of office, he shall not possess the dignities that he has acquired, and if he has erected a synagogue, he shall know that he has labored for the profit of the Catholic Church. Furthermore, if any of these persons has stolen into a position of honor, he shall be considered, as previously, of the lowest condition, even though he should have obtained an honorary dignity. If any one of them should begin the building of a synagogue, not with the desire merely to repair it, in addition to the loss of fifty pounds of gold, he shall be deprived of his audacious undertaking. Besides, he shall perceive that his goods are pro-

scribed and that he himself shall immediately be destined to the death penalty if he should overthrow the faith of another by his perverted doctrine.

(6) Since it behooves Our Imperial Majesty to embrace all contingencies in such a provision that the public welfare may not be injured in any way, We decree that the decurions of all municipalities and also the gubernatorial apparitors shall be bound to their onerous duties, even those of the imperial service, or to the various obligations of their resources and the duties of their personal compulsory services, and they shall adhere to their own orders, of whatsoever sect they may be. Thus We shall not appear on account of the contumely of corrupt solicitation to grant the favor of exemption to men who are execrable, since it is Our will that they shall be condemned by the authority of this constitution.

(7) The following exception shall be observed, namely, that apparitors who are members of the aforesaid sects shall execute the sentences of judges only in private suits, and they shall not be in charge of the custody of prisons, lest Christians, as customarily happens, may at times be thrust into prison by the hatred of their guards and thus suffer a second imprisonment, when it is not certain that they appear to have been rightfully imprisoned.

(8) Hence Our Clemency perceives that We must exercise watchfulness over the pagans also and their heathen enormities, since with their natural insanity and stubborn insolence they depart from the path of the true religion. They disdain in any way to practice the nefarious rites of their sacrifices and the false doctrines of their deadly superstition in the hidden solitudes, unless their crimes are made public by the nature of their profession, to the outrage of the Supernal Majesty and to the contempt of Our times. A thousand terrors of the laws that have been promulgated, the penalty of exile that has been threatened, do not restrain them, whereby, if they cannot be reformed, at least they might learn to abstain from their mass of crimes and from the corruption of their sacrifices. But straightway they sin with such audacious madness and Our patience is so assailed by the attempts of these impious persons that even if We desired to forget them, We could not disregard them.

---

[1] Of Hippocrates.

Therefore, although the love of religion can never be secure, although their pagan madness demands the harshness of all kinds of punishments, nevertheless We are mindful of the clemency that is innate in Us, and We decree by an unshakable order that if any person of polluted and contaminated mind should be apprehended in making a sacrifice in any place whatsoever, Our wrath shall rise up against his fortunes, against his life. For We must give this better victim, and the altar of Christianity shall be kept inviolate. Shall we endure longer that the succession of the seasons be changed and the temper of the heavens be stirred to anger, since the embittered perfidy of the pagans does not know how to preserve these balances of nature? For why has the spring renounced its accustomed charm? Why has the summer, barren of its harvest, deprived the laboring farmer of his hope of a grain harvest? Why has the intemperate ferocity of winter with its piercing cold doomed the fertility of the lands with the disaster of sterility? Why all these things, unless nature has transgressed the decree of its own law to avenge such impiety? In order that we may not hereafter be compelled to sustain such circumstances, by a peaceful vengeance, as We have said, the venerable majesty of the Supernal Divinity must be appeased.

(9) It remains to be said, O Florentius, dearest and most beloved Father, that all inaction shall cease and that the regulations shall be put into swift execution that have been issued in innumerable constitutions against the Manicheans, always odious to God; against the Eunomians, authors of heretical folly; against the Montanists, the Phrygians, the Photinians, the Priscillianists, the Ascodrogians, the Hydroparastatae, the Borboritae, and the Ophitans.

(10) Therefore, since it is dear to your heart to exercise implicit obedience to both the divine and the imperial commands, Your Illustrious and Magnificent Authority, by duly posting edicts of Your Excellency shall cause to come to the knowledge of all that which We have decreed for the insatiable honor of the Catholic religion. You shall also direct that these commands shall be announced to the governors of the provinces, so that by their like solicitude they may make known to all the municipalities

and provinces what We have necessarily sanctioned (438).

VALENTINIAN'S NOVELLA 18

ON THE MANICHEANS

Emperors Theodosius and Valentinian Augustuses to Albinus, Praetorian Prefect for the Second Time

That superstition that was condemned also in pagan times, which is hostile to the public discipline and an enemy to the Christian faith, has not undeservedly provoked Our Clemency to its own destruction. We are speaking of the Manicheans, whom the statutes of all the former emperors have adjudged execrable and worthy of expulsion from the whole world. Their crimes, which have been recently detected, do not permit Us to disregard them. For what things that are obscene to tell and to hear have been revealed by their very manifest confession in the court of the most blessed Pope Leo, in the presence of the most august Senate! Thus even the man who was also said to be their bishop both betrayed with his own voice and wrote out all the secrets of their crimes. This matter could not escape Our notice, since it is not safe for Us to disregard so detestable an outrage to the Divinity of God and to leave unpunished a crime whereby not only the bodies of deluded persons, but also their souls, are inexpiably polluted.

(1) Whence, O Albinus, dearest and most beloved Father, Your Illustrious and Excellent Magnificence shall know that We have decreed by this law, which shall live forever and which you shall cause to come to the knowledge of all the provinces by posting edicts, that if any of the Manicheans should be apprehended anywhere in the world, he shall receive, by the authority of the public severity, the penalties that the laws have sanctioned against persons guilty of sacrilege.

(2) This heresy shall be a public crime, and every person who wishes shall have the right to accuse such persons without the risk attendant upon an accusation.

(3) It shall not be licit and safe for any person either to conceal such persons or to connive at them,

since all the constitutions of the former emperors in regard to such heretics have been confirmed by Us, so that all men shall know that by this edictal law that has been published the Manicheans shall be deprived of the dignity of the imperial service and of the right of residence in the cities, in order that no innocent person may be ensnared by the intercourse and association of such persons. They shall neither take nor leave inheritances, but such inheritances shall be added to the resources of Our fisc. They shall not seek by any fraud that which We publicly forbid them. They shall forfeit the right of action for outrages against them; they shall have no freedom of contract at all.

(4) The primates of every branch of the imperial service and of every office staff shall be punished with a fine of ten pounds of gold, which shall be exacted by your apparitors, if they should permit any person polluted by this superstition to perform imperial service. For it does not appear that anything too severe can be decreed against those persons whose unchaste perversity, in the name of religion, commits crimes that are unknown and shameful even to brothels (445).

CHAPTER 5

Becoming a Christian

The North African Christian writer Tertullian noted in the second century, "Christians are not born, but made." Christians from the beginning construed their religious affiliation as a matter of choice and felt the imperative to spread the message and persuade as many others as possible to make the same choice. Even in established Christian communities in the fourth and fifth centuries, Christians continued to be "made": an infant born of Christian parents still had to be formally brought into the religion, through education and initiation. As the example of Augustine shows (see Text 11), even in the late fourth century it could be expected that a child of Christian parents would explore and study before officially entering the Christian fold.

"Making" a Christian was perceived in both internal and external terms. On the one hand, following the legalization of Christianity, when the profession of Christian faith could no longer lead to potential torture and execution, Christian devotion became an increasingly internalized matter. Public profession of faith was imagined to reflect a profound inner orientation to God that eclipsed all other loyalties. Even a man or woman who had been raised in a Christian family might therefore value an experience of conversion, a radical turning away from the old life and embracing the new life of Christian dedication. The circulation of conversion narratives in this period provided an important (if often overly idealized) touchstone by which to measure this internal reorientation of the self.

But the making of a Christian was also an arduous external process: doctrinal and scriptural formation, under the care of experts, preceded full entry into the Christian fold. In some respects, Christianity retained many of the characteristics of Greco-Roman "mystery cults": participation in secretive communion with the deity (through the Eucharist) could only come after a rigorous and detailed period of instruction (catechesis), followed by a culminating rite of initiation (baptism). In the centuries after our period, as societies in the eastern and western ends of the Mediterranean world grew uniformly Christian, baptism of infants became the norm, and the intense experiences of conversion and instruction were transferred into the daily rhythms of liturgical and sacramental life. In the fourth and fifth centuries, however, a profound sense of *becoming* still permeated the making of Christians.

FOR FURTHER READING

Dujarier, Michael. *A History of the Catechumenate: The First Six Centuries,* trans. Edward J. Haasl. New York: Sadlier, 1979.

Ferguson, Everett, ed. *Conversion, Catechumenate, and Baptism in the Early Church.* New York: Garland Press, 1993.

Finn, Thomas M. *Early Christian Baptism and the Catechumenate,* 2 vols. Collegeville, Minn.: Liturgical Press, 1992.

————. *From Death to Rebirth: Ritual and Conversion in Antiquity.* New York: Paulist Press, 1997.

MacMullen, Ramsay. *Christianizing the Roman Empire.* New Haven, Conn.: Yale University Press, 1984.

Nock, Arthur Darby. *Conversion: The Old and the New in Religion from Alexander the Great to Augustine of Hippo.* Oxford, England: Clarendon Press, 1952.

Stark, Rodney. *The Rise of Christianity: A Sociologist Reconsiders History.* Princeton, N.J.: Princeton University Press, 1996.

Conversion: The Texts

In the fourth and fifth centuries, as Christianity became the majority religion of the Roman Empire, narratives of conversion instructed Christians on the profound significance of their religious affiliation. Christians composed and circulated stories of their own conversions and those of others to understand what their entry into Christian life could and should entail. These narratives became especially significant in this era during which Christianity achieved legitimacy and prominence: as emperors patronized the religion, and conversion came to be viewed as a politically savvy move, the emphasis on the spiritual vitality of conversion seemed more important than ever.

Three different types of conversion narratives are reproduced here. In them, we see conversion to Christianity as a consequence of personal introspection, often belabored and drawn out; as a consequence of persuasion and deliberation; even as a consequence of violence and coercion. In most conversion narratives of this period, we find the turn to Christianity idealized as a moment of excruciating awareness of both self and God, a "lightbulb" moment (drawing, to be sure, on the experience of Paul on the road to Damascus as narrated in Acts 9). It is, of course, impossible to verify to what extent people really experienced their religious identity in such a sudden, dramatic manner; sociologists of religion debate whether even first-person accounts of conversion, written after the fact, can be taken as reliable, influenced as they are by subsequent religious enculturation. In such accounts, we nonetheless catch sight of a widely circulated ideal of what it meant to embrace Christian identity, whether as the culmination of decades of searching or as the result of a sudden and unexpected encounter with the Christian God.

11. Augustine: Confessions

Augustine (354–430), who served as bishop of the small North African city of Hippo Regius from 396 until his death, is one of the most significant figures of early Christian history; his writings on sin and grace, good and evil, and society and humanity evolved into authoritative doctrine for western Christianity. The *Confessions* stand out among Augustine's enormous literary output as a curious and, at times, brilliant synthesis of theology, devotion (addressed to God in the second person), exegesis, and personal reflection. Augustine wrote the *Confes-*

From *Saint Augustine's Confessions,* trans. Henry Chadwick. Oxford, England: Oxford University Press, 1991. Used with permission.

sions in 397, more than a decade after his baptism by Ambrose of Milan. During this decade, Augustine had gone from private intellectual (as recorded in the philosophical dialogues he penned in the years immediately following his baptism) to public theological seeker. The *Confessions* should not then be read as an entirely accurate report of Augustine's thoughts, feelings, and actions in the mid-380s but, rather, as his mature reflections and reformulations on the nature of conversion itself and on the obstacles that the newly ordained Bishop Augustine conceived of as hindering the soul's desire for union with God.

The *Confessions* relate a torturous journey from spiritual dissatisfaction to the emotional surrender to God. Along the way, Augustine recounts many religious wrong turns: as a youth he embraced the intellectualism of the ancient Roman orator Cicero; as an adolescent, he was drawn to the radically dualist Manichean movement (which he later repudiated with gusto and takes pains to renounce even in this selection); later still he read the "books of the Platonists" and admired the cosmic scope of their philosophy; finally, drawing ever closer to the Catholic orthodoxy to which his mother had always belonged, Augustine heard the sophisticated preaching of Ambrose, bishop of Milan, and gained new respect for Christian thought.

Here, the pivotal eighth book of the *Confessions* is reproduced, at the end of which Augustine describes his emotional decision to embrace fully an abstinent form of Christian life. Tortured by his own inability to commit to God, Augustine recounts his famous inspiration by a child's sing-song voice to pick up a volume of Paul's letters and finally understand sin and redemption. Augustine was, by his own account, in his early thirties at this time. His conversion is prefaced by the tales of other converts: the prominent Roman philosopher Marius Victorinus; the famous desert monk Antony (inspired, like Augustine, by a felicitous line of Scripture); and several Roman civil servants who were, in turn, inspired by the *Life of Antony*. Together they form a cluster of men who surrender their worldly selves (emblematized for Augustine by his sexuality) to the simple embrace of God. Themes that would haunt Augustine's later theological career are also evident in this series of conversion accounts: God's grace, humanity's defective will, sin, and the power of evil.

1 (1) My God, in my thanksgiving I want to recall and confess your mercies over me. Let my bones be penetrated by your love and say, "Lord who is like you?" (Ps 35:10). "You have broken my chains, I will sacrifice to you the sacrifice of praise" (Ps 116:16–17). I will tell how you broke them. Let all who adore you say when they hear these things: "Blessed is the Lord in heaven and in earth; great and wonderful is his name" (Ps 72:18–19, 135:6).

Your words stuck fast in my heart and on all sides I was defended by you. Of your eternal life I was certain, though I saw it "in an enigma and as if in a mirror" (1 Cor 13:12). All doubt had been taken from me that there is indestructible substance from which comes all substance. My desire was not to be more certain of you but to be more stable in you. But in my temporal life everything was in a state of uncertainty, and my heart needed to be purified from the old leaven (1 Cor 5:7–8). I was attracted to the way, the Savior himself, but was still reluctant to go along its narrow paths. And you put into my heart, and it seemed good in my sight that I should visit Simplicianus. It was evident to me that he was a good servant of yours; your grace shone in him. I had also heard that from his youth he had lived a life dedicated to you. By this time he had become an old man, and after a long life of saintly zeal in pursuing your way, he appeared to me a man of much experience and much learning. So indeed he was. Accordingly, I wanted to consult with him about my troubles, so that he could propose a method fitted for someone in my disturbed condition, whereby I could learn to walk in your way.

(2) I saw the Church full, with one going this way, another a different way. My secular activity I held in disgust, and now that I was not burning with my old ambitions in hope of honor and money it was burdensome to me to tolerate so heavy a servitude. By now those prizes gave me no pleasure in comparison with your gentleness and "the beauty of your house which I loved" (Ps 26:8). But I was still firmly tied by woman. The apostle did not forbid me to marry, though he exhorted me to something better and very much wished that all men were as unattached as he himself (1 Cor 7:7). But I being weaker chose a softer option, and because of this one factor, I was inconstant in other respects and was wasting away with nagging anxieties. Moreover, there were other matters that were a tiresome distraction to me, but which I was compelled to put up with because they go with married life; once tied by that, I was restricted. From the mouth of truth I had heard that there are "eunuchs who have castrated themselves for the kingdom of heaven's sake." But, he says, "let him who can accept this accept it" (Matt 19:12).

"Assuredly all men are vain in whom there is no knowledge of God; not even from the things which appear good can they find him who is" (Wis 13:1). But now I was not in vanity of that kind. I had climbed beyond it, and by the witness of all creation I had found you our Creator and your Word who is God beside you and with you is one God, by whom you created all things (John 1:1–3).

There are impious people of another sort who "not knowing God, have not glorified him as God nor given thanks" (Rom 1:21). In this respect also I had fallen; but "your right hand sustained me" (Ps 18:36). You took me thence and placed me where I could recover my strength. For you said to man "Behold piety is wisdom," and "Do not wish to appear wise" (Job 28:28; Prov 26:5). "Those who asserted themselves to be wise have been made foolish" (Rom 1:22).

And now I had discovered the good pearl. To buy it I had to sell all that I had, and I hesitated (Matt 13:46).

2 (3) So I visited Simplicianus, father to the then bishop Ambrose in the receiving of grace. Ambrose truly loved him as one loves a father. I told him the story of my wanderings in error. But when I mentioned that I had read some books of the Platonists, which had been translated into Latin by Victorinus, at one time rhetor in the city of Rome who had, I had heard, died a Christian, he congratulated me that I had not fallen in with the writings of other philosophers full of fallacies and deceptions "according to the elements of this world" (Col 2:8), whereas in all the Platonic books God and his Word keep slipping in. Then, to exhort me to the humility of Christ hidden from the wise and revealed to babes (Matt 11:25), he recalled his memory of Victorinus himself, whom he had known intimately when he was at Rome. He told me a story about him that I will not pass over in silence. For the story gives occasion for me to confess to you in great praise for your grace.

Victorinus was extremely learned and most expert in all the liberal disciplines. He had read and assessed many philosophers' ideas and was tutor to numerous noble senators. To mark the distinguished quality of his teaching, he was offered and accepted a statue in the Roman forum, an honor that the citizens of this world think supreme. Until he was of advanced years, he was a worshipper of idols and took part in sacrilegious rites. At that time almost all the Roman nobility was enthusiastic for the cult of Osiris and "Monstrous gods of every kind and Anubis the barking dog, Monsters who once bore arms against Neptune and Venus and against Minerva" (Vergil, *Aeneid* 8.698–700), gods that Rome once conquered but then implored for aid. The old Victorinus had defended these cults for many years with a voice terrifying to opponents. Yet he was not ashamed to become the servant of your Christ and an infant born at your font, to bow his head to the yoke of humility and to submit his forehead to the reproach of the cross.

(4) Lord God, "you have inclined the heavens and come down, you have touched the mountains and they have smoked" (Ps 144:5). By what ways did you make an opening into that heart? Simplicianus said Victorinus read holy Scripture, and all the Christian books he investigated with special care. After examining them, he said to Simplicianus, not openly but in the privacy of friendship, "Did you know that I am already a Christian?" Simplicianus replied: "I shall not

believe that or count you among the Christians unless I see you in the church of Christ." Victorinus laughed and said: "Then do walls make Christians?" He used frequently to say "I am a Christian already," and Simplicianus would give the same answer, to which he equally often repeated his joke about walls. He was afraid to offend his friends, proud devil worshippers. He thought that from the height of Babylonish dignity, as if from the cedars of Lebanon that the Lord had not yet broken (Ps 29:5), the full weight of their hostility would land on him. But after his reading, he began to feel a longing and drank in courage. He was afraid he would be "denied" by Christ "before the holy angels" (Luke 12:9). He would have felt guilty of a grave crime if he were ashamed of the mysteries of the humility of your Word and were not ashamed of the sacrilegious rites of proud demons, whose pride he imitated when he accepted their ceremonies. He became ashamed of the emptiness of those rites and felt respect for the truth. Suddenly and unexpectedly he said to Simplicianus (as he told me): "Let us go to the church; I want to become a Christian." Simplicianus was unable to contain himself for joy and went with him. Not long after he had received his instructions in the first mysteries, he gave in his name for baptism that he might be reborn, to the amazement of Rome and the joy of the church. The proud "saw and were angry. They gnashed with their teeth and were sick at heart" (Ps 112:10). But the Lord God was the hope of his servant; "he paid no regard to vanities and lying follies" (Ps 40:4).

(5) Finally the hour came for him to make the profession of faith, which is expressed in set form. At Rome these words are memorized and then by custom recited from an elevated place before the baptized believers by those who want to come to your grace. Simplicianus used to say that the presbyters offered him the opportunity of affirming the creed in private, as was their custom to offer to people who felt embarrassed and afraid. But he preferred to make profession of his salvation before the holy congregation. For there was no salvation in the rhetoric that he had taught, yet his profession of that had been public. How much less should he be afraid in proclaiming your word, when he used to feel no fear in using his

own words before crowds of frenzied pagans? When he mounted the steps to affirm the confession of faith, there was a murmur of delighted talk as all the people who knew him spoke his name to one another. And who there did not know him? A suppressed sound came from the lips of all as they rejoiced, "Victorinus, Victorinus!" As soon as they saw him, they suddenly murmured in exaltation and equally suddenly were silent in concentration to hear him. All of them wanted to clasp him to their hearts, and the hands with which they embraced him were their love and their joy.

3 (6) God of goodness, what causes man to be more delighted by the salvation of a soul who is despaired of but is then liberated from great danger than if there has always been hope or if the danger has only been minor? You also, merciful Father, rejoice "more over one penitent than over ninety-nine just persons who need no penitence" (Luke 15:4). We too experience great pleasure when we hear how the shepherd's shoulders exult when they carry the lost sheep and as we listen to the story of the drachma restored to your treasuries while the neighbors rejoice with the woman who found it. Tears flow at the joy of the solemnities of your house (Ps 26:8) when in your house the story is read of your younger son "who was dead and is alive again, was lost and has been found" (Luke 15:32). You rejoice indeed in us and in your angels who are holy in holy love. You are always the same, and you always know unchangeably the things that are not always the same.

(7) What then is it in the soul that causes it to take more pleasure in things that it loves when they are found and recovered than if it has always had them? There are other examples that attest this fact, and everyday life is full of instances where the evidence cries out: "That is the case." A victorious emperor celebrates a triumph. He would not have conquered if he had not fought. The greater the danger in the battle, the greater the joy in the triumph. A storm throws people about on a voyage and threatens shipwreck. All grow pale at the imminence of death. Sky and sea become calm, and the relief is great because the fear has been great. A dear person is sick, and his pulse reveals he is in a serious condition. All who wish him

to recover his health feel sick in mind at the same time. He takes a turn for the better, and although he may not walk with his former strength, yet now there is joy as there was not before when he walked in good health and strength. Human beings obtain normal pleasures of human life not as they come on us unexpectedly and against our will, but after discomforts that are planned and accepted by deliberate choice. There is no pleasure in eating and drinking unless they are preceded by the unpleasant sensation of hunger and thirst. Drunkards eat salty things to make their desire uncomfortable. As drinking extinguishes the desire, there is delightful sensation. It is established custom that betrothed girls are not immediately handed over, lest the husband hold the bride being given to him to be cheaply gained if he has not sighed after her, impatient at the delay.

(8) The same phenomenon appears in acts that are demeaning and execrable, in acts that are allowed and lawful, in the sincerest expressions of honorable friendship, and in the case of the one "who was dead and is alive again, was lost and is found" (Luke 15:32). In every case the joy is greater, the worse the pain that has preceded it. Why is this, Lord my God? You are eternal to yourself, you are your own joy; and beings round you continually rejoice in your society. Why is it that this part of the creation alternates between regress and progress, between hostilities and reconciliations? Or is that a restriction placed on them, a limit you have imposed, when "from the highest heaven" (Ps 113:4) down to the lowest things on earth, from the beginning to the end of the ages, from an angel down to a worm, from the first movement down to the last, you have assigned to its proper place and time all kinds of good things and all your just works?

You are so high among the highest, and I am low among the lowest, a mean thing. You never go away from us. Yet we have difficulty in returning to you.

4 (9) Come Lord, stir us up and call us back, kindle and seize us, be our fire and our sweetness. Let us love, let us run. Surely many return to you from a deeper hell of blindness than Victorinus. They approach and are illuminated as they receive light. Those who receive it obtain from you "power to be-

come your sons" (John 1:9, 12). But if they are less well known to the people, there is less rejoicing over them even among those who know them. When many share in the joy, individuals also feel a richer delight. They kindle excitement among themselves and are inflamed by one another. Then those who are known to many are to many a personal influence toward salvation. Where they lead, many will follow. That is why on their account even those who have preceded them feel great joy; for their rejoicing is not only for them.

But God forbid that in your tabernacle the rich be preferred to the poor or the noble to those of low origin. You have chosen in preference the weak things of the world to confound the powerful, and you have chosen the low of this world and things that are despised and things that have no existence as if they had being, to bring to nothing things that have being (1 Cor 1:27–29). Yet the very same writer, the least of your apostles (1 Cor 15:9), by whose tongue you uttered those words, was the person who by combat humbled the pride of Paul the proconsul under the gentle yoke of your Christ and commissioned him as a provincial governor of the great king (Acts 13:7–12). Thereafter he himself, formerly named Saul, loved to be called Paul as a reminder of that great victory. The enemy suffers a severer defeat when he is overcome in a man upon whom he has a greater hold and by whose influence he dominates many. Pride in aristocratic nobility enables him to hold sway especially over the upper class, and by their title and authority he dominates many more. Special pleasure, therefore, was felt at the conversion of Victorinus's heart in which the devil had an impregnable fortress, and of Victorinus's tongue, which he had used as a mighty and sharp dart to destroy many. Your children had good reason to rejoice the more jubilantly because our king had bound the strong man (Matt 12:29) and they saw his vessels being snatched away to be cleaned and made fit for your honor to be "useful to the Lord for every good work" (2 Tim 2:21).

5 (10) As soon as your servant Simplicianus told me this story about Victorinus, I was ardent to follow his example. He had indeed told it to me with this object in view. Later on, he added, in the time of the emperor Julian, when a law was promulgated forbidding Christians to teach literature and rhetoric,[1] Victorinus welcomed the law and preferred to abandon the school of loquacious chattering rather than your word, by which you make "skilled the tongues of infants" (Wis 10:21). I felt that he was not so much courageous as fortunate to find occasion for dedicating all his time to you. I sighed after such freedom, but was bound not by an iron imposed by anyone else but by the iron of my own choice. The enemy had a grip on my will and so made a chain for me to hold me a prisoner. The consequence of a distorted will is passion. By servitude to passion, habit is formed, and habit to which there is no resistance becomes necessity. By these links, as it were, connected one to another (hence my term a chain), a harsh bondage held me under restraint. The new will, which was beginning to be within me a will to serve you freely and to enjoy you, God, the only sure source of pleasure, was not yet strong enough to conquer my older will, which had the strength of old habit. So my two wills, one old, the other new, one carnal, the other spiritual, were in conflict with one another, and their discord robbed my soul of all concentration.

(11) In this way I understood through my own experience what I had read, how "the flesh lusts against the spirit and the spirit against the flesh" (Gal 5:17). I was split between them, but more of me was in that which I approved in myself than in that which I disapproved. In the latter case, it was "no more I" (Rom 7:17), since in large part I was passive and unwilling, rather than active and willing. But I was responsible for the fact that habit had become so embattled against me, for it was with my consent that I came to the place in which I did not wish to be. Who has the right to object if a just penalty pursues a sinner? I no longer had my usual excuse to explain why I did not yet despise the world and serve you, namely, that my perception of the truth was uncertain. By now I was indeed quite sure about it. Yet I was still bound down to the earth. I was refusing to become your soldier, and I was as afraid of being rid of all my burdens as I ought to have been at the prospect of carrying them.

(12) The burden of the world weighed me down with a sweet drowsiness such as commonly occurs during sleep. The thoughts with which I meditated about you were like the efforts of those who would like to get up but are overcome by deep sleep and sink back again. No one wants to be asleep all the time, and the sane judgment of everyone judges it better to be awake. Yet often a man defers shaking off sleep when his limbs are heavy with slumber. Although displeased with himself he is glad to take a bit longer, even when the time to get up has arrived. In this kind of way I was sure it was better for me to render myself up to your love than to surrender to my own cupidity. But while the former course was pleasant to think about and had my notional assent, the latter was more pleasant and overcame me. I had no answer to make to you when you said to me "Arise, you who are asleep, rise from the dead, and Christ shall give you light" (Eph 5:14). Though at every point you showed that what you were saying was true, yet I, convinced by that truth, had no answer to give you except merely slow and sleepy words: "At once"—"But presently"—"Just a little longer, please." But "At once, at once" never came to the point of decision, and "Just a little longer, please" went on and on for a long while. In vain I "delighted in your law in respect of the inward man, but another law in my members fought against the law of my mind and led me captive in the law of sin that was in my members" (Rom 7:22). The law of sin is the violence of habit by which even the unwilling mind is dragged down and held, as it deserves to be, since by its own choice it slipped into the habit. "Wretched man that I was, who would deliver me from this body of death other than your grace through Jesus Christ our Lord?" (Rom 7: 24–25).

6 (13) Lord, my helper and redeemer, I will now tell the story, and confess to your name, of the way in which you delivered me from the chain of sexual desire, by which I was tightly bound, and from the slavery of worldly affairs. I went about my usual routine in a state of mental anxiety. Every day I sighed after you. I used to frequent your church whenever I had

---

[1] See Julian's rescript, Text 6.

time off from the affairs under whose weight I was groaning. With me was Alypius, unemployed in his work as a lawyer after a third period as assessor and waiting for someone else to whom he could again sell his advice, just as I was selling the art of public speaking—if oratory is something that can be conveyed by teaching. Nebridius, however, had yielded to the pressure of his friendship with us and was assistant teacher to Verecundus, a close friend to all of us, a citizen of Milan and instructor in literature there. Verecundus was in urgent need of reliable assistance and by right of friendship claimed from our group the supply he badly wanted. So Nebridius was not attracted to this work by desire for the profits, for had he so wished, he could have made more money on his own as a teacher of literature. He was a most gentle and kind friend and recognizing the duty of generosity would not scorn our request. He performed his task most prudently and took care not to become known to important people, as this world reckons them, so avoiding anything likely to distract his mind. He wanted to keep his mind free and to devote as many hours as possible to the pursuit of wisdom by investigating some problem or listening to conversation.

(14) One day when Nebridius was absent for a reason I cannot recall, Alypius and I received a surprise visit at home from a man named Ponticianus, a compatriot in that he was an African, holding high office at the court. He wanted something or other from us. We sat down together to converse. By chance he noticed a book on top of a gaming table that lay before us. He picked it up, opened it, and discovered, much to his astonishment, that it was the apostle Paul. He had expected it to be one of the books used for the profession that was wearing me out. But then he smiled and looked at me in a spirit of congratulation. He was amazed that he had suddenly discovered this book and this book alone open before my eyes. He was a Christian and a baptized believer. He often prostrated himself before you, our God, at the church with frequent and long times of prayer. When I had indicated to him that those Scriptures were the subject of deep study for me, a conversation began in which he told the story of Antony the Egyptian monk,

a name held in high honor among your servants, though up to that moment Alypius and I had never heard of him. When he discovered this, he dwelt on the story, instilling in us who were ignorant an awareness of the man's greatness and expressing astonishment that we did not know of him. We were amazed as we heard of your wonderful acts very well attested and occurring so recently, almost in our own time, done in orthodox faith and in the Catholic Church. All of us were in a state of surprise, we because of the greatness of the story, he because we had not heard about it.[2]

(15) From there his conversation moved on to speak of the flocks in the monasteries and their manner of life well pleasing to you and the fertile deserts of the wilderness. Of these we knew nothing. There was a monastery full of good brothers at Milan outside the city walls, fostered by Ambrose, and we had not known of it. He developed the theme and talked on while we listened with rapt silence. Then it occurred to him to mention how he and three of his colleagues (the date I do not know but it was at Trier), when the emperor was detained by a circus spectacle in the forenoon, went out for a walk in the gardens adjacent to the walls. There they strolled in couples, one as it turned out with Ponticianus, the other two separately wandering off on their own. In their wanderings they happened on a certain house where there lived some of your servants, poor in spirit: "of such is the kingdom of heaven" (Matt 5:3). They found there a book in which was written the Life of Antony. One of them began to read it. He was amazed and set on fire, and during his reading began to think of taking up this way of life and of leaving his secular post in the civil service to be your servant. For they were agents in the special branch. Suddenly he was filled with holy love and sobering shame. Angry with himself, he turned his eyes on his friend and said to him: "Tell me, I beg of you, what do we hope to achieve with all our labors? What is our aim in life? What is the motive of our service to the state? Can we hope for any higher office in the palace than to be Friends

---

[2] See excerpts from the *Life of Antony,* Text 46.

of the Emperor? And in that position what is not fragile and full of dangers? How many hazards must one risk to attain to a position of even greater danger? And when will we arrive there? Whereas, if I wish to become God's friend, in an instant I may become that now." So he spoke, and in pain at the coming to birth of new life, he returned his eyes to the book's pages. He read on and experienced a conversion inwardly where you alone could see and, as was soon evident, his mind rid itself of the world. Indeed, as he read and turned over and over in the turbulent hesitations of his heart, there were some moments when he was angry with himself. But then he perceived the choice to be made and took a decision to follow the better course. He was already yours and said to his friend: "As for myself, I have broken away from our ambition and have decided to serve God, and I propose to start doing that from this hour in this place. If it costs you too much to follow my example, do not turn against me." His friend replied that he would join him and be associated with him for such great reward and for so great a service. And both men, already yours, were building their tower at the right cost of forsaking all their property and following you (Luke 14:28). Then Ponticianus and his companion who were walking through other parts of the garden in search of them came to the same place and, on finding them, suggested returning home since the daylight had already begun to fade. But they told him of their decision and purpose and how this intention had started and had become a firm resolve. They begged the others, if they did not wish to be associated with them, not to obstruct them. Ponticianus and his friend, however, did not change from their old career; nevertheless, as he told us, they wept for themselves. They offered their friends devout congratulations and commended themselves to their prayers. Then, dragging their hearts along the ground, they went off into the palace. The others fixed their hearts on heaven and stayed at the house. Both had wives. When later their wives heard this, they also dedicated their virginity to you.

7 (16) This was the story Ponticianus told. But while he was speaking, Lord, you turned my attention back to myself. You took me up from behind my own back where I had placed myself because I did not wish to observe myself, and you set me before my face so that I should see how vile I was, how twisted and filthy, covered in sores and ulcers. And I looked and was appalled, but there was no way of escaping from myself. If I tried to avert my gaze from myself, his story continued relentlessly, and you once again placed me in front of myself; you thrust me before my own eyes so that I should discover my iniquity and hate it. I had known it, but deceived myself, refused to admit it, and pushed it out of my mind.

(17) But at that moment the more ardent my affection for those young men of whom I was hearing, who for the soul's health had given themselves wholly to you for healing, the more was the detestation and hatred I felt for myself in comparison with them. Many years of my life had passed by—about twelve—since in my nineteenth year I had read Cicero's *Hortensius* and had been stirred to a zeal for wisdom. But although I came to despise earthly success, I put off giving time to the quest for wisdom. For "it is not the discovery but the mere search for wisdom that should be preferred even to the discovery of treasures and to ruling over nations and to the physical delights available to me at a nod." But I was an unhappy young man, wretched as at the beginning of my adolescence when I prayed you for chastity and said: "Grant me chastity and continence, but not yet." I was afraid you might hear my prayer quickly and that you might too rapidly heal me of the disease of lust that I preferred to satisfy rather than suppress. I had gone along "evil ways" (Sir 2:12) with a sacrilegious superstition, not indeed because I felt sure of its truth, but because I preferred it to the alternatives, which I did not investigate in a devout spirit but opposed in an attitude of hostility.

(18) I supposed that the reason for my postponing "from day to day" (Sir 5:7) the moment when I would despise worldly ambition and follow you was that I had not seen any certainty by which to direct my course. But the day had now come when I stood naked to myself, and my conscience complained against me: "Where is your tongue? You were saying that because the truth is uncertain, you do not want to abandon the burden of futility. But look, it is certain

now, and the burden still presses on you. Yet wings are won by the freer shoulders of men who have not been exhausted by their searching and have not taken ten years or more to meditate on these matters." This is how I was gnawing at my inner self. I was violently overcome by a fearful sense of shame during the time that Ponticianus was telling his story. When he had ended his talk and settled the matter for which he came, he went home, and I was left to myself. What accusations against myself did I not bring? With what verbal rods did I not scourge my soul so that it would follow me in my attempt to go after you! But my soul hung back. It refused and had no excuse to offer. The arguments were exhausted, and all had been refuted. The only thing left to it was a mute trembling, and as if it were facing death, it was terrified of being restrained from the treadmill of habit by which it suffered "sickness unto death" (John 11:4).

8 (19) Then in the middle of that grand struggle in my inner house, which I had vehemently stirred up with my soul in the intimate chamber of my heart, distressed not only in mind but in appearance, I turned on Alypius and cried out: "What is wrong with us? What is this that you have heard? Uneducated people are rising up and capturing heaven (Matt 11:12), and we with our high culture without any heart—see where we roll in the mud of flesh and blood. Is it because they are ahead of us that we are ashamed to follow? Do we feel no shame at making not even an attempt to follow?" That is the gist of what I said, and the heat of my passion took my attention away from him as he contemplated my condition in astonished silence. For I sounded very strange. My uttered words said less about the state of my mind than my forehead, cheeks, eyes, color, and tone of voice.

Our lodging had a garden. We had the use of it, as well as of the entire house, for our host, the owner of the house, was not living there. The tumult of my heart took me out into the garden where no one could interfere with the burning struggle with myself in which I was engaged, until the matter could be settled. You knew, but I did not, what the outcome would be. But my madness with myself was part of the process of recovering health, and in the agony of death I was coming to life. I was aware how ill I was, unaware how well I was soon to be. So I went out into the garden. Alypius followed me step after step. Although he was present, I felt no intrusion on my solitude. How could he abandon me in such a state? We sat down as far as we could from the buildings. I was deeply disturbed in spirit, angry with indignation and distress that I was not entering into my pact and covenant with you, my God, when all my bones (Ps 35:10) were crying out that I should enter into it and were exalting it to heaven with praises. But to reach that destination, one does not use ships or chariots or feet. It was not even necessary to go the distance I had come from the house to where we were sitting. The one necessary condition, which meant not only going but at once arriving there, was to have the will to go—provided only that the will was strong and unqualified, not the turning and twisting first this way, then that, of a will half wounded, struggling with one part rising up and the other part falling down.

(20) Finally, in the agony of hesitation, I made many physical gestures of the kind men make when they want to achieve something and lack the strength, either because they lack the actual limbs or because their limbs are fettered with chains or weak with sickness or in some way hindered. If I tore my hair, if I struck my forehead, if I intertwined my fingers and clasped my knee, I did that because to do so was my will. But I could have willed this and then not done it if my limbs had not possessed the power to obey. So I did many actions in which the will to act was not equaled by the power. Yet I was not doing what with an incomparably greater longing I yearned to do and could have done the moment I so resolved. For as soon as I had the will, I would have had a wholehearted will. At this point the power to act is identical with the will. The willing itself was performative of the action. Nevertheless, it did not happen. The body obeyed the slightest inclination of the soul to move the limbs at its pleasure more easily than the soul obeyed itself, when its supreme desire could be achieved exclusively by the will alone.

9 (21) What is the cause of this monstrous situation? Why is it the case? May your mercy illuminate me as I ask if perhaps an answer can be found in the hidden punishments and secret tribulations that befall the sons of Adam? What causes this monstrous fact, and why is it so? The mind commands the body and is instantly obeyed. The mind commands itself and meets resistance. The mind commands the hand to move, and it is so easy that one hardly distinguishes the order from its execution. Yet mind is mind, and hand is body. The mind orders the mind to will. The recipient of the order is itself, yet it does not perform it. What causes this monstrosity, and why does this happen? Mind commands, I say, that it should will and would not give the command if it did not will, yet does not perform what it commands. The willing is not wholehearted, so the command is not wholehearted. The strength of the command lies in the strength of will, and the degree to which the command is not performed lies in the degree to which the will is not engaged. For it is the will that commands the will to exist, and it commands not another will but itself. So the will that commands is incomplete, and therefore what it commands does not happen. If it were complete, it would not need to command the will to exist, since it would exist already. Therefore there is no monstrous split between willing and not willing. We are dealing with a morbid condition of the mind, which, when it is lifted up by the truth, does not unreservedly rise to it but is weighed down by habit. So there are two wills. Neither of them is complete, and what is present in the one is lacking to the other.

10 (22) "Let them perish from your presence" (Ps 68:2) O God, as do "empty talkers and seducers" of the mind (Titus 1:10) who, from the dividing of the will into two in the process of deliberation, deduce that there are two minds with two distinct natures, one good, the other bad.[3] They really are evil themselves when they entertain these evil doctrines. Yet the very same people would be good if they held to the true doctrines and assented to the truth. As your apostle says to them "You were at one time darkness, but now are light in the Lord" (Eph 5:8). But they wish to be light not in the Lord but in themselves be-

cause they hold that the nature of the soul is what God is. They have in fact become a thicker darkness in that by their horrendous arrogance they have withdrawn further away from you—from you who are "the true light illuminating every man coming into this world" (John 1:9). They should give heed to what you say and blush: "Come to him and be illuminated, and your faces will not blush" (Ps 34:5).

In my own case, as I deliberated about serving my Lord God (Jer 30:9) which I had long been disposed to do, the self that willed to serve was identical with the self that was unwilling. It was I. I was neither wholly willing nor wholly unwilling. So I was in conflict with myself and was dissociated from myself. The dissociation came about against my will. Yet this was not a manifestation of the nature of an alien mind but the punishment suffered in my own mind. And so it was "not I" that brought this about "but sin that dwelt in me" (Rom 7:17, 20), sin resulting from the punishment of a more freely chosen sin because I was a son of Adam.

(23) If there are as many contrary natures as there are wills in someone beset by indecision, there will be not two wills but many. If a person is deliberating whether to go to the Manicheans' conventicle or to the theater, they cry: "Here are two natures, a good one leads one way, a bad one leads the other way. How otherwise explain the opposition of two wills to one another?" But I affirm that they are both evil, both the will to attend their meeting and the will to go to the theater. They think that the intention to go along to them can only be good. What then? If one of us Catholic Christians were deliberating and, with two wills quarrelling with one another, fluctuated between going to the theater or to our church, surely the Manicheans would be quite undecided what to say about that. Either they will have to concede that to go to our Church is an act of goodwill, as is the case with those worshippers who are initiated into its sacraments and feel the obligation thereby imposed, or they will have to think two evil natures and two evil minds are in conflict within a single person. This argument will prove untrue their usual assertion that one is good, the other bad. The alternative for them will be to be converted to the true view and not to

---

[3] Augustine is speaking of Manicheans.

deny that in the process of deliberation a single soul is wavering between different wills.

(24) Accordingly, when they note two wills in one person in conflict with each other, let them no more say that two conflicting minds are derived from two rival substances and that two conflicting principles are in contention, one good, the other evil. God of truth, you condemn them and refute and confound them. For both wills are evil when someone is deliberating whether to kill a person by poison or by a dagger; whether to encroach on one estate belonging to someone else or a different one, when he cannot do both; whether to buy pleasure by lechery or avariciously to keep his money; whether to go to the circus or the theater if both are putting on a performance on the same day, or (I add a third possibility) to steal from another person's house if occasion offers, or (I add a fourth option) to commit adultery if at the same time the chance is available. Suppose that all these choices are confronted at one moment of time, and all are equally desired, yet they cannot all be done simultaneously. They tear the mind apart by the mutual incompatibility of the wills—four or more according to the number of objects desired. Yet they do not usually affirm that there is such a multiplicity of diverse substances.

The same argument holds for good wills. For I ask them whether it is good to delight in a reading from the apostle, or if it is good to take pleasure in a sober psalm, or if it is good to discourse upon the gospel. In each case they will reply "good." What then? If all these offer equal delight at one and the same time, surely the divergent wills pull apart the human heart while we are deliberating which is the most attractive option to take? All are good and yet are in contention with each other until the choice falls on one to which is then drawn the entire single will that was split into many. So also when the delight of eternity draws us upward and the pleasure of temporal good holds us down, the identical soul is not wholehearted in its desire for one or the other. It is torn apart in a painful condition, as long as it prefers the eternal because of its truth but does not discard the temporal because of familiarity.

11 (25) Such was my sickness and my torture as I accused myself even more bitterly than usual. I was twisting and turning in my chain until it would break completely: I was now only a little bit held by it, but I was still held. You, Lord, put pressure on me in my hidden depths with a severe mercy wielding the double whip of fear and shame, lest I should again succumb and lest that tiny and tenuous bond that still remained should not be broken, but once more regain strength and bind me even more firmly. Inwardly I said to myself: Let it be now, let it be now. And by this phrase I was already moving toward a decision; I had almost taken it, and then I did not do so. Yet I did not relapse into my original condition, but stood my ground very close to the point of deciding and recovered my breath. Once more I made the attempt and came only a little short of my goal; only a little short of it—yet I did not touch it or hold on to it. I was hesitating whether to die to death and to live to life. Ingrained evil had more hold over me than unaccustomed good. The nearer approached the moment of time when I would become different, the greater the horror of it struck me. But it did not thrust me back or turn me away, but left me in a state of suspense.

(26) Vain trifles and the triviality of the empty-headed, my old loves, held me back. They tugged at the garment of my flesh and whispered: "Are you getting rid of us?" And "from this moment we shall never be with you again, not for ever and ever." And "from this moment this and that are forbidden to you for ever and ever." What they were suggesting in what I have called "this and that"—what they were suggesting, my God, may your mercy avert from the soul of your servant! What filth, what disgraceful things they were suggesting! I was listening to them with much less than half my attention. They were not frankly confronting me face to face on the road but, as it were, whispering behind my back, as if they were furtively tugging at me as I was going away, trying to persuade me to look back. Nevertheless they held me back. I hesitated to detach myself, to be rid of them, to make the leap to where I was being called. Meanwhile the overwhelming force of habit was saying to me: "Do you think you can live without them?"

(27) Nevertheless it was now putting the question very halfheartedly. For from that direction where I

had set my face and toward which I was afraid to move, there appeared the dignified and chaste Lady Continence, serene and cheerful without coquetry, enticing me in an honorable manner to come and not to hesitate. To receive and embrace me, she stretched out pious hands, filled with numerous good examples for me to follow. There were large numbers of boys and girls, a multitude of all ages, young adults and grave widows and elderly virgins. In every one of them was Continence herself, in no sense barren but "the fruitful mother of children" (Ps 113:9), the joys born of you, Lord, her husband. And she smiled on me with a smile of encouragement as if to say: "Are you incapable of doing what these men and women have done? Do you think them capable of achieving this by their own resources and not by the Lord their God? Their Lord God gave me to them. Why are you relying on yourself, only to find yourself unreliable? Cast yourself upon him, do not be afraid. He will not withdraw himself so that you fall. Make the leap without anxiety; he will catch you and heal you."

I blushed with embarrassment because I was still listening to the mutterings of those vanities, and racked by hesitations I remained undecided. But once more it was as if she said: "'Stop your ears to your impure members on earth and mortify them' (Col 3:5). They declare delights to you, but 'not in accord with the law of the Lord your God'" (Ps 119:85). This debate in my heart was a struggle of myself against myself. Alypius stood quite still at my side and waited in silence for the outcome of my unprecedented state of agitation.

12 (28) From a hidden depth a profound self-examination had dredged up a heap of all my misery and set it "in the sight of my heart" (Ps 19:15). That precipitated a vast storm bearing a massive downpour of tears. To pour it all out with the accompanying groans, I got up from beside Alypius (solitude seemed to me more appropriate for the business of weeping), and I moved farther away to ensure that even his presence put no inhibition upon me. He sensed that this was my condition at that moment. I think I may have said something that made it clear that the sound of my voice was already choking with tears. So I stood up while in profound astonishment he remained where we were sitting. I threw myself down somehow under a certain fig tree and let my tears flow freely. Rivers streamed from my eyes, a sacrifice acceptable to you (Ps 51:19), and (though not in these words, yet in this sense) I repeatedly said to you: "How long, O Lord? How long, Lord, will you be angry to the uttermost? Do not be mindful of our old iniquities" (Ps 6:3–4). For I felt my past to have a grip on me. It uttered wretched cries: "How long, how long is it to be?" "Tomorrow, tomorrow." "Why not now? Why not an end to my impure life in this very hour?"

(29) As I was saying this and weeping in the bitter agony of my heart, suddenly I heard a voice from the nearby house chanting as if it might be a boy or a girl (I do not know which), saying and repeating over and over again "Pick up and read, pick up and read." At once my countenance changed, and I began to think intently whether there might be some sort of children's game in which such a chant is used. But I could not remember having heard of one. I checked the flood of tears and stood up. I interpreted it solely as a divine command to me to open the book and read the first chapter I might find. For I had heard how Antony happened to be present at the gospel reading and took it as an admonition addressed to himself when the words were read: "Go, sell all you have, give to the poor, and you shall have treasure in heaven, and come, follow me" (Matt 19:21). By such an inspired utterance he was immediately "converted to you" (Ps 51:13). So I hurried back to the place where Alypius was sitting. There I had put down the book of the apostle when I got up. I seized it, opened it, and in silence read the first passage on which my eyes lit: "Not in riots and drunken parties, not in eroticism and indecencies, not in strife and rivalry, but put on the Lord Jesus Christ and make no provision for the flesh in its lusts" (Rom 13:13–14).

I neither wished nor needed to read further. At once, with the last words of this sentence, it was as if a light of relief from all anxiety flooded into my heart. All the shadows of doubt were dispelled.

(30) Then I inserted my finger or some other mark in the book and closed it. With a face now at peace I told everything to Alypius. What had been going on in his mind, which I did not know, he disclosed in this

way. He asked to see the text I had been reading. I showed him, and he noticed a passage following that which I had read. I did not know how the text went on, but the continuation was "Receive the person who is weak in faith" (Rom 14:1). Alypius applied this to himself, and he made that known to me. He was given confidence by this admonition. Without any agony of hesitation, he joined me in making a good resolution and affirmation of intention, entirely congruent with his moral principles in which he had long been greatly superior to me. From there we went in to my mother and told her. She was filled with joy. We told her how it had happened. She exulted, feel-

ing it to be a triumph, and blessed you who "are powerful to do more than we ask or think" (Eph 3:20). She saw that you had granted her far more than she had long been praying for in her unhappy and tearful groans.

The effect of your converting me to yourself was that I did not now seek a wife and had no ambition for success in this world. I stood firm upon that rule of faith on which many years before you had revealed me to her. You "changed her grief into joy" (Ps 30:11) far more abundantly than she desired, far dearer and more chaste than she expected when she looked for grandchildren begotten of my body.

---

12. Sulpicius Severus: The Life of Saint Martin

The "soldier-saint" Martin of Tours (ca. 316–97) promoted asceticism and monasticism during his tenure as bishop (from about 372 to his death). His tale of renunciation combined with ecclesiastical service was written by one of his disciples, the learned monk Sulpicius Severus. In addition to casting Martin in roles familiar from other hagiography—renouncing the world, nearly being martyred, working miracles in Christ's name (see Chapter 11)—Sulpicius also portrays Martin as a bearer of the Christian message in a still largely non-Christian world. In the *Life of Martin*, conversion to Christianity is portrayed as a result of contact with the otherworldly virtue of a saint (even the roadside bandits who capture Martin succumb to his Christian fervor). Although much of the *Life of Martin* is constructed to serve Sulpicius's hagiographic agenda, miraculous deeds as an impetus for Christian conversion may not be far off: in a world in which suffering and illness predominated, the promise of healing and salvation from holy people and their Christian God may indeed have been an effective means of securing new converts.

2 (1) Martin, then, was born in Sabaria, a town in Pannonia, but he was brought up in Italy, at Pavia. His parents were not of the lowest rank as far as worldly status goes, but they were pagans. (2) His father was first a soldier and later a military tribune. Martin himself, as a young man, followed him into the army and fought in the elite cavalry regiment under the emperor Constantius and then under the Caesar Julian. He did not do so willingly, however,

because from just about his earliest years, the holy childhood of this remarkable boy preferred to aspire to God's service. (3) For when he was ten years old, he took refuge in the church against his parents' wishes and demanded to be made a catechumen, (4) and it was not long before he was completely converted, in an extraordinary way, to the work of God. At the age of twelve, he longed for the desert, and he would have satisfied this desire if he had not been

Pp. 136–142 from *Early Christian Lives* by Athanasius et al., translated by Carolinne White (Penguin Classics 1998). Copyright © Carolinne White, 1998. Used with permission.

prevented by the weakness of his young age. Yet his mind was always intent either on the monastic cells or on the church, and already in childhood he was planning what he later carried out with devotion. (5) But when the rulers gave out an edict to the effect that the sons of veterans were to be enrolled in the army, his father, who was hostile to his holy actions, betrayed him: at the age of fifteen Martin was arrested, put in chains, and bound by military oaths. He was content with the company of only one slave—and in fact they exchanged roles so that the master served the slave to such an extent that it was usually Martin who pulled his slave's boots off and cleaned them, and when they took their meals together, it was more often Martin who served at table. (6) He was in the army for about three years before his baptism, but he remained free from the vices in which men of this kind usually become entangled. (7) He showed great kindness to his fellow soldiers, extraordinary love, superhuman patience, and humility. It is unnecessary to praise his frugality, which he practiced in such a way that already at that time he might have been taken to be a monk rather than a soldier. These qualities of his bound all his fellow soldiers so closely to him that they adored him with extraordinary affection. (8) Although he had not yet been born again in Christ, in performing good works he behaved like a candidate for baptism: he supported those in trouble, he brought help to the wretched, he fed the poor, he clothed the naked, and kept nothing of his military salary for himself apart from what he needed for food each day. Already at that time, he was not deaf to the gospel, for he took no thought for the morrow (Matt 6:34).

3 (1) One day, then, in the middle of a winter more bitterly cold than usual (so much so that many perished as a result of the severity of the icy weather), when Martin had nothing with him apart from his weapons and a simple military cloak, he came across a naked beggar at the gate of the city of Amiens. The man begged the people who were passing to have pity on him, but they all walked past him. Then Martin, who was filled with God's grace, understood that this man had been reserved for him, since the others were not showing him any mercy. (2) But what was

he to do? He had nothing apart from the cloak he was wearing, for he had already used up the rest of his things for a similar purpose. So he seized the sword that he wore at his side, divided the cloak in two, gave half to the beggar and then put the remaining piece on again. Some of the bystanders began to laugh because he looked odd with his chopped-up cloak, but many who were more sensible sighed deeply because they had not done the same despite the fact that, because they had more than Martin, they could have clothed the beggar without themselves being reduced to nakedness. (3) The following night, therefore, when Martin had fallen asleep, he saw Christ clothed in the part of his cloak that he had used to cover the beggar. He was told to look very carefully at the Lord and to recognize the clothing that he had given. Then he heard Jesus saying in a clear voice to the host of angels standing all around, "Martin who is still a catechumen covered me with this cloak." (4) Undoubtedly, when the Lord declared that he himself was clothed in the person of this beggar, he was recalling his own words (for he had once said, "As often as you do this to one of the least, you have done it to me" [Matt 25:40]). And he deigned to reveal himself in the clothing that the beggar had received in order to confirm his witness to such a good deed. (5) This most blessed man was not puffed up with human pride by this vision. Instead he acknowledged God's goodness in his deed, and now that he was eighteen years old, he was impatient to be baptized. However, he did not immediately give up his military career, for he was persuaded by the entreaties of his tribune with whom he had a close relationship. In fact the tribune promised that once the period of his tribuneship was over, he himself would withdraw from the world. (6) As Martin was kept waiting for this for about two years, after his baptism he continued as a soldier though only in name.

4 (1) Then the barbarians invaded Gaul, and the Caesar Julian assembled his army at the city of the Vangiones and set about paying the soldiers a bonus. They were called out one by one, as was the custom, until it was Martin's turn. (2) Then he judged that the time was right to request his discharge, for he thought it would be dishonest to accept a bonus payment if he did not intend to serve as a soldier. So he said to the Caesar, (3) "Up till now I have fought for you; allow me now to fight for God. Let someone who intends to fight accept your bonus. I am a soldier of Christ, I am not allowed to fight." (4) The tyrant was furious at these words and claimed that Martin was refusing to do his duty as a soldier, not out of religious conviction but out of fear of the battle that was to take place the next day. (5) But Martin was not intimidated. In fact, he stood all the more firm when terror tactics were used against him. "If," he replied, "you ascribe this to cowardice rather than to faith, tomorrow I shall stand unarmed before the front lines. With neither shield nor helmet but with the sign of the cross to protect me, in the name of the Lord Jesus I will push my way into the enemy's formations without being harmed." (6) The order was therefore given for him to be taken back and thrown into prison so that he would keep his promise to be thrust unarmed at the barbarians. (7) The next day the enemy sent envoys to sue for peace, surrendering themselves and all their belongings. Who then could doubt that this victory was really due to the blessed man to whom it was granted not to be sent unarmed into battle? (8) Although the good Lord could have kept his soldier safe amid the swords and weapons of the enemy, he nonetheless removed the necessity for battle so that the holy man's gaze would not be outraged even by the deaths of others. (9) For it was right that Christ should offer his soldier no other victory than one where no one died and where the enemy was driven to surrender without bloodshed.

5 (1) After leaving the army, Martin went to visit the saintly Hilary, bishop of Poitiers, whose faith in theological matters had been tested and was well known at that time, and spent some time with him. (2) This same Hilary attempted to tie Martin more closely to himself and to bind him to the service of God by making him a deacon, but Martin refused time and time again, pleading that he was unworthy. So Hilary, a man of penetrating intellect, understood that the only way in which Martin could be tied down was if Hilary were to confer on him a position that might seem to involve a degree of humiliation. So he suggested that he should be an exorcist. Martin did

not refuse to be ordained to this position, for he did not want it to look as if he was rejecting it as not sufficiently prestigious. (3) Shortly afterward, he was admonished in his sleep to visit, out of a spirit of loving concern, his native land and his parents who were still in the clutches of paganism. So with St. Hilary's consent he set off, after being made to promise, by means of numerous entreaties and tears, that he would return. It was with sadness, so they say, that he set off on this long journey, testifying to the brothers that he would have to endure many tribulations. Later events proved this to be correct. (4) First of all, while crossing the Alps he lost his way and fell among brigands. When one of these raised his axe and prepared to strike Martin on the head, another restrained his arm as he was about to strike. However, they tied Martin's hands behind his back and handed him over to one of the brigands to be guarded and stripped of his belongings. When this brigand led him to a more remote spot and began to question him as to who he was, Martin replied that he was a Christian. (5) The brigand asked whether he was frightened. Then Martin declared with firm conviction that he had never felt so safe because he knew that the Lord's mercy was closest at hand when one was in danger; instead, Martin felt sorry for him because, being a brigand, he was unworthy of Christ's mercy. (6) Martin undertook to set forth the gospel and preached the word of God to the brigand. To cut a long story short, the brigand was converted to the faith and accompanied Martin to set him on the right road, begging him to pray to the Lord on his behalf. This same man was later seen leading a religious life, and in fact the story I have just related is said to have been heard from him.

6 (1) Continuing on his way, Martin had passed Milan when the devil, taking on human form, came up to him and asked where he was going. Receiving Martin's reply, to the effect that he was going where the Lord called him, he said to Martin (2), "Wherever you go and whatever you attempt, the devil will oppose you." Then Martin answered in the words of the prophet: *The Lord is my helper; I will not fear what a man can do to me* (Ps 118:6). At once the enemy disappeared from his sight. (3) And so he carried out his intention to set his mother free from the error of paganism while Martin's father continued in wickedness. However, Martin saved many by his example. (4) By then the Arian heresy had spread throughout the world and especially in Illyricum. Since Martin was almost the only one to fight most strenuously against the heretical beliefs of the priests and because many tortures were inflicted on him (for he was publicly beaten and finally driven to leave the city), he returned to Italy. When he learned that the church in Gaul had also been thrown into confusion by the departure of St. Hilary who had been driven into exile by the power of the heretics, Martin established a monastic cell for himself in Milan. There too Auxentius, the chief instigator and leader of the Arians, persecuted him relentlessly: he inflicted many injuries on Martin and expelled him from the city. (5) Judging it necessary to yield to circumstances, Martin withdrew to an island called Gallinara, accompanied by a priest, a man of great virtues. Here he lived for a time on the roots of grasses. During that period, he ate some hellebore, a plant said to be poisonous. (6) But when he felt the power of the poison attacking him and death close at hand, he managed by his prayers to repel the danger threatening him, and immediately all the pain left him. (7) Not long afterward, when he learned that the emperor had now repented and had granted St. Hilary permission to return from exile, Martin set out for Rome to try and meet Hilary there.

7 (1) As Hilary had already passed through, Martin followed in his footsteps to Poitiers, where he was most warmly welcomed by Hilary. Martin then erected a monastic cell for himself not far from the town. At that time a certain catechumen attached himself to him, wishing to learn how to live according to the teachings of such a holy man. A few days later this man fell sick, suffering from violent attacks of fever. (2) It happened that Martin had just gone away: after an absence of three days, he returned to find a lifeless body. Death had come so suddenly that the man had departed this mortal life without being baptized. The grieving brothers were performing their sorrowful duties around the body laid out in their midst when Martin came running up, weeping and wailing. (3) But then, as his whole mind became filled with the Holy Spirit, he told the others to leave the little room where the body lay. He locked the door and threw himself down upon the lifeless limbs of the dead brother. And when Martin had lain in prayer for a while and felt that the power of the Lord was present through the spirit, he raised himself a little and stared into the dead man's face, fearlessly awaiting the outcome of his prayers and the Lord's mercy. Two hours had scarcely passed when he saw the dead man slowly move each limb and open his eyes, blinking to regain his sight. (4) Then he turned with a great cry to the Lord, filling the tiny cell with shouts of thanksgiving. On hearing this, those who had been standing outside immediately rushed in. It was an extraordinary sight: they saw the man whom they had left as dead now alive. (5) And so, restored to life, he immediately underwent baptism. He lived for many years afterward and was the first to provide evidence and testimony to Martin's spiritual powers. (6) He used to relate how when he left the body, he was taken to the court of the Judge and that he heard the grim sentence that he was to be condemned to the dark places and to the hordes of common people. Then two angels pointed out to the Judge that this was the man for whom Martin was praying, and so the order was given for him to be taken back by the two angels, handed over to Martin, and restored to his former life. (7) It was from that moment that the name of the blessed man first shone forth so that he who was already considered by everyone to be a holy man was now also considered truly worthy of the apostles.

8 (1) Not long afterward, while Martin was passing through the estate of Lupicinus, a man who was held in high esteem in the eyes of this world, he was greeted by cries of grief from a crowd of mourners. (2) He went up to them in concern and inquired what this wailing was about; they explained to him that a young slave belonging to the household had hanged himself. When he learned of this, he entered the little room in which the corpse was lying, and shutting out all the people, he lay down on the body and prayed for a short while. (3) Soon the face showed signs of life, and the dead boy, his eyelids still heavy, raised himself up toward Martin's face. Slowly and with

great effort he managed to get up, and taking hold of the blessed man's hand, he stood up and then walked with him to the entrance of the house while the whole crowd looked on.

9 (1) At about this time, Martin was considered as a candidate for the bishopric of Tours. But since he could not easily be torn from his cell, a certain Rusticius, one of the citizens, pretending that his wife was ill, threw himself at Martin's feet, thus managing to make him come out. (2) Then, when crowds of citizens had been arranged along the route, Martin was escorted as far as the city more or less under guard. What was extraordinary was that an incredible number of people not only from that town but also from neighboring towns gathered to cast their votes. (3) They all shared one will, one wish, one opinion: Martin was the most worthy to become bishop, and fortunate was the church that had such a bishop! A few, however, including some of the bishops who had been summoned to install the prelate, wickedly rejected him, saying that he was despicable: a person with such a scruffy appearance, dirty clothes, and unkempt hair was unworthy of the episcopate. (4) But those who had a more sensible attitude found such foolishness ridiculous; while wishing to find fault with him, these bishops were actually proclaiming him to be an outstanding person! In fact they were unable to do anything other than what the people were planning in accordance with the Lord's will. However, among the bishops present, someone called Defensor is said particularly to have opposed Martin. In this connection, it was noticed that he was afterward severely reprimanded by a reading from the prophets. (5) For it happened that the reader whose turn it was to read on that day had been prevented by the crowds from arriving, and the men in charge were anxiously awaiting the man who was missing, when one of the bystanders took the psalter and seized upon the first verse he came to. (6) This was the psalm verse: *Out of the mouths of babes and sucklings you have perfected praise because of your enemies, so that you might destroy the enemy and the defender* (Ps 8:2). When he read this, the cries of the people rose up, and the opposition party was thrown into confusion. (7) They believed that it had been by God's will that this particular psalm had been read so that Defensor might hear this testimony to his deeds, he who out of the mouths of babes and sucklings had been at the same time revealed as the enemy and destroyed now that the Lord's praise had been perfected in Martin.

13. Severus of Minorca: Letter on the Conversion of the Jews

The following letter, circulated by the bishop of the small Mediterranean island of Minorca, portrays a wholesale conversion of the island's Jews over an eight-day period in February 418. Following the arrival of relics of Saint Stephen (see Text 45; Orosius, mentioned in the "Letter of Avitus," is the African priest mentioned by Severus), the Christians of the island felt empowered by their new "patron" Stephen to pressure the Jews of the city of Magona, who had lived on the island for centuries, to give up their "unbelief" and embrace Christianity. The bishop traveled with a Christian delegation from the city of Jamona, on the opposite side of the island, to "wage war" (apparently through public debate) against Jewish faithlessness. A long-standing pattern of coexistence on the island was disrupted by the sudden demands of the Christians for religious homogeneity. The Jews slowly capitulated; some

From *Severus of Minorca: Letter on the Conversion of the Jews,* trans. and ed. Scott Bradbury. Oxford, England: Clarendon Press, 1996. Used with permission.

were convinced by dreams, others by the threat of violence, others by miracles, and still others by the examples of their leaders, particularly the noble Jew Theodorus. The Jews ended up tearing down the rubble of their own synagogue (which the ardent Christians had burned down) to make way for a new church.

Severus attributes the conversion of the Jews of Minorca to the hand of God (through Stephen) and anticipates a domino effect throughout the Mediterranean. Forced conversion, however, was rare in antiquity and officially forbidden by papal doctrine throughout the Middle Ages; Christians thought it better to marginalize Jews as a reminder of their faithlessness. Even though forced conversion was not the norm for late ancient Christianity, we should nonetheless recognize the underlying potential for violence and coercion to which this letter bears witness. The entire text is reproduced here, apart from Chapter 18, which recounts the psychologically and physically intense conversion experience of two Jewish nobles, Meletius and Innocentius (mentioned later in the text), as they hid in a cave outside the city.

To the most Holy and Blessed Lord Bishops, Presbyters, Deacons and to the Universal Brotherhood of the whole world, Bishop Severus, needful of God's mercy and most unworthy of all men, sends an eternal blessing in Christ our Redeemer.

(1) Just as the Archangel Raphael warns that it is honorable to acknowledge and reveal the works of God (Tob 12:20), surely it is dangerous to veil in silence or conceal the miracles of Christ. Their proclamation produces greater pleasure, however, if they are recounted in familiar and unadorned language, for the radiant beauty of virtue is somehow obscured if she is rouged and painted with excessive eloquence. Wherefore, it will be with language that is not polished but truthful, that I shall undertake to recount for your Blessedness the miraculous deeds that Christ has performed among us.

(2) Minorca is one of the Balearic Islands, whose name has been spread abroad among all peoples, even in the works of pagan writers. It is located in the open sea almost midway between Mauretania and Spain and is confined within rather narrow boundaries, being thirty miles long and ten miles wide. I have mentioned these facts that it may be recognized how the "lowly things of this world" (1 Cor 1:28) are chosen by the Lord not only in the case of people, but places as well. On this island, the most forsaken of all lands due to its tiny size, dryness, and harshness, two small towns were founded opposite one another by the Carthaginians, as is indicated by the names given them: Jamona looks toward the West, Magona towards the East. In these towns, the burden of episcopal office had recently been placed on me, most unworthy of all mortal men.

(3) But Jamona retains even now an ancient favor from God, namely, that Jews are absolutely unable to live there. Ancient tradition hands down that many Jews, if they rashly dared to try, were prevented by sickness and driven out or laid low by sudden death or even struck down by a thunderbolt. The tale is so well known that it has made the Jews themselves afraid, so that they no longer dare to attempt it. Nor do we consider this fact unworthy of our faith, that we observe, on the one hand, an absence of wolves, foxes, and all harmful animals, while, on the other hand, there is a great abundance of those wild animals that are good to eat. What is even more marvelous is that vipers and scorpions are indeed very plentiful, but have lost all ability to do violent harm. Although none of the Jews, who are rightly compared with wolves and foxes for fierceness and villainy, dares to approach Jamona, not even for the right of hospitality, Magona seethed with so great a multitude of Jews, as if with vipers and scorpions, that Christ's church was being wounded by them daily. But that ancient, earthly favor was recently renewed for us in a spiritual sense, so that, as it is written, that generation of vipers (Luke 3:7), which used to attack with venomous stings, suddenly under the compulsion of divine power has cast aside the lethal poison of unbelief.

(4) At about that same period when I, although unworthy, assumed the title of episcopal office, a certain priest, conspicuous for his sanctity, came from Jerusalem and sojourned for a brief time in Magona. After he was unable to cross over to Spain, as he wished to do, he decided to go back to Africa again. Doubtless at the inspiration of the martyr himself, he placed in the church of Magona some relics of St. Stephen the martyr, which recently had come to light and which he had intended to transport to Spain. When this was done, straightaway the fire of his love was kindled, the fire that the Lord "came to cast upon the earth" (Luke 12:49) and which he wishes to blaze forth. Immediately our complacency heated up, and, as it is written, our hearts were "burning by the way" (Luke 24:32). At one moment, zeal for the faith would fire our hearts; at another moment, the hope of saving a multitude would spur us on.

(5) In the end, even the obligation of greeting one another was suddenly broken off, and not only was our old habit of easy acquaintance disrupted, but the sinful appearance of our long-standing affection was transformed into temporary hatred, though for love of eternal salvation. In every public place, battles were waged against the Jews over the Law, in every house struggles over the faith.

(6) The Jewish people relied particularly on the influence and knowledge of a certain Theodorus, who was preeminent in both wealth and worldly honor not only among the Jews, but also among the Christians of that town [Magona]. Among the Jews he was a teacher of the Law and, if I may use their own phrase, the Father of Fathers. In the town, on the other hand, he had already fulfilled all the duties of the town council and served as *defensor,* and even now he is considered the *patronus* of his fellow citizens. The Christians, however, humble in heart as well as physical strength, yet superior by the force of truth, prayed for the assistance of Stephen, their patron, until the two armies separated, after they had agreed upon a day for their debate and concluded a truce for the present moment.

(7) The Jews were eager for Theodorus, on whose strength the whole synagogue relied, to return from the island of Majorca, where, by chance, he had gone at the time to inspect an estate. Indeed, as soon as an embassy was sent to him, he returned and frightened many people by his authority, and although he did not extinguish our ardor for the struggle, he did calm it for a little while. Blazing up suddenly with greater ferocity, the flame of faith also engulfed the neighboring town [of Jamona]. And that the saying of Solomon might be fulfilled, "A brother helping a brother shall be raised up like a solid and lofty city" (Prov 18:19), many of Christ's servants decided to devote all the strength of their spirit to this war, not objecting in the least to the toil of a journey [to Magona].

(8) Now the tract appended to this letter demonstrates the kinds of weapons we prepared in advance as the battle loomed. It was certainly not for anyone's edification that we wished this tract to be published (for in *that* we are utterly deficient and hope rather to acquire *it* from your Blessedness), but that it might be noticed that we showed considerable concern, in so far as our abilities allowed, for the struggle that had been engaged. But, in truth, Christ, whose "kingdom dwells not in talk but in power" (1 Cor 4:20), achieved everything with his own forces and without us even uttering a word. Without any sweat from the struggle, he granted his army this victory that no one dared hope for and that no one could expect. The Jews meanwhile were exhorting one another with examples from the time of the Maccabees, and, in defense of their religion, they desired even death. Thus, they began not only to consult their sacred books, but also to gather stakes, rocks, javelins, and all kinds of weapons into the synagogue, in order to repulse the Christians by physical force if the situation demanded it, although our battle line was defended by the power of the Holy Spirit.

(9) Meanwhile, as these preparations were being made and the future war was being planned on each side with great zeal, both armies were forewarned by countless dreams that were perfectly clear. If I make absolutely no mention of them, I will appear to have concealed no small part of the divine glory. For if Luke, the writer of sacred history, included the dream of the holy Apostle Paul, reporting that a man from Macedonia stood over him in a night vision and

prayed that he be helped by him, and forewarned by this vision, the Apostle changed the course of his journey for Macedonia (Acts 16:9–10), how much greater is the glory of our Lord Jesus Christ, who deigned to reveal to his most insignificant and most unworthy servants that which was revealed to the blessed Apostle and which Scripture was unwilling to conceal. Therefore, for the sake of brevity and that your Blessedness may not find my account tedious, I will include just two dreams.

(10) There was among us a certain devout and very religious woman with the name of Theodora, who, because of her virginity, her religious way of life, and even the significance of her name ["gift of God"], could rightfully serve as a symbol of the church. She saw in a night vision a certain very noble widow sending a request to me in the form of a letter, in which she humbly offered me all her fields to sow, although I occupy the priesthood not from merit, but from the bounty of divine favor. By a similar dream, Christ also deigned to summon me as well, the last among all sinners, in order that I prepare myself for the sowing: for another very noble widow, who without any doubt symbolized the synagogue, begged me [in the dream] to take over her untilled fields and to cultivate them carefully, since the season for sowing was close at hand. Who then is the noble widow but that widow who, by impiously killing Christ, cruelly widowed herself? The dream is identical in each case. It is well established that I both saw the vision about thirty days before it was fulfilled and, although I knew nothing of its fulfilment, that I recounted it to the brethren.

(11) Among the Jews also, by the wondrous ordering of the divine dispensation, the name "Theodora" and my office were associated and united in one man. Theodorus, the high priest of that faithless people, recounted a dream vision that he had seen not only to Jews, but in particular to a certain kinswoman, a distinguished matriarch of that town, and to many Christians as well. Some time before it was fulfilled, he recounted it with these words, "As I was going into the synagogue in my usual way," he said, "twelve men barred my path with outstretched hands, saying, 'Where are you going? There is a lion

in there.' Although I had begun to tremble at hearing the word 'lion' and was getting ready to flee, nonetheless I searched out a spot from which I might peer in, and I saw monks inside singing with uncanny sweetness. A greater terror was immediately aroused in me, and if I had not first entered the house of a certain Jew named Reuben, and from there raced headlong to the side of my married kinswoman, I could scarcely have escaped the force of that deadly terror. She soothed me, breathless, at her bosom, and rescued me from both danger and fear." His dream is perfectly clear and in need of no interpretation. For who is the lion, but that "Lion of the tribe of Judah, the Root of David" (Rev 5:5)? Who is that kinswoman, if not that one of whom it is written, "My kinswoman is but one"? Therefore, one point alone seemed obscure, namely, that he entered the house of a Jew called Reuben when he was terrified by the Lion. This was indeed explained very plainly to us afterward by the very Lion who terrified him, in order that he might save him. We will treat this matter later in its proper place.

(12) Now, however, to proceed with my narrative, a throng of Christ's servants, greater than was thought to reside in that town, gathered together and prepared for the departure from Jamona. Although it was a very arduous journey, they completed it with such speed that they flew over the thirty miles more lightheartedly than if they were being invited to a banquet at some beauty spot outside the town. And so we arrived at Magona. Immediately, I dispatched some clerics to announce my arrival to the Jews and requested that they do us the honor of entering the church. They, however, sent back to us an unexpected message, announcing that it was inappropriate for them to enter a church on that day, lest, I suppose, they be polluted, since it was the Sabbath. If they should corrupt its observance by any actions, they would be committing a very serious, criminal transgression. Again I made a request, to the effect that they should wait for me at the synagogue if they preferred, since entry into the church seemed a source of pollution, and in any case they were not being forced by us into any menial labor on the Sabbath. On the contrary, the dispute concerning the Law was to be

thoroughly calm, and there should be no stirring up quarrels, but rather a sharing of views in discussion. If, on the other hand, they were not avoiding the debate through a ruse, but were offering a genuine excuse, then let them show us the rule by which it was prohibited for them to engage in discussion on a holy day. Although they replied by stubbornly contradicting me on every point, they were in the end driven by terror of that Lion to gather at the house where I was being lodged. There I said, "I ask you, brothers, why, particularly in a city subject to Roman laws, you have gathered together heaps of stones and all sorts of arms as if you faced brigands? We brought books in order to instruct; you brought swords and clubs to commit murder. We wish to increase; you desire to destroy. In my judgment, our struggle is not on an equal footing and our conflict is very different on the two sides. As I see it, you thirst for our blood, while we thirst for your salvation." They were a little frightened at these words and denied the fact of the matter, and when we affirmed that this was the case, they even began to resist with an oath. Then, to cut the knot of contention, I said, "When the matter can be proved with one's eyes, what need is there for an oath? Let's go to the synagogue, and it will be confirmed with yourselves as witnesses whether your assertion rests on perjury or truth."

(13) Then we set out for the synagogue, and along the way we began to sing a hymn to Christ in our abundance of joy. Moreover, the psalm was "Their memory has perished with a crash and the Lord endures forever" (Ps 9:6–7), and the throng of Jews also began to sing it with a wondrous sweetness. But before we reached the synagogue, certain Jewish women (by God's arrangement, I suppose) acted recklessly, and, doubtless to rouse our people from their gentleness, began to throw huge stones down on us from a higher spot. Although the stones, marvelous to relate, fell like hail over a closely packed crowd, not only was none of our people harmed by a direct hit, but not one was even touched. At this point, that terrible Lion took away for a short while the mildness from his lambs. While I protested in vain, they all snatched up stones, and neglecting their shepherd's warning, since they were united in a plan

suggested more by zeal for Christ than by anger, they decided that the wolves had to be attacked with horns, although no one could doubt that this was done with the approval of him who alone is the true and good shepherd. Finally, lest it seem that he had granted his flock a bloody victory, not one of the Jews pretended even to have been touched, not even to stir up ill will, as usually happens. Admittedly, since we must in every way avoid deceit, one man out of the entire number of Christians was discovered who desired to be like that Achan who, under Joshua son of Nun, coveted spoils from the forbidden things (Josh 7:1). For the slave of a certain Christian, as he himself was later forced to confess, had come to that place, drawn not by love of Christ, but by love of plunder. He alone was greedy to steal something from the synagogue, and he was struck by a stone for his offense. In fact, someone from our group threw the stone, though he was aiming at a Jew, but it struck the slave on the head and admonished him to recall his true head, namely, Christ. Although the wound was not dangerous, it both forced him to confess his greedy desire for theft, and, by its obvious retribution, it put fear in everyone else lest they lapse in a similar way. Therefore, after the Jews had retreated and we had gained control of the synagogue, no one, I won't say, "stole" anything, but no one even considered "looting" anything! Fire consumed the synagogue itself and all of its decorations, with the exception of the books and silver. We removed the sacred books so that they wouldn't suffer harm among the Jews, but the silver we returned to them so that there would be no complaining either about us taking spoils or about them suffering losses.

(14) And so, while all the Jews stood stupified at the destruction of the synagogue, we set out for the church to the accompaniment of hymns, and, giving thanks to the author of our victory, we poured forth our tears and beseeched the Lord to lay siege to the true dens of their unbelief and to expose to the light the faithlessness of their dark hearts.

(15) Nor was there any delay in the accomplishment, for on the following day, a certain Jew called Reuben was chosen by the Lord (that appropriate names be preserved in all matters) to be made the

firstborn of them all. For he delighted the hearts of all with a most holy cry, praying that he be released from the chains of Jewish superstition. And without delay he became the "firstborn of Jacob" (Gen 35:23) and received the sign of salvation. From that moment he remained close to our sides and our counsels, and along with us reviled the stubborn hard-heartedness of all [the Jews].

(16) A span of three days passed, if I am not mistaken, in which our people preserved in prayers and the Jews persevered in faithlessness. After that, Theodorus, hedged round with a contingent of his followers, came to the spot where only the walls of the synagogue, which were later pulled down by Jewish converts, could be seen to survive. In that spot a throng of Christians also gathered along with me. There Theodorus debated boldly about the Law, and after he had mocked and twisted all of our objections, the Christian throng, seeing that he could not be vanquished by human arguments, prayed for assistance from heaven. They all shouted together and cried in thunderous unison, "Theodorus, believe in Christ!" From our most indulgent Lord's marvelous mercy, small favors were still being sought, and he had already granted greater ones. But no! A miracle from the Omnipotent is no "miraculous" thing! He himself transformed the import of this shouting in the ears of the Jews, he who once brought it about that four lepers should seize the camp of the king of Syria, who had laid seige to Samaria (2 Kings 7), and he who routed through Gideon the battle lines of the Midianites and who granted a great, effortless victory to three hundred of his men, bringing it about through terror that a multitude of the enemy should kill one another with self-inflicted wounds (Judg 7:19–22). Similarly in the present instance, the Jewish bystanders misinterpreted the phrase spoken by our people, for they all thought they had heard, "Theodorus has believed in Christ!" As a result, since they all thought that the leader of their faithlessness had been converted to faith in Christ, they were all equally afraid, and where there was no cause for fear, they were terrified. Racing together with disheveled hair and wild howling, their women assailed Theodorus with repeated cries, "Theodorus, what have

you done?" As for the men, however, some fled to pathless groves and mountain ravines, while others scattered through the streets of the town in their desire to discover a place where they could hide. Theodorus himself was stunned and shocked, and he perceived that among his people the divine judgment was being fulfilled: "The wicked man runs away with no one in pursuit" (Prov 28:1). But wait, it was not "no one"! That terrible Lion was pursuing them, who from the site of the synagogue, as had been revealed to Theodorus, had unleashed through the monks the roar by which he put fear in our resisting enemies. Thus, Theodorus was standing on the very same spot where previously in his dream he had been smitten with terror of the Lion, and although he searched for the source of his great anxiety and heard only the name of our Lion, he saw nothing fierce there, as he feared he would. All he saw was monks singing psalms. And since he had been abandoned by the whole multitude of his people and he too was preparing to slip away, he began to look for an escape route on foot. Now when Reuben, that most holy man, had caught sight of Theodorus, gripped with terrible fear, and not only pale but unable even to speak, he quickly approached him, addressing the trembling man with coaxing words and encouraging him toward faith in Christ. And by offering him the example of his own faith as a refuge from fear, he seemed somehow to open up the house of his faith, to which Theodorus was fleeing from fear of the Lion. Still, in order that we may recount every detail faithfully and that you may listen eagerly, you who seek not rhetorical adornment, but the truth, I will include the words of Reuben himself and suppress none of the frankness of his speech. Reuben said, "What do you fear, Lord Theodorus? If you truly wish to be safe and honored and wealthy, believe in Christ, just as I, too, have believed. Right now you are standing, and I am seated with bishops; if you should believe, you will be seated, and I will be standing before you." After pondering these words deep in his mind, Theodorus replied to us, "I shall do what you wish," he said. "Accept this promise, but allow me first to address my people, so that I may reap a greater reward for my conversion by the conversion of the others as well."

His pledge was received by everyone with incalculable joy. Some ran to him affectionately and caressed his face and neck with kisses, others embraced him in gentle arms, while still others longed to join right hands with him or to engage him in conversation. And so Theodorus set out for his own home, happy at every sign of affection from our people, but nevertheless not completely free of anxiety, for although he seemed by now to have come to the house of Reuben by making his promise, nonetheless he was still at that point frightened, since he had not yet come to his kinswoman, who after three days took him to her maternal bosom and freed him from all confusion and fear. We, on the other hand, set out for the church to the usual accompaniment of hymns, chanting and singing: "Blessed is the Father of Mercies and the God of all Consolation" (2 Cor 1:3), who granted water for our heads and a font of tears for our eyes, in order that we might lament the wounded among our people (Jer 9:1).

(17) After the completion of our holy rites, we left the church and observed that a good-sized crowd of Jews had gathered to meet us. All of them with singleness of spirit pleaded that they might receive the symbol of Christ from me, unworthy shepherd that I am. So we went back into the church, gave thanks to our merciful God, and there on the spot marked the sign of salvation on their foreheads. . . .

(19) After the third day, while Theodorus was making arrangements to address the assembled people and call them to faith in Christ, he suffered a revolt from Jews who were going to offer themselves for conversion of their own accord. For there was almost no one who did not testify that he had openly felt the power of Christ. In fact, in their first public meeting, a certain youth, a cousin of Theodorus himself, by the name of Galilaeus (that the mystery of events, as has often been said already, may be revealed to the end with appropriate names) began to proclaim with great indignation, "I call you all to witness that I cannot be a Jew. For on my estate I have Christian partners by whose hatred I may be killed if I wish to persevere in Judaism. Therefore, I will heed the danger to my life and will set out right now for the church to escape the death being prepared for me."

Although Galilaeus thought he was devising these remarks for the present moment, inasmuch as he seemed to have explained the reasons for his conversion, and although he then gave no thought to the eventual end of the present age, he was unwittingly speaking the truth. Caecilianus, a worthy man, and so eminent not only among the Jews but also in the town that even now he has been elected *defensor,* all but snatched Galilaeus's speech away from him, affirming that Galilaeus spoke the truth and that he himself had a similar motive and feared a similar fate. With these words, he instilled such great confidence in the youth that before everyone's eyes, with a quick dash, as if to carry off the prize of faith (1 Cor 9:24), he flew to the aid of our Galilaean [Christ] and from my own humbleness requested that henceforth he be enrolled under his name. Caecilianus, however, since he was a Father of the Jews, after holding a rather hurried consultation with his brother Florianus, who was likewise a Father of the Jews, addressed the synagogue, as we learned, with words of this sort, "Since in the synagogue I am second only to Theodorus in honor, I am not advising you and making an appeal, all aflutter, as it were, like the young Galilaeus; rather I exhort you and warn you and proclaim that all of us together must abandon the error of our misguided way, if it can be done, and unite together in the faith of the church. But even if his great power does not draw you to Christ, my brother, Florianus, and I, while we cannot use force against you in your rejection of such great salvation, nonetheless we, with our entire households, will abandon the mockery of this religion, which we lack the strength to defend, and we will join in alliance with the faithful ranks of the Christians. They certainly could never vanquish, with their countless citations from the Scriptures, not only you, brother Theodorus, who are thought to be more learned than the others, but everyone else as well, if they were not pursuing the truth, which cannot be defeated." With such reasoning, we learned, Caecilianus addressed his people, and on that day we received with ineffable joy many Jews who came running with him to faith in Christ.

(20) Although I lack the ability to speak eloquently about the prodigies that occurred in the sky at

that time, I do not dare to be silent. At about the seventh hour, we began solemnly to celebrate the Lord's Mass. The greater part of the day passed, while we were either offering encouragement to or putting on record (for we copied down their names) Jews who were arriving to confess faith in Christ, and the people were spiritually sated with such a banquet of joy that they gave no thought to earthly food. The whole congregation was waiting for Mass with me in the church, which is located a short distance from the town in a secluded spot and in which repose the relics of the blessed martyr Stephen, which were recently deposited there. Meanwhile two monks, whom the Lord chose as witnesses to his miracles, were lying in the grassy field that stretched out in front of the church doors. There was as well a man of rank by the name of Julius seeking the church with another man from the town. When they had started to pass by, suddenly one of the monks, distracted by the sight of a miraculous sign, uttered a garbled cry and, when they turned around toward him, pointed with an outstretched hand, since he could not describe in words what he saw. There was a ball of very brilliant light, approximately the size of a man in height and with the shape of the jugs commonly called *orcae*. The vision was of such clarity and brilliance that it appeared to the brother who noticed it first, as we learned from his own account, that the sun was sinking. It appeared to them to be sinking in a slow descent over the church where the entire congregation remained with me. Indeed, they thought it was so close that that same brother, after being jolted out of his stupor, set out at a run, since he thought that it had sunk behind the church, but he checked his step, held back by his fellow monk. The latter added that it had also appeared to him but that it was farther away, though he was not positive and only guessing. However, certain women who were still Jews at the time, among whom was the wife of the Meletius mentioned above, confirmed that, as they were looking out of an upper story, the same thing appeared to them as if it had descended over the church. But it is still today unclear whether this thing was an angel or St. Stephen himself or what it really appeared to be. At around the fourth hour on that same day, that is,

slightly before this sign was revealed, there fell a light dusting of very fine hail, which the island's inhabitants in their local dialect call *argistinum*. After the air began to grow fragrant with the smell of honey, it was tasted by many who had been struck by it on the road, and it was found to be sweeter than honey. When many people tasted it and saw that on that same day the sons of Israel [viz., the Jews of Minorca] departed from the Egypt of their unbelief and from slavery, they compared what had happened to those wonders we read about in Exodus. They believed that the manna had been renewed for this people who, by their contemplation of God with a heart ready to believe, now merited the name of the true Israel (Exod 16). They also judged that the column of fire, which preceded the Fathers in the desert, had been revealed in order to furnish spiritual guidance for the sons who had departed from the true Egypt and, as it is written, from the iron furnace (Deut 4:20). And in truth, as a reading of Exodus confirms, the similarity of the signs was very close. For what we believe to have been hail corresponded to the tiny coriander seed and recalled honey with its taste, and it is clear that what had appeared [in the sky over the church] was like a fiery column. Moreover, we have learned that both wonders were also revealed to the brethren who remained in Jamona. For many people, who had been granted the ability and disposition to inquire into this matter, attested the rain of honey, and that column of very brilliant light revealed itself to the gaze of many people whom the Lord judged worthy. From which it may be inferred that Jews throughout the whole world are to be visited with the light of faith, since indeed so great a splendor of heavenly grace has shone upon us, who live on this island and, if I may use the phrase, in "this little world," so that the revelation of signs should extend to the utmost boundaries of our world.

(21) Accordingly, on the following day, everyone reminded Theodorus with great anticipation that he should make good his pledge. He believed, for what seemed to him justifiable reasons, that the vows of all the Jews should be postponed, saying that first he wanted to bring his wife here, whom he had left on the island of Majorca. His concern was that she

might, if she learned that her husband had converted without her agreement, remain firm in her faithlessness, as usually happens. Further, she might become confused in her judgment and, at the instigation of her mother in particular, who was still alive, abandon both the marriage and her husband's religion. When Theodorus had made these pleas, the Christians were amenable, but the Jews who had converted persisted in a bitter disturbance. The delay was cut short, and Theodorus himself flew swiftly to the bosom of his kinswoman, as he had seen [in the dream]. After him, the whole synagogue, as if a stumbling block had been removed, flowed together to the church. Marvelous to relate, aged teachers of the Law began to believe, without any verbal wrangling, without any dispute over the Scriptures. After debating for so long whether they were willing to accept faith in Christ, they professed that they believed in Christ and desired to be made Christians without delay.

(22) One man, so they say, was 102 years in age and in faithlessness. Although decrepit, he was nimble in his hope for the future life, and without exchanging three words, he proclaimed that he hoped to return at the end of his days to a spiritual infancy through faith in Christ, and he presented to us his limbs, by now feeble with decay, that he might be renewed through baptism as quickly as possible.

(23) There were certain Jews who, as they sailed past, were driven to the island and were waiting for an appropriate moment and favorable winds. Even though the freedom to set sail was granted them, they preferred to believe.

(24) Consequently, only three women, although very noble women among the Jews, did Christ permit to hold out a little longer, in order to extend the glory of his power amid the hardheartedness of their unbelief. Artemisia, the daughter of Litorius, who recently governed this province and who is now said to be a count, was distraught at the conversion of her husband Meletius. Without any thought for feminine frailty and with just one friend, a nurse, and a few servant girls, she deserted her husband's house and escaped to a cave, which, though located in a vineyard, was none the less in quite a remote spot. In the vineyard, there was a small, new winepress, and a newly

made vat, which seemed somehow to serve as a symbol of a faithful people. For we either believe or can see that the Jews have received the "must" of the New Testament not like "old wineskins" but like "new winevats" (Luke 5:37). This woman had passed two days in that spot, implacable and angry with her husband. As soon as the third day dawned, she ordered a maidservant to draw water for her so that she could wash her face in her usual way. The water came from the winevat, which was full from a rainshower. When she realized that the water resembled honey in the sweetness of its taste and smell, at first she began to grow angry with the servant and asked indignantly why she had put honey in the pitcher. Afterward, however, as if to disprove the servant's denials, she went to the vat, drew forth a little water with cupped hands, and found that the water she had been using for two days was changed into the sweetest, most delightful honey. Then she called over all the women present and told them to taste the water, lest by chance a falsely sweet taste was deceiving her throat alone. All of them tasted it and were stirred with such marvelous delight that they decided it was not water infused with honey, but the purest honey with only a resemblance to water. Struck with wonder, they investigated more carefully while they were preparing to return to town and discovered that the dew, which was on much of the grass, also had a similar taste. Accordingly, the previously mentioned lady set out for the town, reported these things to her husband, and through him made them known to everyone, and immediately, without resistance, she assented to faith in Christ. However, on the same day when Meletius's wife was compelled by the honey to cast away the bitterness of her unbelief, on the same day, I say, when this daughter of Israel was placed as if in a desert and perceived that ancient lake of Marah grow sweet when the "log of the cross" was thrown into it (Exod 15:23–25), the entire church grew fragrant with such a marvelous and truly heavenly odor that nearly all the brethren sensed the presence of the Holy Spirit, which we had also sensed sometimes in the past, but only a few of us.

(25) It was also counted a marvel in everyone's mind that although the sky was for the most part clear

during those days, quite frequent showers did occur. And the rain would precede by a short interval Jews who were coming to confess faith in Christ. We actually noticed it and would say to one another half-jokingly, "Look, it's raining now. Mark my words, some Jews are sure to accept faith in Christ!" Miraculously, often while we were saying such things, there would be a knock on the church door by some Jews. And not in vain did those most joyful showers announce that a people would believe, since, as it is written, "The Lord sets apart a plentiful rain for his inheritance" (Ps 68:9).

(26) There still remained two women who refused to race to the fragrance of Christ's unguents: the wife of that Innocentius whom we mentioned above, along with her sister, a widow of excellent reputation. Yet the moment she learned that her sister's husband, Innocentius, had been converted, she boarded ship. We not only permitted her to do this, we even encouraged her, because she could not be turned to faith in Christ by either words or miracles.

(27) Moreover, Innocentius's wife for nearly four days rejected with deaf ears the word of salvation that we were administering. Since she was overwhelmed by the incurable sickness of her unbelief and refused all our medicine and could not be swayed by Innocentius's threats nor his prayers nor his tears, the whole crowd of the brethren, at Innocentius's request, gathered together at the house where he lived, feeling great pain in their spirits because so great an abundance of happiness was being opposed by a single woman (since her sister was thought already to have set sail). After we had forced vain words on deaf ears for a long time and had accomplished nothing, we hastened to the known assistance of prayer and turned toward heavenly mercy the prayers that mortal impiety rejected. And so our army sweated until nearly the third hour in contests of hymns and prayers against Amalek, the enemy of our leader Jesus (Exod 17:8–17). When we had become (it must be confessed) nearly desperate and were preparing our departure, we ordered everyone to regather their strength and to pray. Stretched out on the floor, we wept for a long time. And when the people had exclaimed "Amen" at the end of the prayer, that woman

added that she believed and that she wanted to be made a Christian. Thereupon, we returned to our houses, delighted that this woman too had been freed from the snares of the devil.

(28) On the following day, that is, the eighth day after we had come, we decided to return to Jamona, carrying back the rich spoils of our joy from our splendid victory. But when we had made ourselves ready and were already leaving the city, the Lord added for his people as a kind of traveling allowance the one joy that appeared to be lacking. For that widowed kinswoman of Innocentius was carried back from the open sea. Suddenly, she wrapped herself about my knees and begged with tears for the assistance of our faith. "Why woman," I asked, "did you wish to desert your brothers in such foolhardiness?" To which she replied, "Even the prophet Jonah wished to flee from the countenance of God, and yet he fulfilled, although unwillingly, the will of God (Jonah 1:1–4). Therefore, receive not just myself, but these orphans, too, and nourish them in Christ." While she was making this pitiful plea, she led her two little daughters to me. Who did not weep for joy? From whom did this abundance of happiness not wring tears? To be sure, I accepted the sheep (the only one from the whole flock we knew to have wandered off), and I recalled her with her twin offspring to the fold of Christ.

(29) Although the eight days in which these events occurred were before the beginning of Lent, they were celebrated by us as if it were Easter. For it is confirmed that 540 souls were added to the church. Moreover, I do not think it frivolous or superfluous (though I will have omitted many things due to my endless supply) to recollect in closing that of the great multitude of people from Jamona who had come so many days before on a journey of thirty miles, not one placed concern for his house, or plans for his daily sustenance, or personal affections before this task.

(30) All the more joy should be felt at the following marvel, namely, that we see the land of the Jewish people, barren for so long, producing manifold fruits of righteousness, now that the thorns of unbelief have been cut down and the seed of the Word im-

planted, so that we rejoice for ourselves in the hope of new crops. Where we uprooted an infamous forest of unbelief, the most fertile works of faith have flourished. For not only are the Jews bearing the expense, first, for leveling the very foundations of the synagogue and then for constructing a new basilica, but they even carry the stones on their own shoulders.

(31) May your Blessedness know that these things were begun on February 2 by the power of our Lord Jesus Christ and were completed on the eighth day hence, in the year after the eleventh consulship of the Emperor Honorius and the second consulship of Constantius, a man of *clarissimus* rank. Wherefore, if you accept respectfully the word of an unworthy sinner, take up Christ's zeal against the Jews, but do so for the sake of their eternal salvation. Perhaps that time predicted by the Apostle has indeed now come when the fullness of the Gentiles will have come in and all Israel shall be saved (Rom 11:25–6). And perhaps the Lord wished to kindle this spark from the ends of the earth, so that the whole breadth of the earth might be ablaze with the flame of love in order to burn down the forest of unbelief.

Catechesis and Initiation: The Texts

Even though conversion was often portrayed as a sharply defined moment of sudden illumination, the process of becoming a full Christian was relatively drawn out. By the third century, this process was described by the technical term *catechumenate*. It comes from the Greek word *katecheō*, "to instruct" (implying oral instruction); someone engaged in Christian instruction was a *catechumen*, and the instruction itself was *catechesis*.

By the third and fourth centuries, the catechumenate served as a dividing line, separating the Christian community into degrees of initiation. The uninitiated members of the community would hear preaching and general instruction from the priest and then depart; next, the catechumens would receive special instruction on doctrine, sacred history, and liturgy and then depart; finally, those Christians who had been baptized would remain and receive the "mystery," the Eucharist. Opinion differed as to the appropriate duration of the catechumenate; the average term of instruction seems to have been three years, although some Christians remained on the roster of the catechumenate for most of their adult lives, while others might be "fast-tracked," through catechesis, baptism, and even clerical ordination in the space of days or weeks.

Once sufficiently instructed, a catechumen might then register for baptism. Final instruction would usually occur during the forty-day period of Lent, and baptisms would then take place during Easter week under the bishop's supervision (creating an annual sense pageantry, particularly in urban churches). The newly baptized were now full members of the Christian community, initiated into the "mysteries of the church." The examples included here of catechetical instruction from the beginning and end of the process: Augustine's examples of speeches to be given to the newly enrolled catechumens and an oration of John Chrysostom delivered to candidates who were registered for imminent baptism.

14. Augustine: On Catechizing the Unlearned

Although Augustine famously renounced his secular career as a professor of rhetoric in order to serve the church (see Text 11), his talent as an orator remains clear in his hundreds of sur-

Adapted from *A Select Library of the Nicene and Post-Nicene Fathers of the Christian Church*, series 1, vol. 3: *Saint Augustin: On the Holy Trinity, Doctrinal Treatises, Moral Treatises*, ed. Philip Schaff. Grand Rapids, Mich.: Wm. B. Eerdmans, 1989.

viving sermons. His oratorical skill also made him particularly valuable to the churches of North Africa. It was recounted that, in the 380s, the elderly Bishop Valerius of Carthage pressed Augustine into the priesthood precisely to have someone capable of expounding true Christian doctrine in language that was comprehensible and engaging to the common folk (Valerius himself had trouble communicating with his flock in their North African Latin). It is to Augustine, the doctrinal and rhetorical expert, that Deogratis, a deacon in Carthage, wrote some time around 400 requesting assistance in preparing his catechetical lectures.

In response, Augustine composed a rhetorical and theological manual, distilling the "how" and "what" of primary catechetical instruction. In the first part of the treatise, a reader can catch a glimpse of Augustine the retired professor: he advises Deogratis on tone, delivery, and even how to adapt himself to the educational level of his audience. In the second half of the treatise (included here), Augustine gives two "sample" catechetical lectures, long and short versions of what he believes to be the essential historical, doctrinal, and spiritual message of Christian instruction. Augustine takes the catechumens out of the mundane context of everyday living—filled with sin, spectacle, and selfishness—and situates them in the broad sweep of salvation history: the Fall in Paradise (Genesis 1–3), the Flood (Genesis 6–9), the call of Abraham (Genesis 12–17), slavery and liberation from Egypt (Exodus-Deuteronomy), the establishment of Israel and the Temple (Samuel-Kings), the Babylonian Exile (prophets), the rise of the Roman Empire and the coming of Jesus (Gospels), the advent of the Holy Spirit (Acts), and the age of apostles, martyrs, and Christian triumph. Through this creative restructuring of the Bible, Augustine conveys the majestic scope of Christian history. We also find embedded in this "primary" instruction some of Augustine's trademark theological concerns: God's grace and human will, the city of God and the city of man, the "mixed" church of the saved and the reprobate, and the ultimate deferment of human perfection to the time of the judgment and resurrection.

16 (24) Let us suppose that someone has come to us who wishes to be made a Christian and who belongs to the order of private persons, not of the class of rustics, but of the city bred, such as those whom you cannot fail to come across in numbers in Carthage. Let us also suppose that on being asked whether the inducement leading him to desire to be a Christian is any advantage looked for in the present life or the rest that is hoped for after this life, he has answered that his inducement has been the rest that is yet to come. Then perhaps such a person might be instructed by us in an address like this:

"Thanks be to God, my brother; heartily I wish you joy, and I am glad on your account that, amid all the storms of this world, which are at once so great and so dangerous, you have considered true and certain insurance. For even in this life people go to great lengths to seek rest and security, but they do not find

it because of their wicked desires. They wish to find rest in restless things that do not last. And these things, since they are taken from them and pass away over time, agitate them with fears and griefs and will not let them be restful. For if a person seeks to find rest in wealth, he is rendered proud, rather than secure. Do we not see how many have lost their riches suddenly? How many, too, have perished because of them, either because they desired to possess them or they have been oppressed and stripped of them by others more desirous than themselves? And even should they remain with the person all his life long and never leave their lover, he himself would leave them at his death. For how long is a person's life, even if he lives to old age? Or when people want old age for themselves, what else do they really want but long illness? So, too, with the honors of this world: what are they but pride and emptiness and the peril of ruin? For thus says Holy Scripture: 'All flesh is grass, and human glory is as the flower of grass. The grass withers, the flower falls away; but the word of the Lord endures forever' (Isa 40:6–7; 1 Pet 1:24–25). Consequently, whoever longs for true rest and true happiness ought to lift his hope from mortal and transitory things and fix it on the word of the Lord, so that, cleaving to that which endures forever, he may himself, together with it, endure forever.

(25) "There are also others who neither crave to be rich nor go about seeking the vain pomps of honors, but who nevertheless wish to find their joy and rest in dainty meats and in fornications and in those theaters and spectacles that are at their disposal in great cities for free. But so it is also with these people: they waste their small means in luxury and subsequently are forced by exigency into thefts and burglaries and, at times, even into highway robberies, and so they are suddenly filled with many great fears, and those who a little before were singing in the house of revelry are now dreaming of the sorrows of the prison. Moreover, in their eager devotion to the public spectacles, they come to resemble demons, as they incite people with their cries to wound each other and instigate those who have done them no hurt to engage in furious contests with each other, while they seek to please an insane people. And if they consider them to be peaceful, then they hate them and persecute them and raise an outcry, asking that they should be beaten with clubs, as if they had been in collusion to cheat them; and this iniquity they force even the judge, who is the (appointed) avenger of iniquities, to perpetrate. On the other hand, if they observe them exerting themselves in horrid hostilities against each other (whether *sintae*,[1] or theatrical actors and players or charioteers or hunters, those wretched people who fight and struggle, not only men with men, but even men with beasts), the fiercer the fury with which they perceive these unhappy creatures rage against each other, the better they like them, and the greater the enjoyment they have in them; and they favor them

---

[1] A colloquial Greek loan word that seems to mean "roughnecks" or "bruisers."

when thus excited, and by so favoring them, they excite them all the more, the spectators themselves striving more madly with each other as they espouse the cause of different combatants than is the case even with those very people whose madness they madly provoke, while at the same time they also long to be spectators of the same in their mad frenzy. How, then, can that mind keep the soundness of peace that feeds on strifes and contentions? For just as is the food that is received, such is the health that results. Ultimately, although mad pleasures are no pleasures, nevertheless let them be what they are, and it still remains the case that whatever their nature may be and whatever the measure of enjoyment yielded by the boasts of riches and the inflation of honors and the spendthrift pleasures of the taverns and the contests of the theaters and the impurity of fornications and the lechery of the baths, one little fever takes them all away, and even for the living, it takes away the whole false happiness of their life. Then there remains only a void and wounded conscience, destined to apprehend that God as a Judge whom it refused to have as a Father and destined also to find a severe Lord in him whom it scorned to seek and love as a tender Father. But you, inasmuch as you seek that true rest that is promised to Christians after this life, will taste the same sweet and pleasant rest even here among the bitterest troubles of this life if you continue to love the commandments of him who has promised the same. For quickly will you feel that the fruits of righteousness are sweeter than those of unrighteousness and that a person finds a more genuine and pleasurable joy in the possession of a good conscience in the midst of troubles than in that of an evil conscience in the midst of delights. For you have not come to be united to the Church of God with the idea of seeking from it any temporal advantage.

17 (26) "For there are some who wish to become Christians either so that they may gain the favor of people to whom they look for temporal advantages or because they are reluctant to offend those whom they fear. But these are reprobate, and although the church bears them for a time, as the threshing floor bears the chaff until the period of winnowing, yet if they fail to amend and begin to be Christians sincerely in view of the everlasting rest that is to come, they will be separated from it in the end. And don't let them flatter themselves because it is possible to be in the threshing floor along with the grain of God. For they will not be together with it in the barn, but are destined for the fire, which is their due. There are also others of better hope, but nevertheless in no less danger. I mean those who now fear God and don't mock the Christian name and don't enter the church of God with an feigned heart, but they still look for their happiness in this life, expecting to have more happiness in earthly things than is enjoyed by those who refuse to worship God. And the consequence of this false anticipation is that when they see some wicked and impious people well established and excelling in this worldly prosperity, while they themselves either possess it in a smaller degree or miss it altogether, they are troubled with the thought that they are serving God without reason, and so they readily fall away from the faith.

(27) "But as for that one who has in view that everlasting blessedness and perpetual rest that is promised for the saints after this life and who wishes to become a Christian in order that he may not pass into eternal fire with the devil, but enter into the eternal kingdom together with Christ (cf. Matt 25:41, 34), such a one is truly a Christian, on his guard against every temptation, so that he may neither be corrupted by prosperity nor be utterly broken in spirit by adversity, but remain at once modest and temperate when the good things of earth abound with him and brave and patient when tribulations overtake him. Such a one will also advance in success until he has such a soul as will make him love God more than he fears hell, so that even were God to say to him, 'Avail yourself of carnal pleasures forever and sin as much as can, and you will neither die nor be sent into hell, but you will only not be with me,' he would be terribly upset and would not sin at all, not just so that he will not incur that which he feared, but so as not to offend him whom he loves so, in whom alone there is also the rest 'that eye has not seen, neither has ear heard, neither has it entered into the heart of humans' (1 Cor 2:9), the rest that God has prepared for those who love him.

(28) "Now, on the subject of this rest, Scripture is significant and is not silent when it tells us how, at the beginning of the world and at the time when God made heaven and earth and all things that are in them, he worked during six days and rested on the seventh day (Gen 2:1–3). Indeed, it was in the power of the Almighty to make all things even in one moment of time. For he had not labored in the view that he might enjoy rest, since indeed 'he spoke, and they were made; he commanded, and they were created' (Ps 148:5); but that he might signify how, after six ages of this world, in a seventh age, as on the seventh day, he will rest in his saints; inasmuch as these same saints shall rest also in him after all the good works in which they have served him (which he himself, indeed, works in them, who calls them, and instructs them, and puts away the offenses that are past, and justifies the person who previously was ungodly). For as, when by his gift they do good works, he is himself rightly said to be working, so, when they rest in him, he is rightly said to rest himself. For, as regards himself, he seeks no cessation because he feels no labor. Moreover he made all things by his Word, and his Word is Christ himself, in whom the angels and all those purest spirits of heaven rest in holy silence. Humanity, however, fallen (*lapsus*) by sin, lost the rest that it possessed in his divinity and receives it again by his humanity. So he became human and was born of a woman at the opportune time when he knew it should be done. Certainly, he couldn't be contaminated by the flesh, being himself rather destined to purify the flesh. Of his future coming, the ancient saints, in the revelation of the Spirit, had knowledge and prophesied. And thus were they saved by believing that he was to come, even as we are saved by believing that he has come. Hence we ought to love God who has so loved us as to have sent his only Son (cf. John 3:16) in order that he might clothe himself with the lowliness of our mortality (cf. Phil 2:7–8) and die both at the hands of sinners and on behalf of sinners. For even in times of old and in the opening ages, the depth of this mystery ceases not to be prefigured and prophetically announced.

18 (29) "Whereas, then, the omnipotent God, who is also good and just and merciful, who made all things—whether great or small, whether highest or lowest, whether things that are seen (such as are the heavens and the earth and the sea; and, in the heavens, in particular, the sun and the moon and other luminaries; and, in the earth and the sea, again, trees and shrubs and animals each after their kind; and all bodies celestial or terrestrial alike) or things that are not seen (such as those spirits by which bodies are animated and endowed with life)—made also humans after his own image, in order that, as he himself, in virtue of his omnipotence, presides over universal creation, so humans, in virtue their intelligence by which they come to know even their Creator and worship him, might preside over all the living creatures of earth. He also made woman as a helper for him: not for carnal desire (since, indeed, they did not have corruptible bodies then before the punishment of sin invaded them in the form of mortality), but so that the man might also possess the glory of the woman (cf. 1 Cor 11:7), since he went before her to God, and present in himself an example to her for imitation in holiness and piety, even as he himself was to be the glory of God since he followed his wisdom.

(30) "So he set them in a certain place of perpetual blessedness, which the Scripture calls Paradise, and he gave them a commandment. If they did not violate it, they were to continue forever in that blessedness of immortality; on the other hand, if they transgressed it, they were to suffer the penalties of mortality. Now God knew beforehand that they would transgress it. Nevertheless, because he is the author and maker of everything good, he chose rather to make them as he also made the beasts, in order that he might replenish the earth with the good things proper to earth. And certainly humanity, even sinful humanity, is better than a beast. And the commandment, which they were not to keep, he still preferred to give them, in order that they might be without excuse when he should begin to vindicate himself against them. For whatever a person may have done, he finds God worthy to be praised in all he does: if he acted rightly, he finds him worthy to be praised for the righteousness of his rewards; if he sinned, he finds him worthy to be praised for the righteousness of his punishments; if he confessed his sins and returned to an upright life, he finds him worthy to be praised for the mercy of his pardoning favors. Why, then, should God not make humanity, although he foreknew that he would sin, when he might crown him if he stood, and set him right if he fell, and help him if he rose, himself being always and everywhere glorious in goodness, righteousness, and mercy? Above all, why should he not do so, since he also foreknew this, namely, that from the race of that mortality there would spring saints, who should not seek their own, but give glory to their Creator and who, obtaining deliverance from every corruption by worshipping him, should be counted worthy to live forever and to live in blessedness with the holy angels? For he who gave free will to humans, in order that they might worship God not of slavish necessity, but with ingenuous inclination, gave it also to the angels, and so the angel who, in company with other spirits who were his followers, forsook in pride the obedience of God and became the devil, did not damage God but himself. For God knows how to dispose of souls that leave him and out of their just misery to furnish the lower parts of his creatures with the most appropriate and befitting laws of his wonderful dispensation. Consequently, neither did the devil in any manner harm God, whether in falling himself or in seducing humans to death, nor did man himself in any degree impair the truth or power or blessedness of his Maker when his partner was seduced by the devil to do that which God had forbidden and he consented of his own volition. For by the most righteous laws of God, all were condemned, God himself being glorious in the equity of retribution, while they were shamed through the degradation of punishment: to the end that man, when he turned away from his Creator, should be overcome by the devil and made his subject and that the devil might be set before man as an enemy to be conquered, when he turned again to his Creator, so that whoever consents to the devil, even to the end, might go with him into eternal punishments, whereas those who humble themselves to God and, by his grace, overcome the devil might be counted worthy of eternal rewards.

19 (31) "Neither ought we to be moved by the consideration that many consent to the devil and few follow God, for the grain, too, in comparison with the chaff, is much less numerous. But even as the husbandman knows what to do with the mighty heap of chaff, so the multitude of sinners is nothing to God, who knows what to do with them, so as not to let the administration of his kingdom be disordered and dishonored in any part. Nor is the devil to be thought victorious merely because he has drawn away more with him than the few by whom he may be overcome. There are two cities—one of sinners, another of saints—that continue from the beginning of the human race even to the end of the world, which are at present commingled in respect of bodies, but separated in respect of wills, and which, moreover, are destined to be separated also in respect of bodily presence in the day of judgment. For those who love pride and temporal power with vain elation and arrogant pomp and all spirits who set their affections on such things and seek their own glory in the subjection of others are bound fast together in one society. Even though they frequently fight against each other on account of these things, nonetheless by an equal weight of desire they are cast into the same depths and are united with each other by similarity of manners and merits. And, again, all persons and all spirits who humbly seek God's glory, and not their own, and who follow him in piety belong to one society. And, notwithstanding this, God is most merciful and patient with impious people and offers them a place for penitence and correction.

(32) "For even though he destroyed all people in the flood, with the exception of one righteous man together with his house, whom he wished to be saved in the ark, he knew that they would not correct themselves; yet, nevertheless, as the building of the ark went on for the space of a hundred years, the wrath of God that was to come upon them was certainly preached to them (Gen 6:7), and if they only had turned to God, he would have spared them, as later he spared the city of Nineveh when it repented, after he had announced to it, by means of a prophet, the destruction that was about to overtake it (Jonah 3). Thus, moreover, God acts, granting a space for repentance even to those who he knows will persist in wickedness, in order that he may exercise and in-

struct our patience by his own example, whereby also we may know how greatly it befits us to bear evil people with long-suffering, since we do not know not what sort of people they will be, seeing that he (who knows everything they will do) spares them and lets them live. By the sacramental sign of the flood, when the righteous were rescued through wood, was foretold the future Church, which Christ, its King and God, has raised on high by the mystery of his cross, in safety from the submersion of this world. Moreover, God was not ignorant of the fact that even of those who had been saved in the ark, there would be born wicked men, who would cover the face of the earth a second time with iniquities. But, nevertheless, he both gave them a pattern of the future judgment and foretold the deliverance of the holy by the mystery of the wood. For even after these things, wickedness did not cease to sprout forth again through pride and lusts and illicit impieties, when humans, forsaking their Creator, not only lapsed toward the creature that God established, so as to worship instead of God that which God made, but even bowed their souls to the human handiwork and to the contrivances of craftsmen. Through this, a more shameful triumph was to be won over them by the devil and by those evil spirits who rejoice in finding themselves adored and reverenced in such false devices, while they feed their own errors with human errors.

(33) "But in truth there was then no lack of righteous men who sought God piously and overcame the pride of the devil, citizens of that holy city, who were healed by the humiliation of Christ their King, still to come and revealed by the Spirit. From among these, Abraham, a pious and faithful servant of God, was chosen, in order that he might be shown the sacrament of the Son of God (cf. Eph 1:9), so that, in virtue of the imitation of his faith, all the faithful of all nations might be called his children in the future (Gal 3:7). Of him was born a people, by whom the one true God who made heaven and earth would be worshipped when all other nations served idols and evil spirits. In that people, plainly, the future Church was quite evidently prefigured. For in it there was a carnal multitude that worshipped God with a view to visible benefits. But in it there were also a few who thought

of the future rest and looked longingly for the heavenly homeland. To these people the future humiliation of God, in the person of our King and Lord Jesus Christ, was revealed through prophecy, in order that they might be healed of all pride and arrogance through that faith. And with respect to these saints who existed before the Lord's birth, not only their speech, but also their life and their marriages and their children and their doings, constituted a prophecy of this time in which the Church is being gathered together out of all nations through faith in the passion of Christ. By the instrumentality of those holy patriarchs and prophets to this carnal people of Israel (who in a later period were also called Jews) were ministered visible benefits that they eagerly desired of the Lord in a carnal manner and those chastisements, in the form of bodily punishments, which were intended to terrify them for the time, as befit their obstinacy. And in all these, nevertheless, spiritual mysteries were also signified, which pertained to Christ and the Church, of which Church those saints also were members, although they existed in this life previous to the birth of Christ, the Lord, according to the flesh. For this same Christ, the only-begotten Son of God, the Word of the Father, equal and coeternal with the Father, by whom all things were made, was himself also made human for our sakes, in order that of the whole Church, as of his whole body, he might be the head. But just as when the whole man is in the process of being born, although he may put the hand forth first in the act of birth, still that hand is joined and compacted together with the whole body under the head, even as also among these same patriarchs some were born with the hand put forth first as a sign of this very thing (cf. Gen 25:26, 38:27–30); so all the saints who lived upon the earth previous to the birth of our Lord Jesus Christ, although they were born prior, were nevertheless united under the head with that universal body of which he is the head.

20 (34) "That people, then, having been brought down into Egypt, were in bondage to the harshest of kings, and taught by the most oppressive labors, they sought their deliverer in God, and there was sent to them one belonging to the same people, Moses, the holy servant of God, who, in the might of God, terrified the impious nation of the Egyptians in those days by great miracles and led forth the people of God out of that land through the Red Sea, where the water parted and opened up a way for them as they crossed it. When the Egyptians pressed on in pursuit, the waves returned to their channel and overwhelmed them, so that they perished. Thus, then, just as the earth through the agency of the flood was cleansed by the waters from the wickedness of the sinners, who in those times were destroyed in their inundation, while the righteous escaped by means of wood, so the people of God, when they went forth from Egypt, found a way through the waters by which their enemies were devoured. Nor was the sacrament of the wood wanting there. For Moses struck with his rod, in order to effect the miracle. Both of these are signs of holy baptism, by which the faithful pass into the new life, while their sins are done away with like enemies and perish. But more clearly was the passion of Christ prefigured in the case of that people when they were commanded to slay and eat the lamb and to mark their doorposts with its blood and to celebrate this rite every year and to designate it the Lord's Passover. For surely prophecy speaks with the utmost plainness of the Lord Jesus Christ, when it says that 'he was led as a lamb to the slaughter' (Isa 53:7). And with the sign of his passion and cross, you are this day to be marked on your forehead, as on the doorpost, and all Christians are marked with the same.

(35) "Thereafter this people was conducted through the wilderness for forty years. They also received the law written by the finger of God (Exod 31:18), under which name the Holy Spirit is signified, as it is declared with the utmost plainness in the Gospel (Luke 21:20). Now God is not defined by the form of a body, neither should we think of him having limbs and fingers as we ourselves do. But, inasmuch as it is through the Holy Spirit that God's gifts are apportioned to his saints, in order that, although they vary in their capacities, they may nevertheless not deviate from love's harmony, and inasmuch as it is especially in the fingers that there is especially a certain degree of division but no breach of unity. But whether this may be the case, or whatever other reason may be

assigned for the Holy Spirit being called the 'finger of God,' we ought not at any rate to think of the form of a human body when we hear this expression used. The people in question, then, received the law written by the finger of God, plainly written on stone tablets, to signify the hardness of their hearts because they would not fulfill the law. For, as they eagerly sought from the Lord gifts meant for the uses of the body, they were held by carnal fear, rather than by spiritual charity. But nothing fulfills the law save charity. Consequently, they were burdened with many visible sacraments, so they could feel the pressure of the yoke of bondage in the observances of meats and in the sacrifices of animals and in other innumerable rites. These things, at the same time, were signs of spiritual matters related to the Lord Jesus Christ and to the Church. Furthermore, at that time, they were also understood by a few holy men as the fruit of salvation and observed by them in accordance with the fitness of the time, while by the multitude of carnal men they were observed only and not understood.

(36) "In this manner, then, through many varied signs of things to come (which it would be tedious to enumerate in complete detail and which we now see in their fulfillment in the Church) that people was brought to the land of promise, in which they were to reign in a temporal and carnal way in accordance with their own longings. This earthly kingdom, nevertheless, sustained the image of a spiritual kingdom. There Jerusalem was founded, that most celebrated city of God, which, while in bondage, served as a sign of the free city, which is called the heavenly Jerusalem (Gal 4:26) (this latter term is a Hebrew word, and means the 'vision of peace'). Its citizens are all sanctified men, who have been, who are, and who are yet to be and all sanctified spirits, even as many as are obedient to God with pious devotion in the exalted regions of heaven, who do not imitate the impious pride of the devil and his angels. The King of this city is the Lord Jesus Christ, the Word of God, by whom the highest angels are governed and, at the same time, the Word that took unto himself human nature, in order that humanity might also be governed by him, who, in his fellowship, shall reign all together in eternal peace. As a prefiguration of this King in that earthly kingdom of the people of Israel, King David stood forth preeminent (1 Kings 11:23), of whose seed according to the flesh that truest King was to come, that is, our Lord Jesus Christ, 'who is over all, God blessed for ever' (Rom 9:5). In that land of promise, many things were done as figures of Christ who was to come and of the Church, with which you will have it in your power to acquaint yourself little by little in the holy books.

21 (37) "After a few generations, another type was presented especially pertinent to the matter at hand. For that city was brought into captivity, and a large section of the people were carried off into Babylonia. Now, as Jerusalem signifies the city and fellowship of the saints, so Babylonia signifies the city and fellowship of the wicked, since the word means *confusion*. On the subject of these two cities, which have been running their courses, mingling with each other through all the changes of time from the beginning of the human race and which will continue on together until the end of the world, when they are destined to be separated at the last judgment, we have already spoken. That captivity, then, of the city of Jerusalem, and the people thus carried into Babylonia in bondage were so ordained to proceed by the Lord, by the voice of Jeremiah, a prophet of that time (Jer 25:18, 29:1). And there appeared kings of Babylon, under whom they were in slavery, who in those times were so moved by certain miracles that they came to know the one true God who founded universal creation and worshipped him, and commanded that he should be worshipped. Moreover the people were ordered both to pray for those by whom they were detained in captivity and, in their peace, to hope for peace, with the result that they should beget children and build houses and plant gardens and vineyards (Jer 29:4–7). But at the end of seventy years, release from their captivity was promised to them (Jer 25:12). All this, furthermore, signified figuratively that the Church of Christ in all his saints, who are citizens of the heavenly Jerusalem, would have to do service under the kings of this world. For the apostolic teaching also says: 'every soul should be subject to the higher powers,' and there 'should be rendered all things to all men, tribute to whom tribute [is due], custom to whom custom' (Rom 13:1, 7), and other things that, without detriment to the worship of our God, we render to the rulers of human societies, for the Lord himself also, in order to set before us an example of this sound doctrine, did not deem it unworthy of himself to pay tribute (Matt 17:27) on account of that human individuality with which he was clothed. Again, Christian servants and good believers are also commanded to serve their temporal masters in equanimity and faithfulness (Eph 6:5). For one day they, in turn, will judge them, if at the end they find them wicked, they will one day reign with them in equality if they have also been converted to the true God. Still all are commanded to be subject to human, earthly powers even until, at the end of the predetermined time that the seventy years signify, the Church shall be delivered from the confusion of this world, as Jerusalem was to be set free from the captivity in Babylonia. Out of the circumstance of that captivity, however, earthly kings have also been led to forsake the idols on whose behalf they used to persecute the Christians and have come to know and now worship, the one true God and Christ the Lord, and it is on their behalf that the Apostle Paul commands prayer to be made, even if they should persecute the Church. For he speaks in these terms: 'I entreat, therefore, that first of all supplications, adorations, intercessions, and thanksgivings be made for kings, for all men, and all that are in authority, that we may lead a quiet and peaceable life, with all godliness and charity' (1 Tim 2:1–2). Accordingly, peace has been given to the Church by these same persons, although it is of a temporal sort—a temporal quiet for the work of building houses after a spiritual fashion and planting gardens and vineyards. In the same way we are engaged, by means of this discourse, in building you up and planting you. And this is going on throughout the whole world, in virtue of the peace of Christian kings, even as the same apostle says: 'You are God's husbandry; you are God's building' (1 Cor 3:9).

(38) "And, indeed, after the seventy years of which Jeremiah had mystically prophesied so that he might prefigure the end of time, in order that the same figure might be filled out, the restoration of the structure of God's Temple was accomplished in Jerusalem. But since everything happened figuratively, no settled peace and liberty were conceded to the Jews. So they were conquered subsequently by the Romans and made tributary. From that period, in truth, at which they received the land of promise and began to have kings, in order to preclude the supposition that the promise of the Christ who was to be their Liberator had met its complete fulfillment in the person of any one of their kings, Christ was prophesied of with greater clarity in a number of prophecies, not only by David himself in the book of Psalms, but also by the rest of the great and holy prophets, even on to the time of their going into captivity in Babylonia; and in that same captivity, there were also prophets whose mission was to prophesy of the coming of the Lord Jesus Christ as the Liberator of all. And after the restoration of the Temple, when the seventy years had passed, the Jews sustained grievous oppressions and sufferings at the hands of the kings of the gentiles, so they would understand that the Liberator had not yet come, whom they failed to apprehend as one who was to effect for them a spiritual deliverance and whom they fondly longed for on account of a carnal liberation.

22 (39) "Five ages of the world, accordingly, having been now completed. Of these ages, the first is from the beginning of the human race, that is, from Adam, who was the first man that was made, down to Noah, who constructed the ark at the time of the flood (Gen 6:22). Then the second extends from that period on to Abraham, who was called the father of all nations who would follow the example of his faith (Gen 17:4), but was also, by carnal propagation, the father of the future people of the Jews, who, before the entrance of the gentiles into the Christian faith, was the one people among all the nations of all lands that worshipped the one true God. From these people also Christ the Savior was decreed to come according to the flesh. For these turning points of those two ages occupy an eminent place in the ancient books. Moreover, the other three ages are declared in the Gospel (Matt 1:17), where the descent of the Lord Jesus Christ according to the flesh is commemorated. Now the third age extends from Abraham to David the king, the fourth from David to that captivity in which the people of God moved to Babylonia, and the fifth from that migration down to the advent of our Lord Jesus Christ. With his coming, the sixth age has begun, so that now the spiritual grace, which in previous times was known to a few patriarchs and prophets, may be made manifest to all nations, so that no one should worship God except freely, desiring of him not the visible rewards of his services and the happiness of this present life, but that eternal life alone in which he is to enjoy God himself; so, in this sixth age, the human mind may be renewed according the image of God, even as on the sixth day man was made according the image of God (Gen 1:27). For then, too, is the law fulfilled, when all that it has commanded is done, not in the strong desire for things temporal, but in the love of him who has given the commandment. Who, then, would not be earnestly disposed to return the love of a God of supreme righteousness and also of supreme mercy, who has first loved people of the greatest unrighteousness and the loftiest pride, and that, too, so deeply as to have sent on their behalf his only Son, by whom he made all things, and who, being made man, not by any change of himself, but by the assumption of human nature, was designed thus to become capable not only of living with them, but also of dying for them and by their hands?

(40) "Now on to the demonstration of our everlasting inheritance, the New Testament, in which humanity was to be renewed by the grace of God and lead a new life, that is, a spiritual life; and the Old Testament is shown to be the first one, in which a carnal people acting out the old man (with the exception of a few patriarchs and prophets, who had understanding, and some hidden saints), and leading a carnal life, longed for carnal rewards from the Lord God and received them as the figures of spiritual blessings. Therefore, the Lord Christ, when he made man, despised all earthly goods, in order that he might show us how these things ought to be despised, and he endured all earthly ills, which he warned must be endured, so that happiness would not be sought in earthly goods or unhappiness feared from earthly ills. For, born of a mother who—although she conceived without being touched by a man and always re-

mained untouched, in virginity conceiving, in virginity bearing, in virginity dying—had nevertheless been married to a carpenter, he extinguished all the inflated pride of carnal nobility. Moreover, being born in the city of Bethlehem, which among all the cities of Jews was so insignificant that even in our own day it is designated a village, he wanted no one to glory in the exalted position of any earthly city. He, too, who possesses all things and by whom all things were created, was made poor, in order that no one, while believing in him, might dare to exalt himself because of earthly riches. He refused to be made a king by humans because he displayed the pathway of humility to those unhappy ones whom pride had separated from him, and yet universal creation attests to his everlasting kingdom. He hungered, who feeds all men; he thirsted, by whom is created every drink, and who in a spiritual manner is the bread of the hungry and the fountain of the thirsty (cf. John 6:51, 4:10); on his earthly journey he became weary, who made of himself a road for us into heaven (cf. John 14:6); he was dumb and deaf in the presence of his revilers (Isa 53:7), he through whom the dumb spoke and the deaf heard; he was bound who freed us from the bonds of sickness; he was scourged who expelled from human bodies the scourges of all distresses; he was crucified (*crucifixus*) who ended our tortures (*cruciatus*);[2] he died, he who raised the dead. But he also rose again, no more to die, so that no one should learn from him to condemn death as if he were never to live again.

23 (41) "Thereafter, having confirmed the disciples and having sojourned with them forty days, he ascended up into heaven as these same persons were beholding him. And on the completion of fifty days from his resurrection, he sent to them the Holy Spirit (for so he had promised), through whom love was diffused through their hearts (cf. Rom 5:5), so that without burden and even with joyfulness, they might be able to fulfill the law. This law was given to the Jews in the Ten Commandments, which they call the

---

[2] Augustine's wordplay between "crucified" and "tortures" does not translate well into English.

Decalogue. And these commandments, again, are reduced to two, namely, that we should love God with
all our heart, with all our soul, with all our mind, and
that we should love our neighbor as ourselves. For on
these two precepts hang all the law and the prophets,
as the Lord himself declared in the Gospel and
showed in his own example (Matt 22:37–40). So also
the people Israel, from the day when they first celebrated the Passover in a figure, slaying and eating the
sheep whose blood marked their doorposts to secure
their safety (Exod 12)—from that day, the fiftieth day
in succession was completed, and then they received
the law written by the finger of God (Exod 34:28), by
which phrase we have already stated that the Holy
Spirit is signified (Luke 11:20). And in the same
manner, after the passion and resurrection of the
Lord, who is the true Passover, the same Holy Spirit
was sent to the disciples on the fiftieth day: not now,
however, by stone tablets signifying the hardness of
their hearts, but when they were gathered together in
one place in Jerusalem, suddenly there came a sound
from heaven, like a violent blast going off, and there
appeared to them tongues split like fire, and they
began to speak with tongues so that all those who had
come to them recognized each his own language
(Acts 2) (for in that city, the Jews were in the habit of
assembling from every country to which they had
been scattered abroad and had learned the diverse
tongues of diverse nations); and thereafter, preaching
Christ with all boldness, they performed many signs
in his name—so much so that, as Peter was passing
by, his shadow touched a certain dead person, and the
man rose in life again (cf. Acts 5:15).

(42) "But when the Jews perceived so many signs
being performed in the name of him, whom, partly
through ill will and partly in ignorance, they crucified, some of them were provoked to persecute the
apostles, who were his preachers, while others, on
the contrary, marveling the more at this very circumstance, that so great miracles were being performed
in the name of him whom they had derided as one oppressed and conquered by themselves, repented and
were converted, so that thousands of Jews believed in
him. For these parties were not bent now on craving
temporal benefits and an earthly kingdom from God,

neither did they look any more for Christ, the promised king, in a carnal manner, but they continued in
immortal fashion to apprehend and love him, who in
mortal fashion endured on their behalf at their own
hands sufferings so heavy and imparted to them the
gift of forgiveness for all their sins, even down to the
iniquity of his own blood, and by the example of his
own resurrection revealed immortality as the object
that they should hope for and long for at his hands.
Accordingly, now mortifying the earthly cravings of
the old man and inflamed with the new experience of
the spiritual life, as the Lord had commanded in the
Gospel, they sold all that they had and laid the price
of their possessions at the feet of the apostles, in
order that they might distribute to each according to
his need; and living in Christian love harmoniously
with each other, they did not affirm anything to be
their own, but they had all things in common and
were one in soul and heart toward God (Acts 2:44,
4:34). Afterward these same persons also themselves
suffered persecution in their flesh at the hands of the
Jews, their carnal fellow-countrymen, and were dispersed abroad, so that, because of their dispersion,
Christ would be preached more extensively and that
they themselves at the same time would follow the
patience of their Lord. For he who in meekness had
endured them, commanded them in meekness to endure for his sake.

(43) "Among those same persecutors of the saints
the Apostle Paul had once also ranked, and he especially raged against the Christians. But, subsequently,
he became a believer and an apostle and was sent to
preach the gospel to the gentiles, suffering more
grievous things on behalf of Christ's name than he had
done against Christ's name. Moreover, in establishing
churches throughout all the nations where he was
sowing the seed of the gospel, he earnestly instructed
that since these converts (coming as they did from the
worship of idols and uninstructed in the worship of the
one God) could not readily serve God by selling and
distributing their possessions, they should make offerings for the poor among the saints of churches of
Judea that believed in Christ (cf. Acts 11:29–30,
24:17; Rom 15:25–27). In this manner, apostolic doctrine established some to be soldiers and others to be

provincial tributaries, setting Christ among them like the cornerstone (in accordance with what had been announced previously by the prophet) (Ps 118:22, Isa 28:16), in whom both parties, like walls advancing from different sides, that is to say, from Jews and from gentiles, might be joined together in the affection of kinship. But at a later period, heavier and more frequent persecutions arose from the unbelieving gentiles against the Church of Christ, and day by day was fulfilled that prophetic word that the Lord spoke when he said, 'Behold, I send you as sheep in the midst of wolves' (Matt 10:16).

24 (44) "But that vine, which was spreading forth its fruitful shoots throughout the world, as had been prophesied about it and as had been foretold by the Lord himself, sprouted all the more luxuriantly as it was watered with richer streams of the blood of martyrs. And as these died on behalf of the truth of the faith in countless numbers throughout all lands, even the persecuting kingdoms themselves desisted and were converted to the knowledge and worship of Christ, with the neck of their pride broken. Moreover it was fitting that this same vine should be pruned in accordance with the Lord's repeated predictions (John 15:2) and that the unfruitful twigs should be cut out of it, by which heresies and schisms were occasioned in various places, under the name of Christ, on the part of men who sought not his glory but their own, whose oppositions, however, also served more and more to discipline the Church and to test and illustrate both its doctrine and its patience.

(45) "All these things, then, we now perceive to be realized precisely as we read of them in predictions uttered so long before the event. And insofar as the first Christians, who could not yet see these things come to pass, were moved by miracles to believe them, so it is with us: inasmuch as all these things have now been brought to pass exactly as we read of them in those books, which were written long before these things were fulfilled, where the whole future was described, even as they are now seen to be present, we are edified for faith, so that, enduring and persevering in the Lord, we believe without any hesitation in the destined accomplishment even of those things that still remain to be realized. For, indeed, in the same Scriptures, tribulations yet to come are read of, as well as the final day of judgment itself, when all the citizens of these two cities shall receive their bodies again and rise and give account of their life before the judgment seat of Christ. For he will come in the glory of his power, who of old condescended to come in the lowliness of humanity, and he will separate all the pious from the impious—not only those who have utterly refused to believe in him, but also those who have believed in him to no purpose and without fruit. To the former, he will give an eternal kingdom with himself, while to the latter he will award eternal punishment with the devil. But just as no joy from worldly things can be found in any way comparable to the joy of eternal life that the saints will receive, so no torment of worldly tortures (*cruciatus*) can be compared to the everlasting tortures of the sinners.

25 (46) "Therefore, brother, confirm yourself in the name and help of him in whom you believe against the tongues of those who mock at our faith, about whom the devil speaks such seductive words, wishing especially to mock the faith in resurrection. But, based on your own self, believe that you will exist in the future, even as you see that once you did not exist and now you do. For where was the massive bulk of your body, and where this formation and compacted connection of members a few years ago, before you were born or even before you were conceived in your mother's womb? Where was this massive bulk and the stature of your body? Did it not come to light from the hidden secrets of this creation, formed invisibly by the Lord God, and did it not rise to its present magnitude and fashion by the determined increments of aging? Is it then in any way a difficult thing for God, who also in a moment brings together out of hidden places the masses of the clouds and veils the heavens in an instant of time, to make this quantity of your body again what it was, seeing that he was able to make it what formerly it was not? Consequently, believe strongly and unshakably that all those things that seem to be withdrawn from human eyes as if to perish are safe and intact to the omnipotence of God, who will restore them, without any delay or difficulty, when he is so minded—those of them at least who are judged by his justice to merit restoration—in order that people may give account of their deeds in the same bodies in which they have done them and that in these they may be deemed worthy to receive either the exchange of heavenly incorruption in accordance with the deserts of their piety or the corruptible condition of body in accordance with the deserts of their wickedness, not in a form to be dissolved by death, but such as will provide material for everlasting pains.

(47) "Flee, therefore, by steadfast faith and good manners; flee, brother, those torments in which neither the torturers fail nor the tortured die, for whom it is death without end, to be unable to die in their tortures (*cruciatus*). And be kindled with love and longing for the everlasting life of the saints, in which action will not be burdensome or will rest be lazy; in which the praise of God will be without tedium and without defect; in which there will be no weariness in the soul, no exhaustion in the body; in which also there will be no need, neither for yourself, so that you should crave for relief, nor for your neighbor, whom you hasten to relieve. God will be the whole enjoyment and satisfaction of that holy city, which lives in him and of him, in wisdom and blessedness. For as we hope and anticipate what has been promised by him, we shall be made equal to the angels of God (Luke 20:36), and together with them we shall enjoy that Trinity now by sight, in which now we move through faith (2 Cor 5:7). For we believe in what we do not see, in order that through these same merits of faith we may be counted worthy to see that in which we believe and to abide in it, so that these mysteries—the equality of the Father, the Son, and the Holy Spirit and the unity of this same Trinity and the manner in which these three are one God—need no longer be sounded out by us in words of faith and sibilant syllables, but may be imbibed in purest and most ardent contemplation in that silence.

(48) "Hold these things fixed in your heart and call upon the God in whom you believe to defend you against the temptations of the devil, and be careful, lest that adversary come stealthily upon you from a strange quarter; as the most malevolent solace for his own damnation, he seeks others to be damned with him. He dares to tempt Christians, not only through those who hate the Christian name or who are aggrieved to see the world occupied by that name and still long to serve idols and the curious rites of evil spirits, but also through those whom we mentioned a short while ago, those who have been severed from the unity of the Church, like twigs lopped off when the vine is pruned, who are called heretics or schismatics. Sometimes he also attempts to tempt and seduce through the Jews. But what must be most guarded against is that no individual should let himself be tempted and deceived by those who are within the Catholic Church itself and who are carried in it like the chaff that is sustained against the time of its winnowing. For in being patient toward such persons, God has this end in view: to exercise and confirm the faith and prudence of his elect by means of the perverseness of these others, while indeed many of their number progress and are converted with great ardor to pleasing God and pitying their own souls. For not all store up wrath as treasure for themselves, through the patience of God, on the day of the wrath of his just judgment (Rom 2:5), but many are brought by the same patience of the Almighty to the most wholesome pain of repentance (cf. Rom 2:4). And until that is done, they are made the means of exercising not only the forbearance, but also the compassion, of those who are already holding to the right path. Accordingly, you will have to witness many drunks, covetous men, deceivers, gamesters, adulterers, fornicators, men who wear sacrilegious charms and others given up to sorcerers and astrologers, and diviners practiced in all kinds of impious arts. You will also have to observe how those very crowds that fill the theaters on pagan festivals also fill the churches on the Christian festivals. And when you see these things, you will be tempted to imitate them. Why should I say *you will see,* since you're already quite familiar with it? You are not ignorant of the fact that many who are called Christians do all the evil things I have mentioned. Nor are you ignorant that at times, perhaps, men whom you know to be called Christians are guilty of even more serious offenses than these. But if you have come to the opinion that you can act in this way with surety, you are greatly in

error; neither will the name of Christ do you any good when he begins to judge most severely, who once condescended to relieve us most mercifully. For he himself has foretold these things and speaks to this effect in the Gospel: 'Not every one that says unto me, Lord, Lord, shall enter into the kingdom of heaven, but he that does the will of my Father. Many shall say unto me in that day, Lord, Lord, in your name we have eaten and drunk' (Matt 7:21–22). For all, therefore, who persevere in such works, the end is damnation. Consequently, when you see many not only doing these things but also defending and recommending them, hold firmly to the law of God; don't follow its willful transgressors. For it is not according to their mind, but according to his truth, that you will be judged.

(49) "Associate with good people, whom you see love the King along with you. For you will discover many if you also begin to cultivate that character yourself. For if in the public spectacles you wished to be in congenial company and to attach yourself closely to men who are united with you in a liking for some charioteer or some hunter or some actor or other, how much more ought you to find pleasure in associating with those who are at one with you in loving that God, with regard to whom no one that loves him shall ever have cause for the blush of shame, inasmuch as not only is he himself incapable of being overcome, but he will also render those unconquerable who are affectionately disposed toward him. At the same time, not even in those same good men, who either anticipate you or accompany you on the way to God, ought you to place your hope, any more than you should place it on yourself, however great may be the progress you have made, but, rather, place it in him who justifies both them and you and thus makes you what you are. For you are secure in God because he does not change, but in people no one prudently considers himself secure. But if we ought to love those who are not righteous as yet, with the view that they may be so, how much more warmly ought those to be loved who already are righteous? At the same time, it is one thing to love humanity and another thing to set one's hope in humanity, and the difference is so great that God commands one and forbids

the other. Moreover, if you have to sustain any insults or any sufferings in the cause of the name of Christ and neither fall away from the faith nor decline from the good path, you are certain to receive the greater reward, whereas those who give way to the devil in such circumstances lose even the smaller reward. But be humble toward God, in order that he may not permit you to be tempted beyond your strength."

26 (50) At the conclusion of this address, the person is to be asked whether he believes these things and longs to observe them. And when he answers, then certainly he is to be solemnly signed and treated in accordance with church custom. On the subject of the sacrament that he receives, it should first be impressed upon him that the signs of divine things are, it is true, things visible, but that the invisible things themselves are also honored in them and that that sort of thing, which is sanctified then by blessing, should not be regarded merely in the way in which it is regarded in any common use. And then he ought to be told what is also signified by the form of words to which he has listened and what in him is seasoned by that of which this material substance presents the likeness. Next we should take the opportunity of that ceremony to admonish him that if he hears anything even in the Scriptures that may carry a carnal sound, he should, even though he fails to understand it, nevertheless believe that something spiritual is signified by it that bears upon holiness of character and the future life. Moreover, in this way he learns briefly that whatever he may hear in the canonical books of such a kind as to make him unable to refer it to the love of eternity and of truth and of sanctity and to the love of our neighbor, he should believe it to have been spoken or done with a figurative significance, and that, consequently, he should endeavor to understand it in such a way that it refers to that twofold love. He should be further admonished, however, not to take the term *neighbor* in a carnal sense, but to understand by it everyone who may ever be with him in that holy city, whether there already or not yet apparent, and not to despair of the correction of any person whom he perceives to be living under the patience of God for no other reason, as the apostle says (Rom 2:4), than that he may be brought to repentance.

(51) If this discourse, in which I have supposed myself to have been teaching some uninstructed person in my presence, appears to you to be too long, you are at liberty to expound these matters more briefly. I do not think, however, that it ought to be longer than this. At the same time, much depends on what the particular case makes advisable and what the actual audience can not only bear, but also appreciate. When, however, rapid dispatch is required, the whole matter can be easily explained. Suppose once more that someone comes before us who desires to be a Christian and, accordingly, suppose further that he has been interrogated and that he has returned the answer that we have taken the former catechumen to have given, for even should he decline to make this reply, it must at least be said that he ought to have given it. Then all that remains to be said to him should be put together in the following manner:

(52) "Of a truth, brother, that is great and true blessedness that is promised to the saints in a future world. All visible things, on the other hand, pass away, and all the pomp and pleasure and solicitude of this world will perish, and (even now) they drag those who love them along with them onward to destruction. The merciful God, willing to deliver humanity from this destruction, that is to say, from everlasting pains, if they should not prove enemies to themselves, and if they should not withstand the mercy of their Creator, sent his only-begotten Son, that is to say, his Word, equal with himself, by whom he made all things. And he, while abiding indeed in his divinity and neither receding from the Father nor being changed in anything, did at the same time, by taking on himself human nature and appearing to humanity in mortal flesh, come to humanity in order that, just as death entered among the human race by one man, to wit, the first that was made, that is to say, Adam, because he consented to his wife when she was seduced by the devil so that they transgressed the commandment of God; even so by one man, Jesus Christ, who is also God, the Son of God, all those who believe in him might have all their past sins done away with and enter into eternal life.

27 (53) "For all those things that at present you witness in the Church of God and that you see taking place under the name of Christ throughout the whole world were predicted long ago. And even as we read of them, so also we now see them. And by means of these things, we are edified by faith. Once there occurred a flood over the whole earth, the object of which was that sinners might be destroyed. And, nevertheless, those who escaped in the ark exhibited a sacramental sign of the Church that was to be, which at present is floating on the waves of the world and is delivered from submersion by the wood of the cross of Christ. It was predicted to Abraham, a faithful servant of God, a single man, that it was determined that a people should be born of him who would worship one God in the midst of all other nations who worshipped idols, and all things that were prophesied as destined to happen to that people have come to pass exactly as they were foretold. Among that people Christ, the King of all saints and their God, was also prophesied as destined to come of the seed of that same Abraham according to the flesh, which flesh he took unto himself in order that all those also who became followers of his faith might be sons of Abraham. So it has come to pass: Christ was born of the Virgin Mary, who belonged to that people. It was foretold by the prophets that he would suffer on the cross at the hands of that same people, the Jews, of whose lineage, according to the flesh, he came, and thus it has come to pass. It was foretold that he would rise again: he has risen again, and, in accordance with these same predictions of the prophets, he has ascended into heaven and has sent the Holy Spirit to his disciples. It was foretold not only by the prophets, but also by the Lord Jesus Christ himself, that his Church would exist throughout the whole world, extended by the martyrdoms and sufferings of the saints, and this was foretold at a time when as yet his name was at once undeclared to the gentiles and made a subject of derision where it was known; and, nevertheless, in the power of his miracles, whether those that he performed by his own hand or those that he performed by means of his servants, as these things are being reported and believed, we already see the fulfillment of that which was predicted and behold the very kings of the earth, who formerly persecuted the Christians, even now brought into subjection to the name of

Christ. It was also foretold that schisms and heresies would arise from his Church and that under his name they would seek their own glory instead of Christ's, in such places as they might be able to command, and these predictions have been realized.

(54) "Will those things, then, that yet remain fail to come to pass? It is clear that just as the former predictions have come to pass, so will these latter also come to pass. I refer to all the tribulations of the righteous, who yet wait for fulfillment, and to the day of judgment, which will separate all the wicked from the righteous in the resurrection of the dead; and not only will it separate those wicked men who are outside the Church, but also it will set apart for the fire, which is their due, the chaff of the Church itself, which must be tolerated with utmost patience until the last winnowing. Moreover, those who deride the resurrection because they think that this flesh, inasmuch as it becomes corrupt, cannot rise again, will certainly rise in it for punishment, and God will make it plain to them that he who was able to form these bodies when they did not yet exist is able in a moment to restore them as they were. But all the faithful who are destined to reign with Christ will rise with the same body in such a way that they may also be counted worthy to be changed into angelic incorruption, so that they may be made equal to the angels of God, even as the Lord himself has promised (Luke 20:36), and that they may praise him without any failure and without any weariness, ever living in him and of him, with such joy and blessedness as can be neither expressed nor conceived by humans.

(55) "Believe these things, therefore, and be on your guard against temptations (for the devil seeks others to perish with him), so that not only may that adversary fail to seduce you by the help of those who are outside the Church, whether they be pagans, or Jews, or heretics, but you yourself also may decline to follow the example of those within the Catholic Church itself whom you see leading an evil life, either indulging in excess pleasures of the belly and the throat or unchaste or given up to the vain and unlawful observances of curious superstitions, whether they are addicted to public spectacles or charms or divinations of devils or living in the pomp and in-

flated arrogance of covetousness and pride or pursuing any sort of life that the law condemns and punishes. But rather join yourself to good people, whom you will easily discover if you yourself become like them, so that you may unite with each other in worshipping and loving God for his own sake. For he himself will be our complete reward, so that we may enjoy his goodness and beauty in that life (cf. Zech 9:17). He is to be loved, however, not in the way in which any object that is seen with the eyes is loved, but as wisdom is loved and truth and holiness and righteousness and charity and whatever else may be mentioned as similar, and, further, with a love conformable to these things not as they are in humans, but as they are in the very fountain of incorruptible and unchangeable wisdom. Whoever, therefore, you may observe to be loving these things, attach yourself to them, so that through Christ, who became human in order that he might be the Mediator between God and humanity, you may be reconciled to God. But as regards the perverse, even if they find their way within the walls of the Church, don't assume that they will find their way into the kingdom of heaven, for in their own time they will be set apart if they have not improved themselves. Consequently, follow the example of good people, bear with the wicked, love all, since you don't know what he will be tomorrow who today is evil. Nevertheless, don't love their unrighteousness; but love the persons themselves with the express intent that they may apprehend righteousness, for not only are we commanded to love God, but also to love our neighbor. On these two commandments hang all the law and the prophets (Matt 22:37, 39). And this is fulfilled by no one save the man who has received the gift, the Holy Spirit, who is indeed equal with the Father and with the Son, for this same Trinity is God, and on this God every hope ought to be placed. We shouldn't hope in a person, of whatever character he may be. For he, by whom we are justified, is one thing, and they, together with whom we are justified, are another. Moreover, it is not only by lusts that the devil tempts, but also by the terrors of insults and pains and death itself. But whatever a person suffers on behalf of the name of Christ and for the sake of the hope of eternal life and endures in faithfulness, the greater reward shall be given him. However, if he gives way to the devil, he will be damned along with him. But works of mercy, joined with pious humility, procure this from God: that he will not let his servants be tempted more than they are able to bear" (1 Cor 10:13).

15. John Chrysostom: Second Baptismal Instruction

John (ca. 347–407) earned the posthumous nickname Chrysostom ("Golden Mouth") for his clear and compelling oratorical style. He received a thorough classical education (he studied with the famous Greek rhetorician Libanius), but eschewed a career in public office to serve the church. After a brief stint among the monks of the Syrian desert, which contributed a distinct moral rigor to his preaching, John entered the clerical hierarchy. He was ordained as a priest in Antioch in 386, and for twelve years preached on Scripture, morality, theology, and Christian society. He was a noted advocate of the poor. John's fame as a preacher led to his appointment as patriarch of Constantinople in 398, where his preaching against wealth and ostentation made him enemies in the imperial court. Religious and political antipathies, particularly the resentment of Bishop Theophilus of Alexandria, led to John's deposition in 404. Although popular acclaim from the people of Constantinople ensured his brief reinstatement, the Emperor Arcadius, whose wife Eudoxia had borne the brunt of several of John's moralizing sermons, had John sent into exile, where he died.

The following baptismal homily was likely delivered during John's days as a priest in Antioch. It would have been delivered during Lent, as part of the final instruction to the catechumens who were about to complete their initiation. John urges the catechumens to view the mystery with the "eyes of faith": to see not just water and a priest, but death, resurrection, and the grace of the Holy Spirit. John goes through each and every stage of the imitation ceremony (exorcism, sponsorship, renunciation of the devil, chrism and anointing, and the baptism itself), in order to instill awe in his audience, but also to convey gratitude and anticipation of their full entry into the Christian community.

(1) Today I am going to speak a few more words to those who have been enrolled among the household of Christ, to teach them the power of the weapons that they are about to receive and the indescribable goodness of the love God shows to the human race. I hope that as a result, they may approach him with great faith and confidence and enjoy his generosity more liberally.

GOD'S GENEROSITY EVEN TOWARD SINNERS

Consider, my beloved, the abundance of God's goodness from the beginning. For if without your having worked for it or shown any qualification, he thinks you worthy of such a gift and pardons all the sins you have committed in your life, what return are you

From *The Awe-Inspiring Rites of Initiation: The Origins of the R.C.I.A.,* 2nd ed., trans. Edward Yarnold. Collegeville, Minn.: Liturgical Press, 1994. Used with permission.

likely to merit from a loving God if after such great kindness you learn to be grateful and determine to make a contribution of your own?

(2) In human affairs nothing similar has ever been seen. On the contrary, many men on many occasions, after undergoing many labors and troubles in hope of recompense, return home empty-handed. Those from whom they expected a return have proved ungrateful for all their exertions, or else they have themselves often been snatched away from this world before they could fulfill their own aim. But in the service of our Master we need never suspect anything of the sort. Even before we begin our efforts and offer anything of our own, he forestalls us and shows his own generosity, so that his many kindnesses may induce us to take thought for our own salvation.

(3) And so from the very beginning, he has never ceased to bless the human race. For as soon as he created the first man, at once he put him to dwell in the garden of Paradise and gave him a life of ease, allowing him the freedom of all that was in the garden except for a single tree. But once the man had intemperately allowed himself to be deceived by the woman, he rode roughshod over the command that was given to him and abused the great honor that had been paid him.

(4) Here, too, you see the extent of God's love for man. It would have been just if one who had been so ungrateful for the benefits prepared for him had been judged unworthy of any further pardon and set outside God's providence. Not only did God not do this, but he was like a loving Father with an undisciplined son. In his instinctive love for the boy, he does not measure punishment by the fault, nor does he completely let him go free, but chastises him with moderation so as not to drive him to greater evil and the shipwreck of his life. In the same way, God in his goodness expelled man for his great disobedience from this comfortable way of life and condemned him to toil and hardship so as to check his pride for the future in case he should kick over the traces again.

It is almost as if God had said to him:

(5) "This ample ease and freedom that you enjoyed has led you to this act of grave disobedience and has made you forget my commandments. You had nothing to do, and this has given you thoughts above your own nature ('It is idleness that is the teacher of all vices' [Sir 33:29]). Consequently I am condemning you to toil and hardship, so that by working the land, you may have a continual reminder of your own disobedience and of the worthlessness of human nature. For since you have had great dreams and refused to remain within your own limits, I order you to go back to the dust from which you have been taken. 'You are dust and to dust you shall return' (Gen 3:19)."

(6) To increase his sorrow and make him perceive his own fall, God made him dwell not far from Paradise and walled off his entry into it, so that the continual sight of what he had forfeited by his heedlessness might serve as a perpetual warning and make him in future more careful to keep the commands that were given to him. For when we do not remember as we should how fortunate we are in the enjoyment of some blessing, as soon as we are deprived of it, the sense of loss makes us take great notice of it and increases our distress. And this is just what happened then in the case of the first man.

(7) If you wish to learn of the evil demon's treachery and our Master's resourceful plan, consider what the devil has tried to effect in man by his deceit and what kindness our Master and Protector has shown toward man. That evil demon, in envy of man's home in Paradise, by promising him greater hopes, deprived him even of what he had already. In leading him to dream of an equality with God, he brought him to the punishment of death. Such are his incitements: he not only deprives us of the blessings we have, but attempts to face us with a fall from a greater height. But even so, God in his love did not abandon the human race. He showed the devil the futility of his attempts and showed man the extent of the care he has for him—through death he gave him immortality. Just think. The devil threw man out of Paradise; the Master brought him into heaven. The profit is greater than the loss.

(8) But as I said at the start—and this is the reason for these remarks—God considered that one who was heedless of such blessings was worthy once

more of his great kindness. So if you, who are the soldiers of Christ, try to be grateful for these indescribable gifts that are being granted to you and if you are vigilant to preserve them once they are granted, who can say what kindness you will win from him if you succeed in preserving them? He it was who said: "To everyone who has will more be given, and he will have abundance" (Matt 25:29). One who makes himself worthy of what he has already received deserves to enjoy greater blessings still.

THE NEED OF FAITH

(9) I ask all of you who have been found worthy to be inscribed in this heavenly book to bring a generous faith and a firm resolve. What is performed here requires faith and the eyes of the soul; we are not merely to notice what is seen but to go on from this to imagine what cannot be seen. Such is the power of the eyes of faith. The eyes of the body can see only what falls under the sense of sight, but with the eyes of faith, it is just the reverse. They see nothing that is visible, but they see what is invisible just as if it lay before their eyes. For faith is the capacity to attend to the invisible as if it were visible. "Now faith is the assurance of things hoped for, the conviction of things not seen" (Heb 11:1).

(10) What is the meaning of these words? Why have I said that one must not attend to the visible but develop spiritual eyes? I will tell you. I said it so that when you see the font with its water and the hand of the priest touching your head, you will not think that this is mere water or that it is simply the hand of the bishop that is laid upon your head. It is not a man who performs the rites, but the gracious presence of the Spirit who sanctifies the natural properties of the water and who touches your head along with the hand of the priest. I was right, then—was I not?—to speak of the need we have of the eyes of faith if we are to believe in what is unseen instead of despising what our sense perceives.

(11) As you know, baptism is a burial and a resurrection: the old self is buried with Christ to sin, and

the new nature rises from the dead "that is being renewed after the image of its creator" (Col 3:10). We are stripped and we are clothed, stripped of the old garment that has been soiled by the multitude of our sins, clothed with the new that is free from all stain. What does this mean? We are clothed in Christ himself. St. Paul remarks: "As many of you as were baptized into Christ have put on Christ" (Gal 3:27).

EXORCISMS

(12) Since you are on the threshold of the time when you are to receive these great gifts, I must now teach you, as far as I can, the meaning of each of the rites, so that you may go from here with knowledge and a more assured faith. So you need to know why it is that after the daily instruction we send you off to hear the words of the exorcists. This rite is neither a simple one nor pointless. You are about to receive the heavenly King into your house. So those who are appointed for this task, just as if they were preparing a house for a royal visit, take you on one side after our sermon and purify your minds by those fearful words, putting to flight all the tricks of the evil one, and so make the house fit for the presence of the King. For no demon, however fierce and harsh, after these fearful words and the invocation of the universal Lord of all things, can refrain from flight with all speed. And, in addition, the rite imprints great reverence in the soul and leads it to great sorrow for sin.

(13) The wonderful, unbelievable thing is that every difference and distinction of rank is missing here. If anyone happens to be in a position of worldly importance or conspicuous wealth, if he boasts of his birth or the glory of this present life, he stands on just the same footing as the beggar in rags, the blind man, or the lame. Nor does he complain of this, since he knows that all such differences have been set aside in the life of the spirit; a grateful heart is the only requirement.

(14) Such is the effect of these marvelous, awesome words and invocations. But something else is made known to us by the outward attitude—the bare

feet and the outstretched hands. Just as those who suffer bodily captivity show by the appearance they present their dejection at the disaster that has struck them, so do those men who have been captives of the devil. As they are about to be freed from his tyranny and go beneath the yoke that is easy, first of all they remind themselves by their appearance of their previous situation and try to understand what they are being saved from and what they are hastening to. This then becomes for them a reason for greater gratitude and thankfulness.

THE DUTIES OF SPONSORS

(15) Will you allow me now to address some words to your sponsors, so that they may know the rewards they are worthy of if they show great care for you and the punishment that will ensue if they become negligent? Consider this, my beloved. Those who act as guarantors for money accept a greater responsibility than the debtor who receives the money. If the borrower proves generous, he lightens the load of the guarantor, but if not, he prepares a greater crash for him. It is for this reason that the wise man offers his advice: "If you offer yourself as surety, be concerned as one who must pay" (Sir 8:13). If those who stand as surety for money are responsible for the full sum, those who guarantee that others will pay their account of virtue in matters of the spirit have an even greater duty to show vigilance, advising, counseling, correcting with a paternal affection.

(16) They should not consider that what they are doing is a routine action. Rather, they should be fully aware that they will share the credit if they guide their charges to the path of virtue by their advice, but that if they are negligent, then grave condemnation will fall upon them. For this reason, it is the custom to call them "spiritual fathers," in order that they may learn from their office the affection they owe to their charges in giving them spiritual instruction. For if it is a noble thing to lead those who are in no way connected with us to a desire of virtue, we have a much greater duty to fulfill this obligation to one whom we have received to the position of our spiritual son. To

sum up, negligence brings no small danger to those of you who are acting as sponsors.

RENUNCIATION OF SIN AND PROFESSION OF FAITH

(17) I turn now to the sacraments and the covenant between yourself and the Lord into which you are about to enter. In business, when a man wishes to entrust his affairs to another, it is necessary for a contract to be signed between the two parties. The same is true now, when the Lord of all things is about to entrust to you affairs that are not mortal and passing away and decaying, but spiritual and heavenly. The contract is also called a pledge of faith, since we are doing nothing that can be seen, but everything can be discerned by the eyes of the spirit. Meanwhile it is necessary for the contract to be signed, not with ink on paper but with the spirit in God. The words that you pronounce are inscribed in heaven; the agreement spoken by your lips remains indelibly before God.

(18) Now consider once again the posture of captivity. The priests who introduce you first of all tell you to kneel down and pray with your hands raised to heaven and, by this attitude of body, recall to your mind the one from whom you have been delivered and the other whom you are about to join. After that the priest approaches each in turn and demands your contracts and confessions and instructs each one to pronounce those fearful and awesome words: *I renounce you, Satan.*

(19) Tears and deep sighs now force themselves upon me. I have recalled the day on which I, too, was judged worthy to pronounce these words. As I reckon up the weight of the sins that I have gathered from that day to this, I am confused in mind and stung in conscience as I reflect upon the shame with which I have covered myself by my subsequent negligence. And so I beg all of you to show some generosity toward me, and since you are about to approach our king—he will receive you with great alacrity, he will dress you in the royal robe, and will grant every kind of gift that you desire, at least if you seek spiritual gifts—beg a favor for me, too. Pray that God may not

ask an account of my sins but grant me pardon and for the future count me worthy of his support. I have no doubt that you will do this in your affection for your teachers.

(20) But I must not allow myself to lose the thread of my argument any more. The priest then instructs you to say, *I renounce you, Satan, your pomp, your worship, and your works.* There is great power in these few words. For the angels who are present and the invisible powers rejoice at your conversion and, receiving the words from your lips, carry them to the common master of all things, where they are inscribed in the books of heaven.

(21) Have you seen the terms of the contract? After the renunciation of the Evil One and all the works he delights in, the priest instructs you to speak again as follows: *And I pledge myself, Christ, to you.* Do you see the overwhelming goodness of God? From you he receives only words, yet he entrusts to you realities, a great treasure. He forgets your past ingratitude; he remembers nothing of your past; he is content with these few words.

ANOINTING WITH CHRISM

(22) Then once you have made this covenant, this renunciation and contract, since you have confessed his sovereignty over you and pronounced the words by which you pledge yourself to Christ, you are now a soldier and have signed on for a spiritual contest. Accordingly the bishop anoints you on the forehead with spiritual myron, placing a seal on your head and saying: *N. is anointed in the name of the Father, the Son, and the Holy Spirit.*

(23) Now the bishop knows that the Enemy is enraged and is sharpening his teeth going around like a roaring lion, seeing that the former victims of his tyranny have suddenly defected. Renouncing him, they have changed their allegiance and publicly enlisted with Christ. It is for this reason that the bishop anoints you on your forehead and marks you with the seal, to make the devil turn away his eyes. He does not dare to look at you directly because he sees the light blazing from your head and blinding his eyes.

From that day onward, you will confront him in battle, and this is why the bishop anoints you as athletes of Christ before leading you into the spiritual arena.

STRIPPING AND ANOINTING WITH OIL

(24) Then after this, at the appointed hour of the night, he strips you of all your clothes, and as if he were about to lead you into heaven itself by means of these rites, he prepares to anoint your whole body with this spiritual oil so that his unction may armor all your limbs and make them invulnerable to any weapons the Enemy may hurl.

BAPTISM

(25) After this anointing, he takes you down into the sacred waters, at the same time burying the old nature and raising "the new creature, which is being renewed after the image of the creator" (Col 3:10). Then by the words of the priest and by his hand, the presence of the Holy Spirit flies down upon you, and another man comes up out of the font, one washed from all the stain of his sins, who has put off the old garment of sin and is clothed in the royal robe.

(26) To give you a further lesson that the substance of the Father, the Son, and the Spirit is one, baptism is conferred in this form. As the priest pronounced the words, *N. is baptized in the name of the Father and of the Son and of the Holy Spirit,* he plunges your head into the water and lifts it up again three times, by this sacred rite preparing you to receive the descent of the Holy Spirit. For the priest is not the only one who touches your head; Christ also touches it with his right hand. This is shown by the actual words of the one who baptizes you. He does not say, "I baptize N.," but rather, "N. is baptized." This shows that he is only the minister of the grace and merely lends his hand, since he has been ordained for this by the Spirit. It is the Father, Son, and Holy Spirit, the indivisible Trinity, who bring the whole rite to completion. It is faith in the Trinity that bestows the grace of remission of sin, and the con-

fession of the Trinity that grants us the adoption of sons.

THE GREETING

(27) The ceremonies that follow are well able to teach us the afflictions from which those who have been counted worthy to receive this sacred rite have been set free and the blessings that they have been granted. As soon as they come up from those sacred waters, all present embrace them, greet them, kiss them, congratulate and rejoice with them, because those who before were slaves and prisoners have all at once become free men and sons who are invited to the royal table. For as soon as they come up from the font, they are led to the awesome table that is laden with all good things. They taste the body and blood of the Lord and become the dwelling place of the Spirit; since they have put on Christ, they go about appearing everywhere like angles on earth and shining as brightly as the rays of the sun.

CONCLUSION

(28) It is not without good reason and careful thought that I have explained all these things to you in advance, my loving people. Even before you actually enjoy them, I wanted you to feel great pleasure as you fly on the wings of hope. I wanted you to take up a disposition of soul worthy of the rite and, as the blessed Paul advised you, to "set your mind on things that are above" (Col 3:2), raising your thoughts from earth to heaven, from the visible to the invisible. We see such things more clearly with the eyes of the spirit than the perceptions of the senses.

(29) But since you have come near the royal entrance hall and are about to approach the very throne where the king sits distributing his gifts, show complete unselfishness in your requests. Ask for nothing worldly or natural, but make a request that is worthy of the giver. As you step out of the sacred waters and express your resurrection by the act of coming up from them, ask for alliance with him so that you may show great vigilance in guarding what has been given to you and so be immune from the tricks of the Enemy. Pray for the peace of the churches. Intercede for those who are still wandering. Fall on your knees for those who are in sin so that we may deserve some pardon. You were once diffident; God has given you great assurance. You were once slaves; he has enrolled you among the chief of his friends. You were once captives; he has raised you up and adopted you as sons. He will not refuse your demands; he will grant them all, true again in this to his own goodness.

(30) In this way, too, you will draw God to still greater kindness. When he sees you showing such concern for those who are your own members and anxious about the salvation of others, because of this he will count you worthy to receive great assurance. Nothing so warms his heart as our compassion for our members and the affection that we show for our brothers, the great forethought we show for the salvation of our neighbor.

(31) And so, dearly beloved, in this knowledge, prepare yourselves with joy and spiritual delight to receive this grace so that you may enjoy the gift in its abundance. And so may we all together, living lives that are in keeping with the grace we have received, be counted worthy to win the eternal and indescribable blessings through the grace and loving kindness of our Lord Jesus Christ with whom to the Father and the Holy Spirit be glory, power, honor now and always, for ever and ever. Amen.

CHAPTER 6

Christian Leadership

Following the legalization of Christianity, the institutional leaders of the Christian church (the clergy) became increasingly entrenched in the public world of the Roman Empire. Clerical hierarchies were integrated into the political landscape: the bishop of the provincial capital (the "metropolitan") acquired authority over his provincial peers, while the bishops of major imperial cities (Antioch, Rome, Alexandria, and Constantinople) became known as "patriarchs," first among equals, setting the stage for later medieval developments of the papacy in the West and ecumenical patriarchate in the East. The ranks of Christian clergy also proliferated: in addition to bishops, priests, and deacons ("ordained" ranks), we find subdeacons, readers, exorcists, deaconesses, porters, and so forth. Although these nonordained clerical posts existed before the legalization of Christianity, they now became more visible as positions to be filled by the members of Christian families who desired the prestige of church service without having to give up one or more of their children to lifelong ecclesiastical service.

Imperial patronage ensured close, if at times, strained, relations between political and religious leadership (see, for instance, Text 8). While Christian leaders continued to serve their local communities as guides to the sacred, they also became more public figures: patrons of the poor, spokesmen for the city or province, advocates, and judges. The rise of asceticism during this period also affected the perception of Christian leaders (see Chapter 9). Although we gain a sense of occasional conflicts of authority between clergy and monks, more often we see how clergy adopted the sanctity of asceticism to their own institutional roles. Priests and bishops took on the trappings of "holy men" and sanctified their own clerical calling.

The public prominence of Christian leaders could at times blur distinctions between secular and ecclesiastical status. Some bishops were drawn directly from the aristocratic nobility, while others bolstered their own civic status by taking on the trappings of a cultured elite (as Gregory of Nazianzus incisively critiques in Text 18). Clergy walked a fine line: erudition and rhetorical skill were praised in a bishop, but so were simplicity and humility. Great responsibility fell on episcopal shoulders, but so did increased suspicion of power mongering and secular politicking. Nonetheless, beneath the controversy and contestation, it seems that the majority of institutional Christian leaders acted most often in the role that their congregations expected from them: as guides to the sacred mysteries of Christian salvation, particularly intitiation (baptism) and communion (Eucharist). Christian leaders continued to draw on biblical models—Moses; Joshua; the apostles; and, of course, Jesus—to provide a spiritual framework for their endeavors.

In this chapter are several different snapshots of Christian institutional leaders (for views of noninstitutional leaders, see especially Chapters 9 and 11). The two examples of "church orders"—compilations of canons and rules for the regulation of Christian communities, attributed pseudepigraphically to apostolic and subapostolic times—give us perhaps idealized images of the various ranks of clergy and their roles in church servies. Gregory of Nazianzus and Aphrahat, on the other hand, take us out of the church and into the service (or disservice) done by Christian leaders in the wider world.

See also the canons treating clerical hierarchy in Chapter 8.

FOR FURTHER READING

Brown, Peter. *Power and Persuasion in Late Antiquity: Towards a Christian Empire.* Madison: University of Wisconsin Press, 1992.

Chadwick, Henry. *The Role of the Christian Bishop in Ancient Society.* Berkeley: Center for Hermeneutical Studies in Hellenistic and Modern Culture, 1980.

Drake, H. A. *Constantine and the Bishops: The Politics of Intolerance.* Baltimore: Johns Hopkins University Press, 2000.

Ferguson, Everett, ed. *Church, Ministry, and Organization in the Early Church Era.* New York: Garland Press, 1993.

Van Dam, Raymond. *Leadership and Community in Late Antique Gaul.* Berkeley: University of California Press, 1992.

The Texts

16. Canons of Hippolytus

Although it is attributed in the manuscript tradition to the second- or third-century Roman Hippolytus, this collection of church rules (*kanones*) probably dates in its present form from the fourth century or later. Like much of the "orders" literature from Late Antiquity, the *Canons of Hippolytus* were likely compiled from diverse sources; ironically, the intensely detailed description of church ranks, ordination ceremonies, and liturgical concerns may not reflect any single ancient church, but rather an ideal composite. Nonetheless, we can learn even from this synthesized ideal what a fourth- or fifth-century Christian might have looked for, in terms both of the formalities of ordination and of the functions and duties of ordained clergy. The almost comical poignancy of canon 29, which pictures clergy guarding the Eucharist cup against insects and piously disposing of altar dust, gives a sense of where Christian clergy were at their most effective: at the altar of the mysteries, performing baptisms and creating communion, bridging the mundane and the celestial worlds of the Christian.

CANON 1

Concerning the Holy Faith

Before all else we speak of the holy and true faith in our Lord Jesus Christ, Son of the living God. And we have set it down faithfully, and we are firmly in agreement [with it], and we say, we, that the Trinity, equal and perfect in honor, is equal in glory. He has no beginning or end, the Word, the Son of God, and he is also the creator of every creature, visible and invisible. This we have set down and we truly agree with it.

And those who have dared to say what they ought not about the Word of God, according to what our Lord Jesus Christ said concerning them, we have assembled ourselves, being the great majority, in the power of God, and we have cut them off because they are not in accord with the holy Scriptures, the word of God, or with us, the disciples of the Scriptures. That is why we have cut them off from the Church, and we have handed over their case to God, who judges every creature with justice.

Those who do not know them, we teach them those things without ill will, so that they may not fall into a bad death, as some heretics, but may be worthy of eternal life and teach their children and those who will come after them this holy faith.

CANON 2

Concerning Bishops

Let the bishop be chosen by all the people, and let him be without reproach, as it is written concerning

From *The Canons of Hippolytus,* ed. Paul Bradshaw, trans. Carol Bebawi. Bramcote, England: Grove Books, 1987. Used with permission.

him in the Apostle. The week when he is ordained, all the clergy and the people say, "We choose him." There shall be silence in all the flock after the approbation, and they are all to pray for him and say, "O God, behold him whom you have prepared for us." They are to choose one of bishops and presbyters; he lays his hand on the head and prays, saying:

CANON 3

Prayer Over Him Who Becomes Bishop, and Order of the Liturgy

"O God, Father of our Lord Jesus Christ, Father of mercies and God of all comfort, dwelling on high and looking upon the lowly, knowing everything before it comes to pass, you who have fixed the boundaries of the Church, who have decreed from Adam that there should exist a righteous race—by the intermediary of this bishop—that is [the race] of great Abraham, who have established authorities and powers, look upon N. with your power and mighty Spirit, which you have given to the holy apostles by our Lord Jesus Christ your only Son, those who have founded the Church in every place, for the honor and glory of your holy name.

"Since you know the heart of everyone, make him shepherd your people blamelessly, so that he may be worthy of tending your great and holy flock; make his life higher than [that] of all his people, without dispute; make him envied by reason of his virtue by everyone; accept his prayers and his offerings that he will offer you day and night; and let them be for you a sweet-smelling savor. Give him, Lord, the episcopate, a merciful spirit, and the authority to forgive sins; give him power to loosen every bond of the oppression of demons, to cure the sick and crush Satan under his feet swiftly; through our Lord Jesus Christ, through whom be glory to you, with him and the Holy Spirit, to the ages of ages. Amen."

And all the people say, "Amen."

After that they are all to turn toward him and give him the kiss of peace because he is worthy of it.

Then the deacon brings the offerings, and he who has become bishop lays his hand on the offerings with the presbyters, saying, "The Lord be with all."

The people reply, "And with your spirit."

He says, "Lift up your hearts."

They reply, "We have [them] to the Lord."

He says, "Let us give thanks to the Lord."

They reply, "It is fitting and right," that is to say, "it is fitting."

After that, he says the prayer and completes the liturgy.

If there is any oil, he prays over it in this manner, though not the same expressions, but the same meaning. If there are any firstfruits, anything edible, which someone has brought, he prays over it, and blesses the fruit that is brought to him, in his prayer.

In each prayer that is said over each thing, there is said at the end of the prayer, "Glory to you, Father, Son, and Holy Spirit, to the ages of ages. Amen."

CANON 4

Concerning the Ordination of Presbyters

When a presbyter is ordained, one is to do for him everything that one does for the bishop, except the sitting on the seat. One is to pray over him all the prayer of the bishop, except only the name of bishop. The presbyter is equal to the bishop in everything except the seat and ordination because to him is not given the power to ordain.

CANON 5

Concerning the Ordination of Deacons

When a deacon is ordained, one is to do for him according to the same rules, and one is to say this prayer over him.

He is not appointed for the presbyterate, but for the diaconate, as a servant of God. He serves the bishop and the presbyters in everything, not only at the time of the liturgy, but he serves also the sick of the people, those who have nobody, and he informs the bishop so that he may pray over them or give to them what they need, or also to people whose poverty is not apparent but who are in need. They are to serve also those who have the alms of the bishops, and they are able to give to widows, to orphans, and to the poor. He is to perform all the services. So this in truth is the deacon of whom Christ has said, "He who serves me, my Father will honor him" (John 12:26). The bishop lays his hand on the deacon and prays over him, saying:

"O God, Father of our Lord Jesus Christ, we beseech you, pour out your Holy Spirit on *N.;* count him among those who serve you according to all your will like Stephen and his companions; fill him with power and wisdom like Stephen; make him triumph over all the powers of the devil by the sign of your cross with which you sign him; make his life without sin before all men and an example for many, so that he may save a multitude in the holy Church without shame; and accept all his service; through our Lord Jesus Christ, through whom be glory to you, with him and the Holy Spirit, to the ages of ages. Amen."

CANON 7

Concerning the Choice of Reader and of Subdeacon

When one chooses a reader, he is to have the virtues of the deacon. One is not to lay the hand on him before, but the bishop is to give him the Gospel.

The subdeacon [is to be appointed] according to this arrangement: he is not to be ordained still celibate and if he has not married, unless his neighbors bear witness for him and testify that he has kept himself away from women during the time of his maturity.

One is not to lay the hand on someone in the state of celibacy, unless he has reached his maturity or is entering into mature age and is thought [worthy], when one bears witness for him.

The subdeacon and the reader, when they pray alone, are to keep themselves behind, and the subdeacon is to serve behind the deacon. . . .

CANON 29

Concerning Vigilance Over the Altar So That Nothing Falls into the Cup: Nothing is to Fall [into It] by [the Fault of] the Priests or the Faithful, for Fear That an Evil Spirit Should Have Power Over It. One Is Not to Say Anything Behind the Veil, Except in Prayer. When They Have Finished Communicating, the People, All Those Who Enter into The [Holy] Place, Are to Recite The Psalms in Place of the Bells. And Concerning the Sign of the Cross and the Dust of the Sanctuary that Is to be Thrown into the Stream

The clergy are to stand with all their attention on the altar when it has been prepared. They are to stand watching over it, so that no insect climbs on to it and nothing falls into the cup: that would be a mortal sin for the presbyters. That is why every one is to stand watching over the holy place: he who gives the mysteries and those who partake are to watch with great care that nothing falls on the ground, for fear that an evil spirit should have power over it.

One is not to speak at all inside the veil, except a prayer only and the things necessary for the service. One is not to do anything [else] in this place. After having finished communicating to the people, they are to enter. They are to sing hymns each time they enter because of the powers of the holy place. The psalms are to replace for them the bells that were on the garment of Aaron. No one is to sit down in that place. [One is] only [to do there] prayer, genuflexion, and prostration before the altar.

The dust that is swept from the holy place is to be thrown into the water of a flowing stream, and one is not to delay for fear that it will be trodden on by people.

Be pure at all times and mark your forehead with the sign of the cross, being victorious over Satan and glorifying in your faith. Moses did that with the blood of the lamb with which he smeared the lintels and the two doorposts, and it healed whoever lived there. How should the blood of Christ not purify more and protect more those who believe in him and manifest the sign of the salvation that is for all the world, which has been healed by the blood of the perfect lamb, Christ?

All the mysteries concerning life, resurrection, and the sacrifice, the Christians alone [are] those who hear them. This is because they have received the seal of baptism because they are the participants [in it].

17. Testament of the Lord

Like the *Canons of Hippolytus,* the *Testament of the Lord* is a fourth-century (or later) composite of earlier traditions about the orderly running of the church. This text is set as a conversation between Jesus (thus, it is the Lord's testament, his "will") and the apostles, by which we are to imagine that ecclesiastical orders and ceremonies were laid out at the dawn of Christianity, filling in an ecclesiastical gap of the canonical Gospels. In this detailed (and, again, perhaps idealized or synthesized) description of the ceremonies of the Eucharist and priestly ordination, we gain a sense of the pageantry of Christian ceremony: the parades of priests, deacons, subdeacons, widows, virgins, monks (here, in the Syriac translation, called the "children of the covenant," or *qyama*; see Text 41), filing up and down from the altar, gesturing in profound silence or leading the congregants in long and involved responsive prayers. Here we see the clergy as participants in a majestic drama, the theater of salvation, moving through intricately scripted entrances, lines, cues, and exits. Even if no eucharistic ceremony was conducted with precisely this staging, the solemnity and theatricality of salvation are evident here, as are the roles played by the attendant clergy.

I.23. THE EUCHARISTIC LITURGY

On the Sabbath let him [i.e., the bishop] offer three breads for the fullness of the Trinity. On Sunday let him offer four breads for the fullness of the Gospel.

Because the ancient people went astray, when he offers, let the veil in front of the door be drawn. Within it let him offer together with the presbyters, deacons, and canonical widows and subdeacons and deaconesses, readers who possess [spiritual] gifts. Let the bishop stand first in the midst [of them] and the presbyters immediately after him; after them, the widows immediately behind the presbyters on the left side, the deacons behind the presbyters on the right side, then the readers behind them, the subdeacons behind the readers, the deaconesses behind the subdeacons.

Let the bishop place his hand upon the breads that have been placed upon the altar in this way, the presbyters placing [their hands on the breads] at the same time. Let the rest be standing only.

Let the bread of the catechumens not be received, not even if he has a believing son or wife and wants to offer on their behalf. Let him not offer until he is baptized.

Before the bishop or presbyter offers, let the people give the Peace to each other. Then, when there is a great silence, let the deacon say as follows.

ADMONITION OF THE DEACON OVER THE EUCHARIST

[Let] your hearts [be] in heaven.

If anyone bears a grudge against his neighbor, let him be reconciled.

If anyone has a faithless mind, let him confess.

If anyone has a mind foreign to the commandments, let him depart.

If anyone has fallen into sin, let him not hide. He cannot hide.

If anyone has infirm reasoning, let him not draw near.

If anyone is defiled, if anyone is not steadfast, let him give place.

From *The Testamentum Domini,* trans. and ed. Grant Sperry-White. Bramcote, England: Grove Books, 1991. Used with permission.

If anyone is a stranger to the commandments of Jesus, let him depart.

If anyone treats the prophets with contempt, let him separate himself. Let him deliver himself from the wrath of the Only begotten.

Let us not despise the Cross.

Let us avoid threatening.

We have our Lord [as] spectator, the Father of lights with the Son; the angels are visiting.

Look to yourselves, that you are not bearing a grudge against those near you.

See that no one is angry: God sees.

Lift up your hearts to offer for the salvation of life and holiness.

In the wisdom of God let us receive the grace that has been bestowed upon us.

I.23. ANAPHORA

Then let the bishop, confessing and giving thanks, say with a loud voice: Our Lord be with you.

And let the people say: And with your spirit.

Let the bishop say: Lift up your hearts.

Let the people say: They are with the Lord.

Let the bishop say: Let us give thanks to the Lord.

And let all the people say: It is meet and right.

And let the bishop cry out: Holy things for holy people.

And let the people shout: In heaven and on earth without end.

EUCHARIST, OR THANKSGIVING OVER THE OFFERING

Preface

We give you thanks, O God, the Holy One and confirmer of our souls, giver of our life, treasure of incorruptibility, and Father of your Only begotten, our Savior, whom you sent to us in the last times as Savior and proclaimer of your will. For it is your will that we be saved in you. Our heart gives you thanks, O Lord, [our] mind, [our] soul, along with every thought, that your grace, O Lord, may come upon us, [so] that we may praise you continually, and your

Only begotten, and your Holy Spirit, now and always and to the ages of ages. Amen.

You, Lord, [are] the power of the Father, the grace of the nations, knowledge, true wisdom, exaltation of the meek, medicine of souls. [You are] the confidence of us who believe, for you are the strengthening of the righteous, the hope of the persecuted, the harbor of those who are buffeted, the illuminator of the perfect.

O Son of the living God, make to shine upon us from your gift that cannot be inquired into, fortitude, valor, confidence, wisdom, steadfastness, unlapsing faith, unshaken hope, knowledge of your Spirit, meekness, integrity, so that always we your servants, Lord, and all the people may purely praise you, bless you, give you thanks at all times, Lord, and supplicate you.

And also let the bishop say: You, Lord, [are] the founder of the heights and King of the luminous treasuries, visitor of the heavenly Zion, King of the archangelic orders: of dominions, praises, thrones, raiments, lights, joys, delights. [You are] Father of kings, you who hold all things in your hand, you who provide by your thought, through your Only-begotten Son who was crucified for our sins. You, Lord, being pleased with him, sent your Word, who is the son of your counsel and son of your promise, through whom you made all things, into a virgin womb; who when he was conceived and became incarnate, being born from the Holy Spirit and the Virgin, was shown to be your Son, who, fulfilling your will and preparing a holy people, stretched out his hands to suffering so that he might free those who have hoped in you from sufferings and corruption of death,

Institution Narrative

Who, when he was betrayed to voluntary suffering so that he might set straight those who had stumbled and find the lost and raise the dead and undo death and burst the bonds of the devil and fulfill the will of the Father and tread upon Sheol and open a way of life and lead the righteous to light and fix a boundary and lighten the darkness and nurture infants and reveal the Resurrection, taking bread, he gave [it] to his disciples, saying, "Take, eat; this is my body that is broken for you for the forgiveness of sins. When you do this, you make my resurrection." Also the cup of wine that he mixed he gave for a type of the blood that he shed for us.

And also let him say: Remembering, therefore, your death and resurrection, we offer you bread and cup, thanking you who alone are the eternal God and our Savior, since you have promised to us to stand before you and serve you as priests. For this we give you thanks, we your servants, O Lord.

And let the people say likewise.

Oblation

And also let him say: We offer you this thanksgiving, eternal Trinity, Lord Jesus Christ, Lord Father, from whom all creation and every nature trembles, fleeing into itself; Lord Holy Spirit, we have brought this drink and this food of your holiness; make it be for us not for condemnation, not for reproach, not for destruction, but for the healing [and] support of our spirit. Indeed, O God, grant us that through your Name every thought of what is unpleasing to you may flee. Lord, grant that every proud thought may be driven away by your Name written within the veil of your lofty sanctuaries, [your Name, at] which Sheol, hearing [it], is dismayed. [By your Name] the depth is rent, spirits are expelled, the dragon is crushed, unbelief is driven away, disobedience is subdued, anger is appeased, jealousy achieves nothing, arrogance is reproved, avarice is uprooted, boastfulness is removed, pride is brought low, and every nature giving birth to bitterness is destroyed.

Intercessions and Doxology

Therefore, O Lord, allow our inner eyes to see you, praising and glorifying you, commemorating you, serving you, having a portion in you alone. O Son and Word of God, to whom all things are subdued, sustain to the end those who have [spiritual] gifts of revelations. Make firm those who have a gift of healing; embolden those who have the power of tongues; direct those who have the word of teaching; care always for

those who do your will; visit the widows succor the orphans, remember those who have fallen asleep in the faith, grant us an inheritance with your saints, and bestow upon us the power to please you, just as they were pleasing to you. Shepherd the people in uprightness. Sanctify us all, O God; grant that all those who partake [and] receive your holy things may be united with you, that they may be filled with the Holy Spirit for the confirmation of faith in truth, so that they may always offer you a doxology, and your beloved Son Jesus Christ, through whom to you be praise and power with your Holy Spirit, to the ages of ages.

And let the people say, Amen.

I.23. POSTANAPHORA

Deacon: Let us earnestly beseech our Lord and our God, that he bestow upon us *homonoia*[1] of spirit.

Bishop: Give us *homonoia* in the Holy Spirit, and heal our souls through this offering, that we may live in you in all the ages of ages.

People: Amen.

Let the people also pray in the same [words].

And after these things, let the seal of the thanksgiving [be] thus:

Blessed be the name of the Lord for ever. People: Amen.

Priest: Blessed is he who has come in the name of the Lord. Blessed [be] the name of his glory.

And let all the people say: So be it, so be it, so be it.

Let the bishop say: Send the grace of the Spirit upon us.

If the bishop has a wet dream, let him not offer, but let the presbyter offer. Nor let him partake of the mystery, not as if he were polluted, but because of the honor of the altar. But after he fasts and washes in pure water, let him come near and minister. Similarly also [for] a presbyter. Also, if a widow is menstruous, let her not come near. Similarly if a woman or lay

---

[1] Greek, "like-mindedness"; preserved in Greek transliteration in non-Greek versions.

person or anyone else from the *qyama*[2] [is polluted], let him not approach because of the honor [of the altar], unless after fasting and washing.

Let the priests receive first in the following way: bishop, presbyters, deacons, widows, readers, sub-deacons. After them, those who have [spiritual] gifts, the newly baptized, little children. The people [receive] in the following way: the elderly, virgins. After them, the rest. The women [receive in the following way]: deaconesses, after them, the rest.

Let each one, when he receives the thanksgiving, say amen before partaking.

Afterward, let him [or her] pray in the following way; after he receives from the eucharist let him say: Holy, Holy, Holy, ineffable Trinity. Grant me to receive this body for life, not for condemnation. And grant me to bear fruits pleasing to you, that I may appear pleasing to you. May I live in you as I perform your commandments, and may I call you Father with courage. When I call [down] upon myself your kingdom and your will, may your name be sanctified in me because you are mighty and glorious, and praise [be] to you forever. Amen.

After the prayer, let him [or her] receive.

When he receives the cup, let him say amen two times for the fullness of the body and blood.

After all have received, let them pray, confessing and giving thanks for receiving, while the deacon says: Praise the Lord when we receive his holy things, that the reception may be for our own life and salvation. We pray and beseech, raising a doxology to the Lord our God.

Then the bishop says: Lord, giver of eternal light, pilot of our souls, guide of the holy: give us understanding eyes that always heed you and ears that listen to you alone, that our soul may be filled with your grace. From in us a pure heart, [O] God, that we may always recognize your greatness. Wondrous God, and lover of humankind: amend our souls; through this Eucharist we receive establish our minds [to be] undeviating, we your unworthy servants. For blessed is your Kingdom, Lord God, and praised and glori-

fied in the Father and in the Son and in the Holy Spirit, both from before the ages, and now and always, and for ever and ever, and to the unending ages of ages.

People: Amen.

I.24. BLESSING OF OIL

If there is oil for the healing of those who suffer, let it be sanctified in the following way. Let him say quietly, setting the vessel before the altar:

Lord God, you who bestowed on us the Spirit, the Paraclete: Lord, [whose] name is salvific and unshaken, hidden to the foolish but revealed to the wise: Christ, you who have sanctified and made wise in your mercy us your servants whom you in your wisdom have chosen, who sent the knowledge of your Spirit to us sinners through your holiness, when you bestowed the power of the Spirit upon us, you are the healer of all who are ill and all who suffer. You who gave the gift of healing to those you deemed worthy of this [gift]: send the deliverance of your compassion upon this oil, which is a type of your richness, that it may deliver those who are diseased and [that] it may heal the sick and sanctify those who return, as they draw near to your faith.

For you are powerful and glorious for ever and ever.

People: amen.

I.25. BLESSING OF WATER

Similarly, the same [prayer] over water. . . .

I.30. PRAYER OF THE *CHEIROTONIA*[3] OF A PRESBYTER

Then let the ordination of a presbyter be thus: after all the priestly *qyama* have brought him, while the

---

[2] That is, a monk (see Text 41).

[3] Greek, "ordination."

bishop lays his hand on his head and the presbyters are touching him and holding him, let the bishop begin, saying thus:

O God, Father of our Lord Jesus Christ, the Ineffable, the Luminary, who has neither beginning nor end, Lord, you who have ordered all things, and set [them] in a limit, and in thought have determined the order for all things you have created:

Hear us and turn toward this your servant and make [him] a partaker and grant him the spirit of grace and of reason and of strength, [the] spirit of the presbyterate that does not age, indissoluble, homogeneous, loving the faithful, admonishing, [in order] to help and govern your people in labor, in fear, with a pure heart, in holiness, and in excellency, and in wisdom, and by the operation of your Holy Spirit through your care, Lord.

In like manner as when you attended to your chosen people, you commanded Moses to ask for the elders, when you filled [them with] Holy Spirit you bestowed your minister; and now, O Lord, bestow your unfailing Spirit upon him, which you gave to those who became disciples through you and to all those who through them truly believed in you; and make him worthy (being filled with your wisdom and with your hidden mysteries) to shepherd your people in the holiness of a pure and true heart, praising, blessing, lauding, acknowledging, always offering a doxology, day and night, to your holy and glorious name, laboring in cheerfulness and patience, so that he might be an instrument of your Holy Spirit, always having and bearing the cross of your only-begotten Son, our Lord Jesus Christ, through whom to you be glory and might, with the Holy Spirit, to all the ages of ages.

Let the people say, Amen.

Let them give him the Peace, both priests and people, with a holy kiss.

I.38. PRAYER OF THE *CHEIROTONIA* OF A DEACON

Then let the ordination of a deacon be thus: let the bishop alone lay his hand on him because he is ordained not to the priesthood but to the ministry of attending to the bishop and the Church. Therefore, let the bishop say thus over the deacon:

O God, you who created all things and who adorned [them] by the Word, you who rest in the pure ages, you who ministered eternal life to us through your prophets, you who have enlightened us with the light of your knowledge;

O God who do great things, the maker of all glory, the Father of our Lord Jesus Christ, whom you sent to minister to your will so that all the human race might be saved; you made known to us and revealed your Thought, your Wisdom, your Action, your beloved Son Jesus Christ, the Lord of light, the Prince of princes, and God of gods:

Bestow the spirit of grace and diligence upon this your servant, so that there might be given to him diligence, serenity, strength, [and] power to please you. Grant him, O Lord, to be a lawful laborer without shame, kind, a lover of orphans, a lover of the pious, a lover of widows, fervent in spirit, a lover of good things.

Enlighten, Lord, the one you have loved and have appointed to minister to your Church to offer in holiness to your sanctuary those things offered to you from the inheritance of your high-priesthood, so that he may minister without blame and in purity and holiness, and with a pure conscience may [he] be proved worthy of this high and exalted rank through your will, praising you continuously through your only-begotten Son Jesus Christ our Lord, through whom be praise and might to you for ever and ever. The people: Amen.

18. Gregory of Nazianzus: On Himself and the Bishops

Gregory (ca. 330–ca. 390) was one of the three great fourth-century Christian thinkers known to historians as the "Cappadocian Fathers," along with Basil of Caesarea and Basil's brother Gregory of Nyssa. Together, they were considered the architects of fourth-century Christian theology (see Chapter 7). Educated in his native Cappadocia and then in Alexandria and Athens, Gregory was an extraordinarily erudite and sensitive thinker. His theological acumen made him both admirers and enemies: at the Council of Constantinople in 381 (see Text 34), Gregory was first appointed Patriarch of the capital city and then deposed by his theological and political enemies. In bitterness, he retired to his native Cappodocia, where he eventually served as bishop of the insignificant village of Nazianzus, where his father had also been bishop.

In addition to theological treatises and orations (see Text 23), Gregory wrote a series of learned and biting autobiographical poems about his disillusioned experience in the overly politicized world of church hierarchy. In this following poem (translated into prose), Gregory acidly critiques the foolish criteria by which Christians choose their leaders: bishops nowadays, Gregory charges, are all style and no substance, riddled with hypocrisy, serving themselves instead of their God and their congregants. At best they are ignorant, at worse self-serving, and all have lost the original apostolic fervor for God: "Today's Simon Peter is the Simon Magus of yesterday" (cf. Acts 8). While we may suspect Gregory of claiming that the grapes of high episcopacy were sour (even as he coveted the patriarchate), his insight into the degree to which church hierarchy—less then a century after the end of persecution—had become subject to intricate plays for power and prestige nonetheless sheds light on the evolution of Christian leadership.

INTRODUCTION

It may be that just as I modeled myself after the commandments of him who suffered and bore with ill use, so, too, after ill use, I should restrain my language: in the hope, that is, of the more perfect reward that recompenses a more demanding struggle. For reward is according to quality of performance, for the perfect, perfect; for the lesser, something less than perfect. However I should not wish the wicked to be altogether triumphant or their path made smooth without a protesting voice being raised.

I am content to leave their ultimate fate to the final conflagration because it will test and purge all things impartially, however much people manage to escape in this world by subterfuges. For my part, I propose to give a minor tongue-lashing to my assassins, for that is what they are, those framers of monstrous judgments, who shed the blood of innocent souls I myself molded and developed. I shall say what I have to say without fear of recrimination, though that is something everyone wishes to avoid and that I find particularly hateful. In the course of my remarks, I do not propose to mention names, lest I seem to be in-

From *Saint Gregory of Nazianzus: Three Poems,* trans. Denis Molaise Meehan. Washington, D.C.: Catholic University of America Press, 1987.

dulging in criticism in domains that ought to be confidential. And for fear my tongue should run away with me, I shall not recount all details at equal length.

BAD AND GOOD BISHOPS

I realize that there are many persons who deserve high commendation. At the present juncture, the one who must be apprehended and subdued is the one who is in the camp of the wicked or worse than wicked. The sword of the tongue shall smite the miscreant, and who the miscreant is you will make manifest. You shall stand as your own accuser if you find yourself at variance with this account. Since this is my attitude, let whoever wishes open fire because long ago I have become inured to stonings. Now of the lion one need have no fear, the leopard is a gentle creature, and even the snake you are terrified by is likely to turn in flight; but there is one thing you must beware of, I assure you. Bad bishops. Don't be overawed by the dignity of the throne. All have the dignity, yes; but not all have the grace. Discard the outer clothing; watch for the wolf. Words do not convince me; I must have deeds.

Teachings that are rendered null by lives I abominate. I must praise the outer coloring of the sepulcher; but the stench of rotten bodies within disgusts me. But how and why, you say? How can a man like you, who invariably deals in fair speech, fail to do so also now? Indeed, it is with pain that I set down this wretched story for God, for friends, for parents, for neighbors, for strangers, and if for them, also for the generations yet to come.

I shall go back some distance in the story. No one should ever say that laborers have any profit from their toil; that is a delusion. It is all a weary pilgrimage through darkness and mist. God tries some by fire, and over some he casts a darkness until the day when fire casts light on all things. You have, on the one hand, a man who has eked out a life of toil. Groans, vigils, limbs wasted by tears, the constraints of fasting and of a hard pallet by night, anxieties of the spirit, study of sacred writ, constant laceration by interior scourges—did I escape any of these things?

Was I guilty of a single untoward act? On the other hand, you have the man who plucked the joys of youth. He sported, he sang, he pandered to the appetites of the belly, he surrendered to all pleasures, unlocked the door to all sensations, was a colt without restraint. And in the end it is the former who is dogged by disaster. Nay, not disaster. Common estimation has it that the wise man is impervious to the calamities of life, but common estimation makes away with even the semblance of wisdom. Our friend who had the smooth course all the way is successful in the domain of reputation, too. He's considered virtuous. The author of the tale that follows can bear witness that the pattern is so.

CALL TO CONSTANTINOPLE

There was a time when I was set on high, above all things of perception, my mind concerned with the intelligibles only. Renown had been laid aside, as well as possessions, prospects, and eloquence. My luxury was to eschew luxury: I sweetened my life with frugal leaven. I was safe from contumely because however wise one may be, one must expect anything.

But, unexpectedly, an upright person whose name I cannot mention snatched me away and exiled me. Was it the Holy Spirit or just my sins that I might pay the penalty of eminence? There was an ostensible occasion, indeed, a synod of bishops and a congregation that was orthodox but limited as yet. Recently the congregation had been raising their gaze a little to the rays of the sun, so that some measure of confidence should be restored to true doctrine and a respite gained from the encircling evils of babbling tongues and complicated errors, before the onset of which they were defenseless. This was the manner of my coming, a godly stranger, to bloom like a fragrant rose in the midst of brambles or a single ripe grape in an unripe cluster. It was their protestations and prayers of every kind that swayed me; to have resisted them would be unduly proud.

I left the land of Cappadocia, that bastion of orthodoxy in the eyes of everyone, and arrived unequipped with any of the things I needed (lying stories to the contrary are the concoctions of enemies to furnish a crude cloak for their spite).

The rest of the story I should like you people to tell, you who can bear witness to my labors. For three years now have I said or done anything harsh, untoward, or injurious? It is true, of course, that I did show one weakness: I spared those miscreants at whose hands I endured stoning at the very outset. When subjected to the same sufferings as Christ, it seemed the more Christian thing to emulate his patience. You see, then, the sort of offering to God that is within the gift of the poor. Another matter, too, might indeed be construed as a fault. Someone has remarked that an anxious mind is a moth that gnaws the bones (Prov 14:30 [LXX]); that is something I've come to realize by experience. This frame of mine, once stalwart, has withered under anxiety and grown bent already. My strength is exhausted, and even when I put forth every effort, I am less than adequate. What a fate it is to be yoked to a friend-body that is unsound.

HIS EARLY MINISTRY

But I must return to the story I had begun. I received my call. In the midst of wolves I built up a congregation. I watered this parched flock with doctrine, and I sowed the seeds of a faith that is rooted in God. I lit the lamp of the Trinity for people hitherto in darkness; a persuasive tongue made me a potent flavor in the milk. Some I had already firmly attached to myself; others were on the point of attachment, and others still were due to come. The temper of the general body, which had been turbulent formerly, had become mild, and teaching was sweetened with charity. A little impetus, and there were prospects of complete success.

The flourishing city of Rome is well aware of this, especially, I maintain, the prominent people there, who held me in no small esteem. And so much superior to all others are such folk that to have even slight repute with them means more than primacy of honor elsewhere. May they live long! They held me in respect while I was there, and now that I am gone they

blame my opponents. It is all that they can do indeed, nor should I require them to do more. Alas, poor city, if I may indulge in tragic exclamation.

RESIGNATION

Envy, however, rent apart those gentlemen, my fellow bishops. You know the character of Thracians, a provincialism that is impervious to training. To bolster their case, they used my bodily infirmity, which had been brought on by overwork. People who had labored even a little for the Lord ought, of course, to have respected this circumstance. They should have reflected that with the world split in acrimonious dispute, the eminence of such a throne held no attraction. Under the impulse of the demon though, they avidly seized upon the pretext and sent me forth. Like ballast from an overloaded ship, I was jettisoned because my moderate sentiments proved a nuisance for the enemy. And, after all that, they presume to raise their hands in righteousness to God, to send up purifying oblations from the heart, to sanctify with mystic words the faithful, those very people who wickedly got rid of me. But I was a willing victim indeed: the shame of being associated with such hucksters of the faith would be intolerable.

Some of them are the offspring of tribute mongers, whose only concern is falsification of accounts. Some come straight from the tax booth and the sort of statutes you get there; some from the plow, with their sunburn still fresh; some again from day-long exertions with the mattock and the hoe; some have just left the galleys or the army. They are still redolent of the bilge water or exhibit the brand on their bodies; but they have blossomed into captains of the people and generals resolved not to yield an inch. Then there are those who, as yet, have not washed the soot of their fiery occupations from their persons, slave material who ought to be in the mills. In the old days, before they could scrape together a ransom for their masters, they would get little enough respite from hard labor. But now you can't hold them back, and either by persuasion or intimidation they've succeeded in filching away a section of the people. So these heaven-bound dung beetles continue their ascent; but their vehicle is no longer from the dung heap, nor are they upside down like in the old days. They think they have the power of heavenly beings themselves and keep spouting pernicious stuff, though they're unable to count their hands or their feet.

WHAT IS A BISHOP

I ask you, is not all this outrageous and unworthy of the office of a bishop? However much we are concerned about humility, let's not be so silly as to take a lowly view of that office, which is no mean thing. A bishop should be from among the best; indeed, let me say it openly, he should be the very best! It follows that he should certainly not be the very worst. Especially so, if my opinion is of any value, at this time of unbridled tongues where the most formidable cities and assemblies are in debate. If they hold steadfast, the gain is great, and if they do not, the loss is proportionately serious. Accordingly good people must be chosen. A person of average equipment will have to struggle very hard to overcome people of that ilk; honest assessment can lead to no other conclusion.

APOSTLES AS BISHOPS

But I shall be confronted, of course, by the fishermen and publicans who were evangelists. Though barren of eloquence, their simple preaching drew the universe into the net, and even the wise were caught, which makes the miracle of preaching greater still. Such a line of argument is very ready on the lips of many. My reply is brief indeed, but unmistakeable.

Let me have someone with the qualities of faith of an apostle. He is without money, without wallet, without staff, half-naked, unshod as well, living for the day, rich only in hope. He is not the sort of man to court the reputation of persuasive speaker, lest he seem to depend on that for his effect. He has no time for secular learning. Give me such a man, and I

shall swallow all deficiencies; he may be inarticulate, base, lowly, a herdsman. His character veils every failing. And if you be a man like that, I shall raise you to the choirs of angels, even though you be a fisherman of frogs. Just tell me one thing: can you exorcise devils, deliver a man from leprosy, or the dead from the tomb; does the paralytic have his limbs restored by you, or does the touch of your hand on the ailing drive out disease? It is by those means that you will persuade me to hold learning in small esteem.

But when two elements go to make up something, one commendable, the other to be deprecated, and you take account of one only, deliberately passing over the other, you are straining the similitude very reprehensibly. True, Matthew was a publican; but he was respected not in his capacity as publican, but because he was suffused by the Spirit. Peter was the head of the disciples; but he was Peter, not in his capacity as netsman, but because he was full of zeal. Even the net I can respect because of his character. From you, however, I turn away, even though you have dignified trappings, which amount to a snare and hunter's trap. You're like a painter who's capable only of reproducing the blemishes and defects of a beautiful model. Reproduce all the beauty, or leave the model alone.

Furthermore, answer me this: Can you describe as untutored the authors of writings the tiniest obscurity of which I, who have long been trained in letters, must labor to elucidate? On those writings so much study and labor have been expended that the whole world is filled with commentaries in every language, works of superior quality, fruitful, the highest flights of exegesis. If the authors had not a measure of the cultivation you are unprepared to allow them, how did they succeed in persuading kings and cities and assemblies, people who accused them, questioned them in their words, before tribunals, in crowded theaters? Their audiences were composed of wise men, lawyers, haughty Greeks, but their timely speech was persuasive; they confuted with full confidence. If only they had not been sharers of a doctrine that you would deny.

The power of the Spirit, you might retort, and you would be right. But consider the implications. Are not you a sharer in the Spirit as well; surely that is your proudest boast? When people come seeking doctrine then, why do you begrudge them? You are prepared to allow inspiration to the Spirit, and to these men the quality of being inspired that made them appear wise. But such concession is futile really. You simply get hopelessly involved in your own arguments, by making facile assertions about things that were better kept private and unspoken. Silent, indeed I know, is the spirit of the adversary, and better silence than evil speech. O Word of God, that you would loose the tongues of those who speak justice and bear down upon those who give vent to the hissings of serpents and to fratricidal venom.

WELL-FORMED, CANDID SPEAKERS

So much for your argument, which is the sort one expects from the ignorant. Let me give a brief exposition of what one must take as the real facts here. Those men *were* well trained, outstandingly so, but not in the sense of making a display. It works this way. All composition is twofold really, made up of thought and expression. Expression is like an outer garment; thought is the body that it clothes.

In some compositions, both elements are good; in others, one element or the other; or it may happen that the whole thing is bad, like its author's training. When we compose, the outer element gets little consideration but the inner one a great deal because for us salvation depends upon that inner element, the thought.

But it must of course be expressed and communicated. A stopped-up spring is not of much use or sunlight obscured by clouds, so with wisdom that is inarticulate. When a rose is sheathed by its calyx, the beauty does not appear, but when the winds dissolve the calyx and the bud is displayed, then we perceive its charm. If the beauty were always sheathed, what would become of the celebrated charms of spring?

The expression we require is simply that of straightforward speakers. If your style is otherwise,

let me discern in you the inspiration of the apostles—I should like a tincture of your enlightenment. If the doctrine set down in writing amounts to nothing, then how did I waste so much time counting in vain the sands of the sea, joining night to day in my endeavor to bring some learning to these wrinkles. If those writings are worthwhile, as indeed they are, then do not abandon to the spiders the works the good have wrought.

Your style may be pedestrian, your speech rustic; it makes no difference to me. I, too, know the lowly pathways. A frugal table often pleases me more than one decked out artificially with dainties. The same with clothes; natural beauty is so much superior to what artifice can produce. Give full rein to the thought, and I am satisfied: let those who like that sort of thing have ornament; it counts for nothing.

Don't entangle me in the language of a Sextus or a Pyrrho; deuce take Chrysippus, and let the Stagirite stay far away; don't attempt to imitate the smooth style of Plato. If you disapprove of a person's ideas, reject his ornamental style as well. Do your philosophizing in simple language, and, however untutored your style, you will satisfy me.

Provided you instruct me, then you may teach in any style you wish. Tell me what the Trinity is, how God is one but yet divided, one majesty, one nature, a unity and a trinity. What is the nature of angels, of the twofold world, how providence is righteous even though much seems unjust to the multitude? What is the principle of soul, of body, of the old and new testaments? What is this incarnation that so far transcends understanding, this mingling of disparate elements toward a single glory, the dying toward resurrection, the return to heaven? How explain the resurrection itself, the judgment: what will be the life of the just, of sinners? Tell me, if in the Spirit you have any glimmering of an explanation, what is the principle of change in the universe, of stability? A full explanation, a partial one, or a deficient one, according to the limits of your mental purification; don't deny me this. But if you are completely blind, why in your sightless state presume to guide? What a darkness besets people whose teacher is himself blind. How both are doomed to fall together into the pit of ignorance.

BISHOPS NOW

Well, that is one group. They constitute indeed a lesser evil because ignorance, though bad, is a lesser evil. What is one to say, though, when one thinks of the really evil people? Because there are such: there are certain wretched folk, miserable and abominable monsters, ambiguous with regard to their faith, whose norm is opportunity, not the law of God. In them as channels, doctrine will flow either way; they are twisted growths, flatterers of women, disseminators of seductive venom, lions among little folk, craven before the powerful. At every table they make mighty fine parasites, and the thresholds worn by them are not those of the wise but those of the powerful. What wins favor is their concern, not what does good, because they want to make their neighbor evil like themselves.

Would you like a specimen of their brand of wisdom? This one boasts about his noble birth, that one about his eloquence, another about his wealth, still another about his family. Those distinguished for nothing else get noted for their villainy. Ignorant themselves, to have succeeded in muzzling the articulate was a clever dodge. So clever of you, gentlemen. I daresay if you felt your hands or your eyes challenged, you'd see to it that we were deprived of those faculties, too.

Is not this sort of thing a manifest outrage, downright injurious, and is it to be tolerated? What a mystery really: the splendid wave of salvation from God that pervades practically the whole universe in our day, as against the very wretched bishops who constitute our lot. I am going to make a statement that is far from pleasant, but only too true. The ordinary stage, alas, is better conducted than we are, and though I blush at having to describe the state of affairs, I shall do so. The empty masks of yesterday are the actors of today, and we who are set up as masters of virtue constitute a den of thieves. Should we seem to hold our tongues, our very silence would be eloquent: "Villainy is at the helm; let no one exert him-

self, just be a villain; it's the best and shortest way." The norm is what people are wont to do. Even with the shaping of good mentors, it's difficult enough for people to get directed toward higher things. But should a man have a villainous model, as inevitably as water must flow downward, he is caught.

HASTY CHOICE

And the cause? The eagle, they say, when he sees his young in the light of the sun, can make an admirable judgment, distinguishing the legitimate from the other.[1] The latter he casts out, but becomes a father to the former. Now we, on the other hand, indiscriminately elevate to bishoprics anyone and everyone, provided only they are willing. We pay no attention to previous performance, recent or long standing; to behavior; to learning; to associations—not even the attention one needs to distinguish the rattle of a false coin.

People whose worth has not been demonstrated by the test of time or fire appear spontaneously as candidates for thrones. If he only realized that, for the most part, people elevated are worsened by power, who in his right senses would put forward a person he does not know? Considering that the control of oneself throughout the crises of life is such a great task, can you possibly entrust the fate of so many people to the chance comer, unless the idea be deliberately to wreck the whole craft? How is it that precious stones are hard to find, fertile land rare, bad horses everywhere, and good ones bred only in rich stables, but that you can find a bishop anywhere, totally untrained, but all ready-made in dignity?

EXAMPLES

What a sudden change of role is made. The business of the Lord depends upon a roll of dice, or a comic mask is suddenly thrust upon some utterly trivial and in-

---

[1] Cf. Aristotle, *On animals* 9.34: The sea eagle kills its young if they cannot be trained to stare at the sun.

significant creature, and behold we have an infant prodigy, a saint. With a beloved Saul like that among the prophets, the grace of the Spirit must indeed be considerable. You, sir, were a mime in the public theater yesterday (I leave to others the investigation of your career outside the theater); today you provide us with an extraordinary spectacle all by yourself. And you, sir, a horse lover the other day, sending clouds of dust to high heaven, instead of the prayers and pious sentiments others send. And this is the reason: some jockey fell, I dare say, or some horse got only a second, and when you got a whiff of equine air, you took leave of your senses. But you're a solid citizen these days, nothing but decorum in your mien—if you don't take a secret canter back along the old trail, that is. A branch that is being trained will revert to its original state, I rather think, once the restraint is removed.

And you, sir, were a pleader up to recently. You did good business in the courts, twisting the law this way and that. You were proficient at ruining people whom justice might have delivered because your standard for justice was the fattest fee. And now you're a judge, a Daniel all of a sudden. You, who used to dispense justice under the sign of the naked sword, making legitimist brigandry of the bench, tyrannizing most of all over the very law itself, have become all gentle now. Apparently you change your character as readily as other people [change] their clothes. The other day you went about with effeminate dancers, you performed at weddings with a chorus of Lydian girls, crooning ditties and getting high in your cups. And now you're the counselor of virgins and matrons, but your former behavior makes your virtue somewhat questionable I fear. Today's Simon Peter is the Simon Magus of yesterday; it's all too precipitate, this transformation from fox to lion.

And you, my good man, a tax official or ex-military man of some kind, do tell me how a poor man like you came to surpass in income Cyrus the Mede or Croesus or Midas? Your house is enriched by the miseries of others. You changed over to the sanctuary, got hold of the throne, and proceeded to plunder indiscriminately. You wind up by lording it over the very mysteries of God, which one should only have

the courage even to contemplate after lengthy preparatory training.

But you were transformed perhaps by the purification of baptism? Wait and see. Why should I begrudge you, the gain is all mine? Let time have its say. I'm only asking you to stipulate a reasonable period. You are cleansed today, yes, by the gift of God. But should you be careless enough to plunge into the same abyss, should the fount of previous wrongdoing continue to exist, be very sure that tears can be shed over your salvation. (Baptism is not by any means a transformation of character, nor does it purge the growths that spring from character.) Furthermore, prior to baptism one still has high expectations, but subsequent to it not even these. One God, one grace.

WHAT IS NECESSARY

Not to be evil; is that sufficient in itself? We are pleased at the obliteration of a previous impression on wax, provided a good one be substituted. You must be like Zachaeus. Be good enough to make restoration to those you have wronged. The exact amount, not a penny more, because you are really unequal to doing what the law enjoins. Give whatever sum you wish to the poor. Then you will be entertaining Christ in a worthy fashion. But to store up spoils and give but stingily to the poor, thinking yourself generous the while, amounts to simony, if I may say so without blasphemy. Would it be fair if my wounds should remain unhealed, while grace in your case has the effect of releasing you from obligations contracted through your wrongdoing? You have grace? Then keep away from what is not yours, and your purification will be complete. You may be full of grace, but if instead of divesting yourself completely, you continue to hold on to what is not yours, I shudder for the outcome. And I think it's quite clear to everyone.

You desire the state of grace. But, however high you happen to be raised by the throne, I know you to be a debtor in fact. It is our past sins, not our present ones, that are wiped out by baptism. It would be well for you to get completely purified, instead of this grotesque performance: presuming, while sullied yourself, to purify others. You're surely not going to claim you have a special privilege from God, like a special indulgence from a monarch, of commendation for the tyranny you exercise. If then, as I said, not even baptism itself will absolutely purify those in the bond of its grace (for God is never outwitted by anyone and will deal with the clever by being cleverer still), who will cleanse from postbaptismal sins? People become sullied again in the abyss of filth. They desecrate the dignity of the image from above with the forms of beasts and creeping things, for by imitation we are formed into the likeness of these. And our character, too, continues to mold us; it is a difficult task to uproot this and cast it away. There is no second purifying.

One (baptismal) birth was vouchsafed me, and at that time I was molded unto God. Perhaps, hereafter, when cleansed by the beneficial fire, I may be molded in another shaping; but in this world I know no remedy except tears. They do produce, but with difficulty, some healing for the wounds. In my view though, the scars continue to remain, as evidence of what once were gaping wounds. If someone has more confidence in the mercy of God than I do, all the better for me, but he must prove his point. It might be argued perhaps that there is a sort of purifying grace in the episcopal ministrations themselves, in public proclamation, the sort of things that, all unworthy, we promulgate. That is to attribute cleansing power to the ceremony and to the overpowering influence doubtless of the Spirit. It is the view of good and wise bishops.

I am inclined to think, however, that the likelihood of contracting defilement is greater than that of gaining further brilliance. It's easier to get involved in evil than in good. How true this is you can realize from the statement of Micah:[2] that, should consecrated meat touch any other food or drink, it will never sanctify what it touches, whereas the touch of the unholy will render what is holy common. Saint Paul, too, in the epistle to Timothy is firmly convinced of this (cf.

1 Tim 5:22). He lays down the principle that hands are not to be imposed on another lightly, nor is one to communicate in his evil ways because our own failings are burden enough for us.

If you wish though, let's grant you this baptismal purification. Who is going to guarantee your character until sufficient time has elapsed to indicate that grace has gone down to the depths, that the shining front is not only skin-deep, like one of those herbal dyes where the beauty can be washed away? Granted even that the purification be absolute. Your elevation has transformed you, yes, and I'm confronted by an angel. This, one of the faithful, who observes the laws that I do and accepts the teaching, will readily concede. A nonbeliever, however, has only one yardstick for measuring the quality of religious faith, good reputation. He may not take the slightest reckoning of his own shortcomings, but he is a stringent critic of yours. And, tell me, how can we set up in his eyes a reputation other than the one we had before? By what arguments can we stop his mouth? On my principles, this is an aspect we cannot overlook: I would have the image of the bishop a polished one from every angle, lest the faithful suffer.

IS GRACE SUFFICIENT?

But grace is stronger than reputation; even this I shall allow to pass. All stand in awe of you; not a shadow of blame falls on you; on those presumptuous premises of yours, you're second only to Elijah. You take your lofty seat, completely ignorant and unaware of considerations that cause many people concern and anxiety. I should be astonished indeed if they were of concern to you; your vanity, by which you are so easily persuaded to baseless pretensions, doesn't allow you to become aware of them.

But you're clear on this score. Very well: can you avoid, though, being master and pupil at one and the same time, whetting the whetstone, like hogs with their tusks? Your obligation is first thoroughly to learn the law and then to teach. A nice mess it all now is, however, did doctrine get reduced to this cheap level? There aren't any boxers who haven't had pre-

[2] Actually Haggai 2:12–14.

vious training and made a study in good time of contests. Do you find a track runner who hasn't exercised his legs? Did anyone in his senses ever cut pipes, shape them, and enter a contest all on the same day? Did you ever hear of a first-rate painter who did not initially experiment with several colors? Of a rhetor without experience of speeches, a doctor without experience of diseases? If the mere wish were sufficient for their possession, skills like these would be of very little value, indeed.

A bishop, however, only needs the call, and he is an expert straightway. It's a signal instance of the saying being the doing. Christ commands, and something springs into being! There's a consideration, too, that I don't want to labor. How can you presume to raise your head and aspire to the power of the throne, when you are conscious of a servant of God continuing to sit below you? You ought to tremble and cower where you sit because you may be leading a flock who are better than their shepherd.

THE GOOD SHEPHERD

Give yourself time to consider what I am here depicting: You have this man who sleeps on the ground and is all befouled with dust. He has worn his body away with keeping vigils, with psalmody, with standing night and day. He has drawn his mind away from all crassness toward the heights, there being no point, he thinks, in bringing the whole carcass to the tomb, just to provide more elaborate nourishment for the worms it shall produce and nourish when produced. He has washed away all the stains with rivers of tears and any tiny speck he retained of that mud of life that spatters even the wise. He bears the noble seal of flesh that has been worn by prayer and countless hardships, the hardships that men returned again to lowly mother earth must endure since the ancient tasting.

In cold, in hunger, and in wretched garments, he yearns to put on the clothing that is imperishable. With insufficient food he does violence to the belly's pride, each day summoning death to mind, because he has knowledge of God, the simple nourishment of the angels. Once he was a rich man, but now he is poor, for he is making life's voyage without cargo. That he decided to jettison, not to the depths, but to the poor. From cities, from the plaudits of the mob, from the whirl in which all public life is tossed, he is a fugitive. His fair soul he has molded toward God and in his absolute solitude partakes of heavenly things only. His body's beauty (and could the body of the best be other than beautiful) he has enclosed, oysterwise, in the secret adornment of iron chains. He, though completely guiltless, has put himself in bonds, for fear his freedom should ever give offense, and his wandering senses he has put in thrall within himself. To him the Spirit has disclosed the deeper meaning of Holy Writ, uncovering all that is sealed to the understanding of the multitude.

THE UNWORTHY SHEPHERD

Can you claim that such a picture describes you? No, what you have is a complete establishment, an attractive wife to be the mother of your children, property, stewards, collectors of tribute, clamor, lawsuits, anxiety, and activity everywhere. Your table groans under the most recherché artifices and menus of cooks, who titivate your appetite with the fruits of land and sea, that combine to submerge and circumscribe the spirit. Perfumes and gaity surround you and the sort of psalms that go with cymbals and foot tapping.

Or there are those who are slaves to the natural lusts. Indulgence with women makes them sleek and swollen; husbands who have anticipated the bridal bower is the kindest description of them. They may be already in dalliance with premarital loves, though their cheeks are still unadorned with the manly ornament of hair. In their first down indeed, they are immature in body, but in character still more immature. Or, at the other extreme, they are ancient of days and full of vices. And they set themselves up as leaders for children who are not of the flesh, children whom the Spirit, that is stranger to the flesh, brings forth. The passions they have themselves experienced they have learned to appreciate, and in dealing with the sins of others, they become advocates for themselves, at once allowing, and being allowed, license.

Such is the pattern. People like that might perhaps improve their conduct, but their thrones stand in the way. Folly is simply intensified by power. Meanwhile there stands your man of self-control in obscurity. He is modestly bowed, his gaze directed exclusively to God, and he chooses the role of disciple though his master of the moment (unless we make position the touchstone of authority) is not perhaps worthy to be even his disciple. To such extent has the evil one come to hold sway among us; by such clever wiles he makes his inroads whenever he has the whim to ensnare a people or a city. As well as tempting each individual, he popularizes vice by means of some fashionable custom. Gold is simply a veneer for bronze; color, chameleon fashion, is changed. We have the beard, the humble mien, the bowed head, the subdued voice, the contrived sincerity, the measured gait—everything that goes with wisdom indeed, except a wise mind.

BISHOPS' FASHIONS

Among fashionable affectations of our time the venerable ephod comes first. Then there's the linen apron of Samuel, an inconspicuous litter not fully caparisoned, headdress in virginal linen, with sackcloth to give the outward semblance of prayer. It's difficult to avoid resorting to language foreign to my style. I cannot help it, any more than I can contain my indignation. Your life of luxury or your hairstyle: one or the other, sir, you should curtail. Don't try to affect simultaneously what is native to you and what is not; the lands of the Mysians and the Phrygians are much divided, the waters of Merra and of Siloe far apart. The former are undrinkable, but when an angel moves the latter, even diseases are cured. Yours is a double sowing, an ambiguous vine. You've made your coat of two materials and are trying to stitch together what won't go together. What was compounded was forbidden under the law you realize: it was averse to duplicity. Between proper adornment for women and for men there is a distinction or between the highest reach of crows and that of eagles. Aping the great is disgrace-

ful when one is an insignificant person. It's just improper, a lesson you could well have learned from the poisons of the Pharaohs if you knew their history.

If you're anxious to be one of the wise, it's not enough just to change the rod into a serpent; you must be the great Aaron as well. I look for a complete transformation. And if you belong to the ranks of Egyptian magicians, be wholehearted in your practice of the art, if that's a good thing to do. No one is going to find fault with your expertise. However, if it's a bad thing, then stay away from it. And do spare my flock because, for your information, however cleverly you play your part, you're depriving me of my one ewe lamb. What Nathan will denounce your counterfeit style? That sober garment of yours I shall rend if I get a chance; you have resort to it occasionally for a change just as one turns to coarser fare from satiety with finer foods. You, in turn, may rend a garment of mine, could anything be fairer? That is, if you ever find me in the softer, meretricious kind. Yes, Laban must have the white garments; the stained ones are the portion of the shepherd who has labored much, who has shivered by night and been scorched by the day's heat. The most despicable trait of despicable people is the character they don, but be consistent in that character, and I'm prepared to commend you.

Does the following anecdote have relevance in this context, by the way, how about it? One can, I dare say, in the midst of serious business indulge in some playful fancy—tears are diversified by laughter. The story goes that a cat got into a bride's boudoir, and being all decked out in wedding garb, she looked like a bride. There was a fine wedding, marriage gifts, rounds of applause, great fun. However, bride though she was, when the cat saw a mouse dart on the floor she pounced on it, and instead of a wedding had supper.[3] Your counterfeit teacher is always like that; he doesn't easily change his nature.

OBJECTION ANSWERED

"But (someone objects) this man you're disparaging has an aptitude for affairs; judged either on old-fash-

---

[3] One of Aesop's fables, usually called "Venus and the Cat."

ioned methods or up-to-date maneuvers, he's a capable leader, whereas the other type of man may be saintly indeed, but he's useless to anyone but himself." Now that's a thoroughly wretched argument. No one, in fact, good, bad, or indifferent, can be confined to himself alone. Just as air will absorb foul odors or fragrance, according to what it happens to encounter, so we, too, are molded by those about us, less intensely indeed by the good, but by the wicked a very great deal. Wickedness is much more readily imitated.

Now if our bishop happens to be a thorough scoundrel, we have an instance of the rod controlling the trees, whereas if he's a man of high quality, once more great Israel, guided by the pillar of fire, makes its way toward the land of promise that everyone is seeking. The good bishop may not go about much or be continually in the agora or be a veritable Proteus when it comes to adapting himself. He may not be a real Melampus, indeed, or any other model of versatility you like, in the ease of his adjustment to circumstances, whatever the sudden crisis happens to be. Can you reasonably describe as useless someone whose example is capable of improving us? Or describe as a good and efficient bishop someone whose example leads you to contempt for the men I praise? With really discerning people, the overly impressive person does not find favor: what counts is genuine sincerity. However, you must have your model, and I mine. Now in the case of painting, do you regard as master, not people like Zeuxis, Polycleitus, or Euphranor who depict living figures with simple colors, but someone who uses florid and variegated hues to produce forms without vitality? Callimachus and Calais were like that I think, in their labored attempts to give us images of images. So indeed is every flamboyant performer.

It is because of the standards you adopt that you have grown tired looking for a bishop. But your efforts have been so puny that I blush for them. You've been considering a bishop as you would an accountant, laying stress on mere rubbish, where I've been concerned with important issues. A priest should have one function and one only: the sanctification of souls by his life and teaching. He should raise them toward the heights by heavenly impulses. He should be serene, high-minded, reflecting like a mirror the godly

and unspotted images that he has inside. For his flock he should send up holy offerings, until the day when he, too, shall perfect them into an offering. Other matters he should relinquish to those skilled in them. It is on such terms that our lives could become secure.

To be sure, you lay great stress on fearless speech, and for me, too, this is no small matter, provided that reason and common sense be observed. In actual fact the truth is this: a wise man's silence is more effective than all your eloquence because in your case, boldness is substituted for courage, whereas, in his, native restraint makes for fewer words. However, should an occasion arise for really fearless speech, you will see the mild man transformed into a warrior, and you will realize what a champion he can be. When your puny human efforts, weighted by the burden of a guilty conscience, meet with rejection while his blameless life wins him ready acceptance, you will understand the distinction between a monkey's scream and a lion's roar. A man's character is the most persuasive thing of all.

Consequently, even in this domain, your paragon comes off second best. True, he occupies a prominent public position: he is regaled at tables not his own; he regards everyone else as parvenu in the very measure that he himself merits contempt. The big city is the one and only thing he can crow about, and that's the very place will bring you to a bad end because miscreants are multiplied there. Whenever did a city ass seek to be of more consequence than a country one? To be sure, he lives in the city, but he is what he is.

What a senseless mess: we might as well have everything definitely arranged to suit the scoundrels and ruination appointed for the decent people! Because when the course is smooth for the wicked while the blameless encounter trouble, a wise man has his wisdom taxed severely. In such a general chaos, with all values topsy-turvy, the best policy is to alter course, find security for one's brief allotment of days, and arrange a serene closure for old age.

CONCLUSION

Accordingly, you may have your thrones and your dominions, if these be the values that hold first place for you. I bid you farewell, you may go on hurling invectives, parceling out patriarchies. Let the whole universe give way before you, and one incumbency be exchanged for another, one man ejected and another elevated, if you enjoy that sort of thing. On with the show. As for me, I propose to withdraw to God. It is for him I live and breathe, to him alone that I turn my gaze. Before I was born, my mother promised me to him, and to him dangers and a fair vision in the night have united me. To him I shall offer in sacrifice the pure motions of the mind, conversing with him, person to person, in so far as one can attain that state.

Such then, on behalf of decent people, is my message for the miscreants. Should anyone take offense at my remarks, they will have found their target. For you, my friends, my message will be delivered in a better place. At the moment, I offer you a brief valediction, brief indeed, but from which you can profit. Please accept it in the spirit in which people receive their father's final words, advice worth remembering.

The words sink all the deeper into memory because after them, one hears no more at all.

Should you, my friends, find another Gregory, be kinder to him. Should you not, it only remains for you to be upright in dealings with your colleagues and yourselves because your agreement has been proportionate only to the sway of the same ambitions among you. Cling always to the peace for which I strove and lay aside those private failings by which the whole world is miserably confused. I shall, for my part, overlook the treatment I received. Who knows, perhaps I am wiser than others; perhaps my great age makes me irritable and morose; perhaps when a man is drunk all by himself, all the sober ones seem drunk to him? Pass laws as you please, but be mindful of all I endured because my friends are what they are. My good sense indeed proved very helpful, and my great age provided the way out of troubles. When all this conflict which brings envy in its train is over, perhaps some friendly spirit will bring about a peace.

19. Aphrahat: Demonstration 10: On Pastors

The Syriac author known as Aphrahat wrote twenty-three "demonstrations" of Christian faith for a non-Roman, Persian Christian audience between 337 and 345 (which would mean he probably survived the persecution of Shapur II; see Chapter 14). The *Demonstrations* treat various aspects of Christian piety and belief, and many express direct conflict (whether actual or imagined) with the criticisms of Persian Jews. Aphrahat seems to have been a member of the *bnay qyama,* the established ascetics of Syrian churches (see Text 41, his demonstration on the *qyama;* they are also addressed directly at the end of this *Demonstration*). His writing is highly influenced by Syriac lyricism and scriptural imagery (like his fellow Syrian, Ephraim), but we should not conclude from this that he was a simplistic or uninspired thinker. His writings give us insight into the spiritual development of non-Roman Christian churches.

Aphrahat's demonstration "On Pastors," reproduced here, focuses on the spiritual qualities of Christian leadership, taking numerous scriptural exemplars of shepherding and pastoral care. It is care for the "sheep" (the Christian community) that characterizes the real Christian leader, just as it characterizes the "Great Pastor," Jesus Christ.

From *Aphrahat Demonstrations I,* trans. Kuriakose Valavanolickal. Kerala, India: HIRS Publications, 1999. Used with permission.

(1) The pastors takes their place at the head of the flock and give the sheep the food of life. Whoever keeps vigil and takes trouble on behalf of his sheep is concerned for his flock, and he is the disciple of our Good Shepherd, who gave himself for his sheep (John 10:13). But he who does not lead his flock well is like the hireling who has no concern for the sheep. O pastors, imitate those former upright pastors.

Jacob fed, guarded, toiled and kept watch over the sheep of Laban, and he received a reward. For Jacob said to Laban, "Behold I have been twenty years with you. I have not taken advantage of your sheep and your flock, I have not eaten the males of your flock; I have not brought any broken to you, so that you might make exaction for it from my hands. The parching heat devoured me in the day and the cold in the night; my sleep departed from my eyes" (Gen 31:38–40). Look, you pastors, how this pastor was concerned for his flock. He was awake at night to guard (them) and he kept vigil; he labored in the day to feed (them).

Jacob was a pastor, Joseph was a pastor, his brothers were pastors, Moses was a pastor, David was also a pastor, and Amos was a pastor. All these were pastors who fed the sheep and led (them) well.

(2) But why, my beloved, did these pastors first shepherd the sheep and (only) then were chosen to feed the people?—if not so that, they should learn how a shepherd cares for his sheep, watches and toils on behalf of his sheep. Once they had learned the practices of pastors, they were chosen for leadership.

Jacob shepherded the sheep of Laban, he toiled, watched, and led (them) well (Gen 31:38–41). Then he shepherded and led well his sons and taught them the manner of shepherding.

Joseph together with his brothers shepherded the sheep (Gen 37:2), and he was a leader for a numerous people in Egypt. He led them as does a good shepherd with his flock.

Moses fed the sheep of his father-in-law Jethro (Exod 3:1). He was chosen from the flock to shepherd his people, and he led them as a good shepherd. Moses took his staff on his shoulder and went at the head of the people whom he was leading and shepherding for forty years. He watched and toiled for his flock (as) a diligent and good shepherd. When his Lord wished to blot them out on account of their sins, because they worshiped the calf, Moses prayed and sought of his Lord, saying, "Either forgive the people their sins or blot me out from your book, which you have written" (Exod 32:32). This is the diligent pastor, who handed himself over on behalf of his sheep. This is the brilliant leader who gave himself for his people. This is the merciful father who hovered over his children and brought them up.

Moses, the great and wise pastor who knew how to lead the flock, taught Joshua, the son of Nun, a man of the spirit who led the flock, the whole camp of Israel. He destroyed kings, conquered the land, and gave the land to them as a feeding place; he distributed a cote and fold to his sheep.

Again David fed the sheep of his father (1 Sam 16:11), and he was taken from the flock to lead his people: "He led them according to the integrity of his heart and according to the skillfulness of his hands" (Ps 78:72). When David counted the flock of his sheep, the (divine) anger came against them, and they began to be brought to destruction. Then David handed himself over on behalf of his sheep, praying and saying, "Lord, God I have sinned, in that I have counted Israel. Let your hand be against me and against the house of my father. These innocent sheep, what have they sinned?" (2 Sam 24:17). So also all the diligent pastors gave themselves up on behalf of their sheep.

(3) But those pastors who have not cared about the sheep, these are hired servants who fed themselves alone. On account of this, the prophet proclaimed to them, saying to them, "O you pastors, who destroy and disperse the sheep of my flock. Hear the word of the Lord. Thus says the Lord, Behold, I care for my sheep as a shepherd cares for his flock on the day of violent rain with wind. I will demand my sheep from your hands. O you foolish pastors, you clothe yourselves with the wool of the sheep, and you devour the flesh of the fatlings, yet you do not feed the sheep, you have not healed the one that was sick, you have not bound up the one that was broken, you have not strengthened the one that was weak, you have not gathered in the one that was lost and scattered. You

have not kept the strong ones and the fatlings, but you subdued them with violence. You yourselves graze the good pasture, and you trample with your feet what is left over. You drink the pleasant water, and you muddy with your feet what is left over. My sheep have fed on that which is trampled, what your feet have trampled, and they have drunk the water that your feet have muddied" (Ezek 34:2–4, 9–12, 18–19).

These are the greedy and wretched pastors, the hired servants who did not feed the sheep or lead (them) well. They did not rescue them from the wolves. But when the Great Pastor comes, the chief of the pastors, he calls and inspects his sheep, and he commands his flock, he will bring those pastors and make an account with them, and condemn them according to their deeds. But the Chief Pastor will cause those who have fed the sheep well to rejoice, and he will make them inherit life and rest. "O stupid and foolish pastor, on your right hand and for your right eye I have left my sheep because you have said about the sheep, that which dies, let it die; that which perishes, let it perish; whatever is left, let it eat the flesh of the others. Behold on account of this I will put out your right eye, and I will wither up your right arm. Your eye that looked on the bribe shall become blind. Your hand that has not led in justice shall be destroyed" (Zech 11:9, 17). "As for you, my sheep, you, the people, are the sheep of my pasture, and I am the Lord your God" (Ezek 34:31). "Behold, henceforward, I will feed you on a good and fertile pasture" (Ezek 34:14).

(4) "The Good Shepherd gives himself for the sake of his sheep" (John 10:11). Again he said, "I have other sheep, and it is proper for me to bring them also hither. The whole (flock of) sheep shall become one, with one shepherd; on account of this my Father loves me, because I give myself over for the sake of the sheep" (John 10:16–17). He said again, "I am the door of the sheep. Every one enters through me shall live, and he will come in, and go out, and will find pasture" (John 10:9). O you pastors, you should be like this diligent pastor, the head of the whole flock, who cares so much for his flock: He brought near the distant, brought back the strayed,

visited the sick, strengthened the weak, bound up the broken, and kept the fatlings (Ezek 34:2–4). He handed over himself for the sake of the sheep. He chose and taught the brilliant pastors and delivered the sheep into their hands and gave them power over all his flock. Indeed he said to Simon Peter, "Feed my sheep, my lambs and my ewes for me" (John 21: 15–17). Simon fed his sheep; when his time was fulfilled, he handed over the flock to you and he went away. You also should feed (them) and lead (them) well. For a pastor who takes care of his sheep has no other occupation together with it: he neither sets up a vineyard nor plants gardens; nor does he fall also into the difficulties of this world. We have never seen a pastor who left his sheep in the field and became a merchant or who became a farmer and caused his flock to wander. If he leaves his flock and does these things, (then) he has handed over his flock to wolves.

(5) Remember, my beloved, what I have written to you about our forefathers who learned first the customs of the sheep, and they received from it the testing of diligence. And (only then) were they chosen for leadership so that they should learn and observe how a shepherd cares for his flock. As they led the sheep carefully, so also they would be perfected in this leadership.

For, Joseph was chosen from the sheep so that he might lead the Egyptians in a time of distress (Gen 37:2).

Moses was chosen from the sheep so that he might lead his people and feed them (Exod 3:1).

David was taken from following the sheep so that he might become the king over Israel (1 Sam 16:11).

The Lord carried away Amos from following the sheep, and he made him prophet over his people (Amos 1:1, 7:14).

Elisha also was taken from following the yoke so that he might become a prophet in Israel (1 Kings 19:19).

Moses neither returned to his sheep nor did he leave his flock which had been delivered to him.

David did not return to the sheep of his father, but he led his people in the innocence of his heart (Ps 78:72).

Amos did not return to feed the sheep or to collect wood, but he took the office of the prophet and fulfilled it.

Elisha did not return to his yoke but served Elijah and filled his place.

But in the case of a deputy pastor, who loves farmsteads, merchandise, vineyards, olive trees, and cultivation, he does not wish to become a disciple, and (so) he (Christ) did not deliver into his hands the flock.

(6) I beseech you, pastors, that you should not be over the flock as foolish and stupid pastors or be greedy and lovers of possessions. Everyone who feeds the sheep may eat of its milk (1 Cor 9:7). Everyone who guides the yoke may make use of his labor. It is right for the priests to take a share from the altar and that the Levites should receive their tithes. Whoever eats from the milk, let his heart be upon the flock. He who makes use of the labor of his yoke, let him be diligent in his cultivation. The priests who share from the altar should serve the altar with honor. And the Levites who receive the tithes should have no share in Israel. Oh pastors, the disciples of our Chief Pastor, you should not be like hired servants, for the hired servant does not care for the sheep (John 10:13). You should be like our Kind Pastor whose life was not more beloved to him than his sheep. Bring up the young, exalt the virgins, love the lambs, let them grow up in your bosoms, so that when you go to the Chief Priest, you may offer to him all your sheep in full, and he may give to what he promised: "Where I am you also shall be" (John 12:26). But these few matters are sufficient for good pastors and leaders.

(7) However, I have written above to remind you, my beloved, of the manners of life that are suitable to the whole flock. In this sermon I have written to you about the pastors, the leaders of the flock. These memoirs I have written to you, my beloved, as you asked me in your beloved letter.

(8) The steward has brought me into the treasury of the King and shown me the many blessed things there. When I saw them, my mind was captivated by the great treasure. When I looked at it, it dazzled the eyes and captivated the thoughts and distracted the mind with many colors. Whoever takes from it will grow rich and make rich. It is open and permitted before all who seek it. When many take from it, it does not decrease in anything at all. When they give from that which they have taken, their own is greatly multiplied. Those who receive freely, let them give freely as they have received (Matt 10:8). For it is not bought for a price because there is nothing that is comparable to it. For the treasure does not diminish, nor do those who take it ever get sated. They drink, but they thirst (for more); they eat, but they hunger (for more). Whoever is not thirsty cannot drink. Whoever is not hungry cannot eat. The hunger for it satisfies many. And from the thirst of it proceeds (many) springs. For the man who comes near to the fear of God is like the man who is thirsty and approaches the spring, drinks, and is satisfied. The spring is not diminished at all. The land that is in need of water to drink, drinks from the spring, and its water is not dried up. When the land drinks, it again has need to drink, but the spring is not diminished from its flow. The knowledge of God is likewise; when all people receive from it, no loss occurs in it, nor is it brought to an end by sons of flesh. He who takes from it cannot take (all of it), but when he gives (of it), he lacks nothing. When you take fire with a lamp from a flame and you light many lamps by it, the fire does not diminish when you take from it, nor does the lamp wane when it lights many. One single man cannot take the whole treasure of the king, nor does the water fail when a thirsty person drinks from the spring. Nor when someone stands on a high mountain (can) his eye perceive (both) the near and the distant. Nor when he stands and counts the stars of heaven, can he limit the powers of heaven. When someone comes near to the fear of God, he cannot bear the whole of it. Even if he takes a great deal, it is not perceived that it is diminished (at all). When someone gives from that which he has taken, it is not finished up for him or arrived at its end.

Remember, my beloved, what I have written to you in the first sermon about Faith, that whoever has freely received, it is proper for him to give freely as he has received (Matt 10:8), as our Lord said, "You have received freely so give freely" (Matt 10:8). For whoever withholds from that which he has taken (Matt 25:29), even that which he has received will be taken away from him. On this account, my beloved, in as much as I was able to take at this time from that treasure that does not fail, I have sent to you from it. Although I have sent (it) to you, the whole of it remains with me. For the treasure does not diminish, for it is the wisdom of God. The steward is our Lord Jesus Christ as he witnessed and said, "Everything is handed over to me by my Father" (Matt 11:27). When he is the steward of wisdom, he is the wisdom, as again the Apostle said, "Christ is the power of God and his wisdom" (1 Cor 1:24). This wisdom is divided up among many, but it lacks nothing, as I have instructed you above. For the prophets received from the spirit of Christ, but Christ was not diminished in anything.

(9) Ten discourses, I have written to you, my beloved; on what you have asked me, I have explained to you without you. (Also) that which you have not sought from me I have given to you. I have asked your name, and I have written to you. I have asked myself your question, and I have replied to you as that which I can for your knowledge. These things that which I wrote to you, meditate on them at all times and labor to read the books that are read in the Church of God. These ten small books that I have written to you, take one from another and build up one with another; do not separate them from one another. I have written to you from *aleph* until *yod,*[1] one letter after another. Read and learn, you, the brethren, the *bnay qyama* and the members of our faith, those from whom mockery is far off, as I have written to you above. Remember that which I have indicated to you, that I have not brought these discourses up to the end, but (only) so much yet of the whole. These are not enough, but hear these things from me without dispute and discuss about them with our brethren, who are of the same conviction. Everything that you hear that builds up, accept; everything that builds up other doctrines, pull down and utterly destroy. For dispute cannot build up. But I, my beloved, as a stonecutter have brought along the stones for the building; let the wise master-builders carve them and place them in the building. All those workers who toil in the building will receive a wage from the Lord of the house.

The end of the Demonstration on Pastors.

---

[1] That is, "one" to "ten."

CHAPTER 7

Heresy and Orthodoxy

Although the distinction of correct from incorrect belief and practice is found in the earliest Christian literature, it took some time for the ideal of orthodoxy ("right belief" that has been transmitted from Jesus through the apostles to the present-day church) versus heresy (deliberate subversion of that one true belief) to become normative among ancient Christians. In the second century, the philosophical term *hairesis* (a "school of thought," from the Greek word for choice) was being used to describe Christian groups that (it was claimed) had maliciously deviated from a single norm. Most of the surviving literature from the second and third centuries comes from the "proto-orthodox," that is, those Christians who would eventually achieve theological and ecclesiastical dominance in the fourth and fifth centuries. (The discovery of the Nag Hammadi texts in Egypt in 1945 provided an invaluable collection of writings from the non-proto-orthodox side.) The ferocity and frequency with which these proto-orthodox writers compiled their heresiologies (writings about or against heretics) suggests, however, a state of plurality in the early Christian world that argues against a single, unified Church in continuous existence from the time of Jesus onward. These early heresiologists were not so much defending their pristine Truth from the onslaught of corrupting elements as constructing an entirely new notion of "right thinking" that demanded absolute and total uniformity of belief and practice.

The conversion of Constantine and his subsequent patronage of Christianity added new institutional force to this call for uniformity. Constantine found Christianity rife with division: North African and Italian Christians were divided by beliefs over the nature of the Church, while Christians in Egypt were divided by debates over the nature of God. Theological opponents depicted heretics as demonic and insane, absolutely opposed to and exterior to the true Church. Scriptural interpretation and disputation became a cornerstone of orthodox controversy. In addition, intricate philosophical concepts were applied with increasing frequency to theological categories. Invective, exegesis, and philosophy had energized orthodox controversy in earlier centuries, but now they were employed with a new vigor to attract the patronage of the emperor. As Christianity became increasingly embedded in society, the language of orthodoxy and heresy was deployed across the social spectrum. Christians rioted, rebelled, and rose up in the name of orthodoxy, and violence erupted over accusations of heresy.

We must resist the temptation to assume that a single, continuous line of theological and ecclesiastical opinion—orthodoxy—stood its ground and battled for supremacy in Late Antiquity. When we examine a debate over orthodox truth and heretical falsehood, we are witnessing Christianity struggling to come to terms with a variety of possibilities and truths concerning God, Christ, human nature, religious and political difference, and the mechanics of salvation. We have included in this chapter, therefore, both writings against heresy and writings that productively construct orthodox positions, with the understanding that they were all part of the same effort by late antique Christians to arrive at a uniform, normative system of truth. The topics of orthodox/heretical debate presented here are standard (Trinity, Christology, human salvation, the church, and "judaizers"), but they by no means exhaust the field of debate. They are given to provide a sense of the diversity of opinion and strategies that Christians used as they moved from earlier anxiety over difference to implacable insistence on the enforcement of truth and unity.

FOR FURTHER READING

Bauer, Walter. *Orthodoxy and Heresy in Earliest Christianity,* ed. Robert Kraft and Gerhard Krodel, trans. Robert Kraft et al. Philadelphia: Fortress Press, 1971.

Evans, Robert. *Pelagius: Inquiries and Reappraisals.* New York: Seabury, 1968.

Frend, W. H. C. *The Donatist Church in North Africa: A Movement of Protest in Roman North Africa.* Oxford, England: Clarendon Press, 1952.

Gregg, Robert, and Groh, Denis. *Early Arianism: A View of Salvation.* Philadelphia: Fortress Press, 1971.

Hanson, R. P. C. *The Search for the Christian Doctrine of God: The Arian Controversy, 318–381.* Edinburgh: T. & T. Clark, 1988.

Jones, A. H. M. *Were Ancient Heresies Disguised Social Movements?* Philadelphia: Fortress Press, 1966.

Klijn, A. F. J., and Reinink, G. J. *Patristic Evidence for Jewish-Christian Sects.* Leiden, the Netherlands: Brill, 1973.

Tilley, Maureen. *The Bible in Christian North Africa: The Donatist World.* Philadelphia: Fortress Press, 1997.

Wiles, Maurice. *Archetypal Heresy: Arianism Through the Centuries.* Oxford, England: Clarendon, 1996.

Trinitarian Controversy: The Texts

Already Christians in the second and third centuries had debated the paradoxical assertions of a single Godhead comprising three Persons (Father, Son, and Holy Spirit). Some Trinitarian propositions were rejected and labeled as heretical, such as the idea that the three persons of the Trinity were facets or activities of a single, coherent Godhead ("modalism"). By the fourth century, intense philosophical speculation and scriptural interpretation added layers of complexity and ferocity to these contests for orthodoxy.

Speculation on the nature of the three-in-one Godhead was intimately connected to Christian doctrines of salvation (soteriology). Understanding the mechanics, or economy, of human salvation necessitated understanding how the perfect Creator could connect to and redeem his imperfect creation. The Alexandrian priest Arius, who gave his name to the century of debate over the Trinity, was concerned precisely with this question of salvation. He proposed a graduated hierarchy of the Godhead, by which the Son and Holy Spirit were inferior or subordinate to God the Father while constituting with him a single Godhead. For Arius, this stratified understanding of the Trinity provided a model of connection between creation and Creator (see Texts 20 and 22). Arius's soteriological solution to the problem of the triune God was rejected, however, by Alexandrian theologians (such as his bishop, Alexander) who were anxious to preserve the total divinity of Christ and the absolute equality of all persons of the Trinity.

The course of debate following Arius's confrontation with Alexander (see Text 21) set a pattern for future theological controversy as debate devolved into name-calling and fierce rhetorical condemnation. Arius was depicted as the leader of a deviant party of heretics, "Arians" (or, as Alexander's successor Athanasius called them, "Ariomaniacs"), the latest in a diabolical genealogy of subversive teachers bent on infecting all good Christians with their madness. Imperial authority intervened at the Council of Nicaea (see Text 33), during which Arius's opponents formulated a creed emphasizing the equality and distinctiveness of the three persons of the Trinity.

The Council of Nicaea, however, did not resolve debate so much as it hardened the lines of theological warfare. The terminological precision the bishops attempted to secure through such phrases as "of one substance" (*homoousion*) and "begotten not made" often led to more controversy. Emperors throughout the fourth century, with the obvious exception of Julian the Apostate, vacillated between support of Nicaea and various non-Nicene theologies as partisans and opponents of Nicaea produced theological treatises that leveled ferocious attacks on their "heretical" enemies. Despite the complexity of the arguments involved, the Trinitarian debates demonstrate how deeply the division between orthodoxy and heresy penetrated into society. Gregory of Nyssa remarked: "If you inquire at the moneychanger's, he philosophizes about the Begotten and the Unbegotten; if you ask about the price of bread, you get the answer: 'The Father is greater and the Son is subordinate'; if you remark, 'This bath is pleasant,' it is declared, 'The Son came into being out of nothing!'" The impact of heretical discourse on the streets, as well as among elites, was another enduring pattern laid down by the Trinitarian controversies.

The Nicene partisans secured a final victory through heresiological rhetoric and the support of the Emperor Theodosius I at the Council of Constantinople (see Chapter 8). The stage had been set, however, for continuing theological debate to be conducted within the absolute and totalizing discourses of orthodoxy and heresy.

20. Arius: Thalia

Arius (ca. 260–336) was a popular teacher and theologian who was raised to the priesthood around 312 in Alexandria. Alexandria had long been home to philosophical and theological speculation, from such figures as Clement (ca. 160–215) and Origen (ca. 185–ca. 251). We should not, therefore, imagine Arius as a renegade priest, willfully flouting orthodox theology to spread subversive ideas about the Trinity. Arius articulated the relation between divinity and humanity according to philosophical categories, while still providing a meaningful description of the workings of salvation. The Son, Arius taught, was appointed by God to demonstrate how human beings might approach a divine essence that must remain incomprehensible to the created order. Arius viewed salvation as the union of two absolutely dissimilar essences—the divine and the human—and the Son, by nature distinct from God but still truly God through the will of God the Father, was the model of that union.

The *Thalia* (literally, "festivity") was circulated by Arius and his supporters after his break with Bishop Alexander of Alexandria (around 319). The use of verse (perhaps even set to music) to promote a theological stance suggests that debates over divinity, humanity, and salvation were not restricted to philosophically trained clergy, but were also conducted "on the ground" among deeply invested laypeople. The *Thalia* does not survive intact; the following extracts have been pulled from the rebuttal of Arius's later theological opponent, Alexander's successor Athanasius.

In accordance with the faith of the elect of God, God's sage servants,
holy and orthodox, who had received God's holy Spirit,
I learned these things from participants in wisdom,
skillful, taught by God in every way and wise.
In their steps came I, stepping with the same opinions,

the notorious, the one who suffered much for God's glory;
having learned from God I myself know wisdom and knowledge.

God then himself is in essence ineffable to all.
He alone has neither equal nor like, none comparable in glory;

From *A New Eusebius: Documents Illustrating the History of the Church to AD 337,* trans. Stuart Hall, ed. J. Stevenson, rev. ed. W. H. C. Frend. London: SPCK, 1987. Used with permission.

We call him Unbegotten because of the one in nature
begotten;
We raise hymns to him as Unbegun because of him
who has beginning.
We adore him as eternal because of the one born in
time.

The Unbegun appointed the Son to be Beginning of
things begotten,
and bore him as his own Son, in this case giving birth.
He has nothing proper to God in his essential property,
for neither is he equal nor yet consubstantial with him.

Wise is God, since he himself is Wisdom's teacher.
There is proof enough that God is invisible to all,
and to those through the Son and to the Son himself
the same (God) is invisible.
I will say exactly how the Invisible is seen by the Son:
By the power by which (a) God can see, and in proper
measures,
the Son sustains the vision of the Father as is right.

Or rather there is a Trinity with glories not alike;
Their existences are unmixable with each other;
One is more glorious than another by an infinity of
glories.

The Father is essentially foreign to the Son because he
exists unbegun.
Understand then that the Unity was, but the Duality
was not, before he existed.
So straight away when there is no Son, the Father is
God.

Thus the Son who was not, but existed at the paternal
will,
is only-begotten God, and he is distinct from
everything else.
Wisdom existed as wisdom by the will of a wise God.

He is conceived by so many million concepts,
as spirit . . . , power, wisdom,
glory of God, truth and image and word.
Understand that he is conceived also as effulgence and
light.
One equal to the Son the Supreme is able to beget,
but more excellent, superior or greater he cannot.
How old and how great the Son is by God's will—
since when, and from what point, even since then he
existed from God.
For being a mighty God he hymns the Supreme in
part.

To sum up, God exists ineffable to the Son,
for he is to himself what he is, that is, unutterable,
so that none of the things said . . . will the Son
know how to express comprehensively; for it is
impossible for him
to explore the Father who exists by himself.
For the Son himself does not know his own essence;
for being Son he truly came to be at his Father's
will.
What logic then permits the one who is from a Father
to know by comprehension the one who begot him?
For clearly for what has a beginning to encompass
by thought or apprehension the one who is unbegun,
is impossible.

21. Alexander of Alexandria: Letter to Alexander of Constantinople

Alexander (bishop of Alexandria, 312–28) presided over a fractured Egyptian church. In addition to combatting the rigorist positions of Melitius, a schismatic bishop of Lycopolis, he found himself embroiled in a controversy over the nature of the Trinity with the popular priest and teacher named Arius (see Texts 20 and 22). The conflict between Alexander and Arius (outlined in the letter reproduced here to his fellow bishop in Constantinople) quickly

From *Kirchengeschichte Theodoretus,* ed. Léon Parmentier and Günter Christian Hansen. Berlin: Akademie Verlag, 1998. (Translated by Andrew S. Jacobs.)

spread beyond the provincial boundaries of Egypt as both sides gained support for their ecclesiastical positions.

Alexander's letter sets the tone for much of the ensuing theological debate of the fourth century: instead of engaging Arius's interest in a meaningful theory of salvation, Alexander emphasizes the need to articulate the metaphysical relationship between God the Father and Son, between the Creator and the created order. We see the debate becoming a full-blown controversy over the Trinity. In addition, we get a clear sense of how heresiological debates progressed. As important as his doctrincal emphases is Alexander's method of painting his opponents (primarily Arius) as devious and deranged; they are divisive, mischievous, deceitful, "Jewish" (see Judaizing Heresies), insane, and embedded in a chain of heretical predecessors (Ebion, Artemas, Paul of Samosata), all drawing their venom from the devil. Alexander also, though, takes time to promote a sophisticated and scripturally justified Trinitarian theology, using the language of being (ōn) and subsistence or entity (hypostasis). This combination of constructive theology and zealous attack would become the standard format of Alexander's equally fervent successor, Athanasius.

To my most honored brother and soul mate Alexander; I, Alexander, greet you in the Lord.

(1) The ambitious and greedy plot of scoundrels has been hatched against those provinces that have always seemed more important, through various pretexts inflicted by certain people on ecclesiastical piety. Driven mad by the devil operating within them, galloping away from all reverence into whatever desire happens to grip them, they trample the fear of God's judgment. (2) I found it necessary in my suffering to clarify these matters to Your Reverence, so that you may guard against these people, lest some of them should dare even to set foot in your provinces, either on their own (for these swindlers are handy at perpetrating fraud) or through letters ingeniously forged, capable of hoodwinking someone who has offered himself in simple and undiluted faith.

(3) For Arius and Achillas recently joined together in a conspiracy, and they rivaled the ambition of Collouthos—although they're much worse. Collouthos found a pretext for his own miserable choices by leveling charge against Arius and Achilles, but they, in turn, having observed the way Collouthos "marketed Christ" (cf. *Didache* 12.5), could no longer bear to remain under the control of the church. Instead they have established their own robbers' dens (cf. Matt 21:23, Jer 7:11), in which they hold interminable meetings and where night and day they devise slanders against Christ and against us. (4) Speaking against every pious and apostolic opinion, they have cobbled together a Christ-fighting gang in a Jewish fashion: they deny the divinity of our Savior and proclaim that he is equal to all humans. By selecting all the verses about the humility of his saving dispensation for our sake (cf. Phil 2:8), they attempt to assemble the preaching of their own impiety. They shy away from those passages about his original divinity and his indescribable glory alongside the Father. (5) Since they affirm the impious doctrine of the Greeks and the Jews concerning Christ, they pursue their praise in particular, undertaking all those things for which we are mocked by them, inciting battles and harassment against us every day. They forge lawsuits using the petitions of brazen women whom they have duped, even as they draw ridicule on Christianity when their young women sashay down every street without dignity (cf. 1 Tim 5:11–13, Acts 13:50). What's more, Christ's undivided cloak, which the executioners did not even wish to divvy up (cf. John 19:23–25), they have dared to rip apart. (6) When we came to understand, though long unaware, the character of their life and their unholy sophistry, we drove them out by the unanimous vote of those churches venerating Christ's divinity.

(7) Using their meanderings, they have manipulated sympathetic ministers into turning away from

us. They claim to discuss under the cloak of peace and unity, but in reality they are hastening to draw some of them into the same disease through pretty speeches. They also request very wordy letters from them so that, when they read them to those whom they have already deceived, they may establish themselves as entirely unrepentant before those whom they have tripped up, utterly inflamed with impiety, claiming that they have bishops who are of the same mind and opinion. (8) They did not confess what they taught and did so vilely in our presence—these things for which they were even expelled! But they either pass them on in silence, or they mislead through the shades of figurative and fantastic speech. (9) By concealing the destructiveness of their own teaching with more persuasive and base language, they snatch a fellow into deception. They don't refrain from misrepresenting our own piety to everyone, and for this reason it even happens that some people, signing on to their letters, have received them into their churches. Now, as I see it, a great slander has been committed by those fellow ministers who have dared not to yield to this apostolic rule, but instead inflame this devilish activity on their behalf against Christ.

(10) Because of these matters and without delay, beloved, I have roused myself to show you the faithlessness of those who say that there was a time when the Son of God did not exist and that the one who did not exist previously came to be later, and when this one came to exist, even then he came into existence just as every human has come into existence. (11) "For," they say, "God made all things out of nothing," including in this creation all things rational and irrational, even the Son of God. Consequently, they say also that he is of a mutable nature, capable of virtue and of evil. And by supposing that he came out of nothing, they utterly abolish the sacred writings about his eternal being, which indicate the immutability of the Word and the divinity of the wisdom of the Word, which is Christ (cf. 1 Cor 1:24). These wretches say: "So we can also become Sons of God, just like he did," (12) because it is written, "I have begotten and exalted them" (Isa 1:2). But when the next part of this passage is pointed out to them—"and they have broken my faith"—which is not innate to the

Savior, who is by nature immutable, they desert all reverence and say that God, knowing through foresight and foreknowledge that he would not break faith, singled him out from all the others. (13) For not by nature and not because he had some trait that the other sons did not (for they say he is not the Son of God by nature or by any distinctive trait of his own), but even though he happened to be mutable by nature, he was singled out for his diligent ways and his discipline (askēsis), which did not worsen. (14) Just so if Paul and Peter exhibited such force, their sonship would be no different from his. To lay out this deranged teaching, they abuse the Scriptures and set out the passage from the Psalms concerning Christ that goes like this: "You loved righteousness and you hated injustice: on this account God anointed you, your God, with the oil of exultation among your fellows" (Ps 45:7, Heb 1:9).

(15) That the Son of God did not come into existence out of nothing and that there was no time when he did not exist, the evangelist John suffices to instruct us, writing in this manner about him: "The only-begotten Son, who was in the bosom of his Father" (John 1:18). The divine teacher, planning ahead to show that the two matters, the Father and the Son, are indivisible from each other specifies that he is in the bosom of the Father. (16) But the Word of God is not counted among those that came into being out of nothing, since the same John says that all things came into existence through him. For John demonstrates that the Word has its own particular subsistence (hypostasis) when he says, "In the beginning was the Word and the Word was with God and the Word was God. All things came to be through him, and apart from him not one thing came to be" (John 1:1–3). (17) For if all things came to be through him, what use would have been to those coming into being when he did not yet exist? For the term "to make" is not applied to those that come into being out of the same nature. If he was in the beginning and all things came to be through him, then he made them out of nothing. (18) It seems that being is the opposite of things that came into being out of nothing and especially distinct. For on the one hand, it is clear that there is no gap between the Father and the Son, not to

any degree that the mind can contemplate. But on the other hand, the creation of the world out of nothing implies a later and more recent origin for this subsistence, since all things partake of this substantification (*housiōsis*) by the Father through the Son. (19) Having long contemplated the "was" of the Word of God and how it surpasses the contemplation of created things, most reverend John deemed it worthless to speak about his beginning and his making, not daring to label his making with the same syllables as those that were brought into being. It is not that he was unbegotten (for the Father alone is unbegotten) but that the subsistence (*hypostasis*) of the ineffable, only-begotten God is beyond the ability of the evangelists, perhaps even beyond the grasp of the angels. I don't think that those who dare press their investigations in any way to this point should be considered pious, since they don't heed the warning to "seek not after very difficult matters, ask not after things higher than you" (Sir 3:21). (20) For if the knowledge of many other things, even of things immeasurably simpler than this, has been hidden from the grasp of humans (as likewise we learn from Paul: "What the eye has not seen and the ear has not heard likewise do not enter into the human heart, what God has prepared for those who love him" [1 Cor 2:9], but God even says to Abraham that he is unable to count the stars [cf. Gen 15:5], and he also says, "the sand of the seas and the drops of rain, who can count them?" [Sir 1:2]) (21) how can anyone waste his time on the subsistence of the Word of God, unless he happens to have a particularly cantankerous disposition? About this the prophetic spirit says: "Who will describe his birth?" (Isa 53:8). For even our Savior, when he was being beneficent to the pillars of the whole universe, was eager to unburden them of this knowledge about this matter. On the one hand, he told all of them that this was not naturally in their grasp, but that to the Father alone could understanding of this most divine mystery be ascribed, when he said: "For no one knows who the Son is except the Father, and no one has known the Father except for the Son" (Matt 11:27). Concerning this I think the Father also said, "This mystery for me and mine" (Isa 24:16 [Vulg]).

(22) That it is madness to think that the Son came to be out of nothing, having been established in time, is straightaway clear from the "out of nothing," even though the witless remain unaware of the madness of their statement. For "he was not" must be situated temporally or in some interval of ages. (23) But if it is true that "all things came to be through him," then it is clear that every age and time and interval and the "then" in which it is claimed "he was not" came into being through him. And how is it not improbable to say that he who also made the times and ages and periods, in which this "he was not" has been confused, did not then exist? For it is also idiotic and full of every kind of ignorance to claim that the cause of something's origin came to be *after* its beginning. (24) According to them, that interval during which the Wisdom of God created all things preceded that in which they say the Son of God was not begotten by the Father, so, according to them, Scripture is proclaiming falsely concerning all creation to say that he was "the first born" (Col 1:15). (25) Yet even Paul, in his mightiest voice, shouts out in agreement with these Scriptures, saying about him: "the one whom he established as heir of all things, through whom he even made the ages" (Heb 1:2), but also "in him were all things created, both in heaven and on earth, the seen and the unseen, principalities and powers and dominions and thrones: all were created through him and in him, and he is prior to all" (Col 1:16–17).

(26) Since the theory of "out of nothing" appears to be most impious, it is necessary that the Father is always the Father. But then the Father is always with the Son, through whom he acquires the title of "Father." Since the Son is always with him, the Father is always complete, being without deficit in his goodness, having begotten his only-begotten Son not in time or out of an interval or "out of nothing." (27) What then? Is it not unholy to say that the Wisdom of God did not exist then, when it says: "I was joined together with him, I was that in which he took delight" (Prov 8:30) or that the Power of God did not then abide with him or that his Word was then mutilated or all other things by which the Son is made known and the Father is distinguished? Saying that "the brilliant

glory" (Heb 1:3) did not exist utterly destroys even that original light from which the brilliance came. For if the "image of God" (2 Cor 4:4) did not always exist, clearly he whose image this was did not always exist. (28) But even in the claim that "the imprint of the subsistence of God" did not exist, that one who is entirely imprinted by it is utterly destroyed. From this we can see that the sonship of our Savior has nothing in common with the sonship of anyone else. (29) As in the manner in which his subsistence is shown to be indescribable by its incomparable preeminence, surpassing all things that he has graced with being, so also his sonship, being according to nature of his Father's divinity, differs by an ineffable preeminence from those who have been made into sons through his decree. For he is of an immutable nature, perfect and lacking in nothing, but since they are deficient in every way, they need assistance from him. (30) What progress might the Wisdom of God have to make (1 Cor 1:24) or the Truth itself to receive more of? Or how might God the Word be able to improve or Life or True Light (John 14:6, 1, 4, 9)? If this is so, then is it not even more unnatural that wisdom should become open to foolishness at some time or that the power of God should be connected with weakness or that the Word (*Logos*) be impaired by irrationality (*alogia*) or that shadow should become mixed up with the True Light, since the Apostle himself says, "What has the shadow in common with the light, and what agreement is there between Christ and Beliar?" (2 Cor 6:14–15), and Solomon says that he would be unable in his mind to find "the serpent's path on the rock" (Prov 30:19), that is, what Christ is, according to Paul (cf. 1 Cor 10:4)? But those who are his creations, humans and angels, have received his blessings to progress in virtue, having heard his lawful commandments not to sin. (31) Accordingly our Lord, who is by nature the Son of the Father, is revered by all. Those who have escaped "the spirit of slavery" (cf. Phil 2:11) and, through brave deeds and personal progress, have received the "spirit of adopted sonship" (Rom 8:15), they have become sons by decree through beneficence of the one who is Son by nature.

(32) Indeed that his sonship is legitimate and particular and natural and exceptional, Paul has thus given his opinion, saying about God: "He did not spare his own Son, but for us"—that is, those who are his sons *not* by nature—"he handed him over" (Rom 8:32). (33) In distinction from those who are not his own sons, he says the he is "*his own* Son." In the Gospel: "He is my beloved Son, with whom I am pleased" (Matt 3:17, 17:5). In the psalms the Savior says: "The Lord said to me: You are my Son" (Ps 2:7). Emphasizing his legitimacy, he distinguishes those others who are not his legitimate sons from himself. (34) What also of "I begot you from my womb before the morning-star" (Ps 109:3 [LXX])? Does he not openly indicate the natural sonship of the paternal childbirth, not by careful behavior or the discipline (*askēsis*) of progress, but obtaining this by his own particular nature? Accordingly, also the only-begotten Son of the Father possesses his sonship in an unchangeable fashion. The adopted sonship of rational creatures, which abides in them not according to nature but by the suitableness of their behavior and the gift of God, reason knows that it is changeable: "For the sons of God saw the daughters of humans, and they took them as wives" (Gen 6:2–4). (35) And elsewhere also: "I have begotten sons and exalted them, but they have broken faith with me" we have been taught that God spoke through Isaiah (Isa 1:2).

Although I have many things to say, beloved, you will think it tiresome to be reminded of so many like-minded teachers. "For you have been taught by God" (1 Thess 4:9), and you are not unaware that the teaching that has recently risen up within the piety of the church is that of Ebion and Artemas and imitates that of Paul of Samosata in Antioch, who was publicly banished from the church by the synod and the judgment of bishops everywhere. (36) Lucianus, whom he taught, remained out of communion with three of these bishops for a period of many years. Those who gulp down the dregs of this impiety now have been "born out of nothing" among us: their hidden offshoots, Arius and Achillas, and the band of evildoers (cf. Ps 22:16) with them. (37) Three bishops in Syria—how they were ordained, I have no idea—

through accord with them have fanned the flames higher. Concerning them let judgment be reserved for your discernment. They have committed to memory those verses about the Savior's suffering, his humiliation, his emptying, how he was called poor (Phil 2:7–8, 2 Cor 8:9) and all those traits the Savior took on for us, and they produce them like a legal brief against the primacy and eternity of his divinity. Yet how forgetful they become of those passages that signal his natural glory and his nobility and how he abides with the Father! One such passage is: "I and my Father are one" (John 10:30). (38) When the Lord says this, he is not proclaiming that he himself is the Father, nor is he clarifying that in his subsistence (*hypostasis*) their two natures (*physeis*) have become one, but rather that the Son of the Father has come forth to preserve the paternal likeness precisely, modeling his similarity in all ways out of his nature and being the exact image of the Father and the deeply engraved impression of the original. (39) So it was the Lord explained fondly to Philip (at the time when he wanted to see and he said, "Show us the Father") saying to him: "Whoever has seen me has seen the Father" (John 14:8–9), as though through a spotless and living mirror the Father was contemplated through his divine image. (40) Something like this is in the Psalms, when the holiest ones say: "In your light we shall see light" (Ps 36:9). So indeed, "He who honors the Son honors the Father" (cf. John 5:23), and sensibly: for every impious thing that they dare to say against the Son refers also to the Father.

What else astounding have I yet to write, beloved, if I expose the false accusations against me and against our most pious people? (41) For those who are arrayed in battle against the divinity of the Son of God do not beg forgiveness for speaking ungracious vulgarities against us. Those who do not consider it fitting that they should be judged along with anyone venerable likewise do not bear that they should be placed on equal footing alongside those teachers with whom we have conversed since childhood. They do not even consider any of our fellow ministers anywhere now to have a measure of wisdom. Only they are wise and humble and discoverers of doctrine, and to them alone have things been revealed that have

never even *occurred* to any other person born under the sun! (42) O unholy humbug and immoderate madness, strange beliefs in a discordant key, Satanic arrogance that has hardened over their unholy hearts! (43) The God-loving clarity of the ancient Scriptures has not dawned upon them, nor has the harmonious reverence of our fellow-ministers concerning Christ impaired their boldness against him. Not even demons will dare unholiness of this sort, as they guard against saying anything blasphemous against the Son of God.

So let these matters be raised by us, according to our present ability, against those who pelt Christ with clods of matter through their lack of education, as they set out to slander us for our piety toward him. (44) For those who invent babbling stories say that by rejecting their impious and illiterate "out of nothing" blasphemy against Christ, we teach two unbegottens. These idiots say that one of these two options must be the case: either to think that he was created out of nothing or to say that both [Father and Son] are entirely unbegotten. These undisciplined people are unaware of how long a distance there could be between the unbegotten Father and those things created by him, rational and irrational beings. (45) Between these the only-begotten nature mediates, through which the Father of God the Word made everything out of nothing, who was begotten out of the Father's very being (*ōn*). The Lord himself even bears witness to this somewhere, when he says: "Everyone who loves the Father also loves the Son who was begotten out of him" (1 John 5:1).

(46) Here is what we believe concerning these matters, as seems right to the apostolic church: in one unbegotten Father, who has no cause for himself, immutable and unchangeable, being always in this way the same, admitting neither waxing nor waning, giver of the law and the prophets and the gospels, Lord of the patriarchs and apostles and all the saints, and in one Lord Jesus Christ, only-begotten Son of God, begotten not out of nothing but out of the Father's being (*ōn*), not by excisions, in the likeness of bodies, nor by emanations out of divisions, as it seems to Sabellius and Valentinus, but in an unutterable and ineffable manner, just as in the saying that we set out

above: "Who will describe his birth?" (Isa 53:8). His subsistence is not to be figured out by any created nature, even as also the Father himself is not to be figured out, because the nature of rational beings lacks the capacity for knowing the Father's method of divine generation. (47) But men who are moved by the spirit of truth have no need to learn these things from me, since the voice of Christ about this matter from long ago still resounds within us and teaches: "No one knows who the Father is except for the Son, and no one knows who the Son is except for the Father" (Matt 11:27). We have learned that he is immutable and unchangeable like the Father, perfect Son lacking in nothing in resemblance to his Father, except for the fact that the Father is unbegotten. (48) For he is the accurate and precise image of the Father. It is clear that the image is full of all those things through which the resemblance is greater, as the Lord himself instructed: "My father is greater than I am" (John 14:28). And according to this, we also believe that the Son has always existed out of the Father: "For he is the brilliance of the glory and the imprint of the Fatherly subsistence" (cf. Heb 1.3). But no one should take "always" to mean that he was unbegotten, as they think whose inner senses have been calcified. (49) That "he was," or "always" or "before the ages" does not mean "unbegotten." No human intellect could seriously make a term that might clarify "unbegotten" (as even I believe you have taken it in this way and I have been inspired by your correct stance concerning all this). In no way can any of these terms be taken to mean "unbegotten." (50) It seems as if these terms signify the extension of time, incapable, as it were, of distinguishing sufficiently the divinity of the only begotten or its antiquity. Yet holy men were constrained to clarify the mystery according to the ability of each, and they asked forgiveness of the audience through a sensible defense, saying: "insofar as we have managed." (51) But if those men expect something better than that which passed through human lips, those men who say that "those things that have been known in part" (cf. 1 Cor 13:8–12) have been abolished for them, it is clear that the terms "was" and "always" and "before the ages" leave much to be desired. But whatever the case may be,

this does not mean "unbegotten." (52) Therefore, this particular dignity must be reserved for the Father as the unbegotten, and nothing is said to be his cause. But a congruous honor must be assigned to the Son, referring to his generation by the Father as outside time. As we have already said, imparting majesty to him, only piously and auspiciously using for him the terms "was" and "always" and "before the ages," not, as it were, demeaning his divinity, but affirming his exact resemblance in the image and the imprint of the Father in all things, while supposing still the particularity of being unbegotten is set aside for the Father alone, as indeed the Savior himself says of him: "My father is greater than me" (John 14:28).

(53) Besides this pious doctrine concerning the Father and the Son, just as the divine Scriptures teach us, we confess one Holy Spirit, renewing the holy people of the Old Testament and the divine teachers of the one called New, and in only one catholic, apostolic church, always unassailable, even if the whole world should wish to do war against her, triumphant against all the most impious uprisings of the heterodox, encouraging us through the battle cry of her master: "Take heart, I have conquered the world!" (John 16:33). (54) After this, we recognize resurrection from the dead, of which our Lord Jesus Christ became the "first fruit" (1 Cor 15:22), bearing a body truly and not in a semblance, out of Mary the Mother of God,[1] at the consummation of the ages sojourning among the human race for the remission of sin, crucified and dying, but not through this becoming inferior in his divinity, rising from the dead, taken up into heaven, sitting "at the right hand of greatness" (cf. Heb 9:26).

(55) I have recorded these things, in part, in this letter, not wishing (as I said) to be tiresome by writing about each point in precise detail, because these things have not escaped the notice of your holy zeal. We teach these things, we proclaim these things, these are the apostolic teachings of the church, on behalf of which we would even die, thinking little of

---

[1] That is, *Theotokos;* later a controversial term (see Texts 24 and 25), this may be its earliest extant usage.

those who would constrain us to denounce them. Even if they compelled us through torture, we would not desert our hope in them. (56) Having become our enemies, the partisans both of Arius and of Achillas and those who battle against the truth with them have been fought back from the church; they have become foreigners to our pious teachings, according to the blessed Paul: "If someone preaches to you a gospel other than this which you have received, let him be anathema" (Gal 1:9), even if he makes himself out to be an angel from heaven. (57) But also: "If anyone teaches differently and does not come near to the healing words of our Lord Jesus Christ and his teaching according to piety, he is deluded and knows nothing" (1 Tim 6:3–4), and so forth.

Let none of you receive those who have been anathematized by the brotherhood or receive anything that has been said or written by them, for they are swindlers who lie about everything; they do not speak the truth. (58) They go around to the cities, eager for nothing other than to deliver and receive letters through hypocrisy and flattery under the cloak of friendship and the name of peace, using their deceptions to mislead a few "silly women piled high with sins" (2 Tim 3:6), and so forth.

(59) So those who have dared such things against Christ, who have disparaged Christianity in public, eagerly seeking to make a public display in the courts, inciting persecution against us in such a time of peace, enfeebling the ineffable mystery of the begetting of Christ—reject them, beloved, my brothers and soul mates! Be of one mind against their daring madness, like some of our fellow ministers who were incensed and wrote to me against them and agreed to sign on to our side.

I have sent these messages to you through my son Api the deacon—one massage from all of Egypt and Thebes, another from Libya and the Pentapolis and Syria, and also Lycia and Pamphylia, Asia, Cappadocia, and all the outlying countries. I am certain I can expect something similar from you. (60) I have supplied many remedies for the impaired, and I have discovered this speedy cure for a deceived people: to come eagerly into repentence through being persuaded by the agreements of our fellow ministers. Greet each other with the brotherhood that is in you. I pray that you will be strong in the Lord, beloved, and that I might benefit from your Christ-loving soul.

(61) These are the heretics who have been anathematized: from the priests, Arius; from the deacons, Achilles, Euzoios, Aithales, Lucius, Sarmates, Julius, Menas, another Arius, Helladios.[2]

---

[2] Compare this list to the signatories of Arius's letter to Alexander (Text 22), written (probably) the next year or so.

22. Arius: Letter to Alexander of Alexandria

In this letter of response to the accusations of his bishop Alexander, we see in Arius an equally capable (if more circumspect) heresiological opponent. Arius, too, constructs a positive theology interwoven with slurs on the integrity and piety of his opponents (among whom Alexander must number). He answers Alexander's doctrine of divine unity with his own theology of distinction of the divine persons (*hypostaseis*). In addition, just as Alexander had embedded Arius in a pedigree of heretics who had denigrated the absolute divinity of Jesus Christ—Ebion, Artemas, Paul of Samosata—so Arius insinuates his opponent into a line of heretics determined to blur the lines between God's remote divinity and the created order: the gnostic Valentinus, Mani, Sabellius (who taught a form of "modalism"), and others who promoted the Son so high that they inevitably dragged the Father down.

To our blessed pope and bishop Alexander the presbyters and deacons send greeting in the Lord.

Our faith that we received from our forefathers and have also learned from you is this. We know there is one God, the only unbegotten, only eternal, only without beginning, only true, who only has immortality, only wise, only good, the only potentate, judge of all, governor, dispenser, unalterable and unchangeable, righteous and good, God of the Law and the Prophets and the New Covenant. Before everlasting ages he begot his unique Son, through whom he made the ages and all things. He begot him not in appearance, but in truth, constituting him by his own will, unalterable and unchangeable, a perfect creature of God, but not as one of the creatures—an offspring, but not as one of things begotten. Neither [was] the offspring of the Father a projection, as Valentinus taught, nor, as Mani introduced, was the offspring a consubstantial part of the Father, nor [was he], as Sabellius said, dividing the Monad, a Son-Father, nor, as Hieracas [taught], a lamp [kindled] from a lamp, or like a torch [divided] into two; nor did he first exist, later being begotten or re-created into a Son—as you also, blessed pope, in the midst of the Church and in council often refuted those who introduced these [ideas]. But as we said, by the will of God [he was] created before times and before ages and received life and being and glories from the Father, the Father so constituting him. Nor did the Father in giving him the inheritance of all things deprive himself of what he possesses unbegottenly in himself, for he is the fount of all things. Thus there are three *hypostases*. God being the cause of all things is without beginning and most unique, while the Son, begotten timelessly by the Father and created before ages and established, was not before he was begotten—but, begotten timelessly before all things, he alone was constituted by the Father. He is neither eternal nor coeternal nor co-unbegotten with the Father, nor does he have his being together with the Father, as some say "others with one," introducing [the idea of] two unbegotten sources. But as Monad and cause of all, God is thus before all. Therefore he is also prior to the Son, as we learned from what you preached in the midst of the Church.

So therefore, as he has being and glories from God, and life and all things were given him, accordingly God is his source. For he precedes him as his God and as being before him. But if the [phrases] "of him" and "out of the womb" and "I came forth from the Father and am come" (cf. Rom 11:36; Ps 110:3; John 16:28) are understood by some as [meaning] a part of the consubstantial himself and a projection, then according to them the Father is compound and divisible and alterable and a body, and according to them presumably, the bodiless God [is thought of as] suffering what belongs to a body.

We pray that you may fare well in the Lord, blessed pope. Arius, Aeithales, Achilleus, Carpones, Sarmatas, Arius, presbyters. Deacons, Euzoius, Lucius, Julius, Menas, Helladius, Gaius. Bishops, Secundus of Pentapolis, Theonas of Libya, Pistus.

23. Gregory of Nazianzus: Third Theological Oration

Despite the "triumph" over Arius at the Council of Nicaea (see Text 33), theological dispute over the Trinity continued throughout the fourth century. Often benefiting from imperial support, theologians who taught that the three persons of the Trinity were neither consubstantial nor coeternal achieved ecclesiastical prominence throughout the East. When Gregory of Nazianzus came to Constantinople (see Text 18), the capital city had long been under the influence of various "neo-Arian" parties (who, of course, did not refer to themselves as such).

From *Faith Gives Fullness to Reason: The Five Theological Orations of Gregory Nazianzen,* trans. Lionel Wickham and Frederick Williams. Introduction and commentary by Frederick W. Norris. Leiden, the Netherlands: E. J. Brill, 1991. Used with permission.

Gregory preached a series of five theological orations in 381 soon before Theodosius convoked the Council of Constantinople and reinstated Nicene orthodoxy in the capital (see Text 34).

As this third oration, "On the Son," demonstrates, Trinitarian debate had evolved into a complex array of philosophical propositions and contradictions, often propped up by endless strings of scriptural citations. Gregory's own discussion of the relation between Father and Son (focused particularly on the notion of "begetting" and foreshadowing the Christological debates of the next century) is heavily informed by Platonic, Stoic, and Aristotelian argumentation (such as the famous "liar's paradox" found in section 9). The importance of logical argumentation and terminological specificity—equally prized by both sides of the debate—almost overtakes substantive argument in this oration, as Gregory tears down the "logic choppers" who twist scriptural interpretation and philosophy (as Gregory charges) to their own ends. Gregory himself must concede that the precise nature of the Son's "begottenness" is a mystery that philosophy will never fully disclose: "faith," he concludes, "gives fullness to our reasoning." He is content to deconstruct his opponents' so-called logic and reiterate the mystery of Trinitarian consubstantiality and coeternity.

(1) Yes, these are the replies one can use to put a brake upon this hasty argumentativeness, a hastiness that is dangerous in all matters, but especially in theological topics. To censure, of course, is a trivial task—anyone so minded can do it quite easily. But to substitute one's own view takes a man of true religion and sound sense. So, come now, let us put our confidence in the Holy Spirit *they* dishonor but *we* worship. Let us bring our convictions about the Godhead—convictions of some significance and standing—into broad daylight, like an offspring of good stock ripe for birth. Not that we have held our peace at other times—here is the one point we become brash and arrogant on—but now we express the truth even more outspokenly, in order that, as Scripture puts it, we may not suffer the condemnation of God's disfavor by balking the issue (cf. Heb 10:38).

Every speech has two parts to it. One part aims at establishing one's own position; the other refutes the opposing case. This is the method we shall try, expounding our own before refuting our opponents' arguments. Both parts will be as brief as possible, so that there may be as good a conspectus of our views as the introductory treatise they have invented for the deception of simpler or more gullible souls provides. Besides which, we do not want our thoughts to be dissipated through the length of discussion, like water without a channel to hold it in, running to waste over flat ground.

(2) The opinions about Deity that hold pride of place are three in number: atheism, polytheism, and monotheism. With the first two, the children of Greece amused themselves. Let the game go on! Atheism, with its lack of a governing principle, involves disorder. Polytheism, with a plurality of such principles, involves faction and hence the absence of a governing principle, and this involves disorder again. Both lead to an identical result—lack of order, which, in turn, leads to disintegration, disorder being the prelude to disintegration. Monotheism, with its single governing principle, is what *we* value—not monotheism, defined as the sovereignty of a single person (after all, self-discordant unity can become a plurality) but the single rule produced by equality of nature, harmony of will, identity of action, and the convergence toward their source of what springs from unity—none of which is possible in the case of created nature. The result is that though there is numerical distinction, there is no division in the being. For this reason, a one eternally changes to a two and stops at three—meaning the Father, the Son, and the Holy Spirit. In a serene, nontemporal, incorporeal way, the

Father is parent of the "offspring" and originator of the "emanation"—or whatever name one can apply when one has isolated them from things visible. We shall not venture, as a non-Christian philosopher rashly did, to talk of an "overflowing of goodness," "as though a bowl had overflowed"—these were the plain terms he used in his disquisition on primary and secondary causes.[1] We ought never to introduce the notion of involuntary generation (in the sense of some sort of unrestrained natural secretion), notions that are completely out of keeping with ideas about the Godhead. This is why we limit ourselves to Christian terms and speak of "the Ingenerate," "the Begotten," and (as God the Word himself does in one passage) "what Proceeds from the Father" (cf. John 15:26).

(3) *So when did these last two originate?*

They transcend "whenness," but if I *must* give a naive answer—when the Father did.

When was that?

There has not been [a time] when the Father has not been in existence. This, then, is true of the Son and of the Holy Spirit. Put another question, and I will answer it.

Since when has the Son been begotten?

Since as long as the Father has *not* been begotten.

Since when has the Spirit been proceeding?

Since as long as the Son has *not* been proceeding but being begotten in a non-temporal way that transcends explanation. We cannot, though, explain the meaning of "supra-temporal" *and* deliberately keep clear of any suggestion of time. Expressions like "when," "before x," "after y," and "from the beginning" are not free from temporal implications however much we try to wrest them. No, we cannot explain it, except possibly by taking the world-era as the period coinciding with eternal things, being a period that is not, as "time" is, measured and fragmented by the Sun's motion.

How is it, then, that these latter are not like the Father in having no origin, if they are coeternal with him?

Because they are *from* him, though not *after* him. "Being unoriginate" necessarily implies "being eternal," but "being eternal" does not entail "being unoriginate," so long as the origin referred to is the Father. So because they have a cause they are not unoriginate. But clearly a cause is not necessarily prior to its effects—the Sun is not prior to its light. Because time is not involved, they are to that extent *unoriginate*—even if you do scare simple souls with the bogey-word; for things which produce Time are beyond time.

(4) *How, then can the process of begetting not involve subjection to change?*

Because a body is not involved. If corporeal begetting implies subjection to change, an incorporeal one must be free of it. Let me put a question to you in return: how can he be God if he is a creature? What is created is not God. Not to mention the fact that if "creating" is given a corporeal interpretation, emotion and change are to be found here as well—for instance, time, desire, imagination, thought, hope, distress, risk, failure, and success. All these factors, and more besides, as everybody knows, are involved in creating. I wonder why you do not go the full length of envisaging mating, periods of gestation and risks of miscarriage as necessarily involved if he were to beget at all, or why you do not list the ways in which birds, beasts, and fish produce offspring and put the divine and unutterable generation down on one of these, or else use your new-fangled scheme to get rid of the Son. You are incapable of understanding that one who has a distinctive fleshly birth—what other case of a Virgin Mother of God do you know?—has a different spiritual birth, or rather, one whose being is not the same as ours has a different way of begetting as well.

(5) *Can anyone be a "father" without beginning to be one?*

Yes, one who did not begin his existence. What begins to exist begins to be a father. *He* did not begin to be Father—he did not begin at all. He is "Father" in the true sense because he is not a son as well. In our case, the word "father" cannot be truly appropriate because we must be fathers *and* sons—the terms carry equal weight. We also stem from a pair, not a

---

[1] Gregory may be referring to the neo-Platonic philosopher Plotinus.

single being, making us be divided and become human beings gradually and maybe not even human beings of the kind we are intended to be. The ties are dissolved by one side or the other, so that only the relationships remain, bereft of the realities.

But, it may be said, *"he begat" and "he has been begotten" can and must bring in the idea of a beginning of this process of generation.*

Why not say then instead, "he has existed as begotten from the beginning," and so avoid your labored objections with their penchant for time? Will you accuse us of falsifying a scriptural truth? Is it not clear to everybody that there are plenty of examples of tenses being employed in an opposite sense, especially in biblical usage? This is true not only of the past tense, but of the present and the future as well. For example: "Why did the heathen rage?" (Ps 2:1)—the raging had not yet occurred, and, "They will cross the river on foot" (Ps 66:6)—which means, "they *have* gone through it." It would be a long task to list all the expressions of this kind on which scholars have bestowed their attention.

(6) So much for that objection! This next one of theirs is like it in being outrageously provocative.

Has the Father, they ask, *begotten the Son voluntarily, or involuntarily?*

They now bind us round with what they think are strong cords, but are really feeble ones.

If, they say, *it was involuntary, he was in someone's power. Who exercised the power? How could God be under someone's power? But if it was voluntary, the Son is son to a will; so how can he stem from the Father?*

They make the will into a new kind of mother in place of the Father.

First, it is certainly a point in their favor if they say this. It means that they are deserting passivity to take refuge in the will. Volition is not, after all, a passive experience. Second, let us take a look at what they put as their strong point. They had best now be grappled with at closer quarters. You who coolly assert what you will, did *you* come into existence as a result of your father's willing it or without his will? If without his will, he must have been in someone's power. What an act of violence! And who exercised that

power over him? You cannot answer, "Nature"—nature is also capable of self-control. If it was voluntary, a few syllables have lost you your father—you are evidently a son of his will, not of your father. Let me pass on to the subject of God and creatures and address this question of yours to your own intelligence. Did he create the universe voluntarily or under compulsion? If it was under compulsion, then external domination and a dominator are involved. If voluntarily, then creatures have been deprived of their God, and you most of all who invent sophistries of this kind. God is walled off from his creation by his will. No, if we are sober, we make a distinction, I think, between "willing" and "a will," between "begetting" (as a participle) and "begetting" (as a noun) between "speaking" and "speech." The participles refer to a subject of motion, the nouns designate the motion itself. What is willed does not *belong* to a will—it is not a necessary concomitant of it. Nor does what is begotten *belong* to a begetting, nor what is heard to an act of speech. They belong instead to the subject who willed, who begat, who speaks. What belongs to God transcends all these cases even. For him, begetting may well just be the will to beget—but without any superiority of begetting to willing either. If we accept this last proposition without reservation, nothing will intervene.

(7) Do you want me to take the game on to the Father? You make me do rash things like that! The Father is God either voluntarily or involuntarily. Now (if you do not want to be trapped by your own expertise) when, if it was involuntary, did he begin to will it? Not, of course, before he actually was God—there being nothing prior to that. Or is he partly the subject, partly the object of an act of will? In that case, he must be divided. According to you, there is a problem how he can avoid belonging to a will. But if it was involuntary, what forced him into being God? How can he be God if he is forced, forced into nothing less than being God?

How, then, has the Son been begotten?

How has he been created, if, as you say, created he has been? Indeed, this is part of the same puzzle.

Perhaps you will answer: *by his will and his reason.*

But your explanation is so far incomplete, for how will and reason can have the power to effect anything remains unexplained—in the case of human beings, after all, they do not.

(8) How, then has he been begotten? This begetting would be a triviality if it could be understood by you, who have no knowledge of how you yourself procreate and are ashamed to explain in full the limited understanding you have. Do you really think you know it all? It will cost you much effort before you discover the principles involved from conception through formation to delivery and the linking of soul to body, of intellect to soul, and of reason to intellect, and can explain the rest of your makeup—movement, growth, assimilation of food, perception, memory, and recollection and what belongs jointly to soul and body, what separately to one, and what involves their interplay. Faculties, after all, whose maturity belongs to a later stage, have principles that accompany the procreative process. Explain these, and even then you are not able to treat of God's begetting. That would be risky. For if you know your own, it by no means follows that you know God's, and unless you know your own, how could you know God's? The heavenly begetting is more incomprehensible than your own, to the same extent that God is harder to trace out than Man. If you make its incomprehensibility a ground for denying the fact, it is high time you ruled out as nonexistent a good number of things you do not understand, the chief of which is God himself. However audacious, however enthusiastic you are, you cannot explain what *he* is at all. Drop your ideas of flux, division, and cleavage, drop the habit of treating the incorporeal nature as if it were a body, and you might well get a worthy notion of God's begetting. How has he been begotten?—I reutter the question with loathing. God's begetting ought to have the tribute of our reverent silence. The important point is for you to learn that he has been begotten. As to the way it happens, we shall not concede that even angels, much less you, know that. Shall *I* tell you the way? It is a way known only to the begetting Father and the begotten Son. Anything beyond this fact is hidden by a cloud and escapes your dull vision.

(9) *Well then, he either existed or did not exist when the Father begat him?*

What drivel! That dilemma might have relevance to you and me. Like Levi in Abraham's loins (cf. Heb 7:9–10) we did have some sort of being, and yet we have *come* into being as well, so that, in a certain fashion, our condition is a product of being and nonbeing. This is the opposite of primeval matter, which obviously came into existence from nonbeing, despite the fact that some people imagine it to be uncreated. In the present case, being begotten coincides with existence and is from all eternity, so where are you going to put this cleft stick of a question? What point is there prior to eternity to fix the existence or nonexistence of the Son? Either way the notion of eternity will be destroyed. Unless, when we put the question whether the Father comes from being or nonbeing, you risk the answers *either* that he has a double being, partly existing, partly preexisting, *or* that he is in the same case with the Son, being a product of nonbeing. This is what your puerile conundrums lead to. Sandcastles, they cannot stand a puff of wind.

No, I allow neither supposition. I say that the question presents an absurdity, not the answer a difficulty. If you follow your logical presuppositions and hold that in every case one of the pair of alternatives must be true, then I shall put you a little question. Is Time *in* Time, or not? If it is, what is the Time it is in? What is the difference between them? How does one contain the other? If Time is not in Time, how acute your wits are to get us nontemporal Time! What about the proposition: "I am now making a false statement"? You must concede one of the alternatives; it is either true or false—we cannot allow both. But that is impossible. If the statement is false, it will be true, and if it is true, it will be false, by logical necessity. Is there anything remarkable then in the fact that two contradictories can both be true in the case under discussion, just as they are both false here, and thus your sophistry will be shown up for the silliness it is? Here is another teaser for you to solve: were you present to yourself when you were being begotten, and are you present to yourself now, or are both propositions false? If you were and are present, who is present to whom? How did the pair of you come to be a single whole? If both alternatives are false, how is it that you came to be parted from yourself, and what caused the separation? No, it is stupid to stir up a dust about whether a thing is present to itself or not. The expression "is present" is used to imply a relationship with other things not with itself. You must appreciate that it is even stupider to be correcting people on the subject of whether or not what has been begotten from eternity existed prior to its begetting. That question only arises in connection with temporally determined beings.

(10) *But,* it may be said, *the ingenerate and the generate are not the same thing. If that is the case, the Father and the Son cannot be the same thing.*

It goes without saying that this argument excludes either the Father or the Son from the Godhead—if ingeneracy is the essence of God, generacy is not his essence, and vice versa. There is no gainsaying this, is there? Make your choice of the alternative blasphemies, you empty-headed theologian, if you are fully intent on blaspheming. Still, what are your grounds for denying that ingenerate and generate are the same? If you had said uncreated and created, I should agree—what has no origin and what is created cannot be identical in nature. But if you are talking about begetter and begotten, this is a false statement—these must be the same; it is in the nature of an offspring to have a nature identical with its parent's. Here is another objection: what do you mean by "the ingenerate" and "the generate"? If you mean ingenerate*ness* and generate*ness*—no, these are not the same thing, but if you mean the things that have these properties in them, why should they not be the same? Lack of intelligence and intelligence are not identical, but they can be predicated of the same thing, a man. They do not mark out separate beings, they are separate qualities of the same being. Do immortality, purity, and immutability each constitute God's being? No, if that were so, there would be a plurality of "beings" of God, not a single being. Or is Deity a composite resulting from these?—if these are "beings" or substances, there would have to be composition.

(11) They do not hold that view because these are properties of other beings besides God. The substance of God is what belongs to him particularly and uniquely. The people who allege that "matter" and "form" are ingenerate would not agree that ingeneracy is uniquely a property of God—we will put the Manichean darkness in the further background. But suppose it does belong uniquely to God, what was Adam? Was he not uniquely a creation formed by God?

Yes, you will say.

Was he a unique human being as well?

Of course not.

Why?

Because manhood does not consist of being formed by God; what has parentage is also man.

In the same way, it is not the case that the ingenerate and only the ingenerate is God (though only the Father is ingenerate) but you must allow that the Begotten too is God. The Begotten stems from God, however fond you are of unbegottenness. Next, how are you to talk of the being of God, when what is said about that being is not a positive assertion but a negation? "Unbegotten" means that he has no parent. It does not state his nature, but simply the fact that he was not begotten.

So what is the being of God?

You must be mad to ask the question, making such a fuss about begottenness! We count it a high thing that we may perhaps learn what it is in the time to come, when we are free of this dense gloom. That is the promise of one who cannot lie (cf Tit 1:2). Yes, this is what men, who purify themselves for it, must think of and hope for. As for us, we can confidently affirm that if it is a high thing for the Father to have no origin, it is no lesser thing for the Son to stem from such a Father. He must share in the glory of the uncaused because he stems from the uncaused. That he has been begotten is a further fact about him, as significant as it is august, for men whose minds are not totally earthbound and materialistic.

(12) *But,* they say, *if the Son is the same in substance as the Father, and the Father is unbegotten, then the Son must be unbegotten, too.*

True—provided that ingeneracy constitutes God's being. That would give us an outlandish mixup—an unbegotten-begotten. But supposing the difference lies outside the substance of God, what validity has your argument got? Must you be your father's father if you are to avoid missing anything he has, when you are the same in being as he? Surely it is clear that when we are looking, if look we can, for what God's being consists of, a personal characteristic must be left out of account. This is the way to find out that God and ingeneracy are not identical. If they were identical, both "God" and "ingenerate" would have to be relational terms, or, since "ingenerate" is an absolute term, "God" would have to be one, too, seeing that logical equivalents can be used interchangeably. But what does "ingenerate" relate itself to, what is it the ingenerate *of*? God has such terms—he is God *of* all. So how can "God" and "ingenerate" be identical? And again since ingeneracy and begottenness are mutually opposed, as condition and privation, it follows that mutually opposed beings or substances have been brought in—which is impossible. Or again, since conditions are prior to privations, and privations take away conditions, not only must the Father's substance be prior to the Son's, but it must also be in the process of destruction by the Father on your presuppositions.

(13) What is left of their invincible arguments? Perhaps they will take a last refuge in this argument:

Unless God has ceased to beget, the begetting must be unfinished and at some time stop, but if it has stopped, it must have started.

Here again we have crude, bodily ideas from crude, bodily people. For my own part, I am not committing myself to saying whether or not the process of being begotten is eternal until I have made a close examination of the text: "Before all the hills, he begets me" (Prov 8:25). But I see no necessity in their argument.

If, as they say, *what is going to stop must have started, what is not going to stop cannot have started.*

What, on that showing, will the soul or angels be? If they have a beginning, they must cease, but if they are not going to end, obviously, according to these people, they have no beginning either. But in fact

they did begin, and they will not end. Their argument then, that something that is going to end requires a beginning, is untrue. Our position, of course, is that horses, man, oxen, and each item that comes under the same species have a single concept. Whatever shares in the concept is rightly called by that name, and whatever does not share in it is not properly called by the name. Thus in the same way there is a single being, nature, and name of God, even though the titles are distinguished, along with the distinct ideas about him. Whatever is properly called "God" *is* God, and whatever he is in his nature is a true name for him—granted that real truth is contained in facts, not in names. These people, though, act as if they were afraid of leaving any opposition to the truth untried. They acknowledge the Son as "God," when forced by reason and proof-texts to do so, but only in an equivocal sense. He shares the name and the name alone!

(14) When we make them the rejoinder, "Well, do you really mean that the Son is not 'God' in the proper sense of the word, in the same way that a picture of an animal is not an animal? In that case, how can he be God, supposing he is not 'God' in the proper sense?" they answer,

Why should not the names be the same and used in the proper sense in either case?

They instance the Greek word for "dog," which can be used in the proper sense to mean both a dog and a shark[2] (there being this sort of case of equivocal terms) and any other case where something bears the same title it shares equally with something else of a different nature.

In these instances, dear fellow, you are putting two natures under the same name, not making one superior to, or prior to, the other or one more true to its name than the other. There is nothing attached to the names to force that conclusion—the animal and the fish are equally entitled to the same Greek name, "dog"—and why not? No, things of the same and things of different status can have the same name. Yet

---

[2] The Greek *kuōn* means "dog" and "dog-shark."

when it comes to God, you attach an awe-inspiring solemnity to him, a transcendence of every essence and nature that constitutes the unique nature of God's deity, so to say. You ascribe this to the Father but then rob the Son of it and make him subordinate. You give the Son second place in reverence and worship. Even if you endow him with the syllables that make up the word "similar," you in fact truncate his godhead and make a mischievous transition from parity to disparity in the usage of a common name. The result is that a pictured and a living man are apter illustrations for you of the Godhead of Father and Son than the dog and shark you used. Alternatively, you must concede that the fact that they have a common name puts their natures on the same level, even if you are making out that they are different; in that case, you have ruined your "dog"example, which you hit on to illustrate a disparity of natures. What does it matter that the animals you distinguish have the same name, "dog," if they are on the same level? The point, after all, of having recourse to "dogs" and ambiguous names was to prove disparity, not parity. How could anyone stand more clearly convicted of self-confuting blasphemy?

(15) If we say that the Father is *qua* cause superior to the Son, they add the minor premise *but he is cause by nature* and hence conclude that *he is superior by nature.*

I do not know whom the fallacy misleads—themselves or their opponents. For it is not the case that all the predicates affirmed of some particular being can be affirmed without further qualification of his basic substance. No, plainly they are affirmed of some particular thing, in some particular respect. Is there anything to stop me also taking as my minor premise, "but 'being superior by nature' does not entail 'being Father'" and then concluding either that "being superior" does not entail "being superior" or that "being the Father" does not entail "being Father." Or take another example: God is being, but being is not necessarily God. Draw the conclusion for yourself—God is not necessarily God. No, the fallacy here arises from arguing, as the logicians call it, "from the particular to the general." We concede, of course, that it belongs to the nature of the cause to be superior, but

they infer that the superiority belongs to the nature—which is like our saying "X is a dead man" and their drawing the inference that "Man," without qualification, is dead.

(16) How could we bypass this next point of theirs, which is quite as dumbfounding as the rest of what they say?

"Father," they say, *is a designation either of the substance or the activity; is it not?*

They intend to impale us on a dilemma, for if we say that it names the substance, we shall then be agreeing that the Son is of a different substance, there being a single substance and that one, according to them, preempted by the Father. But if we say that the term designates the activity, we shall clearly be admitting that the Son is a creation not an offspring. If there is an active producer, there must be a production, and they will declare themselves surprised at the idea of an identity between creator and created. I should have felt some awe myself at your dilemma, had it been necessary to accept one of the alternatives and impossible to avoid them by stating a third, and truer, possibility. My expert friends, it is this: "Father" designates neither the substance nor the activity, but the relationship, the manner of being, which holds good between the Father and the Son. Just as with us these names indicate kindred and affinity, so here, too, they designate the sameness of stock, of parent and offspring. But to please you, let it be granted that "the Father" names a substance. That idea will bring in the Son along with it, not alienate him, if we follow common sense and the meaning of terms. Suppose, if you like, it stands for his activity; you will not catch us out that way either. He will actively have produced that very consubstantiality, even if the assumption of active production's being involved here is decidedly odd.

You see how we get clear of your twists and turns, even though you mean to fight foul. Now that we know just how invincible you are in logical twists, let us see what strength you can muster from Holy Scriptures. Perhaps you may undertake to win us over with them.

(17) We, after all, understand and preach the Son's Godhead on the basis of their grand and sublime lan-

guage. What do we mean here? Expressions like "God," "Word," "he who is in the beginning," who was "with the beginning," who was "the beginning," "In the beginning was the Word and the Word was with God and the Word was God" (John 1:1) and "with you is the beginning" (Ps 109:3 [LXX]) and "who calls it the beginning from the generations of old" (Isa 41:4). Then he is the Only-begotten Son: "The Only-begotten Son, who is in the bosom of the Father, he has declared him" (John 1:18). He is "way," "truth," "life," and "light:" "I am the way, the truth, and the life" and "I am the light of the world" (John 14:6, 8:12). He is "wisdom" and "power:" "Christ the power of God and the wisdom of God" (1 Cor 1:24). He is the "effulgence," "stamp," "image," and "seal:" "Who being the effulgence of his glory and the stamp of his person" (Heb 1:3) and "image of goodness" (Wis 7:26) and "for him did God the Father seal" (John 6:27). He is "Lord," "King," "he who is," and "almighty:" "The Lord rained down fire from the Lord" (Gen 19:24) and "A scepter of righteousness is the scepter of your kingdom" (Ps 45:6) and "who is and was and is to come and the almighty" (Rev 1:8). Plainly these, and all the expressions synonymous with them, refer to the Son. None of them is a later acquisition, none became attached at a later stage to the Son or to the Spirit any more than to the Father, for perfection does not result from additions. There never was [a time] when he was without his word, when he was not Father, when he was not true, or when he was without wisdom and power, or when he lacked life, splendor, or goodness.

(18) Count up the phrases that in your ignorance you set over against these—"My God and your God" (John 20:17), "greater" (John 14:28), "he created" (Prov 8:22), "he made" (Acts 2:36), and "he sanctified" (John 10:36). Reckon in, if you like, "slave" (Phil 2:7) and "obedient" (Phil 2:8), "he gave" (John 18:19), "he learned" (Heb 5:8), "he was commanded" (John 15:10), "he was sent" (John 5:36), "he could do nothing" (John 5:19), "speak nothing" (John 12:49), "judge nothing" (John 8:15–16), "give nothing" (Mark 10:40), "will nothing of himself" (John 5:19, 30; 8:28). You may add these: his "ignorance" (Matt 24:36), his "subjection" (Luke 2:51),

his "praying" (Luke 3:21, 6:12), his "asking" (John 11:34; Luke 2:46); his "progress" and "growing up" (Luke 2:52). Put in, if you like, all the even lowlier expressions used about him—the fact that he "slept" (Matt 8:24), "was hungry" (Matt 4:2), "got tired" (John 4:6), "wept" (John 11:35), "was in agony" (Luke 22:44), was subject to things (cf. 1 Cor 15:28). Maybe you reproach him for his cross and death—I expect you will let his Resurrection and Ascension go free, seeing that here there is something on our side. You can pick up many more scraps besides these if you mean to go on fabricating this intruder of yours, this namesake of God. For us he is true God and on the same level as the Father. Yes, one could easily go through each of these expressions in detail and give you the truly religious interpretation. It is not a hard task to clear away the stumbling block that the literal text of Scripture contains—that is, if your stumbling is real and not just willful malice. In sum: you must predicate the more sublime expressions of the Godhead, of the nature that transcends bodily experiences, and the lowlier ones of the compound, of him who because of you was emptied became incarnate and (to use equally valid language) was "made man" (cf. Phil 2:7). Then next he was exalted, in order that you might have done with the earthbound carnality of your opinions and might learn to be nobler, to ascend with the Godhead and not linger on in things visible but rise up to spiritual realities, and that you might know what belongs to his nature and what to God's plan of salvation.

(19) He whom presently you scorn was once transcendent over even you. He who is presently human was incomposite. He remained what he was; what he was not, he assumed. No "because" is required for his existence in the beginning, for what could account for the existence of God? But later he came into being because of something, namely, your salvation, yours who insult him and despise his Godhead for that very reason because he took on your thick corporeality. Through the medium of the mind he had dealings with the flesh, being made that God on earth which is Man. Man and God blended; they became a single whole, the stronger side predominating, in order that I might be made God to the same extent

that he was made man. He was begotten—yet he was already begotten—of a woman. And yet she was a virgin. That it was from a woman makes it human, that she was a virgin makes it divine. On earth he has no father (Matt 1:20), but in heaven no mother (cf. Ps 2:7). All this is part of his Godhead. He was carried in the womb (cf. Luke 1:31), but acknowledged by a prophet as yet unborn himself, who leaped for joy at the presence of the Word for whose sake he had been created (Luke 1:41). He was wrapped in swaddling bands (Luke 2:7, 12), but at the Resurrection he unloosed the swaddling bands of the grave (cf. John 20:6–7). He was laid in a manger (Luke 2:7, 16), but was extolled by angels, disclosed by a star, and adored by Magi (Matt 2:2, 7, 9–11). Why do you take offense at what you see, instead of attending to its spiritual significance? He was exiled into Egypt (Matt 2:13–14), but he banished the Egyptian idols. He had "no form of beauty" (Isa 53:2) for the Jews, but for David he was "fairer than the children of men" (Ps 45:2), and on the mount he shines forth, becoming more luminous than the Sun (Matt 17:2), to reveal the future mystery.

(20) As a man he was baptized (Matt 3:16), but he absolved sins as God (John 1:29, Matt 9:2); he needed no purifying rites himself—his purpose was to hallow water. As man he was put to the test, but as God he came through victorious (Matt 4:1–11)—yes, he bids us to be of good cheer because he has conquered the world (John 16:33). He hungered (Matt 4:2)—yet he fed thousands (Matt 14:20–21). He is indeed "living, heavenly bread" (John 6:51). He thirsted (John 19:28)—yet he exclaimed: "Whosoever thirsts, let him come to me and drink" (John 7:37). Indeed, he promised that believers would become fountains (cf. John 7:38). He was tired (John 4:6)—yet he is the "rest" of the weary and the burdened (Matt 11:28). He was overcome by heavy sleep (cf. Matt 8:24)—yet he goes lightly over the sea, rebukes winds, and relieves the drowning Peter (Matt 14:25–32). He pays tax—yet he uses a fish to do it (Matt 17:24–27); indeed, he is emperor over those who demand the tax. He is called a "Samaritan, demonically possessed" (John 8:48)—but he rescues the man who came down from Jerusalem and fell

among thieves (cf. Luke 10:30). Yes, he is recognized by demons (Luke 4:33–34), drives out demons (cf. Matt 8:16), drowns deep a legion of spirits (Mark 5:9), and sees a prince of demons falling like lightning (cf. Luke 10:18). He is stoned, yet not hit (John 11:35); he prays, yet he hears prayer (cf. Mark 1:35; Matt 8:13). He weeps (John 11:35), yet he puts an end to weeping (cf. Luke 7:13). He asks where Lazarus is (John 11:34)—he was a man, yet he raises Lazarus (John 11:43–44)—he was God. He is sold, and cheap was the price—thirty pieces of silver (Matt 26:15), yet he buys back the world at the mighty cost of his own blood (cf. 1 Cor 6:20; 1 Pet 1:19). A sheep, he is led to the slaughter (Acts 8:32; Isa 53:7)—yet he shepherds Israel (Ps 80:1) and now the whole world as well (cf. John 10:11, 16). A lamb, he is dumb (Isa 53:7)—yet he is "word" (John 1:1), proclaimed by "the voice of one crying out in the wilderness" (John 1:53). He is weakened, wounded (Isa 53:5)—yet he cures every disease and every weakness (Matt 9:35). He is brought up to the tree (1 Pet 2:24) and nailed to it (cf. John 19:17)—yet by the tree of life he restores us (cf. Gen 2:9; Rev 2:7). Yes, he saves even a thief crucified with him (Luke 23:43); he wraps all the visible world in darkness (cf. Matt 27:45). He is given vinegar to drink (Matt 27:48), gall to eat (Matt 27:34)—and who is he? Why, one who turned water into wine (John 2:7–9), who took away the taste of bitterness (cf. Exod 15:25), who is all sweetness and desire (Song 5:16). He surrenders his life, yet he has power to take it again (John 10:17–18). Yes, the veil is rent, for things of heaven are being revealed, rocks split, and dead men have an earlier awakening (Matt 27:51–52). He dies (Matt 27:50), but he vivifies (John 5:21) and by death destroys death (2 Tim 1:10). He is buried (Matt 27:60), yet he rises again (John 20:8–9). He goes down to Hades, yet he leads souls up (cf. Eph. 4:8–9), ascends to heaven (Mark 16:19), and will come to judge quick and dead (2 Tim 4:1) and to probe discussions like these. If the first set of expressions starts you going astray, the second takes your error away.

(21) This is the answer we make perforce to these posers of puzzles. Perforce—because Christian people find long-winded controversy disagreeable and

one Adversary (cf. 1 Pet 5:8) enough for them. Yet our attackers made it essential, since remedies, too, must be made for diseases if they are to learn that their wisdom is not complete and that they are not invincible in their lavish attempts to nullify the Gospel. For when we abandon faith to take the power of reason as our shield, when we use philosophical inquiry to destroy the credibility of the Spirit, then reason gives way in the face of the vastness of the realities. Give way it must, set going, as it is, by the frail organ of human understanding. What happens then? The frailty of our reasoning looks like a frailty in our creed. Thus it is that, as Paul, too, judges, smartness of argument is revealed as a nullifying of the Cross (1 Cor 1:17). Faith, in fact, is what gives fullness to our reasoning.

But may he who "expounds hard questions and solves difficulties" (cf. Dan 5:12), who puts it into our minds to untie the twisted knots of their strained dogmas, may he, above all, change these men and make them believers instead of logicians, Christians instead of what they are currently called. Indeed this is our entreaty. "We beseech you, for Christ's sake; be reconciled to God and quench not the Spirit" (2 Cor 5:20; 1 Thess 5:19)—or rather let Christ be reconciled with you, and may the Spirit at long last illuminate you. Bent on quarrel though you may be, yet we have the Trinity in our safekeeping and by the Trinity can be saved, abiding pure and blameless (Phil 1:10) until the more complete revelation of what we long for in Christ himself, our Lord, to whom be glory for ever and ever. Amen.

Christological Controversy: The Texts

The resolution of the nature of the Trinity at the Council of Constantinople (381) introduced as many questions as it answered, as sophisticated and philosophically trained theologians struggled with more intricate questions of God's nature. Controversies arose, and heresies (once more) emerged in the struggle to define orthodox Christology (i.e., definitions of the nature of Christ). Apollinaris of Laodicea (ca. 315–392) proposed what one scholar has (facetiously) dubbed "space-suit" Christology: the Word of God entered into the human realm cloaked in human flesh, without the frailty of a human mind. Apollinaris wanted to combat "Arian" tendences to diminish Christ's divinity; nevertheless, at the Council of Constantinople, his position was condemned as heretical for denying Christ's full humanity.

Subsequent Christological controversy was constrained by these heretical poles: impairing Christ's divinity or impairing Christ's humanity. Terminology played a central, albeit confusing, role. Person (Greek *prosōpon*), subsistence or entity (*hypostasis*), and nature (*physis*) were all used in different ways to describe the resulting union of Christ's full humanity and full divinity. Some claimed that the union was at the level of "nature"; others placed it at the level of "personhood." Some tried to argue that divine nature was ultimately indescribable, but one lesson of the Trinitarian controversies had stuck: imprecision led to heresy.

Political rivalries also figured in Christological controversy, specifically the struggle for primacy between the bishops of Constantinople and Alexandria. The respective bishops of these cities in the fifth century, Nestorius and Cyril, led the theological factions that came to a head at the Council of Ephesus in 431. The touchstone for their Christological disagreement was a statement about the Virgin Mary: Nestorius objected to calling Mary *Theotokos,* "bearer" or "mother of God." To ascribe human characteristics to God (being contained in a womb, growing, eating, sleeping, dying) marred God's unchangeable incorruptibility. Nestorius emphasized the distinction between Christ's two "natures." Cyril found this position intolerable: if God was not totally and fully joined to humanity in the single person of Christ, then what use was the incarnation?

Both Nestorius and Cyril were deposed during the Council of Ephesus (see Text 35), with the most extreme facets of their theologies condemned. Cyril worked his way back into power (through such tactics as bribery), while Nestorius accepted deposition and exile. The debate, however, was far from over. Well into the sixth century, theologians continued to argue about the relation of human and divine natures in Christ's person, thus complicating orthodoxy and multiplying heresy. Those who took Nestorius's position to an extreme, insisting on a firm distinction between the human and divine in Christ, were labeled "dyophysites" (from Christ's "two natures") and were accused by their opponents of positing two distinct "Sons." Cyril's hard-line supporters, on the other hand, were dubbed "monophysites"; they insisted on "one, united nature" of Christ, a union of the human and divine natures in the incarnate Christ that seemed to allow the dominance of the divine over the human. The compromise that was reached at the conciliatory Council of Chalcedon in 451 (see Text 36), affirming the title *Theotokos* while also affirming that Christ was "one person in two [distinct] natures," was rejected by hardline Cyrillians and Nestorians. Debate and schism continued throughout the sixth century as Christological refinements, such as "theopaschitism" (God suffered on the cross), "monotheletism" (Christ's two natures operated with a single will), or "aphthartodocetism" (Christ's human body was incapable of corruption), were proposed and condemned as heretical. To this day, different branches of Eastern Orthodox and Oriental Orthodox Christianity continue to disagree over the Chalcedonian definition.

24. Nestorius: Letter to Cyril of Alexandria

Nestorius (ca. 381–ca. 451), like John Chrysostom the generation before him (see Text 15), preached in Antioch before being chosen to serve as bishop of Constantinople in 428. Like Chrysostom, Nestorius preached harshly against heresy and religious laxity and, like Chrysostom, he soon found himself embroiled in controversy. When Nestorius argued against calling Mary "the Mother of God" (in Greek, *Theotokos*), Bishop Cyril of Alexandria perceived this to be a direct attack on the full divinity of Christ. Within a few years, Nestorius had lost the support of the imperial house (particularly Pulcheria, sister of Emperor Theodosius II) and was condemned at the ecumenical Council of Ephesus (see Text 35). His writings were burned, and he lived out his life in exile in Egypt, during which time he wrote memoirs defending his life and theology (the *Bazaar of Heracleides,* surviving only in a Syriac translation).

In this letter to Cyril (written before his deposition at the Council of Ephesus), Nestorius presents his understanding of Cyril's Christology, a "single-nature" Christ that he saw as intolerably blurring the boundaries between the divine and the human, negating the salvific power of Christ's divinity. Nestorius attempts to "correct" his fellow bishop through a quick overview of the consensus of the "Fathers" (i.e., those bishops who had met at Nicaea: see Text 33) and the witness of Scripture. Nestorius's perception of Cyril's Christology as "single nature" is something of an exaggeration (although Cyril is guilty of the same ploy). Nevertheless, in this letter Nestorius's theological concern is clear: to preserve the distinction between the two natures (*physeis*) or entities (*hypostaseis*) that formed the person of Christ: God's eternal Word and the human person in which that Word dwelled.

From *Saint Cyril of Alexanderia, Letters 1–50,* ed. and trans. John I. McEnerney. Washington, D.C.: Catholic University of America Press, 1987. Used with permission.

To his most pious and God-loving fellow bishop, Cyril, Nestorius sends greetings in the Lord.

(1) I dismiss the outrages against me of your amazing letters as deserving healing forbearance and of being answered in due season through circumstances themselves. But as to that which does not permit of silence, since it involves great danger if silence be kept, of this, as far as I may be able, I shall attempt to make a concise statement without exerting myself to wordiness, being on my guard against the nausea of obscure and indigestible tediousness. I shall begin from the very wise utterances of your charity, citing them in your very words. Which, therefore, are the utterances of the amazing teaching of your letters?

(2) The holy and great council says that he, the only begotten Son, was begotten by nature of God the Father, true God of true God, light of light, through whom the Father made all things, that he descended, was made flesh and became man, suffered and rose. These are the words of your reverence, and perhaps you recognize your own.

(3) But hear also our words, a brotherly exhortation to piety and that which the great Paul solemnly stated to his beloved Timothy, "Be diligent in reading, in exhortation, and in teaching. For in so doing, you will save both yourself and those who hear you" (1 Tim 4:13,16). What, pray tell, does "be diligent" imply? It means that in reading the teaching of those holy Fathers without due attention, you failed to recognize a pardonable misconception. You thought that they had said that the Word, who is coeternal with the Father, is able to suffer. Look closely, if you please, at the precise meaning of their words, and you will find that the inspired chorus of the Fathers has not said that the consubstantial divinity is able to suffer nor that divinity, coeternal with the Father, was begotten nor that divinity rose from the dead when raising his destroyed temple. If you give ear to brotherly correction, by citing for you the very utterances, I shall rid you of your misinterpretation of those holy Fathers and through them of the inspired Scriptures.

(4) I believe, therefore, in our Lord Jesus Christ, his only begotten Son. Notice how they place first as foundations the words, Lord, Jesus, Christ, only begotten, and Son, the words common to divinity and humanity. Then they build upon it the tradition of the Incarnation, the Resurrection, and the Passion. They do so once the terminology signifying what is common to both natures has been presented, so that what belongs to filiation and lordship may not be separated, and what belongs to the natures be in no danger of confusion in the oneness of filiation.

(5) For in this Paul himself has been their teacher. When mentioning the divine Incarnation and about to go on to the Passion, he uses first the name Christ, a name common to both natures, as I said a short time earlier, and then he adds a specific term. What are his words? "Have this mind in you that was also in Christ Jesus, for though being in the form of God, he did not consider being equal to God a thing to be clung to, but (to omit details) became obedient to death, even to death on a cross" (Phil 2:5–8). When he was about to mention his death, in order that no one might assume from this that God the Word was subject to suffering, he put the word Christ first as a name signifying the substance capable of suffering and of the nature incapable of suffering in one person, so that without danger Christ may be called incapable and capable of suffering, incapable because of his divinity and capable because of the nature of his body. I could say much about this and, as said earlier, that the holy Fathers mentioned not a begetting according to the "economy," but an incarnation, but I perceive that the promise of brevity in my exordium curbs my speech and calls forth the second topic of your charity.

(6) In it, I praise the distinction of the natures according to the definition of humanity and divinity, and the conjunction of them into one person, and not saying that God the Word had need of a second begetting from a woman, and the profession that the divinity does not admit of suffering. In truth such doctrines are orthodox and opposite to the infamous opinions of all heresies concerning the natures of the Lord. But if the rest bring on some arcane wisdom incomprehensible for your audience to understand, it is for you to scrutinize. To me, at least, they seem to overthrow the first, for they introduced, I do not know how, him who was proclaimed in the first statements as incapable of suffering and not capable of receiving

a second begetting, as, in turn, capable of suffering and newly created. This is as if the properties belonging to God the Word according to nature were destroyed by the union with his temple; or as if it is considered of little import to men that the temple, which is without flaw and inseparable from the divine nature, for the sake of sinners endured both birth and death; or as if the voice of the Lord ought not to be believed when saying to the Jews, "Destroy this temple, and in three days I shall raise it up" (John 2:19). He did not say, "Destroy my divinity, and in three days I will raise it up." Although I would like to amplify my statements, I am restrained by recalling my promise. Nevertheless, this has to be said, though I am observing brevity.

(7) Everywhere in sacred Scripture whenever it makes mention of the "economy" of the Lord, the birth for our sake and the Passion are ascribed, not to the divinity, but to the humanity of Christ. So according to the most precise appellation, the Holy Virgin is called the Mother of Christ, not the Mother of God. Listen to these words of the Gospels that say, "The book of the generation of Jesus Christ, the son of David, the son of Abraham" (Matt 1:1). It is plain that God the Word was not the son of David. Accept another testimony, if you please, "Jacob begot Joseph, the husband of Mary, and of her was born Jesus who is called Christ" (Matt 1:16). Notice yet another voice testifying for us, "Now the origin of Christ was in this wise. When Mary his mother had been betrothed to Joseph, she was found to be with child by the Holy Spirit" (Matt 1:18). Whoever would assume that the divinity of the only begotten was a creation of the Holy Spirit? What need to say, "The mother of Jesus was there" and again, "with Mary the Mother of Jesus" and, "that which is begotten in her is of the Holy Spirit" and, "take the child and his mother and flee into Egypt" and, "concerning his Son who was born according to the flesh of the offspring of David" (John 2:1; cf. Acts 1:14; cf. Matt 1:20; Matt 2:13; Rom 1:3)? And again concerning his Passion, "Since God sent his Son in the likeness of sinful flesh, and concerning sin he has condemned sin in the flesh" and again, "Christ died for our sins" and, "since Christ suffered in the flesh" and,

"This is (not my divinity, but) my body, which is broken for you" (cf. Rom 8:3; 1 Cor 15:3; cf. 1 Pet 4:1; cf. Luke 22:19). And heed the countless other voices testifying to the human race that they should not think that the divinity of the Son was recent, or capable of receiving bodily suffering, but that the flesh was, which was joined to the nature of the divinity. Wherefore, also, Christ calls himself both David's Lord and Son, for he says, "What do you think of the Christ? Whose son is he?" They say to him, "David's." Jesus answered and said to them, "How then does David in the Spirit call him Lord saying, 'The Lord said to my Lord, sit at my right hand,'" (cf. Matt 22:42–44) as he is the Son of David by all means according to the flesh, but his Lord according to his divinity.

(8) Therefore, it is right and worthy of the Gospel traditions to confess that the body is the temple of the Son's divinity and a temple joined to the divinity according to a certain sublime and divine union, and that his divine nature makes his own the things of his body. But in the name of this relationship to attribute also to his divinity the properties of the united flesh, I mean birth, suffering, and death, is, my brother, the act of a mind truly led astray like the pagans or diseased like the minds of that mad Apollinaris, Arius, and the other heresies, but rather more grievously than they. For it is necessary that such as are dragged into error by the word relationship make the Word God partake of the nourishment of milk through the relationship and have a share in growing, little by little, and of fear at the time of his Passion, and be in need of angelic assistance. And I pass over in silence that circumcision, sacrificing, sweat, hunger, and thirst, which happened to his body on account of us, are worshipfully united to the divinity. If these are taken with reference to the divinity, and falsely, there is a cause for just condemnation against us as slanderers.

(9) These are the teachings handed down by the holy Fathers; these are the precepts of the Holy Scriptures. Thus one teaches about God the actions of the divine benevolence and majesty. "Meditate on these things, give yourself entirely to them, that your progress may be manifest to all and toward all," as Paul says (1 Tim 4:15).

(10) But you do well to cling to your anxiety for those scandalized, and I give thanks that your spirit, anxious over things divine, took thought of our affairs. But realize that you have been led astray by those condemned by the holy synod as Manichean sympathizers of the clerics who perhaps share your opinions. For the affairs of the church daily go forward, and the numbers of the faithful are so increasing through the grace of God that those who behold the multitudes of them repeat the words of the prophet, "The earth will be filled with the knowledge of the Lord, as much water would veil the seas" (cf. Isa 11:9), since the teaching has shed its light upon the interests of the emperor, and, to put it briefly, one would very joyfully find fulfilled day by day among us the famous saying with regard to all the ungodly heresies and the correct teaching of the church, "The house of Saul went forth and grew weak. And the house of David went forth and was strengthened" (2 Sam 3:1). These are our counsels, as of a brother to a brother. "But if anyone is disposed to be contentious," as Paul shall cry out against such a one through us, "we have no such custom, neither have the churches of God" (1 Cor 11:16).

(11) I and those with me greet especially all the brotherhood with you. May you continue to be vigorous in Christ and pray for us, my most God-loving friend who is dear to me in every way.

25. Cyril of Alexandria: Third Letter to Nestorius

Cyril (ca. 378–444) was the nephew of Bishop Theophilus of Alexandria and had watched his uncle lead the charge to depose John Chrysostom, bishop of Constantinople. Cyril succeeded his uncle in 412 and became a brilliant but (some would argue) ruthless defender of the faith. He produced biblical commentaries, doctrinal treatises, polemical works (notably a lengthy refutation of long-dead Julian the Apostate), and his episcopacy witnessed the lynching of the pagan philosopher Hypatia and religious unrest resulting in the expulsion of the city's ancient Jewish community.

In the following letter (the third written to Nestorius, delivered soon before the Council of Ephesus), Cyril accuses Nestorius of denying a true union of human and divine in Christ; Nestorius, he claims, merely believes in a "juxtaposition," such that the Gospels might be read as the account of two persons: God performed miracles, but Jesus (the man) wept, ate, and died. Like Nestorius, Cyril marshals scriptural citations, references to the "Fathers" at Nicaea, and theological reasoning; he also invokes the bishop of Rome, Celestine, who would become a powerful ally in the upcoming Council of Ephesus.

Appended to this letter are twelve anathemas ("curses"), condemning a variety of theological positions that might be held to separate Christ into two persons or "entities" (*hypostaseis*). In them, Cyril reaches the pinnacle of his "one-nature" Christology when he claims (anathema 12) that "the Word of God suffered, was crucified, and died." Although perceived even by his contemporaries as perhaps extreme in its formulation, Cyril's theology seeks above all to preserve the truly saving "economy" of Christ's God-man nature: anything less than full union, Cyril believed, would entail less than full salvation.

From *Saint Cyril of Alexanderia, Letters 1–50,* ed. and trans. John I. McEnerney. Washington, D.C.: Catholic University of America Press, 1987. Used with permission.

To the most pious and most God-loving fellow bishop Nestorius, Cyril and the synod assembled in Alexandria from the diocese of Egypt send greetings in the Lord.

(1) Since our Savior distinctly says, "He who loves father or mother more than me is not worthy of me, and he who loves son or daughter more than me is not worthy of me" (Matt 10:37), what shall we suffer who are demanded by your reverence to love you more than Christ, the Savior of us all? Who on the day of judgment will be able to help us? What kind of defense shall we find, if we valued silence so long about the blasphemies that came to be on your part against him? If you injured only yourself by thinking and teaching such things, our concern would be less. You have scandalized the whole church, and you have cast a leaven of strange and foreign heresy among the people, not only among those there (i.e., at Constantinople) but everywhere.

(2) The books of your statements were handed round. What kind of an account will suffice for the silence of those with us, or how is it not necessary to remember Christ saying "Do not think that I have come to send peace upon the earth but a sword. For I came to set a man at variance with his father, and a daughter with her mother" (Matt 10:34–35)? When the faith is being injured, let reverence toward parents be dismissed as obsolete and unstable! Let the law of warm affection toward children and kinsmen be silenced! Let death hereafter be better for the pious than life, "that they might find a better resurrection" (Heb 11:35) according to the Scriptures!

(3) Therefore, together with the holy synod, which has been assembled in the great city of Rome with our most holy and God-revering brother and fellow servant, Celestine the bishop, presiding, we also solemnly charge you by this third letter, advising you to desist from the doctrines, so wicked and perverted, which you think and teach. Choose instead the true faith, the one handed down to the churches from the beginning through the holy apostles and evangelists, who have been eyewitnesses and servants of the word. If your reverence does not do this, according to the time defined and limited in the letter of the aforementioned most holy and most God-revering brother and fellow minister of ours, Celestine, the bishop of the Church of Rome, know you that you have no clerical office among us, nor place, nor esteem among the priests of God and the bishops.

(4) It is not possible for us to disregard churches so disturbed and people scandalized and true faith being set aside and flocks being torn asunder by you who ought to preserve them if you were with us a lover of the true faith and following the piety of the holy Fathers. But we are all in communion with all those, both lay persons and clerics, who were excommunicated for the faith by your reverence or deposed. It is not just that they who have been known to hold true doctrines be injured by your decrees because they, in doing the right, have contradicted you. You have made known this very thing in your letter, written by you to our most holy fellow bishop of the great city of Rome, Celestine.

(5) But it shall not suffice for your reverence to confess with us just the profession of the faith set forth in the Holy Spirit during critical times by the holy and great synod assembled in the city of Nicaea. You have not understood and have not interpreted it rightly, but rather perversely, even if you confess the text with your lips. But you must follow up in writing and under oath confess that you also anathematize, on the one hand, your abominable and profane teachings, and, on the other hand, you will teach and think what we, all the bishops throughout the West and the East, teachers and leaders of the laity, [think and teach]. The holy synod in Rome and we all agreed that the letters to your reverence from the Church of Alexandria were orthodox and blameless. But we subjoined to these writings of ours what it is necessary to think and teach and the teachings from which it is necessary to desist.

(6) For this is the faith of the Catholic and Apostolic Church to which all the orthodox bishops throughout the West and East agree. We believe in one God, the Father almighty, creator of all things both visible and invisible, and in one Lord Jesus Christ, the only begotten Son of God, begotten of the Father, that is of the same substance as the Father, God of God, light of light, true God of true God, begotten not made, consubstantial with the Father, by

whom all things were made, both those in heaven and those on earth, who for us humans and our salvation descended, and was incarnate, and was made man, suffered and rose on the third day, ascended into heaven, and is coming to judge the living and the dead; and in the Holy Spirit.

(7) But those who say: there was a time when he was not, and he was not before he was begotten, and that he was begotten from what was not or who say that he is of some other *hypostasis* or substance and say that the Son of God was mutable or subject to change, these the Catholic and Apostolic Church anathematizes. Following in every way the confessions of the holy Fathers, which they made by the Holy Spirit speaking in them, and following the meaning of the thoughts in them, and, as it were, going along a royal road, we say that he, the only begotten Word of God, begotten of the very substance of the Father, true God of true God, light of light, by whom all things were made both those in heaven and those on earth, having descended for our salvation, and having come down to an emptying of himself (cf. Phil 2:7–8), was incarnate and was made man, that is, having taken flesh from the Holy Virgin and having made it his own from the womb, he endured our birth and came forth as man from a woman, not having lost what he was, but even though he was born in the assumption of flesh and blood, even so he remained what he was, God manifestly in nature and in truth.

(8) We say also that the flesh was neither turned into the nature of the divinity nor, indeed, that the ineffable nature of the Word of God was altered into the nature of the flesh, for he is immutable and absolutely unchangeable, always being the same, according to the Scriptures. But when he was visible and still remained an infant in swaddling clothes and in the bosom of the Virgin who bore him, he filled the whole of creation as God and was coruler with the one who begot him. For the divine is both without quantity and without magnitude and does not admit of limitation.

(9) Confessing that the Word was united to flesh substantially, we adore one Son and Lord Jesus Christ. We do not set up a division and distinguish the man and God, nor do we say that they are conjoined to one another by dignity and authority, for this is idle chatter and nothing more. Nor do we speak of the Word of God separately as Christ and, likewise, the one born of woman separately as another Christ, but we acknowledge only one Christ, the Word of God the Father, with his own flesh. As man he has been the anointed among us, although he gives the Spirit to those worthy of receiving it, and not by measure, as the blessed evangelist, John, says (cf. John 3:34). Neither do we say that the Word of God dwelled, as in an ordinary man, in the one born of the Holy Virgin, in order that Christ might not be thought to be a man bearing God. For even if the Word both "dwelt among us" (cf. John 1:14), and it is said that in Christ "dwells all the fullness of the Godhead bodily" (Col 2:9), we do not think that, being made flesh, the Word is said to dwell in him just as in those who are holy, and we do not define the indwelling in him to be the same. But united according to nature (*physis*) and not changed into flesh, the Word produced an indwelling such as the soul of man might be said to have in its own body.

(10) Therefore Christ is one, both Son and Lord, not by reason of a man having simply a conjoining to God, as God, by a unity of dignity or indeed of authority. For the equality of honor does not unite the natures, and indeed Peter and John were equal in honor to each other, insofar as they were both apostles and holy disciples, except that the two were not one. Neither indeed do we think that the manner of the "conjoining" is according to a "juxtaposition," for this is not sufficient for a personal union, nor indeed according to a nonessential participation, as we also, who cleave to the Lord according to the Scripture, are one spirit with him, but rather we reject the term "conjoining" as not being sufficient to signify the union. Neither do we speak of the Word of God the Father as the God or Lord of the Christ, in order that we may not again openly cut into two the one Christ, the Son and Lord, and may not fall foul of the charge of blasphemy by making him his own God and Lord. The Word of God united, as we already said before, to flesh according to *hypostasis* is God of all and is Lord of all, and neither is he servant of himself nor master of himself. To think and say this is absurd and rather impi-

ous as well. He said God is his Father, although he is God by nature and of his Father's substance. But we have not failed to perceive that while he continued to be God, he also became man under God according to the law proper to the nature of the humanity. But how might he become God or master of himself? Therefore, as man, and as far as concerns what is proper to the limits of the emptying of himself, he says that he himself is under God as we are. Thus he also was "born under the law" (cf. Gal 4:4), although he proclaims the law and is the lawgiver as God.

(11) But we refuse to say of Christ, "Because of the one who clothed him with flesh, I worship the one clothed; because of the invisible, I adore the invisible." It is abhorrent to say this also, "God, the one assumed, is associated with the one assuming him." Whoever says these things severs him again into two christs and, in turn, sets the humanity and divinity apart also. Whoever says these things admittedly denies the union, according to which one is worshipped together with the other, not as one in another. Indeed, God is not associated with another, but one Christ Jesus is meant, the only begotten Son, who is revered along with his flesh by one act of adoration. We confess that he, the Son begotten of God the Father and only begotten God, though being incapable of suffering according to his own nature, suffered in his own flesh for our sake, according to the Scriptures, and that he made his own the sufferings of his own flesh in his crucified body impassibly, for by the grace of God and for the sake of all he tasted death by having surrendered to it his own body although by nature he was life, and was himself the Resurrection. In order that by his ineffable power, after having trampled upon death in his own flesh first, he might become "the first born from the dead" (Col 1:18) and "the first fruits of those who have fallen asleep" (1 Cor 15:20), and in order that he might prepare the way for the rise to immortality for the nature of man, by the grace of God, as we said just now, for the sake of all he tasted death, but on the third day he came back to life after despoiling hell. Wherefore, even if the resurrection of the dead may be said to be through a man, still we mean that the man is the Word begotten of God and that the power of death has been de-

stroyed through him, and he will come at the right time as the one Son and Lord in the glory of the Father to judge the world in justice, as it is written (cf. Acts 17:31).

(12) But of necessity we shall add this also. Proclaiming the death according to the flesh of the only begotten Son of God, that is, of Jesus Christ, and confessing his Resurrection from the dead and his Ascension into heaven, we celebrate the unbloody sacrifice in the churches, and we thus approach the spiritual blessings and are made holy, becoming partakers of the holy flesh and of the precious blood of Christ, the Savior of us all. And we do this, not as men receiving common flesh, far from it, nor truly the flesh of a man sanctified and conjoined to the Word according to a unity of dignity, or as one having had a divine indwelling, but as the truly lifegiving and very own flesh of the Word himself. For, being life according to nature as God, when he was made one with his own flesh, He proclaimed it life giving. Wherefore even if he may say to us, "Amen, I say to you: Except you eat the flesh of the Son of Man and drink his blood" (cf. John 6:53), we shall not conclude that his flesh is of some one as of a man who is one of us (for how will the flesh of a man be life-giving according to its own nature?), but as being truly the very flesh of the Son who was both made man and named man for us.

(13) Moreover, we do not allocate the statements of our Savior in the Gospels either to two *hypostaseis* or indeed to two persons, for the one and only Christ is not twofold, even if he be considered as from two entities and they different, which had been made into an inseparable unity, just as, of course, man also is considered to be of soul and body yet is not twofold, but rather one from both. But, because we think rightly, we shall maintain that the statements as man and also the statements as God have been made by one person.

(14) When as God he says about himself, "he who has seen me has seen the Father" (John 14:9), and, "I and the Father are one" (John 10:30), we think of his divine and ineffable nature according to which he is one with his Father through identity of substance and is his likeness and image and the brightness of his

glory (cf. Heb 1:3). But when, not despising the full measure of his humanity, he said to the Jews, "But now you are seeking to kill me, one who has spoken the truth to you" (John 8:40), again nevertheless even from the full measure of his humanity we recognize the Word who is God in both equality and likeness to his Father. If we must believe that although he was God by nature, he was made flesh, that is to say, he was made man animated by a rational soul, what reason would anyone have for being ashamed at statements by him if they had been made by him as man? For if he declined the words that are proper to a man, what necessary reason was there for him becoming man as we are? For what reason would he, who descended for us into a voluntary emptying of himself, decline words proper to the emptying? Therefore to one person must all the statements in the Gospels be ascribed, to the one incarnate *hypostasis* of the Word, for the Lord Jesus Christ is one, according to the Scriptures.

(15) But if he may be called the "apostle and high priest of our confession" (cf. Heb 3:1) as the one offering to God the Father the confession of the faith being conveyed by us to him and through him to God the Father, and also to the Holy Spirit, again we say that he is by nature the only begotten Son of God. And we do not assign to a man different from him the name and reality of his priesthood, for he became mediator of God and men and conciliator unto peace having offered himself to God the Father for an odor of sweetness. Wherefore he also said, "Sacrifice and oblation you did not want: but a body you have fitted to me. In holocausts and sin offerings you have had no pleasure. Then said I, 'Behold I come (in the head of the book it is written of me) to do your will, O God'" (Heb 10:5–7). For he has offered his own body for an odor of sweetness for our sake, rather than his own. What oblation or sacrifice did he need for his own sake, who, since he is God, is superior to all sin? For "if all have sinned and have need of the glory of God" (cf. Rom 3:23) consequently we are apt to fall, and the nature of man was weakened toward sin. But he was not so, and we are inferior to his glory because of this. How then would there be a doubt remaining that the true lamb has been sacrificed through us and for our sake? The statement that he has offered himself for his own sake and for ours in no way would escape an accusation for impiety. He has erred in no fashion, nor did he commit sin. Of what sacrifice, therefore, did he have need, since there existed no sin for which, and very reasonably, a sacrifice might exist?

(16) But when he says concerning the Spirit: "He will glorify me" (John 16:14), we, rightly, do not say that the one Christ and Son of God, because he was in need of glory from another, gained glory from the Holy Spirit, since his Spirit is not superior to him nor above him. But since he used the Holy Spirit as a proof of his divinity for the performance of great works, he says that he was glorified by him, just as if anyone of us might say, concerning perhaps the strength within him, or the understanding of some subject, "they will glorify me."

(17) For even if the Spirit exists in his own *hypostasis,* and moreover is considered by himself insofar as he is the Spirit and not the Son, yet he is not therefore alien from the Son, for he is called the Spirit of truth and Christ is the truth, and the Spirit proceeds from him, just as undoubtedly he also proceeds from God the Father. Wherefore the Spirit even through the hand of the holy apostles worked miracles after our Lord, Jesus Christ, ascended into heaven, and thereby glorified him. For it is believed that he is God according to nature, and again that he acts through his own Spirit. For this reason he also said, "because he will receive of what is mine and will declare it to you" (John 16:14). And we do not in any way say that the Spirit is wise and powerful from a participation, for he is all-perfect and without want of any good. But since he is the Spirit of the power and wisdom of the Father that is of the Son, he is in very truth wisdom and power.

(18) And since the Holy Virgin brought forth as man God united to flesh according to the *hypostasis,* we say that she is the Mother of God, not because the nature of the Word had a beginning of existence from the flesh, for, "In the beginning was the Word, and the Word was with God, and the Word was God" (John 1:1), and he is the creator of the ages, coeternal with the Father, and creator of all things. As we have stated

before, having united the human to himself according to *hypostasis* he even endured birth in the flesh from the womb. He did not require because of his own nature as God a birth in time and in the last stages of the world. He was born in order that he might bless the very beginning of our existence, and in order that, because a woman bore him when he was united to the flesh, the curse against the whole race might be stopped. This was sending our bodies from the earth to death, and by him abolishing the saying, "in pain shall you bring forth children" (Gen 3:16), the words of the prophet might be shown to be true, "strong death has swallowed them up" (Isa 25:7 [LXX]) and again "God has taken away every tear from every face" (Isa 25:8). Because of this, we say that according to the "economy" he himself both blessed the marriage and attended it when invited in Cana of Galilee along with his holy apostles.

(19) We have been taught to have these thoughts by the holy apostles and evangelists and by all the divinely inspired Scripture and by the true confession of the saintly Fathers. It is necessary that your reverence also consent to all these and agree to every one without deceit. What your reverence must anathematize has been subjoined to this letter from us.

1. If anyone does not confess that the Emmanuel is God in truth and because of this does not confess that the Holy Virgin is the Mother of God (for she bore according to the flesh the Word of God made flesh), let him be anathema.

2. If anyone does not confess that the Word of God the Father was united to flesh substantially and that there is one Christ with his own flesh and that he manifestly is God, the same one as is man, let him be anathema.

3. If anyone separates the *hypostaseis* in the one Christ after the union, joining them together only by a conjunction according to dignity, that is, by authority or power, and not rather by a combination that is according to a real union, let him be anathema.

4. If anyone attributes to two persons, that is, to

two *hypostaseis,* the sayings in the Gospels and apostolic writings, either those made by the saints in reference to Christ or those made by him concerning himself, and ascribes some to a man considered separately from the Word of God and ascribes others, as proper to God, only to the Word of God the Father, let him be anathema.

5. If anyone dares to say that Christ is a God-bearing man, and not, rather, that he is God in truth, as the one Son and by nature, in so far as the Word was made flesh and has flesh and blood just as we do, let him be anathema.

6. If anyone says that the Word of God the Father is God or master of the Christ and does not confess rather that he is God, the same one as is man, since the Word was made flesh, according to the Scriptures, let him be anathema.

7. If anyone says that Jesus as man was activated by the Word of God and that the glory of the only begotten was attributed as if the only begotten was separate from him, let him be anathema.

8. If anyone dares to say that the man assumed must be adored with God, the Word, and be glorified with him, and be called God by the same name, as if one existed in the other (for the word "with," which has always been added, forces this to be the meaning), and does not rather honor the Emmanuel with one adoration only and does not send up to him one hymn of praise only, as the Word was made flesh, let him be anathema.

9. If anyone says that the one Lord Jesus Christ has been glorified by the Spirit, and the Lord was using the power that was through the Spirit as if it belonged to someone else, and says that the Lord received from the Spirit the power to act against unclean spirits and to complete among men the miracles and does not rather say that the Spirit is his very own through whom he has performed the miracles, let him be anathema.

10. The divine Scripture says that Christ is the

high priest and apostle of our confession (cf. Heb 3:1), and has offered himself for us in an odor of fragrance to God the Father (cf. Eph 5:2). If anyone therefore says that our high priest and apostle is not the very Word of God when he was made flesh and man as we are, but as another man apart from him born of a woman, or if anyone says that he offered himself as the sacrifice for his own sake also, and not rather for us only (for he who has not known sin would have no need of a sacrifice), let him be anathema.

11. If anyone does not confess that the flesh of the Lord is life giving and is the very own flesh of the Word from God the Father, but says that it is the flesh of someone else other than him joined to him according to dignity, that is, as having had only a divine indwelling, or does not rather confess that his flesh is life giving, as we said, because it was made the very flesh of the Word, who is able to endow all things with life, let him be anathema.

12. If anyone does not confess that the Word of God suffered in the flesh and was crucified in the flesh and tasted death in the flesh, and became the firstborn from the dead, since he is life and life giving as God, let him be anathema.

The Nature of Humanity: The Texts

Scripture taught early Christians that humanity had lost an original perfection in the Garden of Eden through sin and that Jesus Christ had come to redeem humanity from that Fall. As significant to this economy of salvation as the nature of Christ and the rest of the Trinity, therefore, was the nature of humans. What had humans lost in the Fall, and what had Christ come to restore? Controversy over the nature of God and Christ led to controversy over the nature of humanity.

Much of this controversy revolved around the question of humanity's potential to participate in its own redemption. Had the sin of Adam and Eve somehow irreparably damaged the nature of all humans, or did they still retain the full and glorious "image and likeness of God"? Were the seemingly negative aspects of humanity (sin, passion, mortality) original to human nature or a consequence of the Fall? Could humans ever rid themselves of the taint of evil, sex, and death in this life? Was sin itself now endemic to humanity, an internal defect, or was it rather a cosmic force that Christ had battled and against which humans now possessed the weapons to fight?

Interpretation of Scripture played a vital role in determining the possibility of humans' participation in their own salvation, particularly the narratives of sin and redemption in the Old Testament (Genesis) and the sin-laden preaching of the apostle Paul (Romans). Intertwined with these theological and interpretive complications was the religious culture of late ancient Christianity. During this period, Christians were undertaking extraordinary feats of physical and spiritual devotion to participate more fully in their own salvation (see Chapter 9). The prominence of this ascetic elitism brought into sharper relief questions of human potential for sinlessness and the relation between ability and divine assistance.

As was the case for debates about God's nature, many Christians found it easier to determine error (heresy) than truth (orthodoxy). Some of the most popular "heresies" of the fourth and fifth centuries emerged out of precisely these questions of human nature and redemption: the Manicheans, a quasi-Christian movement that viewed the human person as the battleground for cosmically opposed forces of good and evil; the Origenists (followers of the speculative theology of the third-century exegete Origen), who believed in the ultimate restoration of the entire created order (including angels, demons, and perhaps even the devil) into a total union with God; and the Pelagians, who insisted on the capacity of humans to exert their own will in cooperation with the grace of God to effect salvation. Even though these "heresies" were condemned by orthodox partisans, their persistent questioning of human participation in divine redemption forced the church to find other answers to the vexing question of human fault, responsibility, and possibility.

26. Athanasius: On the Incarnation of the Word

Athanasius (ca. 298–373) spent most of his ecclesiastical career engaged in theological struggles. As a young man, he was an assistant to Bishop Alexandria of Alexandria, accompanying him to the Council of Nicaea in 325. He succeeded Alexander as bishop in 328. During Athanasius's long episcopacy, political and theological fighting led to his deposition (removal from office) by antagonistic emperors no fewer than five times. Athanasius is most often recalled as a champion of orthodox Trinitarian theology, as an unyielding and (at times) ferocious defender of the Nicene Creed (see "Trinitarian Controversy" at the beginning of this chapter). His two-part apologetic treatise *Against the Gentiles* and *On the Incarnation of the Word* seems to date from early in Athanasius's career, perhaps the first decade of his episcopacy. In the first part of the treatise, he takes up the familiar themes of second- and third-century Christian apology: attacking the idolatry and mythology of the Greeks and the stubbornness and faithlessness of the Jews.

The second part of the treatise, *On the Incarnation of the Word,* reaches beyond this apologetic framework to give a detailed examination of the rationale behind the incarnation of the Son of God. Although the treatise does not mention Nicaea, *homoousios,* or Arius, the strict separation of the corruptible created order—humans—and the incorruptible Creator—God the Father, the Word, and the Spirit—gives a clear sense of Athanasius's theological standpoint. There is a subtle argument against the Arian party, whose understanding of the Son led to a particular understanding of human nature in the scheme of salvation. For Athanasius, humans are sunk in corruptibility, as a result of their created nature and their original disobedience to God. All of humanity suffers, and only the Word (*Logos*) of God can restore incorruptibility to the rational (*logikoi*) creations of God. The human body of Christ incarnate, Athanasius explains, was an "instrument" by which God restored his creations: "He became human that we might become divine." Although nominally a treatise on the divine incarnation, this is really a sophisticated theological statement on the nature of human existence at its origins, in its present state, and in its future incorruptibility, a complex demonstration of how theologies of God engender theologies of humanity.

(1) We have discussed in the preceding part, sufficiently though briefly, the error of the gentiles concerning idols and their superstition, how they invented them from the beginning and that it was out of wickedness that men thought up for themselves the worship of idols. We also by the grace of God made a few remarks concerning the divinity of the Word of the Father and his providence for and power in the universe: that the good Father disposes all things through him, and the universe is moved by him and is given life through him. Well then, my friend and true lover of Christ, let us next with pious faith tell of the incarnation of the Word and expound his divine manifestation to us, which the Jews slander and the Greeks mock, but which we ourselves adore, so that from the apparent degradation of the Word you may

From *Contra Gentes and De Incarnatione,* trans. and ed. R. W. Thomson. Oxford, England: Clarendon Press, 1971. Used with permission.

have ever greater and stronger piety toward him. For the more he is mocked by unbelievers, the greater witness he provides of his divinity because what men cannot understand as impossible he shows to be possible, and what men mock as unsuitable by his goodness he renders suitable, and what men explain away and mock as human by his power he shows to be divine, overthrowing the illusion of idols by his apparent degradation through the cross and invisibly persuading those who mock and do not believe to recognize his divinity and power.

For the explanation of these matters one must remember what was said earlier, that you may be able to know the reason for the manifestation in the body of the Word of such and so great a Father, and lest you think that the Savior put on a body as a consequence of his nature, but rather that although he is incorporeal by nature and Word, yet through the mercy and goodness of his Father he appeared to us in a human body for our salvation. But as we proceed in our exposition of this, we must first speak about the creation of the universe and its creator, God, so that in this way one may consider as fitting that its renewal was effected by the Word who created it in the beginning. For it will appear in no way contradictory if the Father worked its salvation through the same one by whom he created it.

(2) The making of the world and the creation of the universe have been understood by many in various ways, and everyone has defined them according to his individual liking. Some say that the universe came into being of its own accord and by chance, such as the Epicureans who pretend that there is no providence in the world, though their theory is contrary to the obvious facts of experience. For if, as they claim, the universe came into being by chance without providence, then everything would have had to be uniform and identical and undifferentiated. Everything would have been as in a single mass sun or moon, and among humans the whole would have been a hand or eye or foot. Now this is not the case. We see here the sun, there the moon or earth; and again as for human bodies, here a foot, there a hand or head. And such order indicates that they did not come into being of their own accord, but shows that

a cause preceded their creation, from which cause one can apprehend the God who ordered and made the universe.

But others, among whom is that great philosopher among the Greeks, Plato, claim that God made the world from preexistent and uncreated matter: God would not have been able to make anything unless matter already existed, just as a carpenter must have wood first in order to be able to fashion it. But they do not realize when they say this that they are imputing weakness to God. For if he is not the cause of the matter but simply makes things from preexistent matter, then he is weak, since he cannot fashion any of the things that exist without matter—just as the weakness of the carpenter consists in his inability to fashion any necessary object without wood. For, according to the argument, unless matter existed, God would not have made anything. But how, then, could he be called Maker and Creator if his creative ability had come from something else, I mean from matter? And if this is the case, according to them God would be merely a craftsman and not the creator of their existence if he fashions underlying matter but is not himself the cause of the matter. For he could in no way be called Creator if he does not create the matter from which created things come into being.

Others again among the heretics devise for themselves another creator of the universe apart from the Father of our Lord Jesus Christ. These are exceedingly blind in what they say. For the Lord said to the Jews: *Have you not read that he who created them in the beginning made them male and female?* And he said: *For this cause a man will leave his father and mother and will cleave to his wife, and the two will be one flesh.* Then referring to the Creator he added: *What then God has joined together let not man put asunder* (Matt 19:4–6). How then do they introduce a creation alien to the Father? But if, according to the all-inclusive saying of John, *all things were made by him and without him was nothing made* (John 1:3), how could there be another creator apart from the Father of Christ?

(3) These are their notions. But the divinely inspired teaching of faith in Christ refutes their vain talk as impiety. It teaches that the world did not come

into being of its own accord because it did not lack providence, and that neither was it made from preexistent matter since God is not weak, but that through the Word God brought the universe, which previously in no way subsisted at all, into being from nonexistence, as he says through Moses: *In the beginning God made heaven and earth* (Gen 1:1), and through the most helpful book of the Shepherd: *First of all believe that God is one, who created and fashioned the universe and brought it from nonexistence into being,* (*Hermas* Sim. 1). This Paul too indicates when he says: *By faith we understand that the worlds were formed by the word of God, so that the visible was not made from what is apparent* (Heb 11:3). For God is good—or rather the source of goodness—and the good has no envy for anything. Thus, because he envies nothing its existence, he made everything from nothing through his own Word, our Lord Jesus Christ. And among these creatures, of all those on earth he had special pity for the human race, and seeing that by the definition of its own existence it would be unable to persist forever, he gave it an added grace, not simply creating men like all irrational animals on the earth, but making them in his own image and giving them also a share in the power of his own Word, so that having as it were shadows of the Word and being made rational, they might be able to remain in felicity and live the true life in paradise, which is really that of the saints. Furthermore, knowing that human faculty of free will could turn either way, he first secured the grace they had been given by imposing a law and a set place. For he brought them into his paradise and gave them a law, so that if they kept the grace and remained good, they would enjoy the life of paradise, without sorrow, pain, or care, in addition to their having the promise of immortality in heaven. But if they transgressed and turned away (from the law) and became wicked, they would know that they would suffer the natural corruption consequent on death and would no longer live in paradise, but in future dying outside it would remain in death and corruption. This also the Divine Scripture foretells, speaking in God's words: *Of all the trees in paradise you shall eat, but of the tree of knowledge of good and evil you shall not eat. On the day you eat of*

it, you shall die by death (Gen 2:16–17). And this "you shall die by death," what else is it save not merely to die, but to remain in the corruption of death?

(4) Perhaps you are wondering why, when we proposed to speak about the incarnation of the Word, we are now treating of the beginning of humanity. But this is not irrelevant to the purpose of our exposition. For we must, when speaking of the manifestation of the Savior to us, speak also of the beginning of humanity, in order that you may know that our own cause was the reason of his coming and that our own transgression called forth the mercy of the Word, so that the Lord came even to us and appeared among humans. For we were the cause of his incarnation, and for our salvation he had compassion to the extent of being born and revealed in a body. God, then, had so created man and willed that he should remain in incorruptibility. But when humans had disregarded and turned away from the understanding of God and had thought of and invented for themselves wickedness, as was said in the first part, then they received the condemnation of death, which had been previously threatened, and no longer remained as they had been created, but as they had devised, were ruined. And death overcame them and reigned over them. For the transgression of the commandment turned them to what was natural, so that, as they had come into being from nonexistence, so also they might accordingly suffer in time the corruption consequent to their nonbeing. For if, having such a nature as not ever to exist, they were summoned to existence by the advent and mercy of the Word, it followed that because humans were deprived of the understanding of God and had turned to things that do not exist—for what does not exist is evil, but what does exist is good since it has been created by the existent God—then they were also deprived of eternal existence. But this means that when they perished, they would remain in death and corruption. For man is by nature mortal in that he was created from nothing. But because of his likeness to him who exists, if he had kept this through contemplating God, he would have blunted his natural corruption and would have remained incorruptible, as the book of Wisdom says: *The keeping of the*

law is the assurance of incorruptibility (Wis 6:18). But being incorruptible, he would thenceforth have lived as God, as also somewhere the Divine Scripture declares, saying: *I said that you are gods and all sons of the Highest: but you die like men and fall as one of the princes* (Ps 82:6).

(5) For God did not only create us from nothing, but he also granted us by the grace of the Word to live a divine life. But humans, turning away from things eternal and by the counsel of the devil turning toward things corruptible, were themselves the cause of the corruption in death. They are, as I said above, corruptible by nature, but by the grace of the participation of the Word, they could have escaped from the consequences of their nature if they had remained virtuous. For on account of the Word who was in them, even natural corruption would not have touched them, as the book of Wisdom says: *God created man for incorruption, and made him the image of his own eternity, but by the envy of the devil death entered the world* (Wis 2:23–24). Since this happened, men died, and corruption thenceforth took a strong hold on them and was more powerful than the force of nature over the whole race, the more so as it had taken up against them the threat of God concerning the transgression of the law. For in their trespasses humans had not stopped at the set limits, but gradually moving forward, at length had advanced beyond all measure. In the beginning they had been inventors of evil and had called upon themselves death and corruption, and in the end they turned to vice and exceeded all iniquity, and not stopping at one wickedness but inventing ever more new things, they became insatiable in sinning. For adulteries and thefts were committed everywhere; the whole earth was filled with murders and violence; there was no care for the law, but for corruption and vice; and every wickedness, singly and in concert, was committed by all. Cities warred with cities, and peoples rose up against peoples; the whole world was torn apart by seditions and battles; and everyone competed in lawlessness. Not even acts against nature were alien to them, but as the witness of Christ, the Apostle, said: *Their women changed the natural use for that which is contrary to nature; and in the same*

way also the men, leaving the natural use of the woman, burned with their desire for each other, men with men doing what is shameful, and they received in themselves the recompense that their error deserved (Rom 1:26–27).

(6) For these reasons death held greater sway and corruption stood firm against humans; the human race was being destroyed, and man who was rational and who had been made in the image was being obliterated; and the work created by God was perishing. For indeed, as I said above, by the law death thenceforth prevailed over us. And it was impossible to flee the law, since this had been established by God because of the transgression. And these events were truly at once absurd and improper. For it was absurd that, having spoken, God should lie, in that he had established a law that man would die by death if he were to transgress the commandment, and man did not die after he had transgressed, but God's word was made void. For God would not have been truthful, if after he had said we would die, man had not died. And furthermore, it would have been improper that what had once been created rational and had partaken of his Word, should perish and return again to nonexistence through corruption. For it would not have been worthy of the goodness of God that what had been brought into existence by him should be corrupted on account of the deceit that the devil had played on men. And it would have been especially improper that the handiwork of God in humanity should come to nought, either through their neglect or through the deceit of demons.

Therefore, since rational creatures were being corrupted and such works were perishing, what should God, who is good, have done? Allow corruption to hold sway over them and death to capture them? Then what need would there have been for them to have been created in the beginning? For it was more fitting that they should not be created than that having come into being, they should be neglected and perish. For by their neglect, the weakness of God rather than his goodness would be made known, if after creating he had abandoned his work to corruption, rather than if he had not created man in the beginning. For if he had not created him, there would have been no one to consider his weakness. But after he had made him and brought him into existence, it would have been most improper that his works should perish, especially in front of him who created him. So it was not right that he should permit humans to be destroyed by corruption because this was neither proper nor fitting for the goodness of God.

(7) But as this had to be, so again on the other hand lies opposed to it what was reasonable for God, that he should appear truthful in passing the law about death. For it would have been absurd that for our benefit and permanence God, the Father of truth, should appear a liar. What therefore in this matter had to occur, or what should God have done? Demand repentance from humans for the transgression? For one might say that this was fitting for God, that as they had become subject to corruption by the transgression, so by repentance they might return to incorruption. But repentance would not have saved God's honor, for he would still have remained untruthful unless humans were in the power of death. Repentance gives no exemption from the consequences of nature, but merely looses sins. If, therefore, there had been only sin and not its consequence of corruption, repentance would have been very well. But if, since transgression had overtaken them, humans were now prisoners to natural corruption, and they had been deprived of the grace of being in the image, what else should have happened? Or who was needed for such grace and recalling except the Word of God, who also in the beginning had created the universe from nothing? For it was his task both to bring what was corruptible back again to incorruption and to save what was above all fitting for the Father. For since he is the Word of the Father and above everyone, consequently he alone was both able to re-create the universe and be worthy to suffer for all and to be an advocate on behalf of all before the Father.

(8) For this reason the incorporeal and incorruptible and immaterial Word of God came to our realm; not that he was previously distant, for no part of creation is left deprived of him, but he fills the universe, being in union with his Father. But in his benevolence toward us, he condescended to come and be made

manifest. For he saw that the rational race was perishing and that death was reigning over them through corruption, and he saw also that the threat of the transgression was firmly supporting corruption over us and that it would have been absurd for the law to be dissolved before it was fulfilled. He saw also the impropriety of what had occurred, that the creatures he himself had made should perish, and he saw the excessive wickedness of humans and that they were gradually increasing it against themselves and making it intolerable, and he saw, too, the liability of all humans in regard to death. Therefore he had pity on our race and was merciful to our infirmity and submitted to our corruption and did not endure the dominion of death. And lest what had been created should perish and the work of the Father among humans should be in vain, he took to himself a body, and that not foreign to our own. For he did not wish simply to be in a body, nor did he wish merely to appear, for if he had wished only to appear, he could have made his theophany through some better means. But he took our body, and not simply that, but from a pure and unspotted virgin ignorant of a man, a body pure and truly unalloyed by intercourse with men. For he, although powerful and the creator of the universe, fashioned for himself in the virgin a body as a temple and appropriated it for his own as an instrument in which to be known and dwell. And thus taking a body like ours, since all were liable to the corruption of death, and surrendering it to death on behalf of all, he offered it to the Father. And this he did in his loving kindness in order that, as all die in him, the law concerning corruption in humans might be abolished—since its power was concluded in the Lord's body and it would never again have influence over humans who are like him—and in order that, as humans had turned to corruption, he might turn them back again to incorruption and might give them life for death, in that he had made the body his own, and by the grace of the resurrection had rid them of death as straw is destroyed by fire.

(9) For since the Word realized that the corruption of humans would not be abolished in any other way except by everyone dying—but the Word was not able to die, being immortal and the Son of the Fa-

ther—therefore he took to himself a body that could die, in order that, since this participated in the Word who is above all, it might suffice for death on behalf of all, and because of the Word who was dwelling in it, it might remain incorruptible, and so corruption might cease from all humanity by the grace of the resurrection. Therefore as an offering and sacrifice free of all spot he offered to death the body that he had taken to himself and immediately abolished death from all who were like him by the offering of a like. For since the Word is above all, consequently by offering his temple and the instrument of his body as a substitute for all humans, he fulfilled the debt by his death. And as the incorruptible Son of God was united to all humans by his body similar to theirs, consequently he endued all humans with incorruption by the promise concerning the resurrection. And now no longer does the corruption involved in death hold sway over humans because of the Word who dwelled among them through a body one with theirs. As when a great king has entered some great city and dwelled in one of the houses in it, such a city is then greatly honored, and no longer does any enemy or bandit come against it, but it is rather treated with regard because of the king who has taken up residence in one of its houses; so also is the case with the King of all. For since he has come to our realm and has dwelled in a body similar to ours, now every machination of the enemy against humans has ceased and the corruption of death, which formerly had power over them, has been destroyed. For the human race would have perished unless the Lord of all and Savior, the Son of God, had come to put an end to death.

(10) Truly this great deed particularly befitted the goodness of God. For if a king has constructed a house or a city and brigands attack it through the negligence of its inhabitants, he in no wise abandons it, but avenges and rescues it as his own work, having regard not for the negligence of its inhabitants but for his own honor. So all the more, when the human race that had been created by himself had descended to corruption, God the Word of the all-good Father did not neglect it, but effaced the death that had fallen upon it by the offering of his own body and corrected its negligence by his teaching and reformed all hu-

manity's estate by his own power. This one can verify from the theologians who speak of the Savior himself, by reading in their writings where they say: *For the love of Christ forces us, as we judge this, that if one died for all, then all died; and he died for all in order that we should no longer live for ourselves but for him who died for us and rose* (2 Cor 5:14–15) from the dead, our Lord Jesus Christ. And again: *We see him who was made a little less than the angels, Jesus, crowned with honor and glory because of the passion of death, that by the grace of God he might taste death on behalf of all* (Heb 2:9). And then, indicating the reason why no other save God the Word himself should be incarnate, he says: *For it was fitting that he, for whom are all things and through whom are all things and who brought many sons to glory, should make the leader of their salvation perfect through sufferings* (Heb 2:10). By this he means that it was the task of no one else to bring humans, from the corruption that had occurred save God the Word, who also in the beginning had created them. And that for a sacrifice on behalf of the bodies similar to his the Word himself had also taken to himself a body, this also they declare, saying: *So, since the children have partaken of blood and flesh, he equally partook of them, that by death he might destroy him who held the power of death, that is the devil, and might free all those who by the fear of death were condemned to servitude all the length of their lives* (Heb 2:14–15). For by the sacrifice of his own body he both put an end to the law that lay over us and renewed for us the origin of life by giving hope of the resurrection. For since by humans death had laid hold of humans, so for this reason by the incarnation of God the Word were effected the overthrow of death and the resurrection of life. For the man who put on Christ says: *Since by man came death, also by man came the resurrection of the dead; for as in Adam all die, so also in Christ all will be made alive* (1 Cor 15:21–22), and so on. For now no longer as condemned do we die, but as those who will rise again we await the general resurrection of all, which God *in his own time will reveal* (1 Tim 6:15), he who also made and granted it to us. This, therefore, is the primary cause of the incarnation of the Savior. One could also recognize that his blessed manifestation among us was justified from the following.

(11) God, who has dominion over all, when he made the human race through his own Word, saw that the weakness of its nature was not capable by itself of knowing the Creator or of taking any thought of God, in that he was uncreated, whereas it had been made from nothing, and he was incorporeal, but humans had been fashioned here below with a body, and he saw the creatures' complete lack of understanding and knowledge of him who made them. So having pity on the human race, in that he is good he did not leave them destitute of knowledge of himself, lest even their own existence should be profitless for them. For what advantage would there be for those who had been made, if they did not know their own Maker? Or in what way would they be rational, being unaware of the Word of the Father by whom they had also been created? For indeed they would in no way have differed from irrational creatures if they had known nothing more than terrestrial things. And why would God have made creatures by whom he did not wish to be known? Therefore, lest this should happen, since he is good, he bestowed on them of his own image, our Lord Jesus Christ, and he made them according to his own image and likeness, in order that, understanding through such grace the image, I mean the Word of the Father, they might be able through him to gain some notion about the Father and recognizing the Maker, might live a happy and truly blessed life.

But humans, foolish as ever, so despised the grace that had been given them and so turned away from God, and so fouled their souls, that not only did they lose the concept of God, but even formed others for themselves instead. They fashioned idols for themselves instead of the truth and honored beings who do not exist more than the God who is, and *they worshipped creation more than its creator* (Rom 1:25); and what was worst, they even transferred to wood and stones and all kinds of matter and humans the honor due to God. And they did more than this, as has been said above. So impious were they that they even worshipped demons and called them gods, accomplishing their desires. For they made sacrifices of dumb animals and slayings of humans as their due, as was said above, ensnaring themselves all the more in their frenzies. So therefore they learned magic from them, and divination in various places led humans astray, and they attributed the causes of their birth and of their existence to the stars and all the heavenly bodies, taking no thought of anything more than appearances. Everything was completely filled with impiety and vice, and only God was ignored and his Word, although he had not hidden himself invisibly from humans or given them knowledge of himself in one way only, but had unfolded it to them in various fashions and in manifold ways.

(12) The grace of being in the image was sufficient for one to know God the Word and through him the Father. But because God knew the weakness of humans he anticipated their negligence, so that if they failed to recognize God by themselves, through the works of creation they might be able to know the Creator. But because the negligence of humans sank gradually to the worse, God again provided for such weakness of theirs and sent the law and the prophets, who were known to them, so that if they were reluctant to raise their eyes to heaven and know the Creator, they would have schooling from those close by. For humans can learn more directly from other humans about more advanced things. So they could lift their eyes to the immensity of heaven, and discerning the harmony of creation know its ruler, the Word of the Father, who by his providence in the universe makes the Father known to all humans, and for that reason moves the universe, in order that by him all humans should know God. Or if they were reluctant to do this, they could meet the saints and through them learn of God the Creator of the universe, the Father of Christ, and that the worship of idols was godless and full of all impiety. They could also, by knowing the law, desist from all wickedness and lead lives of virtue. For the law was not for the Jews only, nor on their account only were the prophets sent—though they were sent to the Jews and persecuted by the Jews—but they provided holy instruction for the whole world about the knowledge of God and the conduct of one's soul. Although, therefore, such was the goodness and mercy of God, nevertheless hu-

mans, being overcome by their present desires and the illusions and deceits of demons, did not look toward the truth, but sated themselves with many vices and sins, so that they no longer appeared rational beings, but from their behavior were considered to be irrational.

(13) Since humans had become so irrational and the deceit of evil spirits was casting such a wide shadow everywhere and hiding the knowledge of the true God, what was God to do? Be silent before such things and let humans be deceived by demons and be ignorant of God? But then what need would there have been for man to have been created in the image from the beginning? For he should have been made simply irrational, or else, having been created rational, he should not live the life of irrational creatures. But what need was there at all for him to gain an idea about God from the beginning? For if he is not now worthy to receive it, neither ought it to have been given him from the beginning. And what advantage would there be to God who made him, or what glory would he have, if humans who had been created by him did not honor him, but thought that others had made them? For then God would seem to have created them for others and not for himself.

Furthermore, a king—who is a man—does not permit the realms that he has founded to be handed over and become subject to others and escape from his power, but reminds them with letters and frequently also sends to them through friends, and if there be need he himself finally goes to them to win them over by his presence, only lest they become subject to others and his work be in vain. Will then God not have much greater pity on his creatures, lest they stray from him and serve those who do not exist? Especially as such an error is the cause of their ruin and destruction, and it would not be right for those who had once partaken of the image of God to perish? What then was God to do, or what should have happened, except that he should renew again that which was in his image, in order that through it humans might be able once more to know him? But how could this have been done unless the very image of God were to come, our Savior Jesus Christ? For neither by humans was it possible, since they had been

created in the image, nor by the angels, for neither were they images. So the Word of God came in his own person, in order that, as he is the image of his Father, he might be able to restore humanity who is in the image. In any other way it could not have been done without the destruction of death and corruption. So he was justified in taking a mortal body, in order that in it death could be destroyed and humans might be again renewed in the image. For this, then, none other than the image of the Father was required.

(14) For as when a figure that has been painted on wood is spoilt by dirt, it is necessary for him whose portrait it is to come again so that the picture can be renewed in the same material—for because of his portrait the material on which it is painted is not thrown away, but the portrait is redone on it—even so the all-holy Son of the Father, who is the image of the Father, came to our realms to renew humanity who had been made in his likeness and, as one lost, to find him through the forgiveness of sins; just as he said in the gospels: *I have come to save and find that which was lost* (Luke 19:10). Therefore he also said to the Jews: *Unless a man be born again* (John 3:5), not referring to the birth from women as they supposed, but indicating the soul that is born again and restored in being in the image. But because the madness of idolatry and impiety had hold of the world and knowledge of God was hidden, whose task was it to teach the world about the Father? A man's, someone might say. But it was not in humans' capacity to traverse the whole earth, nor were they able naturally to run so far or to inspire belief about this, nor were they capable of resisting by themselves the deceit and illusion of the demons. For since all had been confounded in their souls and disturbed by the deceit of demons and vanity of idols, how would they have been able to convert the soul of humanity and the mind of humans, when they could not even see them? For how can a man convert what he cannot see? But perhaps someone might say that creation was sufficient. But if creation had been sufficient, such evils would not have occurred. Now creation did exist, yet humans were no less confused in the same error about God. So again, who was needed but God the Word, who sees both soul and mind, and who moves all things in

creation and by them makes known the Father? For it was the task of him who by his providence and regulation of the universe teaches about the Father, also to renew the same teaching. How then could this be done? Perhaps one might say that it was possible through the same means, so that he could show the facts about him once more through the works of creation. But that was no longer a certainty. Not at all, for humans had neglected it previously, and their eyes were no longer directed upward but downward. So as it was right for him to wish to be of help to humans, he came as a man and took to himself a body like theirs of humble origin (I mean through the works of the body) in order that those who were unwilling to know him by his providence and government of the universe, yet by the works done through the body might know the Word of God who was in the body, and through him the Father.

(15) For as a good teacher who cares for his pupils always condescends to teach by simpler means those who cannot profit by more advanced things, so does the Word of God, as Paul says: *Because in the wisdom of God the world did not know God through wisdom, it pleased God to save those who believed through the foolishness of the gospel* (1 Cor 1:21). For because humans had turned away from the contemplation of God and were sunk as it were in an abyss with their eyes cast down, and they were seeking God in creation and sensible things, and had set up mortal men and demons as gods for themselves; for this reason the merciful and universal Savior, the Word of God, took to himself a body and lived as a man among men and took the senses of all humans in order that those who supposed that God was in corporeal things might understand the truth from the works that the Lord did through the actions of his body and through him might take cognizance of the Father. And because they were humans and thought of everything in human terms, wherever they directed their senses they saw a comprehensible universe, and they learned the truth from all sides. For if they were struck at creation, yet they saw it confessed Christ as Lord; and if their minds were preconceived toward humans so that they supposed them gods, yet when they compared the works of the Savior with theirs, it appeared that the Savior alone among humans was

the Son of God, since humans had no such works as those done by God the Word. But if they were prejudiced for the demons, yet when they saw them being put to flight by the Lord, they recognized that only he was the Word of God and that the demons were not gods. And if their minds were by then fixed on the dead, so that they worshipped the heroes and those said to be gods by the poets, yet when they saw the resurrection of the Savior they confessed that the former were false and that only the Word of the Father was the true Lord, he who has power over death. For this reason he was born and appeared as a man and died and rose again, weakening and overshadowing by his own works those of all humans who ever existed, in order that from wherever humans were attracted, he might lift them up and teach them his true Father, as he himself says: *I have come to save and find that which was lost* (Luke 19:10).

(16) For since human reason had descended to sensible things, the Word submitted to being revealed through a body, in order that he might bring humans to himself as a man and turn their senses to himself, and that thenceforth, although they saw him as a man, he might persuade them through the works he did that he was not merely a man but God and the Word and Wisdom of the true God. This Paul wished to indicate when he said: *Be firm and grounded in love, that you may be able to understand with all the saints what is the breadth and length and height and depth, and that you may know the love of Christ which transcends knowledge, in order that you may be filled with all the fullness of God* (Eph 3:17–19). For the Word spread himself everywhere, above and below and in the depth and in the breadth: above, in creation; below, in the incarnation; in the depth, in hell; in breadth, in the world. Everything is filled with the knowledge of God. For this reason, not as soon as he came did he complete the sacrifice on behalf of all and deliver his body to death, and resurrecting it make himself thereby invisible. But by means of it he rendered himself visible, remaining in it and completing such works and giving signs as made him known to be no longer a man but God the Word. For in two ways our Savior had compassion through the incarnation: he both rid us of death and renewed us; and also, although he is invisible and indiscernible,

yet by his works he revealed and made himself known to be the Son of God and the Word of the Father, leader and king of the universe. . . .

(54) So just as if someone wishes to see God, who is invisible by nature and in no way visible, he understands and knows him from his works, so he who does not see Christ with his mind, let him learn of him from the works of his body, and let him test whether they be human or of God. And if they be human, let him mock; but if they are recognized to be not human but of God, let him not laugh at what are not to be mocked but, rather, wonder that through such simple means these divine things have been revealed to us, and that through death immortality has come to all, and through the incarnation of the Word the universal providence and its leader and creator the Word of God himself have been made known. For he became human that we might become divine, and he revealed himself through a body that we might receive an idea of the invisible Father, and he endured insults from humans that we might inherit incorruption. He himself was harmed in no respect because he is impassible and incorruptible and the very Word and God, but he cared for and saved suffering humans, for whom he endured these things, by his impassibility. And, in short, the achievements of the Savior effected through his incarnation are of such a kind and so great, that if anyone wished to expound them he would be like those who gaze at the vast expanse of the sea and wish to count the number of its waves. For as one cannot grasp all the waves with his eyes, since the successive waves elude the perception of him who tries to count them, so also he who tries to comprehend all the accomplishments of Christ in the body is unable to grasp them all in his reckoning, for those that pass before his mind are more than he thinks he has grasped. So it is better not to view or speak of all of which one cannot even express a part, but to recall one part, leaving you to wonder at the whole. For they are all equally amazing, and wherever anyone looks, there to his exceeding wonder he sees the divinity of the Word.

(55) So after what has been said above, this you must learn and consider as the principle of what remains unmentioned and marvel at greatly: that when the Savior came, idolatry no more increased, but even

that which existed is diminishing and gradually ceasing. No longer does the wisdom of the Greeks prosper, but even that which does exist is now disappearing. And the demons no longer deceive with fantasies and oracles and magic, but as soon as they dare and try, they are put to shame by the sign of the cross. To sum up, see how the teaching of the Savior increases everywhere, while all idolatry and all opposition to the faith of Christ day by day diminish and weaken and fall. And seeing this, worship the Savior *who is over all* (Rom 9:5) and the powerful God the Word, but condemn those whom he causes to diminish and disappear. For just as when the sun is present darkness no longer has any strength, but even if there is some darkness left anywhere it is put to flight, even so, since the divine manifestation of God the Word has occurred, the darkness of idols has no more strength, but all parts of the world everywhere are illuminated by his teaching. And just as if someone is king and is not seen anywhere but remains inside his palace, frequently seditious men, taking advantage of his absence, proclaim themselves, and each one of them deceives the simple by pretending to be king; and thus humans are led astray by a name, for they hear that there is a king but do not see him because they cannot possibly enter the palace. But when the real king comes forth and is revealed, then the deceitful revolutionaries are refuted by his presence, while the citizens, seeing the real king, abandon those who formerly deceived them. In like fashion, demons and humans previously exercised deceit and paid to themselves the honor due to God. But after the Word of God was revealed in the body and made known to us his Father, then the deceit of the demons disappears and vanishes, while humans, looking to the true divine Word of the Father, abandon idols and henceforth recognize the true God. This is a proof that Christ is God the Word and the Power of God. For since these human things cease yet the word of Christ remains, it is clear to all that the things that cease are temporal, but he who remains is God and the true Son and only-begotten Word of God.

(56) These remarks, O lover of Christ, we briefly offer you as the rudiments and paradigm of the faith of Christ and his divine manifestation to us. But if you take the opportunity they present and read the

words of the Scriptures and really apply your mind to them, you will learn from them more completely and more clearly the accuracy of what has been said. For the Scriptures were spoken and written by God through men versed in theology, and we have learned from the teachers of theology who are found therein, who were also witnesses of the divinity of Christ, and we pass on our knowledge to your own love of learning. You will learn also of his second glorious and truly divine manifestation to us, when he will come no more with simplicity but in his own glory, no more with humility but in his own greatness, no more to suffer but thenceforth to bestow the fruit of his own cross on all—I mean the resurrection and incorruption—no more judged but judging all according to the works each one has done in the body, whether good or evil; wherefrom for the good is reserved the kingdom of heaven, but for those who have done evil, eternal fire and outer darkness. For so the Lord himself says: *I say to you that hereafter you will see the Son of Man sitting on the right hand of power and coming on the clouds of heaven in the glory of the Father* (Matt 26:64). For this reason the saying is salutary that prepares us for that day and says: *Be ready and keep watch, for he will come in an hour that you do not know* (Matt 24:42). For according to the blessed Paul: *We must all stand before the tribunal of Christ, that each may receive according to what he has done in the body, whether good or evil* (2 Cor 5:10).

(57) But in addition to the study and true knowledge of the Scriptures are needed a good life and pure soul and virtue in Christ, so that the mind, journeying in this path, may be able to obtain and apprehend what it desires, in so far as human nature is able to learn about God the Word. For without a pure mind and a life modeled on the saints, no one can apprehend the words of the saints. For just as if someone wishes to see the light of the sun, he cleanses and clears his eye and purifies it until it is similar to what he desires, so that as the eye thus becomes light it may see the light of the sun, or as when someone wishes to see a city or a country, he goes to that place for the sight; so he who wishes to grasp the thought of the theologians must first cleanse and wash his soul by his conduct and approach the saints in the imitation of their deeds, so that, being included in their company through the manner of his life, he may understand those things that have been revealed to them by God, and thenceforth, as if joined to them, may escape the danger that threatens sinners and the fire that consumes them on the day of judgment, and that he may receive what has been reserved for the saints in the kingdom of heaven, *which eye has not seen, nor ear heard, nor have they ascended into the heart of man* (2 Cor 5:10), all the things that have been prepared for those who live in virtue and love God and the Father, in Jesus Christ our Lord, through whom and with whom, to the Father with the Son himself in the holy Spirit, be honor and power and glory forever and ever, Amen.

27. Jerome: Letter to Ctesiphon (Against Pelagius)

Jerome (ca. 347–ca. 420) rose from modest social origins to become one of the dominant voices of fourth- and fifth-century theology and ascetic theory. Following his education and early embrace of the monastic life, Jerome moved through the ecclesiastical circles of Antioch, Constantinople, and Rome before leaving the West and settling in Bethlehem in 386 with his wealthy ascetic patrons, Paula and her daughter Eustochium (see Text 37). There he

From *Hieronymus: Epistulae, pars III*, ed. I. Hilberg. Vienna: Verlag der Österreichischen Akademie der Wissenschaften, 1996. (Translated by Andrew S. Jacobs.)

produced numerous translations and commentaries on the Bible (translating the Old Testament from its original languages) and became embroiled in the major theological controversies of his day.

Two such controversies that drew in Jerome were the "Origenist controversy" (of the 390s) and the "Pelagian controversy" (of the 410s–430s). Both controversies were fueled by rival ascetic experts who were keen to elaborate the role of spiritual elitism in human salvation. Jerome loaned his fierce polemical style to the ultimate condemnation of both the Origenists and the Pelagians. In the letter presented here, written in reply to Ctesiphon (possibly a wealthy supporter of Pelagius), Jerome creates a sinister genealogy of Christian heresies (reaching back into philosophical schools) that have all sought to uplift human potential at the expense of divine glory. Through torturous interpretation of Scripture, slippery sophistry, and outright lying, Jerome claims, the most recent version of this godless heresy, the Pelagians, has risen up and taken theological prisoners in the East. (When Jerome makes accusations in the second person in this letter, we may assume the "you" is Pelagius.) Particularly prone, Jerome suggests, are female believers: he lays out a vicious dual genealogy of heresy, by which every infamous heresiarch has been assisted by a woman (a curious and malicious rhetorical move for Jerome, whose own life of religious scholarship was financed by Roman noblewomen). This letter is also peppered with the scriptural interpretation and pedantic use of non-Christian classical writers that were Jerome's hallmarks.

SALUTATION: NEW HERESY, ANCIENT ROOTS

(1) Not with audacity, as you falsely think, but with love and zeal have you acted in sending me a new dispute born of an old one. Even before your letter came, this dispute had deceived many in the East, as they teach pride through false humility, and they say along with the devil, "I shall ascend into heaven; I shall set my throne above the stars of heaven, and I will be like the Most High" (Isa 14:13–14). What could be more daring than for me to say not that I am in the likeness of God but to claim to be his equal, and in a brief statement to combine the poisons of all the heretics, which flow from the source of the philosophers, particularly Pythagoras and Zeno, the prince of the Stoics?

What the Greeks call *pathē* [passions] (we might call them "disturbances," such as sickness and joy, hope and fear, of which two relate to the present and two to the future) they assure us we can purge from our minds and have no leaf or root of vices reside anywhere in a person, through contemplation and the assiduous exercise of virtues. Against these even the Peripatetics, who derive from the source of Aristotle, argue strongly; also the new Academics, whom Cicero followed, overturn their—well, I won't call them *facts,* because they are nothing but shadows and conceits. This is even to raise up humanity out of humanity and to reconstitute the human without a body; it is to *want* rather than to *teach,* as the Apostle says: "I am a poor human, who will free me from this mortal body?" (Rom 7:24). But since the brevity of the letter writer cannot comprehend all things, I shall describe summarily what you must avoid. So even Vergil said:

> They fear and desire and grieve and rejoice and the heavens
> They do not perceive, shut up in shadows and the blind prison.[1]

Who, then, is able not to be moved by joy or contracted with grief or exalted by hope or shaken by fear? For this reason, too, that most serious poet Horace wrote in his *Satires:*

---

[1] *Aeneid* 6.733–34.

For no one is born without vices; that man is the best
Who is least driven by them.[2]

SINLESSNESS

(2) One of our own says it nicely: "philosophers, the
forefathers of heretics."[3] With perverse teaching have
they defiled the church's purity, since they do not
know that saying about human weakness: "Why does
earth and ash take pride?" (Sir 10:9). Particularly
since the Apostle himself says: "I see another law in
my limbs, revolting to the law of my mind, and leading me into captivity" (Rom 7:23). And again: "I do
not do what I want, but what I do not want, this I
bring to pass" (Rom 7:29). But if he brings to pass
what he does not want, how can it be said that a
human is able to be without sin should he wish it? By
what rationale can he be what he wishes, when the
Apostle has assured us that he cannot fulfill his own
desires?

Whenever we ask them who are those people
whom they consider to be apart from sin, they try to
evade the truth with a new trick: they do not say that
there are, or have been, such people, but that there
could have been. Extraordinary teachers! They say
that something is possible that they show has never
existed, even though Scripture says, "Everything that
will be has already been in an earlier time" (Eccl
1:9). Now I don't have to go through every one of the
saints, as if to point out every little wart and mole on
their beautiful bodies. Many on our side do this simply, and with a few little lines of Scripture they can
overcome the arguments of the heretics and, through
them, the philosophers.

What does the vessel of election say? "God has
enclosed all things under sin, so that he might be
merciful to all" (Rom 11:32). And in another place:
"Indeed all have sinned, and they are unworthy of
God's glory" (Rom 3:23). Even Ecclesiastes, through

whom Wisdom herself sang forth, freely declares:
"There is no just person on the earth, who does good
and does not sin" (Eccl 7:20), and again: "If the people sin, for there is no person who has not sinned" (1
Kings 8:46). And: "Who boasts that he has a chaste
heart" (Prov 20:9). And "there is nothing clean from
filth, even if his life on earth has been a single day"
(Job 14:4–5). So also David says: "Behold I was conceived in sin, and in transgression my mother conceived me" (Ps 51:5). And in another psalm: "No one
of all those living will be made righteous in your
sight" (Ps 143:2).

This last testimony they mock through a new form
of argument under the name of piety. Indeed they
say that *compared to God,* no one is perfect, just as
Scripture has said. But it does not say, "No one of all
those living will be made righteous *in comparison to
you,*" but "no one of all those living will be made
righteous *in your sight.*" When it says "in your sight,"
this means that even though they may seem saintly to
humans, by no means are they saintly in the knowledge and familiarity of God. For a person just sees
the face; God looks into the heart (1 Sam 16:7).
Moreover, if to God, seeing and contemplating all the
secrets of the heart that do not escape his notice, no
one is righteous, clearly it is shown that these heretics
do not raise up humanity to new heights but, rather,
detract from the power of God. But if I were to gather
all the many other points from sacred Scriptures that
I wanted to, I would not be writing a letter but would
exceed the bounds of a book.

(3) Those who deceive the simple and unlearned in
this sort of self-congratulatory treachery are not gaining anything new. But they can't deceive those men of
the church who meditate on God's law day and night.
Therefore it should shame their leaders and companions who say that, if he wanted to, a person could be
without sin,[4] which the Greeks call *anamartētos.*
Since ears in the eastern churches cannot bear this,
they pretend that they merely said "apart from sin,"[5]
but that they would never dare to say *anamartētos,* as

---

[2] *Satires* 1.3.68–69.
[3] The reference is to a phrase from Tertullian's *Against
Hermogenes* 8; the sentiment is common among early
Christian writers on heresy.

[4] *Sine peccato.*
[5] *Absque peccato.*

if one were "apart from sin" and the other *ana-martētos* and that the Latin language didn't express in two words what the Greek language merely composed into one. If you say *apart from sin,* and you deny that you say *anamartētos,* then condemn those who preach *anamartētos.* But you don't do this. For you know what you teach your disciples inwardly, saying one thing with your mouth and concealing another in your conscience: to us, the outsiders and uninitiated, you speak in parables, but to your own, you confess deep secrets. And you brag that you do this according to Scripture, since it says: "Jesus told them many things in parables" (Matt 13:3), and he said to his disciples in private: "To you it is given to know the mysteries of the kingdom of heaven, but to them it is not given" (Matt 13:11).

CATALOG OF HERETICS

But, as I was saying: I shall briefly set out the names of your leaders and companions, so you might consider what sort of company you boast of. Mani says of his chosen ones, whom he arranges among Plato's vaults in the heavens,[6] that they lack every sin and that they couldn't sin if they wanted to. Furthermore, they have reached such heights of virtue that they make fun of the works of the flesh. Priscillian was Mani's Spanish counterpart; many of his disciples adore you for your foulness, rashly claiming for themselves the greatest distinction of perfection and knowledge; alone, they shut themselves up with women by themselves and chant this to them amid their sexual embraces:

> Then All-Powerful Father Sky with fertile rains
> Descends into the depths of his happy bride; and all
> Their offspring the great one nourishes, mingling with
> the great body.[7]

They share a part in the gnostic heresy coming from impious Basilides. Like him, you assert that those who have no knowledge of the law cannot avoid sin. What can I say about Priscillian, who was condemned by the secular sword and the whole world's opinion?

Evagrius of Ibera, in Pontus, who wrote to virgins, wrote to monks, and wrote to her whose name testifies to the blackened shadows of her foulness,[8] also edited a book of phrases *peri apatheias,* which we might translate as *without suffering* or *without disturbance:* when the mind is no longer moved by any thought or vice; to put it simply, it has become like a stone or like God. They read his books in Greek throughout the East, and now many in the West read it in the Latin translation of his disciple, Rufinus.

Rufinus also wrote a book as if it were about monks, even though many of those people in it were never any such thing, and he even describes those who were Origenists and who were doubtless condemned by the bishops.[9] That is, Ammonius, and Eusebius, and Euthymius, and Evagrius himself, Or also and Isidore and many others whom it would be boring to list. But even as Lucretius recommends:

> And just as when they try to treat boys
> With foul wormwood, first around the mouths of the
> vessels
> They dab sweet honey and golden liquid[10]

so that one placed at the front of his book John, about whom there is no doubt as to his catholic and saintly nature, and used him as an excuse to introduce others established as heretics to the church. Who can explain with a straight face that rashness—indeed, his madness—that entitled a book of Xystus the Pythagorean, a person lacking Christ and a gentile, with the altered name of Sixtus the martyr, bishop of the church of Rome? In this, according to the teaching of Pythagoreans, who make themselves equal to God

---

[6] For vaults, Jerome writes the Greek word *hapsidas;* see Plato, *Phaedrus* 247b.
[7] Vergil, *Georgics* 2.325–27.

[8] Melania the Elder, whose name (in Greek) means "black" or "dark."
[9] Jerome refers to the *History of the Monks of Egypt* (see Text 48), which Rufinus translated into Latin.
[10] Lucretius, *On the Nature of Things* 1.4.

and of his same substance, many things are said about perfection, with the result that whoever doesn't know that this is a philosopher's book, drinks from the golden chalice of Babylon (cf. Rev 17:4) under the martyr's name. Then in this same book not a single mention is made of the prophets, of the patriarchs, of the apostles, or of Christ, so that he claims that a bishop and martyr was without Christ's faith. From this you seize so much proof against the church!

He did the same thing against the name of the holy martyr Pamphilus: he ascribed the first of six books in defense of Origen, by Eusebius of Caesarea (whom everybody *knows* was an Arian) to the name of Pamphilus alone. He did this even while pouring those four outrageous volumes of Origen's *peri archōn* [*On First Principles*] over Latin ears.

Do you want to get to know yet another leader of your error? Your teaching is an offshoot of Origen. In that psalm where it is written (so I may refrain from other examples), "Well even into the night my heart has instructed me" (Ps 16:7), he asserted that a holy man (among whom indeed even you number!) when he has reached the pinnacle of virtue, does not suffer in the night those things that are characteristic of humans and is in no way titillated by the thought of sins. You shouldn't blush to be in such company, denying their names, as you join in their blasphemies! The teaching of your intellect is Jovinian's second proposition.[11] That which served as his response must serve as your response. It is impossible that the outcome should be different when there is one single opinion.

HERETICS AND WOMEN

(4) Things being as they are, what is the desire of these miserable little women decked out in sin, who are borne about by every breeze of teaching, always learning and never coming to knowledge of the truth

---

[11] That is, the possibility of sinlessness; Jerome wrote *Against Jovinian* in the 390s.

(cf. 2 Tim 3:6–7), and the other companions of these little women, ears pricked up, not even knowing what they hear, what they say, who admire the most ancient filth as if it had just been concocted: who, according to Ezekiel, seal up a wall without the correct mixture and, when the rain of truth comes down, are washed away (cf. Ezek 13:10)?

Simon Magus established heresy, joined by the aid of his whore Helena. Nicholaus of Antioch, deviser of all sorts of filthiness, led female choruses. Marcion sent a woman ahead to Rome who prepared souls for him to deceive. Apelles had in Philumela a companion of his own teachings. Montanus, preacher of the Unholy Spirit, through Prisca and Maximilla, noble and wealthy women, first corrupted many churches with gold and then polluted them with heresy.

I shall leave behind old news and pass on to more recent events. Arius, so he might take in the world, first deceived the emperor's sister. Donatus was assisted by Lucilla's riches so he might pollute so many unhappy souls in stinking waters throughout Africa. In Spain, the blind woman Agape led the blind man Elpidus into a pit (cf. Matt 15:14). He had Priscillian as his successor, a very eager Zoroastrian mage, and from mage a bishop, to whom Galla (that was her name, not her nationality) was joined, and she left a sister running here and there as the heir of another related heresy. Now indeed the mystery of sin is working! Both sexes trip up each other, such that we are forced to recall that prophecy: "The partridge claimed and collected what it did not bear, making its fortune unjustly. In the middle of her days she will abandon them, and at the end of the line they will be fools" (Jer 17:11).

GRACE AND FREE WILL

(5) But in order to deceive those people, they have also tacked on this phrase—"not apart from God's grace"—to the first, which deceives readers up front but cannot deceive when examined and very carefully pored over. Even as they establish God's grace,

we are not guided by its aid as we strive through individual works, but they mean by it free will and the precepts of the law, laying out that saying of Isaiah: "God indeed established the law as a helper" (Isa 8:20 [LXX]), such that in this are thanks[12] to be conferred on God, because he established in us the ability to choose good or to avoid evil by our own will. They don't even understand that when they say this, the devil hisses intolerable blasphemy through their mouths. If indeed God's grace is merely this, that he established in us our own volition and we are content with free will, then we require no more of his assistance, unless we should demand that free will be abolished. Therefore we should no longer pray or appeal to his clemency with pleas, so we may daily receive what once and for all has been received into our power. Such people annul prayer and boast that through free will, they have been made not persons of their own volition, but even of Godlike power, who require no support. Fasts are also rendered null and all continence. Why should I bother to toil to receive through hard work the ability that has once and for all been given to me? I am not putting forth my own argument: one of his disciples—rather, one who is already master and leader of his army and the vessel of ruin opposite the Apostle, scurrying through the thickets of solecism (and not, as they boast of him, of "syllogism")—philosophizes and argues in this way: "If I do nothing apart from God's aid, and every single work I have done is his, it is therefore not I who toil, but the aid of God in me will earn the crown, and he gave the power of free will in vain, since I cannot make full use of it unless he himself gives me constant aid. Indeed, volition is destroyed if it requires the support of another. But God gave free will, and it isn't really 'free' unless I do what I want. And so either once and for all I use the ability that was given to me, and so free will is preserved, or if I require another's support, freedom of will is destroyed in me."[13]

---

[12] A pun: "thanks" in Latin is *gratia*, the same as "grace."
[13] Jerome is probably quoting Celestinus, who wrote a treatise on *Definitions and Syllogisms*.

(6) What blasphemy is not exceeded by the one who says these things? What heretical poison has he not surpassed? They are certain that through the freedom of will, they no longer need God. But they ignore what is written: "What do you have that you have not received? Moreover, if you have received it, why do you boast as if you did not receive it?" (1 Cor 4:7). He gives God great thanks when, through "freedom of the will," he becomes rebellious against God! Rather, we freely embrace, as far as that goes, the fact that we always give thanks for his generosity, and we know that we are nothing except what he has given to us, what he himself preserves inside us, as the Apostle says: "it is not of will or exertion, but of merciful God" (Rom 9:16). To want and to exert are mine, but they are not *really* mine unless God grants me his continual assistance. Indeed, the same Apostle says: "It is God who is at work in you both to desire and to perfect" (Phil 2:13). And in the Gospel the Savior says: "My Father is still working, and I am working" (John 5:17). He is always generous and always giving. It is not enough for me that once he gave if he will not always give. I ask that I may receive, and when I have received, I ask again. I am greedy to receive God's favors; he does not fail in his giving, and I am not satisfied in my receiving. The more I drink, the thirstier I become. I have read what the psalmist sang: "Taste and see how sweet is the Lord" (Ps 34:8). Every good thing we have is a taste of the Lord. Whenever I think I have reached the finish line of virtues, I have only just begun. "The beginning of wisdom is fear of the Lord" (Ps 111:10), which is expelled and destroyed by love. The only perfection humans possess is the knowledge that they are imperfect. "And you," he says, "when you have done all things, you say 'We are useless slaves, we have done what we were supposed to do'" (Luke 17:10). If the person who does everything is useless, what should we say about the person who couldn't get it done? So the Apostle says that he has received in part and he has understood in part, but that he is still not perfect and that he has forgotten what has gone by and that he reaches into the future (cf. 1 Cor 13:10, Phil 3:13). The one who always forgets what has gone by and

longs for the future shows that he isn't happy with the way things are.

Moreover, because they are boasting up and down that free will is being destroyed by us, let them hear just the opposite: *they* destroy freedom of the will because they abuse it so poorly against the goodness of the one who generously gave it. Who destroys the will? The person who always gives God thanks and attributes back to its source whatever small stream flows down? Or the one who says, "Withdraw from me for I am clean (cf. Isa 65:5), I don't need you? For you gave me once and for all freedom of the will, so I might do as I wish; why should you inflict yourself once more on me, such that I can't do anything at all unless you keep cramming your gifts into me?" Fraudulently do you claim God's grace, such that you fall back on the human condition and do not require God's aid in every single task, lest you should seem to cast off free will. And since you condemn God's support, you end up seeking human aid.

(7) Listen, I beg you, listen to the sacrilege. He says: "If I wanted to bend my finger, to move my hand, to sit, to stand, to walk, to run around, to spit, to pick snot from my nose with two fingers, to relieve my bowels, to expel urine, would I always need God's help?" Listen, ingrate—rather, sacrilegious one, to the Apostle's preaching: "Whether you chew, whether you drink, or whether you do anything, you do all things in God's name" (1 Cor 10:31). And this point of James: "Look, now, you who say, 'Today or tomorrow I shall go forth into that city, and I shall spend one year there, and I shall do business and make money,' you know nothing about tomorrow. What is your life? It is a breeze or a mist appearing for the briefest time: then it dissipates. For this you ought to say: 'If the Lord wishes it, and I am alive, I shall do this or that.' Now even though you leap about in your pride, this is the worst kind of boasting" (Jas 4:13–16). Do you think you're being hurt and that freedom of will is being destroyed if you always run back to God as the creator, if you depend on his volition, and if you say: "My eyes go always to the Lord, since he pulls my feet from the snare" (Ps 25:15)? How do you even dare to say such rash things, that each and every person is ruled by his own will? If he is ruled by his own will, where is God's help? If he doesn't need Christ as his ruler, why does Jeremiah write: "Humanity's way is not its own" and "a person's steps are guided by the Lord" (Jer 10:23)?

GOD'S COMMANDS

You say God's commands are easy, and yet you can't put forth anyone who has fulfilled them all. Answer me: Are they easy, or difficult? If they are easy, show me someone who has fulfilled them. Explain why David sings in the psalm: "You who make grief in the commandment" (Ps 94:20) and again: "Because of the words from your lips I have guarded hard roads" (Ps 17:4). And the Lord in the Gospel: "Enter through the narrow gate" (Matt 7:13), and "Love your enemies; pray for those who persecute you" (Matt 5:44)? If these are difficult, why have you dared to say that God's commands—which no one has fulfilled—are easy? Don't you understand that your own opinions contradict themselves? Either they are easy, and the multitude of people who have fulfilled them is boundless, or they are difficult, and you have been rash to say that something difficult is easy.

(8) You also tend to say that either the commands are possible and were correctly given by God, or they are impossible and that the blame is not in those who receive, but in the one who gave impossible commands. Has God somehow commanded me that I should be what God is, so that there is no distance between me and the Lord Creator, so that I am greater than the highest angel, so that I possess what angels do not? About this it is written that it belongs to him alone: "Whoever does not sin, no malice is found in his mouth" (Isa 53:9). If Christ and I have this in common, why does he possess it as his own? In this respect your opinion demolishes itself.

You assert that a person can be without sin if he wishes it. And after coming out of the deepest sleep, you tack this on, attempting in vain to deceive clumsy souls: "Not apart from God's grace." If a person were able to be without sin, once and for all, why would God's grace be necessary? But if he can't do anything without his grace, why was it necessary to say he can do what he can't? He says: "He can be without sin, he can be perfect, if he wishes it." What Christian doesn't want to be without sin? Who would turn down perfection if all he had to do was *want* it, if ability followed desire? No Christian doesn't want to be without sin; therefore, they will all be without sin, since they all *desire* to be apart from sin! And so unwillingly you are caught: since you can produce no one, or the rare person, who is without sin, while you profess that everyone can be apart from sin.

He says: "God gave possible commands." Who denies this? But how this opinion should be understood is taught most clearly by the vessel of election, who says: "What was impossible for the law, which was weakened through the flesh, God, sending his Son in the likeness of the flesh of sin and because of sin, condemned sin in the flesh" (Rom 8:3). And again: "No flesh is made righteous from the works of the law" (Rom 3:20). And so you won't think he's talking only about the law of Moses, and not about all commands that are contained under the single name of "law," the same Apostle writes: "I agree with God's law according to my interior person, but I see another law in my limbs, rejecting the law of my mind and keeping me captive in the law of sin, which is in my limbs. I am a poor man, who will free me from this body of death? God's grace through out lord Jesus Christ" (Rom 7:22–25). Why he has said this, he shows us in another speech. "We know that the law is spiritual, but I am fleshly, sold under sin. What I do I do not understand. I do not what I wish, but what I hate, that is what I do. But even though I do what I do not want, I consent to the law, since it is good. But now it is no longer I who act, but that sin which dwells in me. I know that good does not dwell in me, that is, in my flesh. To want lies near me, but I cannot find out how to accomplish the good; but the evil I do not will, this I do. Moreover, that which I do not wish, this I do, but no longer do I do it, but the sin which dwells in me" (Rom 7:14–20).

EVIL NATURE(S)

(9) You will protest and say that I follow the teaching of the Manicheans and of those who wage wars against the church concerning diverse natures, of those who assert that there is an "evil nature" that can in no way be transformed. Don't level this charge at me, but at the Apostle, who knew the difference between God and humanity, between the weakness of the flesh and the strength of the spirit. "Indeed, the flesh desires against the spirit, and the spirit against the flesh, and these are enemy to each other, as we do not want to do those things we do" (Gal 5:17). You will never hear from me that there is an "evil nature." But how the weakness of the flesh should be discussed we should learn from the one who wrote to teach us. Ask him why he says: "What I don't want, this I do; but that evil I hate, this I do." What necessity impedes his volition, what sort of force drives him to do things worthy of hatred, compels him to do not what he wants, but what he hates and not what he wants? He will answer you: "O human being, who are you to talk back to God? Does the pot say to the potter, why did you make me thus? Doesn't the potter have power over the clay to make from this lump either a vessel for honor or else another for shame?" (Rom 9:20–21). Bring yet a stronger charge against God: Ask why, when Esau and Jacob were in the womb, he said: "I loved Jacob, but for Esau I had hatred" (Mal 1:2–3). Accuse him of unfairness, asking why Charmi's son Achan stole some spoils from the people of Jericho, and why so many thousands of people were slaughtered for his vice (Josh 7). Because Eli's sons sinned, so nearly all the people were destroyed and the ark was captured (1 Sam 4). David sinned, when he counted the populace, but why did so many thousands of people throughout Israel have to die (2 Sam 24)? And, finally (because your drinking companion Porphyry likes to raise this objection against us), for what reason would a merciful and compassionate God permit all the nations of the world, from Adam to Moses and from Moses to the coming of Christ, to perish in ignorance of the Law and the commandments of God? For Britain, that province so rich in tyrants, and the Scythian peoples, and all the barbarian nations until the circle of the Ocean knew nothing of Moses and the prophets. Why was it necessary for him to come at the last minute, and not before an uncountable multitude of people

had died? The blessed Apostle very wisely lays this question out when writing to the Romans. You plead ignorance of these things and yield to God's knowledge. It is fitting, then, that you also should not know the answer to your question. Yield to God his own power; he in no way needs you as his defender. I am wretched, awaiting your smears, I who read always this message: "You were saved by grace" (Eph 2:8). And "Blessed are they whose transgressions are forgiven and whose sins are covered over" (Ps 32:1). So I shall speak of my own weakness, how I wish to know many things that are holy, and yet I am unable to accomplish them. For the strength of the spirit leads to life, but the weakness of the flesh leads to death. And I hear the Lord warning me: "Be vigilant and pray, lest you should enter into temptation. For the spirit is willing but the flesh is frail" (Matt 26:41).

(10) In vain do you blaspheme and heap ignorance on their ears and say that I condemn free will. Whoever condemns it is damned. Still, not in this do we differ from wild animals, that we have been endowed with free will. As I have said, that free will relies upon God's assistance and needs his support in everything, something you do not want. But you want it to be the case that, whoever possesses free will once and for all has no need of God as an assistant. Free will gives free volition, but it does not make you a God who has no need of support. But *you,* who boast that humans have perfect righteousness equal to God, but who confess that you are a sinner, answer me: Do you or don't you want to be without sin? If you do, why, according to your own opinion, do you not fulfill your own desire? But if you don't want to be, you show that you have scorn for God's commands. If you have such scorn, so, too, are you a sinner. If you are a sinner, listen to what Scripture tells you: "God said to the sinner: Why do you recount my righteousness and take my covenant into your mouth? Yet you hate the teaching, and you cast my words behind you" (Ps 50:16). While you do not wish to do God's words, you cast them behind you. But as a new apostle, you decree what should and should not be done for the whole world. But despite what you say, something else occupies your mind. Indeed, when you say that you are a sinner and that a

person can be without sin, if he wishes, you want people to think that you, too, are a saint and free from all sin but that, out of humility, you take on the name "sinner," praising others more while demeaning yourself.

BEING AND BEING ABLE

(11) Who can stand this next part of your argument? You say in so many words: "To be is one thing, to be able another. To be is not within our abilities, but to be able to be is, generally speaking. Just because no one has happened to be so, nevertheless it is possible to be so for whomever wishes to be so." I ask you, what kind of reasoning is this? To be able to be, but never to have been? To be able to be done, yet you swear no one has done it? To ascribe this to *someone,* although you do not know if he will ever exist? And to give to any random person that which you cannot agree existed in the patriarchs, prophets, and apostles? Hear some churchly simplicity—or boorishness or unlearnedness or however it seems to you. Say what you think. Preach publicly what you say in secret to your disciples. You who claim to have freedom of will, why don't you freely say what you think? The hiding places of your little rooms hear one thing, but the people at the public docket another. Perhaps the unlearned crowd can't bear the burden of your secret teachings, so they do not receive solid food but are content with infant's milk (cf. 1 Cor 3:2).

I have not yet written, but you threaten me with the thunders of your replies, so that, perhaps, shaken with this fear, I will not dare to open my mouth. But you don't realize that I am writing so that you will be forced to respond, to say something openly at some point, what you speak about and what you remain silent about, depending on the time, persons, and places. I do not want you to be *free* to deny what you have once written down. It is the church's victory for you to say openly what you think. Either you are going to respond with what I am saying, and we will no longer be enemies, but friends; or if you propose teachings contrary to mine, I will at least have this victory: all the churches will know what you think.

To bring forth your opinions is to overcome them. Blasphemy is clear at first glance. There is no need to be convinced because in the very profession of it there is already blasphemy. You threaten me with a response, but no one avoids that except he who doesn't write at all.

How do you know what I'm going to say, so that you might prepare a response? Maybe I should take up your side, and you will have sharpened the pen of your genius in vain. Eunomians, Arians, Macedonians, distinct in name but of like-minded impiety, are short work for me. Because they *say* what they *think!* This is the only heresy that blushes to say publicly what it doesn't fear to teach in secret! But the disciples' madness exposes the teachers' silence. What they hear in secret rooms, they preach from rooftops (cf. Matt 10:27). The result is that if what they have said has pleased their audience, they defer to the glory of their teachers, but if it has displeased, the fault lies with the disciples, not the teachers. Accordingly, your heresy sprang up and you deceived many people, especially those who cling to women and know that they cannot sin! You are always teaching, you are always denying, you deserve to hear that prophecy: "In the throes give glory to those in the throes of labor, Lord. What will you give them? A barren womb and dry breasts" (Hos 9:11, 14 [LXX]). My ire is up, and I can't hold back my words. The constraints of letter writing will not allow a work of great magnitude. No one's proper name appears in this little work. I have spoken against the teacher of twisted teaching. If he becomes angry and responds, he will be betrayed by a clue like a mouse, opening himself up to more serious wounds in open battle.

(12) Over the course of many years, from my youth even into the present age, I have written diverse little works and have always zealously conveyed to my readers what I taught publicly in the church: not to be split by the arguments of philosophers, but to concede before the simplicity of the apostles, knowing what is written: "I shall ruin the wisdom of the wise and bring to nothing the prudence of the prudent" (Isa 29:14 and 1 Cor 1:19). And: "God's folly is wiser than humans" (1 Cor 1:25). Since this is the case, I call upon my enemies to read back over all my books, and if they discover anything sinful in my poor intellect, they should make it public. What I have said will either be good, and I shall refute their charge, or reprehensible, and I shall confess my mistake. Better to correct wrongdoing than to persist in depraved opinion. So you, too, extraordinarily learned man, either defend what you have said and add to the keenness of your opinions with subsequent eloquence—and do not deny what you have said when it pleases you—or if you have clearly erred, as a person, confess *freely* and bring agreement to those who have disagreed. Think of how the Savior's cloak was not even torn by the soldiers (cf. John 19:23–24). When you see quarrels between brothers, you laugh and you make fun because some are called by your name while others are called by Christ's. Imitate Jonah and say: "If this storm is because of me, take me up and cast me into the sea" (Jonah 1:12). He was tossed into the sea because of humility, so he might rise up more gloriously as a figure of our Lord. You are raised up through pride to the stars, as Jesus said about you: "I saw Satan like a flash of lightening falling from heaven" (Luke 10:18).

SINS OF THE RIGHTEOUS

(13) Although many in the holy Scriptures are called righteous, such as Zechariah, Elizabeth, Job, Josaphat, and Josiah, and many whose names are contained in the sacred Scriptures, I shall speak of these in that fuller work I promised (if the Lord is gracious to me); nevertheless, in the present letter it should suffice to have examined this briefly, that they are called righteous and that they are not free of all sin, but that they are credited with a greater part of virtue. Indeed, even Zechariah was condemned to silence (cf. Luke 1), and Job is accused by his own speech, and with respect to Josaphat and Josiah, who were without doubt called righteous, it is told how they displeased God. One of them took the aid of that impious man (1 Kings 22) and was punished by the prophet; the other, against the Lord's command out of Jeremiah's mouth, went up against Necho, king of Egypt, and was killed (2 Kings 23); and yet both are

called righteous. Of the rest there is no time to write, for you did not ask me for a book, but a letter. What must be written will come out of leisure, and all their quibbles will be destroyed with Christ's help. For this, it is appropriate for me to use the witnesses of holy Scriptures, in which God speaks daily to his believers.

And this, through you, I beg of the little assembly of your holy and noble house, and I give warning, lest through one, or more, even three of these little dum-mies, they should receive such heretical rubbish or (at the least) notoriety. For there, where first was virtue, and sanctity was praised, there the foulness of the filthiest and diabolical company would be created. And tell those who supply such people with wealth, to gather together the hordes of heretics is also to make an enemy of Christ and to nourish his enemies; it's no use for them to claim one thing with the tongue, when they demonstrate with their actions that they feel something else.

The Nature of the Church: The Texts

The trauma of the Great Persecution led some Christians to create a sharper distinction between Christianity and "the world." In North Africa, where religious rigor had always been popular, the church was viewed by many of the faithful as a pristine body of saints, which must reject unrepentant Christians who had renounced their religion under duress (the *lapsi*) and condemn Christian leaders who had cravenly handed over sacred books and objects to the persecutors (the so-called *traditores,* "betrayers"). The sacraments of the church and clerical ordination, they argued, should likewise be restricted to bishops and priests who had proved their loyalty by refusing to capitulate to or collaborate with the persecutors. Caecilian, ordained bishop of Carthage in 311, was rejected by these rigorists when one the bishops who presided at his ordination was accused of being a *traditor.* The installation of a series of rival bishops (the second of whom, Donatus, gave his name to the controversy) inaugurated a split in the church that would continue in full strength until the 410s and linger on until the arrival of Islam in the seventh century.

At some points during the fourth century, partisans of Donatus (Donatists) were actually the majority Christians in North Africa. Their popularity was due, in part, to their ability to harness an image of the Christian church that appealed to many believers, of a church body defined by personal and communal holiness. The partisans of Caecilian (who claimed the name "Catholic," meaning "universal") promoted a notion of the Church not as the refuge of saints but, rather, as a "mixed body" of sinners and penitents struggling for salvation. Sacraments and ordinations, the Catholics argued, were effective regardless of the moral state of the cleric performing the office. Baptism and rebaptism were sacramental flashpoints of the debate, which at times exploded into violence across North Africa.

Debates on the nature of the Church were deeply implicated in controversies over the nature of humanity and divinity, but employed different terminology and tactics. The Catholic and Donatist opponents called each other *schismatics* (from schism, or division), instead of *heretics.* Heretics inspired by the devil deliberately corrupted the church through false doctrine and practice; schismatics, on the other hand, were "brothers" of a single Mother Church. Imperial support was sought by both sides of the schism. Constantine, eager to restore harmony to the Western church at the beginning of his reign, originally ruled in favor of Caecilian, but the Donatists secured the support of subsequent emperors and officials. In the end, Augustine managed to have the Donatist clergy deposed and their flocks reintegrated into the Catholic churches through coercion by imperial forces. This heavy-handedness created an outward semblance of unity and, perhaps ironically, reinforced Augustine's own theology of the church as a "mixed body" of sinful and striving Christians locked in a perilous struggle for salvation.

28. Optatus: Against the Donatists

We know little about Optatus other than that he was the bishop of the town of Milevis in Numidia (present-day Algeria) and that he wrote a detailed condemnation of the Donatists in six books sometime around 367 (he later added a seventh book, complete with supporting documents). The work is addressed to Parmenianus, the Donatist bishop of Carthage from 362 to 392, whom Optatus calls "brother." Optatus provides what would become the classic distinction between heresy and schism: heretics, vicious purveyors of lies, stand resolutely "outside the church," while schismatics have been disaffected by anger and in-fighting but are still Christians. While Optatus treats the theological implications of schism (particularly the question of sacramental efficacy), he is more concerned in the following excerpt with undermining the Donatists' specific arguments. The Donatists had claimed superiority on the basis of the moral laxity of Catholic clergy during and after the persecution; the truth, Optatus crows, is that the Donatists' founding bishops were guilty of collaboration with the persecutors, a charge he supports with official documents and records. The real roots of this schism lie in jealousy, cowardice, and the petty resentment of a wealthy Roman woman (as in heretical discourse, women emerge as particular targets of invective). If the Donatists wish to exclude morally inferior "schismatics" from the ranks of the saved, Optatus writes, they must begin with their own ecclesiastical forebears.

(11) The catholic church is made known by simplicity and truth in knowledge, singleness and absolute truth in the sacrament, and unity of minds. A schism, on the other hand, is engendered when the bond of peace is shattered through discordant sentiments, nourished by bitterness, strengthened by rivalry and feuds, so that the impious sons, having deserted their catholic mother, go out and separate themselves, as you have done, and, having been cut off from the root of the mother church by the blade of bitterness, depart in erratic rebellion. Nor are they able to do anything new or anything else, except what they have long since learned from their own mother.

(12) Heretics, on the other hand, exiles from the truth who have deserted the sound and truest creed, fallen from the bosom of the church through their impious sentiments, contemptuous of their good birth, have set out to deceive the ignorant and unlearned by claiming to be born of themselves. And whereas they had previously fed on wholesome foods, through the corruption of a bad digestion they vomited forth lethal poisons in their impious disputations to destroy their wretched victims. You therefore see, brother Parmenianus, that heretics, being wholly estranged from the house of truth, are the only ones who have different and false baptisms, by which he who is soiled cannot wash, nor the unclean cleanse, nor the subverter restore, nor the condemned bring freedom, nor the criminal bestow pardon, nor the condemned grant absolution. You have rightly closed the garden to the heretics, you have rightly recalled the keys to Peter, you have rightly taken away the power of cultivation lest those who are patently alien to the garden and paradise of God should cultivate their trees; you have rightly taken away the ring from those who are not allowed to admit to the font. To you schismatics, on the other hand, although you are not in the catholic church, these things cannot be denied, because you have administered with us the true and common sacraments. So, whereas all these things are

From *Optatus: Against the Donatists,* trans. Mark Edwards. Liverpool: Liverpool University Press, 1997. Used with permission.

rightly denied to heretics, why did you think it proper to desire that these be denied to you also, who are manifestly schismatics? For you stand without. So far as in us lies, our wish was that only heretics should be damned; so far as in you lies, you have desired that we strike you together with them in a single judgment.

(13) But now, that we may return to dealing with the several points in the proposed order, hear in the first place, who the collaborators were and learn more fully who were the authors of the schism. In Africa it is well known that two evils of the worst kind were committed, one in collaboration, the other in schism, but both evils were apparently committed at the same time and by the same people. You should learn, then, brother Parmenianus, what you clearly do not know. For a full sixty years ago and more, the storm of persecution spread throughout the whole of Africa, which made martyrs of some, confessors of others, laid low not a few in grievous death, but let those who hid go unharmed. Why should I recall the laity, who at that time were supported by no office in the church? Why recall the great number of ministers? Why recall the deacons who stood in the third, or the presbyters in the second, rank of priesthood? The very foremost, the leaders of all, certain bishops of that time, in order to procure a few minute extensions to this uncertain light at the cost of life eternal, impious gave over the instruments of the divine law. Among them were Donatus of Mascula, Victor of Russicade, Marinus from the Aquae Tibilitanae, Donatus of Calama, and the murderer Purpurius of Limata, who, when interrogated about the sons of his own sister, because he was said to have confessed to having ordered their execution in the prison of Milevis, said: "I both killed them and kill, not only them, but also everyone who has acted against me." Also there was Maenalius, who, in order not to be convicted of offering incense by his fellow citizens, shrank from attending a conference of his own people by feigning a disease of the eyes.

(14) These and others, whom we shall prove a little further on to have been your leaders, assembled after the persecution in the city of Cirta, since the churches had not yet been restored, at the house of

Urbanus Carisius on March 13, as the writings of Nundinarius, then a deacon, testify and as is witnessed by the antiquity of the documents that we shall be able to produce for those who doubt it. For we have appended to the last part of this book a complete record of these matters as a full confirmation. These bishops, on interrogation by Secundus of Tigisis, confessed their collaboration. Purpurius alleged against Secundus himself that he also stayed a long time with those who remained and did not flee, yet was released and had not been released without reason but, rather, because he had collaborated. Forthwith all stood and began to murmur, and Secundus, fearing their vehemence, took the advice of the younger Secundus, his brother's son, that he should commit a case like this to God. Those who had remained were consulted: that is, Victor of Garba, Felix from Rotarium, and Nabor from Centuriona. These replied that a case like this should be committed to God. And Secundus said: "Be seated, all of you"; then all said: "Thanks be to God," and sat. So now you know, brother Parmenianus, who were the manifest collaborators.

(15) Then shortly after this, all these people—such as they were, collaborators, sacrificers, and murderers—went to Carthage and after the ordination of Caecilian, created a schism by ordaining Majorinus, whose see you occupy. And since it has been demonstrated that your leaders were guilty of collaboration, it follows that these same people were the authors of the schism. So that this fact may be clear and manifest to all, it must be shown from what root the branches of error stretch forth even up to the present day and from what font this rivulet of foul water, creeping secretly, has diffused right up to our own times. It must be said whence and where this other evil is known to have arisen, what causes conspired, what persons were active, who the authors of this evil were, who nourished it, whose judgments between the parties were sought by the emperor, what judges sat, where the council took place, what verdicts were uttered.

Our subject is a division, and in Africa, as in the other provinces, there was one church, before it was divided by those who ordained Majorinus, whose hereditary see you occupy. It must be seen who remained in the root with the whole world, who went out, who occupied another see, who erected altar against altar, who performed an ordination in the face of another valid ordination, who lies under the sentence of the Apostle John: *For they were not of us,* he says, *for if they had been of us, they would have remained with us* (1 John 2:19). Therefore he who has chosen not to remain at one with his brethren has followed heretics and, like the Antichrist, has gone out.

(16) No one is unaware that this took place at Carthage after the ordination of Caecilian and indeed through some factious woman or other called Lucilla, who, while the church was still tranquil and the peace had not yet been shattered by the whirlwinds of persecution, was unable to bear the rebuke of the archdeacon Caecilian. She was said to kiss the bone of some martyr or other—if, that is, he was a martyr—before the spiritual food and drink, and since she preferred to the saving cup the bone of some dead man, who if he was a martyr had not yet been confirmed as one, she was rebuked, and went away in angry humiliation. As she raged and grieved, a storm of persecution suddenly arose to prevent her submitting to discipline.

(17) At the same time a certain deacon called Felix, who was arraigned as a criminal because of a notorious letter about some tyrannical emperor or other, is said to have taken refuge in fear of danger at the house of Mensurius. When he was asked for, Mensurius publicly refused; a report was sent, and the reply was that if Mensurius did not give up Felix the deacon, he was to be brought to the palace. The congregation was greatly distressed because the church had a great many ornaments of gold and silver that it could not bury in the ground or carry with it. He entrusted these as if to faithful seniors, making an inventory that he is said to have given to a certain old woman with the proviso that if he did not return, that woman should give it, when peace was restored to the Christians, to the person whom she found in occupation of the episcopal see. He went off to plead his cause, was ordered to return, but was unable to reach Carthage.

(18) The storm of persecution was finished and concluded. When Maxentius, at God's bidding, ex-

tended indulgence to Christians, liberty was restored. It is said that in Carthage Botrus and Celestius, craving ordination, took pains to ensure that only local bishops should be sought to perform ordinations in Carthage, the Numidians being absent. Then by the vote of the whole populace, Caecilian was elected and ordained bishop by the hand of Felix of Abthugni. Botrus and Celestius were disappointed of their hopes. When Caecilian took his seat, an account of the gold and silver was handed to him, with witnesses in attendance, just as it had been entrusted by Mensurius. The aforesaid seniors, who had lapped up the prey committed to their avaricious jaws, were called together, and, since they were under pressure to return it, withdrew from communion. So also did those who had not succeeded in being ordained by bribery, and Lucilla, who had long been unable to endure discipline. This powerful and factious woman, with all her crew, refused to join in communion. Thus three causes and persons conspired to ensure that malignity worked its effect.

(19) The schism of that time, then, was brought forth by the anger of a humiliated woman, nourished by ambition, strengthened by avarice. By these three parties charges were fabricated against Caecilian so that his ordination might be declared improper. A summons to come to Carthage was sent to Secundus of Tigisis. Hither came all the collaborators mentioned above, receiving hospitality from the avaricious, the ambitious, and the angry, but not from catholics, by whose petition Caecilian had been ordained. Meanwhile none of the above-named came to the church, where the whole city was gathered with Caecilian. Then Caecilian issued a command: "If there is anything to be proved against me, let an accuser come forth and prove it." At that time nothing could be fabricated against him by all these enemies, but he suffered defamation on account of the one who ordained him, who was falsely said by these men to be a collaborator. Once again Caecilian commanded that if Felix, as they believed, had conferred nothing upon him, they themselves should ordain Caecilian as though he were still a deacon.

Then Purpurius, relying on his wonted malice, as though Caecilian too were the son of his sister, spoke as follows: "Let him come forth hither," as though he would lay hands on him to make him bishop and shake his head in repentance. When this was known, the whole church held Caecilian back from handing himself over to the brigands. Either he should have been expelled from the see at that time as a criminal or they should have communicated with him as being innocent. The church was filled by the populace, the episcopal see was filled, the altar was in its place, in which previous peaceable bishops—Cyprian, Lucian, and others—had made their offerings in the past. Thus it was that some went out and altar was erected against altar and an ordination was performed illicitly, and Majorinus, who had been a reader in the diaconate of Caecilian, a domestic of Lucilla, was ordained bishop with her approval and by collaborators who, as we have said above, had confessed their own crimes to each other and had then granted each other indulgence. It is therefore manifest that those who left the church were the ones ordaining, who had been collaborators, and Majorinus, who was ordained.

(20) Meanwhile they decided that from the fountain of their own crimes, which their numerous atrocities had turned to overflowing streams, the single charge of collaboration should be diverted against the one who ordained Caecilian; they expected that rumor would not be able to proclaim two similar stories at the same time. So that they might consign their own wrongdoing to silence, they undertook to defame the life of another, and when they themselves could be confuted by the innocent, they made efforts to confute the innocent, sending letters everywhere that had been written at the dictation of bitterness; these we have appended among other actions. While they were still based at Carthage, they sent letters before them, so that they might instill false rumors into the ears of all. Rumor spread the lie among the people, and while false charges concerning one were widespread, the extremely real crimes of the above-named persons were concealed in silence. Often crime causes blushes, but at that time there was no one to prompt the blushes, since, apart from a few catholics, all had sinned and among many an admitted wrong was like the picture of innocence. The outrage of collaboration, which was patently admitted by Donatus of Mascula and the others named above, was not enough; to their collaboration they added the great atrocity of schism.

(21) You see therefore, brother Parmenianus, that these two great crimes of collaboration and schism, evil and weighty as they are, belong to your leaders. Acknowledge then, late though it is, that you have assailed your own party, when you were pursuing the other; and even when it is patent that your party are the architects of this other wrong, you still strive to follow them with iniquitous footsteps, so that what they were the first to do in the name of schism, you also have visibly been doing for a long time and still are. They shattered the peace in their own time, you extinguish unity. Of your parents and of yourselves it can deservedly be said: *if the blind leads the blind, both fall into the ditch* (Matt 15:14). Rancorous bitterness blinded the eyes of your fathers, emulation has deprived your own of vision. You, too, are the last who would be able to deny that schism is the worst evil, yet without any qualms you have imitated Dathan and Abiram and Korah (cf. Num 16), your abandoned masters, nor have you been willing to set before your eyes the fact that this evil is both forbidden by the word of God and severely avenged when committed. Furthermore, the distance between sins is attested either by the remission or by the punishment. To conclude, among other precepts, the divine command has prohibited these three things also: *You shall not kill, you shall not follow after strange gods, and at the head of the ordinances: you shall not create a schism* (Exod 20:13; cf. Exod 20:5; *Didache* 4:4). Let us see which of these three ought to be punished and which forgiven. Parricide is the chief offense; and yet, even though Cain was guilty, he was not struck by God but avenged when killed (cf. Gen 4:15). In the city of Nineveh 120,000 people were sacrilegious, who were seen to follow strange gods; after the wrath of God and the preaching of the prophet Jonah, a brief fast and a prayer earned indulgence (Jonah 3:5–10). Let us see whether such results accrued to those who dared to cause the original schism among the people of God.

When God had cast the yoke of servitude from the necks of so many thousands of the children of Israel, he had set none but Aaron over them as their holy priest (cf. Num 16:40). But when his acolytes, holding thuribles in their desire for a priesthood that was not theirs by right, had seized it by deluding part of the people, they set before the face of the deluded people 200 and more acolytes, doomed to perish like themselves in imitation of the sacred rites. God, who hates schism, could not look kindly on this. In a sense they had declared war on God, as if there were another god who would accept another sacrifice. Therefore God was angry with a great anger because of the schism that had occurred, and what he had not done to sacrilegious men and parricides he did to the schismatics. There stood the line of priests and the sacrilegious multitude, doomed to perish there with their forbidden sacrifices; the time of repentance was denied to them and taken away because the fault was not of such a kind as to merit pardon. Famine was decreed upon the earth: all at once, it opened its throat against the dividers of the people and yawned greedily to swallow the despisers of God's commands. In the space of a moment, the earth opened to ingest these men; it snatched them away and closed. And lest it seem that they obtained a benefit from the reward of death, as they were not worthy to live, these men were not even allowed to die. Suddenly imprisoned in a Tartarean dungeon, they were buried before they died. And you are surprised that any such severity has been meted out to you, who either create or cultivate a schism, when you see what suffering was earned by the instigators of the original schism. Is it because such punishments have ceased now that you adjudge yourself and your party innocent? God has set forth a form of punishment in particular cases in order that he may have cause to blame the imitators. Immediate punishment overtook the first sins for an example; the second he will reserve for judgment. What are you going to say in answer to this, you who, having usurped the name of a church, covertly nourish a schism and brazenly defend it?

(22) But because I hear that some of your company with a zeal for litigation have records of some kind, it must be asked which ones should be trusted as according to reason and concurring with truth. Yours, if there are any, will perhaps appear to be stained with lies. The proof of our records is the forensic strife, the debates of parties, and the outcome of adjudications and of Constantine's letter. For as to what you say concerning us—"what have Christians to do with kings? Or what have bishops to do with the palace?"—if knowing kings is something to be blamed, the whole opprobrium falls on you. For your ancestors, Lucianus, Dignus, Nasutius, Capito, Fidentius, and the rest, petitioned Constantine with these prayers, of which a copy follows while he yet know nothing of these matters:

> "We petition you, Constantine, best of emperors, since you are of upright stock, as your father did not carry on the persecution in company with the other emperors and Gaul was immune from this outrage, seeing that in Africa there are dissensions between us and other bishops: we petition that your piety should make haste to have judges given to us from Gaul. Given by Lucian, Dignus, Nasutius, Capito, Fidentius, and the other bishops of Donatus's party."

(23) Having read this, Constantine replied with extreme acerbity, in which response he also exposed their prayers when he said: "You are petitioning me for a temporal judgment, when I myself am awaiting the judgment of Christ." Nonetheless, judges were given: Maternus from the city of Agrippina, Reticius from the city of Autun, Marinus from Arles. These three Gauls and fifteen others from Italy arrived at the city of Rome. They convened at the house of Fausta in the Lateran, when Constantine was consul for the fourth and Licinius for the third time, on October 2, the sixth day of the week, the session consisting of Miltiades, the bishop of the city of Rome; Maternus, Reticius, and Marinus, the Gaulish bishops; and Merocles from Milan, Florianus from Siena, Zoticus from Quintianum, Stennius from Rimini, Felix from Tuscan Florence, Gaudentius from Pisa, Constantius from Faventia, Proterius from Capua, Theophilus from Beneventum, Sabinus from Tarracina, Secundus from Praeneste, Felix from Tres Tabernae, Maximus from Ostia, Evandrus from Ursinum, and Donatianus from Forum Claudii.

(24) With these nineteen bishops in session, the case between Donatus and Caecilian was brought into

the open, and they severally pronounced the following verdicts against Donatus, that he had confessed that he had rebaptized and laid hands on lapsed bishops, which is alien to the custom of the church. The witnesses brought in by Donatus had confessed that they had nothing to say against Caecilian. Caecilian was pronounced innocent by the verdicts of all those enumerated above and also by the verdict of Miltiades, which judgment closed with these words:

> "Since it is patent that Caecilian has not been accused in respect of his calling by those who came with Donatus, and it is patent that he has not been convicted in any regard by Donatus, I judge that he should continue to be held in good standing by his eccesiastical communion."

(25) It is clear enough, then, that so many adverse judgments were inflicted on Donatus and that Caecilian was cleared by such a great tribunal, and yet Donatus thought it proper to appeal. To this appeal the Emperor Constantine's response was as follows: "O what a madman will dare in his rage! Just as if this were a common case of heathen litigation, a bishop thought it proper to appeal! etc."

(26) At this time the same Donatus petitioned for the right to return . . . arrive at Carthage. Then Philumenus, a supporter of his, suggested to the emperor that Caecilian be detained at Brixia for the sake of peace; and so it was done. Then two bishops, Eunomius and Olympius, were sent to Africa, so that, in the absence of both, they might ordain one. They arrived and stayed at Carthage forty days, so that they might declare where the catholic church was. This the seditious party of Donatus would not allow to happen, and every day riots were caused by partisan zeal. What we read as the final sentence of the same bishops, Eunomius and Olympius, is a declaration that the catholic church was the one that was spread throughout the whole world and that the verdict of nineteen bishops, given long before, could not be annulled. They communicated with Caecilian's clergy and returned. We have a book of the proceedings over these issues, which anyone who wishes may read in the final sections. While these events were taking place, Donatus, of his own accord, was the first to return to Carthage. On hearing this, Caecilian hurried to join his own folk. In this way the parties were renewed for a second time. It is however patent that so many adverse judgments were inflicted on Donatus and that Caecilian was pronounced innocent by the same number of verdicts.

(27) But since in this same case there seemed to be two people's names on trial in the catholic church, that of the one ordained and that of the one ordaining, once the one ordained had been cleared, the one who ordained still needed to be cleared. Then Constantine wrote to the proconsul Aelianus that he should set aside public business and hold a public inquiry into the life of Felix of Abthugni. As enjoined, he held a session. Those brought in were Claudius Saturianus, the curator of the common weal, who at the time of the persecution had been in the city of Felix, and the curator at the present time of debating the case, Callidius Gratianus, and the magistrate Alfius Caecilianus, but also Superius the constable was dragged in, and Ingentius the public scribe hung in fear of imminent tortures. All of them gave answers that yielded nothing of the kind that might incriminate the life of Bishop Felix. A book of the proceedings is in our possession, which contains the names of those who were present in the case of Claudius Saturianus, the curator, and Caecilianus, the magistrate, and Superius, the constable, and the scribe Ingentius and Solon, the public official of that time.

After their answers, the proconsul mentioned above spoke this part of his verdict:

> "Felix the pious bishop is manifestly innocent of the burning of the sanctifying instruments, since no one has been able to prove anything against him to the effect that he handed over or burned the most venerable scriptures. For the manifest [result of the] interrogation of all those named above is that no sanctifying Scriptures at all were found to have been either adulterated or burned. The content of our proceedings is that Felix the pious bishop was not present at that time, nor was a conscious accessory, nor commanded anything of the kind."

Obloquy, routed and wiped out, retired from that tribunal amid great acclamation. Opinion had wavered for a long time while truth seemed hidden in the mists exhaled by bitterness and rancor. But every writing also has been put on record and is published in the books of the proceedings and in the letters that were either put on record or read.

(28) You see, brother Parmenianus, that you were wrong to inveigh against the catholics, hurling at them the false name of collaborators; clearly, you have mixed up the names and transferred the deserts. You have closed your eyes, so as not to perceive that your parents were the criminals; you have opened them in order to make incriminating attacks on innocents who did not deserve it. Everything is said for the occasion, nothing for the truth, so that the most blessed Apostle Paul might say of you: *Some indeed have turned to vain speaking, aspiring to be teachers of the law, and not understanding what they say or what they speak of* (1 Tim 1:7). A little earlier we showed that your parents were collaborators and schismatics, and you, the heir of these same people, have desired no mercy for schismatics or collaborators. Now, therefore, by the documents put on record above, all the weapons that you treacherously wished to cast at others, repulsed by the shield of truth, have recoiled with a backward impetus on your own parents. All that you have been able to say against collaborators and schismatics, therefore, belongs to you, for it does not belong to us, since we have remained in the root and are on the side of everyone throughout the whole world.

29. Augustine: Sermon on the Dispute with the Donatists

Augustine delivered this sermon, ostensibly on the verse from the Wisdom of Ben Sirach that he cites at the beginning on "brotherly concord," in late 411, soon after an episcopal council in Carthage secured a definitive condemnation of the Donatists from an imperial agent named Marcellinus. The enforcement of the condemnation, issued as an imperial edict the following year, had evidently begun: Augustine speaks of Donatists who had given up their struggle and allowed themselves to be disciplined. The struggle was also, evidently, ongoing: Augustine refers to Donatists who still stubbornly resist the pull of fraternal accord, and he mentions a recent and shocking incident of Donatist violence against a Catholic priest. Augustine's framing of the schism as a question of fraternal dispute coheres with the distinction between heresy and schism laid out by Optatus. While heretics might be portrayed as suffering from an incurable and debilitating "madness," the Donatists are described as suffering from a "fever" that can be cured by careful ministration. Augustine is notably less eager than Optatus to lay blame for the schism. Even had Caecilian been found to be a *traditor* (he was, in fact, exonerated, as Augustine firmly notes), Augustine would still welcome him as a brother. This difference in opinion may reflect Augustine's more mature theological reflection on the nature of the church. It may also be a sign of the turning tide: Optatus had written his books *Against the Donatists* as a minority Catholic bishop in a Donatist stronghold (Numidia), while Augustine preached his sermon on "fraternal accord" mere months after securing the cooperation of imperial soldiers in enforcing "Catholic" unity.

From *The Works of Saint Augustine: A Translation for the 21st Century*, Part III, Volume 10: *Sermons*, trans. Edmund Hill, O.P. Hyde Park, N.Y.: New City Press, 1995. Used with permission.

(1) The first reading from the divine Scriptures, from the book called Ecclesiasticus, commended three excellent things to us that are most worthy of consideration: *concord between brothers, and the love of neighbors, and a husband and wife in agreement with each other* (Sir 25:1). These things are certainly good, delightful, and admirable in purely human affairs. But in divine matters they are much more significant. Is there anyone, after all, who doesn't rejoice over brothers in concord with each other? And what is indeed deplorable is that such a great thing is so rare in human affairs; the thing is admired by all, actually practiced by so few. Happy indeed are those who embrace in themselves what they cannot help admiring in others. There are no brothers who don't admire brothers living in concord with each other. And what makes it so difficult for brothers to live in concord with each other? The fact that they are at odds about earth, that they want to be earth. Right at the beginning, you see, the man who was a sinner heard, *Earth you are, and to earth you shall go* (Gen 3:19). From this we should be able to work out and examine the words that the man who is just ought to hear in the opposite sense. If the sinner was rightly told, *Earth you are and to earth you shall go,* the just man is rightly told, "Heaven you are and to heaven you shall go."

Or aren't the just the heavens, seeing that it is most plainly said about the evangelists, *The heavens tell of the glory of God?* And indeed that this is being said about them is made sufficiently clear by what follows: *And the firmament proclaims the works of his hands.* The ones he called heavens he also called the firmament. *Day bellows the word to day, and night to night points out knowledge. There are no languages or dialects in which their voices may not be heard.* You ask whose, and the only answer you can get is, the heavens'. So it was said about the apostles, said about those who proclaimed the truth. Thus it continues, *Into all the earth their sound went forth, and to the ends of the wide world their words* (Ps 19:1–4).

There are no languages or dialects in which their voices may not be heard. When the Holy Spirit came upon them, and God began to dwell in the heaven that he had made out of earth, they spoke, with the Holy Spirit generously filling them, in the tongues of all nations (cf. Acts 2:1–4). That's why it says, *there are no languages or dialects in which their voices are not heard.* And because they were sent from there to preach the gospel throughout all nations, *into all the earth their sound went forth, and to the ends of the wide world their words.* Whose? Those of the heavens, who are rightly told "Heaven you are, and to heaven you shall go," just as the sinner was rightly told, *Earth you are, and to earth you shall go.*

(2) So if brothers wish to live in concord with each other, they should not love earth. But if it is their wish not to love earth, they must not be earth. Let them seek possession of a property that cannot be divided, and they will always live in concord. What does discord between brothers spring from, the upsetting of natural family feeling? How is it there is one womb between them, and not one spirit, if not because their souls are bent double (cf. Luke 13:11), and each of them only has eyes for his own portion, and spends all his efforts on improving and adding to his own portion, and wishes to have unity in the possession of his own piece, while possessing division with his brother?

"This is a fine property; whose is it?"

"It's ours."

"A large property." That's the sort of thing that is usually said. "Is it all yours, brother?"

"No; I have a partner here; but if God wills, he will sell me his share."

The flatterer replies, "May God see to it." May God see to what? That the squeeze may be put on the neighbor, and he may sell his share to his neighbor?

"May God see to it. You have the right idea, may God bring it about for you."

Since the sinner is praised in the desires of his soul, and the one who practices iniquity is blessed (Ps 10:3).

What could be more iniquitous than to wish to get rich through the other person's poverty? And yet there's so much of this going on; *the one who practices iniquity is blessed.* And perhaps he has succeeded, perhaps he has put the pressure and the squeeze on, turned the screw, twisted the arm, not of any old partner, but maybe of his own brother: "It's better that I should buy it, rather than a stranger." And the other one, squeezed out so easily, has some consolation if he's a just man. He should listen to the Scripture, which he heard just now. He is weighed down with want, his brother is full of fatness—but he's full of earth, empty of justice. Notice, earth, what that poor man hears: *Do not be afraid when a man becomes rich or when the glory of his house is multiplied, since when he dies, he will not take it all with him* (Ps 49:16–17).

As for you, poor man, hold on to what you won't leave behind when you die and what you will possess while living forever. Hold on to justice; don't regret it. Does it depress you that you are poor on earth? The one who created the earth was poor here, too. The Lord your God is consoling you, your creator is consoling you, your redeemer is consoling you. Your brother, who is not grasping, is consoling you. That Lord of ours, you see, was prepared to be our brother, the only brother completely to be trusted without a shadow of doubt, with whom concord is to be possessed. I said he isn't grasping, and possibly I find he is. Yes, he's grasping, but it's us he wants to grab, us he wants to get possession of. It was for us that he paid such a huge price, himself, a price to which nothing can be added. He gave himself up as our price and became our redeemer. He didn't give himself up as the price, after all, in such a way that the enemy would let us go, and keep possession of him. He gave himself to death in order to slay death. Yes, by his death he slew death; he wasn't slain by death, and with death slain, he delivered us from death. Death, you see, was alive and kicking while we were dying; it will die when we are living, when it will be told, *Where, death, is your striving?* (1 Cor 15:55).

(3) So that was the sort of brother who was appealed to by one brother against his brother, brothers between whom, on account of earth, there was no concord, and he said to him, "*Lord, tell my brother to divide the inheritance with me* (Luke 12:13). He took the lot, he doesn't want to give me my share, he ignores me; he may at least listen to you." What concern was it of the Lord's? The way we think, though,

low people thinking low thoughts, crawling on the earth, fixed in this life, and not wishing to hurt anybody, and frequently thereby hurting them all the more gravely, what would we have said? "Come, brother, give your brother back his share." That's not what the Lord said. And where could better justice be found than with him? Who could hope to find such a judge to appeal to against the avarice of his brother? Wasn't that man delighted at finally discovering such a great relief to his wrong? Undoubtedly he was hoping for really effective assistance, when he said to such a judge, *Lord, tell my brother to divide the inheritance with me.* Yet what did the judge say? *O man, who appointed me a divider of the inheritance between you?* (Luke 12:14). The Lord repulsed him, he didn't give him what he was being asked for, he didn't grant him a gratuitous favor.

What was the problem? What was he to lose by it? What in any case was so difficult about doing such a favor? He didn't give him what he wanted. And what about, *To everyone who asks you, give* (Luke 6:30)? He didn't do this, the one who has given us an example of how we should live. How are we, then, going to do it? Or how shall we give what costs us something if we don't grant a favor that costs us nothing, by which we spend nothing, lose nothing? The Lord didn't give this particular thing; nevertheless, he didn't give nothing. He refused a lesser favor, but bestowed something more than he was asked for. He said, he said quite plainly, *To everyone who asks you, give.* What if someone asks of you, I'm not saying something that it's unprofitable to give, but that it's disgraceful to give? What if some woman asks for what a woman asked of Joseph (cf. Gen 39:7–12)? What if some man asks for what the false elders asked of Susanna (Sus 1:20)? Does that apparently general rule have to be followed even here? Perish the thought! So shall we in such a case act against the instructions of the Lord?

On the contrary, let us act according to the Lord's instructions, and not give bad things to those who ask for them, and even so we shall not be acting against this maxim. What was said, after all, is, *To everyone who asks you, give;* what was not said, is, "Give everything to one who asks you." *To everyone who asks you, give.* Most certainly, give; give him something. He's asking for something bad, it's for you to give him good things. That's what Joseph did. He didn't give the shameless woman what she was asking for, and yet he did give her what it was right she should hear, so that she wouldn't have his example to justify her shamelessness; he both avoided falling into the pit of lust and also gave her sound advice about chastity. This, you see, was his answer: *Far be it from me to do this thing to my master, that I should defile his bed, though he has entrusted to me all that is in his house* (Gen 39:8–9). If a slave bought for cash kept such faith with his master, what sort of faith should a wife keep with her husband? This was to admonish her: "I, a slave, will not do this to my master; ought you, his wife, to be doing this to your husband?"

Susanna too gave something and didn't send them away empty-handed, if they had been willing to take her advice about chastity. Not only, you see, did she not consent to them, but she did not, either, keep quiet about why she didn't consent. *If I consent to you,* she said, *I am lost to God; if I do not consent, I cannot escape your hands; it is better, though, to fall into your hands than to be lost to God* (Sus 1:22–23). But what's the meaning of, *it is better to fall into your hands than to be lost to God?* You are already lost to God, simply by seeking such things.

So hold on to this rule: give whenever you are asked, even if not precisely what you are asked for. That's what the Lord did. That man was asking for—what? The division of the inheritance. The Lord gave him—what? The death knell of greed. What did he ask for? *Tell my brother to divide the inheritance with me.* What did he receive? *Tell me, man, who appointed me a divider of the inheritance between you? I though, have this to say to you both.* What? *Beware of every kind of greed* (Luke 12:13–15). And I'll tell you why. Perhaps, you see, you are asking for half the inheritance precisely in order to get rich. Listen: *A certain rich man's territory was successful,* that is, it showed great profits and was blessed with many crops. *And he thought to himself, saying, What am I to do, where am I to store my crops?* And thinking hard, *I have realized,* he said, *what I must do; I shall*

pull down the old barns, I shall put up new ones, I shall fill them. You see, I shall make them bigger than the old ones were. And I shall say to my soul, You have many goods; take your fill, enjoy yourself. God said to him, Fool, you think you're so very shrewd. You know indeed how to pull down old structures and build new ones; you, though, have remained in the old, worn-out ruins of yourself, where you should have been pulling down the old structures in yourself, so that you would no longer savor the things of earth. *Fool,* what have you said, who have you said it to? You have said to your soul, *Enjoy yourself, you have many goods. This very night your soul will be required of you, to which you have made such promises. Whose shall they be, the things you have promised?* (Luke 12:16–20). So then, *do not be afraid when a man becomes rich because he will not, when he dies, take it all with him* (Ps 49:16–17).

(4) There you have the kind of advice on how to achieve concord, which the Lord gave brothers who were at loggerheads; they should lay aside greed and would straightaway have their fill of truth. So let us acquire an inheritance like that. How long shall we go on talking about concord between brothers over earthly matters, which is rare enough, unreliable enough, difficult enough? Let's talk about that brotherly concord that ought to be, and can be, very real. Let all Christians be brothers, let all the faithful be brothers, let those be brothers who have been born of God and of the womb of mother Church by the Holy Spirit; let them be brothers, let them too have an inheritance to be possessed and not divided. Their inheritance is God himself. The one whose inheritance they are is himself in turn their inheritance. How are they his inheritance? *Ask of me, and I will give you the nations as your inheritance* (Ps 2:8). How is he their inheritance? *The Lord is the portion of my inheritance and my cup* (Ps 16:5). In this inheritance concord is preserved; for this inheritance there is no litigation. Any other inheritance may be acquired by litigation; this one is lost by litigation. Those who don't wish to lose this inheritance avoid the wrangling of litigation.

And when perhaps they seem to be wrangling over it, they are not in fact doing so. But perhaps they appear to be wrangling or are assumed to be wrangling when what they are wishing to do is to consult the interests of their brothers. Notice in what a concordant spirit they wrangle or litigate, with what peaceable intentions, what goodwill, what justice, what fidelity. We, too, after all, seem to be wrangling or litigating with the Donatists, but in fact we are not. A man is litigating, you see, when he wishes his opponent ill; he's litigating when he wishes his opponent's loss to be his own gain, for something to be snatched from the other and to accrue to himself. That's not what we are like. You people know this, too, you that are litigating outside the unity; you, too, know this, you that have been acquired as a result of division; you know that this lawsuit is not an action of that sort because it is not prompted by ill will, because it is not aiming at the opponent's loss, but rather at his gain.

What we were hoping for, you see, was that those with whom we appeared to be litigating, or even still appear to be doing so, should acquire the inheritance together with us, not that they should lose it in order that we might acquire it for ourselves. In a word, our tone is quite different from that brother's, who appealed to Christ as he was walking this earth. Because we, too, are appealing to him in this case, as he is seated in heaven, and we are not saying, *Lord, tell my brother to divide the inheritance with me* (Luke 12:13); but, "Tell my brother to possess the inheritance with me."

(5) That such are our wishes is also borne out by the published *Acts* of the Conference. That such were our wishes is indicated not only by our speeches, but by our letters that were given to them. Do you value the episcopate? Keep it together with us. In you there is nothing that we hate, nothing we detest, nothing we abominate, nothing we condemn, except human error. It's human error, we said, that we detest, not divine truth. But what you have that is God's, we acknowledge; what you have as your own deviation, we wish to correct. The sign of my Lord, the sign of my emperor, the mark of my king I acknowledge in the deserter; I go looking for the deserter, I find him, approach him, accost him, take him by the hand, bring him along, correct him; I do no violence to his regi-

mental mark or badge. To anyone really paying attention and being observant, this is not a matter of litigating, but of loving.

We said that it is possible in one Church, for the sake of peace, for brothers to be in concord with each other; concord between brothers is, surely, a beautiful thing. Is it not possible, after all, we said, for there to be two bishops, so that they both take their seats in one single basilica, one on the bishop's throne, the other as a visitor; one on the bishop's throne, the other seated next to him as a colleague? Or again that one should preside over his brother's congregation, the other in turn over his?

We said that *repentance for the forgiveness of sins had been preached through all nations by the apostles, beginning from Jerusalem* (Luke 24:47). We said: "Let us suppose that Caecilian had an entirely bad case; is one man having a bad case, are two, five, ten men going to prejudice the salvation of so many thousands of the faithful, spread in the most variegated abundance throughout the whole world?" We said all that. Abraham believed, and he was promised all nations (cf. Gen 12:3); Caecilian sinned, and are all nations lost, so that the wrong he did should outweigh what Truth had promised? These things were said; they are there to be read. Against the divine examples, the testimonies which assert that the Church is to be spread throughout the whole wide world, the Church whose unity we hold fast to in the name of the Lord, they themselves were able to answer precisely nothing.

(6) So then, saving the case of the Church, confirmed and unchangeably fixed and established, as on a foundation of rock so that the gates of the netherworld may not defeat it, so saving this then, we also came to the case of Caecilian, not in the least worried now about whatever he might be found to have done wrong. After all, could we possibly be going to argue that if as a man he were found to be in any way to blame, judgment would be given that we were all to be either condemned or rebaptized because of one man's fault? And we said, "Saving the case of the Church, which is not prejudiced at all by the sin of Caecilian—the Church is neither given the prize for

Caecilian's virtue nor declared the loser for Caecilian's fault—let us also see what sort of case there is against him."

We agreed to look into it, but as the case of a brother, not of a father or mother. Our father is God, our mother the Church; Caecilian was our brother, or is our brother; if good, a good brother, if bad, a bad brother, still a brother. If we find him to be innocent, where will you now be, who have also fallen into the vice of human calumny? But if he's found to have done wrong, if he's found guilty, not even in that event have we been defeated because what we take our stand on is the unity of the Church, which is undefeated. Let him be found guilty through and through, I condemn the man, I don't desert Christ's Church. That, we said, is what we have guaranteed; from then on, we will not recite his name at the altar among the bishops whom we believe to have been faithful and innocent. That is all we have guaranteed; are you going to rebaptize the whole world just because of Caecilian?

So with this assurance firmly settled, the case of Caecilian was opened for investigation. He was found to be innocent; he was found to have been attacked by false accusers. He was condemned once in his absence, three times absolved when he was present; condemned by a faction, absolved by true judgment of the Church. All this was read out, all of it duly attested as genuine. They were asked whether they had anything to say in rebuttal. When they had used up all the twists and turns of their false accusations, or when they were able to offer nothing against the plain evidence of the documents or against the innocence of Caecilian himself, judgment was given against them. And still they go on saying, "We won." I hope they do win, but over themselves, so that Christ may obtain possession of them; may he win the case against them, the one who has redeemed them.

(7) And yet there are many of them over whom we can rejoice. Many of them were profitably defeated because in fact they were not defeated. Human error was defeated; the human being was saved. The doctor, after all, is not striving against the patient; even if the patient is doing so against the doctor, it's the fever that is defeated, while the patient is cured. The doctor's intention, surely, is to win, and that is also the fever's intention, to win. The patient is kind of placed in the middle; if the doctor wins, the patient is saved; if the fever wins, the patient will die.

So in our struggle, the doctor was striving for a cure and health; the patient was on the side of the fever. Those who took some notice of the doctor's advice won the day; they overcame the fever. We have them with us in the Church, in good health and glad of it. They used to speak ill of us before because they didn't acknowledge us as their brothers; the fever, you see, had disturbed their wits. We, though, love them even while they abominate us and rave against us, and we were putting ourselves at the service of the raving patients. We were standing up to them, struggling with them, and in a kind way wrangling and litigating; and yet we were doing it out of love. All who serve invalids of that sort, after all, make nuisances of themselves, but it is for their welfare and salvation that they do so.

(8) We have found some, though, who are sluggish and reluctant to move and who say, "It's true, my lord, it's true; there's nothing more to say."

So what are you waiting for? Come over, act.

"My dead father is there, my mother is buried there."

You've mentioned someone dead and buried. You're alive, there's still someone here to talk to. Your parents were Christians of the party of Donatus; perhaps their parents, too, were Christians; their grandparents or great-grandparents were certainly pagans. So those who first became Christians, did they freeze up against the truth when they carried out their pagan parents for burial? Did they bow to the authority of their dead parents and not rather prefer the living Christ to their dead parents? So if it's here that true unity is to be found, outside of which you are bound to die forever, why do you wish to follow your dead parents, dead to you and to God? What have you got to say? Answer!

"What you say is true. There's nothing more to be said. What do you want me to do?"

Goodness knows what kind of habit is holding

such people in its grip. They are lethargic, suffering from the opposite kind of disease; they are going to die of sleep. Others are frenzied; they are very troublesome. Because even if the lethargic ones are going to die, at least they don't make trouble for those who are trying to serve them. The frenzied ones make a great deal of trouble, and being quite out of their minds, they roam about, insane and raving and armed, looking for people they can kill, people they can blind. Yes, we have just received the news, they cut out the tongue of one of our priests. These people are in a frenzy. It's a test of charity; they, too, must be loved. Many of them, seeing the light, have wept bitterly; many have seen the light. We know this, a number of these frenzied people have come to us. Every day they weep over their past deeds, nor can they have enough of tears when they observe the fury of those who are still raving, still drunk on their futile nonsense. So what do we do? Charity obliges us to be at the service of such people. And although we are a troublesome nuisance to both sorts, both by shaking the lethargic and by restraining the frenzied, still we love them both all the same.

(9) A good thing indeed it is, *concord between brothers; but notice where: in Christ. And the love of neighbors* (Sir 25:1). What if even now he's not a brother in Christ? Because he's human, he's a neighbor; you should love him, too, in order to gain him, too. So there you are, in concord with your brother Christian and loving your neighbor, even though you are not yet in concord with him, because he's not yet your brother in Christ, not yet born again in Christ, doesn't yet know about the sacraments of Christ; he's a pagan, he's a Jew; still he's a neighbor because he's a human being. So if you love him, you have also attained another strand of love, by another gift, and in this way there are two things in you: *concord between brothers, and the love of neighbors.* And it is of all those who maintain concord between brothers and who love their neighbors that the Church consists, wedded to Christ and submissive to her husband, so that we get the third strand, *a husband and wife in agreement with each other* (Sir 25:1).

Which is why I am admonishing your graces and urging you in the Lord to think lightly, my brothers

and sisters, of things present, which you can't carry with you when you die. Be on your guard against sin, on your guard against injustice of all sorts, on your guard against worldly appetites and greed. It is only then, you see, that our profit from you is undiminished, and our reward full of joy in the Lord. I mean, even if we say what has to be said, even if we preach what has to be preached and absolve ourselves of our debt to the Lord in the Lord's sight, because we haven't kept quiet about what we fear, haven't kept quiet about what we love, so that the sword of the Lord's vengeance, whoever it may fall upon, will not find anything to charge the lookout with (cf. Ezek 33:1–6); still, we don't want our reward to be assured with all of you being lost, but with all of you being found. I mean, the apostle Paul too was sure of his reward, and yet what did he say to the people? *Now we live, if you stand fast in the Lord* (1 Thess 3:8).

I am talking to all of you, and to your graces, fathers and brothers, by the Lord's command. I am also speaking on behalf of my brother, your bishop, whose joy you ought to be by obeying the Lord our God. Certainly this church has been constructed for you, in the Lord's name, by his labors, thanks to the generous contributions and the sympathetic and devout assistance of faithful brothers and sisters. This church has been put up for you, but it is you, rather, who are the Church. What has been built for you is a place for your bodies to enter, but it's your minds that ought to be the place for God to enter. You have honored your bishop by wishing to call this basilica the Florence. But it's really you that are his Florence or flowering. Because that's what the apostle says: *My joy and my crown is what you are in the Lord* (Phil 4:1).

Whatever there is in the world, it fades away, it passes. As for this life, what is it but what the psalmist said: *In the morning it will pass like the grass, in the morning it will flower and pass away; in the evening it will fall, it grows hard and withers* (Ps 90:5–6). That's what *all flesh is* (Isa 40:6). That's why Christ, that's why the new life, that's why eternal hope, that's why the consolation of immortality has been promised us, and in the flesh of the Lord has already been given us. It was from us, after all, that that flesh was taken that is now immortal and that has shown us what he accomplished in himself. It was on our account, you see, that he had flesh. I mean, on his own account *in the beginning was the Word, and the Word was with God, and the Word was God* (John 1:1). Look for flesh and blood; where is it to be found in the Word? Because he wished really and truly to suffer with us and to redeem us, he clothed himself in *the form of a servant* (Phil 2:7) and came down here though he was here, in order to be plainly visible though he had never been absent; and he that had made man wished to be made man; to be created of a mother, though he had created his mother. He mounted the cross, he died, and showed us what we already knew about, being born and dying. In his humility he went through with these hoary old experiences of ours, so familiar, so well known.

We knew all about being born and dying; what we didn't know about was rising again and living forever. So in his humility he took to himself our two old things; in his sublimity he accomplished two other great and new things. He raised up flesh, he lifted flesh up to heaven, he is seated as flesh at the right hand of the Father. He wished to be our head; the head has pleaded for the members because even when he was here, he said, *Father, it is my wish that where I am, there these also may be with me* (John 17:24). Let us hope firmly for all this with respect to our flesh, too, resurrection, transformation, inperishability, immortality, an eternal abode; and let us so conduct ourselves that we achieve it. That will be Florence, the real flowering Florence.

Judaizing Heresies: The Texts

The Christian problem of Jewish origins is inscribed in the oldest Christian writings, the New Testament. Jesus' confrontation with the "scribes and Pharisees" (Matthew) and "the Jews" (John), Paul's conflict with the "circumcisers" (Galatians), and Peter's relaxation of Jewish custom (Acts) all point to an early and abiding dilemma: How should Christians (of Jewish and gentile origins) distinguish themselves from nonbelieving Jews, even as they shared a history, a Bible, and a theological vocabulary? Early Christians, such as Marcion (ca. 84–160), sought a clean break by throwing out the Jewish Scriptures and the Jewish God; this rejection of Jewish roots, however, was deemed extreme and "heretical" (although evidence suggests that Marcionite Christianity survived in remote pockets for centuries after his death). Other Christians chose to contrast Jewish adherence with Christian "spiritualization" (i.e., rejection and reinterpretation) of Old Testament Law.

In the third and fourth centuries, Jewish difference was seen as increasingly doctrinal in nature. Jews were not just "stubborn" in their retention of the Law and refusal to accept Christ's divinity: they were theologically deficient. Trinitarian and Christological controversies preyed on this deficiency: both Arius and Nestorius were decried as "Judaizers" for (supposedly) denying Christ's Godhood. "Judaizing" or "Jewish-Christian" heresies were isolated, labeled, and condemned: Ebionites, Nazoraeans, Naasenes, Elkasaites, and Cerinthians were attacked by the "orthodox" for their Judaizing. Scholars often call these groups "Jewish Christians," a label that does not distinguish between Jews confessing some belief in the messiahship of Jesus and Christians incorporating some aspect of Jewish ritual into their observance. We know almost nothing about these groups apart from the accusations made against them, including to what extent all of them comprised recognizable groups distinct from mainstream Christians. John Chrysostom's panicked attack on Judaizers, reproduced here, may indicate that social, religious, and even theological interaction between Jews and Christians continued well into the fourth century, or it may highlight the marginal activities of a few Christians, deliberately skating the thin edge of religious difference.

Writings against "Judaizing" Christians, therefore, may not give us clear insight into the social relations of Jews and Christians. They do, however, point to an ongoing anxiety about Christian identity, which erupted into a flurry of heresiological writings in the fourth and fifth centuries. The inscription of doctrinal, practical, and social boundaries between orthodox Christians and Judaizing heretics provided a more nuanced way to approach the persistent problem of Jewish-Christian difference. The rhetorical license of heretical discourses, moreover, would inevitably spill over into Christian language about Jews as well as "Judaizers," setting the stage for antagonism and violence during the Middle Ages.

30. John Chrysostom: First Speech Against the Judaizers

John Chrysostom preached eight sermons "Against the Judaizers" (sometimes called, perhaps erroneously, "Against the Jews") while still a priest in Antioch (for Chrysostom's rhetorical and ecclesiastical career, see the introduction to Text 15). Famous for their scathing invective, these homilies provided unfortunate fodder for rabid anti-Judaism throughout the Middle Ages. In this first sermon, Chrysostom's reasons for preaching so vehemently against Jewish custom and belief is placed in a specific context: Antiochene Christians who treated Jewish synagogues as holy places, appropriate for making vows and seeking supernatural healing. While Chrysostom has only loathing for Jews, his primary concern is for Christians seeking to "Judaize" Christianity by attending Jewish festivals, approving of their scriptural interpretation, and ignoring their slanders against Christ. This last accusation places the Jews and Judaizers, for Chrysostom, squarely in the camp of the theological heretics who denied Christ's full divinity. Chrysostom, in fact, interrupted a series of anti-Arian (Anomoean) homilies to preach these sermons against the Judaizers.

Chrysostom's venomous homily draws on standard heretical metaphors: the attraction to Judaism is a "disease" that must be healed, and the Jews who lure Christians to their polluted synagogues are infested with "demons" attempting to defile Christianity purity. Chrysostom's famous rhetorical prowess is vividly, and distressingly, evident in the speech, particularly when he attempts to portray Jews as negatively as possible. His near-hysterical tone has been read as a combination of oratorical fancy and genuine alarm at the attraction of Judaism to his congregants. This speech also demonstrates how discourses of heresy could be used not just in internal theological debates, but to sharpen the divide between all Christians and religious "others."

(1) Today I wanted to finish the topic we were discussing recently and to show as clearly as possible that God is incomprehensible. Last Sunday I spoke in detail and at length on this topic, and at that time I brought forth the testimony of Isaiah, of David, and of Paul. From Isaiah I cited the words, "Who can describe his generation?" (Isa 53:8). The psalmist, giving him thanks because of his incomprehensibility, says, "I will praise you, for you fill me with awe and your works are wonderful" (Ps 139:14). And again, "Such knowledge is beyond my understanding, so high that I cannot reach it" (Ps 138:6). And Paul, chary of inquiring into the essence of God, speaks only of his providence and only of a single aspect of his providence, namely, that which is seen in the calling of the gentiles. Gazing on God's providence as a vast and yawning sea, he cries out, "O depth of wealth, wisdom, and knowledge in God: How unsearchable his judgments, how untraceable his ways!" (Rom 11:35).

Although these testimonies were sufficient proof, I was not satisfied with the prophets, nor did I stop with the apostles. I went up to heaven itself and displayed the chorus of angels singing, "Glory to God in highest heaven, and on earth peace, goodwill to men" (Luke 2:14). Moreover you heard the seraphim, trembling and filled with awe, cry out, "Holy, Holy, Holy is the Lord of Hosts, the whole earth is full of his glory" (Isa 6:3). To which were added the cherubim, crying, "Blessed is the glory of the Lord in his place" (Ezek 3:12). Three testimonies from earth, three from heaven declare the unapproachable glory of God. When I finished and the proof was irrefutable, the congregation broke into thunderous applause, shaking the building and setting the people afire with enthusiasm. I was delighted not because they were praising me, but because they glorified my Lord. Your applause and your praise showed what love you have for God. Just as affectionate servants, when they hear someone praising their master love the one who praises him because they love him, too, so also you did the same on Sunday. The excessiveness of your applause showed your love for the Lord.

Today I wanted to return to the same contest. For if the enemies of truth have not had their fill of blaspheming their benefactor, how much more have we not been satisfied with honoring the supreme God. But what can I do? Another more terrible sickness beckons, and our tongue must be turned to heal a disease that is flourishing in the body of the church. First, we must root this out and then return to those who are outside the church. We must first heal our own members and then busy ourselves with outsiders.

What is this sickness? The festivals of the wretched and miserable Jews that follow one after another in succession—trumpets, booths, the fasts— are about to take place.[1] And many who belong to us and say that they believe in our teaching attend their festivals and even share in their celebrations and join in their fasts. It is this evil practice I now wish to drive from the church. Sermons against the Anomoeans [Arians] can be delivered at another time, and the delay would not work any harm. But if those who are sick with Judaism are not healed now when the Jewish festivals are "near, at the very door" (Matt

24:33), I am afraid that some, out of misguided habit and gross ignorance, will share in their transgressions, and sermons about such matters would be pointless. If the offenders are not present to hear what we say today, afterward medicine would be applied in vain because they would already have committed the sin. This is the reason I am in a hurry to take up this matter before the festivals. That is the way doctors do things. They deal with the most urgent and acute sicknesses first.

Of course this struggle [with the Jews] is related to the previous struggle [with the Anomoeans]. And since there is kinship between the impiety of the Anomoeans and the impiety of the Jews, there is a relation between the present and the former controversies. For that which the Jews have long charged us, the Anomoeans also accuse us. What do they charge? That by calling God his own father, Jesus claimed equality with God (John 5:18). This accusation— though not really an accusation—is rather an attempt to eliminate this text and its meaning completely, if not with the hand, then with the mind.

(2) Do not be surprised if I have called the Jews wretched. They are truly wretched and miserable, for they have received many good things from God yet they have spurned them and violently cast them away. The sun of righteousness rose on them first, but they turned their back on its beams and sat in darkness. But we, who were nurtured in darkness, welcomed the light, and we were freed from the yoke of error. The Jews were branches of the holy root, but they were lopped off. We were not part of the root, yet we have produced the fruits of piety. They read the prophets from ancient times, yet they crucified the one spoken of by the prophets. We had not heard the Holy Scriptures, yet now we worship the one about whom the prophets speak. This is why they are wretched, because when others embraced and welcomed the good things given to them, the Jews refused them.

They were called to sonship, but they degenerated to the level of dogs. But we who were dogs were, by the grace of God, able to cast off our former irrationality to be elevated to the dignity of sons. How do I know this? "It is not right to take the children's

---

[1] That is, New Year's, the Day of Atonement, and Sukkoth.

bread and throw it to the dogs" (Matt 15:26). Jesus was speaking there to the Canaanite woman, and he called the Jews "beloved children" and the gentiles "dogs." But note how the order is reversed later; they have become "dogs," and we are "beloved children." Paul said this about them, "Beware of those dogs and their malpractices. Beware of those who insist on mutilation—'circumcision' I will not call it; we are the circumcised" (Phil 3:2–3). Don't you see how those who were formerly beloved children have become dogs?

Do you want to know how we who were once dogs have become beloved children? "To all who received him, he gave the right to become children of God" (John 1:12). Nothing is more miserable than those who always kick against their own salvation. When it was required to keep the law, they trampled it under foot; now when the law has been abrogated, they obstinately observe it. What could be more pitiful than people who provoke God's anger not only by transgressing the Law, but also by observing the Law. This is why the Scripture says, "You stiff-necked and uncircumcised in heart; you always fight against the Holy Spirit" (Acts 7:51). They not only transgressed the Law, but they want to observe it at the wrong time. They are rightly called "stiff-necked" for they did not bear the yoke of Christ, although it was neither grievous nor burdensome but gentle. "Learn from me, for I am gentle and humble hearted," and "Bend your necks to my yoke, for my yoke is good to bear, my load is light" (Matt 11:29–30).

Nonetheless they did not bear it; they smashed it and broke it. "Ages ago you broke your yoke and snapped your traces" (Jer 2:20). It was not Paul who said these things, but the prophet, using "yoke" and "traces" as symbols of dominion because the Jews rejected the Lordship of Christ. "We have no king but Caesar," they said (John 19:15). When you broke the yoke and snapped the traces, you cast yourself out of the kingdom of heaven and subjected yourself to human rulers.

Consider with me how the prophet intimates that they are unmanageable. For he did not say, "You threw off my yoke," but "you broke my yoke." This is the shortcoming of wild animals, unused to the reins,

who refuse to be tamed. Where does this stiffness come from? From gluttony and drunkenness. Moses himself said, "Israel ate, and he was well fed and grew fat, and the beloved became recalcitrant" (Deut 32:15). Just as animals, when they are allowed to eat as much as they want, grow fat and become stubborn and hard to hold, and neither the yoke, nor the bridle, nor the hand of the driver can restrain them, so also the Jewish people, by drunkenness and overeating have been driven to the ultimate evil. They have kicked up their hooves, refusing to bear the yoke of Christ and to draw the plow of his teaching. One prophet intimated this when he said, "Israel has run wild, wild as a heifer" (Hos 4:16). Another called Israel an "unbroken calf" (Jer 31:18). Such animals, unfit for any useful work, are fit only for slaughter. This is what has happened since they made themselves unsuitable for any task. They are suited only for slaughter. This is why Christ said, "Those enemies of mine who did not want me for their king, bring them here and slaughter them" (Luke 19:27).

You should have fasted, O Jew, when your drunkenness was doing you such harm and when your gluttony bred impiety, but not now. Now the time for fasting is past. Fasting has become abominable. Who says these things? Isaiah cries out with a loud voice, "Is not this what I require of you as a fast? says the Lord." Why? "Since your fasting leads only to wrangling and strife and dealing vicious blows with the fists" (Isa 58:4, 5). If your fast was abominable when you beat your fellow servants, how can your fast be acceptable when you murder your master? What logic is there to that?

One who fasts should be restrained, subdued, humble, not drunk with anger. Are you still beating your fellow servants? Once their fasting led only to wrangling and strife, now it leads to wanton violence and extreme licentiousness, to dancing with naked feet in the marketplace. They are supposed to be fasting, but they are really having a drunken party. Listen to what the prophet says about fasting: "Sanctify a fast" (Joel 1:14). Don't make a pompous spectacle of fasting. "Announce a day of abstinence; gather the elders" (Joel 1:14). But they gather rabble—effeminate men and prostitutes—and they drag the crowd from the theater and the actors to the synagogue. There is no difference between the theater and the synagogue. I know that some condemn me for daring to say that the synagogue is no different from the theater, but I reply that it is audacious of them to disagree with what I said. Condemn me if I declare this on my own authority, but if I cite the words of the prophet, accept what I say.

(3) I know that many have high regard for the Jews, and they think that their present way of life is holy. That is why I am so anxious to uproot this deadly opinion. I said that the synagogue is no better than the theater, and I submitted proof from the prophet. The Jews are not more trustworthy than the prophets. What did the prophet say? "Yours was a harlot's brow, and you were resolved to show no shame" (Jer 3:3). A place where a prostitute offers her wares is a house of prostitution. But the synagogue is not only a house of prostitution and a theater, it is also a hideout for thieves and a den of wild animals. "Your house has become for me a hyena's den" (Jer 7:11). But it is not simply the den of a wild animal but of an unclean one at that. Further, "I have forsaken my house; I have cast off my inheritance" (Jer 12:7). When God leaves, what hope of salvation remains? When God forsakes a place, it becomes a dwelling place for demons.

Surely they say that they worship God. Away with such talk! No Jew worships God. Who says these things? The son of God. "If you knew me, you would know my father as well. You know neither me nor my father" (John 8:19). What testimony can I offer that is more trustworthy than this one?

If they are ignorant of the Father, if they crucified the Son and spurned the aid of the Spirit, can one not declare with confidence that the synagogue is a dwelling place of demons? God is not worshipped there. Far from it! Rather, the synagogue is a temple of idolatry. Nevertheless, some go to these places as though they were sacred shrines. I am not imaging such things. I know them from my own experience.

Three days ago (believe me, I am not lying), I saw a noble and free woman, who is modest and faithful, being forced into a synagogue by a coarse and senseless person who appeared to be a Christian (I would not say that someone who dared to do such things was really a Christian). He forced her into a synagogue to make an oath about certain business matters that were in litigation. As the woman passed by, she kept calling out for help, hoping someone would stop this lawless show of force (for she would not be allowed to participate in the sacred mysteries [Eucharist] if she went into the synagogue). Enraged and burning with anger, I roused myself and rescued her from this unjust abduction so that she would not be dragged into such lawlessness. When I asked her abductor whether he was a Christian, he admitted he was. I reproached him severely, accusing him of stupidity and a complete lack of understanding, and I told him that he was no better than a jackass if he thinks that one can worship Christ and, at the same time, drag someone to the haunts of the Jews who crucified him.

Then I went on to exhort him further. First, I said that it is not permissible to make oaths at all or to require someone else to make an oath, as the holy gospels teach. Further, one should not force an unbaptized person to do such a thing, much less a woman who is baptized and a faithful Christian. Then, as I expunged with many arguments these erroneous ideas from this soul, I asked him why he had walked by the church and dragged this woman to a gathering place of the Hebrews. He replied that many had told him that oaths that were taken there were more awesome. When I heard this, I shouted at him and was again consumed by anger. But then I began to laugh. When I saw the villainy of the devil, and with what skill he was able to deceive men, I groaned. When I thought of the gullibility of those who are deceived, I was filled with anger. But when I saw just how great was the stupidity of those who were deceived, I could only laugh.

I tell you these things and recount my experience because your attitude toward people who do such things, as well as to those to whom they are done, is insensitive and unfeeling. If you see one of your brothers falling into such sins, you consider it to be someone else's trouble, not your own. And if someone accuses you, you attempt to defend yourself by saying, "What business is it of mine?" or "What do I have in common with that person?" uttering words of utter contempt with the cruelty of Satan. Do you realize what you are saying? You are a man, and you share the same human nature. Even more, if one must speak about sharing the same nature, you have one head, Christ, and you dare to say that you have nothing in common with your own members. How can you confess Christ to be the head of the church? For the head knits together all the members, ensuring that each looks after the other and that all are united. If you have nothing in common with your limbs, neither do you have anything in common with your brother, nor do you have Christ as your head.

The Jews frighten you as though you were little children, and you don't even realize it. For just as coarse slaves will show ridiculous and terrifying masks to children (the masks themselves are not terrifying, but they appear so to childish minds) and make them laugh loudly, so also the Jews terrify simple Christians. How can the Jewish synagogues be considered worthy of awe when they are shameful and ridiculous, offensive, dishonored, and contemptible?

(4) Our places of worship, however, are not of this sort; they are truly places of awe and are filled with religious fear. For where God, who has authority over life and death, is present, that place is terrifying. For there one hears countless sermons about eternal punishments, about fiery rivers, about the poisonous worm (cf. Isa 66:24; Mark 9:48), about unbreakable chains, about outer darkness. But the Jews have not the faintest idea of such things, living for their stomachs, all agape about the present, no better off than pigs and goats, ruled only by licentiousness and excessive gluttony. One thing only they know—how to stuff themselves and get drunk, to come to blows over dancers, and to get beat up in brawls over chariot drivers. Tell me, are these things holy and awesome? Who would claim this? How can they appear awesome to us unless one considers dishonored servants who have lost their privileges and been banished from their master's house more worthy of respect than servants who are held in honor and good favor? But that is not the way things are—they simply aren't. If an inn is not more august than the halls of kings, so a synagogue is less honorable than any

inn. For it is not simply a gathering place for thieves and hucksters, but also of demons; indeed, not only the synagogue, but the souls of Jews, are also the dwelling places of demons. And at the conclusion of this sermon I will try to prove this to you. This is why I ask you especially to remember my words. I am not saying these things to show off or to win your applause, but to heal your souls. What is there left to say if there are as many doctors as there are sick?

There were only twelve apostles, and they won the whole world. The greater part of this city is Christian, yet there are some who are sick with Judaism. What sort of defense can we who are healthy put up? Of course, the sick deserve the blame themselves, but we who overlook their infirmity are not completely free of blame; it is inconceivable that they would remain ill if we gave them our full attention. In anticipation of that, I am now saying these things, that each of you can attempt to persuade your brother, whether by force, by striking him, by insulting him, or by arguing with him. Do anything to rescue him from the devil's snare and deliver him from the fellowship of Christ killers. Tell me: if you see someone in the marketplace being led away and who has been condemned justly and you had authority to release him from the hands of his executioners, wouldn't you do everything to free him from his sentence? But now you see your brother being dragged unjustly and iniquitously to the pit of destruction, not by an executioner but by the devil, and you don't make the slightest effort to rescue him from that iniquity. What kind of excuse can you offer? That he is stronger and more powerful. Show him to me. I would rather have my head cut off than allow him to enter the doors of the church if he is contentious and will not change his ways. What do you have in common with the "free Jerusalem," with the "heavenly Jerusalem?" You chose the earthly; be a slave just like she is. For "she and her children are in slavery" (Gal 4:25), as the apostle says.

Do you fast with Jews? Then take off your sandals with the Jews and go barefoot into the marketplace and join in their disgraceful and ridiculous behavior. But you'd be too ashamed and embarrassed to do this. If you are ashamed to participate in their indecorous dances, are you not ashamed to participate in their impiety? What kind of mercy do you expect to receive when you are only a half-Christian? Believe me—if I see anyone sick with this disease, I would rather have my head cut off than overlook them. On the other hand, if I don't know anything about them, God will forgive me. I want each of you to mull over these things; don't consider this thing to be a peripheral matter.

Haven't you noticed that in the mysteries the deacon frequently calls out, "Acknowledge one another"? In saying this he entrusts you with the responsibility of carefully examining your brother. Do the same things with those about whom you have question. If you know someone who is Judaizing, grab him and take note of him, so that you yourself will not be exposed to peril. In frontier army camps, if someone is found among the soldiers who sympathizes with the barbarians or the Persians, not only is he in danger, but also anyone who knew him and did not report him to the general is in danger. Since you belong to the camp of Christ, carefully examine and take pains to see whether someone is mixed in with you from the other side; make clear to them, however, that you do so not to kill them or punish them, as they do in the army, or to take vengeance on them, but to deliver them from error and impiety and make them completely one of us. But if you refuse to do this and conceal what you know, you can be assured that you will receive the same punishment as the Judaizer. For Paul does not correct and punish only those who do evil, but also those who tolerate evildoers. And the prophet condemns not only those who steal but also their accomplices. For if someone has knowledge of an evildoer and protects and hides him, he only gives greater opportunity for his indulgence and allows him to do evil with less restraint.

(5) But we must return again to the sick. Do you realize that those who are fasting have dealings with those who shouted, "Crucify him! Crucify him!" (Luke 23:21) and with those who said, "His blood be on us and on our children" (Matt 27:23, 25)? If a band of would-be revolutionaries were apprehended and then condemned, would you dare to go to them and talk with them? I certainly don't think so! Is it not

absurd to be zealous about avoiding someone who sinned against mankind, but to have dealings with those who have affronted God? Is it not folly for those who worship the crucified to celebrate festivals with those who crucified him? This is not only stupid—it is sheer madness.

But since there are some who consider the synagogue to be a holy place, we must say a few things to them as well. Why do you reverence this place when you should disdain it, despise it, and avoid it? "The Law and the books of the prophets can be found there," you say. What of it? You say, "Is it not the case that the books make the place holy?" Certainly not! This is the reason I especially hate the synagogue and avoid it, that they have the prophets but do not believe in them, that they read these books but do not accept their testimonies. This makes their effrontery all the worse. Tell me, if you see a distinguished man, one who is honored and respected being led into a tavern or into a den of robbers, and he is assaulted there and beaten up by a bunch of drunks, would you admire the tavern or the robber's den because once a noble and distinguished man had been there and was beaten up by drunks? I doubt it! Instead, for this very reason, you would all the more hate it and avoid it. The same applies to the synagogue. They brought the prophets and Moses with them into the synagogue, not in order to honor them but to insult and dishonor them. When they say that the prophets and Moses did not know about Christ, nor did they say anything about his coming, what greater insult can there be against these holy men? When they accuse them of not knowing their Lord, they make them accomplices in their impiety. For this reason, we should all the more hate them and their synagogue because they offend these holy men.

But why am I speaking about books and places? In times of persecutions, executioners seize the bodies of the martyrs to beat and whip them. Are their hands holy because they have touched the bodies of holy men? Far from it! Such hands, although they have held the bodies of the saints, remain impure for the very reason that they have held them for evil ends. Similarly, those who handle the writings of the saints and mistreat them no less than executioners mistreat the bodies of the martyrs—should they be venerated for this reason? Is not this the height of irrationality? For those who seize bodies for the purpose of harming them not only are not sanctified by touching them, but they are made even more cursed. How much less are writings read with unbelief able to help those who read them. Indeed, the extent of their impiety is evident in that they possess the books with evil intentions. They would not be worthy of such condemnation if they did not possess the prophets; they would not be so unclean and impure if they did not read these books. Now they are deprived of any forgiveness because they possess the heralds of truth and have maliciously resisted them as well as the truth. For this reason, they are impure and accursed, because having the prophets at their disposal they consult them with an evil purpose. Therefore I beg you to shun them and avoid their gatherings.

The harm to our weaker brethren is not a small matter, nor is the opportunity for them to flaunt their arrogance a minor matter. For when they see you, who worship the Christ who was crucified by them, observing Jewish customs and reverencing Jewish ways, how can they not think that everything done by them is the best? How can they not think that our ways are not worth anything when you, who confess to be a Christian and to follow the Christian way, run to those who degrade these same practices. It is written, "If a weak character sees you sitting down to a meal in a heathen temple—you who have knowledge—will not his conscience be emboldened to eat food consecrated to heathen deity?" (1 Cor 8:10). And I say: If a weak character sees you arriving at a synagogue to watch them blow trumpets [for the New Year's festival]—you who have knowledge—will not his conscience be emboldened to marvel at the Jewish practices? One who falls is punished not only because of his own fall, but also for tripping others up. Similarly, the one who stands firm is honored not only for his virtue, but also because he inspired others to emulate him. Therefore stay away from their gatherings and from their synagogues and do not praise the synagogue on account of its books. Rather, hate it and avoid it for that very reason, for they have mangled the saints because they do not believe their words and they accuse them of extreme impiety.

(6) That you may learn that books do not make a place holy and that the disposition of those who gather there defiles it, let me tell you a story from ancient history. When Ptolemy Philadelphus, who was collecting books from all over the world, learned that among the Jews there were books that philosophized about God and the best way of life, he sent for men from Judaea and commissioned them to translate these books. Ptolemy placed the books in the temple of Serapis. He was a Greek, and this translation of the prophets is in use to this very day. Now then, are we to consider the temple of Serapis holy because of these books? Of course not! While books do have a holiness of their own, they do not impart it to a place if those who frequent it are defiled. You should think about the synagogue in the same way. Even if there is not an idol there, demons inhabit the place. And I say this not only about the synagogue here in the city but also about the one in Daphne. For the pit of destruction there, which they call Matrona's, is even more evil. For I heard that many of the faithful have gone up there to practice incubation in the shrine. But I should not be calling such people "faithful." Both the shrine of Matrona and the temple of Apollo are equally impure to me.

If someone condemns my audacity in speaking this way, I condemn his utter madness. Tell me, if demons dwell there, is it not a place of impiety even if there is not a statue of an idol standing there? Where Christ killers gather, the cross is ridiculed, God blasphemed, the father unacknowledged, the Son insulted, the grace of the Spirit rejected. Indeed, is not the harm even greater where demons are present? In a pagan temple, the impiety is open and obvious and can hardly seduce or deceive one who has his wits about him and is soberminded. But in the synagogue they say that they worship God and abhor idols. They read and admire the prophets and use their words as bait, tricking the simple and foolish to fall into their snares. The result is that their impiety is equal to that of the Greeks, but their deception is much worse. They have an altar of deception in their midst that is invisible and on which they sacrifice not sheep and calves, but the souls of men. In a word, if you admire the Jewish way of life, what do you have in common with us? If the Jewish rites are holy and venerable, our way of life must be false. But if our way is true, as indeed it is, theirs is fraudulent. I am not speaking of the Scriptures. Far from it! For they lead one to Christ. I am speaking of their present impiety and madness.

But it is now time to show that demons dwell in the synagogue and not only in the place, but also in the souls of the Jews. "When the unclean spirit comes out, it wanders over the deserts seeking a resting place. If it finds none, it says, 'I will go back into my own house.' So it returns and finds the house unoccupied, swept clean and tidy. Off it goes and collects seven other spirits more wicked than itself, and they all come in, and in the end the man's plight is worse than before. This is how it will be in this generation" (Matt 12:43–45). Can you see that demons inhabit their souls and that the present demons are worse than before? But that is hardly surprising. Then they sinned against the prophets; now they insult the Lord of the prophets. Tell me, how can you gather together in a place with men possessed by demons, whose spirits are so impure and who are nurtured on slaughters and murders—how can you do this and not shudder? Instead of exchanging greetings with them and addressing one word to them, ought one not rather avoid them as a pestilence and disease spread throughout the whole world? Haven't they been the cause of all kind of evil? Haven't the prophets wasted many words condemning them time after time? What kind of tragedy, what manner of lawlessness, has not been hidden in their blood guiltiness? "They sacrificed their sons and daughters to demons" (Ps 106:37), ignoring nature, forgetting the pangs of birth, trampling on child rearing, turning the laws of kinship upside down, and they became wilder than wild beasts. Wild beasts often give up their lives and disregard their own safety to protect their young. But the Jews, without any compulsion, slaughtered their offspring with their own hands to appease the avenging demons who are enemies of life itself. Which of these things astonishes more? Their impiety or their brutality and inhumanity? That they sacrificed them to demons? Their licentiousness has overshadowed the lechery of animals. Listen to what the prophet says about their intemperance. "They became as lusty stallions, each neighed after his neighbor's wife" (Jer 5:8). Instead of saying, "Each desires his neighbor's wife," he expresses vividly their inborn madness and licentiousness by using the sound of animals.

(7) What more can I say? Rapacity, greed, betrayal of the poor, thefts, keeping of taverns. The whole day would not suffice to tell of these things. But you ask, "Aren't their festivals holy and venerable?" Even these they have made impure. Listen to the prophet or, rather, listen to God who is repelled by their festivals: "I hate, I spurn your feasts" (Amos 5:21). God hates them, and you have fellowship with them. Furthermore, he did not say this feast or that one, but all of them. Don't you realize that he hates worship by means of kettledrums and lyres and psalteries and other musical instruments? "Spare me the sound of your songs," he says. "I cannot endure the music of your lutes" (Amos 5:23). God says "Spare me," and you run off to hear trumpets. Are their sacrifices and offerings not an abomination? "If you offer me wheat cakes, they are useless; the reek of sacrifice is abhorrent to me" (Isa 1:13). How can the reek of sacrifices be abhorrent and the place not be abhorrent? When was it abhorrent? Before they committed the height of iniquity, before they killed their Lord, before the cross, and before the abomination of killing Christ. Is it not much more abhorrent now? What is more fragrant than incense? God does not look at the nature of the gifts but the disposition of those who offer them, and in this way he judges the offerings. He looked at Abel and regarded his gifts with favor. "But he looked at Cain and did not receive his sacrifices" (Gen 4:5). He had no regard for Cain and his sacrifices. Noah brought sacrifices to God, sheep and calves and birds, and Scripture says, "The Lord smelled the soothing odor" (Gen 8:21). That is, he accepted the offerings. God has, of course, no nostrils because the divine is incorporeal. Moreover, there is nothing fouler than the smoke and odor of burning flesh that comes from offerings, yet God accepts the sacrifices of one and rejects those of another in order that you might learn that God is concerned about the disposition of those who offer. The odor and smoke

of one he calls an odor of sweetness, but the incense of the other he calls an abomination, since the disposition of the latter is full of foul odors.

Don't you realize that because of those who enter it God rejects the temple with its sacrifices and musical instruments and festivals and incense? He has shown this especially through his actions, first handing it over to the barbarians, later destroying it completely. Likewise even before the catastrophe, he cried out through the prophet saying, "You keep saying, 'This place is the temple of the Lord, the temple of the Lord!' This catchword of yours is a lie; put no trust in it. It will do you no good" (Jer 7:4).

The temple does not sanctify those who enter, but those who enter make the temple holy. If the temple was of no benefit even when the cherubim and the ark were present, how much less value is it when it is deprived of all these things, when God has turned his back completely and there is even greater reason for his enmity. What sort of folly, what kind of madness, to participate in the festivals of those who are dishonored, abandoned by God, and provoked the Lord? If someone killed your son, tell me, could you bear the sight of him? Could you stand to hear his name? Would you not rather flee from him as from an evil demon, as from the devil himself? They killed the son of your Lord, and you dare to gather with them in the same place? When the one who was killed by them honors you by making you a brother and fellow heir, you dishonor him by revering his murderers, those who crucified him, and by attending their festival assemblies. You enter their defiled synagogues, you pass through impure gates, and you share in the table of demons. That is what I am persuaded to call the Jewish fast after the God slaying. What else can one call those who set themselves against God than worshippers of demons?

Are you hoping to be healed by demons? When Christ allowed demons to enter the swine (Matt 8:31–33), without a moment's notice they drowned the swine in the sea. Do you think they will spare you because you are human? Would that they did not kill, would that they did not plot against us! However, if they drove man out of paradise and deprived him of his celestial glory, do you think they will heal his body? That is ridiculous! Foolish myths! Demons know how to scheme, to harm, but not to heal. If they do not spare the soul, tell me, will they spare our bodies? If they drive men out of the kingdom, will they attempt to deliver them from diseases? Have you not heard the word of the prophet (i.e., the word of God through the prophet), that they can neither do harm nor good? Even if they are able to heal and wish to— which is impossible—you must not exchange a small and fleeting benefit for an interminable and eternal loss. Will you have your body healed only to lose your soul? Hardly a good bargain. You anger God who created your body and beseech your enemy to heal you.

Might it not happen that a man devoted to Greek superstition, but skilled in medicine, could lead you easily to worship his gods? For the Greeks (through their skill) have often driven out many diseases and restored many sick people to health. What shall we make of this? That this is reason to have converse with impiety? Of course not! Listen to what Moses said to the Jews. "If a prophet or a dreamer appears among you and offers you a sign or a portent and calls on you to follow other gods whom you have not known and worship them, even if that sign or portent should come true, do not listen to the words of that prophet or that dreamer" (Deut 13:1–2). What he means is this: If a prophet arises among you, he says, and does a sign or raises the dead or cleanses a leper or heals a cripple, and after doing the sign he invites you to embrace a false religion, don't trust him just because he did a sign. Why? "God is testing you through him to discover whether you love the Lord your God with all your heart and soul" (Deut 13:13). Whence it is evident that demons do not heal. If once in a while God allows healing to take place, it is to test you. This is not because God is ignorant of you, but that you might be trained to stay clear from demons even when they heal. And why am I speaking of the healing of the body? If someone threatens you with hell unless you deny Christ, pay no attention to him. If someone promises you a kingdom only if you apostasize from the only son of God, avoid and despise him. Become a disciple of Paul and emulate the sentiments that the blessed and noble soul of the apostle expressed: "For I am convinced," he said, "that there is nothing in death or life, in the realm of spirits or superhuman powers, in the world as it is or the world as it shall be, in the forces of the universe, in heights or depths—nothing in all creation that can separate us from the love of God in Christ Jesus our Lord" (Rom 8:38–39). Neither angels, nor anything in the realm of spirits or superhuman spirits, nor the world as it is or the world as it shall be, nor anything in all creation could separate Paul from the love of God in Christ Jesus. And the healing of the body separates you! What kind of mercy can we expect? Christ is surely more terrifying to us than Gehenna and more desirable than a kingdom.

If we become sick, it is better to remain sick than to fall into impiety simply to be healed of our illness. For if a demon heals us, the healing does us more harm than good. It helps the body, that insignificant part of man that will surely die in a short time and rot, but it damages your immortal soul. Just as slavedealers show sweets and cakes, dice, and similar things to small children to entice them and deprive them of their freedom and even of their lives, so also demons, promising to heal the sick limbs of our body, completely destroy the health of the soul. Let us not give in, brethren; rather, let us seek to free ourselves from all manner of impiety. Could not Job, urged by his wife to blaspheme God, have been delivered from the calamity that was brought on him? "Curse God," she said, "and die" (Job 2:9). But he chose rather to suffer and to waste away, to bear that intolerable calamity than to blaspheme and be delivered from his present misfortunes. Imitate Job. If a demon promises to release you from a myriad of evils that beset you, don't trust him, don't give in, just as the righteous Job did not give in to his wife. Choose rather to endure the illness than to lose your faith and the health of your soul. God is not abandoning you when he often allows you to get sick; rather, he wishes to make you an object of admiration. Keep strong, then, that you may hear the words, "Do you think I am speaking to you for any other reason than to show that you are a righteous man?" (Job 40:8).

(8) There are still many other things to say, but to ensure you will not forget what has been said, I will end this oration with the words of Moses. "I summon heaven and earth to witness against you this day" (Deut 30:19). If someone who is present or someone who is absent goes to watch the blowing of trumpets or enters the synagogue or visits the shrine of Matrona or shares in the fast or keeps the Sabbath or observes any other Jewish custom, be it significant or insignificant, "I am innocent of the blood of all of you" (Acts 20:26). These words will stand you and me in good stead in the day of our Lord Jesus Christ; if you heed them they will give you great confidence; if you spurn them, and you do not expose those who dare to do such things, these same words will turn against you and become your stern accusers. "For I have kept back nothing; I have disclosed to you the whole purpose of God" (Acts 20:27). In a word, I have deposited money in the hands of bankers. Your responsibility is to let that deposit increase, to put to use for the salvation of your brothers what you have heard. It is disagreeable and burdensome to have to denounce those who have sinned in these ways. But it is also tedious and burdensome to keep silent. This same silence that angers God brings destruction both on those of you who conceal [your brothers] as well as those among them who escape notice. How much better to incur the enmity of your fellow servants than to provoke the Lord's anger. For if your brother is angry with you now, he cannot hurt you and will thank you later because you helped him to be healed. But if you are silent, supposedly doing your fellow servant a favor—which, of course, will only hurt him—God will condemn you eternally. So that if you are silent, you make yourself an enemy of God and you hurt your brother, but if you denounce him and expose him, God will be gracious; you will win your brother back, and you will earn a devoted friend, who has learned by experience of the favor you have done him. Don't think you are doing your brothers a favor, if, when you see them participating in such absurd matters, you don't reprove them vigorously. If you lose a coat, don't you consider not only the one who stole it but also anyone who knew he did it but did not denounce him? Aren't both considered enemies? Our mother whom we both share has not lost a coat but one of our brothers. The devil abducted him and

holds him now in Judaism. You know the kidnapper, and you know the victim. You see me as a torch, setting afire the word of our teaching, dashing about and looking everywhere. Are you going to stand there mute, saying not a word? What kind of forgiveness do you expect to receive? How else can the church think about you except as one of the worst of its enemies, a hostile spoiler? God forbid that anyone who heard this advice would be guilty of the sin of betraying a brother for whom Christ died. Christ poured out his blood for him. But you can't even bring yourself to utter a word on his behalf. Come now, I exhort you! Leave this place at once and set out on the hunt. Each of you bring me one of those who are sick with this disease; rather—God forbid that there should be so many sick—two or three of you or groups of ten or twenty, bring me one, so that on that day when I see the prey trapped in the net, I can set a more bountiful

table for you. If I see you putting into effect the advice given you today, I will attend to their healing with high enthusiasm, and both you and they will profit more. Don't make light of what I say. Women should go after women, men after men, slaves after slaves, freemen after freemen, children after children. In a word—let everyone join with diligence in the hunt for those afflicted with this disease and then return to our next service to receive our praise. But you are worthy of more than my eulogies, for you will deserve a splendid and ineffable reward from God, a reward that far exceeds the labors of those who are successful.

May we well earn this reward by the grace and loving kindness of our Lord Jesus Christ, through whom and with whom be glory to the Father and the Holy Spirit, now and forever, to ages unending. Amen.

31. Epiphanius: Medicine Chest Against Heresies: The Nazoraeans

Epiphanius (ca. 315–403) was a monk in Palestine before becoming a bishop in Cyprus in 367. Unyielding in his ascetic and theological strictness, Epiphanius was instrumental in igniting the Origenist controversy that resulted in (among other things) the deposition of John Chrysostom. He is most famous as a heresiologist, and his *magnum opus* was the *Panarion,* or *Medicine Chest:* a series of 80 chapters describing all known heresies and their "antidotes" (the number 80 is derived from Song of Songs 6:8; the conceit of poisons and antidotes is drawn from medical literature). To craft his descriptions of the heresies, Epiphanius built on the work of previous heresiologists and church historians, as well as on his own experience and inventiveness. Like all heresiologists, he attributed heretical deviance to willful subversion (as opposed to honest disagreement), often through the contamination of Christian truth by the falsehoods of outsiders, such as Greeks, Jews, or barbarians.

The twenty-ninth heresy in his catalog, against the "Nazoraeans," provides a paradigmatic description of what modern scholars have come to call "Jewish-Christianity": a movement merging Jewish practice and Christian belief, subsequently rejected by "orthodox" Christians and Jews alike (Epiphanius's reference to a Jewish prayer against the Nazoraeans is often taken, despite its context, as proof that Jews in synagogues prayed against all Christians). This selection is also typical of Epiphanius's heresiological style: writing against

From *The Panarion of Epiphanius of Salamis,* trans. Frank Williams. Leiden, the Netherlands: E. J. Brill, 1987. Used with permission.

heresy becomes a venue for scriptural exegesis (on Jesus' genealogy), Christian history (the reference to Philo's *Therapeutae*), and antiquarianism (Matthew's "original" Hebrew Gospel). Thus, antiheretical writing was more than just a means of defending theological orthodoxy; it also provided a means of defining the broad sweep of Christian culture, belief, practice, and identity.

1 (1) After these [the Cerinthians] come Nazoraeans, who originated at the same time or even before or in conjunction with them or after them. In any case they were their contemporaries. I cannot say more precisely who succeeded whom. For, as I said, these were contemporary with each other and had similar notions.

(2) For this group did not name themselves after Christ or with Jesus' own name, but "Nazoraeans." (3) However, at that time all Christians were called Nazoraeans in the same way. They also came to be called "Jessaeans" for a short while before the disciples began to be called Christians at Antioch. (4) But they were called Jessaeans because of Jesse, I suppose, since David was descended from Jesse, but Mary from David's line. This was in fulfillment of sacred Scripture, for in the Old Testament the Lord tells David, "Of the fruit of your belly shall I set upon your throne" (Ps 131:11).

2 (1) At each topic of discussion I am afraid of making its treatment very long. I therefore give this sketch in brief—though the truth makes me anxious to give some indication of the subjects (that arise) in the discussion itself—so as not to cover too much ground in composing the narrative. (2) Since the Lord has told David, "Of the fruit of your belly shall I set upon your throne," and, "The Lord swore unto David and will not repent" (Ps 110:4), it is plain that God's promise is an irreversible one. (3) In the first place, what does God have to swear by but "By myself have I sworn, says the Lord?" (Gen 22:16)—for "God has no oath by anything greater" (cf. Heb 6:13). What is divine does not even swear; yet the statement has the function of providing confirmation.

For God swore with an oath to David that he would set the fruit of his belly upon his throne. (4) And the apostles bear witness that Christ had to be born of David's seed, as our Lord and Savior Jesus Christ indeed was. As I said, I shall pass over most of the testimonies, to avoid a very burdensome discussion.

(5) But someone will probably say, "Since Christ was physically born of David's seed, that is, of the Holy Virgin Mary, why is he not sitting on David's throne? For the Gospel says, 'They came that they might anoint him king, and when Jesus perceived this, he departed . . . and hid himself in Ephraim, a city of the wilderness'" (cf. John 6:15, 11:54). (6) But now that I reach the place for this, and I am asked about this text, and why it is that the prophecy about sitting on David's throne has not been fulfilled physically in the Savior's case—for some have thought that it has not—I shall still say that it is a fact. Not a word of God's holy Scripture can come to nothing.

3 (1) David's throne and kingly seat is the priesthood in the holy church. The Lord has combined this rank, which is both that of king and high priest, and conferred it on his holy church by transferring David's throne to it, never to fail. (2) Formerly David's throne continued by succession until Christ himself, since the rulers from Judah did not fail until he came "for whom are the things prepared, and he is the expectation of the nations" (Gen 49:10), as Scripture says.

(3) For at Christ's arrival, the rulers in succession from Judah came to an end. Until his time the rulers were anointed priests, but after his birth in Bethlehem of Judaea, the order ended and changed with Alexander, a ruler of priestly and kingly stock. (4) After Alexander this heritage from the time of Salina—also known as Alexandra—died out under King Herod and the Roman Emperor Augustus. (Though Alexander was crowned also, since he was one of the anointed priests and rulers. (5) For with the union of the two tribes, the kingly and priestly—I mean Judah's and Aaron's and the whole tribe of Levi—kings also became priests; nothing based on a hint in

holy Scripture can be wrong.) (6) But then finally a gentile, King Herod, was crowned, and not David's descendants any more.

(7) But because of the change in the royal throne, the rank of king passed, in Christ, from the physical house of David and Israel to the church. The throne is established in God's holy church forever and has both the ranks of king and high priest for two reasons. (8) The rank of king from our Lord Jesus Christ, also in two ways: because he is descended from King David physically and because, in Godhead, he is in fact a greater king from all eternity. But the rank of priest because Christ is high priest and chief of high priests—(9) since James, called the brother and apostle of the Lord, was made the first bishop immediately. Actually he was Joseph's son, but was said to be in the position of the Lord's brother because they were reared together.

4 (1) For James was Joseph's son by Joseph's first wife, not Mary, as I have said, and discussed with greater clarity, in many other places. (2) And moreover I find that he was of Davidic descent because he was Joseph's son, and that he was born a nazirite—for he was Joseph's firstborn, and hence consecrated. But I find further that he also functioned as a priest in the ancient priesthood. (3) For this reason he was permitted to enter the Holy of Holies once a year, as Scripture says the Law commanded the high priests. For many before me—Eusebius, Clement, and others—have reported this of him. (4) He was allowed to wear the priestly mitre besides, as the trustworthy persons mentioned have testified in the same historical writings.

(5) Now as I said our Lord Jesus Christ is "priest forever after the order of Melchizedek" (Heb 5:6) and at the same time king after the order on high, and so may transfer the priesthood with its legal charter. (6) But since David's seed through Mary is seated on a throne, his throne endures forever, and of his kingdom there will be no end. He would need now to reposition the former crown, for his kingdom is not earthly, as he said to Pontius Pilate in the Gospel, "My Kingdom is not of this world" (John 18:36). (7) For since Christ fulfills all that was said in riddles, the beginnings have reached a limit.

For he who is always king did not come to achieve sovereignty. Lest it be thought that he advanced from a lower estate to a higher, he granted the crown to those whom he appointed. (8) For his throne endures, and there will be no end of his kingdom. And he sits on the throne of David and has transferred David's crown and granted it, with the high priesthood, to his own servants, the high priests of the catholic church.

(9) And there is much to say about this. However, since I have come to the reason why those who came to faith in Christ were called Jessaeans before they were called Christians, I have said that Jesse was the father of David. And they had been named Jessaeans, either because of this Jesse or from the name or our Lord Jesus, since, as his disciples, they were derived from Jesus or because of the etymology of the Lord's name. For in Hebrew Jesus means "healer" or "physician" and "savior." (10) In any case, they had acquired this additional name before they were called Christians. But at Antioch, as I have mentioned before and as is the essence of the truth, the disciples and the whole church of God began to be called Christians (cf. Acts 11:26).

5 (1) If you enjoy study and have read about them in Philo's historical writings, in his book entitled "Jessaeans," you may discover that, in his account of their way of life and hymns and his description of their monasteries in the vicinity of the Marean marsh, Philo described none other than Christians. (2) For he was edified by his visit to the area—the place is called Mareotis—and his entertainment at their monasteries in the region. (3) He arrived during Passover and observed their customs and how some of them kept the holy week of Passover (only) after a postponement of it, but others by eating every other day—though others, indeed, ate each evening. But Philo wrote all this of the faith and regimen of the Christians.[1]

(4) So in that brief period when they were called Jessaeans—after the Savior's ascension and after

---

[1] Epiphanius refers to first-century Jewish writer Philo's description of an ascetic Jewish sect, the Therapeutae (confused here with the Essenes); later Christians believed Philo was actually writing about early Christians.

Mark had preached in Egypt—certain other persons seceded, though they were followers of the apostles if you please. I mean the Nazoraeans, whom I am presenting here. They were Jewish, were attached to the Law, and had circumcision. (5) But it was as though people had seen fire under a misapprehension. Not understanding why, or for what use, the ones who had kindled this fire were doing it—either to cook their rations with the fire or to burn some dead trees and brush, which are ordinarily destroyed by fire—they kindled fire, too, in imitation, and set themselves ablaze.

(6) For by hearing just the name of Jesus and seeing the miracles the apostles performed, they came to faith in Jesus themselves. But they found that he had been conceived at Nazareth and brought up in Joseph's home, and for this reason is called "Jesus the Nazoraean" in the Gospel as the apostles say, "Jesus the Nazoraean, a man approved by signs and wonders" (Acts 2:22), and so on. Hence they adopted this name, so as to be called Nazoreans.

(7) Not "nazirites"—that means "consecrated persons." Anciently this rank belonged to firstborn sons and men dedicated to God. Samson was one, and others after him, and many before. Moreover, John the Baptist, too, was one of these persons consecrated to God, for "he drank neither wine nor strong drink" (Luke 1:15). (This regimen, befitting their rank, was prescribed for persons of that sort.) 6 (1) They did not call themselves Nasaraeans either; the Nasaraean sect was before Christ and did not know Christ.

(2) But besides, as I indicated, everyone called the Christians Nazoraeans, as they say in accusing the apostle Paul, "We have found this man a pestilent fellow and a perverter of the people, a ringleader of the sect of the Nazoraeans" (Acts 24:5). (3) And the holy apostle did not disclaim the name—not to profess the Nazoraean sect, but he was glad to own the name his adversaries' malice had applied to him for Christ's sake. (4) For he says in court, "They neither found me in the temple disputing with any man, neither raising up the people, nor have I done any of those things whereof they accuse me. But this I confess unto you, that after the way that they call heresy, so worship I, believing all things in the Law and the prophets" (Acts 24:12–14).

(5) And no wonder the apostle admitted to being a Nazoraean! In those days everyone called Christians this because of the city of Nazareth—there was no other usage of the name then. People thus gave the name of "Nazoraeans" to believers in Christ, of whom it is written, "He shall be called a Nazoraean" (Matt 2:23). (6) Even today, in fact, people call all the sects, I mean, Manicheans, Marcionites, Gnostics, and others, by the common name of "Christians," though they are not Christians. However, although each sect has another name, it still allows this one with pleasure, since it is honored by the name. For they think they can preen themselves on Christ's name, not on faith and works!

(7) Thus Christ's holy disciples called themselves "disciples of Jesus" then, as indeed they were. But they were not rude when others called them Nazoraeans, since they saw the intent of those who called them this. They did it because of Christ, since our Lord Jesus was called "the Nazoraean" himself—so say the Gospels and the Acts of the Apostles—(8) because of his upbringing in Joseph's home in the city of Nazareth, which is now a village. (Though he was born in the flesh at Bethlehem, of the ever-virgin Mary, Joseph's betrothed. Joseph had settled in Nazareth after leaving Bethlehem and taking up residence in Galilee.)

7 (1) But these sectarians whom I am now sketching disregarded the name of Jesus and did not call themselves Jessaeans, keep the name of Jews, or term themselves Christians—but "Nazoraeans," from the place-name, "Nazareth," if you please! However they are simply complete Jews.

(2) They use not only the New Testament but the Old Testament as well, as the Jews do. For unlike the previous sectarians, they do not repudiate the legislation, the prophets, and the books Jews call "Writings." They have no different ideas, but confess everything exactly as the Law proclaims it and in the Jewish fashion—except for their belief in Christ, if you please! (3) For they acknowledge both the resurrection of the dead and the divine creation of all

things and declare that God is one and that his Son is Jesus Christ.

(4) They are trained to a nicety in Hebrew. For among them the entire Law, the prophets, and the so-called Writings—I mean the poetic books, Kings, Chronicles, Esther, and all the rest—are read in Hebrew, as they surely are by Jews. (5) They are different from Jews and different from Christians, only in the following. They disagree with Jews because they have come to faith in Christ, but since they are still fettered by the Law—circumcision, the Sabbath, and the rest—they are not in accord with Christians. (6) As to Christ, I cannot say whether they, too, are captives of the wickedness of Cerinthus and Merinthus and regard him as a mere man—or whether, as the truth is, they affirm his birth of Mary by the Holy Spirit.

(7) Today this sect of the Nazoraeans is found in Beroea near Coelesyria, in the Decapolis near Pella, and in Bashanitis at the place called Cocabe—Khokhabe in Hebrew. (8) For that was its place of origin, since all the disciples had settled in Pella after they left Jerusalem—Christ told them to abandon Jerusalem and withdraw from it because of its coming siege. And they settled in Peraea for this reason and, as I said, spent their lives there. That was where the Nazoraean sect began.

8 (1) But they too are wrong to boast of circumcision, and persons like themselves are still "under a curse" (cf. Gal 3:10), since they cannot fulfil the Law. For how can they fulfil the Law's provision, "Thrice a year thou shalt appear before the Lord your God, at the feasts of Unleavened Bread, Tabernacles, and Pentecost" (cf. Exod 23:14–17), on the site of Jerusalem? (2) As the site is closed off and the Law's provisions cannot be fulfilled, anyone with sense can see that Christ came to be the Law's fulfiller—not to destroy the Law, but to fulfill the Law—and to lift the curse that had been put on transgression of the Law. (3) For after Moses had given every commandment, he came to the point of the book and "included the whole in a curse" (cf. Gal 3:22) with the words, "Cursed is he that continues not in all the words that are written in this book to do them" (Gal 3:10).

(4) Hence Christ came to free what had been fettered with the bonds of the curse. In place of the lesser commandments that cannot be fulfilled, he granted us the greater, which are not inconsistent with the completion of the task as the earlier ones were. (5) For I have discussed this many times before, in every sect, in connection with the Sabbath, circumcision and the rest—how the Lord has granted something more perfect to us.

(6) But how can people like these defend their disobedience of the Holy Spirit, who has told gentile converts, through the apostles, "Assume no burden save the necessary things, that you abstain from blood, and from things strangled, and fornication, and from meats offered to idols?" (Acts 15:28–29). (7) And how can they fail to lose the grace of God, when the holy apostle Paul says, "If you be circumcised, Christ shall profit you nothing . . . whosoever of you do glory in the Law are fallen from grace?" (Gal 5:2–4).

9 (1) In this sect, too, my brief discussion will be enough. People like these are refutable at once and easy to cure—or rather, they are nothing but Jews themselves. (2) Yet these are very much the Jews' enemies. Not only do Jewish people have a hatred of them; they even stand up at dawn, at midday, and toward evening, three times a day when they recite their prayers in the synagogues, and curse and anathematize them. Three times a day they say, "God curse the Nazoraeans." (3) For they harbor an extra grudge against them, if you please, because despite their Jewishness, they preach that Jesus is the Christ—the opposite of those who are still Jews, for they have not accepted Jesus.

(4) They have the Gospel according to Matthew in its entirety in Hebrew. For it is clear that they still preserve this, in the Hebrew alphabet, as it was originally written. But I do not know whether they have removed just the genealogies from Abraham to Christ.

(5) But now that we have also detected this sect—like an insect that is small, yet still causes pain with its poison—and have squashed it with the words of the truth, let us pray for help from God, beloved, and go to the next.

CHAPTER 8

Canons and Creeds

Legalization and imperial patronage encouraged early Christians to standardize their beliefs and practices. Certainly before 312, Christians had prized uniformity and structure: our earliest Christian history, the Acts of the Apostles, recounts a meeting of the apostles to settle matters of practice and belief (Acts 15, anachronistically referred to as "the Jerusalem Council"). Christian leaders in the second and third centuries adopted common Greco-Roman municipal practice by convening authoritative councils to resolve issues of communal concern. Some of these pre-Constantinian synods treated local issues (controversies over ordinations, for instance), while others addressed broader matters (such as the date of Easter or the reintegration of heretics).

The entry of Christianity onto the stage of imperial politics, however, brought institutional coherence into sharper focus. Constantine was supposedly disturbed to find "the Church" of the 310s in such a splintered state; in 314 he instructed Western bishops to assemble at Arles to resolve the Donatist schism (unsuccessfully: see "The Nature of the Church" in Chapter 7). Other Christian leaders internalized this impulse to tighten ecclesiastical structure without direct pressure from the emperor. Local synods met and issued sweeping directives on church practices (called rules, or canons) and settled theological disputes by crafting mandatory public confessions of faith (creeds). One such example of a local synod is given here—the early fourth-century Council of Elvira. Its canons are included here neither for their universality nor their originality: if enforced at all, they would have been applicable only in Spain; and similar, if not identical, church canons were issued in the early decades of the fourth century in Arles (southern France), Ancyra (Ankara, central Turkey), and Neocaesarea (eastern Turkey). But Elvira gives a sense of the issues that ecclesiastical leadership now felt authorized and compelled to address.

The provincial and local quickly gave way to the imperial and universal. In 325 Constantine called for a meeting of church leaders to settle questions of practical and doctrinal division within Christianity. With a mandate from the emperor, the canons and creed of this Council of Nicaea were soon declared to be "ecumenical" (from the Greek word *oikoumenē*, "inhabited world"), that is, effective for all Christians in the Roman Empire. A new age of totality and conformity (which may have existed previously in theory but rarely, if ever, in practice) was ushered in, an institutionalization of the stepped-up rhetoric of heresy and orthodoxy that marked fourth-century Christianity. Henceforth emperors claimed the right to call ecumenical councils of bishops empowered to dictate theology and practice for all Christians. Four councils met between 325 and 450 that were declared, at the time or subsequently, to enjoy this ecumenical status (other councils that claimed universal authority met during this time, but their decrees were later overturned): the Councils of Nicaea, Constantinople, Ephesus, and Chalcedon. The creeds (where applicable) and canons of these four councils are reproduced here. We can never be entirely sure that the uniformity of confession and practice that these canons and creeds attempted was ever achieved. Often it seems they raised as much controversy as they settled. But perhaps the display and exercise of authority (by both emperors and bishops) was as important to Christian development in this period as the effort made for compromise and ecclesiastical peace.

FOR FURTHER READING

Davis, Leo Donald. *The First Seven Ecumenical Councils (325–787): Their History and Theology.* Collegeville, Minn.: Liturgical Press, 1990.

Hefele, C. J. *A History of the Councils of the Church from the Original Documents,* 5 vols. Edingburgh: Clark, 1896; repr. New York: AMS, 1972.

Kelly, J. N. D. *Early Christian Creeds,* 3rd ed. London: Longman, 1972.

Laeuchli, Samuel. *Power and Sexuality: The Emergence of Canon Law at the Synod of Elvira.* Philadelphia: Temple University Press, 1972.

L'Huillier, Peter. *The Church of the Ancient Councils: The Disciplinary Work of the First Four Ecumenical Councils.* Crestwood, N.Y.: St. Vladimir's Seminary Press, 1995.

The Texts

32. Canons of Elvira

We know little about the provincial synod that met sometime between 305 and 310 in Elvira (in southern Spain, near modern Granada) other than the rulings (*kanones*) they issued. The synod was attended by twenty-six local priests and nineteen local bishops. The only signatory about whom we have outside knowledge is Hosius of Cordova. Hosius would, in ensuing decades, become the religious confidant of Emperor Constantine, advising him on the convocation of the Council of Nicaea. These canons, however, give a clear sense of the impulse to total social and ecclesiastical organization that characterized Christian communities in the wake of the Great Persecution: questions of religious distinction and conversion, ethical propriety (particularly regarding sex), and liturgical and clerical conduct are addressed in severe and unequivocal terms. The council is, perhaps, most famous for issuing the first extant blanket mandate for clerical celibacy (Canon 33). Thus, in the unyielding social ideals of the Council of Elvira we glimpse a Christian community emerging from the shadow of religious marginalization with moral vigor and a desire for sharp communal boundaries.

CANON 1

It is decided that anyone of a mature age, who, after the faith of saving baptism, approaches a temple as an idolater and commits this major crime, because it is an enormity of the highest order, is not to receive communion even at the end.

CANON 2

Flamines[1] who, after the faith of font and regeneration, have sacrificed, since they have thereby doubled their crimes by adding murder or even tripled their evil deed by including sexual offense, are not to receive communion even at the end.

CANON 3

At the same time, flamines who have not actually sacrificed but simply performed their function may, since they have refrained from the deadly sacrifices, be offered communion at the end, provided that the required penance has been done. If, however, after the penance they commit a sexual offense, it is decided to accord them no further communion, lest they seem to make a mockery of the Sunday communion.

---

[1] That is, pagan priests.

From *Power and Sexuality: The Emergence of Canon Law at the Synod of Elvira,* by Samuel Laeuchli. Philadelphia: Temple University Press, 1972. Used with permission of Samuel Laeuchli.

CANON 4

Again, flamines who are catechumens and who have refrained from sacrifices shall be admitted after a period of three years.

CANON 5

If a woman overcome with rage whips her maidservant so badly that she dies within three days, and it is doubtful whether she killed her on purpose or by accident: provided that the required penance has been done, she shall be readmitted after seven years, if it was done purposely, and after five years if accidentally; in the event that she becomes ill during the set time, let her receive communion.

CANON 6

If anyone kills another by sorcery, communion is not to be given to him even at the end, since he could not have accomplished this crime without idolatry.

CANON 7

If one of the faithful, after a sexual offense and after the required period of penance, should again commit fornication, he shall not have communion even at the end.

CANON 8

Again, women who, without any preceding cause, leave their husbands and take up with other men are not to receive communion even at the end.

CANON 9

Further, a baptized woman who leaves her adulterous baptized husband and marries another is forbidden to marry him; if she does, she shall not receive communion until the death of her former husband unless, by chance, the pressure of illness demand that it be given.

CANON 10

If a woman who has been deserted by her catechumen husband marries another man, she may be admitted to the font of baptism; this also applies to female catechumens. But if the man who leaves the innocent woman marries a Christian woman, and this woman knew he had a wife whom he had left without cause, communion may be given to her at death.

CANON 11

If that female catechumen should grow seriously ill during the five-year period, baptism is not to be denied her.

CANON 12

A mother or female guardian or any Christian woman who engages in pandering, since she is selling another's body—or even her own—she shall not receive communion even at the end.

CANON 13

Virgins who have consecrated themselves to God, if they break their vow of virginity and turn to lust instead, not realizing what they lose, shall not be given communion at the end. If, however, corrupted by the fall of their weak body only once, they do penance for the rest of their lives and abstain from intercourse so that they only seem fallen, they may receive communion at the end.

CANON 14

Virgins who have not preserved their virginity, if they marry those who violated them and keep them as husbands, they must be reconciled without penance after a year, since they have broken only the nuptials. If, however, they have been intimate with other men—becoming guilty of real sexual offense—they ought to be admitted to communion only after five years, having fulfilled the required penance.

CANON 15

No matter the large number of girls, Christian maidens are by no means to be given in matrimony to pagans lest youth, bursting forth in bloom, end in adultery of the soul.

CANON 16

Heretics, if they are unwilling to change over to the Catholic church, are not to have Catholic girls given to them in marriage, nor shall they be given to Jews or heretics, since there can be no community for the faithful with the unfaithful. If parents act against this prohibition, they shall be kept out for five years.

CANON 17

If any should perchance join their daughters in marriage to priests of the idols, they shall not be given communion even at the end.

CANON 18

Bishops, presbyters, and deacons, if—once placed in the ministry—they are discovered to be sexual offenders, shall not receive communion, not even at the end, because of the scandal and the heinousness of the crime.

CANON 19

Bishops, presbyters, and deacons are not to abandon their territories for commercial reasons, nor shall they run around the provinces seeking after profitable business; in order to procure their livelihood, let them rather send a son or freedman, an employee, a friend, or whomever they want; if they want to pursue business, let them do it within their own province.

CANON 20

If anyone of the clergy has been discovered practicing usury, he shall be degraded and kept away. If a layman, too, is shown to have practiced usury and, after having been accused, promises to stop and no longer to exact interest, he shall be granted pardon; if, however, he should persist in this wickedness, he is to be cast out of the church.

CANON 21

If anyone living in the city does not go to church for three Sundays, he shall be kept out for a short time in order that his punishment be made public.

CANON 22

If anyone goes over from the Catholic church to heresy and returns again, penance shall not be denied to him, since he has recognized his sin. He shall do penance for ten years, and after these ten years, communion shall be offered to him. If, however, as children they were carried away, they shall be received back without delay, since they have not sinned on their own.

CANON 23

The extensions of the fast shall be celebrated through each month—except for the days of the two months of July and August, because of some people's weakness.

CANON 24

All those who have been baptized away from home, since their life has scarcely been examined, shall not be promoted to the clergy in foreign provinces.

CANON 25

Anyone who carries a letter of a confessor should be given instead a letter of communion eliminating the title "confessor," since all those sharing in the glory of this title at times upset the simple people.

CANON 26

In order to correct the erroneous practice, it is decided that we must celebrate the extension of the fast every Saturday.

CANON 27

A bishop or any other cleric may have living with him only a sister or a virgin daughter dedicated to God; by no means shall he keep any woman unrelated to him.

CANON 28

A bishop shall not take a gift from one who is not in communion.

CANON 29

A possessed man who is tormented by an erratic spirit shall not have his name read out at the altar with the offering, nor shall he be permitted to serve personally in the church.

CANON 30

Those who in their youth have sinned sexually are not to be ordained subdeacons inasmuch as they might afterward be promoted by deception to a higher order. Furthermore, if any have been ordained in the past, they are to be removed.

CANON 31

Young men who after the faith of saving baptism have committed sexual offense shall be admitted to communion when they marry, provided the required penance is done.

CANON 32

If anyone, through grave sin, has fallen into fatal ruin, he shall not do penance before a presbyter but rather before the bishop; however, under the pressure of illness, it is necessary that a presbyter shall offer communion, and even a deacon if a priest orders him.

CANON 33

Bishops, presbyters, and deacons and all other clerics having a position in the ministry are ordered to abstain completely from their wives and not to have children. Whoever, in fact, does this, shall be expelled from the dignity of the clerical state.

CANON 34

Candles shall not be burned in a cemetery during the day, for the spirits of the saints are not to be disturbed. Those who do not observe this are excluded from the communion of the church.

CANON 35

Women are forbidden to spend the night in a cemetery, since often under the pretext of prayer they secretly commit evil deeds.

CANON 36

There shall be no pictures in churches, lest what is worshipped and adored be depicted on walls.

CANON 37

Those who are tormented by unclean spirits, if they have reached the point of death, shall be baptized; if they are already baptized, communion shall be given them. Furthermore, these people are forbidden to light candles publicly. If they want to act against the prohibition, they shall be kept away from communion.

CANON 38

On the occasion of a trip or if a church is not near, a baptized Christian who has kept his baptism intact and who is not married a second time can baptize a catechumen who is critically ill, as long as he takes him to the bishop if he survives, so that it can be completed through the laying on of hands.

CANON 39

Pagans, if in sickness they wish to have the laying on of hands and if their life has been at least partially decent, shall have the laying on of hands and become Christians.

CANON 40

It is forbidden that landholders, when they receive their payments, shall account as received anything offered to idols. If after this prohibition they do so anyway, they shall be served from communion for the space of five years.

CANON 41

The faithful are warned to forbid, as far as they can, that idols be kept in their homes. If, however, they fear violence from their slaves, they must at least keep themselves pure. If they do not do this, they are to be considered outside the church.

CANON 42

Those who arrive at the first stage of faith, if their reputation has been good, shall be admitted to the grace of baptism in two years, unless under the pressure of illness reason compels help more rapidly for the one approaching death or at least the one begging for grace.

CANON 43

The perverted custom shall be changed in accordance with the authority of the scriptures, so that we all celebrate the day of Pentecost, lest anyone who does not conform be regarded as having introduced a new heresy.

CANON 44

A prostitute who once lived as such and later married, if afterward she has come to belief, shall be received without delay.

CANON 45

As for one who was a catechumen and for a long time did not go to church at all, if one of the clergy acknowledged him to be a Christian or if some of the faithful come forward as witnesses, baptism shall not be denied him since he appears to have cast off the old man.

CANON 46

If one of the faithful, having forsaken his religion, has not come to church for a long time but should then return, as long as he has not been an idolater, he shall receive communion after ten years.

CANON 47

If a baptized married man commits adultery, not once but often, he is to be approached at the hour of death. If he promises to stop, communion shall be given him; if he should recover and commit adultery again, he shall nevermore make a mockery of the communion of peace.

CANON 48

The custom of placing coins in the baptismal shell by those being baptized must be corrected so that the priest does not seem to sell for money what he has received freely. Nor shall their feet be washed by priests or clerics.

CANON 49

Landholders are warned not to allow the crops, which they have received from God with an act of thanksgiving, to be blessed by Jews lest they make our blessing ineffectual and weak. If anyone dares to do this after the prohibition, he shall be thrown out of the church completely.

CANON 50

If any of the clergy or the faithful eats with Jews, he shall be kept from communion in order that he be corrected as he should.

CANON 51

If a baptized person has come from any heresy, by no means is he to be promoted to the clergy; if any have been ordained in the past, they shall be deposed without any question.

CANON 52

Those who have been caught placing derogatory writings in church shall be anathematized.

CANON 53

It is agreed by all that a person is to receive communion from that bishop by whom he was denied it for a particular crime. If another bishop presumes to admit him without the participation or consent of the bishop by whom he was deprived of communion, let him know that in this way he is going to create cause for dissent among the brethren and bring danger to his own position.

CANON 54

If parents break the betrothal agreement, they shall be kept away for three years. But if either the groom or the bride has been caught in a serious crime, the parents are excused. If, however, the sin was mutual and the betrothed have defiled each other, the former penalty holds.

CANON 55

Priests who simply wear the wreath and who neither sacrifice nor offer any of their income to idols shall receive communion after two years.

CANON 56

A magistrate is ordered to keep away from the church during the one year of his term as duumvir.[2]

CANON 57

Matrons or their husbands are not to lend their finery to enhance a procession in a worldly fashion, and if they do so, they are to be kept away for three years.

CANON 58

We have resolved that everywhere, and especially where the principal episcopal chair has been established, those who present letters of communion shall be interrogated to determine whether everything is verified by their testimony.

CANON 59

It is forbidden for any Christian to go up to the idol of the capitol, as a pagan does in order to sacrifice, and watch. If he does, he is guilty of the same crime. If he was baptized, he may be received, having completed his penance, after ten years.

CANON 60

If someone has broken idols and on that account was put to death, inasmuch as this is not written in the Gospel nor is it found ever to have been done in the time of the apostles, he shall not be included in the ranks of the martyrs.

CANON 61

If a man after the death of his wife marries her sister and she was baptized, he shall be kept away from communion for five years, unless perchance the pressure of illness demands that peace be given more quickly.

CANON 62

If a charioteer or pantomime wants to believe, they shall first renounce their professions and only then be accepted on the condition that they do not later return to their former professions; if they attempt to violate this decision, they shall be expelled from the church.

---

[2] Duumvir was the title of a local magistrate.

CANON 63

If a woman, while her husband is away, conceives by adultery and after that crime commits abortion, she shall not be given communion even at the end, since she has doubled her crime.

CANON 64

If a woman remains in adultery with another man up to the end of her life, she shall not be given communion even at the end. But if she should leave him, she may receive communion after ten years, having completed the required penance.

CANON 65

If the wife of a cleric has committed adultery, and her husband knew of it but did not immediately throw her out, he shall not receive communion even at the end, lest it appear as though instruction in crime is coming from those who should be the model of a good life.

CANON 66

If a man marries his stepdaughter, inasmuch as he is incestuous, he shall not be given communion even at the end.

CANON 67

It is forbidden for a woman, whether baptized or a catechumen, to have anything to do with long-haired men or hairdressers; any who do this shall be kept from communion.

CANON 68

A catechumen, if she has conceived a child in adultery and then suffocated it, shall be baptized only at the end.

CANON 69

If a married man happens to fall once, he shall do penance for a period of five years and thus be recon-ciled, unless the pressure of illness compels that communion be given before that time: this is also binding for women.

CANON 70

If a wife, with her husband's knowledge, has committed adultery, he shall not be given communion even at the end; but if he gets rid of her, he may receive communion after ten years, if he kept her in his home for any length of time once he knew of the adultery.

CANON 71

Men who sexually abuse boys shall not be given communion even at the end.

CANON 72

If a widow has intercourse with a man and later marries him, she shall be reconciled to communion after a period of five years, having completed the required penance; if she marries another man, having left the first, she shall not be given communion even at the end; however, if the man she marries is one of the faithful, she shall not receive communion except after ten years, having completed the required penance, unless illness compels that communion be given more quickly.

CANON 73

An informer, if he was baptized and through his denunciation someone was proscribed or killed, shall not receive communion even at the end; if it was a lesser case, he can receive communion within five years; if the informer was a catechumen, he may be admitted to baptism after a period of five years.

CANON 74

A false witness, since he has committed a crime, shall be kept away; but if what he brought about did not lead to death and he has explained satisfactorily why he did not keep silent, he shall be kept away for a period of two years; however, if he cannot prove this to the assembly of the clergy, he shall be excluded for five years.

CANON 75

If anyone attacks a bishop, presbyter, or deacon by accusing them of false crimes, and he is unable to prove them, communion shall not be given him even at the end.

CANON 76

If someone allows himself to be ordained deacon and afterward is discovered in a mortal crime, which he had committed at one time: if he confessed on his own, he shall receive communion after three years, having completed the required penance; but if someone else exposes him, he shall receive lay communion after five years, having done his penance.

CANON 77

If a deacon in charge of common people with no bishop or presbyter baptizes some of them, the bishop shall perfect them by his blessing, but if they leave this world before that, a man can be regarded as justified depending on the faith by which he believed.

CANON 78

If one of the faithful who is married commits adultery with a Jewish or a pagan woman, he shall be cut off, but if someone else exposes him, he can share Sunday communion after five years, having completed the required penance.

CANON 79

If one of the faithful plays dice, that is, on a playing board, for money, he shall be kept away; if, having reformed, he stops, he may be reconciled to communion after a year.

CANON 80

It is forbidden for freedmen whose former masters are still alive to be promoted to the clergy.

CANON 81

Women shall not presume on their own, without their husbands' signatures, to write to lay women who are baptized, nor shall they accept anyone's letters of peace addressed only to themselves.

33. Creed and Canons of Nicaea

When Constantine defeated his Eastern co-Emperor Licinius in 324 and assumed sole control of the Roman Empire, he became aware of the deepening divide in the eastern churches occasioned by Trinitarian debates (see Chapter 7). In 325, he invited around 300 bishops and priests from across the empire to the city of Nicaea, about sixty miles from his newly planned capital, Constantinople. (The reference to 318 assembled "fathers" may be apocryphal,

"Nicene Creed" from *Early Christian Creeds,* 3rd ed., ed. J. N. D. Kelly. Copyright © D. McKay, 1972. Used with permission of Pierson Education Limited. "Canons of Nicaea" used by permission of St. Vladimir's Seminary Press, 575 Scarsdale Rd., Crestwood, NY, 10707, © 1996 *The Church of the Ancient Councils: The Disciplinary Work of the First Four Ecumenical Councils.* Translated and edited by Archbishop Peter L'Huillier, pp. 31–84.

drawing on the number of Abraham's warriors in Genesis 14:14.) Although records from the council itself are fragmented, their mandate from Constantine seems clear: to unify church doctrine, practice, and organization.

The creed, which had to be signed by all attendants, was designed to be the official statement of faith for all Christians, replacing local confessions, which varied considerably. The creed was a matter of great debate, introducing the controversial term *homoousios,* "of the same substance" to describe the relationship between God the Father and God the Son (see "Trinitarian Controversy" in Chapter 7) and underscoring that the Son was "begotten, not made" by the Father. The specific phrases anathematized (i.e., cursed) at the end of the creed were attributed to Arius and his theological followers, making clear the "winners" and "losers" of creedal argument.

The canons do not treat Christian ethical values as severely as do the canons of Elvira, but they do combine concerns for clerical correctness with attempts to unify the practice of worship among all Christians. They also attempt to steer a middle path between moralistic rejection and lax accommodation of the "lapsed" Christians, who had renounced their faith during the Great Persecution. Notable also are attempts to codify empirewide ecclesiastical organization through the hierarchy of metropolitan bishops and patriarchs (see Canons 6 and 7 and Chapter 6) and the institution of regular provincial meetings (synods). Other records from the council indicate that the assembled clerics also addressed a schism over episcopal ordination (the so-called Meletian schism of Egypt) and a controversy over the date of Easter (the so-called Quartodeciman controversy).

Despite its pretensions at theological settlement, the Council of Nicaea ignited decades of further controversy: not until the Second Ecumenical Council of Constantinople (381) were the Trinitarian and episcopal issues proposed at Nicaea finally affirmed, and the creed and canons of Nicaea granted foundational authority for subsequent Christian doctrine and community.

NICENE CREED

We believe in one God, the Father, almighty, maker of all things visible and invisible;

And in one Lord Jesus Christ, the Son of God, begotten from the Father, only-begotten, that is, from the substance of the father, God from God, light from light, true God from true God, of one substance (*homoousios*) with the Father, through whom all things came into being, things in heaven and things on earth, who because of us humans and because of our salvation came down and became incarnate, becoming human, suffered and rose on the third day, ascended to the heavens, will come to judge the living and the dead;

And in the Holy Spirit.

But as for those who say, "There was when he was not" and "Before being born he was not" and that "He came into existence out of nothing" or who assert that the Son of God is of a different hypostasis or substance or is subject to alteration and change—these the Catholic and Apostolic church anathematizes.

NICENE CANONS

The canons of the 318 fathers gathered at Nicaea under the consulate of the illustrious Paulinus and Julian in the year 536 of the Alexandrian era, the 19th of the month of Desius, the 13th day of the Kalends of July.

CANON 1

If anyone has been maimed by doctors at the time of an illness or has been castrated by barbarians, let him remain a cleric; but if anyone, already being a cleric and in good health, castrates himself, he must be excluded from the clergy and in the future no such person shall be ordained. As it is obvious that what has been said above concerns those who castrate themselves, the ruling permits, therefore, those who have been made eunuchs by barbarians or by their masters to become clerics if on other grounds they are judged to be worthy.

CANON 2

Whether by necessity or by the weight of human frailties, several things have come about contrary to the general order of the Church. Thus, spiritual washing has been given and, along with this baptism, the episcopate or the priesthood has been given to men who have only been recently received from pagan life to the faith and have not been sufficiently instructed. It seems right and proper that such things not happen anymore. These men, in effect, must remain catechumens for a certain time and after baptism submit to a still longer period of probation. The apostolic statement in this matter is very clear: "Let him not be a neophyte for fear that by pride he fall into judgment and into the trap of the devil" (1 Tim 3:6). If during this probation period, he is found to be guilty of some fault affecting his soul and that is attested to by two or three witnesses, let him be excluded from the clergy. If anyone acts contrary to this ordinance, as much as he opposes himself in that to the great council, he is in danger of being excluded from the clergy.

CANON 3

The great council absolutely forbids any bishop, priest, deacon, or any other member of the clergy to have a woman living with him, unless she is a mother, a sister, an aunt, or any other woman completely above suspicion.

CANON 4

It is preferable that a bishop be established by all the bishops of a province, but if this appears difficult, because of a pressing necessity or because of the distance to be traveled, at least three bishops should come together, and having the written consent of the absent bishops, they may then proceed with the consecration. The confirmation of what takes place falls to the metropolitan bishop of each province.

CANON 5

Concerning those who have been excommunicated, either among the clergy or among the laity, let the sentence that was given by the bishops of each province remain in force; let this be in conformity with the regulation that requires that those so excluded by the bishops must not be received by others. But let each case be examined to see if those involved were excluded for a cowardly reason, from a quarrelsome spirit, or from some feeling of dislike on the part of the bishop. Therefore, so that a proper inquiry may take place, it seems good and proper that in each province there be a synod two times a year so that all bishops of the province sitting together may examine such questions and thus those who, according to the general opinion, may have disobeyed their bishop will be properly considered as excommunicate by all until such time as all the bishops see fit to render a more merciful sentence. Let the synods be held as follows: one before the fortieth day so that, all cowardly feelings being set aside, a pure offering may be made to God; the second during the fall.

CANON 6

Let the ancient customs be maintained in Egypt, in Libya, and in the Pentapolis so that the bishop of Alexandria has authority over all these territories, since for the bishop of Rome there is a similar practice and the same thing concerning Antioch; and in other provinces, let the prerogatives of churches (of the capitals) be safeguarded.

Moreover, let this matter be completely clear: if anyone becomes a bishop without the consent of the metropolitan, the great council decrees that such a person is not even a bishop. In addition if after a common vote of all has taken place knowingly and in conformity with the church regulation, two or three, for reasons of personal ill will, refuse the decision, then let everyone go along with the majority vote.

CANON 7

Since custom and ancient tradition have prevailed according to which the bishop of Aelia [Capitolina, i.e., Jerusalem] is honored, let him enjoy the honor that flows from his position, while the dignity proper to the metropolitan [in Caesarea] is safeguarded.

CANON 8

Concerning those who have called themselves "the pure ones," if they ever want to come into the catholic and apostolic Church en masse, it seems right and proper to the holy and great council that they, after having received the imposition of hands, should then remain in the clergy. But first it is important that they promise in writing to accept and to follow the rulings of the catholic Church, that is, they will have communion with those who have been married a second time and with those who renounced the faith during persecution for whom a period (of penance) has been established and a date (of reconciliation) set. It is, therefore, necessary that they follow in full the rulings of the catholic and apostolic Church.

Consequently, when in the cities or villages, there are only clerics ordained by these "pure ones," let them keep their status; on the other hand, where there is a bishop or priest of the catholic Church, if certain ones of these "pure ones" want to be admitted, it is evident that the bishop of the Church should keep the dignity of the bishop. As for the person who carried the name of bishop among the so-called pure ones, he is to have the rank of priest unless the bishop consents to allow him to receive the honor of his title. But if he is not so disposed, let the bishop give him a place as a chorepiscopus [i.e., a "circuit bishop"] or of a priest so that he can appear as being integrated into the clergy. Without this provision, there would be two bishops in the city.[1]

CANON 9

If certain men have been made priests without inquiry, or if having been examined, they acknowledged the sins committed by them and despite this confession, some other men acting against the canon impose hands on such people, the canon does not admit them because the catholic Church requires unquestionable conduct and character.

CANON 10

If anyone who has renounced the faith has been promoted to the clergy, whether because the bishops did not know about the apostasy or because they did not take it into account, the church canon is not lessened by either reason, for as soon as these men are discovered, they are to be deposed.

CANON 11

About those who have renounced the faith during the tyranny of Licinius without having been forced, without having lost their property, without having faced dangers or anything of the sort, it has been decided by the holy council that although not being worthy of mercy, nonetheless, we will make use of gentleness in their cases. Consequently, those among them who were baptized and manifest a real repentance must re-

---

[1] The "pure ones" refers to Christian followers of the third-century Roman bishop Novatian, who had been in schism (see Chapter 7, "The Nature of the Church") from other Christians over the question of reintegration of believers who renounced their faith under persecution. The integration of schismatic clergy pronounced here perhaps also looks forward to a settlement of the North African Donatist schism.

main three years among "hearers," and during seven years, they must pray prostrate and then during two years they will participate in the prayers of the people but without participating in the offering.

CANON 12

Those who, being called by grace and being obedient to its first movement, have laid aside their sword belts who have later on, like dogs returning to their vomit, even gone so far as to pay money and give gifts to be reinstated in the military service, all those persons must remain among the prostraters during ten years, after a period of three years as hearers. But it is good and proper to examine their attitudes and their way of being penitent. In effect, those among them who with fear, tears, submission and good works show that their change of mind was real and not simply on the surface, when they have passed the prescribed time among the hearers, then they can participate in the prayers (of the faithful); it is even up to the bishop to treat them with more leniency. As for those who endure their penance with indifference and judge that the procedure set out for being readmitted into the Church is sufficient for expiation, those persons are to be required to do penance for the full time required.

CANON 13

We must now observe the ancient and canonical law with regard to those who are about to die, so that if someone is about to die, he must not be deprived of the last and very necessary sacrament. If, after being in a hopeless state, having received communion and participated in the oblation, he gets well, let him be placed with those who participate only in the prayer.

As a general rule, for all persons about to die and who ask to receive the Eucharist, let the bishop, after inquiry, allow them to participate in the offering.

CANON 14

As for catechumens who renounce the faith, the holy and great council has decided that during three years

they should be only hearers and that after that they may pray with the catechumens.

CANON 15

Because of the great agitation and troubles that have recently occurred, it has been decided to abolish completely the custom that, contrary to the rule, has been introduced in certain places, so that it is forbidden for a bishop, priest, or deacon to go from one city to another. If anyone, after the decree of the holy and great council, dares to attempt such a thing or busies himself in actually doing it, his scheme will be struck with absolute nullity, and he will be reinstalled in the church for which he was ordained bishop, priest, or deacon.

CANON 16

Priests and deacons or, in general, any member of the clergy who have the audacity, not considering the fear of God and not knowing the Church's rule, to abandon their churches, must not under any circumstances be received in another church but, by all means, must be forced to return to their proper communities and, if they refuse, they are to be properly excommunicated.

In addition, if anyone dares to take someone who is under the authority of another bishop and to ordain him in his own church without the consent of the bishop in whose clergy he was enrolled, let the ordination be regarded as null.

CANON 17

Seeing that many of those enrolled in the clergy, being full of greed and of a shameful, money-grubbing spirit, have forgotten the sacred word which says that "he did not give his money out for interest" (Ps 15:5) and who in lending out their money require a certain percentage in return, the holy and great council has judged that if anyone, after the publication of this decree, takes interest for a loan or, for whatever reason, holds back half the loan or invents another thing with the mind to realize a shameful profit, he shall be deposed from the clergy and taken off the clergy list.

CANON 18

It has come to the knowledge of the holy and great council that in certain places and in certain cities, deacons distribute communion to priests, although it is contrary to the rule and custom to allow the Body of Christ to be given to one who has the power to offer it by someone who does not; it has equally been learned that certain deacons take communion even before bishops. Therefore, let all this come to an end, and let deacons stay within the limits of their assigned roles, remembering that, on the one hand, they are the servers of the bishops and, on the other, they are inferior to the priests. Consequently, let them receive the Eucharist according to their order after the priests, whether it be the bishop or the priest who gives it to them. Deacons are likewise not permitted to sit among the priests because that is contrary to the rule and order. If someone after these decisions does not want to submit to them, let him be suspended from the diaconate.

CANON 19

Concerning the Paulinianists who return to the catholic Church, a decree has been adopted according to which they must absolutely be rebaptized. If some of them were before members of their clergy, they may, after being rebaptized, be ordained by the bishop within the catholic Church on condition, however, that they appear without stain and blameless. But if an inquiry shows that they are unacceptable, they are to be properly deposed. The same principle is to be observed for the deaconesses and, in general, for all the members of the clergy. We have mentioned the deaconesses serving in this condition although they have not received the imposition of hands, and they must absolutely be counted among the laity.

CANON 20

Seeing that certain people kneel on Sunday and during the Pentecost season, so that there might be the same practice in all the communities, it has been decided by the holy council that all prayers should be addressed to the Lord standing up.

34. Creed and Canons of Constantinople

Although the Council of Nicaea had condemned the theology of Arius, the following decades witnessed a sharp rise to prominence in various "neo-Arian" theologians who modulated the Nicene formulation with terms such as *homoiousios* ("of similar substance"), *homoios* ("similar"), or even *anomoios* ("dissimiliar"). These opponents of Nicaea, such as Eusebius of Nicomedia (who performed Constantine's deathbed baptism) and Eunomius had more than a little success in swaying Christians, including some emperors, to their Trinitarian interpretation. The Second Ecumenical Council was convened by the Eastern Emperor Theodosius I in 381 to reassert Nicene orthodoxy in the capital city. The 150 bishops at first appointed Gregory of Nazianzus, a champion of Nicene orthodoxy, as patriarch of the city, but in-fighting in later sessions resulted in his removal from office (see Text 18). The council did succeed,

"Constantinopolitan Creed" from *Early Christian Creeds,* 3rd ed., ed. J. N. D. Kelly. Copyright © D. McKay, 1972. Used with permission of Pierson Education Limited. "Canons of Constantinople" used by permission of St. Vladimir's Seminary Press, 575 Scarsdale Rd., Crestwood, NY, 10707, © 1996 *The Church of the Ancient Councils: The Disciplinary Work of the First Four Ecumenical Councils.* Translated and edited by Archbishop Peter L'Huillier, pp. 111–131.

however, in reinstating full Nicene orthodoxy. It also supplemented the creed of Nicaea by affirming the full divinity of the Holy Spirit as "proceeding" from the Father (in distinction to the Son, who was "begotten"), thus defeating the so-called Pneumatomachoi ("Spirit-fighters") who placed the Spirit in a subordinate position. The subsequent "Niceno-Constantinopolitan creed" remains authoritative for most Christian churches today.

Perhaps the most significant of the seven canons preserved from the Council of Constantinople is Canon 1, which declared the absolute authority of the Council of Nicaea and began the tradition of listing those specific heretical camps to be anathematized ("cursed") by all good orthodox Christians. The cataloguing of heresies and the reliance on the "holy Fathers" would henceforth be hallmarks of theological debate. These canons are almost entirely concerned with internal matters of clerical organization and authority.

CONSTANTINOPOLITAN CREED

We believe in one God, the Father, almighty, maker of heaven and earth, of all things visible and invisible;

And in one Lord Jesus Christ, the only-begotten Son of God, begotten from the Father before all ages, light from light, true God from true God, begotten not made, of one substance (*homoousios*) with the Father, through whom all things came into existence, who because of us humans and because of our salvation came down from heaven and was incarnate from the Holy Spirit and the Virgin Mary and became human and was crucified for us under Pontius Pilate and suffered and was buried and rose again on the third day according to the Scriptures and ascended to heaven and sits on the right hand of the Father and will come again with glory to judge the living and the dead, of whose kingdom there will be no end;

And in the Holy Spirit, the Lord and life giver, who proceeds from the Father, who with the Father and the Son is together worshipped and together glorified, who spoke through the prophets;

In one holy Catholic and apostolic church.

We confess one baptism for the remission of sins; we look forward to the resurrection of the dead and the life of the world to come. Amen.

CONSTANTINOPOLITAN CANONS

Here is what we have decided, we the bishops of different provinces gathered together in Constantinople by the grace of God and on the invitation of the pious Emperor Theodosius.

CANON 1

Let no one undermine the faith of the 318 fathers gathered at Nicaea in Bithynia, but let it remain firm and untouched, and let every heresy be anathematized, in particular, that of the Eunomians or Anomoeans, that of the Arians or Eudoxians, that of the Semi-Arians or Pneumatomachoi, that of the Sabellians, that of the Marcellians, that of the Photinians, and that of the Apollinarians.

CANON 2

Let the bishops refrain from interfering in churches outside the limits of a diocese and from causing trouble in the churches, but, in conformity to the canons, let the bishop of Alexandria take care of just the affairs of Egypt; let the bishops of the East only govern the East, the prerogatives recognized by the canons of Nicaea for the church of the Antiochians being preserved; let the bishops of the diocese of Asia take care of just the affairs of Asia; the bishops of Pontus, only the affairs of Pontus; the bishops of Thrace, only the affairs of Thrace. If they are not invited, let the bishops refrain from going outside a diocese for an ordination or for any other ecclesiastical act. The above-mentioned rule about the dioceses being observed, it is obvious that the council of the province will direct the affairs of each province according to what was decided at Nicaea. Concerning the Church of God among the barbarian nations, it is important that they be administered by custom established in the time of the fathers.

CANON 3

As for the bishop of Constantinople, let him have the prerogatives of honor after the bishop of Rome, seeing that this city is the new Rome.

CANON 4

Concerning Maximus the Cynic and the disorder that he caused in Constantinople, we have decided that Maximus has never been and is not now a bishop, nor are those that he ordained, no matter what order of the clergy they were ordained to; everything that was done in his name or done by him is declared null and void.

CANON 5

Concerning the tome of the westerners, we have also received those who in Antioch confess one single divinity of the Father, Son, and Holy Spirit.

CANON 6

Because many people are seeking to sow trouble and confusion in church ranks, being motivated by a hateful and slanderous spirit, they invent accusations against the orthodox bishops who administer the churches; their only intention is to impugn the reputations of the priests and to provoke troubles among peoples living in peace. It has, therefore, seemed right and proper to the holy council of bishops assembled in Constantinople that accusers no longer be accepted without previous inquiry; neither should just anybody be allowed to present himself as an accuser of those who administer the churches. This rul-

ing does not, however, exclude everyone from making accusations. But if someone issues a personal complaint against a bishop, that is, of a private nature, whether the person suffered injury from the bishop or suffered from an illegal action of the bishop, the religion of the complaining person should not be taken into account in matters of this kind. It is absolutely necessary that the conscience of the bishop be clear, and whoever claims to have been injured, regardless of his religion, must be able to obtain justice. But if the complaint against the bishop is about a churchly matter, then the religion of the accusers must be examined, first of all since heretics are not permitted to accuse orthodox bishops in matters that concern the Church. (We mean by heretics those who have already been excluded from the Church for a long time, those who even after such exclusion have been anathematized by us, and those who pretend to profess the true faith but who have separated themselves from the bishops in communion with us and who hold separate assemblies.) In addition, if certain people have been condemned and excluded from the Church or excommunicated, whether they be clerics or laymen, they will not be allowed to accuse a bishop before they have been cleared of the things they have been reproached for. In the same way, those who have been accused cannot turn around and accuse a bishop or other clerics before having shown their innocence as to their alleged misconduct. On the other hand, if some persons who are neither heretics nor excommunicated, who have not received any condemnation and have not been accused in any way, if any of these persons claim to have a complaint against the bishop in a churchly matter, the holy council requires them first to submit their complaint to all the bishops of the province and in their presence to prove their accusations. If, however, the other bishops of the province cannot redress the wrongs imputed to the bishop, let them then appeal to the greater council of bishops of the diocese, convoked just for this reason. These bishops should not, however, present their complaint until they have agreed in writing to accept for themselves the sentence handed down if it is shown that they have slandered the accused bishop.

If anyone, not abiding by these decisions mentioned above, dares to weary the ears of the emperor or to disturb the law courts of the civil authorities or an ecumenical council, thus scorning all the bishops of the diocese, that person should not be allowed to make such an accusation, since he disregards the canons and injures the good order of the Church.

CANON 7

Those heretics who come over to orthodoxy and to the society of those who are saved we receive according to the prescribed rite and custom: Arians, Macedonians, Novatianists who call themselves "pure and better," Quartodecimans or Tetradites as well as Apollinarians. We receive them on condition that they present a written document and that they anathematize every heresy that is not in accord with the thinking of the holy, catholic, and apostolic Church of God, and then they should be marked with the seal, that is, anointed with chrism on the forehead, eyes, nostrils, mouth, and ears. And as they are marked with the seal, we say "seal of the gift of the Holy Spirit."

As for Eunomians who are baptized with only one single immersion, Montanists here called Phrygians, Sabellians who teach the doctrine of "Father-Son" and commit other abominable things, and all the other heresies—for there are many of them here especially among the people coming from the country of the Galatians—all those among them who want to come over to orthodoxy we receive as pagans: the first day, we make them Christians, the second catechumens, the third we exorcize them by blowing three times on their faces and ears; then we teach them, and we make them come to the church for a long time and to hear the Scriptures. After that, we baptize them.

35. Canons of Ephesus

The Council of Ephesus, called by Theodosius II in 431, provides a window into the intersection of theological debate and ecclesiastical politics in the fifth century. No creedal formulation emerges from the debate (Canon 7 affirms the inviolability of the creed of Nicaea) since both parties to the ongoing Christological controversy (see Chapter 7) readily signed on to the Niceno-Constantinopolitan creed while vociferously debating its implications. A formal definition of Christ's nature would have to wait for the Council of Chalcedon (see Text 36).

Instead we have a series of canons that are concerned almost entirely with church administration: the authority of metropolitans and patriarchs, the deposition of heretical clergy, the liberation of orthodox priests from the authority of heretical bishops, and so forth. While there is mention of the excommunication of lay heretics, it is merely a footnote to the central matter: welding all orthodox clergy into a united bulwark against the teachings of the named archheretics, Nestorius and, in some manuscripts, the Pelagian Celestius (see Chapter 7). The Ecumenical Council now serves not so much to define a uniform Christian society but, rather, to erect an unassailable front of orthodox hierarchies and institutions.

Used by permission of St. Vladimir's Seminary Press, 575 Scarsdale Rd., Crestwood, NY, 10707, © 1996 *The Church of the Ancient Councils: The Disciplinary Work of the First Four Ecumenical Councils*. Translated and edited by Archbishop Peter L'Huillier, pp. 154–164.

The canons of the 200 holy fathers gathered together in Ephesus after the 13th consulship of Flavius Theodosius and the 3rd of Flavius Valentinian, the august eternal ones, the 10th of the kalends of July.

CANON 1

Since it was necessary that those who did not at all attend the holy council for a churchly reason or by reason of physical infirmity—whether they live in an urban or a rural area—should not be ignorant of what was decided concerning them, we hereby make known to your Holiness and Love that if the metropolitan of the province, being separated from the holy ecumenical council, joined the assembly of apostasy or joined it later on, or even if he only shared the opinions of Celestius [alternately: Nestorius], he can undertake no action against the bishops of the province, seeing that he has already been excluded from all churchly communion by the council, and thus is suspended. What is more, it is the responsibility of the bishops of the province and of the neighboring metropolitans who are of orthodox opinion to exclude him completely from the rank of bishop.

CANON 2

If certain bishops of a province have abandoned the holy council and have gone over to apostasy or were trying to find ways of getting around the council or after having signed Nestorius's deposition, later on turned to the assembly of apostasy, those bishops, following the judgment of the holy council, are completely separated from the priesthood and deprived of their rank.

CANON 3

If, in any city or rural area, certain clerics have been restrained from exercising their priesthood by Nestorius and his followers because of the rectitude of their opinions, we have deemed it right and proper that they be reintegrated into their rank. As a general rule, we ordain that the clerics who are in agreement with the orthodox and ecumenical council should in no way be submissive to bishops who have gone over to apostasy or will do so.

CANON 4

If any clerics should apostasize and, in private or in public, dare to take the side of Nestorius's or Celestius's ideas, the holy council has thought it good and proper that they be deposed.

CANON 5

Those who have been condemned by the holy council or by their own bishops for culpable actions and those whom Nestorius (contradicting the canons with the indifference that characterizes him) or his followers sought out or may seek out to return to communion or to their rank, we have judged that these persons should in no way profit from these actions and should remain deposed.

CANON 6

Similarly, if, in whatever manner, anyone should want to set aside what was done in each case at the holy council of Ephesus, the holy council has decided that if they are bishops or clerics, they should be completely deposed from their rank, and if they are laypersons, they should be excommunicated.

CANON 7

A resolution adopted by the same holy council after having read the statement of the 318 holy fathers of Nicaea and of the impious symbol altered by Theodore of Mopsuestia and presented by Charisius, priest of Philadelphia, to this same holy council of Ephesus:

Therefore, after their reading of these things, the holy council decreed that no one is permitted to produce, to edit, or to compose another faith than that set out by the holy fathers gathered in Nicaea with the Holy Spirit.

As for those who would dare to compose another faith, present it, or propose it to those who might want to be converted to the knowledge of the truth (whether coming from Hellenism, Judaism, or any other heresy), these persons, if they are bishops or clerics, will be set aside, the bishops separated from the episcopate and the clerics from the clergy; if they are laypersons, they are to be excommunicated. In the same way, if any bishops, clerics, or laypersons are found to admit or to teach the doctrines contained in the statement presented by the priest Charisius on the subject of the incarnation of the only-begotten Son of God, or, what is more, to admit or to teach the impious and perverse dogmas of Nestorius that are joined to the statement, let them fall under the sentence of this holy and ecumenical council: that is, a bishop should be separated from his episcopate and deposed, a cleric equally deposed from the clergy, and a layperson excommunicated, as was said above.

CANON 8

A vote of the Holy Council taken following the presentation of a petition to it by the bishops of Cyprus.

An innovation contrary to the church institutions and the canons of the holy fathers, as well as an attack on the liberty of all, has been reported to us by Rheginus, the very religious fellow bishop, and by those who were with him, the very reverend bishops of the province of the Cypriots, Zeno and Evagrius. Sicknesses that affect everyone need urgent remedies, all the more so because they can cause such great suffering; therefore, if no ancient custom exists according to which the bishop of the city of the Anti-ochians performed the ordinations in Cyprus (we have learned by written and verbal reports that it is so), the very reverend men who have had recourse to the holy council, the heads of the holy churches in Cyprus, without being bothered or exposed to violence, will proceed, according to the canons of the holy fathers and ancient usage, to the ordinations of their own very reverend bishops.

The same thing will also be observed in the other dioceses and everywhere in the provinces, so that none of the bishops beloved of God shall take over another province that, in former times and from the beginning, has not been under his authority or that of his predecessors, and if anyone has thus taken over any province and by force has placed it under his authority, let him give it back so that the canons of the fathers may not be transgressed and so that, under the pretext of holy acts, the pride of worldly power enters and that without or knowing it we may lose little by little the liberty that has been given to us by the blood of our Lord Jesus Christ, the liberator of all persons. It has therefore seemed good and proper to the holy ecumenical council that the rights acquired from the beginning and established according to ancient usage from time immemorial be safeguarded intact and inviolate for each province. Each metropolitan has the leisure to take a copy of the acts as a guarantee for himself.

If anyone produces an ordinance contrary to what has now been defined, the holy ecumenical council with one voice declares it to be null.

36. Definition and Canons of Chalcedon

Cyril's victory at the Council of Ephesus sharpened the rivalry between Alexandria and Constantinople. When Flavian, patriarch of Constantinople, excommunicated a monk named Eutyches for preaching Christ's "one nature," Cyril's successor, Dioscorus, secured the vindication of Eutyches and the condemnation of Flavian at a second Council of Ephesus in 449.

Used by permission of St. Vladimir's Seminary Press, 575 Scarsdale Rd., Crestwood, NY, 10707, © 1996 *The Church of the Ancient Councils: The Disciplinary Work of the First Four Ecumenical Councils.* Translated and edited by Archbishop Peter L'Huillier, pp. 184, 206–265.

In addition to theological argument, Dioscorus employed the physical intimidation of imperial troops on the more stubborn bishops. Flavian himself was beaten so severely that he died soon after the council deposed him. The brute force placed in the service of theological conformity later earned this synod the title "the Robber Council," and it did not enjoy ecumenical status.

Emperor Theodosius II died in 450. The following year his successor, Marcian, and Marcian's wife, Theodosius's sister Pulcheria, called an ecumenical council to Chalcedon, a suburb of Constantinople, to undo the excesses of the Robber Council. Marcian and Pulcheria were determined to reinstate the theological and episcopal primacy of Constantinopole. Dioscorus of Alexandria was deposed and excommunicated, and the council's canons strongly condemn the heavy-handed tactics of the Alexandrian bishops: manipulation of clerical appointments, exercise of authority outside their metropolitan jurisdiction, and the use of zealous monks as "shock troops" in the service of theological controversy. The bishop of Constantinople was given ecclesiastical authority equal to the bishop of Rome. In addition, the strict control over clerical matters was now extended to monks in order to rein in their potential exercise of religious authority outside the bounds of the institutional church.

The Council of Chalcedon affirmed the Niceno-Constantinopolitan creed of the fourth century and produced a supplementary "Definition" of Christ's nature. It has been said that debate over the definition boiled down to a single letter in Greek: Eutyches's partisans preferred Cyril's formulation, that Christ was "one person *out of* (Greek *ek*) two natures," while their opponents claimed Christ was "one person *in* (Greek *en*) two natures." The final language was, in fact, a jumble of monophysite and dyophysite propositions that placated few people, although Nestorius, still alive in exile, was reportedly pleased with it. The term *Theotokos* was affirmed for the Virgin Mary, fast becoming a patron saint of Constantinople. Christ's single person and entity (*prosōpon* and *hypostasis*) were likewise affirmed. The division between the "natures" of Christ was stated in language that sounded, to the hardline Cyrillian camp, like Nestorian heresy. Debate did not end at Chalcedon, and theological division—often erupting into civic violence—continued well into the seventh century, persisting among Eastern churches even until today.

DEFINITION OF CHALCEDON

[*After affirming the creeds of Nicaea and Constantinople:*] Therefore, following the holy fathers, all of us teach unanimously that everyone must confess that our Lord Jesus Christ is one single and same Son, who is perfect according to divinity and perfect according to humanity, truly God and truly man, composed of a reasonable soul and a body, consubstantial (*homoousios*) with the Father according to divinity and consubstantial (*homoousios*) with us according to humanity, completely like us except for sin; he was begotten by the Father before all ages according to his divinity and, in these latter days, he was born for us and for our salvation of Mary the Virgin, the Mother of God (*Theotokos*), according to his humanity; one single and same Christ, Son, Lord, only-begotten, known in two natures, without confusion, without change, without division, without separation; the difference of natures is in no way suppressed by their union, but rather the properties of each are retained and united in one single person (*prosōpon*) and single hypostasis; he is neither separated nor divided in two persons, but he is a single and same only-begotten Son, God the Word, the Lord Jesus Christ, such as he was announced formerly by the prophets, such as he himself, the Lord Jesus Christ, taught us about himself and such as the symbol of the fathers has transmitted to us.

CANONS OF CHALCEDON

The canons of the 630 holy fathers gathered together in Chalcedon under the consulate of Marcian, the eternally glorious and of him who will be designated consul on the eighth of the Kalends of November

CANON 1

We have decided that the canons issues by the holy fathers in each council up to the present time should remain in force.

CANON 2

If a bishop sets a price for ordaining someone and sells the grace of God that has no price and ordains a bishop, a country bishop, a priest, a deacon, or anyone counted among the clergy, or if for money a bishop promotes a treasurer, a defender, a watchman, or anyone else to the service of the Church, such a bishop, being motivated by his own greed in undertaking such a thing, is in danger of losing his position if the deed is uncovered. Let the person not benefit in any way from the ordination or the promotion bought in this fashion, but let him be a stranger to the dignity or the position acquired for a price. Moreover, if any one gets involved in this shameful and illicit business, if he is a cleric, let him be deposed from his position; if he is a layman or a monk, let him be excommunicated.

CANON 3

It has come to the attention of the holy council that some of those on the list of the clergy, by a shameful money-grubbing spirit, take on the management of other people's rental properties and become businessmen dealing with temporal matters; they neglect the service of God, visit the homes of worldly people, and through greed, take on the management of their material possessions.

The holy and great council has therefore decided that from this time on, no bishop, cleric, or monk must manage rental properties or become the administrators of temporal affairs unless he is compelled by the law—not being able to get out of it—to become the guardian of minors or to become responsible for the affairs of the church, orphans, helpless widows, or persons in great need of the church's help: and this only if the bishop of the city asks him and in the fear of the Lord. If anyone from now on goes against these decisions, let him be put under ecclesiastical penalties.

CANON 4

Let those who truly and sincerely lead a monastic life be honored as is proper! But because certain persons, for whom the monastic life is only a pretext, sow trouble in the affairs of the church and state by inconsiderately roaming around in the cities trying even to establish monasteries for themselves, it has seemed good and proper that no one be allowed to build or establish a monastery or an oratory anywhere without the consent of the bishop of the city. In each city and country area, let the monks be subject to the bishop; let them seek peace and apply themselves only to fasting and prayer, remaining in the place where they made their profession of renunciation; let them not cause any troubles in the affairs of the church or state; and let them not get mixed up in such affairs by leaving their monasteries, except if eventually they are permitted to do so by the bishop of the city for some grave necessity. In addition, let no slave be admitted into the monasteries with the intention of becoming a monk without the consent of his own master.

We have decided that whoever goes against the present ruling will be excommunicated, so that the name of God will not be blasphemed.

As for the bishop of the city, he must exercise oversight in the monasteries, as is proper.

CANON 5

Concerning bishops or clerics who wander from one city to another, it has seemed right and proper that the canons issued by the holy fathers with them in mind should remain in force.

CANON 6

In addition, no one is to be ordained at large, either priest or deacon, or any member of the clergy in general, unless the ordinand is attached to a city or village church, to a martyr's shrine, or to a monastery. As for whoever is ordained at large, the holy council has decided that such an ordination is without value and that, to the shame of the ordainer, he will not be able to exercise his function anywhere.

CANON 7

We have decided that those who have been admitted into the ranks of the clergy or who have become monks, from now on, must no longer take service in the army or accept any secular dignity; if they dare to do this and do not repent and return to the state that they previously chose for God, they will be excommunicated.

CANON 8

Let those clerics who serve in centers for the poor, monasteries, and martyrs' shrines remain under the authority of the bishop of each city in conformity with the tradition of the holy fathers, and let them not rebel arrogantly against their own bishops.

Those who dare to go against this ruling in whatever way and who do not submit themselves to their proper bishop, if they are clerics, let them be under canonical sentence, and if they are monks or laymen, let them be deprived of communion.

CANON 9

If a cleric has a dispute with another cleric, let him not bypass his bishop and go to the secular courts, but let him submit the affair first to his own bishop or, of course, on the advice of his bishop, to some agreed-on third party who can judge the case.

If anyone goes against this ruling, let him be subject to canonical penalties.

If, on the other hand, a cleric has a dispute with his own bishop or with another bishop, let him appeal to the synod of the province. Finally, if a bishop or a cleric has something against the metropolitan of the province in question, let him appeal either to the exarch of the diocese or to the see of the imperial city of Constantinople, and let him be given justice there.

CANON 10

It is not permitted for a cleric to be enrolled in the churches of two cities at the same time: the one in which he was first ordained and the other where he later went because the second was more important, and he was motivated by vain feelings. Therefore let those who act in this way be sent back to the church in which they were first ordained, and let them exercise their functions there only.

Whoever has already been transferred from one church to another, he must no longer busy himself with the affairs of the first church or the martyrs' shrines or the centers for the poor or the lodging facilities that are attached to them. After the publication of this present ruling of the great and holy council, for those who dare to do anything that is prohibited by it, the holy council has decided that they should be removed from their rank.

CANON 11

We have decided that all the poor, as well as those who need to be helped, after proper evaluation, will be issued short letters called "ecclesiastical [letters] of peace," and not "of recommendation" because the "letters of recommendation" are issued only to persons of distinction.

CANON 12

It has come to our attention that certain persons, acting against church rules, appeal to the public authorities in order to effect the division of a province in two by imperial decree; this they do so that hence-forth there may be two metropolitans in the same province. The holy council has, therefore, decreed that, in the future, no bishop shall dare to act in this way; if he tries to do so, he must be removed from his rank. As for cities that have already been honored by the title of metropolis by imperial letters, let these cities and the bishops who govern them enjoy only the honor of the title; that is, let the proper rights of the real metropolitan be safeguarded.

CANON 13

Unknown clerics and readers must in no way exercise their functions in a city other than their own, without being issued letters of recommendation from their own bishop.

CANON 14

Since, in some provinces, readers and chanters have been allowed to marry, the holy council has decided that none of them should marry a heterodox woman. As for those who have already had children by such a marriage, if they have these children baptized by heretics, they must present them to the communion of the catholic church; in case they have not been baptized, they must no longer have them baptized by heretics or, what is more, give them in marriage to a heretic, to a Jew, or to a pagan, unless the person they are united to promises to embrace the orthodox faith.

If anyone goes against the decree of the holy council, let him be submitted to a canonical sentence.

CANON 15

A woman must not be ordained deacon before the age of forty and that after a careful inquiry. If, after having received ordination and after having exercised her ministry for some time, she wants to marry, thereby scorning the grace of God, let her be excommunicated, as well as him who has united himself to her.

CANON 16

A virgin who has dedicated herself to the Lord God, as well as a monk, is not permitted to marry. There-fore, if they have gotten married, let them be excommunicated. In addition, we have decided that the bishop of the area has the power to exercise compassion in reference to such persons.

CANON 17

The rural and village communities of each church must without change remain attached to the bishops who possess them, especially if for thirty years one bishop has administered them and had them under his authority without any problems. But if, during these thirty years, anyone has contested or contests this matter, it is possible for those who feel themselves wrong-fully treated to bring the affair before the synod of the province. If, on the other hand, someone has been wrongfully treated by his metropolitan, let him make an appeal either to the exarch of the diocese or to the see of Constantinople, as has been said earlier.

Finally, if by imperial authority a city has been founded or is founded in the future, let the rank of the ecclesiastical communities be in conformity with that of the civil and public arrangements.

CANON 18

Since the crime of plotting and conspiring is re-pressed through all possible means by civil laws, even more so is it proper that it should be forbidden by the Church of God. If, therefore, any clerics or monks are found plotting and conspiring, or even thinking about such improper action against bishops or colleagues in the clergy, let them be completely deposed from their rank.

CANON 19

It has come to our attention that, in the provinces, the bishops' councils required by the canons are not being held, and for this reason much church business that requires attention is being neglected. Thus the holy council has decided that, in conformity with the canons of the holy fathers, the bishops of each province are to gather together two times a year in the place where the metropolitan judges best, and they will attend to all such business that requires attention. The bishops who will not come to the meetings even though they are in good health in their home cities and free from other urgent and necessary duties are to be fraternally reprimanded.

CANON 20

As we have already decreed, clerics serving in one church must not be integrated into the church of another city but must reattach themselves to the church for whose service they were found worthy in the beginning; an exception is to be made for those clerics who have lost their country of origin and therefore are required to go into another church. If after this decree a bishop receives a cleric under the authority of another bishop, it seems right and proper that he who received and him who was received should be excommunicated until the cleric who moved into another church returns to his own church.

CANON 21

Clerics and laypersons who make complaints against bishops or other clergy should not be allowed to make such complaints without first having their reputations examined.

CANON 22

Clerics are not permitted to seize the material goods of the bishop after his death; this has already been forbidden by the ancient canons. Those who do such a thing run the risk of losing their rank.

CANON 23

It has come to the attention of the holy council that certain clerics and monks, without any commission from their bishops, sometimes even excommunicated by them, are going to the imperial city of Constantinople and staying there for a long time; they cause trouble, sow disorder in church affairs, and even shake up some people's houses. The council has therefore decided that such persons should first receive a warning from the Advocate of the very holy church of Constantinople to leave the imperial city; if they persist in their activities, they should be expelled by the same Advocate even if they do not want to go, and they should return to their own countries.

CANON 24

Once monasteries have been consecrated with the consent of the bishop, they must remain forever monasteries, and their material goods must remain in the possession of the monasteries. They must never again become secular habitations. Those who allow them to become secular habitations are to be subjected to the sentence prescribed by the canons.

CANON 25

Since certain metropolitans, as we have learned, neglected the flock that has been given to them and put off the ordination of bishops, it has seemed right and proper to the holy council that the ordinations of bishops take place within three months unless an absolute necessity requires a longer delay. If he does not act in this way, let the metropolitan be subjected to an ecclesiastical sentence. As for the revenue of the widowed church [i.e., without a bishop], let it be maintained intact by the treasurer of this church.

CANON 26

As we have learned, in some churches, the bishops administer the material goods of the church without a treasurer; it has seemed right and proper that every church with a bishop should also have a treasurer taken from the clergy who will administer to the church's goods with the advice of his own bishop. In this way, the administration of the church will not be without checks and balances, the goods of the church will not be dissipated, and the priesthood will be free from all suspicion. Let anyone who will not follow these instructions be subjected to the divine canons.

CANON 27

Those who carry off women by force under the pretext of marriage, as well as those who aid and approve those who carry out such actions, the holy council has decided that if they are clerics they are to be deposed from their position, and if they are laymen, they are to be excommunicated.

CHAPTER 9

Asceticism and Monasticism

Among philosophers of the ancient world, bodily discipline, or *askēsis,* was a common way of pursuing spiritual perfection. For early Christians, who believed that God had employed a human body to effect human salvation, the body was likewise believed to be useful in transforming the soul: fasting, self-denial, voluntary poverty, and sexual renunciation are found early on in the Christian movement. The precise role the body played in the Christian soul's salvation was much debated, however. Some groups, such as Gnostics or Manicheans, promoted a starkly dualistic vision of the world, in which created matter, including the body, was evil and to be combatted by the immaterial soul. Most Christians, however, took a more balanced view, seeing the body as a tool graciously provided by God for the disciplining of the soul, allowing the more rigorous Christians to gain a taste of eschatological perfection in this life.

Monasticism (from the Greek term *monos,* or solitary) describes the rise of organized ascetic forms in the fourth and fifth centuries. For Christians of the period, the ascetic landscape of the Egyptian desert provided a paradigm for male and female monastic vocations (see Text 48). There were the anchorites, of whom Antony became the model, from the Greek word *anachōrēsis* ("withdrawal"): hermits who lived in solitary isolation. And there were cenobites, of whom Pachomius was allegedly the first great organizer, from the Greek *koinos bios* ("common life"): monks who lived together in communities under a common rule and leadership. The options for monastic life were much more varied than this, however, and seem to have emerged simultaneously in Egypt, Syria, Palestine, and the West. We know of groups of women who chose to live together in urban or rural domestic settings, perhaps under the guidance of a male cleric or monk. We also hear suspicious rumblings about the so-called *agapetae* (see Text 37), male and female ascetics living together in chaste companionship. We learn from our Syriac sources (see Text 41) about monastic circles, the *bnay qyama,* that were fully integrated into their local ecclesiastical communities. Monks in the deserts outside Jerusalem lived a form of communal withdrawal ("semianchoritic"), and joint houses of male and female monastic communities sprouted at the holy places. In addition, spectacular (and relatively rare) forms of monastic life emerged: stylites, who lived on pillars (see the description of Symeon in Text 47); dendrites, who lived in trees; and the so-called "grazers" (Greek, *boskoi*), who roamed in the countryside and, it was alleged, ate grass. As rare and extreme as these ascetic forms were, they had in common with more settled forms of monastic life the desire to change one's spiritual status by radically altering one's physical life, constraining the body in order to perfect the soul. As the canons of the Council of Chalcedon also demonstrate (see Text 36), monastic withdrawal often, paradoxically, resulted in a form of religious authority that could operate alongside or against the established institutions of the church. Ascetic elitism also provided opportunities for religious advancement to women, who were otherwise restricted from institutional clerical positions and who were disparaged in Christian theological writings as the "devil's gateway."

Monasticism, and the increasingly public prominence of ascetic athleticism in Late Antiquity, gave a new moral dynamic to Christianity. The desert—the barren, mythical space of absolute renunciation—was viewed with ever-increasing awe as the necessary counterpart to the worldly city in which the majority of Christians lived. Those Christians who chose the path of ascetic withdrawal, whether in solitary isolation or in a community of monks, were part of a religious vanguard that made no (ostensible) distinctions based on class, gender, or family. The literature of monasticism was the literature of moral perfection: even those Christians who might never hope to transcend their mundane lives through extraordinary (and, it must be added, often dangerous) feats of ascetic prowess could still learn the lessons of salvation, embodiment, and perfection honed by a monastic elite (see Chapter 11).

FOR FURTHER READING

Brown, Peter. *The Body and Society: Men, Women, and Sexual Renunciation in Early Christianity.* New York: Columbia University Press, 1988.

Burton-Christie, Douglas. *The Word in the Desert: Scripture and the Quest for Holiness in Early Christian Monasticism.* Oxford, England: Oxford University Press, 1993.

Chitty, Derwas. *The Desert a City: An Introduction to the Study of Egyptian and Palestinian Monasticism Under the Christian Empire.* Oxford, England: Blackwell, 1966.

Clark, Elizabeth A. *Ascetic Piety and Women's Faith: Essays on Late Ancient Christianity.* Lewiston, N.Y.: Edwin Mellen Press, 1986.

Elm, Susanna. *"Virgins of God": The Making of Asceticism in Late Antiquity.* Oxford, England: Clarendon Press, 1994.

Goehring, James E. *Ascetics, Society, and the Desert: Studies in Egyptian Monasticism.* Harrisburg, Penn.: Trinity International Press, 1999.

Krawiec, Rebecca. *Shenoute and the Women of the White Monastery: Egyptian Monasticism in Late Antiquity.* Oxford, England: Oxford University Press, 2002.

Rousseau, Philip. *Ascetics, Authority, and the Church in the Age of Jerome and Cassian.* Oxford, England: Oxford University Press, 1978.

———. *Pachomius: The Making of a Community in Fourth-Century Egypt.* Berkeley: University of California Press, 1999.

Wimbush, Vincent, and Valantasis, Richard, eds. *Asceticism.* Oxford, England: Oxford University Press, 1995.

The Texts

After a brief stint among monks outside Antioch, Jerome made a name for himself as an ascetic and biblical expert in Rome (see the introduction to Text 27). He became an adviser to ascetically minded noblewomen of the city and developed a close relationship with a prominent and wealthy widow named Paula, who became his patron. Jerome wrote the following letter to Paula's daughter, Julia Eustochium during this period in Rome. The letter, as Jerome states, functions as a guide to maintaining sanctified virginal status and was presumably intended for wider circulation.

The letter encapsulates many of the theological, social, and spiritual issues surrounding the ascetic movements of the time: the problem of desire (both physical and spiritual), monastic institutionalization (Jerome gives what would become a standard taxonomy of monastic vocations), appropriate virginal behavior, and the use of Scripture as an ascetic manual (Jerome cites more than forty biblical books in the course of the letter). Jerome also gives us insight into ascetic controversies: accusations of heresy, particularly association with the famously antibody Manicheans; disruption of society, especially as upper-class women chose renunciation over reproduction; suspicions that fell upon male and female ascetics in close proximity (the so-called *agapetae,* cohabitating monks and female virgins, as well as Jerome's own associations with women). The letter also contains Jerome's famous vision in which he is called a "Ciceronian," indicating the difficulties of defining "Christian culture" during this period.

Jerome's strong language about the pitfalls of marriage and the rigors of renunciation drew censure from fellow clergy in Rome, particularly when Eustochium's elder sister, Blaesilla (mentioned in the letter) died from an illness related to her ascetic discipline. Jerome, Paula, and Eustochium moved East soon after, settling in Bethlehem where Jerome and Paula founded joint monasteries. There Jerome continued to dispense ascetic and biblical expertise to monastic devotees across the empire until his death in 420 or 421 (see also Text 27).

(1) *Listen, O Daughter, and see, and incline your ear and forget your people and your father's house and the king shall desire your beauty* (Ps 45:10–11). In this forty-fifth psalm, God speaks to the human soul, saying that following the example of Abraham, it should go out from its own land and from its kindred and should leave the Chaldeans (cf. Gen 12:1), that is, the demons, and should dwell in the country of the

From *Handmaids of the Lord: Contemporary Descriptions of Feminine Asceticism in the First Six Christian Centuries,* trans. Joan M. Petersen. Kalamazoo, Mich.: Cistercian Studies, 1996. Used with permission.

living, for which elsewhere the prophet sighs, *I believe that I shall see the good things of the Lord in the land of the living* (Ps 27:13). But it is not enough for you to go out from your own land, unless you forget your people and your father's house; unless you scorn the flesh and cling to the Bridegroom in a close embrace. *Do not look behind you,* he says, *or remain in the entire region; take refuge on the mountain, lest by chance you be consumed* (Gen 19:17). Anyone who has grasped the plow must not look behind him or return home from the field (Luke 9:62), or, having Christ's tunic, descend from the roof to fetch another garment (Matt 24:17–18). What a marvelous thing, that a father charges his daughter to remember her father. *You are of your father the devil, and it is your will to do the lusts of your father* (John 8:44). So it was said of the Jews—and, in another place, *Someone who commits sin is of the devil* (1 John 3:8). Born, in the first instance, of such parentage, we are naturally black, and even when we have repented, so long as we have not scaled the heights of virtue, we may still say, *I am black and beautiful, daughter of Jerusalem* (Song 1:5). But you will say to me, "I have left the home of my childhood; I have forgotten my father, I am born again in Christ. What reward do I receive for this?" The context shows: *The king shall desire your beauty.* This, then, is the great mystery. *For this a man shall leave his father and mother and shall cling to his wife, and they two shall be,* not as is said there *of one flesh,* but of "one spirit" (Eph 5:31–32). Your bridegroom is not haughty or disdainful; he has *married an Ethiopian woman* (Num 12:1). When once you desire the wisdom of the true Solomon and come to him, he will avow all his knowledge to you. He will lead you into his chamber with his royal hand (Song 1:4). He will miraculously change your complexion, so that it shall be said of you, *Who is this who goes up and has been made white?* (Song 8:5 [LXX]). (2) I write to you thus, my lady Eustochium (I am bound to call my Lord's bride "my lady"), to show you by my opening words that my object is not to praise the virginity that you follow and of which you have proved the value or yet to recount the drawbacks of marriage—the swelling of the womb, of a baby, the torments of a mistress, the cares of house-hold management and all those fancied blessings that death at last cuts short; indeed married women have their own status, that is, honorable matrimony and an undefiled marriage bed (Heb 13:4). My purpose is to show you that you are fleeing from Sodom and should take warning by Lot's wife (Gen 19:26). There is no flattery, I can tell you, in these pages. A flatterer's words are fair, but for all that, he is an enemy. You need expect no rhetorical flourishes setting you among the angels and, while they extol virginity as blessed, putting the world at your feet.

(3) I would have you draw from your monastic vow not pride but fear (cf. Rom 11:20). You walk laden with gold; you must keep out of the robber's way. To us human beings this life is a race course; we contend here, we are downed elsewhere. No one can lay fear aside while serpents and scorpions beset his path. The Lord says, *My sword has drunk deep in heaven* (Isa 34:5), and do you expect to find peace on the earth? No, the earth yields only thorns and thistles, and its dust is food for the serpent (Gen 3:14). *For our wrestling is not against flesh and blood, but against the principalities and powers of this world and of this darkness, against the spirits of wickedness in the heavenly places* (Eph 6:12). We are hemmed in by hosts of foes; our enemies are on every side. The weak flesh will soon be ashes; one against many, it fights against tremendous odds. Not till it has been dissolved, not till the prince of this world has come and found nothing in it (John 14:30), not till then may you safely listen to the prophet's words, *You shall not fear the terror by night or the arrow that flies by day or the activity that surrounds you in darkness or the demon and his attacks at noon day. A thousand shall fall at your side and ten thousand at your right hand, but the terror will not come near you* (Ps 91:5–7). When the hosts of the enemy distress you, when you begin to be aroused to separate attacks of temptation to do wrong, when you say in your heart, "What shall we do?" Elisha's words will supply your answer, *Do not be afraid, for there are more on our side than on theirs* (2 Kings 6:16). He shall pray, "Lord, open the eyes of your handmaid, that she may see," and then, when your eyes have been opened, you will see a fiery chariot like Elijah's waiting to carry you to

heaven (2 Kings 2:11). Then you will joyfully sing, *Our soul has been snatched like a sparrow from the snare of the fowlers; the snare is broken, and we have been set free* (Ps 124:7).

(4) So long as we are held down by this frail body, so long as we have our treasure in earthen vessels (2 Cor 4:7), so long as the flesh lusts against the spirit and the spirit against the flesh (Gal 5:17), there can be no sure victory. *Our adversary the devil goes about like a roaring lion, seeking something to devour* (1 Pet 5:8) . . . *you have placed the darkness and night has been created, when all the beasts of the forest prowl around. The lion cubs roar after their prey and seek their food from God* (Ps 104:20–21). The devil does not look for unbelievers, for those outsiders whose flesh the Assyrian king roasted in the furnace (Jes 29:22). It is the Church of Christ that he *makes haste to spoil* (cf. Isa 8:1). According to Habbakuk, *his food is of the choicest* (Hab 1:16). He desires to overthrow Job, and having devoured Judas, he seeks power to sift the [other] apostles (Luke 22:31). The Savior came not to send peace on the earth but a sword (Matt 10:34). Lucifer fell, Lucifer who used to rise at dawn (Isa 14:12), and he who was bred up in a paradise of delight had the well-earned sentence passed upon him, *If you are borne on high like the eagle, I shall bring you down, says the Lord* (Obad 4). For he had said in his heart, *I will set my throne above the stars of heaven, and I will be like the Most High* (Isa 14:13–14). Therefore God says every day to the angels, as they descend the ladder that Jacob saw in his dream (Gen 28:12), *I have said, you are gods and all of you are children of the Most High. But you shall die like men and fall like one of the princes* (Ps 82:6–7). The devil fell first, and since *God stands in the congregation of the gods and judges among the gods* (Ps 82:1), the Apostle writes to those who cease to be gods, *When there is jealousy and rivalry among you, are you not carnal and do you not live according to human standards?* (1 Cor 3:3).

(5) If then the Apostle, who was a chosen vessel (Acts 9:15) and prepared for the gospel of Christ (Gal 1:15), keeps his body in subjection, on account of the pricks of the flesh and the attractions of vice, lest while preaching to others, he may himself be found to be a fraud (1 Cor 9:27), and yet, for all that, sees another law in his members warring against the law of his mind and bringing him into captivity to the law of sin (Rom 7:23); if after nakedness, fasting, hunger, imprisonment, scourging, and other torments, he turns back to himself and cries, *O wretched man that I am, who shall deliver me from the body of this death?* (Rom 7:24), do you think that you are safe? Take care, I beg you, that God does not say of you someday, *The virgin of Israel is fallen and there is no one to raise her up* (Amos 5:2). I will say it boldly, that though God can do all things, he cannot raise up a virgin once she has fallen. He may indeed relieve someone defiled from the penalty of her sin, but he will not give her a crown. Let us fear lest in us, too, the prophecy will be fulfilled, *Even good virgins shall fail* (Amos 8:13), because there are also bad virgins. *The man who looks on a woman to lust after her,* says the Lord, *is already an adulterer in his heart* (Matt 5:28). Virginity, then, may be lost even by a thought. The virgins who are bad are those who are virgins in the flesh, not in the spirit, the foolish virgins, who having no oil, are shut out by the bridegroom (Matt 25:3).

(6) But if even real virgins, when they have other failings, are not saved by their physical virginity, what shall become of those who have prostituted the members of Christ and have changed the temple of the Holy Spirit into a brothel? They will immediately hear the words, *Come down, O virgin daughter of Babylon, sit on the ground. There is no throne for a daughter of the Chaldaeans; you shall no longer be soft and delicate. Receive the millstone, grind the flour, uncover your head, bare your legs, cross the rivers, and your shame will be uncovered and your dishonor will stand revealed* (Isa 47:1–3). And will she come to this, after the bridal chamber of the Song of God, after the kisses of him who is to her both kinsman and spouse? (Song 5:2). Yes, she of whom the prophecy once sang, *At your right hand stood the queen in a vestment of gold, shot through with varied colors* (Ps 45:9), shall be made naked and the hind parts of her skirts shall be placed over her face. She shall sit by the waters of loneliness, her pitcher laid

aside, and shall stretch out her legs to every passerby, and shall be polluted to the crown of her head (Ezek 16:25). It would have been better for her to have submitted to the yoke of marriage and to have walked in level places, rather than having aspired to loftier heights only to fall like this into the depth of hell. I pray you, do not let Zion, the faithful city, become a harlot (Isa 1:21): do not let it be, where the Trinity has lodged, there demons shall dance and serpents make nests and hyenas build (Isa 34:15). Let us not loose the band that binds the beast. When lust tickles the sense and the soft fire of sensual pleasure sheds its pleasing glow over us, let us immediately break forth and cry, *The Lord is my helper; I shall not fear what the flesh can do to me* (Pss 118:6, 56:4). When, for a little while, the inner person shows signs of wavering between vice and virtue, say, *Why are you sad, O my soul, and why do you distress me? Hope in God, since I shall confess to him that he is the health of my countenance and my God* (Ps 42:11). You must never let suggestions of evil grow in you or a babel of disorder gain strength in your breast. Slay the enemy while he is small. And to avoid having a crop of weeds, nip evil in the bud. Bear in mind the warning words of the Psalmist, *Unhappy daughter of Babylon, happy shall he be who shall reward you as you have been rewarded. Happy shall he be who shall hold your little children and dash them against the stones* (Ps 137:8–9). Because natural heat inevitably kindles sensual passion in a man, he is praised and accounted happy who, when foul suggestions arise in his mind, gives them no quarter, but dashes them instantly against the rock. *Now the rock is Christ* (1 Cor 10:4).

(7) How often, when I was living in the desert, in the vast solitude which, parched by the blazing heat of the sun, gives the hermits a savage dwelling place, did I imagine myself among the pleasures of Rome! I used to sit alone because I was filled with bitterness. I presented a disgusting sight: my filthy skin conveyed the impression of the blackness of an Ethiopian's flesh; tears and groans were my daily portion, and if ever sleep assailed me, though I struggled against it, I beat against the ground my bare bones that scarcely held together. Of my food and

drink I say nothing; for even in sickness, the solitaries have nothing but cold water, and to eat one's food cooked is looked on as self-indulgence. Now, although in my fear of hell I had consigned myself to this prison, where I had no companions but scorpions and wild beasts, I often found myself amongst bevies of girls. My lips were pale and my frame chilled with fasting, yet my mind was burning with desire, and the fires of lust kept bubbling up before me when my flesh was a good as dead. Helpless, I cast myself at the feet of Jesus. I watered them with my tears, I wiped them with my hair, and then I subdued my rebellious body with weeks of abstinence. I do not blush to avow my abject misery. Rather I lament that I am not now what once I was. I remember how I often cried aloud all night until the break of day and did not stop beating my breast until tranquillity returned at the Lord's chiding. I used to dread my very cell as though it knew my thoughts, and, stern and angry with myself, I used to make my way alone into the desert. Wherever I saw hollow valleys, craggy mountains, steep cliffs, there I made my oratory, there the house of correction for my unhappy flesh. There also the Lord himself is my witness when I had shed copious tears and strained my eyes toward heaven, I sometimes felt myself among angelic hosts and for joy and gladness sang, *For the scent of your good ointments we will run after you* (Song 1:3).

(8) Now, if these are the temptations of men who have only evil thoughts to fear, since their bodies are emaciated with fasting, how must it fare with a girl whose surroundings are those of luxury and ease? Surely, to use the Apostle's words, *She is dead while she is alive* (1 Tim 5:6). Therefore, if experience gives me a right to advise or makes my words credible, I urge, first of all, as a most solemn warning that the Bride of Christ shun wine as if it were poison. For wine is the first weapon used by demons against young people. Greed does not shake nor pride puff up nor ambition infatuate as much as this. Other vices we easily escape, but this enemy is shut up within us, and wherever we go, we carry him with us. Wine and youth between them kindle the fire of sensual pleasure. Why do we throw oil on the flame? Why do we add fresh fuel to a miserable body that is already

ablaze? Paul, it is true, says to Timothy, *Do not drink water, but use a little wine for the sake of your stomach and your frequent slight indispositions* (1 Tim 5:23). But notice the reasons for which the permission is given, to cure an aching stomach and a frequent slight indisposition, and lest we overindulge ourselves on the score of our ailments, he commands that only a little be taken. He advises more as a physician than as an apostle (though, indeed, an apostle is a spiritual physician). He evidently feared that Timothy might succumb to this weakness and might prove unequal to the constant moving to and fro involved in preaching the gospel. Besides, he remembered that he had spoken of *wine wherein is lust* (Eph 5:18) and had said, *It is not good for a person either to eat meat or to drink wine* (Rom 14:21). Noah drank wine and became intoxicated in that primitive age after the flood, when the vine was first planted. Perhaps he did not know its power of inebriation. And to let you understand the sacramental significance of Scripture in every respect—for the Word of God is indeed a pearl and can be pierced on every side—after his drunkenness came the uncovering of his thighs, and lust was joined to riotous living (Gen 9:20–21). First came the needs of his belly, and the rest immediately followed. For the people ate and drank and *arose to play* (Exod 32:6). Lot, the friend of God who was saved on the mountain and was found to be the only righteous man out of many thousands of people, was made drunk by his daughters. And although they may have acted as they did more from a desire for children than from love of sinful pleasure—for the human race seemed in danger of extinction—yet they were well aware that the righteous man would not abet their plan unless intoxicated. In fact, he did not know what he was doing, and his sin was not willful. Still his error was a grave one, for it made him the father of Moab and Ammon (Gen 19:30–38), Israel's enemies, of whom it is said, *Even to the fourteenth generation they shall not enter into the community of the Lord forever* (Deut 23:3).

(9) When Elijah, in his flight from Jezebel, lay weary and desolate beneath the oak tree, an angel came and aroused him and said to him, *"Arise and eat," and he looked and behold, there was a scone and a vessel of water at his head* (1 Kings 19:5–6).

Had God willed it, might he not have sent his prophet spiced wine and food flavored with olive oil and meat that had been tenderized by beating? When Elisha invited the sons of the prophets to dinner, he gave them wild herbs to eat. Then he heard a racket coming from all the diners shouting together, "Man of God, there is death in the pot." He did not storm at the cooks—for he was not accustomed to sumptuous meals—but throwing flour into the pot, he sweetened the bitterness of the food (2 Kings 4:38–41). With spiritual strength, as Moses had once sweetened the waters of Marah (Exod 15:23–25). Again, when men sent to arrest the prophet were smitten with physical and mental blindness, that he might bring them without their own knowledge to Samaria, notice the food with which Elisha ordered them to be refreshed. *"Set before them bread and water,"* he said, *"that they may eat and drink and be sent back to their master"* (2 Kings 6:18–23). Quite a rich meal, too, could have been brought over to Daniel from the king's table, but he preferred the mowers' lunch brought to him by Habakkuk, which, I think, was country food (Dan 1:8; Bel 33–39). He was called *a man of desires* (Dan 9:23) because he would not eat the bread of desire or drink the wine of concupiscence.

(10) There are in the Scriptures countless divine answers condemning gluttony and approving simple food, but as fasting is not my present theme and an adequate discussion of it would require a treatise to itself, these few observations, of the many that the subject suggests, must suffice. By them you will understand why the first man, obeying his belly and not God, was cast down from paradise into this vale of tears (Gen 3:6; Ps 84:6), and why Satan used hunger to tempt the Lord himself in the wilderness (Matt 4:2–4); why the Apostle cries, *Food for the belly and the belly for food, but God shall destroy both it and them,* (1 Cor 6:13) and why he speaks of the self-indulgent as men *whose God is their belly* (Phil 3:19). For people invariably worship what they like best. Care must be taken, therefore, that abstinence may bring back to paradise those whom satiety once drove out.

(11) You will tell me, perhaps, that, high born as you are, reared in luxury and always sleeping on a

soft bed, you cannot do without wine and gourmet food and would find a stricter rule of life unendurable. I can only say, "Live by your own rule, then, since God's rule is too hard for you." Not that the Creator and Lord of all takes pleasure in the rumbling of our intestines and the emptiness of our stomachs and a burning fever in our lungs. But there are no other means by which our chastity can be preserved. Job was dear to God and in his eyes a man of unblemished simplicity, but hear what he says about the devil: *His strength is in the loins and his force is in the navel* (Job 40:16).

For the sake of decency the names have been changed, but the reproductive organs of the two sexes are meant. Thus, the descendant of David who, according to the promise, is to sit upon his throne, is said to come from his loins (Ps 132:11), and the seventy-five souls descended from Jacob who entered Egypt are said to come out of his thigh (Gen 46:26). So also when his thigh shrank after the Lord had wrestled with him (Gen 32:24–25), he ceased to beget children. Again, the Israelites are told to celebrate the Passover with their loins girded and mortified (Exod 12:11). God says to Job, *Gird up your loins like a man* (Job 38:3). John wears a leathern girdle (Matt 3:4). The apostles must gird their loins to carry the lamps of the gospel (Luke 12:35). When Ezekiel tells us how Jerusalem is found in the plain of wandering, covered with blood, he uses the words, *Your umbilical cord has not been cut* (Ezek 16:4). In his assaults on men, therefore, the devil's strength is in the loins; in his attacks on women, his force is in the navel.

(12) Do you want proof of my assertions? Take examples. Samson was braver than a lion and tougher than a rock. Alone and unprotected, he pursued a thousand armed men, and yet in Delilah's embrace, his resolution melted away (Judg 16). David was a man after God's own heart, and his lips had often sung of the Holy One, the future Christ. And yet, as he walked on his housetop, he was fascinated by Bathsheba's nakedness and added murder to adultery (2 Sam 11). Notice here how a man cannot use his eyes without danger even in his own house. Then, repenting, he says to the Lord, *Against you alone have*

I sinned and done this evil in your sight (Ps 51:4). Being a king, he feared no one else. So, too, with Solomon. Wisdom used him to sing her praise, and he treated of all plants *from the cedar tree that is in Lebanon to the hyssop that springs out of the wall* (1 Kings 4:33). Yet he withdrew from God because he was a lover of women (1 Kings 11:1–4). And as if to show that near relationship is no safeguard, Amnon burned with illicit passion for his sister Tamar (2 Sam 13).

(13) I cannot bring myself to speak of the many virgins who daily fail and are lost to the bosom of the Church, their mother: stars over which the proud foe sets up his throne (Isa 14:13) and rocks hollowed by the serpent that he may dwell in the fissures. You may see many women dressed as widows before they have married, who try to conceal their miserable fall by adopting a deceitful way of dressing. Unless they are betrayed by swelling wombs or by the crying of their babies, they walk abroad with tripping feet and heads in the air. Some go so far as to take potions to ensure barrenness, and thus murder human beings almost before their conception. Some, when they find themselves pregnant through their sin, use drugs to procure an abortion, and when (as often happens) they die with their offspring, they enter the lower world, laden with the guilt not only of adultery against Christ, but also of suicide and child murder. Yet these are the ones who say, "*To the pure all things are pure* (Tit 1:15). My conscience is guide enough for me. A pure heart is what God looks for. Why should I abstain from food that God has created to be used?" And when they want to appear agreeable and entertaining, they first drench themselves with wine and then, joining the grossest profanity to intoxication, they say, "Far be it from me to abstain from the blood of Christ." When they see another woman looking pale and sad, they call her a "wretch" or a "Manichean," quite logically in fact, for by their principles, fasting involves heresy. When they go out, they do their best to attract notice and, with nods and winks, encourage troops of young men to follow them. To each and all of them the prophet's words apply: *You have a whore's face; you refuse to be ashamed* (Jer 3:3). Their robes have only a narrow

purple stripe,[1] it is true, and their heads are bound somewhat loosely, to leave the hair flowing. Their slippers are cheap, and little capes flutter over their shoulders. Narrow sleeves cling to their arms, and they walk in a mincing manner, with bent knees. This is the extent of their virginity. Let them have their own admirers of this type and let them perish for a higher price under the pretext of their virginity. To virgins such as these I prefer to be displeasing. (14) I am ashamed to speak of it—it is so shocking—but it is true. How comes this plague of the *agapetae* to be in the Church?[2] Whence come these unwedded wives, this new race of concubines, these women who are harlots though they cling to a single partner? They and their partners occupy the same house, the same bedroom, and often the same bed—and then they call us suspicious if we believe something is wrong. A brother leaves his virgin sister; a virgin despises her bachelor brother and seeks a brother in a stranger; but though they both pretend to have the same intention, namely, to seek spiritual consolation from people not related to them, their real aim is to have sexual intercourse. It is on people of this kind whom God in the book of the Proverbs of Solomon pours his reproaches, saying, *Who will bind fire to his bosom and not set his clothes on fire? Or who will walk on coals of fire and not burn his feet?* (Prov 6:27–28).

(15) We cast out therefore and banish from our sight those who wish only to seem and not be virgins. Hereafter, all my speech is directed toward you. Just as it is your fate to be the first virgin of noble birth in the city of Rome, so must you labor the more diligently, in order not to lack both the good things of the present day and the good things to come. You have learned at any rate, from the example of your own family, about the troubles of wedded life and the uncertainty of marriage. Your sister Blesilla, more advanced in age than you but less advanced in her vow, has become a widow in the seventh month after tak-

ing a husband. O how unhappy is our human condition, ignorant of what is to come! She has lost both the crown of virginity and the pleasure of marriage. Although the second degree of chastity is still hers as a widow, can you imagine her bearing her continual crosses, moment by moment, when every day she sees in her sister what she herself has lost and finds it more difficult [than you] to be without the pleasure of marriage, having experienced it, and yet to receive a lesser reward for her present continence? Let her nevertheless feel secure and full of joy. The fruit that is a hundredfold and the fruit that is sixtyfold both spring from the same seed, which is chastity (Matt 13:8).

(16) I do not want you to associate with married women. I do not want you to visit the houses of the nobility. I do not want you to see frequently the things that you spurned in desiring to be a virgin. What if silly little women are in the habit of priding themselves on the fact that their husbands are judges and occupy positions of some dignity, if an eager crowd of visitors collects at the door of the emperor's wife? Why do you, the bride of God, hurry to visit the wife of a mere human being? Learn in this respect a holy pride. Know that you are better than they. I want you not only to avoid social intercourse with those women, who are puffed up by their husbands' honors, who are hedged in by troops of eunuchs, and are clad in robes delicately worked with metallic threads, but also to flee from those who are widows. It is not that they ought to have desired the death of their husbands, but that, their husbands having died, they have not gladly seized the opportunity for continence. As it is, they have only changed their clothes; their former ambition remains unchanged. A row of eunuchs walks in front of their enclosed litters, their cheeks are ruddy and their skin is stretched over such well-nourished flesh that you would think they had not lost husbands, but were looking for them. Their houses are full of flatterers and full of guests. Even the clergy, who ought to be held in authority and respect, kiss their patronesses on the forehead and, putting out their hands in such a way that you would think if you did not know otherwise, that they wanted to confer a blessing, accept fees for their visits. In the

---

[1] A marker of low social status.
[2] Literally "beloved ones," ascetic women who cohabited with celibate men.

meantime, the women, seeing that the priests cannot manage without their protection, are lifted up with pride, and because, having experienced the domination of marriage, they prefer the freedom of widowhood, they are called chaste women and nuns, and, after a dubious dinner, they fall asleep to dream of the apostles.

(17) Let your companions be women who, as you see for yourself, are thin from fasting, whose faces are pale, whose worth is proved by their age and conduct, who daily sing in their hearts, *Where do you feed your flock and where do you bring it to rest at noon?* (Song 1:7), and who say with real earnestness, *I desire to be released and to be with Christ* (Phil 1:23). Be subject to your parents; imitate your Bridegroom. Let your outings be rare, and let the aid of the martyrs be sought in your own room. You will never need a pretext for going out if you always go out when it is necessary. Your food should be moderate in quantity, and your belly should never be overfull. Indeed, very many women, while temperate with wine, are intemperate with food. When you rise at night to pray, let your breath be that of an empty and not of an overladen stomach. Read often and learn as much as you can. Let sleep steal over you as you hold the book and let the holy page catch your head as it falls. Let fasting be a daily occurrence and avoid satiety in your refreshment. It is unprofitable to put up with an empty stomach if, in two or three days' time, the fast is to be compensated for by eating your fill. When clogged, the mind immediately grows sluggish, and when the ground is watered, it puts up thorns of lust. If you feel the outward man sighing for the flower of youth and if, as you lie on your couch after a meal, you are excited by an alluring train of sexual desires, then seize the shield of faith, for it alone can quench the fiery darts of the devil (Eph 6:16). *They are all adulterers,* says the prophet, *their hearts are like an oven* (Hos 7:4, 6). But you, keep close to the footsteps of Christ, and intent upon his words, say, *Did not our heart burn within us on the road, while Jesus opened the Scriptures to us?* (Luke 24:32), and again, *Your word is ablaze and your servant loves it* (Ps 119:140). It is hard for the human soul to avoid loving something, and our mind must necessarily yield to affection of one kind or another. The love of the flesh is overcome by the love of the spirit. Desire is quenched by desire. What is taken from the one increases the other. Therefore, as you lie on your couch, say again and again, *On my bed by night have I sought him, whom my soul loves* (Song 3:1). *Mortify your members on earth,* says the Apostle (Col 3:5). Because he himself did so, he could afterward say with confidence, *I live, yet not I, but Christ, lives in me* (Gal 2:20). Someone who mortifies his members and feels he is walking in a vain show (Ps 39:6) is not afraid to say, *I have become like a wineskin in the frost* (Ps 119:83). Whatever there was in me of the moisture of lust has been dried out of me, and again, *My knees are weak through fasting; I have forgotten to eat my bread. By reason of the voice of my groaning, my bones cleave to my flesh* (Pss 109:24; 102:5).

(18) Be like the grasshopper at night. Wash your bed every night and water your couch with your tears (Ps 6:6). Watch and be like the sparrow in your solitude (Ps 102:7). Sing with the spirit and sing with the understanding (1 Cor 14:15), too, the psalm, *Bless the Lord, O my soul, and do not forget all his benefits. He forgives all your iniquities; he heals all your infirmities and redeems your life from destruction* (Ps 103:2–4). Can we, any of us, honestly make his words our own, *I have eaten ashes like bread and mixed my drink with my tears* (Ps 102:9)? Yet should I not weep and groan when the serpent again invites me to eat forbidden food? When, after ejecting me from the paradise of virginity, he wishes to clothe me with the tunics of skins that Elijah, on his return to paradise, cast down behind him on earth (2 Kings 2:13)? What have I to do with sensual pleasures that soon come? What have I to do with the sweet but deadly song of the sirens? I want you not to submit to that sentence, whereby condemnation is brought upon humankind: *In pain and sorrow, woman, shall you bear children* (Gen 3:16)—say to yourself, "That is not my law"—or its continuation, *and your yearning shall be for your husband.* Let yearning for her husband belong to the woman who has not Christ for her spouse. When at the least God says, *You shall die* (Gen 2:17), that is the end of the union: say to yourself, "My purpose is to be without sex. Let those who

are wives keep their own time and status. For me, virginity is consecrated in the persons of Mary and Christ."

(19) Someone may say, "Do you dare detract from wedlock, which is a state blessed by the Lord?" I do detract from wedlock when I set virginity before it. No one compares a bad thing with a good. Married women are to be congratulated for coming next after virgins. *Increase,* says God, *and multiply and replenish the earth* (Gen 1:28). Anyone who wants to replenish the earth may increase and multiply if he wishes, but the marching column to which you belong is not on earth, but in heaven. The command to increase and multiply first finds fulfillment after the expulsion from paradise, after the nakedness and the fig leaves, which betoken sexual passion. Let marry and be given in marriage the person who eats his bread in the sweat of his brow, whose land produces figs and thistles (Gen 3:18), and whose crops are choked with briars. My seed produces fruit a hundredfold. *Not everyone can receive the word of God, but only those to whom it is given* (Matt 19:11). Some people may be eunuchs from necessity; I am one by free will (cf. Matt 19:12). *There is a time to embrace and a time to withdraw the hands from the embrace. There is a time to cast away stones and a time to gather stones together* (Eccl 3:5). Now that God has raised up children from Abraham out of the hard stones of the gentiles (Matt 3:9), they begin to be *holy stones rolling on the earth* (Zech 9:16 [LXX]). They pass through the world's whirlwinds and roll on in God's chariot on rapid wheels. Let people stitch coats for themselves who have lost the coat woven from the top throughout (John 19:23), who delight in the cries of infants who, as soon as they see the light, lament that they were born. In paradise Eve was a virgin, and it was only after the coats of skins that she began her married life. Now, paradise is your home, too. Keep your birthright therefore and say, *Return to your rest, O my soul* (Ps 116:7). To show that virginity is natural, while wedlock only follows guilt, what is born of wedlock is virgin flesh, and it gives back in fruit what in root it has lost. *There shall come forth a rod out of the root of Jesse, and a flower shall arise from the*

root (Isa 11:1). The rod is the Lord's mother[3]—simple, pure, unsullied, drawing no germ of life from outside herself, but fruitful in singleness, like God himself. The flower of the rod is Christ, who says of himself, *I am the flower of the field and the lily of the valley* (Song 2:1). In another place he is foretold to be *a stone cut out of the mountain without hands* (Dan 2:45), a figure by which the prophet signifies that he is to be born a virgin of a virgin. For the hands here are a figure of wedlock, as in the passage, *His left hand is under my head and his right hand embraces me* (Song 2:6). This agrees, too, with the interpretation that unclean animals were led into Noah's ark in pairs, while of the clean an uneven number were taken (Gen 7:2). Similarly, that Moses and Joshua were ordered to enter on holy ground in their bare feet (Exod 3:5; Josh 5:15), whereas the disciples were appointed to preach the gospel unburdened by sandals or leather shoelaces (Matt 10:10), and also that the soldiers, after Jesus' clothing had been distributed by lot, found no boots they could take away (John 19:23–24). For the Lord could not himself possess what he had forbidden his servants to possess.

(20) I praise wedlock, I praise marriage, but only because they produce virgins for me. I gather the rose from the thorns, the gold from the earth, the pearl from the shell. *Does the plowman plow all day to sow?* (Isa 28:24). Shall he not also enjoy the fruit of his labor? Wedlock is more honored, when what is born of it is more loved. Why, mother, do you envy your daughter? She has been nourished with your milk, she has been brought forth from your womb, and she has grown up at your bosom. Your watchful religious faith has kept her a virgin. Are you angry with her because she wishes to be the wife not of a soldier, but of a king? She has conferred a great benefit on you; you now begin to be the mother-in-law of God. *Concerning virgins,* says the Apostle, *I have no commandment from the Lord* (1 Cor 7:25). Why was this? Because his own virginity was due, not to a command, but to his free choice. Those people who

---

[3] A Latin pun between *virga* (rod) and *virgo* (virgin).

claim that he had a wife should not be listened to, since when he is discussing continence and commending perpetual chastity, he uses the words, *I wish that all men were as I am* (1 Cor 7:7), and farther on, *I say, therefore, to the unmarried and the widowed: "It is good for them if they remain just as I am"* (1 Cor 7:8), and in another place, *Have we no right to be accompanied by a wife, as are the rest of the apostles?* (1 Cor 9:5). Why then has he no commandment from the Lord concerning virginity? Because what is freely offered is worth more than what is extorted by force, and to command virginity would have been to abrogate wedlock. It would have been a hard enactment to compel opposition to nature and to extort the angelic life, and not only that, it would have been to condemn what is a divine ordinance.

(21) The old law had a different ideal of blessedness. There it is said, *Blessed is he who has seed in Zion and a household in Jerusalem* (Isa 31:9 [LXX]), and *Cursed is the barren woman who does not bear children* (Isa 54:1), and *Your children shall be like olive shoots round about your table* (Ps 128:3). Riches, too, are promised to the faithful, and we are told that *there was not one feeble person among their tribes* (Ps 105:37). But now it is said, *Do not say, behold I am a dry tree* (Isa 56:3), for instead of sons and daughters, you have a place forever in heaven. Now the poor are blessed, now Lazarus is set before Dives in purple (cf. Luke 16:19–21). Now a weak person is counted as strong. But in those days the world was still unpeopled: accordingly, to pass over instances of childlessness meant only to serve as types, only those who could boast of children were considered happy. It was for this reason that Abraham in his old age married Keturah (Gen 25:1), that Leah hired Jacob with her son's mandrakes (Gen 30:14–16), and that the beautiful Rachel—a type of the Church—complained of the closing of her womb (Gen 30:1–2). But gradually the crop grew up, and then the reaper was sent forth with this sickle. Elijah lived a virgin life, as did Elisha and many of the sons of the prophets. To Jeremiah came the command, *Do not take a wife* (Jer 16:2). He had been sanctified in his mother's womb (Jer 1:5) and was forbidden to take a wife because the

captivity was near. The Apostle gives the same advice in different words, *I think that it is good on account of the present distress, namely, that it is good for a man to remain as he is* (1 Cor 7:26). What is this distress that does away with the joys of wedlock? The Apostle tells us in a later verse, *The time is short. From now on even those who have wives should be as though they had not* (1 Cor 7:29). Nebuchadnezzar is close by. *The lion is stirring from his lair.* What good will marriage be to me if it ends in slavery to the haughtiest of kings? What good will little ones be to me if their lot is to be that which the prophet sadly describes: *The tongue of the sucking child clings to the roof of its mouth in thirst; the young children asked for bread, and there was no one to break it for them* (Lam 4:4). In those days, as I have said, the virtue of continence was found only in men; Eve continued to give birth in pain. But now that a virgin has conceived in her womb (Isa 7:14) and has borne to us a child of whom the prophet says, *The government shall be upon his shoulder, and his name shall be the mighty God, the everlasting Father* (Isa 9:6), the chain of the curse is broken. Death came through Eve, but life has come through Mary. Thus the gift of virginity has been very richly bestowed on women, in that it had its beginning from a woman. As soon as the Son of God set foot on the earth, he formed a new household for himself there, so that, as he was adored by angels in heaven, angels might serve him also on earth. Then chaste Judith once more cut off the head of Holofernes (Judith 13). Then Haman—whose name means iniquity—was once more burned in a fire of his own kindling (Esth 7:10). Then James and John forsook father and net and ship and followed the Savior, abandoning ties of kinship, bonds of secular life, and the care of their homes. Then were heard the words; *Let the person who chooses to come after me deny himself, take up his cross, and follow me* (Mark 8:34). No soldier goes to battle with a wife. When a disciple wanted to bury his father, the Lord forbade it and said, *Foxes have holes and the birds of heaven have nests, but the Son of Man has nowhere to lay his head* (Matt 8:20–22). So you must not complain if you are lodged in cramped quarters. *The man who is without a wife cares for the things that belong to the Lord and how he may please the Lord, but the married man cares for the things that are of this world and how he may please his wife. There is the difference also between a wife and a virgin. The unmarried woman cares for the things of the Lord, that she may be holy both in body and in spirit, but the married woman cares for the things of this world and how she may please her husband* (1 Cor 7:32–34).

(22) What great inconveniences are involved in wedlock and how many anxieties encompass it I have, I think, described briefly in my treatise—published against Helvidius—on the perpetual virginity of blessed Mary. It would be tedious to go over the same ground now, and anyone who pleases may draw that fountain. But lest I seem wholly to have passed over the matter, I will say now simply that the Apostle bids us pray without ceasing (1 Thess 5:17), and that someone in the married state who gives his wife her due (1 Cor 7:3) cannot so pray. Either we pray always and are virgins, or we cease to pray to fulfill the claims of marriage. Still he says, *If a virgin marries, she has not sinned. Nevertheless she will have trouble of this kind in her flesh* (1 Cor 7:28). At the outset I promised that I should say little or nothing of the embarrassments of wedlock, and now I give you notice to the same effect. If you want to know how many vexations a virgin is free of and how many a wife is fettered by, you should read Tertullian, "To a Philosophic Friend,"[4] and his other treatises on virginity, the blessed Cyprian's noble volume, the writings of Pope Damascus in prose and verse, and the treatises recently written for his sister by our own Ambrose. In these he has poured forth his soul in such a flood of eloquence that he has sought out, set forth, and put in order everything that bears on the praise of virgins.

(23) We must proceed by a different path, for our purpose is not to exalt virginity, but to preserve it. To know that it is a good thing is not enough; when we have chosen it, we must guard it with jealous care. The first requires only judgment, and this we share with many; the second calls for toil, and few compete

with us in it. *The person who perseveres to the end shall be saved* (Matt 24:13), and *Many are called, but few chosen* (Matt 22:14). Therefore I entreat you, before God and Jesus Christ and his chosen angels, so to guard what you have received, not readily exposing to the public gaze the vessels of the Lord's temple (which only the priests are by right allowed to see), that no profane person may look upon God's sanctuary. Uzzah, when he touched the ark, which it was not lawful to touch, was suddenly struck down by death (2 Sam 6:6–7), and assuredly no gold or silver vessel was ever so dear to God as is the temple of a virgin's body. The shadow went before, but now the reality is come. You may indeed speak in all simplicity, and from motives of amiability may treat even strangers with courtesy, but unchaste eyes see nothing aright. They fail to appreciate the beauty of the soul and value only that of the body. Hezekiah showed God's treasure to the Assyrians (2 Kings 20:12–13), who ought never to have seen what they were sure to covet. The consequence was that Judaea was ravaged by continual wars and that the very first things carried away to Babylon were these same vessels of the Lord. We find Belshazzar at his feast and among his concubines drinking out of these sacred cups (Dan 5:1–3)—vice always glories in defiling what is noble.

(24) Never incline your ear to words of mischief. Men often say an improper word to try a virgin's steadfastness, to see if she hears it with pleasure, and if she is ready to unbend at every silly joke. Such persons applaud whatever you affirm and deny whatever you deny; they speak of you as not only holy, but accomplished and say that in you there is no guile. "Behold a true handmaid of Christ," they say. "Behold her complete singleness of heart. She is not like that uncouth, ill-bred country bumpkin of frightful appearance, who perhaps for that reason could not find a husband." Led by our sinful nature, we readily favor those who flatter us, and although we reply that we are unworthy, and a warm blush suffuses our cheeks, nevertheless our inmost heart rejoices at our own praise.

Like the ark of the covenant, Christ's spouse should be overlaid with gold within and without

---

[4] This treatise is not extant.

(Exod 25:11). She should be the guardian of the law of the Lord. Just as the ark contained nothing but the tables of the covenant (1 Kings 8:9), so in you there should be no thought of anything that is outside. The Lord wishes to sit on this mercy seat—your thoughts—as on the cherubim (Exod 25:22). He sends his disciples so that they may loose you from worldly cares, as they loosed the colt, the foal of an ass (Matt 21:5), in order that you may leave the bricks and straw of Egypt (Exod 5), follow Moses into the wilderness, and enter the promised land (Deut 27–32). Let no one forbid you to do this, not your mother or your sister or your kinswoman or your brother. The Lord needs you (Matt 21:1–3). If they want to hinder you, let them fear the scourges that fell upon Pharaoh, who, because he would not allow the people of God to depart to worship him, suffered those things that are written in the Scriptures (Exod 7–12). Jesus entering into the temple cast out everything that did not belong in the temple (Matt 21:12). God is jealous and will not allow the father's house to be made into a robbers' den (Matt 21:13). Moreover, where money is counted; where doves are sold; where simplicity is stifled; where, that is, a virgin's breast glows with the cares of this world, the veil of the temple is immediately rent (Matt 27:51), and the Bridegroom rises in anger, saying, *Your house shall be left desolate* (Matt 23:38). Read the Gospel and see how Mary, sitting at the feet of the Lord, is preferred to the zealous Martha. In her eagerness to be hospitable, Martha was preparing a meal for the Lord and his disciples, yet Jesus said to her, *Martha, Martha, you are worried and distressed about many things, but few things, or one, are necessary. Mary has chosen the good part, which shall not be taken away from her* (Luke 10:41–42). Be like Mary, then. Prefer spiritual knowledge to bodily food. Leave it to your sisters to run to and fro and to seek how they may receive Christ as their guest. Having once and for all flung away the burden of the world, sit at the Lord's feet and say, *I have found him for whom my soul was seeking; I will hold him, and I will not let him go* (Song 3:4). And he will reply, *My dove, my perfect one is my only one; she is the only one of her mother, the chosen one of her who bore her, that is, the heavenly Jerusalem* (Song 6:9; Gal 4:26). (25) Always let the privacy of your bedroom keep guard over you; always let your Bridegroom disport himself with you within it. You pray, you speak to him there, and you read there. There he speaks to you, and, when sleep assails you, he will come behind the wall and put his hand through an opening and will touch your belly. You will arise, trembling, and will say, *I am wounded by love* (Song 5:2, 4, 8). *My sister, my betrothed, is a garden enclosed, a fountain sealed* (Song 4:12).

Be careful not to leave your home and do not wish to see the daughters of a foreign country when you have the patriarchs for your brothers and rejoice in Israel as your father. Dinah went out and was corrupted (Gen 34). I do not want you to search for your Bridegroom in the thoroughfares or to go around the nooks and crannies of the city. For though you may say, *I will rise and walk around in the city, in the marketplace and in the main streets, and search for him whom my soul loves,* and you may inquire, *Have you seen him whom my soul loves?* (Song 3:2–3), no one will condescend to answer you. The Bridegroom cannot be found in the streets. *Straight and narrow is the way that leads to life* (Matt 7:14). Then there follows [in the Song of Songs], *I have sought him and I have not found him; I have called him and he has not responded to my call* (Song 3:2, 5:6). If only failure to find him were all! You will be wounded, you will be stripped naked, and you will groan, as you relate, *The watchmen who patrol the city found me; they struck me; they wounded me; they took my cloak away from me* (Song 5:7). Now if someone who could say, *I am asleep, but my heart is awake* (Song 5:2), and *My brother is a bunch of myrrh for me; he shall remain all night between my breasts* (Song 1:13), if someone who could say such things suffered so much when she went out from her house, what will happen to us, who are still young girls and who still remain outside, when the bride goes in with the Bridegroom? Jesus is jealous. He does not want your face to be seen by others. Although you may make excuses and say, "I have covered my face closely with a veil and have sought you and have said to you, *Tell me, you whom my soul loves, where you feed your flock, where you sleep at midday, lest I may ever become as one covered with a veil in the presence of the flocks of your companions* (Song 1:7)," he will be angry and will swell with rage and will say, "*If you do not know yourself, fairest of women, go forth in the steps of my flocks and feed your goats in the shepherds' tents* (Song 1:8). You may be fair and of all faces yours may be the dearest to the Bridegroom. Yet, unless you know yourself (Song 1:9) and keep your heart with utmost diligence (Prov 4:23), unless also you avoid the eyes of young men, you will be turned out of my bride chamber to feed the goats, which shall be set on the left hand (Matt 25:33)."

(26) These things being so, my Eustochium, daughter, lady, fellow servant, sister—these names refer, the first to your age, the second to your rank, the third to your religious vocation, the last to the place you hold in my affection—hear the words of Isaiah, *My people, enter into your bedrooms and shut your doors; hide yourself for a brief moment, until the anger of the Lord has passed over* (Isa 26:20). Let foolish virgins stray outside; you be indoors with your Bridegroom because if you shut your door and, in accordance with the precept of the Gospel (Matt 6:6), pray to your Father in secret, he will come and knock and say, *Behold, I stand at the door and knock. If anyone will open it to me, I will enter and dine with him and he with me* (Rev 3:20). Then at once you will eagerly reply, "It is the voice of my kinsman, who knocks: open the door to me, my sisters, my nearest and dearest, my dove, my perfect one." It is impossible that you should refuse and say, *I have taken off my tunic; how shall I put it on? I have washed my feet; how shall I defile them?* (Song 5:3). Get up at once and open the door. Otherwise he may pass on as you linger, and you may have mournfully to say, *I opened the door to my kinsman, but my kinsman has passed by* (Song 5:6). Why do the doors of your heart need to be closed to the Bridegroom? Let them be open to Christ, but closed to the devil, according to the saying, *If the spirit of him who has power rises up against you, do not leave your place* (Eccl 10:4). Daniel, in that upper room to which he withdrew when he could no longer continue below, had its windows open toward Jerusalem (Dan 6:10). Keep your windows open, too, but only on the side where light may enter and from which you may see the city of God. Do not open those other windows, of which the prophet says, *Death has entered through our windows* (Jer 9:21).

(27) You must also take care to avoid being seized with a passion for vainglory. *How,* says Jesus, *can you believe, when you receive glory from men?* (John 5:44). See how evil a thing it is, when the person who possesses it cannot believe. Instead, let us say, *You are my glory* (Jer 9:24), and *Let anyone who glories, glory in the Lord* (1 Cor 1:31), and *If I still pleased people, I should not be the servant of Christ* (Gal 1:10). *Far be it from me to glory, save in the cross of my Lord Jesus Christ, through whom the world has been crucified to me and I to the world* (Gal 6:14), and finally, *In you we boast all the day long; my soul shall make her boast in the Lord* (Pss 44:8, 34:2). When you give alms, let God alone see you. When you fast, let your face be cheerful (Matt 6:3, 16). Let your dress be neither overly neat nor overly careless. Neither let it be so remarkable as to draw the attention of passersby and to make people point their fingers at you. Is a brother dead? Has the body of a sister to be carried to burial? Take care lest while you perform these offices, you yourself die. Do not wish to seem very devout or more humble than need be, lest you seek glory by shunning it. Many who screen their poverty, charity, and fasting from public view want to excite admiration by their very disdain of it and strangely look for praise while they profess to keep out of its way. From the other disturbing influences that make people rejoice, despond, hope, and fear, I find many free, but this is a defect that few are without, and he is best, whose character, like a beautiful body, is spotted with only very rare disfigurements and blemishes. I do not think it necessary to warn you against boasting of your riches or against priding yourself on your birth or against setting yourself up as superior to others. I know your humility; I know that you can say with sincerity, *Lord, I am not haughty nor do my eyes gaze proudly* (Ps 131:1). I know that in your case, as in your mother's, the pride through which the devil fell has no place in the depths of your being. It would be a waste of time to

write to you about it, for there is no greater folly than to teach a pupil what he already knows. But now that you have despised the boastfulness of the world, do not let the fact inspire you with new boastfulness. Do not harbor the secret thought that, having ceased to court attention in garments of gold, you may begin to do so in mean attire. And when you come into a room full of brothers and sisters, do not sit in too low a place or plead that you are unworthy of a footstool. Do not deliberately lower your voice, as though worn out with fasting, or, leaning on the shoulder of another, mimic the tottering gait of someone who is faint. Some women, it is true, disfigure their faces that they may appear unto men to fast (cf. Matt 6:16). As soon as they catch sight of anyone, they groan and look down; they cover up their faces, except for one eye, which they keep free to see with. Their dress is somber, their belts are made of sackcloth, their hands and feet are dirty; only their stomachs—which cannot be seen—are hot with food. Of these the psalm is sung daily, *God has scattered the bones of men who please themselves* (Ps 53:5). Others change their clothes and assume the appearance of men, being ashamed of being what they were born to be—women. They cut off their hair and shamelessly set themselves up to look like eunuchs. Some clothe themselves in goat's hair and, putting on hoods so they may return to their childhood, make themselves look like night owls and horned owls.

(28) But I want to discuss not only women. Shun men also, when you see them loaded with chains and wearing their hair long like women, contrary to the Apostle's precept (1 Cor 11:14), not to mention beards like those of goats, black cloaks, and bare feet braving the cold. All these things are tokens of the devil. Such were Antimus, over whom Rome groaned some time ago, and Sophronius more recently. Such persons, when they have once gained admission to the houses of the nobility and have deceived *silly little women laden with sins, always learning and never arriving at knowledge of the truth* (2 Tim 3:6–7), assume a gloomy appearance and pretend to undertake long fasts, whereas at night, they feast in secret. Shame forbids me to say more, for my language might appear more like invective than admonition.

There are others—I speak of those of my own order—who seek the priesthood and the diaconate simply to be able to see women with less restraint. Such men think of nothing but their clothing. They use perfumes freely and see that there are no creases in their leather shoes. Their curly hair shows traces of the tongs; their fingers glisten with rings; they walk on tiptoe across a damp road to avoid splashing their feet. When you see men acting this way, think of them as bridegrooms, rather than as clergy. Certain persons have devoted the whole of their energies and lives to the single object of knowing the names, houses, and characters of married ladies. I will here briefly and cursorily describe someone who is at the head of this profession, that from the master's portrait you may more easily recognize his disciples. He rises and goes forth with the sun. The order of his visits is arranged; he seeks the shortest routes and importunately forces his way almost into the bedrooms of ladies while they are still asleep. If he sees a pillow or an elegant tablecloth or some article of domestic furniture, he praises it, admires it, takes it into his hand, and complaining that he lacks such a thing himself, not so much requests as extorts it from its owner because each and every woman [he visits] is afraid to offend the news carrier of the city. Chastity and fasting are alike distasteful to him. For lunch a plump bird with a savory smell—a crane, commonly called a "cheeper"—meets with his approval. He changes his horses every hour, and they are so sleek and spirited that you would take him for a brother of the Thracian king.[5]

(29) Many are the stratagems that the wily enemy employs against us. The serpent was wiser than all the beasts that the Lord God had made upon earth (Gen 3:1). Then the Apostle says, *We are not ignorant of his devices* (2 Cor 2:11). Neither an affected shabbiness nor a stylish smartness becomes a Christian. If there is anything of which you are ignorant, if you have any doubt about the Scriptures, ask someone whose life commends him, whose age places him

---

[5] A reference to the legendary hero Diomede's fierce horses.

above suspicion, whose reputation does not belie him, and who can say, *I have espoused you to one husband, to present you as a chaste virgin to Christ* (2 Cor 11:2). Or if there is no one like this, who can explain things, it is better to be safe but ignorant than to expose yourself to danger in learning. Remember that you walk in the midst of snares and that many virgins of long standing and of a chastity never called into question have, on the very threshold of death, let their crowns fall from their hands.

If any of your handmaids share your purpose, do not set yourself against them or pride yourself because you are their mistress. You have all chosen the same Bridegroom. You sing psalms to Christ at the same time; you receive his Body at the same time. Why, then, should there be a different table for them? Let others, too, receive the challenge. Let the office of virgin be an invitation to the rest. If you find one of them weak in the faith, be attentive to her, comfort her, caress her, and make her chastity your treasure. But if a girl pretends to have a vocation because she wants to escape from service, read aloud to her the words of the Apostle, *It is better to marry than to burn* (1 Cor 7:9).

Shun like the plague those women, whether virgins or widows, who go from house to house calling on married women from idle curiosity and who display an unblushing effrontery like that of a parasite on the stage. For *evil communications corrupt good manners* (1 Cor 15:33), and women like this care for nothing but their bellies and what is nearest to their bellies. They will often exhort you this way, saying, "My pet, make the best of your advantages and live while you are alive," and "Surely you are not laying up money for your children." Given to wine and wantonness, they instill all kinds of evil and induce stern minds to indulge in soft pleasures, and *when they have begun to run riot against Christ, they wish to marry and incur damnation because they have rejected their original pledge* (1 Tim 5:11–12).

Do not seek to appear overly eloquent or to trifle with verse or to amuse yourself with lyric songs. And do not, from affectation, follow the feeble taste of married ladies, who now clenching their teeth together, now keeping their lips wide apart, speak with a lisp and purposely clip their words, thinking that anything natural is a sign of rusticity. Therefore an adultery of the tongue is what pleases them. For *what have light and darkness in common? And what agreement is there between Christ and Belial?* (2 Cor 6:14–15). How can Horace go with the psalter, Vergil with the Gospels, Cicero with the Apostle? Is not a brother made to stumble if he sees you reclining at table in an idol's temple? Although *to the pure all things are pure* (Tit 1:15) and *nothing is to be refused, which is received with thanksgiving* (1 Tim 4:4), still we ought not to drink the cup of Christ and, at the same time, the cup of devils. I will tell you the story of my own unhappy experience.

(30) Many years ago, when, for the kingdom of heaven's sake, I had cut myself off from my home, my parents, my sister, my relatives, and—still more difficult than this—from the exquisite food to which I had been accustomed, and when I was on my way to Jerusalem to wage my warfare, I still could not bring myself to forgo the library that I had collected with great care and toil for myself at Rome. Miserable man that I was, I used to fast for the purpose of reading Cicero. After frequent nightly vigils, after tears that the recollection of my past sins brought forth from the depths of my heart, I took Plautus in my hands. If ever I returned to my right mind and began to read a prophet, his uncultivated style caused me to shrink from him with horror. Because I failed to see the light with my blinded eyes, I attributed the fault not to them but to the sun. While the old serpent was playing with me this way, about the middle of Lent a deep-seated fever attacked my body, which was worn out and totally lacked rest. It is almost incredible to say this, but it so wasted my unhappy limbs that my flesh scarcely clung to my bones. As preparations for my funeral were going on, my body gradually grew colder, and the warmth of life lingered only in my throbbing breast. Suddenly I was caught up in the spirit and dragged before the tribunal of the Judge. And here the light was so bright, and those who stood around were so radiant, that I threw myself to the ground and did not dare to look up. Asked who and what I was, I replied, "I am a Christian." But he who was sitting there said, "You lie; you

are a follower of Cicero and not of Christ. For *where your treasure is, there will your heart be also* (Matt 6:21)." Instantly I became dumb, and amid the strokes of the lash—for he had ordered me to be scourged—I was tortured still more severely by the fire of conscience, considering within myself that verse, *In the grave who shall give you thanks?* (Ps 6:5). Yet for all that, I began to cry and to bewail myself, saying, "Have mercy upon me, O Lord: have mercy upon me." Amid the sound of the scourges this cry still made itself heard. At last the people who were standing by fell down before the knees of him who presided and prayed that he would have pity on my youth and would give me space to repent of my error. He might still, they urged, inflict torture on me, should I ever again read pagan literature. By the stress of that awful moment, I should have been ready to make still larger promises than these. Accordingly, I swore an oath and called upon his name, saying, "Lord, if ever again I possess worldly books, or if ever again I read them, I have denied you." Dismissed, on taking this oath, then, I returned to the upper world, and to everyone's surprise, I opened on them eyes so drenched with tears that my distress served to convince even the incredulous, and that this was no sleep or idle dream, such as those by which we are often mocked, I call to witness the tribunal before which I lay and the judgment that I feared. May it never be my lot to fall under such an inquisition! I profess that my shoulders were bruised, that I felt the bruises long after I awoke from my sleep, and that thereafter I read the holy books with an enthusiasm greater than I had previously given to human writings.

(31) You must also avoid the sin of covetousness, not only by not seizing what belongs to others—for that is punished by the laws of the state—but also by not keeping your own property, which has now become no longer yours. *If you have not been faithful regarding the property of another,* says the Lord, *who will give you your own property?* (Luke 16:12). "The property of another" is a quantity of gold or silver, while our own property is the spiritual heritage, of which it is said elsewhere, *The ransom of a man's life is his riches* (Prov 13:8) . . . *No one can serve two*

masters, for either he will hate the one and love the other, or else he will hate the one and love the other, or else he will bear with one and despise the other. You cannot serve God and Mammon (Matt 6:24)—riches, that is, for in the pagan tongue of the Syrians, riches are called Mammon. The *thorns* that choke our faith are *taking thought for our life* (Matt 6:25); the root of covetousness is *care for what the Gentiles seek* (Matt 6:32).

"But," you will say, "I am a girl who has been delicately nurtured, and I cannot work with my hands. If I live to old age and then fall sick, who will take pity on me?" Hear Jesus speaking to the apostles, *Do not ponder in your heart over what you will eat or yet over what clothes you will put on your body. Is not the soul more than food and the body more than clothes? Look at the birds in the sky, for they do not sow or reap or gather food into barns, yet your heavenly Father feeds them* (Matt 6:25–26). Should you lack clothing, set the lilies before your eyes. Should hunger seize you, think of the words in which the poor and hungry are blessed. Should pain afflict you, read, *Therefore I take pleasure in my infirmities* (2 Cor 12:10), and *There has been given me a thorn in my flesh, a messenger of Satan, to buffet me, lest I should become proud* (2 Cor 12:7). Rejoice in all God's judgments. Does not the psalmist say, *The daughters of Judah rejoiced in all your judgments, O Lord* (Ps 97:8). Let these words be always sounding on your lips, *I came naked out of my mother's womb, and naked shall I return to it* (Job 1:21), and *We brought nothing into this world, and we shall carry nothing out of it* (1 Tim 6:7).

(32) Nowadays you see a number of women cramming their cupboards with clothes and changing their tunics daily, but still unable to conquer the moths. A woman who is more scrupulous may wear out one dress, yet she is in rags while her chests are full. Parchments are tinted purple, liquid gold is poured out for lettering, and manuscripts are decked with jewels, and yet the naked Christ perishes on their doorsteps. When they stretch out their hands [to give alms], they sound a trumpet (Matt 6:2); when they summon guests to a love feast, a town crier is employed. I recently saw the noblest of Roman ladies—

I suppress her name, for fear you should think I am being satirical—with eunuchs preceding her into the basilica of Saint Peter, distributing a penny apiece to the poor with her own hand, so that she might be thought more religious. While this was happening, as is quite a familiar occurrence, an old woman, full of years and rags, ran forward to receive a second coin, but when her turn came, she received not a coin but a blow from a fist, and guilty blood flowed from her veins.

Covetousness is the root of all evil (1 Tim 6:10), and the Apostle speaks of it as idolatry (Col 3:5). *Seek first the kingdom of God, and all these things will be added to you* (Matt 6:33). The Lord will not slay the soul of a righteous man by hunger. *I was young,* says the psalmist, *and now I am old, and I have never seen the righteous man forsaken or his seed begging bread* (Ps 37:25). Elijah was fed by the ministering ravens (1 Kings 17:4). The widow of Sarepta, who with her sons expected to die the same night, went without food herself so she could feed the prophet. He who had come to be fed then turned feeder, for by a miracle, he filled the empty barrel (1 Kings 17:9–16). The apostle Peter says, *Silver and gold have I none, but what I have I give you. In the name of Jesus Christ, get up and walk* (Acts 3:6). But many, though they do not say it in words, do so in deeds: "Faith and pity I have none, but what I have, gold and silver, I do not give you. *As we have food and clothing, we are content with these* (1 Tim 6:8)." Hear what Jacob asks in his prayers: *If the Lord God will be with me and preserve me on this road by which I am traveling and will give me bread to eat and clothing to wear,* [then shall the Lord be my God] (Gen 28:20–21). He prayed only for what was necessary, yet twenty years later, he returned to the land of Canaan a rich master and richer still as a father (Gen 33:5, 10). Innumerable examples are available from the Scriptures, which also teach us to shun covetousness (cf. Luke 12:15).

(33) But since something is now being said on covetousness as a side issue—and it will be treated in a book to itself, if Christ permits—I will relate what took place at Nitria not very many years ago. A brother, who was thrifty rather than covetous and was

unaware that the Lord had been sold for thirty pieces of silver (Matt 26:15), left behind him a hundred pieces of money that he had earned by weaving flax. The monks took counsel together—there were about five thousand of them living at the same place in as many separate cells—as to what they ought to do. Some said that the coins should be distributed to the poor, others that they should be given to the Church, and yet others that they should be sent back to the relatives of the dead monk. Macarius, Pambo, Isidore, and the rest, whom they call Fathers, at the prompting of the Holy Spirit speaking within them, decided, however, that they should be buried with their owner, with the words, *May your money go with you to perdition* (Acts 8:20). Nor was each monk to think harshly of what had been done; so great a fear has assailed all monks throughout Egypt that it is now a crime to leave behind oneself a single *solidus.*

(34) Since we have made mention of the monks, and I know that you like to hear about what is holy, lend an ear to me for a few moments.

There are in Egypt three classes of monks. First, there are the cenobites, whom in their pagan language they call *Sauses,* but whom we can call men living in community. Second, there are the anchorites, who live in the desert, each man by himself, and are so-called because they have withdrawn from human society. Third, there is the class called *Remnuoth,* a very inferior and little regarded type, though in my own province this is the main, if not the only, sort. These live together in twos and threes, but seldom in larger numbers, and are bound by no rule but do exactly as they choose. A portion of their earnings they contribute to a common fund, out of which food is provided for all. In most cases they reside in cities and strongholds, and as if it were their skill that is holy and not their life, everything they sell is extremely dear. There are often quarrels among them because living as they do on their own food, they do not allow themselves to be subordinate to another. It is true that they vie with one another in their fasting, and they make what should be secret an occasion for boasting. Everything about them is affected: their sleeves are loose, their boots bulge, and their clothing is very coarse. They sigh frequently; they pay visits to virgins; they run down the secular clergy; and whenever a feast day occurs, they eat until they are sick.

(35) Having therefore rid ourselves of these people as though they were so many pests, let us come to that more numerous sort who live together and who are called, as we have said, cenobites. Among these, the first principle of agreement is to obey the elders and to do whatever they command. They are divided into groups, by tens and by hundreds, so that every tenth man is in authority over nine others, and the hundredth man, in turn, has ten officers placed under him. They live separately, but their cells adjoin one another in groups. Until the ninth hour there is, as it were, a cessation of business. No one may disturb another, except those whom we call deans, so that anyone troubled by wandering thoughts may receive comfort through speaking with them. After the ninth hour, they meet together, psalms ring out, and the Scriptures are read according to custom. When prayers are finished and everyone has sat down, the person whom they call their Father stands up among them and begins to expound the reading. While he is speaking, the silence is so profound that no one dares to look at another or to cough. The speaker's praise is in the weeping of his hearers. Silently their tears roll down their cheeks, but their sorrow does not break out in sobs. Yet when he begins to speak of the kingdom of Christ, of future bliss, and of the glory that is to come, you see all of them sigh gently and, lifting their eyes heavenward, say among themselves, *Who will give me wings like a dove, and I shall fly away and be at rest?* (Ps 55:6). After this the meeting breaks up, and each company of ten goes with its Father to its own table. This they take in turns to serve, each for a week at a time. No noise is made over the food; no one talks while eating. They live on bread, beans, and greens, which are seasoned with salt and oil. Only the old men receive wine. (For them and for children, there is often a meal prepared to sustain the weary old age of the one group and to save the others from premature decay.) When the meal is over, they all rise together and, having recited a hymn, return to their own huts. There each one of them talks until evening with his friends and say, "Do you see so-and-so? How much grace he has! How silent he is! How soberly he walks!" If they see some-

one weak, they comfort him. If they see someone fervent in his love for God, they exhort him to further devotion. And because at night, besides the public prayers, each man keeps vigil in his own sleeping quarters, they go round the cells, one by one, and listening intently to them, carefully ascertain what the occupants are doing. If they find that a man is slothful, they do not scold him, but pretending that they do not know, they visit him more frequently and at first exhort him, rather than compel him, to pray more. A task is allotted for each day, and when this has been given to the dean, he takes it to the steward. The latter, once a month, returns an accurate account to the Father of all the monks in fear and trembling. He also tastes the food after it has been prepared, and as no one is allowed to say, "I have no tunic or blanket or bed of woven rushes," he arranges that no one need ask for or go without what he needs. If a monk falls ill, he is moved to more spacious quarters and there so attentively nursed by the old men that he seeks neither the pleasures of city life nor the affection of a mother. Every Sunday they devote a great deal of time to prayer and reading; indeed, once they have finished their small tasks, they do this all the time. Every day they learn a portion of the Scriptures by heart. They keep the same fasts all year round, with the exception of Lent, in which alone they are allowed to live more strictly. At Pentecost they exchange their evening meal for a midday meal, in order both to satisfy the tradition of the Church and not to burden their stomachs with a double supply of food.

A similar description of the Essenes is given by Philo, the imitator of Plato's discourse, and also by Josephus, the Greek Livy, in his narrative of the Jewish captivity.

(36) As my present subject is virgins, I have said almost too much about monks. I will now come to the third class, whom they call anchorites and who go from monastic communities into the desert and take nothing with them except bread and salt. Paul was the originator of this way of life,[6] Antony made it fa-

---

6 That is, Paul the Hermit, whose saint's life Jerome had written.

mous, and if I may go back farther still, John the Baptist was its pioneer. Jeremiah the prophet describes such a person when he says, *It is good for a man, when he shall have borne the yoke from his youth. He will sit alone and will keep silence because he has borne the yoke upon himself. He will offer his cheek to the man who smites him; he will be filled with reproaches, since the Lord will not cast him away forever* (Lam 3:27–28, 30–31). The struggle of these men and their way of life, in the flesh and yet not in the flesh, I will, if you wish, explain to you some other time. Now let me return to my subject, covetousness, because it was while I was discussing it that I came to the monks. Setting their example before your eyes, you will despise, I will not say gold and silver and other forms of wealth, but the earth itself and heaven. United to Christ, you will sing, *The Lord is my portion* (Lam 3:24).

(37) Furthermore, although the Apostle bids us to pray without ceasing (1 Thess 5:17), and although to the saints their very sleep is prayer, we ought nevertheless to have fixed hours of prayer, so that if we happen to be detained by some piece of work, the time may remind us of our duty. There is no one who does not know that we should pray at the third, sixth, and ninth hours and daybreak and at evening. Take no meal unless it is preceded by prayer, and never depart from the table without returning to the Creator. At night we should get up two or three times and go over the parts of Scripture we know by heart. Let prayer be our armor as we leave the home that shelters us, and when we return from the street, let prayer be said before we sit down, and do not let the puny body rest before the soul is fed. In every act we perform, in every step we take, let our hand trace the cross. Speak against nobody and do not slander your mothers's son (Ps 50:20). *Who are you to judge the servant of another? He stands or falls for his own master; indeed, he shall stand, for God has the power to make him stand* (Rom 14:4). If you have fasted two or three days, do not think yourself better than others who do not fast. You fast and are angry; another eats and wears a smiling face. You work off your irritation and hunger in quarrels; he uses food in moderation and gives God thanks. Daily Isaiah cries, "*Is this the sort of fast I have chosen?*" says the Lord (Isa 58:5), and again, *In the day of your fast you find your own pleasure and goad all those over whom you have power. If you fast in courts and litigation and strike the lowly man with your fist, what kind of a fast do you perform for me?* (Isa 58:3–4). What kind of fast can his be, whose wrath is so great that not only does the night go down upon it, but even the phases of the moon leave it unchanged? (38) Look to yourself and glory in your own success and not in other peoples' failure.

Do not set before yourself the example of those women who take care of the flesh and reckon up their income and daily expenditure. Nor were the eleven apostles crushed by the treachery of Judas, nor when Phygelus and Alexander made shipwreck (1 Tim 1:19–20, 2 Tim 1:15), did the rest stop running in the race of faith. Do not say, "So-and-so enjoys her own property; she is honored by everyone; her brothers and sisters come to see her; does she then cease to be a virgin?" In the first place, it is doubtful whether such a woman as she is a virgin. For *God does not see as human beings see. Man looks upon the outward appearance, but God looks into the heart* (1 Sam 16:7). Again, even if she is a virgin in body, I do not know whether she is a virgin in spirit. The Apostle himself defines a virgin this way: *That she may be holy both in body and in spirit* (1 Cor 7:34). Last, let her glory in her own way. Let her override Paul's opinion and live in enjoyment of her good things. But you and I must follow better examples.

Set before yourself the blessed Mary, whose surpassing purity made her worthy to be the mother of the Lord. When the angel Gabriel came down to her in the form of a man and said, *Hail, lady full of grace, the Lord is with you* (Luke 1:28), she was terror stricken and unable to reply, for she had never been greeted by a man. But when she learned that he was a messenger, she spoke to him, and she, who had feared a man, conversed fearlessly with an angel. You, too, can be the Lord's mother. *Take to yourself a great book, a new book, and write swiftly in it with the pen of a man who destroys the spoils* (Isa 8:1), and when you have approached the prophetess and have conceived in the womb and have brought forth a son (Isa 8:3), say, *Lord, we have conceived a child by your fear, we have been in pain and we have given birth; the spirit of your salvation have we created upon earth* (Isa 26:18 [Vulg]). Then shall your Son replay, *Behold my mother and my brothers* (Matt 12:49). And he whose name you have a short while earlier inscribed on the amplitude of your heart and have written with flying pen on its renewed surface, he—after he has captured the spoil from the enemy and has laid bare principalities and powers, nailing them to his cross—he, having been conceived, grows to manhood, and as he grows older, he regards you no longer as his mother but as his bride. It is a great struggle, but it is also a great prize, to be as the martyrs or the apostles or as Christ. Indeed, all these things are profitable if they are done within the Church, if we celebrate the passover in the same house (Exod 12:46), if we enter the ark with Noah (1 Pet 3:20–21), if Rahab, once pardoned, holds us while Jericho falls (James 2:25). Such virgins, however, as are said to be among the various sects of heretics and at the side of the infamous Mani, must be regarded as prostitutes, not virgins. For if the devil is the originator of the body [as they claim], how can they honor what their enemy has fashioned? No, it is because they know that the word *virgin* has a glorious meaning that they go about as wolves in sheep's clothing. As Antichrist claims falsely to be Christ, so they clothe the baseness of their lives with an honorable, but falsely assumed, name. Rejoice, my sister, rejoice, my daughter, rejoice, my virgin, because you begin really to be what other women pretend to be.

(39) All the things we have gone through here one by one will seem hard to a person who does not love Christ. Yet someone who has come to regard all the splendor of the secular world as offscourings and thinks that everything under the sun is vain (Eccl 1:14), if he may win Christ (Phil 3:8), someone who has died and risen again with his Lord and has crucified the flesh with its affections and lusts (Rom 6:4; Gal 5:24), will boldly cry out, *Who shall separate us from the love of Christ? Shall tribulation or poverty or persecution or hunger or nakedness or danger of the sword?* and again, *I am sure that neither death nor life nor an angel nor principalities nor powers nor the present nor the future nor courage nor height nor depth nor any other created thing can separate us from the love of God, which is in Christ Jesus our Lord* (Rom 8:35, 38–39), the Son of God, who was made Son of Man for our salvation. For ten months he waits in the womb to be born; he endures revolting conditions, he comes forth covered in blood, he is swathed in rags and covered with caresses. He who shuts the world up in his fist is contained within the narrow limits of a manger. I say nothing of the thirty years during which he lives in obscurity, satisfied with the poverty of his parents. When he is scourged, he holds his peace. When he is crucified, he prays for his crucifiers. *What shall I give to the Lord for all the rewards he bestows upon me? I will receive the cup of salvation and call upon the name of the Lord. Precious in the sight of the Lord is the death of his saints* (Ps 116:12–13, 15). The only fitting return we can make to him is to give blood for blood and, as having been redeemed by the blood of Christ, gladly to lay down our lives for our Redeemer. What saint has ever won his crown without first contending for it? The righteous Abel is murdered. Abraham is in danger of losing his wife, and as I must not turn my book into a large volume, look up [other passages] for yourself, and you will find that all holy men have suffered adversity. Only Solomon lived in luxury and that is perhaps why he fell. *For whom the Lord loves, he snatches up, and he punishes every son whom he receives* (Heb 12:6). Is it not better to do battle for a short time, to carry stakes for the palisades, to bear arms and rations, to grow weary under breastplates and later to rejoice as a victor, than to be slaves forever because we cannot endure for a single hour? (cf. Matt 26:40).

(40) Nothing is hard for those who love; no task is difficult for the enthusiast. See how much Jacob bore for Rachel, the wife who had been promised to him. *Jacob,* the Scripture says, *served seven years for Rachel. And they were like a few days in his sight because he loved her* (Gen 29:20). Afterward he himself tells us what he had to undergo. *By day I was burned by the heat and by night by the frost* (Gen 31:40). So we must love Christ and always seek his embraces. Then everything difficult will seem easy; everything long we shall account short, and smitten

with his arrows (Ps 38:2), we shall say every moment, *Woe is me, because my pilgrimage has been prolonged* (Ps 120:5). For *the sufferings of this present time are not worthy to be compared with the future glory that will be revealed in us* (Rom 8:18). For *tribulation bestows patience, patience experience, and experience hope, and hope does not throw us into confusion* (Rom 5:3–5). When your lot seems hard to bear, read Paul's Second Epistle to the Corinthians: *In toil most abundant, in blows beyond measure, in prison frequently, often near death. Five times I was beaten thirty-nine times by the Jews; three times I was beaten with rods; once I was stoned; three times I suffered shipwreck, a night and a day I have been in the depths of the sea. I have often been on journeys, in danger from rivers, in danger from robbers, in danger from my own countrymen, in danger from pagans, in danger in the city, in danger in the wilderness, in danger on the sea, in danger among false brethren, in toil and misery, in frequent vigils, in hunger and thirst, in frequent fasting, in cold and nakedness* (2 Cor 11:23–27). Which of us can claim the merest fraction of the virtues here enumerated? Yet it was these that afterward made him bold to say, *I have finished my course, I have kept the faith. There will be stored up for me a crown of righteousness, which the Lord will give me* (2 Tim 4:7–8). If our food is somewhat insipid, we get gloomy and think we are doing God a favor; if we drink watered-down wine, the cup is smashed, the table overturned, the sound of scourging is heard, and the overwarm water is paid for with blood. *The kingdom of heaven endures violence, and violent men take it by force* (Matt 11:12). Still, unless you use force, you will never seize the kingdom of heaven. Unless you knock importunately (Luke 11:5–8), you will never receive the sacramental bread. Does it not seem to you typical of a violent man that the flesh yearns to be what God is and to ascend to the place from which angels have fallen, for the purpose of judging angels?

(41) Go forth, I beg you, for a little while from your body and picture before your eyes the reward of your present toil, a reward which *neither the eye has seen nor the ear heard, nor the human heart conceived* (1 Cor 2:9). What will be the glory of that day when Mary, the mother of the Lord, will come to meet you, accompanied by choirs of virgins; when Miriam, after the passage through the Red Sea and the drowning of Pharaoh with his army, holding her tambourine, will chant to the answering women, *Sing to the Lord, for he has triumphed gloriously; the horse and its rider has he thrown into the sea* (Exod 15:20–21). Then shall Thecla fly with joy to embrace you. Then shall your Spouse himself come forward to meet you and say, *Rise, my nearest and dearest, my fair one, my dove, for behold! The winter is over, for you the rain has gone away* (Song 2:10–11). Then will the angels say with wonder, *Who is she who looks forth like the dawn, fair as the moon, choice as the sun?* (Song 6:10). . . . *The maidens shall see you and bless you; the queens shall proclaim you and the concubines praise you* (Song 6:9). Then yet another chorus of chaste women shall come to meet you: Sarah will come with the matrons and Anna, the daughter of Phanuel, with the widows (Gen 12–23; Luke 2:36). There, as in different groups, will be your physical mother and your spiritual mother. The one will rejoice because she bore you; the other will exult because she taught you. Then truly will the Lord ride on his she-ass and enter the heavenly Jerusalem. Then the little children—of whom the Savior says in Isaiah, *Look! here I am with the boys whom the Lord has given me* (Isa 8:18)—shall lift up palms of victory and chant with a single voice, *Hosanna in the highest; blessed is he that comes in the name of the Lord; hosanna in the highest* (Matt 21:9). Then shall the hundred and forty four thousand hold their harps before the throne and before the elders and they shall sing a new song, and no one shall be able to recognize that song save those for whom it is appointed. *These are they who have not contaminated themselves with women, for they are virgins. These are they who follow the Lamb wherever he goes* (Rev 14:1–4). As often as this life's idle show tries to charm you, as often as you see in the world some vain pomp, transport yourself in your mind to Paradise. Try to be now what you will be hereafter, and you will hear from your Spouse, *Set me as a seal upon your heart, as a seal on your arm* (Song 8:6). Then, strengthened in both body and mind, you will cry out and say, *Many waters cannot quench love, neither can the floods drown it* (Song 8:7).

38. Pachomian Rules

Pachomius (a Latinized form of the Coptic name Pachōm) is famed as the "founder" of communal (or cenobitic) monasticism in fourth-century Egypt. Although he may not have been the first Egyptian to found a communal monastery in the desert, his influence spread throughout the Christian world, in part because of the translation and circulation of his communal *Rules* reproduced here. He founded his monasteries in Upper (southern) Egypt, far from the metropolitan city of Alexandria. Other communal monastic settlements in the area, particularly the White Monastery under the direction of the fiery abbot Shenoute, seem to have early felt the influence of Pachomius's communal system.

The *Rules* were probably compiled over time and not composed on a single occasion: some rules are repetitive, switch voice (from "you" to "they"), and have opening lines that signal that they may once have stood alone or in separate collections of regulations. However this written text came into existence, it is clear that the Pachomian monasteries (which may have housed as many as 3,000 monks by the time of Pachomius's death in 346) was a highly structured setting for the seeking of spiritual perfection.

We should not interpret this rigid structure as a lack of ascetic enthusiasm, however; rather, the intention seems to have been the construction of an entire separate social order (complete with spiritual "families," "houses," "tribes," and "races") that worked through harmonious fellowship (*koinōnia*) in all details of life. Men and women, Egyptians, Greeks, and Romans of all classes, shed their previous identities and submitted themselves totally to the monastic ideal. These rules may represent an ideal of that monastic fellowship, rather than its daily functioning; nonetheless, the concerns, aims, and obstacles of that life do come into view.

This ideal of communal monastic life not only influenced ascetic endeavors in the East, but also provided a guiding force in the development of cenobitic monasticism in the West. Jerome translated Pachomius's rules into Latin (one source of the version reproduced here), and John Cassian (ca. 365–ca. 433), a westerner who spent many years as a monk in Palestine, further translated (literally and culturally) the ideals of Egyptian cenobitic monasticism by founding communal monasteries in southern Gaul.

Here begin the precepts:

(1) When someone uninstructed comes to the assembly of the saints, the porter shall introduce him according to [his] rank from the door of the monastery and give him a seat in the gathering of the brothers. He shall not be allowed to change his place or rank of sitting until the *oikiakos,* that is, his own housemaster, transfers him to the place he should have.

(2) He shall sit with all modesty and meekness, tucking under his buttocks the lower edge of the goat skin that hangs over his shoulder down his side, and carefully girding up his garment—that is, the linen tunic without sleeves called *lebitonarium*—in such a way that it covers his knees.

(3) As soon as he hears the sound of the trumpet calling the [the brothers] to the *synaxis,* he shall leave his cell, reciting something from the Scriptures until he reaches the door of the *synaxis.*

From *Pachomian Koinonia,* Vol. 2: *Pachomian Chronicles and Rules,* trans. Armand Veilleux. Kalamazoo, Mich.: Cistercian Studies, 1981. Used with permission.

(4) And when he begins to walk into the *synaxis* room, going to his place of sitting and standing, he should not tread upon the rushes that have been dipped in water in preparation for the plaiting of ropes, lest even a small loss should come to the monastery through someone's negligence.

(5) But at night when the signal is given, you shall not stand at the fire usually lighted to warm bodies and drive off the cold, nor shall you sit idle in the *synaxis,* but with a quick hand you shall prepare ropes for the warps of mats, although exception is made for the infirmity of the body to which leave must be given for rest.

(6) When the one who stands first on the step, reciting by heart something from the Scripture, claps with his hand for the prayer to be concluded, no one should delay in rising, but all shall get up together.

(7) Let no one look at another twisting ropes or praying; let him rather be intent on his own work with eyes cast down.

(8) These are the precepts of life handed down to us by the elders. If it happens that during the psalmody or the prayer or in the midst of a reading anyone speaks or laughs, he shall unfasten his belt immediately and with neck bowed down and hands hanging down he shall stand before the altar and be rebuked by the superior of the monastery. He shall do the same also in the assembly of the brothers when they assemble to eat.

(9) When by day the trumpet blast has called [the brothers] to the *synaxis,* anyone who comes after the first prayer shall be punished in the manner described above and shall remain standing in the refectory.

(10) At night however, more is conceded to the body's weakness, and anyone who comes after the third prayer shall be punished in the same manner both in the *synaxis* and at mealtime.

(11) When the brothers are praying in the *synaxis,* let no one go out except by order of the superiors and unless he has asked and been permitted to go out for the necessities of nature.

(12) No one shall divide the rushes for plaiting ropes except the person who does the weekly service. And if he is reasonably detained by some work, the directive of the superior shall be resorted to.

(13) Among the weekly servers from one house, some shall not be chosen to stand on the step and recite something from the Scripture in the assembly of all, but all of them, according to their order of sitting and standing, shall repeat from memory what has been assigned to them.

(14) If any one of them forgets anything and hesitates in speaking, he shall undergo punishment for his negligence and forgetfulness.

(15) On Sunday, or at the time of the Eucharist, none of the weekly servers shall be absent from his seat on the *embrimium* and not responding to the psalmist. They are all [to be] from the same house that does the greater weekly service, for there is another lesser weekly service performed in the individual houses by a smaller number. If a greater number is necessary, others from the same tribe shall be called by the housemaster doing the weekly service. Without his order no one shall come from another house of the same tribe to sing psalms. Likewise, it shall not be permitted anyone at all to serve in the weekly service of a house other than his own, unless it be [a house] of the same tribe. They call a tribe a group of three or four houses—according to the population of the monastery—which we could designate as families or peoples of a single race.

(16) On Sunday and in the *synaxis* in which the Eucharist is to be offered, let no one be allowed to sing psalms apart from the housemaster and the elders of the monastery, who are of some reputation.

(17) If anyone is missing when one of the elders is chanting, that is, reading the psalter, he shall at once undergo the order of penance and rebuke before the altar.

(18) Anyone who, without an order from the superior, leaves the *synaxis* in which the Eucharist is offered shall be rebuked at once.

(19) In the morning in the individual houses, after the prayers are finished, they shall not return right away to their cells, but they shall discuss among themselves the instruction they heard from their housemasters. Then they shall enter their quarters.

(20) An instruction shall be given three times a week by the housemasters. And during the instruction, the brothers, whether sitting or standing, shall

not change their place [which is] according to the order of the houses and of the individual men.

(21) If someone falls asleep while sitting during the instruction of the housemaster or of the superior of the monastery, he shall be forced to get up at once, and he shall stand until ordered to sit.

(22) When the signal is given to assemble and hear the precepts of the superiors, no one shall remain behind. Nor shall the fire be lighted before the instruction has ended.

Anyone who neglects one of these precepts shall undergo the aforesaid punishment.

(23) Without the order of the superior of the monastery, the weekly server shall not have authority to give ropes or any vessel to anyone. And without his order, he shall not be able to give the signal for [the brothers] to gather whether for the midday *synaxis* or for the evening *synaxis* of the Six Prayers.

(24) After the morning prayer, the weekly server on whom this work is enjoined shall ask the superior of the monastery about the various things he believes necessary and about when they ought to go out to work in the fields. And according to his directives, he shall go around the individual houses to find out what each one has need of.

(25) If they seek a book to read, let them have it, and at the end of the week they shall put it back in its place for those who succeed them in the service.

(26) When they are working at mats, the ministers shall ask each of the housemasters in the evening how many rushes are required per house. And so he shall dip the rushes and distribute them in the morning to each in order. If in the morning he notices that still more rushes are needed, he shall dip them and bring them around to each house, until the signal is given for the meal.

(27) The housemaster who is completing the weekly service and the one taking up the service for the coming week and the superior of the monastery shall have the responsibility of observing what work has been omitted or neglected. They shall have the mats that are usually spread out on the floor in the *synaxis* shaken out. And they shall also count the ropes twisted per week, noting the sum on tablets and keeping the record until the time of the annual gathering,

when an account shall be given and sins forgiven everyone.

(28) When the *synaxis* is dismissed, each one shall recite something from the Scripture while going either to his cell or to the refectory. And no one shall have his head covered during recitation.

(29) And when they come to eat, they shall sit in order in [their] appointed places and cover their heads.

(30) When you are ordered by the superior to pass from one table to another, you shall do it at once, without contradicting him at all. Nor shall you dare to stretch out your hand at the table before your housemaster. And you shall not look around at others eating.

(31) Each master shall teach, in his own house, how they must eat with manners and meekness. If anyone speaks or laughs while eating, he shall do penance and be rebuked there at once, and he shall stand until another of the brothers who are eating gets up.

(32) If someone comes late to eat, without [being detained by] an order of the superior, he shall likewise do penance or return to his house without eating.

(33) If anything is needed at table, no one shall dare to speak, but he shall make a sign to the ministers by a sound.

(34) When you come out of the meal, you shall not speak while going back to your own place.

(35) The ministers shall eat nothing but what has been prepared for the brothers in common, nor shall they dare to prepare special foods for themselves.

(36) The one who strikes the signal to assemble the brothers for meals shall recite while striking.

(37) The one who dispenses sweets to the brothers at the refectory door as they go out shall recite something from the Scriptures while doing so.

(38) The one who receives the things that are handed out shall receive it not in his hood, but in his goat skin, and he shall not taste what he has received until he reaches his house. The one who portions out [the sweets] to the others shall receive his portion from the housemaster. In the same way, the other ministers shall receive theirs from another, claiming

nothing for themselves at their own discretion. What they receive shall be enough for three days. And if anyone has anything left over, he shall bring it back to the housemaster, who shall put it back in the store-room to be mixed with the rest and given out to all the brothers.

(39) No one shall give more to one than another has received.

(40) If some sickness is alleged, the housemaster shall proceed to the ministers of the sick and receive from them whatever is necessary.

(41) If one of the ministers is sick himself, he shall not have permission to enter the kitchen or storeroom to get something for himself, but the other ministers shall give him whatever they consider he needs. Nor shall he be permitted to cook for himself what he desires, but the housemasters shall get from the other ministers what they consider he needs.

(42) Let no one who is not sick enter the infirmary. The one who falls sick shall be led by the master to the refectory for the sick. And if he needs a mantle or a tunic or anything else by way of covering or food, let the master himself get these from the ministers and give them to the sick brother.

(43) Nor may a sick brother enter the cell of those who are eating and eat what he wants, unless he is led there to eat by the minister in charge of this matter. Nor shall he be permitted to take to his cell any of the things he has received in the infirmary, not even a fruit.

(44) Those who cook the meals shall themselves serve them in turn.

(45) Let no one touch wine or broth outside the infirmary.

(46) If someone is sent on a journey and falls sick on the road or in the boat and has the need or the desire to eat some fish broth or some other things that are used at meals in the monastery, he shall not eat with the other brothers but by himself. And the ministers shall give to him abundantly so that a sick brother may not be saddened in any way.

(47) No one may dare visit a sick brother without the superior's leave. And except by order of the housemaster, not even a relative or a blood brother shall be authorized to serve him.

(48) If someone omits or neglects any of these [precepts], he shall be corrected with the customary rebuke.

(49) When someone comes to the door of the monastery, wishing to renounce the world and be added to the number of the brothers, he shall not be free to enter. First, the father of the monastery shall be informed [of his coming]. He shall remain outside at the door a few days and be taught the Lord's prayer and as many psalms as he can learn. Carefully shall he make himself known: has he done something wrong and, troubled by fear, suddenly run away? Or is he under someone's authority? Can he renounce his parents and spurn his own possessions? If they see that he is ready for everything, then he shall be taught the rest of the monastic discipline: what he must do and whom he must serve, whether in the *synaxis* of all the brothers or in the house to which he is assigned, as well as in the refectory. Perfectly instructed in every good work, let him be joined to the brothers. Then they shall strip him of his secular clothes and garb him in the monastic habit. He shall be handed over to the porter, so that at the time of prayer he may bring him before all the brothers, and he shall sit where he is told. The clothes he brought with him shall be given to those in charge of this matter and brought to the storeroom; they will be in the keeping of the superior of the monastery.

(50) No one living in the monastery may receive anyone to eat; he shall send him to the guesthouse door to be received by those in charge of this matter.

(51) When people come to the door of the monastery, they shall be received with greater honor if they are clerics or monks. Their feet shall be washed, according to the Gospel precept (cf. John 13:14–15), and they shall be brought to the guesthouse and offered everything suitable to monks. If they wish to join the assembly of the brothers at the time of prayer and *synaxis,* and they are of the same faith, the porter or the guestmaster shall inform the father of the monastery, and they shall be brought in to pray.

(52) If seculars or infirm people or *weaker vessels*—that is, women (cf. 1 Pet 3:7)—come to the door, they shall be received in different places ac-

cording to their calling and their sex. Above all, women shall be cared for with greater honor and diligence. They shall be given a place separate from all areas frequented by men, so there may be no occasion for slander. If they come in the evening, it would be wicked to drive them away, but, as we have said, they shall be lodged in a separate and enclosed place with every discipline and caution, so that the flock of the brothers may freely tend to its duty and no occasion for detraction be given to anybody.

(53) If someone presents himself at the door of the monastery and says he would like to see his brother or his relative, the porter shall inform the father of the monastery, who will call the housemaster and ask him whether the man is in his house. Then, with the housemaster's permission, he shall be given a trustworthy companion and so shall be sent to see his brother or relative. If it happens that the latter brought him some of the foods that are allowed to be eaten in the monastery, he may not receive them himself, but he shall call the porter who shall receive the gifts. If they are of a kind to be eaten with bread, the one to whom they were brought shall receive none of them, but they shall all be taken to the infirmary. But if they are sweets or fruits, the porter shall give him some of these to eat as he is able, and he shall carry the rest to the infirmary. The porter may not eat any of the things brought, but he shall give the donor either some charlock—which is a cheap kind of herb—or some bread or some small vegetables. As for the aforesaid foods brought by parents or relatives, which need to be eaten with bread, the one to whom they have been brought shall be taken by the housemaster to the infirmary, where he will eat from them once only. The rest shall stay in the hands of the minister of the sick, who himself may not eat any of these things.

(54) If it is reported that one of the relatives or family of those living in the monastery is sick, the porter shall first inform the father of the monastery, who will summon the housemaster and question him. They shall choose a man of proved faith and discipline and send him with the brother to visit the sick person. And he shall receive as much provision for the journey as the housemaster decides. If it is neces-

sary for him to remain and eat outside, he shall by no means do this in the house of his parents or relatives. He shall stay instead in a church or in a monastery of the same faith. If his parents and relatives have prepared foods and served them, they shall not accept or eat anything at all except what they customarily eat in the monastery. They shall not taste broth or drink wine or take any of the other things that they do not customarily eat. If they receive anything from the parents, they shall eat just as much as it is necessary for the journey. They shall give the rest that remains to their housemaster, who will take it to the infirmary.

(55) When someone's close relative dies, he shall not be allowed to attend the funeral unless the father of the monastery orders it.

(56) No one should be sent out alone on any errand without a companion.

(57) And if, on their return to the monastery they see at the door someone looking for one of his relatives living there, they shall not dare go tell him or call him. And they may not, in any circumstance, talk in the monastery about what they have done or heard outside.

(58) When the signal is given to go to work, the housemaster shall lead them, and no one shall remain in the monastery except by order of the father. And those who go out shall not ask where they are going.

(59) And when all the houses are gathered, the housemaster of the first house shall go before them all, and they shall proceed according to the order of the houses and of individuals. They shall not speak to each other, but each one shall recite something from the Scriptures. If perhaps someone comes along and wants to speak to one of them, the porter of the monastery whose task it is shall come and answer him, and they shall use him as an intermediary. If the porter is not at hand, the housemaster or another appointed to this task shall answer those who might come along.

(60) At work, they shall talk of no worldly matter, but either recite holy things or else keep silent.

(61) No one shall take his linen mantle with him when going to work, except with the superior's permission. And in the monastery, no one shall walk around wearing that same mantle after the *synaxis*.

(62) At work no one shall sit without the superior's order.

(63) If the leaders of the brothers find it necessary to send someone on a journey, they may not do so without the master's order. And if the leader himself must go off somewhere, he shall delegate his office to the next in rank.

(64) If the brothers who are sent out on business or are staying far away eat outside the monastery, the weekly server who accompanies them shall give them food but without making cooked dishes, and he shall himself distribute water as is done in the monastery. No one may get up to draw or drink water.

(65) When they return to the monastery, no one shall remain out of his rank. When they come to their houses, they shall hand over the tools they used for work and their shoes to the second—the one after the housemaster. He shall take them at evening into a special cell and secure them there.

(66) At the end of the weekly service, all the tools shall be brought to one house, so that those who come next in the service may know what to distribute to each house.

(67) No one apart from the boatmen and the bakers shall wash his tunic or any other monastic clothes except on Sunday.

(68) They shall not go to do laundry unless one signal has sounded for all. They shall follow their housemaster and do the washing in silence and with discipline.

(69) No one shall do the laundry with his clothes drawn up higher than is established. When the washing is done, all shall return together. If someone stays behind or is not present at the time they go to do the laundry, he shall inform his master, who shall send him with someone else. And when he has washed his clothes, he shall return to his house.

(70) In the evening, they shall take up the dry tunics and give them to the second—the one who is after the housemaster—and he will put them in the cell. But if they are not dry, they shall be spread out in the sun the next day until they are dry. But they shall not be left in the heat of the sun after the third hour. And when they are brought in, they shall be lightly softened. The brothers shall not keep them with themselves but shall hand them over to be stored in the cell until Saturday.

(71) No one shall take vegetables from the garden unless he is given them by the gardener.

(72) No one on his own authority shall take palm leaves for basket plaiting, except the one in charge of the palms.

(73) For the sake of discipline, no one should dare eat still unripe grapes or ears of corn. And no one shall eat at all anything from field or orchard on his own before it has been served to all the brothers together.

(74) The cook shall not take any of the food before the brothers eat.

(75) The one in charge of the palm trees shall not eat any of their fruits before the brothers have first had some.

(76) Those who are ordered to harvest the fruits of the palm trees shall receive a few from the master of the harvesters to eat on the spot. And when they have returned to the monastery, they shall receive their portion with the other brothers.

(77) If they find fallen fruits under the trees, they shall not dare to eat them, but they shall put them together at the foot of the trees as they pass by. Also the one who distributes [the fruits] to the other harvesters may not taste them, but shall bring them to the steward, who shall give him his portion after he has given some of them to the other brothers.

(78) Let no one put away in his cell anything to eat, except what he has received from the steward.

(79) As regards the small loaves given to the housemasters to be distributed to those who dedicate themselves to greater abstinence and do not want to eat in common with the others, they must see to it that they give them to no one as a favor, not even to someone going away. Nor shall they be put in common, but they shall be distributed in good order to them in their cells when they want to eat. And with these loaves, they shall eat nothing else except only salt.

(80) No one may cook foods outside the monastery and the kitchen. When they go out, that is, to work in the fields, they shall receive vegetables sea-

soned with salt and vinegar and prepared for long storage in summertime.

(81) In his house and cell, no one shall have anything except what is prescribed for all together by the law of the monastery: no woolen tunic, no mantle, no soft sheepskin with unshorn wool, not even a few coins, no pillow for his head, or various other conveniences. They shall have only what is distributed by the father of the monastery through the housemasters. This is their equipment: two linen tunics plus the one already worn, a long scarf for the neck and shoulders, a goat skin hanging from the shoulder, shoes, two hoods, a belt, and a staff. If you find anything more than this, you shall take it away without contradiction.

(82) No one shall have in his own possession little tweezers for removing thorns he may have stepped on. Only the housemaster and the second shall have them, and they shall hang in the alcove in which books are placed.

(83) If anyone is transferred from one house to another, he may take nothing with him but what we have mentioned above.

(84) No one may go out into the fields, walk around in the monastery, or go outside the monastery wall without requesting and receiving the housemaster's permission.

(85) Let care be taken that no one reports words from house to house, from monastery to monastery, from monastery to field, or from field to monastery.

(86) Anyone who has been journeying by land or water or working outside shall not speak in the monastery about what he has seen happen there.

(87) For sleeping, either in the cell or on the roof—on which they rest at night during times of great heat—or in the fields, one must always use the reclining seat alloted to him.

(88) No one shall speak to another in the place where he sleeps.

No one, after he has been in bed and slept, shall get up in the morning to eat or drink during a time of fast. And no one shall spread anything on his reclining seat except a mat.

(89) No one shall enter the cell of his neighbor without first knocking.

(90) Nor should one go in to eat at noon before the signal is given. Nor shall they walk around in the village before the signal is given.

(91) No one shall walk in the community without his goat skin and his hood, either to the *synaxis* or to the refectory.

(92) No one shall go to oil his hands in the evening unless a brother is sent with him; no one shall oil his whole body unless he is sick or bathe or wash it immodestly contrary to the manner established for them.

(93) No one shall oil or bathe a sick man unless ordered.

(94) No one may speak to his neighbors in the dark.

(95) Nor shall you sit two together on a mat or a carpet.

No one may clasp the hand or anything else of his companion, but whether you are sitting or standing or walking, you shall leave a forearm's space between you and him.

(96) No one shall draw a thorn out of a man's foot, except the housemaster or the second or another so ordered.

(97) No one shall shave his head without his housemaster['s permission], nor shall a man shave another without being ordered, nor shall a man shave another when both are seated.

(98) No one shall change anything in his wardrobe without his housemaster['s permission]. Nor shall they take anything in trade without his approval. And no one shall add anything to his wardrobe contrary to what has been established for them.

(99) All the goat skins shall be belted up, and all the hoods shall bear the sign of the community and the sign of their house.

(100) No one shall leave his book unfastened when he goes to the *synaxis* or to the refectory.

(101) Every day at evening, the second shall bring the books from the alcove and shut them in their case.

(102) Either in the village or in the fields, no one shall go to the *synaxis* or to the refectory with shoes on his feet or clad in his mantle.

(103) No one shall leave his mantle in the sun until the signal is given at noon for the meal.

The one who neglects all these things shall be rebuked.

(104) No one shall take a shoe or any other object to oil it but only the housemasters.

(105) When a brother has been injured and is not bedridden but is up and around, if he needs a garment or a bit of oil, his housemaster shall go to the stewards' place to get them for him until he is well again; then he shall return them to their place.

(106) No one shall receive anything from another without his housemaster['s permission].

(107) No one shall sleep in a locked cell, nor shall anyone get a locked room except by order.

(108) No one, not even the farmers, shall enter the stables without being sent, except the herdsmen.

(109) Two men shall not sit together on a bare-backed donkey or on a wagon shaft.

(110) When you arrive at the monastery mounted on a donkey, you shall dismount and walk ahead of it, except in case of necessity.

(111) No one may go to the shops except those in charge, who go for the needs of their work; nor may they go before the signal is given for eating, except for work needs. In that case the superior of the monastery shall be informed first, and he shall send the weekly server.

(112) No one shall go to the breadboards place, and no one shall enter a house unless he is sent.

(113) No one shall take anything on trust from another man, not even from his own brother.

(114) No one shall eat anything in his cell.

(115) When any man in charge goes away, the housemaster of his tribe shall take care of his house in everything in which the second may need him. He shall give the fast days' instructions, one in his own house, the other in the house of his fellow [master].

(116) About the bakery: No one shall speak when the kneading is done in the evening, nor shall those who work at the baking or at the boards in the morning. They shall recite together until they have finished. If they need anything, they shall not speak, but shall signify it by a knock.

(117) No one shall go to the baking without being ordered. No one shall loiter in the oven house when the bakers are baking, except only those appointed.

(118) About the boats: No boatman shall put out a craft, not even a skiff, from port without [the permission of] the superior of the monastery. Aboard a boat no one shall go to the hold to sleep. Nor may they take a secular aboard to sleep.

(119) Nor [shall they take aboard] any *weaker vessel* (1 Pet 3:7) without the permission of the superior of the monastery.

(120) No one shall light a fire in his house before the brothers have been so commanded.

(121) The one who arrives late for one of the Six Prayers at evening or does not recite, or laughs or talks shall do penance in his house during the Six Prayers.

(122) Sitting in their houses, they shall not speak . . . but they shall reflect on the words spoken by the housemaster.

(123) Reflecting on the instruction, they shall not plait or draw water until the housemaster says so.

(124) No one shall take soaked rushes without [the permission of] the weekly server of the house.

(125) Whoever breaks a clay vessel or who dips a batch of rushes three times shall be rebuked during his Six Prayers.

(126) After the Six Prayers, when all separate for sleep, no one may leave his cell except in a case of necessity.

(127) When a brother dies among the brothers, they shall all together accompany him to the mountain. No one shall remain behind unordered, nor shall anyone sing psalms without being ordered.

(128) Proceeding to the mountain, they shall not sing psalms two by two. No one shall take his mantle with him while going to the mountain. They shall not neglect to respond, but shall maintain unison.

(129) The infirmarian shall remain behind in case a brother should fall sick. This is the way [of doing things] wherever someone may be sent.

(130) No one may walk ahead of his housemaster and his leader.

(131) No one may stay out of his rank. If anyone loses anything, he shall be publicly rebuked before the altar. And if what he has lost is from his own clothing, he shall not receive it for three weeks; in the fourth week, once he has done penance, he shall be given what he has lost.

(132) Whoever finds a thing shall hang it up for three days in front of the *synaxis* of the brothers, so that the one who recognizes it may take it.

(133) For all reproofs and teachings whose measure is determined in writing, the housemasters shall suffice. But if there is any novel fault, it shall be referred to the superior of the monastery.

(134) No one shall make abode in a house without his permission; and any new matter shall be decided by him.

(135) Every rebuke shall be made this way: those who are rebuked shall remove their belt and shall stand in the major *synaxis* and in the refectory.

(136) Anyone who has left the *Koinonia* of the brothers and afterward does penance and comes back shall not return to his rank without the superior's order.

(137) In the same way, if a housemaster or a steward sleeps outside one night without the brothers and afterward does penance and comes to the assembly of the brothers, he shall not be permitted to enter his house or take his rank without the superior's order.

(138) Everything that is taught them in the assembly of the brothers they must absolutely talk over among themselves, especially on the days of fast, when they receive instruction from their masters.

(139) Whoever enters the monastery uninstructed shall be taught first what he must observe, and when so taught, he has consented to it all, they shall give him twenty psalms or two of the Apostle's epistles or some other part of the Scripture.

And if he is illiterate, he shall go at the first, third, and sixth hours to someone who can teach and has been appointed for him. He shall stand before him and learn very studiously with all gratitude. Then the fundamentals of a syllable, the verbs, and nouns shall

be written for him, and even if he does not want to, he shall be compelled to read.

(140) There shall be no one whatever in the monastery who does not learn to read and does not memorize something of the Scriptures. [One should learn by heart] at least the New Testament and the Psalter.

(141) No one shall find pretexts for himself for not going to the *synaxis,* the psalmody, and the prayer.

(142) One shall not neglect the times of prayer and psalmody, whether he is on a boat, in the monastery, in the fields, or on a journey, or fulfilling any service whatever.

(143) Let us speak also about the monastery of virgins: No one shall go to visit them unless he has there a mother, sister, or daughter, some relatives or cousins, or the mother of his own children.

And if it is necessary to see them for any evident reason, and if some paternal inheritance is due them from the time before their renunciation of the world and their entry into the monastery, or if there is some obvious reason, they shall be accompanied by a man of proved age and life; they shall see them and return together. No one shall go to visit them except those we have just mentioned.

When they want to see them, they shall first inform the father of the monastery, and he shall inform the elders appointed to the virgins' ministry. These shall meet [the virgins] and with them see those whom they need with all discipline and fear of God. When they see the virgins, they shall not speak to them about worldly matters.

(144) Whoever transgresses any of these commands shall, for his negligence and his contempt, do penance publicly without any delay so that he may be able to possess the kingdom of heaven.

39. Sayings of the Desert Fathers

The so-called *Sayings of the Desert Fathers,* or *Apophthegmata Patrum,* range from pithy aphorisms to extended anecdotes and enshrine the memory of the monastic heroes of the Egyptian desert, focused particularly on the anchorites and semianchorites of Scetis and Kellia ("The Cells") in Lower (northern) Egypt. The *Sayings* may have begun circulating orally in the fourth century; they were eventually written down in various collections in the fifth and sixth centuries. Reproduced here are selections from the Alphabetical Collection, in which the sayings were categorized under the monk's name to whom they were attributed.

We can discern some aspects of anchorite life from these collections. Of central importance was the master-disciple relationship: ascetic men (as well as some women) sought the guidance of a spiritual master (called an "abba," from the Aramaic term for "father" found in the New Testament; it is the origin of the English word "abbot"). Although these monks had withdrawn from society, their lives were not solitary: they gathered for occasional sacraments, such as the Eucharist, and to seek each other's advice and wisdom, a practice that may have led to the collection of these sayings.

The monastic ideals incorporated into this collection may not entirely reflect the reality of the fourth-century desert. Spiritual athleticism, particularly prayer and manual labor, is given pride of place over intellectual inquiry, yet the *Letters* of Antony (see Text 40) suggest that philosophical sophistication was also prominent among these "simple" monks. Likewise, the idealized split between "desert" and city (in one saying, Antony describes monks out of the desert as fish out of water) reflects an ideology of ascetic renunciation that grew gradually over time (particularly in the late fourth and early fifth centuries) and may not have so clearly defined monastic endeavors at their origins.

ANTHONY

(1) When the holy Abba Anthony lived in the desert, he was beset by *accidie*[1] and attacked by many sinful thoughts. He said to God, "Lord, I want to be saved, but these thoughts do not leave me alone; what shall I do in my affliction? How can I be saved?" A short while afterward, when he got up to go out, Anthony saw a man like himself sitting at his work, getting up from his work to pray, then sitting down and plaiting a rope, then getting up again to pray. It was an angel

---

[1] That is, "sloth" or "languor."

of the Lord sent to correct and reassure him. He heard the angel saying to him, "Do this, and you will be saved." At these words, Anthony was filled with joy and courage. He did this, and he was saved.

(10) He said also, "Just as fish die if they stay too long out of water, so the monks who loiter outside their cells or pass their time with men of the world lose the intensity of inner peace. So like a fish going toward the sea, we must hurry to reach our cell, for fear that if we delay outside we will lose our interior watchfulness."

(31) One day Abba Anthony received a letter from the Emperor Constantius, asking him to come to Constantinople, and he wondered whether he ought

---

From *Sayings of the Desert Fathers,* ed. and trans. Sister Benedicta Ward. Kalamazoo, Mich.: Cistercian Studies, 1975. Used with permission.

to go. So he said to Abba Paul, his disciple, "Ought I to go?" He replied, "If you go, you will be called Anthony, but if you stay here, you will be called Abba Anthony."

ARSENIUS

(5) Someone said to blessed Arsenius, "How is it that we, with all our education and our wide knowledge, get nowhere, while these Egyptian peasants acquire so many virtues?" Abba Arsenius said to him, "We indeed get nothing from our secular education, but these Egyptian peasants acquire the virtues by hard work."

(28) When Abba Arsenius was living at Canopus, a very rich and God-fearing virgin of senatorial rank came from Rome to see him. When the Archbishop Theophilus met her, she asked him to persuade the old man to receive her. So he went to ask him to do so in these words, "A certain person of senatorial rank has come from Rome and wishes to see you." The old man refused to meet her. But when the archbishop told the young girl this, she ordered the beast of burden to be saddled saying, "I trust in God that I shall see him, for it is not a man whom I have come to see (there are plenty of those in our town), but a prophet." When she had reached the old man's cell, by a dispensation of God, he was outside it. Seeing him, she threw herself at his feet. Outraged, he lifted her up again and said, looking steadily at her, "If you must see my face, here it is, look." She was covered with shame and did not look at his face. Then the old man said to her, "Have you not heard tell of my way of life? It ought to be respected. How dare you make such a journey? Do you not realize you are a woman and cannot go just anywhere? Or is it so that on returning to Rome you can say to other women: I have seen Arsenius? Then they will turn the sea into a thoroughfare with women coming to see me." She said, "May it please the Lord, I shall not let anyone come here, but pray for me and remember me always." But he answered her, "I pray God to remove remembrance of you from my heart." Overcome at hearing these words, she withdrew. When she had re-

turned to the town, in her grief she fell ill with a fever, and blessed Archbishop Theophilus was informed that she was ill. He came to see her and asked her to tell him what was the matter. She said to him, "If only I had not gone there! For I asked the old man to remember me, he said to me, 'I pray God to take the remembrance of you from my heart.' So now I am dying of grief." The archbishop said to her, "Do you not realize that you are a woman and that it is through women that the enemy wars against the saints? That is the explanation of the old man's words, but as for your soul, he will pray for it continually." At this, her spirit was healed and she returned home joyfully.

(42) Abba Daniel used to say this about him: "He never wanted to reply to a question concerning the Scriptures, though he could well have done so had he wished, just as he never readily wrote a letter. When from time to time he came to church, he would sit behind a pillar, so that no one should see his face and so that he himself would not notice others. His appearance was angelic, like that of Jacob. His body was graceful and slender; his long beard reached down to his waist. Through much weeping, his eyelashes had fallen out. Tall of stature, he was bent with old age. He was ninety-five when he died. For forty years he was employed in the palace of Theodosius the Great of divine memory, who was the father of the divine Arcadius and Honorius; then he lived forty years in Scetis, ten years in Troë above Babylon, opposite Memphis; and three years at Canopus of Alexandria. The last two years he returned to Troë where he died, finishing his course in peace and the fear of God. He was a good man 'filled with the Holy Spirit and faith' (Acts 11:24). He left me his leather tunic, his white hair shirt and his palm-leaf sandals. Although unworthy, I wear them, in order to gain his blessing."

BESSARION

(8) The same Abba Bessarion said, "For fourteen years I have never lain down, but have always slept sitting or standing."

EVAGRIUS

(7) One day at the Cells, there was an assembly about some matter or other, and Abba Evagrius held forth. Then the priest said to him, "Abba, we know that if you were living in your own country, you would probably be a bishop and a great leader, but at present you sit here as a stranger." He was filled with compunction, but was not at all upset, and bending his head he replied, "I have spoken once and will not answer, twice but I will proceed no further (Job 40:5)."

THEODORA

(3) She also said, "It is good to live in peace, for the wise man practices perpetual prayer. It is truly a great thing for a virgin or a monk to live in peace, especially for the younger ones. However, you should realize that as soon as you intend to live in peace, at once evil comes and weighs down your soul through *accidie,* faintheartedness, and evil thoughts. It also attacks your body through sickness, debility, weakening of the knees, and all the members. It dissipates the strength of soul and body, so that one believes one is ill and no longer able to pray. But if we are vigilant, all these temptations fall away. There was, in fact a monk who was seized by cold and fever every time he began to pray, and he suffered from headaches, too. In this condition, he said to himself, 'I am ill and near to death, so now I will get up before I die and pray.' By reasoning in this way, he did violence to himself and prayed. When he had finished, the fever abated also. So, by reasoning in this way, the brother resisted and prayed and was able to conquer his thoughts."

JOHN THE DWARF

(16) The old man also said this to a certain brother about the soul that wishes to be converted, "There was in a city a courtesan who had many lovers. One of the governors approached her, saying, 'Promise me you will be good, and I will marry you.' She promised this, and he took her and brought her to his house. Her lovers, seeking her again, said to one another, 'That lord has taken her with him to his house, so if we go to his house and he learns of it, he will condemn us. But let us go to the back and whistle to her. Then, when she recognizes the sound of the whistle, she will come down to us; as for us, we shall be unassailable.' When she heard the whistle, the woman stopped her ears and withdrew to the inner chamber and shut the doors." The old man said that this courtesan is our soul; that her lovers are the passions and other men; that the lord is Christ; that the inner chamber is the eternal dwelling; those who whistle are the evil demons, but the soul always takes refuge in the Lord.

ISIDORE THE PRIEST

(8) Abba Isidore went one day to see Abba Theophilus, archbishop of Alexandria, and when he returned to Scetis, the brethren asked him, "What is going on in the city?" But he said to them, "Truly, brothers, I did not see the face of anyone there, except that of the archbishop." Hearing this, they were very anxious and said to him, "Has there been a disaster there, then, abba?" He said, "Not at all, but the thought of looking at anyone did not get the better of me." At these words, they were filled with admiration and strengthened in their intention of guarding the eyes from all distraction.

ISAAC OF THE CELLS

(5) He also said to the brethren, "Do not bring young boys here. Four churches in Scetis are deserted because of boys."

ISIDORE THE PRIEST (II)

(5) He also said, "Disciples must love as their fathers those who are truly their masters and fear them as

their leaders; they should not lose their fear because of love, nor because of fear should love be obscured."

MACARIUS THE GREAT

(1) Abba Macarius said this about himself: "When I was young and was living in a cell in Egypt, they took me to make me a cleric in the village. Because I did not wish to receive this dignity, I fled to another place. Then a devout layman joined me; he sold my manual work for me and served me. Now it happened that a virgin in the village, under the weight of temptation, committed sin. When she became pregnant, they asked her who was to blame. She said, 'The anchorite.' Then they came to seize me, led me to the village, and hung pots black with soot and various other things round my neck and led me through the village in all directions, beating me and saying, 'This monk has defiled our virgin, catch him, catch him,' and they beat me almost to death. Then one of the old men came and said, 'What are you doing, how long will you go on beating this strange monk?' The man who served me was walking behind me, full of shame, for they covered him with insults, too, saying, 'Look at this anchorite, for whom you stood surety; what has he done?' The girl's parents said, 'Do not let him go until he has given a pledge that he will keep her.' I spoke to my servant, and he vouched for me. Going to my cell, I gave him all the baskets I had, saying, 'Sell them and give my wife something to eat.' Then I said to myself, 'Macarius, you have found yourself a wife; you must work a little more in order to keep her.' So I worked night and day and sent my work to her. But when the time came for the wretch to give birth, she remained in labor many days without bringing forth, and they said to her, 'What is the matter?' She said, 'I know what it is, it is because I slandered the anchorite and accused him unjustly; it is not he who is to blame, but such and such a young man.' Then the man who served me came to me full of joy, saying, 'The virgin could not give birth until she had said "The anchorite had nothing to do with it, but I have lied about him." The whole village wants to come here

solemnly and do penance before you.' But when I heard this, for fear people would disturb me, I got up and fled here to Scetis. That is the original reason why I came here."

(23) A brother came to see Abba Macarius the Egyptian and said to him, "Abba, give me a word, that I may be saved." So the old man said, "Go to the cemetery and abuse the dead." The brother went there, abused them, and threw stones at them; then he returned and told the old man about it. The latter said to him, "Didn't they say anything to you?" He replied, "No." The old man said, "Go back tomorrow and praise them." So the brother went away and praised them, calling them, "Apostles, saints, and righteous men." He returned to the old man and said to him, "I have complimented them." And the old man said to him, "Did they not answer you?" The brother said no. The old man said to him, "You know how you insulted them, and they did not reply, and how you praised them, and they did not speak; so you, too, if you wish to be saved must do the same and become a dead man. Like the dead, take no account of either the scorn of men or their praises, and you can be saved."

(33) Abba Bitimius related that Abba Macarius said this: "When I was living at Scetis, two young strangers came down there. One had a beard, the other was beginning to grow one. They came toward me saying: 'Where is Abba Macarius's cell?' I said to them: 'What do you want with him?' They replied, 'We have heard tell of him and of Scetis, and we have come to see him.' I said to them, 'I am he.' Then they bowed low to me and said, 'We want to live here.' Seeing that they were delicate and had been brought up in comfort, I said to them, 'You cannot live here.' The elder said, 'If we cannot live here, we will go somewhere else.' Then I said to myself, 'Why chase them away and be a stumbling block to them? Suffering will make them go away of their own accord.' So I said to them, 'Come and make yourselves a cell, if you can.' They said, 'Show us a place, and we will make one.' The old man gave them an ax, a basket full of bread and salt, and showed them a lump of rock, saying, 'Cut out some stones here and bring wood from the marsh, make a roof, and live here.' He added, 'I

thought they would choose to go away, because of the hardship. But they asked me what work they should do here.' I replied, 'Rope making.' And I took some leaves from the marsh and showed them the rudiments of weaving and how to handle the reeds. I said to them, 'Make some baskets, give them to the keepers, and they will bring you bread.' Then I went away. But they, with patience, did all that I had told them and for three years they did not come to see me. Now I wrestled with my thoughts, thinking, 'What is their way of life? Why do they not come to ask me about their thoughts? Those who live far off come to see me, but those who live quite close do not come. They do not go to anyone else either; they only go to church, in silence, to receive the oblation.' I prayed to God, fasting the whole week, that he would show me their way of life. At the end of the week, I got up and went to visit them, to see how they were. When I knocked, they opened the door and greeted me in silence. Having prayed, I sat down. The elder made a sign to the younger to go out, and he sat plaiting the rope without saying anything. At the ninth hour, he knocked, and the younger one returned and made a little soup and set the table at a sign of his elder brother. He put three small loaves on it and stood in silence. As for me, I said, 'Rise, and let us eat.' We got up to eat, and he brought a small water bottle and we drank. When the evening came, they said to me, 'Are you going away?' I replied, 'No, I will sleep here.' They spread a mat for me on one side, another for themselves in the opposite corner. They took off their girdles and cowls and lay down together on the mat. When they were settled, I prayed God that he would show me their way of life. Then the roof opened, and it became as light as day, but they did not see the light. When they thought I was asleep, the elder tapped the younger on the side, and they got up, put on their girdles again, and stretched their hands toward heaven. I could see them, but they could not see me. I saw the demons coming like flies upon the younger one, some sitting on his mouth and others on his eyes. I saw the angel of the Lord circling round about him with a fiery sword, chasing the demons far from him. But they could not come near the elder one. When early dawn came, they lay down, and I made as though I had just woken up, and they did the same. The elder simply said to me 'Shall we recite the

twelve psalms?' and I said to him, 'Yes.' The younger one chanted five psalms in groups of six verses and an alleluia, and at each verse a tongue of flame came out of his mouth and ascended to heaven. Likewise with the elder, when he opened his mouth to chant, it was like a column of fire that came forth and ascended up to heaven; in my turn, I recited a little by heart. As I went out, I said, 'Pray for me.' But they bowed without saying a word. So I learned that the first was a perfect man, but the enemy was still fighting against the younger. A few days later, the elder brother fell asleep, and three days afterward, his younger brother died, too." When the Fathers came to see Abba Macarius, he used to take them to their cell and say, "Come and see the place of martyrdom of the young strangers."

MOSES

(2) A brother at Scetis committed a fault. A council was called to which Abba Moses was invited, but he refused to go to it. Then the priest sent someone to say to him, "Come, for everyone is waiting for you." So he got up and went. He took a leaking jug, filled it with water, and carried it with him. The others came out to meet him and said to him, "What is this, Father?" The old man said to them, "My sins run out behind me, and I do not see them, and today I am coming to judge the errors of another." When they heard that, they said no more to the brother but forgave him.

(3) Another day when a council was being held in Scetis, the Fathers treated Moses with contempt in order to test him, saying, "Why does this black man come among us?" When he heard this, he kept silence. When the council was dismissed, they said to him, "Abba, did that not grieve you at all?" He said to them, "I was grieved, but I kept silence."

(4) It was said of Abba Moses that he was ordained and the ephod was placed upon him. The archbishop said to him, "See, Abba Moses, now you are entirely white." The old man said to him, "It is true of the outside, lord and father, but what about him who sees the inside?" Wishing to test him, the archbishop said to the priests, "When Abba Moses comes into the sanctuary, drive him out and go with him to hear what he says." So the old man came in,

and they covered him with abuse and drove him out, saying, "Outside, black man!" Going out, he said to himself, "They have acted rightly concerning you, for your skin is as black as ashes. You are not a man, so why should you be allowed to meet men?"

MATOES

(11) A brother questioned Abba Matoes saying, "Give me a word." He said to him, "Go, and pray God to put compunction in your heart and give you humility; be aware of your faults; do not judge others, but put yourself below everyone; do not be friendly with a boy or with an heretical friend; put freedom of speech far from you; control your tongue and your belly; drink only a small quantity of wine, and if someone speaks about some topic, do not argue with him, but if he is right, say, 'Yes'; if he is wrong, say, 'You know what you are saying,' and do not argue with him about what he has said. That is humility."

OLYMPIUS

(2) Abba Olympius of the Cells was tempted to fornication. His thoughts said to him, "Go, and take a wife." He got up, found some mud, made a woman, and said to himself, "Here is your wife; now you must work hard in order to feed her." So he worked, giving himself a great deal of trouble. The next day, making some mud again, he formed it into a girl and said to his thoughts, "Your wife has had a child; you must work harder so as to be able to feed her and clothe your child." So, he wore himself out doing this and said to his thoughts, "I cannot bear this weariness any longer." They answered, "If you cannot bear such weariness, stop wanting a wife." God, seeing his efforts, took away the conflict from him, and he was at peace.

POEMEN

(19) Some brothers told Abba Poemen of a brother who did not drink wine. He said, "Wine is not for monks."

(65) He said that someone asked Abba Paësius, "What should I do about my soul, because it is insensitive and does not fear God?" He said to him, "Go, and join a man who fears God and live near him; he will teach you, too, to fear God."

(150) Abba Poemen said, "In Abba Pambo we see three bodily activities: abstinence from food until the evening every day, silence, and much manual work."

(160) Abba Poemen said, "These three things are the most helpful of all: fear of the Lord, prayer, and doing good to one's neighbor."

(208) A brother asked Abba Poemen, "What can I do about my sins?" and the old man said to him, "Weep interiorly, for both deliverance from faults and the acquisition of virtues are gained through compunction."

(209) He also said, "Weeping is the way that Scripture and our Fathers have handed on to us."

PAMBO

(4) Athanasius, archbishop of Alexandria, of holy memory, begged Abba Pambo to come down from the desert to Alexandria. He went down, and seeing an actress he began to weep. Those who were present asked him the reason for his tears, and he said, "Two things make me weep: one, the loss of this woman, and the other, that I am not so concerned to please God as she is to please wicked men."

(13) They said of Abba Pambo that his face never smiled. So one day, wishing to make him laugh, the demons stuck wing feathers on to a lump of wood and brought it in making an uproar and saying, "Go, go." When he saw them, Abba Pambo began to laugh, and the demons started to say in chorus, "Ha! ha! Pambo has laughed!" But in reply he said to them, "I have not laughed, but I made fun of your powerlessness because it takes so many of you to carry a wing."

PAPHNUTIUS

(4) There was at Scetis with Paphnutius a brother who had to fight against fornication, and he said, "Even if I take ten wives, I shall not satisfy my de-

sire." The old man encouraged him, saying, "No, my child, this warfare comes from the demons." But he did not let himself be persuaded, and he left for Egypt to take a wife. After a time it happened that the old man went up to Egypt and met him carrying baskets of shellfish. He did not recognize him at all, but the other said to him, "I am so and so, your disciple." And the old man, seeing him in such disgrace, wept and said, "How have you lost your dignity and come to such humiliation? No doubt you have taken ten wives?" And groaning, he said, "Truly I have only taken one, and I have a great deal of trouble satisfying her with food." The old man said, "Come back with us." He said, "Is it possible to repent, abba?" He said that it was. And leaving everything, the brother followed him and returned to Scetis, and thanks to this experience he became a proved monk.

SISOES

(25) One day some Arians came to see Abba Sisoes on Abba Anthony's mountain, and they began to speak against the orthodox faith. The old man gave them no answer, but he called his disciple and said to him, "Abraham, bring me the book of Saint Athanasius and read it." Then they were silent as their heresy was unmasked, and he sent them away in peace.

(33) One of the Fathers related of Abba Sisoes of Calamon that wishing to overcome sleep one day, he hung himself over the precipice of Petra. An angel came to take him down and ordered him not to do that again and not to transmit such teaching to others.

SILVANUS

(5) A brother went to see Abba Silvanus on the mountain of Sinai. When he saw the brothers working hard, he said to the old man, "Do not labor for the food that perishes (John 6:27). Mary has chosen the good portion (Luke 10:42)." The old man said to his disciple, "Zacharias, give the brother a book and put him in a cell without anything else." So when the ninth hour came, the visitor watched the door expecting someone would be sent to call him to the meal. When no one called him, he got up, went to find the old man, and said to him, "Have the brothers not eaten today?" The old man replied that they had. Then he said, "Why did you not call me?" The old man said to him, "Because you are a spiritual man and do not need that kind of food. We, being carnal, want to eat, and that is why we work. But you have chosen the good portion and read the whole day long, and you do not want to eat carnal food." When he heard these words, the brother made a prostration saying, "Forgive me, abba." The old man said to him, "Mary needs Martha. It is really thanks to Martha that Mary is praised."

SOPATRUS

Someone asked Abba Sopatrus, "Give me a commandment, abba, and I will keep it." He said to him, "Do not allow a woman to come into your cell and do not read apocryphal literature. Do not get involved in discussions about the image. Although this is not heresy, there is too much ignorance and liking for dispute between the two parties in this matter. It is impossible for a creature to understand the truth of it."

SERAPION

(1) One day Abba Serapion passed through an Egyptian village, and there he saw a courtesan who stayed in her own cell. The old man said to her, "Expect me this evening, for I should like to come and spend the night with you." She replied, "Very well, abba." She got ready and made the bed. When evening came, the old man came to see her and entered her cell and said to her, "Have you got the bed ready?" She said, "Yes, abba." Then he closed the door and said to her, "Wait a bit, for we have a rule of prayer, and I must fulfill that first." So the old man began his prayers. He took the psalter and at each psalm he said a prayer for the courtesan, begging God that she might be converted and saved, and God heard him. The woman stood trembling and praying beside the old man. When he

had completed the whole psalter, the woman fell to the ground. Then the old man, beginning the Epistle, read a great deal from the apostle and completed his prayers. The woman was filled with compunction and understood that he had not come to see her to commit sin but to save her soul, and she fell at his feet, saying, "Abba, do me this kindness and take me where I can please God." So the old man took her to a monastery of virgins and entrusted her to the amma, and he said, "Take this sister and do not put any yoke or commandment on her as on the other sisters, but if she wants something, give it her and allow her to walk as she wishes." After some days the courtesan said, "I am a sinner; I wish to eat every second day." A little later she said, "I have committed many sins, and I wish to eat every fourth day." A few days later she besought the amma saying, "Since I have grieved God greatly by my sins, do me the kindness of putting me in a cell and shutting it completely and giving me a little bread and some work through the window." The amma did so, and the woman pleased God all the rest of her life.

(2) A brother said to Abba Serapion, "Give me a word." The old man said to him, "What shall I say to you? You have taken the living of the widows and orphans and put it on your shelves." For he saw them full of books.

SARAH

(4) Another time, two old men, great anchorites, came to the district of Pelusia to visit her. When they arrived, one said to the other, "Let us humiliate this old woman." So they said to her, "Be careful not to become conceited thinking to yourself: 'Look how anchorites are coming to see me, a mere woman.'" But Amma Sarah said to them, "According to nature I am a woman, but not according to my thoughts."

(8) Some monks of Scetis came one day to visit Amma Sarah. She offered them a small basket of fruit. They left the good fruit and ate the bad. So she said to them, "You are true monks of Scetis."

(9) She also said to the brothers, "It is I who am a man, you who are women."

SYNCLETICA

(9) She also said, "When you have to fast, do not pretend illness. For those who do not fast often fall into real sicknesses. If you have begun to act well, do not turn back through constraint of the enemy, for through your endurance, the enemy is destroyed. Those who put out to sea at first sail with a favorable wind; then the sails spread, but later the winds become adverse. Then the ship is tossed by the waves and is no longer controlled by the rudder. But when in a little while there is a calm, and the tempest dies down, then the ship sails on again. So it is with us, when we are driven by the spirits who are against us; we hold to the cross as our sail, and so we can set a safe course."

(10) She also said, "Those who have endured the labors and dangers of the sea and then amass material riches, even when they have gained much desire to gain yet more and they consider what they have at present as nothing and reach out for what they have not got. We, who have nothing of that which we desire wish to acquire everything through the fear of God."

(12) She also said, "It is dangerous for anyone to teach who has not first been trained in the 'practical' life. For if someone who owns a ruined house receives guests there, he does them harm because of the dilapidation of his dwelling. It is the same in the case of someone who has not first built an interior dwelling; he causes loss to those who come. By words one may convert them to salvation, but by evil behavior, one injures them."

40. Antony: Letters

The image of Antony that emerges from his *Letters* differs dramatically from his portrayal in both Athanasius's *Life of Antony* (Text 46) and the *Sayings of the Desert Fathers* (Text 39). The Antony of the *Life* and *Sayings* was a simple illiterate monk whose ability to combat earthly and demonic opponents sprang from his spiritual talents, not his intellect. The Antony of the *Letters,* however, is philosophically sophisticated, viewing the monastic endeavor in light of complex conceptions of creation and salvation derived from the teachings of the third-century speculative theologian Origen.

Origen had theorized that all rational creatures had existed in a primordial unity with God, but that these preexistent minds at some point were distracted and fell away from God. The degree to which souls fell determined their place in a new created order: angels, powers, humans, demons, and the devil. God provided a material world and bodies (the "coats of skin" of Genesis 3:21) within which humans could discipline their rebellious souls and find a way back to that original unity with God.

Antony, along with other desert monastics (most famously, Evagrius of Pontus), transformed this Origenist cosmology and soteriology into monastic systems of ascetic withdrawal and discipline. The mortification of body and spirit that characterized the ascetic movement were embedded in a rich philosophical framework that has been obscured by subsequent hagiography and heretical controversy. The Origenist monks of Lower Egypt were accused of heresy by some of their fellow monks and Bishop Theophilus of Alexandria and were driven out of the desert at the end of the fourth century (see Text 27). This theological purge has left us with the image of monastic simplicity and anti-intellectualism that survives in the *Sayings of the Desert Fathers.* Of the seven letters of Antony recently reconstructed from a variety of sources, three are reproduced here; they give a sense of the deep intellectual traditions—both philosophical and scriptural—that existed in the early fourth-century desert.

LETTER ONE

First of all, I greet you in the Lord.

I believe that the souls, whether male or female, whom God in his mercy has assembled by his own Word, are of three kinds.

Some were reached by the Word of God through the law of promise and the discernment of the good inherent in them from their first formation. They did not hesitate but followed it readily as did Abraham, our father. Since he offered himself in love through the law of promise, God appeared to him, saying: *Go from your country and your kindred and from your father's house to the land that I will show you* (Gen 12:1). And he went without hesitating at all, but being ready for his calling. This is the model for the beginning of this way of life. It still persists in those who follow this pattern. Wherever and whenever souls endure and bow to it, they easily attain the virtues, since their hearts are ready to be guided by the Spirit of God. This is the first kind.

The second kind we find in those who hear the written law testify of all pain and punishment prepared for the wicked and announce the blessed prom-

From *The Letters of Saint Antony: Monasticism and the Making of a Saint,* by Samuel Rubenson. Minneapolis: Fortress, 1995. Used with permission.

ises for those who progress. Through the testimonies of the written law, their thoughts are aroused, and they try to enter into their calling. David, too, testifies of this, saying: *The law of the Lord is without blemish and vivifies the soul* (Ps 19:8), and elsewhere he says: *The revelation of your words gives light and makes children wise* (Ps 119:130), and of the same more than we are able to recount.

The third kind we find in those whose hearts are hard from the beginning and who persist in the works of sin. God the merciful sends afflictions and chastisement upon them, until through their afflictions they are made aware and repent and return. And if they repent with all their heart, they enter into the calling and attain the virtues, like the others about whom I have already written.

These are the three gates for the souls who come to repent until they obtain grace and the calling of the Son of God.

But I believe that those who have entered with all their heart and have prepared themselves to endure all the trials of the enemy until they prevail are first called by the Spirit, who alleviates everything for them so that the work of repentance becomes sweet for them. He sets for them a rule for how to repent in their bodies and souls until he has taught them the way to return to God, their own Creator. He also gives them control over their souls and bodies in order that both may be sanctified and inherit together:

First the body through many fasts and vigils, through the exertion and the exercises of the body, cutting of all the fruits of the flesh. In this the Spirit of repentance is his guide, testing him through them, so that the enmity does not bring him back again. Then the guiding Spirit begins to open the eyes of the soul, to show it the way of repentance that it, too, may be purified.

The mind also starts to discriminate between them and begins to learn from the Spirit how to purify the body and the soul through repentance. The mind is taught by the Spirit and guides us in the actions of the body and soul, purifying both of them, separating the fruits of the flesh from what is natural to the body in which they were mingled and through which the transgression came to be, and leads each member of the body back to its original condition, free from

everything alien that belongs to the spirit of the enemy.

The body is thus brought under the authority of the mind and is taught by the Spirit, as the words of Paul testify: *I castigate my body and bring it into subjection* (1 Cor 9:27). Then mind sanctifies it in food and drink and sleep and, in one word, in all its movements, even separating itself from the natural union through its own sanctity.

I believe that there are three movements in the body. There is a natural, inherent movement, which does not operate unless the soul consents, otherwise it remains still. Then there is another movement as a result of stuffing the body with a multitude of food and drink. The heat of the blood, caused by excessive eating, stirs up the body, which is now moved by gluttony. Because of this the apostle says: *Be not drunk with wine, wherein is excess* (Eph 5:18). And the Lord enjoined his disciples in the Gospel saying: *Take heed lest at anytime your hearts be overcharged with surfeiting and drunkenness* (Luke 21:34) and pleasures. Especially since they seek the level of sanctity, they should say: *I castigate my body and bring it into subjection* (1 Cor 9:27). The third movement comes from the evil spirits, tempting us out of envy and seeking to divert those who attempt to sanctify themselves.

If the soul perseveres in these three ways and keeps to what the Spirit has taught the mind, it purifies both from the three types of affliction. But if the mind spurns the testimonies that the Spirit has given it, then evil spirits override the [natural] constitution of the body and stir up these movements, until the soul grows weary and asks from where it can receive help and converts and adheres to the testimony of the Spirit and is healed. Then it believes that this is its rest: to abide with God, who is its peace.

This I have said about repentance in the body and the soul and how they are sanctified. And when the mind accepts this struggle, then it prays in the Spirit and begins to expel the afflictions of the soul, which have come upon it through its own greed. The soul is then in communion with the Spirit, since it keeps the commandments it has received. And the Spirit teaches it how to heal all its afflictions and how to expel them one by one, from head to foot, those mingled with what is natural to the body as well as those that are independent of the body, but have been mingled with it through the will.

It sets a rule for the eyes that they may see rightly and purely and never again have anything alien in them and for the ears that they may hear in peace and never again wish to hear anything evil or any slandering of men, but rather all kinds of benevolence and mercy toward all creation, for in [both of] them it was once sick.

It also teaches the tongue its own purity, since its affliction is great. For the one who speaks is sick and gives to the tongue his own works. Thus the afflictions are made abundant through this member, which is the tongue. This is confirmed by James, the apostle, who says: *If someone thinks that he serves God and does not control his tongue but deceives his own heart, his worship is vain* (Jas 1:26). Somewhere else he says that *the tongue is a small member, but it defiles the whole body* (Jas 3:5). And there is more like this than we can quote. But if the mind is strengthened by the Spirit, it is first purified itself; then it examines the words and gives them to the tongue, so that they are free from hypocrisy and self-will. Thus the words of Solomon are fulfilled: *My words are spoken by God. There is nothing twisted or perverse in them* (Prov 8:8), and somewhere else he says, *The tongue of the wise heals* (Prov 12:18), and so on.

And also the movements of the hand, if they were moved disorderly by the will of the soul, are now made firm by the Spirit and destined to move toward purity by prayers and acts of mercy. And on them the word about prayer is fulfilled, stating, *Let the lifting up of my hands be as the evening sacrifice* (Ps 141:2), and also, *The hands of the diligent make rich* (Prov 10:4).

Also the belly is purified in its eating and drinking, although it used to be insatiable in these matters, once it had been moved toward them by the will of the soul. Through desire and greed for food and drink, not a few have fallen in with the demons, and of them it is said by David, *I do not dine with one who has a high look and an insatiable heart* (Ps 101:5).

To those, however, who seek purity, the Spirit assigns this rule of purification: moderation after the power of the body, devoid of any greed or desire. On them this word of Paul is fulfilled saying: *Whether you eat or drink, or whatever you do, do all to the glory of God* (1 Cor 10:31).

Then, in regard to the sexual thoughts moved from below the belly, the mind is again taught by the Spirit how to distinguish between the three types of movements mentioned above and how to strive for purification having the help of the Spirit. All the movements are then quenched by the power of the Spirit, pacifying the entire body and extinguishing the movements. This is the word given by Paul: *Mortify your members that are upon the earth: fornication, uncleanness, and evil desires* (Col 3:5), and so forth.

And then also the feet, which formerly did not walk soundly according to the will of God; the mind, being united under the authority of the Spirit, makes them walk according to the will of the Spirit, that they may minister in good works so that the whole body may be changed and placed under the authority of the Spirit. And I think that [even] now this dwelling has taken on something of that other spiritual body that will be taken on at the resurrection of the just.

This I have said concerning the afflictions of the soul that have become mingled with what is natural to the body, in which the soul moves, so that it has become a guide to the evil spirits working in its members.

But I also say that the soul has some [movements] proper to it alone, which we will now examine: Pride is an affliction apart from the body, self-glorification another, as well as insolence, hatred, envy, wrath, pusillanimity, impatience, and the rest. But if it gives itself to God wholeheartedly, God the merciful gives to it the Spirit of repentance and shows it how to repent in the case of each affliction and also how the enemies prevent her and try to possess her, not allowing her to repent.

If the soul endures and obeys what the Spirit has taught it about repentance, then the Creator has mercy on the weariness of its repentance through the labors of the body, such as prolonged fasts, vigils, much study of the Word of God, and many prayers, as well as the renunciation of the world and human things, humility, and contrition. And if it endures in all this, then God the merciful sees its patience in the temptations and has mercy and helps it.

LETTER FIVE

Antony greets his beloved children, holy Israelite children, in their spiritual essence. I do not need to call you by your names in the flesh, which are passing away, for you are Israelite children. Truly, my sons, the love I have for you is not the love of the flesh, but the love of godliness. Therefore I do not tire of praying for you day and night that you may come to know the grace he has granted you, that God did not visit his creatures just once, but from the beginning of the world God looks after his creatures and he raises up the generations one by one through occasions and gifts of grace.

Now, my children, do not neglect to cry out day and night to God, entreating by the benevolence of the Father, to grant you help from above, and teach you what befits you. Truly, my children, we dwell in our death and stay in the house of the robber, bound by the fetters of death. Therefore, *do not give sleep to your eyes or slumber to your eyelids* (Ps 132:4), that you may in all sanctity *offer yourselves as a sacrifice to God* (cf. Rom 12:1), whom no one can inherit without sanctity.

Truly, my beloved in the Lord, let this word be manifest to you, that you may do good and so give rest to all the saints and readiness to the ministry of the angels and rejoice at the coming of Jesus, for because of us none of them has yet found rest (cf. Heb 11:39–40). Even to my miserable self, dwelling in this house of clay, you will thus bring happiness to my soul.

Truly, my children, this affliction and humiliation of ours gives distress to all the saints. For our sake they weep and moan before the Creator of all. Thus, because of the moaning of the saints, the God of all is angry with all our evil deeds. But our progress and justification stir up the assembly of the saints, and they pray devoutly and make joyful exultation before our Creator, and he himself, the Creator of all, rejoices in our good deeds on the testimony of his saints, and so he grants us great gifts of grace.

That you may know that God always loves his creatures, their essence being immortal, not to be dissolved with the body: Having seen that the spiritual essence had descended into the abyss, being completely dead, and that the law of promise had grown cold, God in his benevolence visited them through Moses. Moses truly founded the house of truth and wanted to heal the great wound and bring them back to their original unity, but he could not, and left them. Then, too, the council of the prophets built upon the foundation of Moses, but they were unable to heal the great wound of their members and realized that their power ceased. Thus the communion of all the saints assembled in unity and offered prayers before their Creator, saying: *Is there no balm in Gilead? Is there no physician there? Why then is not the health of the daughter of my people recovered? O Lord, we would have healed Babylon, and she is not healed. Now let us forsake her and flee from her* (Jer 8:22, 51:9).

And all prayed by the benevolence of the Father for his only begotten, because unless he himself would come, none of the creatures would be able to heal the great wound. For this reason the Father in his benevolence spoke and said: *Son of man, make to yourself vessels of captivity* (Ezek 12:3). For the salvation of us all, the Father *did not spare his Only begotten, but delivered him up for our sins* (Rom 8:32). *Our iniquities humbled him, and by his stripes we were healed* (Isa 53:5), and he gathered us from all lands, from one end of the earth to the other, resurrecting our minds from the earth and teaching us that we are members of one another.

Take heed, children, that the word of Paul may not be accomplished upon us, that: *We have the form of godliness, but deny its power* (2 Tim 3:5). Let each one of you rend his heart and weep before him and say: *What shall I render unto the Lord for all his benefits towards me?* (Ps 116:12). But I tremble, my children, lest the word be accomplished upon us: *What profit is there in my blood, when I go down to corruption?* (Ps 29:10 [LXX]).

Truly, my children, I talk to you *as to wise men* (cf. 1 Cor 10:15), so that you understand what I tell you: Unless each one of you hates all earthly possessions and renounces them and all their workings by all his heart and stretches out the hands of his heart to heaven and to the Father of all, he cannot be saved. But if he does this, God will have mercy because of his labor and grant him the invisible fire that burns up all impurity from him and purifies his mind. Then the Holy Spirit will dwell in us, and Jesus will stay with us, and thus we will be able to worship God as is proper. But as long as we have peace with the natures of this world, we remain enemies of God and of his angels and all his saints.

Now therefore, I beseech you, my beloved, in the name of our Lord Jesus Christ, not to neglect your true life, and not to confound the brevity of this time with time eternal, nor mistake the skin of the corruptible flesh with the reign of ineffable light, and not to let this place of damnation squander the angelic thrones of judgment.

Truly, my children, my heart wonders and my soul is terrified that we are all engulfed as if by a flood and carried away as if drunk by wine. Each one of us has sold himself by his own will, and we are dominated by it. We do not want to lift our eyes to seek the glory of heaven and the works of all the saints and to walk in their footsteps.

Now, therefore, understand that whether it be the holy heavens or angels or archangels or thrones or dominions or cherubim or seraphim or sun or moon or stars or patriarchs or prophets or apostles or devil or Satan or evil spirits or the powers of the air, or (to say no more) whether it be man or woman, in the beginning of their formation they all derive from one, except the perfect and blessed Trinity: Father, Son, and Holy Spirit. Because of the evil conduct of some, it was necessary that God should set names upon them after their works. And those who made the best progress, he gave more abundant glory.

LETTER SIX

Antony greets all his dear brothers, who are at Arsinoë and its neighborhood and those who are with you in the Lord. All of you who have prepared yourselves to come to God, I greet you in the Lord, my beloved, the young and the old, men and women, Israelite children, saints in your spiritual essence.

Truly, my beloved, you are greatly blessed, for great gifts of grace have been given to your generation. Thus, for the sake of him who has visited you, you should not weary in the struggle until you have offered yourselves as a sacrifice to God in all sanctity, without which none can inherit God.

Truly, my beloved, it is great for you to attempt to understand the spiritual essence, in which there is neither man nor woman; rather it is an immortal essence, which has a beginning but no end. You ought to know how it is utterly fallen into this humiliation and great confusion, which has come upon all of us. But since it is an immortal essence that is not destroyed with the body, God, seeing this incurable wound and seeing that it had become grave, visited them in his mercy, and after a time he, in his benevolence, granted them the law as an assistance through Moses, who gave the law. And Moses founded the house of truth and wanted to heal the great wound, but could not complete the building of the house. Then all the host of the saints assembled in unity and prayed by the benevolence of God for our salvation, that he would come to us to save us all, he, who is the great and true high priest and true physician, who is able to heal the great wound. For this reason he, following the will of the Father, divested himself of his glory; *being God, he took the form of a servant and gave himself for our sins, and our iniquities humbled him and through his stripes we were all healed* (Phil 2:6–7; Gal 1:4; Isa 53:5).

Therefore, my beloved in the Lord, I want you to know that it was for our foolishness that he choose to become a fool, for our weakness he accepted the form of weakness, for our poverty he became poor, and for our death he assumed death, and that he endured all this for our sake (cf. 1 Cor 1:18–28, 3:18–19, 4:10; 2 Cor 8:19). Truly, my beloved in the Lord, we ought not *to give sleep to our eyes or slumber to our eyelids* (Ps 132:4), but pray and beseech the benevolence of the Father until he comes to our help and we thus may find rest at the coming of Jesus and strength so that we are able to follow the saints, who are eager to support us in the time of our negligence, making them zealous so that they may help us in the time of our tribulations. Then *he that sows and he that reaps rejoice together* (John 4:36).

I want you to know, my children, the great distress that I have for you, for I see the great disgrace that comes upon us all and contemplate the struggle of the saints and their tears, which they shed at all times before God for our sake, when they see all the labor of their Creator and the evil devices of the devils and their disciples, which they always plan for our perdition, since their part is in the hell to come. Therefore they want us to be lost with them, so that we shall be with the multitude.

Truly, my beloved, *as to wise men I talk to you* (cf. 1 Cor 10:15), that you may know all the dispensations of our Creator, which he made for us, that he has payed visits to us through manifest and secret revelations. Yes, we are called sensible, but have put on an irrational mind, so that we are ignorant of how the secret contrivances and manifold crafts of the devil work and how they might be known. For they know that we have tried to know our disgrace and sought for a way to escape their acts, which they effect in us. And not only do we not obey the evil counsels that they sow in our hearts, but many of us even laugh at their contrivances. They know the indulgence of our Creator, that he died because of them in this world and prepared for them to inherit Gehenna as a result of their own negligence.

I want you to know, my children, that I do not cease to pray to God for you, day and night, that he may open the eyes of your hearts that you may see all the secret evils that they pour upon us every day in this present time. I ask God to give you a heart of knowledge and a spirit of discernment, that you may be able to lift you hearts before the Father as a pure sacrifice in all sanctity, without blemish.

Truly, my children, they are jealous of us at all times with their evil counsel, their secret persecution, their subtle malice, their spirits of seduction, their fraudulent thoughts, their faithlessness that they sow in our hearts every day, their hardness of heart and their numbness, the many sufferings they bring upon us at every hour, the weariness that causes our hearts to be weary at all times, all their wrath, the mutual slander that they teach us, our self-justifications in our deeds, and the condemnations that they sow in our hearts so that we, when we are alone, condemn our fellows, though they are not with us, the contempt they send into our hearts through pride so that we become hard-hearted and despise one another, becoming bitter against each other with hard words, and troubled every hour accusing each other and not ourselves, thinking that our struggle comes from our fellows, judging what is outside while the robbers are all inside our house, and [furthermore, with] the disputes and divisions we have with each other until we have established our own words so that they seem justified in the face of the other, and they incite us to do things that we are unable to do (and whose time it is not) and make us weary of things we do and that are good for us.

Therefore they make us laugh when it is time for weeping and weep when it is time for laughter, simply turning us aside every time from the straight way. Through many other deceits, they make us their slaves, but there is no time now to reveal all of them. But when they fill our hearts with all these and we feed on them and they become our food, then God is wroth with us.

Therefore, do not fail to beseech the goodness of the Father that perchance a helper will come to you so that you may teach yourselves to know what is truly right. Truly, I tell you, my children, that this our vessel in which we dwell is our destruction and a house full of war. In truth, my children, I tell you that every man who delights in his own desires and who is subdued to his own thoughts and sticks to what is sown in his own heart and rejoices in it and thinks in his heart that it is some great chosen mystery, and through it justifies himself in what he does, the soul of such a man is the breath of evil spirits and his counsel toward evil, and his body a store of evil mysteries that it hides in itself: and over such a one the demons have great power, because he has not dishonored them before all men.

Do you to know that they have not one single method of hunting, that we should know it and escape it? And if you seek, you will not find their sins and iniquities revealed bodily, for they are not visible bodily. But you should know that we are their bodies and that our soul receives their wickedness, and when it has received them, then it reveals them through the body in which we dwell. Now, then, my children, let us not give them any place; otherwise we shall stir up the wrath of God against us, and they will move freely [as if] in their home and laugh at us, since they know that our destruction is of our neighbor, and also our life is of our neighbor. For, who has ever seen God and rejoiced with him and kept him within himself, so that he would not leave him, but help him while he dwells in this heaviness? Or, who ever saw a demon fighting against us and preventing us from doing good, or opposing us, standing somewhere in the body, so that we should become afraid and flee from him? No, they are all hidden, and we reveal them by our deeds. They are, moreover, all from one (source) in their spiritual essence, but through their flight from God, great diversity has arisen between them since their deeds are varying.

Therefore all these names have been imposed on them after the deeds of each one. Some of them are called archangels, some thrones and dominions, principalities, powers, and cherubim. These names were given to them since they kept the will of their Creator. But due to the wickedness of the conduct of others, it was necessary to name them devil and Satan, after their own evil conduct. Others are called demons, evil and impure spirits, spirits of seduction and powers of this world, and there are many other varities among them. But there are also those who have opposed them in this heavy body in which we dwell—some of them are called patriarchs, and some prophets and kings and priests and judges and apostles, and there are many others chosen after their good conduct. All these names are given to them, whether male or female, for the sake of the variety of their deeds and in conformity with their own minds, but they are all from one (source).

Therefore, whoever sins against his neighbor sins against himself, and whoever does evil to his neighbor does evil to himself. Likewise, whoever does good to his neighbor does good to himself. For truly, who would there be who could do evil to God, or who

exists who can hurt him, or who is there who can give him rest, or who can ever serve him, or who exists who could ever bless him, as if he would need his blessing, or who could honor him so that he [really] is honored, or who could exalt him so that he [really] is elevated? Therefore, let us raise up God in ourselves by spurring one another and deliver ourselves to death for our [own] souls and for one another, and doing this we shall reveal the essence of our own mercy. Not that we should become self-lovers, lest we come under the power of inconstancy. For he who knows himself knows all, and thus it is written: *who called everything into being out of nothingness* (2 Macc 7:28). Saying this, they speak about their spiritual essence, which is hidden in this corruptible body, which it did not have from the beginning, and which it will be called away from. But he who is able to love himself, loves all.

My dear children, I pray that this will not be a burden to you, nor that you should tire of loving one another. Lift up your body in which you are clothed and make it an altar and lay upon it all your thoughts and leave all evil counsels before God, and lift up the hands of your heart to him, that is to the Creator of the mind, and pray to God that he gives you the great invisible fire, that it may descend from above and consume the altar and all upon it, as well as all the priests of Baal, who are the hostile works of the enemy, that they may fear and flee before you as before the prophet Elijah (cf. 1 Kings 18:38–40). Then you will see as it were the track of a man over the sea, who will bring you the spiritual rain, which is the comfort of the Spirit of comfort.

My dear children in the Lord, Israelite children, there is no need to bless or to mention your transient names in the flesh, for you are not ignorant of the love I have for you, that it is not the love of the flesh, but the love of godliness. Therefore I am confident that it is for you a great blessing that you have tried to know your own shame and to make firm the invisible essence, which does not pass away with the body. Thus I think that your blessing has begun (even) in our time. Let this word be manifest to you, that you should not regard your progress and entry into the service of God as your own work; rather a divine power supports you always. Be eager *to offer yourselves as a sacrifice to God always* (cf. Rom 12:1) and arouse the power that supports you and give rest to the coming of God and to all the host of the saints and to my miserable self, which dwells in this house of dust and darkness.

This is why I speak to you and give you rest and pray: We are all created from one invisible essence, having a beginning but no end; thus, they who know themselves know that the essence of unity is immortal.

I want you to know that our Lord Jesus Christ is the true mind of the Father, by whom all the fullness of every rational nature is made to the likeness of his image, he himself being the head of all creatures and the body of the Church (cf. Col 1:18). *Therefore we are all members of one another and the body of Christ. The head cannot say to the feet, "I do not need you," and if a member suffers the whole body is moved and suffers* (1 Cor 12:21, 26–27). But if a member is estranged from the body, having no contact with the head, but delighting in the passions of the flesh, it has contracted an incurable wound and has forgotten its beginning and its end.

For this reason the Father of creation had mercy upon us for the sake of this wound that none of the creatures could heal, but only the goodness of the Father. And he sent us his Only begotten, who for the sake of our servitude *accepted the form of a servant* (Phil 2:7), and *gave himself up for our sins, and our iniquities humbled him, but through his stripes we were all healed* (Rom 8:32; Gal 1:4; Isa 53:5). And he gathered us from all lands, until he resurrected our hearts from the earth and taught us that we are of one essence and members of one another. Therefore we ought to love one another warmly, for he who loves his neighbor loves God, and he who loves God loves his own soul.

Let this word be manifest to you, my dear children in the Lord, holy Israelite children, and prepare yourselves to go and *offer yourselves as a sacrifice unto God* (Rom 12:1) in all sanctity, for no one can inherit him without sanctity. Do you not know, my dear, that the enemy of virtue always contemplates evil against the truth? Therefore, my dear, take heed, and *do not give sleep to your eyes or slumber to your eyelids* (Ps 132:4), but cry out to you Creator day and night that he may send you a helper from above, who may encompass your hearts and thoughts in Christ.

Truly, my children, we dwell in a house of robbers and are bound by the bonds of death. Truly, I tell you that this our negligence, humiliation, and outward confusion is not only harmful for us, but it is also labor to the angels and all the holy of Christ, since for our sake they have not yet found peace. Truly, my beloved, our humiliation gives pain to all of them, as our salvation and pride give joy and rest to all of them.

And you should know that the goodness of the Father does not cease to do good to us always, from when it was first moved until this day, so as not to make us guilty of our own death, for we are created with a free will, and thus the demons watch out for us always. But for that reason it is written, *the angel of the Lord encamps around those who fear him and delivers them* (Ps 34:7).

Now, my children, I want you to know that from the first movement until now, all who have become estranged from virtue and fulfilled their wickedness are counted as children of the devil, and those who are of them, know it, and so they try to fashion each one of us after his own will. Knowing that the devil has fallen from above because of [his] pride, they, cunning as they are, attack through pride and contempt for one another, first those who have attained a high level. They know that thus they can cut us off from God, knowing that he who loves his neighbor loves God. For this reason the enemies of virtue sow the seed of division in our hearts, so that we become great adversaries of one another and do not at all, even from a distance, speak with our neighbor. Truly, my children, I also want you to know that there are many who have endured great struggle in this way of life, but have been killed by lack of discernment. Truly, my children, I consider it not strange at all that if you neglect yourselves and do not discern your works, you fall into the hands of the devil, and while you think you are close to God, and while you are expecting light, darkness overtakes you.

Why did Jesus gird himself with a towel and wash the feet of his disciples, if not to make this an exam-

ple and teach those who turn back to their first beginning, since pride is the origin of that movement that
was in the beginning. Therefore, if you do not have
great humility throughout your heart and in all your
mind, in all your soul and in all your body, you cannot inherit the kingdom of God. Truly, my children in
the Lord, I pray day and night to my Creator, who has
entrusted me with his spirit, to open for you the eyes
of your hearts that you may know this my love that I
have for you and open the ears of you hearts that you
may perceive your disgrace. For he who knows his
disgrace seeks again his chosen glory, and he who
knows his death also knows his eternal life.

As to wise men I write to you (1 Cor 10:15), my
children, for truly I fear that hunger may overtake
you on the way and in the place where we need to be
made rich. I wanted to see you face to face in the
body, but I now look forward to the time, which is
near, in which we will be able to see for ourselves the
faces of one another, when distress and pain and tears
shall have passed away, when joy will be among all.
There is much more I would have liked to tell, but
*if one gives occasion to a wise man he will be yet
wiser* (Prov 9:9). I greet you all by name, my beloved
children.

41. Aphrahat: Demonstration 6: On Covenanters

The Persian Christian known as Aphrahat (see Text 19) seems to have been a member of a
group known as the *bnay qyama,* or "covenanters" (literally, "sons of the covenant"). The
bnay qyama (and *bnat qyama,* "daughters of the covenant") practiced ascetic renunciation as
active members of their Christian communities. They did not withdraw to the desert, nor did
they partake in some of the more extreme forms of ascetic display found in the Syriac world
(see Text 47). They served their churches and communities and were, in turn, supported in
their ascetic vocations. The covenanters emerged early in the Syriac churches, perhaps by the
third century, and were incorporated in various ways into the ecclesiastical hierarchy.

Aphrahat's concerns resonate with ascetic discourse throughout the Christian world. Like
Jerome (see Text 37), he emphasizes spiritual as well as physical purity and particularly de-
cries cohabitating monks and virgins. Aphrahat's condemnation of the role of women in the
moral fall of humanity is also widespread among ascetic theorists of the fourth century (even
as women achieved prominence for their asceticism). Like Victricius of Rouen (see Text 44),
Aphrahat provides philosophical explanations of the distributive and omnipresent quality of
God in the holy bodies of ascetics. The distinctive terminology preserved in this translation
gives nuance to the theological particularities of Syriac asceticism. The *bnay* and *bnat qyama*
are also called *iḥidaye,* or "solitaries," a term related to the Greek *monachos* (monk), but also
used to describe the "Only-begotten," Christ (the *Iḥidaya*). This "singleness" (*iḥidayuta*) thus
represents not only the solitary life of renunciation, but also imitation of God's "Only-
begotten" Son. The renunciants are also called *qaddiše,* or "holy ones"; in seeking *qaddišuta,*
or sanctification, through renunciation, the covenanters pursue the indwelling of the Holy
Spirit that will fortify them in their battle against evil and guarantee their honored placed at
the end of time.

From *Aphrahat Demonstrations I,* trans. Kuriakose Valavanolickal. Kerala, India: HIRS Publications, 1999. Used with permission.

(1) The words that I speak are appropriate and fitting to be received.

For let us be aroused from our sleep at this time (Rom 13:11)
and raise our hearts along with our hands to heaven toward God.
Maybe all of a sudden the Lord of the house will come so that
when he has come, he will find us in a state of wakefulness (Matt 24:42).
Let us keep the appointed meeting with the Glorious Bridegroom
so that we may enter with him to his bridal chamber (Matt 25:10).
Let us have oil ready for our lamps
so that we may go out to meet him in joy (Matt 25:4).
Let us prepare provisions for our abode
(ready) for the road that is narrow and confined (Matt 7:14).
Let us take off and cast from us all filthiness
so that we may put on the wedding garments (Matt 22:12).
Let us do trade with the money we have received
so that we may be called "diligent servants" (Matt 25:21).
Let us be constant in prayer (Rom 12:12)
so that we may pass by the place of dread.
Let us purify our heart from evil
so that we may see the Exalted One in his glory (Matt 5:8).
Let us be merciful, as it is written (Matt 5:7; Luke 6:36),
so that God may have mercy on us.
Let there be peace among us
so that we may be called "brothers of Christ" (Matt 5:9).
Let us be hungry for righteousness (Matt 5:6)
so that we may have our fill from the Kingdom's table.
Let us be the true "salt" (Matt 5:13)
so that we do not become food for the serpent.
Let us keep our seedlings clear of thorns
so that they may give fruit a hundredfold (Matt 17:7–8; Luke 8:7–8).
Let us set our building upon rock
so that it is not shaken by winds and waves (Matt 7:24–27).
Let us be vessels for his honor
so that we may be required by our Lord for his use (2 Tim 2:21).
Let us sell all that we possess
and buy for ourselves the pearl, so that we may become rich (Matt 13:46).
Let us lay up our treasures in heaven (Matt 6:20; 10:21)
so that when we have gone, he may open to us and we have delight.
Let us visit our Lord in the sick (Matt 25:36)
so that he may call us to stand at his right hand (Matt 25:33).
Let us hate ourselves and love Christ (John 12:25)
just as he loved us and was delivered up for our sake (Eph 5:2).
Let us honor the Spirit of Christ
so that we may receive from him grace.
Let us be aliens from the world
just as Christ was not of it (John 17:14).
Let us be humble and gentle
so that he may cause us to inherit the land of life (Matt 5:5, 11:26; Isa 38:11, 53:8).
Let us be constant in his service
so that he may serve us in the tent of the saints.
Let us pray his prayer in purity
so that it may enter before the Lord of Majesty.
Let us be sharers in his passion
so that in this way we may also have life at his resurrection (Phil 3:10; Gal 6:17).
Let us carry his "mark" on our bodies (Ezek 9:4)
so that we may be delivered from the wrath that is to come (1 Thess 1:10).
For fearful is the day upon which he is coming,
and who is able to endure it? (Joel 2:11; Mal 3:2).
Full of wrath and heated is his anger (Isa 13:9),
and it will destroy all the wicked.
Let us place on our heads the helmet of salvation (Eph 6:17),
so that we may not be wounded and die in the battle.
Let us gird our loins in truth (Eph 6:14)
so that we are not found to be feeble in the contest.
Let us get up and awaken Christ (Matt 8:25–26)
so that he may still the storms from us.
Let us take as a shield against the Evil One
the preparedness of the Gospel of our Savior (Eph 6:16).
Let us receive from the Lord the authority
to trample upon snakes and scorpions (Luke 10:19).
Let us cause anger to rest from us

along with all wrath and evil.
Let words of abuse not issue from our very mouths
    (Jas 3:9–10)
with which we pray to God.
Let us not be people who utter curses
so that we may be rescued from the curse of the Law
    (Gal 3:10).
Let us be diligent workers
so that we may demand our wages along with the first
    (Matt 20:1–16).
Let us take on the burden of the day
so that we can ask for an extra wage (Matt 20:1–16).
Let us not be idle workers
seeing that our Lord has hired us for his vineyard
    (Matt 20:1–16).
Let us be planted as vines in his vineyard,
for he is the true Vine(yard) (John 15:1).
Let us become good vine plants (John 15:6)
lest we be rooted up from the vineyard.
Let us be a sweet scent (2 Cor 2:15)
so that the scent of us wafts to those round about us.
Let us be poor in the world
so that we may enrich many with the teaching of our
    Lord (Jas 2:5).
Let us not call anyone our father,
so that we may be(come) children to the Father who is
    in heaven (Matt 23:9).
While having nothing,
we possess everything (2 Cor 6:10).
While no one knows us,
we ourselves have many friends.
Let us rejoice in our hope at all times (Rom 12:12)
so that our Hope and our Savior may rejoice in us.
Let us judge ourselves with uprightness and find
    ourselves guilty (1 Cor 11:31)
lest we have to bow our faces in the presence of the
    judges who are seated upon the thrones and judge
    the Tribes (Matt 19:28).
Let us take for ourselves as armor for the struggle
the preparedness of the Gospel (Eph 6:16).
Let us knock at the door of heaven
so that it may be opened before us and we can enter in
    (Matt 7:7).
Let us ask for mercy insistently
so that we may receive as much as is needful for us
    (Luke 11:8).
Let us seek for the Kingdom and its righteousness
so that we may receive upon earth what is added (Matt
    6:33).

Let us ponder upon what is above, on things of
    heaven,
and upon them let us meditate,
in the place where Christ has been raised up and
    exalted (Col 3:1–2).
Let us leave behind us the world that does not belong
    to us
so that he may cause us to arrive at the place to which
    we have been invited.
Let us cause our eyes to fly up to the heights
so that we may see the Radiance (Zech 3:8) that is
    going to be revealed.
Let us lift up our wings, like eagles,
so that we may see where the body is (Matt 24:28).
Let us prepare as offerings for the King,
fair fruits consisting of fasting and prayer
Let us guard his surety in purity
so that he may entrust us over all his Treasury.
For the person who acts deceitfully with his surety
will not be allowed to enter his Treasury.
Let us be attentive to the Body of Christ
so that our bodies may arise at the sound of the
    trumpet (1 Thess 4:16).
Let us listen to the voice of the Bridegroom (Matt
    25:6)
so that we may enter the Bridal Chamber with him.
Let us prepare the gift for the wedding
and go out to meet him in joy (Matt 25:6).
Let us put on the holy raiment (Matt 22:12)
and let us become guests, reclining among the chosen
    (Luke 14:10).
The person who is not wearing a wedding garment,
they will cast him out into outer darkness (Matt
    22:13).
He who excuses himself from the wedding feast
will not taste of the banquet (Luke 14:18, 24).
The person who prefers fields and trade
will be deprived of the city of the saints.
He who does not provide fruit inside the vineyard
will be rooted out and cast into torment (Luke 13:6–9).
He who has received money from his master,
let him return it to its donor with its profit (Matt 25:16,
    27).
He who wishes to be a merchant,
let him buy the field with a treasure in it (Matt 13:44).
He who receives good seed,
let him clear his ground from thorns (Matt 13:7; Jer
    4:3).
He who wishes to become a fisherman,

let him be casting his net all the time (Matt 13:47).
He who is trained in the athletic art (1 Cor 9:24–25),
let him keep himself from the world.
He who wants to receive a crown (1 Cor 9:24),
let him run in the contest as victor.
He who wants to enter the stadium and fight,
let him gain knowledge of his adversary.
He who wants to enter the battle,
let him take for himself armor so that he can fight;
let him be polishing it all the time.
He who takes upon himself the likeness of the angels
   (Matt 22:30),
let him become a stranger to human beings.
He who takes upon himself the yoke of the
   "continent,"
let him keep money affairs far from himself.
He who seeks to gain his soul (Matt 10:39),
let him keep far from himself worldly possessions.
He who yearns for a house in heaven,
let him not toil over a building of mud which will fall
   down.
Whoever is waiting expectantly to be snatched up in
   the clouds (1 Thess 4:17)
should not arrange decorated carriages for himself.
Whoever is expectantly awaiting the marriage feast of
   the bridegroom
should not love the marriage feast that belongs to time.
Whoever wishes to take delight in the banquet that is
   reserved
should keep drunkenness at a distance from himself.
Whoever has let himself be invited to the banquet
should not (then) excuse himself and become a
   merchant (Luke 14:18, 19).
The person in whom the good seed has fallen (Matt
   13:24–25)
should not allow the Evil One to sow tares in him.
Whoever has commenced on building a tower
should reckon all of its costs (Luke 14:28).
It is appropriate that he who builds should complete
   (the work)
lest he (it) become a laughing stock to passersby
   (Luke 14:29).
Whoever places his building on the rock
should make its foundations deep
so that it does not collapse as a result of the waves
   (Matt 7:24–25).
Whoever wishes to escape from the darkness,
let him travel while he still has daylight (John 12:35).
Whoever is afraid lest he has to flee in winter,

let him prepare himself from the summer (onward)
   (Matt 24:20).
Whoever expectantly waits to enter into rest,
let him prepare his expenses for that Sabbath (Heb
   4:9–11; John 6:27).
Whoever seeks forgiveness from his Lord
should himself also forgive the person in debt to him
   (Matt 18:24).
Whoever does not demand a hundred denarii (Matt
   18:24)
(will find) his Lord forgiving him ten thousand talents.
Whoever puts his master's money in the bank (Matt
   25:27)
will not be called a bad servant.
Whoever loves humility
will become an inheritor in the land of the living (life)
   (Matt 5:5).
Whoever wishes to make peace
will become one of the children of God (Matt 5:9).
Whoever knows his master's will,
let him do his will lest he be beaten a great deal (Luke
   12:47).
Whoever purifies his heart from deceit (Matt 5:8),
that person's eyes will behold the King in his beauty
   (Isa 33:17).
Whoever receives the Spirit of Christ
should adorn his inner person (Luke 11:25; Rom
   7:22).
Whoever has been called "the Temple of God" (1 Cor
   3:16, 17)
should purify his body of all uncleanness.
Whoever grieves the Spirit of Christ (Eph 4:30)
will not raise up his head from griefs (Ps 110:7).
Whoever receives the Body of Christ,
let him keep his own body from all uncleanness.
Whoever is stripping off the "old person,"
let him not return again to his former deeds (Eph
   4:22).
Whoever is putting on the "new person" (Eph 4:24),
let him guard himself against all impurity.
Whoever has put on armor from the (baptismal) water,
let him not take off his armor
lest he finds himself defeated.
Whoever is taking a shield against the Evil One (Eph
   6:16),
let him guard himself against the arrows he will shoot
   at him.
With the person who gets dispirited (Heb 10:38)
his Lord will not want him.

Whoever ponders on the Law of his Lord
will not be perturbed by the cares of this world.
Whoever meditates on the Law of his Lord
resembles the tree planted by the water (Ps 1:1, 3).
The person whose confidence is in the Lord
again resembles the tree that is firmly (planted) by a
  stream (Jer 17:7, 8).
Whoever puts his confidence in a human being
will receive Jeremiah's curses (Jer 17:5).
Whoever has been invited by the Bridegroom
should make himself ready (Matt 22:1–6).
Whoever has lit his lamp stand (Matt 25:7–8)
should not let the light go out.
Whoever is expectantly waiting the shout (Matt 25:6),
let him take for himself oil in his vessel.
Whoever is guarding the door (Matt 25),
let him wait expectantly for his Lord.
Whoever loves virginity
will be likened to Elijah.
Whoever takes on the yoke (Matt 11:29–30; Lam
  3:27) of the holy,
let him sit down in silence (Lam 3:27–28).
Whoever loves stillness,
let him wait expectantly for the Lord, the hope of
  salvation (Tit 2:13).

(2) My beloved, our Adversary is skillful and cunning in his fight against us. He is at the ready against the valiant and the glorious, in order to get them to weaken. The feeble are his anyhow, and he does not (need to) fight with people he has already taken captive!

Whoever possesses wings will fly off from him without the arrows aimed at him reaching him. Spiritual people can see him as he fights, and his weapon has no power over their bodies. All the children of light have no fear of him, seeing that darkness flees from the presence of illumination (1 John 2:8). The children of the Good (God) are not afraid of the Evil One, for (God) has given him to be trampled under their feet (Gen 3:15; Ps 91:13; Luke 10:19). When he takes on the semblance of darkness to them, they themselves become light, and when he creeps up to them like a snake, they become salt (Matt 5:14), something that he cannot eat.

And if he takes on the semblance of an asp, they become like young children (Isa 11:8). Or if he makes his incursion against them by means of a yearning for food, they vanquish him with fasting, as did our Savior (Matt 4:2–4). Or if he desires to fight with them by means of the eyes' lust (1 John 2:16), they lift up their eyes to the heights of heaven. Or if he wants to overcome them by using blandishments, they do not pay him any attention. And if he wants to fight against them openly, then clothed in armor, they take their stand against him. And if he desires to make his incursion against them by means of sleep, they stay awake and keep vigil, singing (psalms) and praying. And should he entice them through possessions, they (simply) hand these over to the poor. And if he makes his incursion against them under the guise of something sweet, they do not taste it, realizing that it is bitter. And if he should incite them through lust for Eve, they live by themselves and not in the company of the daughters of Eve.

(3) (Satan) made his incursion on Adam by means of Eve, and in his childishness Adam was beguiled (Gen 3:1–7).

He again made his incursion against Joseph (Gen 39:7–20) by means of the wife of his master, but Joseph recognized his cunning and refused to pay any attention to him.

It was by using a woman that he fought against Samson until he (succeeded in) taking away his nazirite status (Jud 16:4–32).

Reuben was the oldest of all his brothers, and it was through his father's wife that (Satan) cast (his) foul mark on him (Gen 35:21–22; 49:3–4).

Aaron was high priest in Israel, but it was because of Miriam his sister that he became jealous of Moses (Num 12:1–2).

Moses was sent to deliver the people from Egypt, and he took with him a woman who gave (him) hateful advice, with the result that the Lord encountered Moses, and wanted to kill him (Exod 4:24–26), until he (decided to) return his wife to Midian (Exod 18:2–3).

David conquered in all his battles, but it was because of a daughter of Eve that blemish was found in him (2 Sam 11).

Amnon was handsome and fair of face, and the (Evil One) bound him with lust for his sister, with the result that Absalom killed him in return for the dishonor to Tamar (2 Sam 13).

Solomon was greater than all the kings of the earth, but in the days of his old age his wives led his heart astray (1 Kings 11:1–13; Sir 47:19–20).

Due to Jezebel, daughter of Ethbaal, the iniquity of Ahab increased, and he acted most foully (1 Kings 21:25).

Again, (Satan) tried (tempted) Job by means of his children and his possessions (Job 1–2); then, being unable to get dominion over him, he went and brought against him his weaponry, bringing along with him a daughter of Eve who had caused Adam to sink; and through her mouth he said to Job, the just man, "Revile God" (Job 2:9), but Job rejected her counsel.

King Asa also vanquished (Satan whose) life is accursed, when the latter wanted to attack him through his mother. For Asa recognized his cunning and so removed his mother from her high position, cut down her idol and threw (it to the ground) (1 Kings 15:13; 2 Chr 15:16).

Take the case of John, the greatest of all the prophets; Herod had him killed because of the dancing of one of Eve's daughters.

Haman was rich, and the king's third in command: his wife counseled him to destroy the Jews (Esth 5:9–14).

Zimri was a chief of the tribe of Simeon, yet Cozbi, a daughter of the chiefs of Midian, ruined him, with the result that because of a single woman twenty-four thousand fell from Israel in a single day (Num 26:6–25).

(4) Therefore, my brethren, any man who is a *bar qyama* or a *qaddiša* who loves *ihidayuta* and wants a woman, who is a *bat qyama* like him, to live with him, in such a case it is better that he should take a wife openly and not be unrestrained in lust (1 Cor 7:9). Likewise, in the case of a woman, it is appropriate for her, if she is not going to separate from a man who is an *ihidaya,* to be openly with a husband. It is fitting that a woman should live with (another) woman, and a man ought to live with (another) man. Even in the case of a man who wants to live in *qaddišuta,* his spouse should not live with him, lest he revert to his former natural state (1 Cor 7:8), and he be accounted

an adulterer. Therefore, this advice that I apply to myself is fitting, proper, and right for you as well, my beloved *ihidaye* who do not take wives, and (you) virgins who are not with husbands, and those who love *qaddišuta:* it is right, proper, and fitting that a person should be alone even if it is in affliction (distress), and in this way it is fitting for him to live in accordance with what is written in Jeremiah, the prophet: "Blessed is the man who shall take your yoke in his youth, and sit down and be silent, because he has received upon himself your yoke" (Lam 3:27–28). For, in this way, my beloved, it is fitting that the person who takes up the yoke of Christ (Matt 11:29–30) should preserve his yoke in purity.

(5) For it is written thus concerning Moses, my beloved, that ever since the time that the Holy One was revealed over him (Exod 3:2), he too loved *qaddišuta.* And ever since the time he was consecrated, his wife did not minister to him; instead, it is written as follows, "Joshua, son of Nun, was the minister to Moses from his youth (childhood)" (Exod 33:11; Num 11:28). And concerning Joshua, it is furthermore written as follows: "he never used to depart from the tent" (Exod 33:11). Now the temporal tent was not ministered to by a woman because the Law did not permit women to enter the temporal tent; rather it was the case that even when they came to pray, they would pray at the door of the tabernacle (Exod 38:8) and then return. (The Law) also prescribed that the priests should be (live) in *qaddišuta* during their period of ministering, and they should not know their wives.

Similarly, in the case of Elijah it is written that he would sometimes reside on mount Carmel, and sometimes in the ravine of the Kerith (1 Kings 17:2–6), being ministered to by his disciple. And because his heart was in heaven, birds of the heaven used to bring him sustenance. And because he had taken upon himself the likeness of the Watchers of heaven, these very Watchers brought him bread and water when he was fleeing from Jezebel's presence (1 Kings 19:5–7). And because he laid all his concern in heaven, he was snatched up in a chariot of fire to heaven (2 Kings 2:11–12), and that became his abode for ever.

Elisha also walked in his master's footsteps and lived in the upper room of the Shilomite (Shunamite) woman, being ministered to by his disciple. Thus the Shilomite woman said, "The prophet of God is holy, and he passes by us all the time. For in this way it is fitting for his *qaddišuta* that we should make (ready for) him the upper room and the service in it" (2 Kings 4:4–10). And what did the "service" in Elisha's upper room consist of, apart from only a bed, a table, a chair, and a lamp?

What can we say about John, who did not live among (other) human beings either; he preserved virginity in purity and received the spirit of Elijah.

The blessed Apostle also said of himself and of Barnabas, "Is it not authorized for us to eat and drink and also women to go around with us? But this is not fitting or right" (1 Cor 9:4–5).

(6) For this reason, my brothers, we recognize and have seen how from the beginning (of creation) the enemy used woman as a means of his entry against humanity, and to the very end he carries out (his deeds) by means of her. For she serves as Satan's weapon, and using her he fights against the athletes. Through her he sings all the time, since she became his lyre from the very first day. On account of her, the Law's curse was imposed, and on account of her, the promise was made of death: for in pains she gives birth to children (Gen 3:16), handing them over to death. On account of her, the earth was cursed, so that it caused thorns and thistles to sprout up (Gen 3:17–18).

Henceforth, at the advent of the Child of the blessed Mary,
the thorns are uprooted,
the sweat is removed,
the fig tree is cursed (Matt 21:19; Gen 3:19),
the dust is made into salt (Matt 5:13),
the curse has been affixed to the cross (Col 2:14),
the sharp sword has been removed from before the tree of life (Gen 3:24),
(and the Tree) has been given as food to the faithful.
While Paradise has been promised to the blessed, to both virgins
and *qaddiše*,
and the fruits of the Tree of Life have been given as food to the faithful,

and to the virgins (Matt 25:1–13) who do the will of God,
the door has been opened (Matt 7:13–14),
and the path lies trodden out,
and the fountain flows (John 7:37–38) giving water to the thirsty,
the table is set out (Ps 23:5; Matt 22:4),
and the banquet is ready,
the fatted ox has been slain,
and the "cup of salvation" is mixed (Ps 116:13),
enjoyment has been prepared,
and the Bridegroom is close at hand to take his place,
the Apostles have sent invitations,
and those invited are many indeed (Matt 22:10; Luke 14:16).
You who are chosen, prepare yourselves;
Light has shone out, resplendent and beautiful,
garments not made by (human) hands are in readiness,
the call is close at hand,
the graves are opened (Matt 25:6; 27:52),
the treasure stores are being revealed,
the dead arise,
and the living take flight to meet the King (1 Thess 4:17).
The feast is set out,
the horn gives courage,
the trumpets urge haste (1 Cor 15:52),
the Watchers of heaven come quickly,
the throne is set out for the Judge:
He who has labored will rejoice (Matt 24:31),
he who has been slack will be in fear.
He who has done wrong will not approach the Judge.
The children of the right hand exult,
but those on the left weep and wail.
Those in the light are resplendent,
those in the darkness groan out that their tongue be wetted (Luke 16:24).
Grace moves on, and uprightness reigns:
no repentance exists in that place.
Winter is close at hand, and the summer has passed on.
The Sabbath of rest is coming, labor is ceasing.
Night is coming to an end, and the day reigns.
The sting of death is broken, and is swallowed up in life (1 Cor 15:54–56).
Those who return to Sheol weep and gnash their teeth (Luke 13:28),
and those who go to the kingdom rejoice, exult, leap for joy, and give praise.

Those who do not take wives are ministered to by the Watchers of heaven.

Those who preserve *qaddišuta* find rest in the sanctuary of the Most High.

The *Iḥidaya* who is from his Father's womb (John 1:18) gives joy to all the *iḥidaye*.

There is no male or female there, no servant or freeborn (Luke 6:35; Gal 3:28),

rather, all are children of the Most High,

and all the pure virgins who are betrothed to Christ will have their lamps shining brightly

there as they enter, with the Bridegroom, to his bridal chamber (Matt 25:7–10).

All those who are betrothed to Christ are far removed from the curse of the Law,

and they are delivered from the punishment of Eve's daughters.

For they do not have husbands, or (as a result) receive the curses and be in pains;

they do not reckon death (to be anything) because they do not hand over children to him.

Instead of a husband who dies, they are betrothed to Christ,

"And because they do not give birth to children, they are given a name that is better than sons and daughters" (Isa 56:5).

Instead of the lamentations of Eve's daughters, these women will utter the Bridegroom's songs.

The wedding feast for Eve's daughters lasts seven days,

but in the case of these women, their Bridegroom never departs.

The adornment of Eve's daughters consists of wool that wears out and is eaten away,

but in the case of these women, their garments never wear out.

Old age causes the beauty of Eve's daughters to fade,

but the beauty of these women is renewed at the time of the resurrection.

(7) O Virgins who have betrothed your souls to Christ, when one of the *bnay qyama* says to one of you, "I will live with you, you minister to me," you should reply, "I am betrothed to a man who is King, and it is him to whom I am ministering; if I leave (this) ministry to him and I minister to you (instead), then my betrothed will become angry with me, write a letter of divorce, and dismiss me from his house. If you want to be held in honor by me, and I, too, (want) to be held in honor by you, (take care) to prevent harm coming to both me and you: do not put fire in your lap lest you burn your clothes (Prov 6:27–8). Rather remain alone in honorable state, and I, too, will be alone in my honorable state. Make yourself a wedding gift out of the things that the Bridegroom has prepared for the eternity of his wedding feast and prepare yourself to meet him; I, in turn, will make ready the oil so that I may enter with the wise virgins and not be kept back outside the door along with the foolish virgins" (Matt 25:1–12).

(8) Listen, therefore, my beloved, to what I am writing to you about—matters that are appropriate for *ihidaye, bnay qyama*, virgins (both male and female) and *qaddiše*. Above all else, it is appropriate that the man upon whom the yoke (of Christ) is laid should have a sound faith, in accordance with what I wrote to you in the first letter; he should be assiduous in fasting and in prayer; he should be fervent in the love of Christ; he should be humble, composed, and alert; his speech should be gentle and kind; he should be sincere minded with everyone; he should speak (carefully); weighing his words; he should make a fence for his mouth against any harmful words; he should distance himself from hasty laughter; he should not have a liking for finery in clothing, nor again should he let his hair grow (long) and adorn it; it is not appropriate for him to use on it scented unguents, nor should he take a seat at banquets. It is not appropriate for him to wear ornate clothing, nor should he impetuously go too far (in drinking) wine.

He should banish any haughty thought, and it is inappropriate for him to see ornate clothing or to wear veils. He should rid himself of deceitful speech and remove from himself overzealousness and quarrelsomeness; he should banish from himself deceitful words, and let him not listen to, or accept without first investigating, any words spoken against someone who is not present, lest (otherwise) he will fall into sin. Jeering is an odious fault, and it is not appropriate that it should reach the heart. He should not lend and receive interest, and he should not love greed.

Let him be wronged, rather than wrong (someone). Let him also keep away from commotion, and let him not utter any scurrilous words.

Let him not scoff at a person who repents of his sins or mock at his brother who is fasting. Nor should he make someone who is unable to fast feel ashamed.

Let him give reproof, where he will be accepted, but where people do not accept him, let him recognize his own dignity.

Let him speak on the occasion when his words will be accepted; otherwise he should remain in silence.

He should not reprove (despise) himself because of his stomach's requests, and let him reveal his secret to the person who fears God, but let him guard himself against the Evil One. He should not say anything in reply to a bad man, not even to his enemy. In this way let him strive not to have any enemy at all.

When people are indignant with him over something good, let him simply add to his good action and not feel harmed because of jealousy.

When he has something and gives it to the poor, let him rejoice.

When he has nothing, let him not be sad.

Let him have no association with an evil person, and let him not speak with an abusive man lest he give himself over to abuse (Prov 1:10–12; Sir 11:33–34).

Let him not argue with a blasphemer, lest his Lord be reviled as a result of him.

Let him keep false accusation at a distance, and let him not seek to please any person at all through flattery.

These are the things appropriate for *iḥidaye* who are receiving the heavenly yoke and are becoming disciples to Christ. For thus it is appropriate for the disciples of Christ to imitate Christ their Master.

(9) Let us take on the likeness from our Savior, my beloved: being rich, he made himself poor (2 Cor 8:9).

Though he was exalted,
he brought low his Majesty.
Though his abode was in the heights,
there was nowhere for him to lay his head (Matt 8:20).
Though he was going to come (Dan 7:13) on the
clouds (Matt 26:64),
he rode on an ass (John 12:15) and (so) entered
Jerusalem.

Though he is God, the son of God,
he took the likeness of a servant (Phil 2:7).
Though he was the resting place from all labors,
yet he became weary from the labor of the journey
(John 4:6).
Though he was a fountain that assuages thirst,
he became thirsty and asked for water to drink (John
4:7).
Though he is satiety and has satisfied our hunger (in
plenty),
(yet) he hungered and went out to the wilderness to be
tempted (Matt 4:2).
Though he was the Watchful One who does not
slumber (Ps 121:4),
yet he slumbered and slept in the boat in the midst of
the sea (Matt 8:24).
Though he was someone ministered to in the
Tabernacle of his Father,
he was ministered to by the hands of human beings.
Though he was the physician of all sick human beings,
yet nails were fixed in his hands (Matt 9:12; Ps 22:17).
Though his mouth uttered (only) good,
(yet) they gave him bitter food to eat (Ps 69:22; Matt
27:34).
Though he neither hurt nor harmed anyone,
he was struck by blows and endured ignominy (Matt
26:67, 26:30).
Though he is Savior of all the mortals,
he handed himself over to death on the cross.

(10) So great a humility did our Savior manifest to us in himself! Let us therefore as well make ourselves humble, my beloved. When our Lord came, he went about in our nature, but outside his (true) nature. Let us remain in our (true) condition, so that on the day of justice he will make us share in his condition. Our Lord took from us a pledge and went off (2 Cor 1:22, 5:5, Eph 1:14), and he left for us a pledge that comes from him and was raised up. He who had no need proved to be the means for fulfilling our need. What belongs to us was his from the very beginning, but as for what belongs to him, who (else) could have given to us? For it is true what our Lord promised us: "Where I am, you too shall be" (John 14:3)—because what he has taken from us is (placed) in honor with him, and a crown is set upon his head (Heb 2:9). Likewise we should hold in honor what we have received of his: what belongs to us is held in honor with

him, though it is not now existing in our nature. Let us honor what belongs to him that is in its nature. If we hold him in honor, we will go to him, since he took of what belonged to us and ascended.

But if we despise him, he will take away from us what he has given to us. And if we disdain his pledge, (then) there he will take what belongs to himself and deprive us of what he promised to us. Let us magnify the King's Son who is with us properly, for a hostage has been taken away from us on his behalf. Whoever holds the King's Son in honor will discover many gifts (emanating) from the King.

What belongs to us that is now with him sits (there) in honor, with a crown set upon his head, and he has seated him with the King. But as for us who are so poor, what can we do for the King's Son who is with us? Nothing else is required by him of us except that we should adorn our temples for him, so that when the time is completed and he goes to his Father, he may acknowledge him, from us, because we have held him in honor. When he came to us, he did not have anything of ours, nor did we have anything of his, though the two natures belonged to him and his Father.

Now when Gabriel announced to the blessed Mary who gave him birth, the Word set off from the height and came, "and the word became body and dwelt in us" (John 1:14). And when he went (back) to his sender, he took off what he had not brought, as the Apostle said: "He has raised us up and caused us to sit with him in heaven" (Eph 2:6). And when he went to his Father, he sent us his Spirit, telling us, "I am with you until the world comes to an end" (Matt 28:20). For Christ is seated at the right hand of his Father, and Christ dwells in human beings.

He is capable (of being) above and below through the wisdom of his Father, and he dwells in many, while yet being one, and he overshadows all the faithful each with a portion of himself, without his being diminished, as is written "I will divide him up among many" (Isa 53:12). Even though he is divided up among many, he is seated at the right hand of his Father (Mark 16:19; Eph 1:20; Heb 10:12). And he is in us and we are in him, just as he said, "you are in me and I am in you" (John 14:20), and in another place he said, "I and my Father are one" (John 10:30).

(11) If someone with a conscience weak in understanding should argue against this and say that since Christ is one and his Father is one, how can Christ and his Father dwell in human beings who are believers? And how can the just (among) human beings become temples for God in which he dwells? If this is then the case, and Christ has individually come to each individual human being who is a believer, along with God who is in Christ—if this is so, then there turn out to be multiple gods and innumerable Christs!

Listen, my beloved, to the refutation that needs (to be made). Let the person who has said this be persuaded from a visible example: Everyone is aware that the sun is fixed in the sky, and its rays are spread out over the earth; something of it enters the many doors and windows of houses, and wherever the sunlight falls—even if it (only covers) the palm of the hand—it is called "sun." Though (while) falling on many different places it is called by this name, yet the sun itself is in heaven. If this is then the case, have there turned out to be many suns? Likewise the waters of the sea are vast, and (yet) when you take a bowlful from them, it is (still) called "water," and when you divide this water up into thousand vessels, it still retains the name "water."

Likewise, when you kindle fire in many different places, (starting) from one (source of) fire, the source from which you take the fire to kindle others does not diminish, and it is (all) called by the single name "fire": just because you divide (the fire) up in many different places, it does not take on a plurality of names. And when you take dust from the earth and scatter it in many different places, the dust does not loose anything, nor can you speak of it as plural.

Similarly in the case of God and his Christ, while being one, nevertheless they dwell in many human beings, while they themselves are in heaven, they do not loose anything by dwelling in many (people), just as the sun in heaven does not loose anything when its power resides on earth. Is not the power of God so much greater seeing that the sun itself exists by the power of God!

(12) I would remind you once again, my beloved, of what is written (in Scripture), for it is written as follows; (telling) how, when it was proving too oner-

ous for Moses to guide the (Israelite) camp by himself, the Lord said to him: "I will take a little of the spirit that is upon you, and I will give (it) to the seventy men (who are) the elders of Israel" (Num 11:17). When he had taken a little of the spirit of Moses and the seventy men had been filled with it, Moses did not lack anything, nor was his spirit recognized as having had a little taken from it.

The blessed Apostle also said, "God has divided up of the spirit of his Christ and sent it among the prophets"[1]—but Christ was not harmed in any way, "for his Father did not give him the Spirit using a measure" (John 3:34). In this sense you be convinced that Christ dwells in human beings (who are) believers, without his suffering any harm by being divided up among many.

For it is from the spirit of Christ that the prophets received, each of them insofar as he was able to bear, and what is being poured out today on all flesh is from the spirit of this same Christ, with the result that sons and daughters, old and young, servants and maid servants are prophesying (Acts 2:17–18; Joel 3:1–2).

Something from Christ is in us, while Christ is (also) in heaven at the right hand of his Father (Eph 1:20). Christ did not receive the spirit in a measured quantity; rather his Father, in his love for him, handed over everything into his hands, giving him authority over his entire treasury. For John said, "It was not in a measured quantity that the Father gave the Spirit to his Son, but in his love for him he has handed over everything into his hands" (John 3:33–34). Our Lord too said, "Everything has been handed over to me by my Father" (Matt 11:27). And again he said, "The Father will not judge anyone, but will give all judgment to his Son" (John 5:22). The Apostle too said, "Everything shall be subjected to Christ apart from his Father, who has subjected everything to him. And once everything has been subjected to him by his Father, then he, too, will be subjected to God his Father

who had subjected everything to him, and God will be all in all and in everyone" (1 Cor 15:27–8).

(13) Concerning John, our Lord testifies how he is greater than the prophets (Matt 11:9–11), but he received the spirit in measured quantity, since John partook of the spirit in the same measure that Elijah received. Just as Elijah dwelt in the wilderness, so, too, the Spirit of God took John, and he was dwelling in the wilderness and on the mountains and in the caves. Birds nourished Elijah, whereas John ate flying locusts (1 Kings 17:6; Matt 3:4), Elijah wore a leather girdle around his waist, and John wore a leather strap around his waist (2 Kings 1:8; Matt 3:4). Elijah was persecuted by Jezebel, and John was persecuted by Herodias (1 Kings 19:1–2; Mark 6:19).

Elijah rebuked Ahab, and John rebuked Herod (1 Kings 18:17, 21:17–24; Mark 6:18; Luke 3:19). Elijah divided Jordan (2 Kings 2:8), and John opened up baptism. Elijah's spirit resided in a double measure on Elisha (2 Kings 2:9); while John laid his hand upon our Savior, and he received the Spirit without measure. Elijah opened up the heaven and ascended (2 Kings 2:11), while John saw the heaven opened and the spirit of God descending and residing on our Savior (Matt 3:16; Mark 1:10; Luke 3:22; John 1:33). Elisha received Elijah's spirit twofold (2 Kings 2:9), while our Savior received both from John and from heaven.

Elisha took up the mantle of Elijah (2 Kings 2:13), while our Savior (took up) the laying on of the hands of priests. Elisha made oil from water (2 Kings 4:1–7), while our Savior made wine from water (John 2:1–11). Elisha satisfied (the hunger) of only 100 men by means of a little bread (2 Kings 4:42–44), while our Savior (again) with a little bread satisfied 5,000 men, apart from children and women (Matt 14:21). Elisha cleansed Naaman the leaper (2 Kings 5:1–14), while our Savior cleansed ten (lepers) (Luke 17:12–19).

Elisha cursed some children, and they were devoured by bears (2 Kings 2:24). Our Savior received praise with hosannas from the children (Matt 21:15–16). Elisha cursed Gehazi his disciple (2 Kings 5:27), and our Savior cursed Judas his disciple (Matt 26:24), but blessed all his (other) disciples

---

[1] This quotation actually comes from the apocryphal Pauline letter *3 Corinthians* 3:10, recognized by some fourth-century Christians as authentic.

(Luke 24:50). Elisha revived only one dead person (2 Kings 4:32–35), whereas our Savior revived three. In Elisha's case, a single dead person came alive by means of his bones (2 Kings 13:21), while our Savior, when he descended to the abode of the dead, revived many and resurrected them. Many are the signs that the spirit of Christ has performed—(the same spirit) from which the prophets had received.

(14) Accordingly we, too, my beloved, have received of Christ's Spirit, and Christ dwells in us, as it is written how the Spirit spoke through the prophet's mouth, saying "I will dwell (Isa 66:2; Lev 26:11) in them and go about in them" (Ezek 36:12, 26:12).

Let us therefore from now on make ready our "temples" for the Spirit of Christ and not grieve her, lest she depart from us. Recall how the Apostle warns you, "Do not grieve the Holy Spirit, with whom you have been sealed for the day of salvation" (Eph 4:30). Now it is from baptism that we receive the Spirit of Christ: for at that moment when the priests invoke the Spirit, (the Spirit) opens up the heavens, descends and hovers over the water (Gen 1:2), while those who are being baptized clothe themselves in her. The Spirit remains distant from all who are of bodily birth until they come to the birth (that belongs to the baptismal) water; only then do they receive the Holy Spirit. For at (their) first birth they are born with an animate spirit that is created inside a person, which is furthermore immortal, as it is said, "Adam became a living soul" (Gen 2:7; 1 Cor 15:45). And at the second birth, which occurs at baptism, they receive the Holy Spirit, from a portion of divinity and this, too, is immortal.

Now when people die, the animate spirit is buried away with the body, and sense perception is removed from the latter, but the heavenly Spirit that we received returns to its natural state with Christ. These two (kinds of Spirit) were indicated by the Apostle, who said: "The body is buried away according to the way of the soul (1 Cor 15:44), whereas it rises according to the way of the Spirit." And the Spirit reverts to Christ, to its natural state. The Apostle further said, "When we depart from the body, we shall be with Christ" (2 Cor 5:8). For it is to our Lord that the Spirit of Christ that spiritual people receive reverts,

while the animate spirit is buried away in its own (natural) condition, and sense perception is taken away from it. In the case of the person who has preserved the Spirit of Christ in purity, when (this) Spirit goes to Christ, she says to him: "The body to which I went and that put me on from the water of baptism has preserved me in purity." And the Holy Spirit will urge on Christ concerning the resurrection of that body that preserved her in a pure manner, asking him that the body be added to her again and that it might rise in glory.

But in the case of that person who receives the Spirit from the (baptismal) water and (then) grieves her, she will leave him before he dies and go back to her natural state, Christ; (there) she will make complaint to him about the person who has grieved her. And when the time of the appointed end has arrived and the time for the resurrection is at hand, the Holy Spirit who has been preserved in holiness will take on great might from her nature and will go in front of Christ and stand at the entrance of the graves where people who have preserved her in purity lie buried, and she will await expectantly for the (last) cry; then, once the angels have opened the gates of heaven in front of the King, the horn will sound and the trumpets will blare (1 Cor 15:52). And when the Spirit as she awaits the cry hears, she will open up the graves in haste and raise up the bodies and that which lay buried in them; she will put on the glory that accompanies her. She herself will be within for the resurrection of the body, while the glory will be outside for the adornment of the body. And the animate spirit will be swallowed up in the heavenly Spirit, and the whole person will become of the Spirit, while his body (exists) in her. And death will be swallowed up in life, and the body swallowed up in the Spirit. And as a result of the Spirit, that person will fly off to meet the King (1 Thess 4:17), who will receive him with joy. And Christ will thank the body for preserving his Spirit in pure fashion.

(15) This Spirit that the prophets received is likewise the one we (received), my beloved. She is not all the time to be found with those who receive her; rather, at times she goes off to him who sent her, and at times she comes back to the person who received

her. Listen to what our Lord said: "Do not despise a single one of these small ones who believe in me, for their angels in heaven continually behold the face of my Father" (Matt 18:10). This same Spirit all the time goes and stands before God and beholds his face, and against the person who harms the temple in which she resides, she will lay complaint before God.

(16) I will convince you (on the basis of) what is written (in Scripture), that the Spirit is not to be found all the time with those who receive it. For it is written as follows: In the case of Saul, the Holy Spirit that he had received when he was anointed (1 Sam 10:1) passed from him because he had grieved her, and God sent him a consuming spirit (1 Sam 16:14) in its place. And whenever he was afflicted by an evil spirit, David would strike upon the lyre, and the Holy Spirit that David had received when he was anointed (1 Sam 16:3) would come along, and the evil spirit that was consuming Saul would flee away from her presence. Now the Holy Spirit that David had received was not to be found with him all the time, (but only) when he struck upon the lyre, then it would come. For had it been with him all the time, it would not have allowed him to commit sin with the wife of Uriah (2 Sam 11). For when he was praying concerning his sins and acknowledging his faults before God, this is what he said, "Take not your holy spirit from me" (Ps 51:13).

Concerning Elisha, too, it is written, "Once he had struck upon his lyre, then the Spirit came to him and he prophesied saying, Thus says the Lord: You shall not see spirit or rain, and this wadi will be made into pits" (2 Kings 3:15–17). Again when the Shilomite (Shunamite) woman came to him concerning her son who had died, he said this to her; "The Lord has concealed (it) from me and not informed me" (2 Kings 4:27).

But when the king of Israel sent (someone) with the intention of killing him, the Spirit informed him before the messenger had reached him, and he said, "look, this son of iniquity has sent (someone) to remove my head" (2 Kings 6:32). He also made known (beforehand) concerning the glut of (food) that would occur in Samaria (2 Kings 7:1–2) the very next day. Again, the Spirit made it known to him when Gahazi stole the money and hid it (2 Kings 5:26).

(17) For this reason, my beloved, when the Holy Spirit departs from a person who has received her, (all the while) she goes of and comes (back) to him, it is then that Satan engages in battle with that person, aiming at making him act wickedly, so that the Holy Spirit will depart from him altogether. For as long as the Spirit is with someone, Satan is afraid to approach him.

Look, my beloved, at the case of our Lord, who was born of the Spirit; he was not tested by Satan until he had received from on high the Spirit at baptism. Only then did the Spirit take him out in order that he might be tempted by Satan.

A person possesses the following means: the moment he perceives in himself that he is not (any longer) fervent in Spirit and his heart falls back into the concerns of this world, (at this point) he should realize that the Spirit is no longer with him; he should get up, pray, and keep vigil so that the Spirit of God may come and he may not be defeated by the enemy.

A thief does not break into a house until he sees that its owner is departing. Likewise Satan, too, is unable to approach this house of our body until the Spirit of Christ is departing from it. You should recognize, my beloved, that the thief has no knowledge whether the owner of the house is at home or not unless he has previously listened to see if he can hear the sound of the voice of the owner of the house inside it. If he hears the voice of the owner of the house (and realizes) that he is inside, then he says, "The way lies open for me to leave." But once he has investigated and seen that the owner of the house has departed in order to see to his affairs, then the thief comes along, breaks into the house, and steals (things). But if he hears the householder's voice giving instructions to the members of his household to keep vigilant and guard his house, telling them, "I, too, am at home," then the thief takes fright and runs away so as not to be apprehended or caught.

Thus, too, with Satan: he does not have any prior knowledge (enabling him) to know and to see when the Spirit departs and he can come along to despoil a person. Rather, he, too, listens in and keeps watch: if he hears the person in whom Christ is dwelling uttering any ugly words or losing his temper or quarreling or fighting, then Satan knows that Christ is not with that person, and he comes along and fulfills his desire upon him. For Christ dwells with the gentle and the humble, residing in those who tremble at his word, just as (Scripture) says the prophet: "Upon whom shall I look and (in whom) shall I dwell, if not in the gentle and humble (of Spirit), who tremble at my word" (Isa 66:2). And our Lord said: In the case of the person who walks in my commandments and preserves my love, we will come and make an abode with him (John 14:23).

Now if by listening he (discovers) that a person is vigilant, praying and meditating on the law of (Ps 1:2) his Lord day and night, then he will turn back from that person, realizing that Christ is dwelling with him.

But if you should say, How great Satan is! seeing that he is fighting with so many people (at the same time), listen, and be convinced by what I pointed out above to you concerning Christ; however much he is divided up among many, he is not diminished in any way. For a house through whose window a little sunlight comes in is entirely illumined by it; (so too) a person into whom a little of Satan enters becomes entirely dark. Listen to what the Apostle said: "If Satan takes on the resemblance of an angel of light, it is no great thing if his ministers can also take on the resemblance of the ministers of righteousness" (2 Cor 11:14–15). Our Lord furthermore said to his disciples: "Look, I have given you the authority to trample down the power of the enemy" (Luke 10:19).

The Scriptures have indicated that he has power and ministers as well. Job, too, said concerning him: "God made him so he could conduct his battle" (Job 40:14). These ministers he has, then, (and) he rushes them into the world to conduct the battle. But realize that he does not fight openly; since (God) has provided authority over him ever since the time of the coming of our Savior, he seizes (people) furtively.

(18) I should (like to) convince you, my beloved, concerning the word(s) that the Apostle spoke whereby false teachings and teachings that serve as vessels for the Evil One are scandalized. For the Apostle said, "There is an animate body and there is a spiritual body; it is written as follows, First Adam

came into being with a living soul, but the second Adam (was) life-giving Spirit" (1 Cor 15:44–45). They say there are two Adams; (the Apostle) said, "Just as we have put on the image of that Adam who (came) from the earth, so we shall put on the image of that Adam who (came) from Heaven" (1 Cor 15:49). For the Adam who is from the earth is the one who sinned, while the Adam from heaven is our Savior, our Lord Jesus Christ. Those therefore who receive the Spirit of Christ are in the likeness of the heavenly Adam who is our Savior, our Lord Jesus Christ, because what belongs to the soul is swallowed up by what belongs to the Spirit, as I described to you above.

And the person who grieves the Spirit of Christ remains with the soul (only) at his resurrection, since the heavenly Spirit is not present with him so that the animate (spirit) might be swallowed up by the heavenly. Instead, once he has risen, he remains in his natural state, naked of the Spirit; since he has put the Spirit of Christ to shame, he is handed over to great shame, whereas the person who honors the Spirit and it is protected by him in purity, on that day (of resurrection) the Holy Spirit will protect him, and he will not be found to be naked, as the Apostle said: "Once we are clothed, we will not be found naked" (2 Cor 5:3). Again he said, "We shall all sleep, but at the resurrection we shall not all be changed" (1 Cor 15:51). He further said: "He who dies is going to put on him who does not die, and he who is subject to corruption (will put on) him who is incorruptible. And when the mortal puts on the immortal, and the corruptible the incorruptible, then the words written will be fulfilled: Death has been swallowed up by victory" (1 Cor 15:53–54).

Again he says, "All of a sudden, like the blinking of an eye, the dead will rise uncorrupted (1 Cor 15:52), and we shall be changed." Those who are changed are those who put on the image of that heavenly Adam, and they become spiritual beings, whereas those who are not changed remain with an animate (spirit) in the natural state of Adam as he was created out of the earth, and they remain in their natural state in the lowest part of the earth. Then the heavenly beings will be snatched up to heaven (1

Thess 4:17), and the Spirit in whom they are clothed will cause them to fly up and they will inherit the kingdom that has been prepared for them from the beginning. But (those left just) animate will remain on earth owing to their being weighed down by their bodies, and they will return to Sheol (Ps 9:18), where there will be weeping and gnashing of teeth (Matt 8:12).

(19) These things have I written to you, my beloved, reminding myself as well as you. Accordingly, have a love for virginity as the heavenly portion that involves communion with the Watchers of heaven. There is nothing comparable to it, and in those who (live) like this Christ dwells. The time of summer is approaching; the fig tree has sprouted, and its leaves have appeared (Matt 24:32; Song 2:13). The signs that our Savior gave have begun to come fulfilment, for he said "one people shall rise up against another, and one kingdom against another,

and there shall be famines, plagues, and terrible (signs) from heaven" (Luke 21:10–11). You can see all these things coming to fulfillment in our own days.

(20) Accordingly, read what I have written to you, both you and the brethren, members of the covenant who love virginity. Beware of the people who jeer. To the person who jeers at or mocks at his brother the words written in the Gospel apply, when our Lord wanted to get an opinion from the greedy and from the Pharisees, for it is written that because they loved money they were jeering at him (Luke 16:14). So now, too, they are jeering at everything they do not agree with. Read, learn, and be diligent in both reading and action. Let the Law of God be your meditation all the time (Ps 119:97). And when you have read this letter, by your life, my beloved, stand in prayer and make mention of my sinful self in your prayer.

The end of the Demonstration on *Bnay Qyama.*

CHAPTER 10

Pilgrims, Relics, and Holy Places

The same interrelation between physicality and spirituality that emerged in the ascetic movements of the period are also evident in the rise of cults of holy places and relics. In the fourth century, especially under the patronage of Constantine and his successors, the holy places associated with the Bible (in Palestine, Syria, and Egypt) emerged as the "holy land." In particular, the previously obscure backwater of Jerusalem (devastated in the first and second centuries by Roman troops) was endowed with lavish churches marking the nativity, crucifixion, and resurrection of Jesus Christ. Monks from around the Mediterranean settled on the Mount of Olives and in nearby Bethlehem. Our first extant pilgrimage text, from the so-called Bordeaux Pilgrim (we do not know his or her name), was written in 333; floods of pilgrims and migrating monks followed his or her path throughout Late Antiquity.

Many sites throughout the Roman Empire were likewise viewed as holy places for their association with the deeds or the tomb of a saint, particularly apostles, martyrs, and ascetic virtuosi. Sacred sites had long been common throughout the ancient Mediterranean: temples, heroes' tombs, healing shrines, places where the earthly and the heavenly were believed to intersect. Christians also came to see the sacred concentrated in the physical world; by the end of Late Antiquity, holy places dotted the ancient landscape, where pious Christians sought spiritual guidance, physical healing, and proximity to the divine.

Closely linked with the veneration of the holy land and holy places is the veneration of relics (literally "leftovers"), the remains of holy persons or their personal items. Although Roman law forbade the exhumation and transfer of human remains or their interment within city limits, the remains of holy persons were frequently uncovered and parceled out to be displayed in churches and shrines throughout the Roman Empire. Pilgrimage and relic veneration went hand in hand; throughout her journey, the pilgrim Egeria collected "blessings," souvenirs of the holy places, such as water or soil (see Text 42). The disbursement of relics also gives a keen sense of the politics of religious traffic. Ambrose, for instance, discovered the remains of Protasius and Gervasius in the midst of his conflict with the Arian clergy and imperial court in Milan. The discovery of Saint Stephen, recounted here, came at a similar moment of crisis among the churches of the East, as Bishop John of Jerusalem presided over a synod examining the beliefs of Pelagius (see Chapter 7). The most prized relics came from the True Cross (the cross on which Jesus was crucified), allegedly discovered by Constantine's mother Helena (see Ambrose's account of this legend, Text 8; Paulinus of Nola mentions his fragment in Text 57).

Deeper philosophical and theological disputes emerge in the veneration of holy places and holy objects, as the belief in divine immateriality came into conflict with the increasingly prominent veneration of the physical. As demonstrated by Gregory of Nyssa's critique of pilgrimage and Victricius of Rouen's defense of the veneration of relics, persistent and conflicting aspects of Christian identity often came into play in the elaborate material manifestations of religious practice and belief.

FOR FURTHER READING

Brown, Peter. *The Cult of the Saints: Its Rise and Function in Latin Christianity.* Chicago: University of Chicago Press, 1981.

Drijvers, Jan Willem. *Helena Augusta: The Mother of Constantine the Great and the Legend of Her Finding of the True Cross.* Leiden, the Netherlands: E. J. Brill, 1992.

Hunt, E. D. *Holy Land Pilgrimage in the Later Roman Empire, AD 312–460.* Oxford, England: Clarendon Press, 1982.

Ousterhout, Robert, ed. *The Blessings of Pilgrimage.* Urbana: University of Illinois Press, 1990.

Vikan, Gary. *Byzantine Pilgrimage Art.* Washington, D.C.: Dumbarton Oaks, 1982.

Wilken, Robert L. *The Land Called Holy: Palestine in Christian History and Thought.* New Haven, Conn.: Yale University Press, 1994.

The Texts

42. Egeria: Travel Journal

Around the year 381, a woman and ascetic from the West (southern France or Spain) set out on an extended journey through the holy land. We know little about her, other than what she tells us about herself: her name was probably Egeria, she traveled for nearly three years (implying a level of economic self-sufficiency, if not outright upper-class status), and she recorded the sights and sounds of the holy places in a long letter written to her "sisters" (perhaps a monastic community) back home. Most scholars have noted the Bible's importance to Egeria's pilgrimage experience. Her pattern was to visit a holy place, say a prayer, read the appropriate scriptural passage about it, and then celebrate the Eucharist. Egeria's guides seem to have been local monks, priests, and bishops (again, perhaps attesting to lofty social connections). To read Egeria's account of fourth-century Palestine, one might conclude that it was populated solely by monks, priests, bishops, and pilgrims: laypeople, much less non-Christians, do not figure in the journal.

Egeria's account does not engage the sort of theological critiques leveled against pilgrimage (see Text 43). Her journal nonetheless provides insight into what, exactly, a pious Christian might seek from the long and costly journey across the entire empire to see the holy places: the chance not only to walk in the footsteps of the saints, the prophets, the apostles, and even Christ, but to immerse oneself in the sacred history culminating in Christian salvation. Reproduced here are the travel portions of Egeria's journal, beginning where the extant manuscript picks up, as her tour party reaches Sinai. (Missing portions probably extended her journey north, into Galilee.) The account is noteworthy, as well, for being one of the few documents written by a Christian woman to survive from antiquity. Appended to the journal, but not included here, were detailed descriptions of the festivals celebrated in Jerusalem, particularly those surrounding Easter week.

1 (1) . . . were shown to us according to Scriptures. Walking along we reached a place where the hills we had been walking through opened up and made an endless valley, huge, absolutely flat and very beautiful, and across the valley appeared the holy mountain of God, Sinai. The place where the mountains open up connects to the place where the "Monuments of Lust" are (cf. Num 11:34). (2) When we got there, our guides, those holy men who were with us, alerted us: "It is customary for those who arrive here to say a prayer when they first catch sight of the Mountain of God." So we did. From there to the Mountain of God, it was perhaps four miles altogether through that valley (I told you, it's huge).

From *Égérie: Journal de voyage (Itinéraire) et Lettre sur la Béatissime Égérie,* ed. Pierre Maraval. Paris: Cerf, 1982. (Translated by Andrew S. Jacobs.)

2 (1) That valley is really huge, lying alongside the bottom of the Mountain of God. It was maybe—and this was just our guess as we eyeballed it, but they said so, too—maybe sixteen miles long, and they said it was four miles along its side. So we had to cross that valley so we could climb the mountain. (2) Now this is the huge and absolutely flat valley where the Israelites kept watch for those days (cf. Exod 19:2) while holy Moses "ascended the mountain" of the Lord "and was there forty days and forty nights" (Exod 24:18). This is also the valley where they made the calf (Exod 32:4), and the place is shown even now (for a big rock stands fixed to that spot). So this is the same valley at the head of which holy Moses, while he was pasturing his father-in-law's flocks, was twice spoken to by God from the burning bush (Exod 3:4–15).

(3) And so we took the following path: first we would climb the Mountain of God, since the side of our approach was better for climbing, and then we would come down from there to that end of the valley where the bush was, since the descent was easier on that side. So it was decided: When we had seen everything we wanted to, we would come down from the mountain and arrive at the bush, and from there we would go back across all the same valley (which stretched far off) on the road with the men of God who would show us every single place that was written about: And so this is what we did. (4) As we went out from that place where, coming from Pharan, we had said a prayer, this was our path: we crossed through the midst from one end of that valley, and so we approached the Mountain of God. (5) Now it looks like it's just one peak when you view it from around, but once you go up inside it, there are many peaks, but the whole thing is called the Mountain of God. But that one particular peak, on whose summit is the place where "God's majesty came down" (cf. Exod 24:16), as it is written, is in the middle of all the others. (6) All those that were around it were as high as any I thought I had ever seen, but that one in the middle—where "God's majesty came down"—was even higher than all the others. When we went up onto it, all those other peaks that had seemed so high were now like little hills below us. (7) That is really

quite remarkable, and I don't think it would happen without God's grace: even though that middle peak is higher than the others, which is called Sinai proper, right where "God's majesty came down," nevertheless, you can't see it until you come right to its base before you go up onto it. Now after you've done what you wanted and you're climbing down from it, you can see it opposite you, but before you go up, it can't be done. I had learned this before we arrived at the Mountain of God from the account of the brothers, and once we got there I knew clearly how this could be.

3 (1) So Saturday evening we were going up to the mountain and we arrived at some monasteries, where we were received quite decently by the monks who lived there, and they offered us every kindness. There is also a church there with a priest. So we stayed the night there, and early on Sunday, with that same priest and the monks who lived there, we undertook to climb every single peak.

You get up those peaks with infinite toil, since you don't go up them slowly, slowly going around, as they say, in spirals; but you have to go up all at once, as if you were climbing straight up a wall, going over each peak until you arrive at the base of that middle mountain, which is Sinai proper. (2) So it was as Christ our God willed, and assisted by the prayers of the holy men who accompanied us and with great toil, since it was necessary for me to climb on foot, since no litter could have been carried up—but still I never felt the toil itself. Indeed, I felt no toil, but had only a desire to fulfill what I saw as God's commandment. At about the fourth hour [ten o'clock], we arrived at the summit of that holy Mountain of God, Sinai, where the Law was given, on that spot where "God's majesty came down" on that day when the mountain was smoking (Exod 19:18). (3) Now there is a church there—not too big, since there isn't a lot of room on the summit of a mountain—but nevertheless the church has a great deal of charm. (4) When, as God willed, we had climbed up that summit and arrived at the entrance of that church, the priest came out of his monastery to meet us, the one assigned to this church, a well-preserved old man, a monk from a young age, an "ascetic" as they say here, and—

what more to say?—just the man for the place. The other priests came out to meet us, and not just them but all the monks who lived around that mountain—at least, all those who were not impeded by their age or sickness. (5) But really no one lives right there on the summit of that middle peak; indeed, there is nothing there except for a lone church and the cave that belonged to holy Moses (cf. Exod 33:22). (6) When the whole passage had been read from the Book of Moses and the offering had been conducted in proper order, we held communion; as soon as we went out of the church, the priests gave us blessings (*eulogiae*) of that place, some fruits that are native to that mountain. Now even though that holy Mount Sinai was so totally rocky that it had no fruit trees, nevertheless down near the foot of those mountains, around that middle peak as well as the peaks around it, there's a tiny bit of soil. On that spot the holy monks diligently plant little bushes and set up little orchards and garden plots alongside the monastery itself. It seems like they picked fruit from the soil of the mountain itself, but nevertheless they have labored for it with their own hands. (7) So then after we held communion and the holy men gave us the blessings and we went outside the church entrance, then I undertook to ask them to show us every single site. Then right away those holy men saw fit to show it all. For they showed us that cave where holy Moses was when, for the second time, he climbed up the Mountain of God (Exod 34:1) to receive the tablets again after he had broken the first ones because of the sinning populace (Exod 32:19). And they saw fit to show us other sites of the sort we wanted to see and those that they knew better. (8) I want you to know this well, my venerable lady sisters, about the place where we stood: around the walls of the church, on the summit of that middle peak, and below us it seemed as if those mountains (which earlier we had scarcely managed to climb), from where we stood, it was as if they were little hills, even though they are almost without limit. I don't think I've ever seen any peaks (except for the middle one) that were any higher. Egypt, Palestine, the Red Sea, the Parthenian Sea (which carries you to Alexandria), not just these, but even the borders of the limitless lands of the Saracens, were all visible down beneath us, which I would scarcely believe possible. But those holy men pointed all of it out to us in turn.

4 (1) When we had fulfilled every desire that had hastened our ascent, we undertook to climb down from the summit of the Mountain of God that we had climbed up—onto another mountain that adjoined it, to a place called Horeb (cf. Exod 17:6), where there is another church. (2) This place Horeb is where the holy prophet Elijah fled from the presence of King Ahab, where God spoke to him saying: "Why are you here, Elijah?" as it is written in the books of Kings (1 Kings 19:9). In addition, the cave where holy Elijah hid is there; today it is shown before the entrance of the church. Also shown there is the stone altar that that same holy Elijah set up to make his offering to God; thus the holy men saw fit to show us everything in turn. (3) So we also made the offering there and a very fervent prayer, and the appropriate passage was read from the book of Kings. This was always my special request for our group, that wherever we went we would always have the appropriate passage read from the Bible. (4) So once the offering had been made, we went again toward the other place, not far off from there, with the priest and monks showing us the way, to the very place where holy Aaron stood with the seventy Elders, when holy Moses received from the Lord the Law for the Israelites (Exod 24:9–14). In that place, even though there is no structure, there is nevertheless a great big round rock, flattened on top, on which (it is said) those holy men stood, and in the middle it is as if a stone altar had been constructed. The appropriate passage was read there from the book of Moses, and a psalm was recited that was fitting for the site. Once we had made the offering, we climbed down from there. (5) Now it was already about the eighth hour [two o'clock], and we still had three miles to go before we had left behind those peaks that we had set out on the evening before. But we weren't to leave from the same side on which we had entered, as I said above, since we also had to walk around and see all the holy places and the local monasteries of that valley (as I said above) and to come out at the other end of the valley that adjoins the Mountain of God. (6) So we had to go out toward that end of the valley, since there were many more monasteries of holy men and churches at the site of the bush. Even today, this bush still survives and grows new shoots.

(7) Once we had climbed down the Mountain of God, we came to the bush at around the tenth hour [four o'clock]. This is the bush I mentioned above, from which the Lord spoke to Moses in fire; at that site there are many monasteries and a church at that end of the valley. In front of that church, there is a very lovely garden, full of the best water; the bush is in that garden. (8) Nearby the place is shown where holy Moses stood when God said to him: "Loosen the straps of your shoes" (Exod 3:5) and so forth. By the time we reached that place, it was already about the tenth hour [four o'clock], and so, since it was already evening, we couldn't make the offering. But we prayed in the church and in the garden before the bush, as well. The appropriate passage was read from the book of Moses, according to our custom. And so, since it was evening, we made our meal there in the garden before the bush with the holy men, and we lodged there. The next day, waking up early, we asked the priests to make the offering there, and so they did.

5 (1) Now since our route took us through the middle of that valley that stretched on for a long way— this is that same valley of which I spoke above, where the Israelites made camp while Moses went up and down the Mountain of God—the holy men with us always pointed out everything there was to see as we passed through the whole valley. (2) On one end of that valley, where we lodged and saw that bush from which God spoke to holy Moses in fire, we also saw that place where holy Moses stood before the bush, when God said to him: "Loosen the straps of your shoes: for the place in which you stand is holy land [*terra sancta*]" (Exod 3:5). (3) And they also undertook to show us other sites as we made our progress away from the bush. They also showed the place where the Israelites made their camp while Moses was on the mountain (Exod 19:2). And they showed us the place where that calf was made (Exod 32:4), for fixed in that place even until today there is a big stone. (4) As we went, we saw opposite us the summit of the peak that overlooks the entire valley; from

this place holy Moses saw the Israelites dancing when they made the calf. They showed us a huge rock, on the site where holy Moses came down with Joshua, son of Nun: on that rock "in anger he broke the tablets" that he was carrying (Exod 32:19). (5) Throughout that valley, they showed us how each of them [the Israelites] had had a house; the foundations of those houses are still visible today where rounded rocks remain. They showed us the place where holy Moses commanded the Israelites to run "from gate to gate" (Exod 32:27) upon his return from the mountain. (6) They also showed us the place where that calf that Aaron had made was burned, on the command of holy Moses (Exod 32:20; Exod 32:4). They also showed us that stream from which holy Moses "had the Israelites drink," as it is written in Exodus (Exod 32:20). (7) They showed us also the place where the seventy men received some of the spirit of Moses (Num 11:25). They also showed us the place where the Israelites felt their lust for food (Num 11:4). They showed us as well that place that is called "Fire," which is a "certain part of the camps" that was burning, and then "the fire ceased" because holy Moses prayed (Num 11:1–3). (8) They showed us also that place where manna and quails rained on them (Num 11:7–9, 31–32). And everything that it is written in the books of holy Moses was done in that place, that is, in that valley that adjoins the Mountain of God, holy Sinai, was shown to us. All these things, one by one, it suffices to write down, since no one could keep all this in their memory. But when Your Affection reads the holy books of Moses, she will perceive more diligently what happened there. (9) For this is the valley where the Passover was celebrated at the end of the year that the Israelites went forth from the land of Egypt (Num 9:1–5), since in that same valley the Israelites waited a very long time while holy Moses went up and came down from the Mountain of God, once and then a second time, and they waited there while the tabernacle was built, along with the other things revealed on the Mountain of God. They showed us also that place where Moses first constructed the tabernacle and completed all the individual things that God commanded him on the mountain to make (cf. Exod 40). (10) We also saw, at the other end of that valley, the "Monuments of Lust" (cf. Num 11:34), at the place where we returned to our path—that is, the place where we went out of that big valley and reentered the road on which we arrived, between the mountains I mentioned above. On that same day also we came to those other very holy monks who, because of their age or sickness could not be present on the Mountain of God to make the offering. Nonetheless, they saw fit to entertain us as we arrived at their monasteries.

(11) Now that we had seen all the holy places that we had wanted as we went to and returned from the mountain of God, as well as all the places where the Israelites had been, and had also seen the holy men who lived there, we returned in God's name to Pharan. (12) Surely, I should always give thanks to God in all things, and I'm not just talking about such great favors as deeming me worthy (although I am unworthy and undeserving) to visit all the places I did not deserve to visit, and I could never thank enough all those holy men who saw fit to receive me, in my insignificance, in their monasteries with generous hearts and to guide us with certainty through all the places that I requested, always according to the holy Scriptures. Many of these holy men who stay near that Mountain of God saw fit to lead us into Pharan, those who were physically stronger.

6 (1) Once we arrived at Pharan (which is thirty-five miles from the Mountain of God), we had to wait there two days to recover. Moving quickly, on the third day we came once more to the lodging post in the desert of Pharan where we had lodged on our way through, as I said above. The next day we once more packed some water. After traveling for a little while between the mountains, we arrived at the lodging post overlooking the sea, where you come out from the mountains and begin again to walk all along the sea. Here's how you travel along the sea: one moment the waves lap against your animals' feet, then suddenly you're one or two hundred paces away, at other times more than fifty paces from the sea, and you're walking through desert.[1] The road is hardly even

there, but it's all sandy desert. (2) So the Pharanites are accustomed to traveling with camels, and they lay markers out from place to place by which they guide themselves by day. By night the camels look out for these markers. What more is there to say? The Pharanites are accustomed to traveling with greater direction and security by night than any other person could travel in those places when the road is clear. (3) On our return trip we came out of the mountain at the place where we had entered into the mountains, and so once again we turned toward the sea. The Israelites, coming back here from Sinai, the Mountain of God, went by the same road that comes out at the place where we left the mountains and joined up again with the Red Sea. From there, we went back on the road that we had taken, but the Israelites (as it is written in the books of holy Moses) took their own path from that place (cf. Num 10:12). (4) By the same road, and through the same lodging posts by which we had come, we returned to Clysma. When we arrived at Clysma, we had to rest there again, since we had just made a long trip across the sandy desert.

7 (1) Now I was already pretty familiar with the land of Goshen because I had previously been to Egypt; nevertheless, so that I could visit all the places where the Israelites had taken shelter as they left Rameses (cf. Exod 12:37) until they arrived at the Red Sea (which is now the site of a military camp that goes by the name of Clysma), I wanted to go out of Clysma through the land of Goshen to the city called Arabia, a city in the land of Goshen. It has taken its name from the same territory, that is, "the land of Arabia, the land of Goshen" (cf. Gen 46:34 [LXX]), which is part of the land of Egypt but is better by far than all of Egypt. (2) From Clysma, on the Red Sea, to the city of Arabia there are four lodging posts through the desert (which, although it is a desert, has stations in the lodging posts with soldiers and officers, who always escorted us from camp to camp). On that road, the holy men who were with us (the clerics and the monks) showed us every single place that I requested of them according to the Scriptures: sometimes on the left, sometimes on the right of our route, sometimes far off from the road, other times close by. (3) Believe me, Your Affection, as far as I

---

[1] A Roman pace (*passus*) is about 1.5 meters; there are 1,000 paces in a Roman mile (*milia*).

could tell, the Israelites traveled in this way: sometimes they went to the right, as often they turned back to the left, and they even traveled back again, until they came to the Red Sea. (4) The Epauleum was shown to me (cf. Exod 14:2), although far off, and we came to Migdol. Now there is a military camp there with an officer and a soldier who are in charge there in the name of Roman authority. As had become customary, they guided us from there to another military camp, where the site of Baalzephon was shown to us, and indeed we went there. For the camp itself is above the Red Sea, along the side of the mountain (as I said above) where the Israelites cried out when they saw the Egyptians coming after them (cf. Exod 14:10). (5) Etham was shown to us (Exod 13:20), which is the place "next to the desert," as it is written, as well as Succoth (Exod 12:37). Succoth is a modest slope in the middle of the valley, a little hill next to which the Israelites established their camps, for this is the place where they received the law of Passover (Exod 12:43). (6) Pithom, the city that the Israelites built (Exod 1:11), was shown to us on that same road, in the place where we crossed the Egyptian border and left behind the lands of the Saracens. Now Pithom is a military camp. (7) The city of heroes (Heroöpolis), which was a city when Joseph came to meet his father Jacob when he arrived (cf. Gen 46:29), as it is written in the book of Genesis, is now a village, but a big one—what we could call a town. That town has a church and martyria and many monasteries of holy monks; we just had to go down there to see every one of them (as had become our custom). (8) Nowadays that town is called Hero. Hero is sixteen miles from the land of Goshen, on the Egyptian border. The place is quite pleasant since a part of the Nile River runs through it. (9) And so leaving Hero, we arrived at the city called Arabia, which is a city in the land of Goshen, about which it is written that Pharaoh said to Joseph: "Settle your father and your brothers in the best part of the land of Egypt, in the land of Goshen, in the land of Arabia" (Gen 47:6).

8 (1) It's four miles from the city of Arabia to Rameses. To get to the lodging post in Arabia, we crossed through the middle of Rameses. The city of Rameses is now a field without a single house. Still you can plainly see that it had a huge perimeter and lots of buildings. Its ruins, even though they have fallen apart, even today seem limitless. (2) But now there is nothing there except for just a single huge Theban stone, from which two giant statues have been carved, which they say are the holy men Moses and Aaron. For they say that the Israelites erected them in their honor. (3) Furthermore, there is a sycamore tree there, which they say was planted by the patriarchs; even though it is very, very old and rather modest in size, nonetheless it seems to bear fruit. Whoever has an injury comes there and picks up its [fallen] branches, and it benefits them. (4) We learned this from the report of the holy bishop of Arabia, for he himself told us the name of this tree, which is called in Greek "Dendros alethiae" (as we would say, "Tree of Truth"). This holy bishop saw fit to come out to meet us at Rameses. He is an older man, but quite religious and a former monk, and he receives pilgrims with a great deal of kindness. He is also very learned in God's Scriptures. (5) He saw fit to take the trouble to meet us there, and he showed us everything and told us about the two statues (as I said) and about that sycamore tree. This holy bishop also told us that when Pharaoh saw the Israelites getting away from him, he set out after them. He went with his whole army into Rameses and burned all of it (which was practically limitless) and from there continued on after the Israelites.

9 (1) We had the most fortunate bit of luck: we arrived at the lodging post of Arabia on the day before the most blessed Epiphany, on the same day that the vigils were being held in the church. And so for two days, we were kept on by the holy bishop, holy and truly a man of God, quite well known to me from the time when I had come down to the Thebaid. (2) That same holy bishop had been a monk; from childhood he had been raised in a monastery, and this is why he was so learned in the Scriptures and also so blameless in his whole life, as I said above. (3) We sent back the soldiers from there, whose assistance had been provided to us in the name of Roman authority for as long as we traveled through suspicious places. But now, since this was a public route through Egypt that crossed through the city of Arabia (the route that goes from the Thebaid to Pelusium), it was no longer necessary to trouble the soldiers.

(4) As we proceeded altogether out of the land of Goshen, our route took us constantly among vineyards that produced grapes and vineyards that produced balsam and among orchards and the most cultivated fields and first-rate gardens. Our road held entirely to the banks of the Nile River, among the very fertile lands that had once been the cities of the Israelites. What else? I think that I have never seen a more beautiful territory than the land of Goshen. (5) So from the city of Arabia, we made our way for two whole days through the land of Goshen, and we arrived at Tanis, the city where holy Moses was born. This same city of Tanis was formerly the capital city of the Pharaoh. (6) I already was familiar with these places, as I said above, from when I had gone to Alexandria and the Thebaid, but since I wished to learn as much as possible about these places—where the Israelites had traveled as they proceeded from Rameses until the Mountain of God (cf. Exod 12:37–38), holy Sinai—it was necessary to return once again to the land of Goshen and from there to Tanis. Proceeding from Tanis, walking on a path we already knew well, we arrived at the border of Palestine. And from there, in the name of Christ our God, after a few more lodging posts through Palestine, I returned to Aelia, which is Jerusalem.

10 (1) Some time passed. As God willed, the wish came once more upon me to go to Arabia, to Mount Nebo, which is there, where God commanded Moses to ascend, saying to him: "Ascend Mount Arabot, Mount Nebo, which is in the land of Moab opposite Jericho, and see the land of Canaan that I give to the Israelites as their inheritance, and you will die on that mountain that you ascend" (Deut 32:49–50). (2) So then Jesus, our God, who does not desert those who have faith in him, again saw fit to bring to pass the granting of my wish.

(3) So proceeding out from Jerusalem, we made our way with the saints—that is, with a priest and deacons from Jerusalem and certain brothers—and we arrived at that place on the Jordan where the Israelites crossed over when holy Joshua, son of Nun,

sent them across the Jordan, as it is written in the book of Joshua, son of Nun (cf. Josh 3–4). Also the site was shown to us (a little higher up) where Reuben and Gad and the half-tribe of Manasseh made an altar (cf. Josh 22:9–10), on the bank of the river where Jericho is located.

(4) So, crossing the river, we arrived at the city called Livias, which is in the field where the Israelites established their camps. Even today in that place are visible the foundations of the Israelites' camps and their homes, where they waited. The field itself is limitless, under the mountains of Arabia and over the Jordan. This is the place about which it is written: "and the Israelites wept for Moses in Arabot Moab and at the Jordan opposite Jericho for forty days" (Deut 34:8). (5) This is also the place where, after the departure of Moses, right away "Joshua son of Nun was filled with the spirit of knowledge: for Moses had laid his hands on him" (Deut 34:9), as it is written. (6) Furthermore, this is also the place where Moses wrote the book of Deuteronomy (cf. Deut 31:24). Here is where "Moses spoke into the ears of the whole assembly of Israel, words of song until his end" (Deut 31:30), as it is written in the book of Deuteronomy (Deut 32:1–43). This is the very same place where holy Moses, "man of God, blessed the Israelites" (Deut 33:1) one by one, in order, before his death. (7) So when we arrived at this field, we made our way to this place; we said a prayer and read a certain part of the book of Deuteronomy there, not just his song, but also the blessings that he pronounced over the Israelites (Deut 33). And we prayed one more time after the reading, and, thanking God, we moved on from there. This was always our custom, whenever we wished to make our way to a place we desired to see: first we said a prayer there, then the appropriate reading was read from the codex, a psalm was recited that was relevant to the matter, and once again a prayer was said. We kept to this custom because God willed it, whenever we had managed to arrive at a place we wished to see.

(8) To accomplish our task, we hurried to arrive at Mount Nebo. As we went, the priest alerted us about this place (that is, Livias, which we were asking to see as we made our way to the lodging post), since he knew these places better than we. So this priest tells

us: "If you want to see water flowing from a rock, which Moses provided for the thirsty Israelites (Num 21:16–18), you can see it if you don't mind troubling yourself to double back from the road at about the sixth mile marker." (9) When he said this, we wanted quite eagerly to go there, and right away we turned from the road and followed the priest who was guiding us. There was a tiny little church under the mountain (not Nebo, but another one farther in but not too far off from Nebo). Many monks resided there, truly holy, whom they call here "ascetics."

11 (1) These holy monks saw fit to receive us very hospitably; they even let us come in and greet them. After we came inside to them, we said a prayer with them, and they saw fit to give us blessings (which they usually give to those whom they hospitably receive). (2) Right there, between the church and the monastery, an enormous amount of water flows from a rock, very beautiful and clear, extremely tasty. Then we also asked those monks who lived there what kind of water was of such quality and so tasty. They replied: "This is the water that holy Moses gave to the Israelites in this desert" (Exod 17:6, Num 20:8). (3) We said a prayer (as was our custom), and the appropriate reading from the books of Moses was read, and a single psalm was recited. And so with those holy clerics and monks who came with us, we set out for the mountain. Many of the holy monks who resided next to that water (that is, those who were able to impose such toil on themselves) saw fit to climb Mount Nebo with us. (4) So as we proceeded from that place, we arrived at the base of Mount Nebo, which was very high, but the greater part of it could be climbed up on the back of a donkey. A small part of it was so steep, however, that it was necessary to climb up on foot with toil, and so we did.

12 (1) So we arrived at the summit of that mountain, where there is now a church that is not very big, on the very peak of Mount Nebo. Inside this church, at the pulpit, I saw a place set slightly higher, taking up as much space as tombs usually have. (2) Then I asked the holy men who were there, and they responded: "This is where Moses was laid to rest by the angels, since, as Scripture says, 'no one knows his grave' (Deut 34:6), so certainly he was buried by an-

gels. For his tomb, where he was buried, is not visible today. But our predecessors, who lived here, showed it to us, and so we show it to you; these same predecessors said that they received this tradition from their predecessors." (3) Quickly we said a prayer, and all the things we usually did in the holy places in order we also did. And so we began to leave the church. Then the local experts (the priest and the holy monks) said to us: "If you want to see the places written about in the books of Moses, proceed outside the entrance of the church and of this summit to a part with good visibility; go out and look, and we'll tell you all the places that are visible." (4) Then we, quite joyously, right away went outside. From the entrance of the Church, we saw a place where the Jordan entered the Dead Sea; this place appeared right below where we stood. We also saw opposite us not only Livias, on this side of the Jordan, but also Jericho, which is across the Jordan, so high was the place where we stood before the church entrance. (5) Most of Palestine, which is the promised land, was visible from there, as well as the land of Jordan, as far as the eyes could perceive. To the left we saw all the lands of the Sodomites, as well as Zoar (Gen 19:22); Zoar is the only one of those five cities that still stands today. (6) There is even a monument there, but of the other cities, nothing is visible except for overturned ruins, insofar as they were turned into ashes. The place that had the notice about Lot's wife was shown to us, the place we read about in Scripture. (7) But believe me, venerable ladies, that pillar [of salt] is no longer visible, but only the site itself is shown, for they say that the pillar itself was swallowed up by the Dead Sea. Certainly, when we saw the place, we saw no pillar, and so I can't deceive you on this matter. The priest of this place (I mean Zoar) told us that it has already been quite a few years since that pillar was visible. Now Zoar is maybe six miles from that place where that pillar stood, but now the water has swallowed it all. (8) Now we moved to the right part of the church (outside, that is), and we were shown two cities opposite us: Heshbon, where King Sihon was king of the Amorites (cf. Num 21:26) and that is now called Exebon, and the other of King Og of Bashan (cf. Num 21:33), which is now called Safdra.

From the same place they showed us Peor, opposite us, was the city of the King of Edom (cf. Num 23:28). (9) All these cities that we saw were set up in the mountains, but below, just a little bit, we saw a flatter site. We were told that, in the time when holy Moses and the Israelites waged war against these cities, they had made their camps there, for markers of military camps are also visible there. (10) But on the side of the mountain (left, I said) that was above the Dead Sea, we were shown a very steep mountain that used to be called Lookout Point. This is the mountain where Balak, son of Beor, set up Balaam, the seer, so he could curse the Israelites, but God didn't allow it, as it is written (Num 23:14–28). (11) And so once we had seen all the things we desired, returning in God's name through Jericho and that whole road we had traveled, we returned to Jerusalem.

13 (1) A little while later I wanted to go to the region of Uz (cf. Job 1:1) so that I could see Job's tomb for the sake of prayer.[2] I saw many holy monks coming from there to Jerusalem to see the holy places for the sake of prayer; all their detailed reports about those sites conveyed a great desire to make the trouble for myself to go to those places (if I can speak of trouble when a person sees her desire fulfilled). (2) So I proceeded from Jerusalem with the holy men who saw fit to provide companionship for my trip, and they also came for the sake of prayer. We made our way from Jerusalem to Carneas by passing through eight lodging posts (Carneas is what Job's city is now called, which used to be called Dinhaba "in the land of Uz, on the border of Idumaea and Arabia" [Job 42:18, LXX]).

Making our way, I saw on the bank of the Jordan River a quite beautiful and pleasant valley, full of vines and trees, since there was quite a lot of good watering there. (3) Now in this valley there was a big town that is now called Sedima. In the middle of that town, which is set in the middle of a plain, there is a little peak, not too big, but formed in the shape of a big tomb. At the top of it is a church, and all around that little hill huge, ancient foundations are visible. But now only a few clusters of people reside in that town. (4) When I saw such a lovely place, I asked what such a lovely place as this might be. I was told: "This is the city of King Melchizedek, which used to be called Salem, but now the language has degraded and this town is called Sedima. On that hill, which is located in the middle of the town, built on the summit you see, is a church. This church is called (in Greek) Opu Melchizedek.[3] For this is where Melchizedek 'offered' pure sacrifices to God, that is, 'bread and wine' (Gen 14:18), as it is written he did."

14 (1) As soon as I heard this, we dismounted from our animals, and behold the holy priest of this place and the clerics came out to meet us. Receiving us right away, they guided us up to the church. When we got there, right away we first made our usual prayer; then the appropriate passage was read from the book of holy Moses, a psalm was also recited befitting that place, and we came down after another prayer was said. (2) When we came down, that holy priest (now older and well versed in Scriptures, who had taken charge of the place while still a monk; about this priest many bishops, as many as we got to know afterward bore great witness to his life, for they said this of him: he was just the person to preside in the place where holy Melchizedek made the pure sacrifices to God at the arrival of holy Abraham)—when we came down (as I said above) from beneath the church, this holy priest said to us: "Look at the foundations around this little hill that you see, these are from the palace of King Melchizedek. Even until today, if someone suddenly decides to make his home near it and collects foundation material from it, he sometimes finds little fragments of silver and bronze. (3) And look at this road, this is that road on which holy Abraham 'returned from the death of Chedorlaomer,' king of the nations, as he made his way back to Sodom, on which holy 'Melchizedek, King of Salem' came out to meet him" (Gen 14:1–18).

---

[2] This phrase *gratia orationis* (for the sake of prayer) is sometimes translated as "pilgrimage"; it seems to be Egeria's way of distinguishing religious travel from secular travel.

[3] That is, "where Melchizedek [offered]."

15 (1) Then, as I recalled that it was written that holy John baptized "in Aenon near Salem" (cf. John 3:23), I asked whether it was far from this place. That holy priest said: "There it is, about 200 paces. If you like, I'll guide you there on foot. The water you see in this town, which is so great and so pure, comes from that spring." (2) Then I began to thank him and ask him to guide us to the site, and so he did. Right away, I began to walk the whole way with him on foot through the most agreeable valley, until we arrived at a very agreeable apple orchard. In the middle of this, he showed us a very good, pure spring of water that gave off water in a single stream. There was a sort of pool in front of that spring, where it was clear that holy John the Baptist did his work. (3) Then that holy priest said to us: "Even today there is no other name for this garden in the Greek language except 'cepos tu agiu Iohanni,' or as you would say in Latin, 'Saint John's garden.'" Now many brothers, holy monks, coming from all sorts of places, stayed there and washed in that place. (4) Once again at that spring, just as in every single place, a prayer was said and the appropriate passage read; a fitting psalm was recited, all in order, as it had become our custom to do whenever we came to holy places, so also we did there. (5) And that holy priest said to us that even into the present day at Easter, everyone who came to be baptized in this town in the church called Opu Melchizedek was baptized in that spring. So they come back from there early, holding candles, with the clerics and the monks, reciting psalms and antiphonal hymns, and all those who were baptized are led early from the spring until the church of holy Melchizedek. (6) We received blessings from the priest from the orchard of John the Baptist, as well as from the holy monks who had a monastery in the apple orchard, and we thanked God continually as we made our way, taking the same route we had come by.

16 (1) And so we went for a while through the Jordan valley on the banks of that river, since our route took some time. Then suddenly we saw the city of the holy prophet Elijah, that is, Tishbe, whence he had the name Elijah the Tishbite (1 Kings 17:1). Today there is in that place a cave, in which that holy man stayed; there is also the tomb of holy Jephtha, whose name we read in the book of Judges (Judges 11–12).

(2) And so thanking God, as was our custom, we set out on our path. As we made our way on that road, we saw a very agreeable valley off to our left, a huge valley sending a boundless stream down into the Jordan. In that valley, we saw that there was now a monastery of a certain brother, that is, a monk. (3) Then—since I'm quite curious—I began to ask what this valley was that a holy monk should now make a monastery for himself there. I thought there must be a reason for it. The holy men who traveled with us, the local experts, said to us: "This is the valley of Cherith, where the holy Elijah the Tishbite stayed in the time of King Ahab, during the famine, and by God's command a raven brought him his food 'and he drank from there the streaming water' (1 Kings 17:2–6). That's the stream you saw rushing through this valley into the Jordan; this is Cherith." (4) And so we thanked God, who showed us all these things we wanted to see, even though we didn't deserve it, and we began to make our way again one day at a time. And so we were making our way one day at a time, when suddenly off to the left, where we could see parts of Phoenicia opposite us, a huge mountain appeared to us, of boundless height, which extended as far as [*a page is missing here, part of which is supplied by a fragment*]. . . .

. . . where Job sat in his pile of filth (cf. Job 2:8), there is now a very tidy place, enclosed all around by iron screens, and a great glass lamp shines there from evening to evening. Now the fountain where he scraped his scabs with the potsherd changes color four times a year: first it has the color of pus, then blood, then gall, and then it becomes entirely clear. . . .

[*the manuscript resumes*] . . . (5) ". . . this holy monk, an 'ascetic' man, after many years of living in the desert, had to stir himself and go down to the city of Carneas to alert the bishop and the clerics of that time to do what had been revealed to him, to dig in that place that had been revealed to him, and so they did. (6) After digging in the place that had been revealed, they found a cave that they followed for about 100 paces; suddenly a stone appeared before the diggers. When they had completely uncovered the stone, they found carved into its cover 'JOB.' So a church was built at that time, in that place, to Job, which you see; but they didn't move the stone with the body to another place, but the body is laid right there where it was found, so that the body lies under the altar. That church, which some tribune or other built, still stands unfinished until today." (7) And so on the next morning, we asked the bishop to say a prayer, which he was kind enough to do, and the bishop proceeded to bless us. After taking communion there, thanking God as always, we returned to Jerusalem, making our way through each lodging post we passed through on the way out.

17 (1) Then, in God's name, some time passed. Already three full years had gone by since I had first come to Jerusalem. I had seen all the holy places for which I had come, for the sake of prayer, and so I was just about ready to return to my native land. I wanted, as God willed, to go to Syrian Mesopotamia to see the holy monks who were said to be numerous and to live such extraordinary lives that they can scarcely be recounted; what's more, to go, for the sake of prayer, to the martyrium of the holy apostle Thomas, where his untouched body was laid out, in Edessa. He's the one our God Jesus promised to send, before he ascended into the heavens, by means of a letter that he sent by Ananias his messenger to King Abgar. This letter is guarded with great reverence in the city of Edessa, where the martyrium is. (2) Believe me, Your Affection, there is no Christian among those who have come all the way to the holy places, to Jerusalem, who has not gone there, too, for the sake of prayer; this place is about twenty-five lodging posts from Jerusalem. (3) And since Antioch is close to Mesopotamia, I thought it quite a good opportunity—as God willed—to make my way through Antioch and go to Mesopotamia through there, and so, as God willed, we did.

18 (1) So in the name of Christ our God I set out from Antioch to Mesopotamia, making my way through the lodging posts and a number of cities of the province of Coele-Syria (where Antioch is); from there, I crossed the border of the province of Augusta Euphratensis, and I arrived at the city of Hierapolis, the capital of this province (I mean, Augusta Euphratensis). Since this city is very beautiful and opulent and has everything in abundance, I had to make a stop there; from there, it wasn't very far to the Mesopotamian border. (2) So I set out from Hierapo-

lis and, at the fifteenth mile marker (in God's name), I arrived at the Euphrates River, of which it is quite well written that the "Euphrates is a great river" (Gen 15:18): it's huge and almost frightening. It has a fast-flowing current, just like the Rhone River, except that the Euphrates is bigger. (3) So since we had to cross it by boat (and only by big boats), I waited there for maybe more than half the day. From there in God's name, once I had traversed the Euphrates River, I crossed the border of Syrian Mesopotamia.

19 (1) And so making my way once again through a number of lodging posts, I arrived at the city whose name we read out in Scripture, Batanis, which is still a city today.[4] It has a church with a bishop, a very holy man, a monk and a confessor, and a number of martyria. That city has a large population, and soldiers are stationed there with their tribune.

(2) Making our way from there once more, we arrived in the name of Christ our God at Edessa. When we arrived there, right away we made our way to the church and to the martyrium of Saint Thomas. As was our custom, prayers were said and so forth, as we had customarily done in the holy places, and what's more we read a number of things of Saint Thomas there.[5] (3) The church there is huge and really pretty and well laid out, as is fitting for God's house. Since there were so many things I wanted to see I had to stay there for three days. (4) And so in that city I saw many martyria, as well as holy monks, some who resided in the martyria and others farther away from the city in more private places that had monasteries. (5) The holy bishop of that city, a truly religious man, a monk and a confessor who received me generously, said to me: "Since I see, daughter, what great trouble you have imposed upon yourself for the sake of religion, such that you have come to this place from the other end of the world, if you like, we shall show you all the places that Christians find pleasing to see." First giving thanks to God and then to him, I eagerly asked him to see fit to do as he said. (6) So he guided me first to the palace of King Abgar; there he showed

---

[4] There is a city of this name (Bathnae) in Josh 19:25, but it cannot be the city Egeria sees in Syria.
[5] Possibly Egeria is talking about readings from the apocryphal *Acts of Thomas*.

me a huge marble portrait of him, which they said was a good likeness, as shiny as if it were made from pearl. Standing opposite, it appeared from Abgar's face that this man had been quite wise and honorable. The holy bishop said to me, "This is King Abgar, who, before he saw the Lord, believed that he was truly God's son." Next to it there was also another similar portrait made out of the same marble, which he said was of his son Magnus, and he also had a certain charm in his face.

(7) We proceeded farther, to the inner part of the palace. There were many fountains full of fish; I had never seen so many, of such great size and so bright and of such good flavor. This city doesn't have any other source of water except this one, which comes out of the palace like a huge silvery river. (8) That holy bishop recounted this to me about that water: "It was at that time after King Abgar had written to the Lord and the Lord wrote back to Abgar through his messenger Ananias, as it is written in this letter. Some time passed, and the Persians invaded and surrounded this city. (9) But right away Abgar carried the Lord's letter to the gate with all his troops and prayed publicly. And afterward he said: 'Lord Jesus, you promised us that no enemy would enter this city and now look: the Persians are attacking us.' When the king said this, holding that open letter in his raised hands, suddenly great shadows fell outside the city, before the eyes of the Persians (now, they had already come close to the city; they were approaching the third mile marker from the city). They were quickly so confused by the shadows that they could barely set up camp and surround the whole city from three miles away. (10) The Persians were so confused that they couldn't see from what part of the city they could gain access, but they kept the city shut in by enemy troops (although from three miles' distance), and they kept them shut in for a number of months. (11) After a while, when they saw that there was no way to gain access to the city, they wanted to kill the people in the city. Now that little hill that you see, daughter, above this city, at that time it served as the city's water source. Seeing this, the Persians diverted that water source from the city and made it turn back to where they had set up their camps. (12) On the

very day, in the very hour, in which the Persians diverted the water, right away these springs that you see right here burst forth at once by God's command. From that day until today, these springs have remained here by God's grace. The water that the Persians diverted dried up in that same hour, so that the people besieging the city didn't have enough drinking water for a single day, and so it appears even today; after then no liquid of any kind has ever appeared there up to the present. (13) And so, as God willed, who had promised this would happen, they had to turn back right away to their own homes in Persia. Afterward, whenever enemies have wanted to come and attack this city, this letter has been carried forth and read in the gates, and right away, with a nod from God, all enemies are repulsed."

(14) The holy bishop also reported that the spot where these springs had burst forth was a field within the city that lay below Abgar's palace: "Abgar's palace had been set up on a site above the city, even as it appears now, as you see. For it was customary in that time, whenever someone built a palace, to set it up on higher elevations. (15) But after these springs burst forth in this site, that same Abgar had a palace built there for his son Magnus (that is, the one whose portrait you saw set next to his father's), so that these springs would be enclosed within the palace." (16) After the holy bishop related all this, he said to me: "Let us now go to the gate through which Ananias, the messenger, entered with that letter of which I spoke." When we came to that gate, the bishop made a prayer as he stood there, and he read to us from those very letters; he then blessed us once again, and a prayer was made a second time. (17) That holy man also told us that from that day, when the messenger Ananias entered through that gate with the Lord's letter, until the present day, it has been ensured that no one unclean or in mourning has passed through that gate, and no dead person's body has been carried out through that gate. (18) The holy bishop showed us the tomb of Abgar and his whole family—very pretty, but made in an antique fashion. He guided us to that elevated palace, which King Abgar had possessed previously, and if there were any sites to see, he showed them to us. (19) Another thing that pleased

me quite a bit: those very letters, from Abgar to the Lord and from the Lord to Abgar, which the holy bishop had read to us there, I received them from that holy man. Even though I have copies of them back home, it seemed much better to me to receive them from him in that place, just in case, perhaps, our copies back home turn out to be less complete. The ones I received there seem to be longer. So if Jesus our God wills it and I return home, you yourselves will read them, my dearest ladies.

20 (1) After I spent three days there, I had to push on even farther to Carrae, as it is called nowadays. In the holy Scriptures it is called Harran, where holy Abraham lived as it is written in Genesis, when the Lord said to Abraham: "Go out from your land and from your father's house and go to Harran," and so forth (Gen 12:1). (2) When we got to Harran, right away I went to the church of that city. I quickly saw the bishop of that place (truly holy and a man of God, as well as a monk and confessor), who quickly saw fit to show us all the places we wanted to see. (3) He guided us right away to the church outside the city, where Abraham used to have a house. It is on the same foundations and from the same stone, as the holy bishop said. When we got to that church, a prayer was said and the appropriate passage was read from Genesis, and a single psalm was recited and another prayer said and, when the bishop had blessed us, we went outside. (4) Then he saw fit to guide us to that well from which holy Rebecca used to carry water (Gen 24:15–20). The holy bishop said to us: "Look, this is the well from which holy Rebecca watered the camels of Abraham's manservant, Eleazar," and he saw fit to show us everything in turn. (5) This church (which I said is outside the city, ladies and venerable sisters) where Abraham formerly had a house has now also been established as a martyrium, of a certain monk named Helpidius. Things turned out quite well for us, for the day before we came to the martyrium was the festival of that holy Helpidius, the ninth of the kalends of May [April 23]. On that day, all the monks from there and from all of Mesopotamia have to come down, even those greater ones who reside in solitude who are called "ascetics." That day is observed quite grandly, also on account of the remembrance of holy

Abraham, whose house this was that is now a church, where the body of that holy martyr has been put. (6) This, too, was quite pleasing beyond anything we had hoped for, that we should see there holy men, truly men of God, the monks of Mesopotamia—what's more, those whose fame and way of life we had long heard about. I would never have guessed that I would be able to see them, not because it would be impossible for God to grant it to me—who has seen fit to grant me all things—but because I had heard that, apart from Easter and this day, they don't come down from their own places, since these are the sort of men who perform many miracles. And I didn't know what day of the month this martyrdom was celebrated, as I said. But as God willed this took place on that same day that we came there, which I could not have hoped for. (7) So we stayed there for two days on account of the martyr's festival and to see those holy men who saw fit to greet me with a generosity of spirit, to receive and converse with me, of which I was not worthy. On the very day after the martyr's festival, they were not seen there, but quickly by night they disappeared back into the desert, each one to his monastery that he had there. (8) Now in that city, apart from a few clerics and holy monks, I did not meet any Christians, should any happen to dwell there; they were all gentiles. Just as we attend with great reverence to the place where holy Abraham first had his house, in his memory, so those gentiles attend with great reverence to the spot about 1,000 paces from the city where the tombs of Nahor and Bethuel are found. (9) Since the bishop of that city was well versed in Scriptures, I asked him about this: "I ask you, lord, to tell me what I would like to hear." He said: "Say, daughter, what you want, and I shall speak if I know." So I said: "I know from Scriptures that holy Abraham came to this place with his father Terah and his wife Sarah and his brother's son Lot. But I have not read when Nahor and Bethuel migrated to this place. The only one I know who came to Harran later is Abraham's manservant, who came seeking Rebecca, the daughter of Bethuel, the son of Nahor, for the son of his master Abraham, Isaac" (cf. Gen 24:15). (10) Then the holy bishop said to me: "Truly, daughter, it is written as you say in Genesis, that holy Abraham migrated here with his family (Gen. 11:31).

And the canonical Scriptures do not say when Nahor and Bethuel came with their families. But clearly, they also migrated here afterward, since their tombs are also here 1,000 paces from the city. And truly Scriptures bear witness to this, since the manservant of holy Abraham came here to take holy Rebecca, and once more Jacob came here when he took the daughters of Laban the Syrian" (cf. Gen 29). (11) Then I asked where that well was found, where holy Jacob watered the flocks that Rachel, daughter of Laban, the Syrian, pastured. The bishop said to me: "Six miles from this place, next to a town that was the estate of Laban, the Syrian, at that time. When you want to go there, we'll go with you and show you, for there are many monks there who are very holy and ascetics, and there is also a holy church there." (12) I asked the holy bishop where the site of the Chaldees was, where Terah had formerly lived with his family. The holy bishop said to me: "That place, daughter, about which you ask, is ten lodging posts from here, inside Persia. There are five lodging posts from here to Nisibis, and from there to Ur, which was the city of the Chaldees, there are another five lodging posts. But Romans have no way of getting there, since all of it is held by Persia. This part of the world is called 'eastern' because it is the Roman border with the Persians and Chaldees." (13) He saw fit to report many more things to us, just as other holy bishops and holy monks saw fit to do, all about God's Scriptures or the deeds of holy men (that is, monks), whether it was the miracles performed by those who had already passed away or of those who are still in bodily form, who perform them daily, those who are called "ascetics." I don't want Your Affection to suppose that the stories monks tell have anything to do with anything other than God's Scriptures or the deeds of ancient monks.

21 (1) After I stayed two days there, our bishop guided us to the well where holy Jacob watered the flocks of holy Rachel (Gen 29:2); this well is six miles from Carrae. To honor this well, a holy church was constructed next to it, huge and very beautiful. When we got to that well, a prayer was said by the bishop; the appropriate passage was read from Genesis; a single psalm was recited befitting the place; and after a second prayer was said, the bishop blessed us. (2) We saw next to the well a stone, lying adjacent to it, really

enormous, which holy Jacob moved away from the well (Gen 29:10), and it's still shown today. (3) No one lives around the well except the clerics of that church there and monks who had their monasteries there. The holy bishop told us about their lives, which are truly incredible. After prayers had been said inside the church, I went with the bishop to the holy monks among their monasteries. Thanks be to God and to them! Whenever I entered their monasteries, they saw fit to receive me with a generous spirit and to engage in the kind of speech that is fitting to come forth from their mouths. They saw fit to give me blessings and all those who came with me, as monks are accustomed to give to those whom they receive with generous spirit in their monasteries. (4) Since that site is on a big plain, the holy bishop showed me, opposite us, a quite huge town, about 500 paces from the well, and we made our way through this town. This town, at least as the bishop said, used to be the estate of Laban, the Syrian; the town is called Fadana. In this town, I was shown the tomb of Laban, the Syrian, Jacob's father-in-law, and I was also shown the place where Rachel hid her father's idols (Gen 31:19). (5) And so, after we had visited all these places in God's name, we said good-bye to the holy bishop and the holy monks who had seen fit to guide us to this place, and we returned by the road and the lodging posts that we had taken from Antioch.

22 (1) When I got back to Antioch, I stayed there a week, the time that was necessary to prepare the trip. Setting out from Antioch, I made my way through a number of lodging posts until I arrived at the province called Cilicia, whose capital is Tarsus, where I had already been when I was going to Jerusalem. (2) But since three lodging posts from Tarsus is Isauria, which has the martyrium of holy Thecla, I was quite pleased to proceed there, especially since it was so close.

23 (1) Setting out from Tarsus, I arrived at a certain city on the sea in Cilicia called Pompeiopolis. Crossing the border of Isauria from there, I lodged in a city called Corycus. On the third day, I arrived in the city of Isaurian Seleucia. When I arrived, I went to the bishop, a truly holy man and former monk; I saw the very pretty church in that city. (2) Now since I had to go about 1,500 paces from the city to get to Saint Thecla's (the site is outside the city on the flat part of a hill), I preferred to go and stay there, since I had to stay somewhere. There is nothing at the holy church except for a monastery with a number of men and women. (3) I met there a certain very dear friend of mine, about whom everyone in the East bore witness to her way of life, a very holy deaconess named Marthana. I got to know her in Jerusalem, where she had gone for the sake of prayer. She was in charge of these monasteries of apotactites and virgins.[6] When she saw me, how great her joy was, and mine—how could I ever describe it? (4) But to get back to the subject: there are many monasteries on that hill and in the middle of a huge wall that encloses the church of the martyrium (the martyrium is quite pretty). Now the wall was erected to guard the church so that the Isaurians (who are quite wicked and frequently make raids) will not try something around the monastery that is highly regarded there. (5) When I got there, in God's name, a prayer was said at the martyrium, and all the *Acts of Thecla* were read; I gave boundless thanks to Christ our God, who saw fit to fulfill my desires, even though I am unfit and undeserving in every way.

(6) After two days there, and after having seen the holy monks and apotactites (as many men as women) who were there, having said prayers and made communion, I made my way back to Tarsus. I stayed there for three days (in God's name), and then I set out on my way. The same day I arrived at the lodging post called Manuscrinae, which is under Mount Taurus, and I lodged there. (7) From there, the next day we went up Mount Taurus and took a familiar path through all the provinces that we had crossed through on our journey: Cappadocia, Galatia, Bithynia. I arrived at Chalcedon, already familiar to me because of its very famous martyrium of holy Euphemia located there; I lodged in that place. (8) And on the next day, after the sea crossing, I arrived at Constantinople, thanking Christ our God that he saw fit to show me such favor despite my unfitness and undeservedness, for he had seen fit to grant me not only the desire to travel, but also the ability to visit everything I wanted to and to return once more to Constantinople. (9) When I arrived, I did not stop thanking our God Jesus in every church, at the apostles' tomb, and at all the martyria (which are numerous there), since he saw fit to bestow such mercy on me. (10) From there, ladies, my light, as I render these matters to Your Affection, it has already been proposed (in the name of Christ our God) that I go up to Asia, to Ephesus, to make prayer at the martyrium of the holy and blessed apostle John. If after this I am still alive, and if I can get to know more places, either in person (if God sees fit to grant it), I shall report it to Your Affection, or, certainly, if some other plan occurs to me, I shall let you know in writing. Ladies, my light, only see fit to remember me, whether I should be "in my body or out of body" (cf. 2 Cor 12:3).

---

[6] The term *apotactite* is Greek and just means "renunciant"; it is unclear whether Egeria knows what the word means or whether she thinks it is a local term for monks (like "ascetic").

43. Gregory of Nyssa: Letter on Pilgrimage

Gregory (ca. 331–ca. 395) was born into an influential Christian family in Cappadocia (in modern Turkey), where he eventually became bishop of Nyssa. Along with his elder brother Basil and their friend Gregory of Nazianzus (see Texts 18 and 23), Gregory of Nyssa vigorously defended Nicene orthodoxy in the later fourth century. His writings attempt to weld scriptural piety with classical Greek philosophy (particularly a late ancient form of Platon-

---

From *Grégoire de Nysse: Lettres*, ed. Pierre Maraval. Paris: Cerf, 1990. (Translated by Andrew S. Jacobs.)

ism). Gregory's writings on the "philosophical life" emphasize physical and spiritual asceticism aimed at achieving virtue (see Text 56).

At about the time that Egeria was traveling through the holy land, Gregory was in Arabia settling ecclesiastical matters there. His trip included a detour to Jerusalem. Although elsewhere Gregory wrote positively of this experience of the holy places, the more severe letter reproduced here became famous for its warnings on the ascetic dangers of pilgrimage. Practically, he questioned whether any ascetic (especially a woman) could expect to survive the open road with her virtue intact; philosophically, he wondered why people should focus their piety on one place, rather than another: was not the spirit of God omnipresent? Did Christians really believe it could be concentrated more in one location? If so, he quipped, then Christians might as well start making pilgrimage to a truly pious province, such as Cappadocia. The only appropriate pilgrimage for an ascetic, Gregory opines, is the spiritual journey to Christ, not the bodily journey to his empty tomb. Gregory's short letter on the pitfalls of pilgrimage condenses many of the concerns shared by other Christians regarding the spiritual gain of visiting holy places and hints at the popularity it nonetheless enjoyed.

(1) Since, my friend, you inquired by letter, I thought it fitting to respond to all points in the order you raised them. I say that those who once and for all have committed themselves to the higher calling[1] would do well to remain focused on the words of the gospel at all times. Just as those who correct what has been laid out with a ruler change the curves of what they have in their hands into straightness, using the straight edge of the ruler, so I think it is appropriate for those who have dedicated themselves to the same sort of firm and unbending rule (I mean the calling of the gospel) to conform themselves, according to that calling, to God. (2) But now there are some who have taken up the solitary life of withdrawal who thought a measure of piety lay in seeing the sites in Jerusalem, in seeing there the signs of the Lord's sojourn in the flesh. They might do well to look at their rule, and if the direction of the commandments wishes such things, to get it done as if the Lord ordered it. But if this lies outside the Master's commandments, I don't know why they should arrange matters however they wish, making a law out of what seems nice for them. (3) When the Lord called the blessed to inherit the kingdom of heaven (cf. Matt 25:34), he didn't include among upright deeds going off to Jeru-

salem. When he preached the beatitudes (Matt 5:3–11), he did not include this kind of effort. For something that neither makes one blessed nor ready for the Kingdom, someone with half a mind might ask, why even bother? (4) And even if such an act were considered useful, it would not be good for such an effort to be exerted by those who are perfect. On the contrary, we observe quite precisely that this act even inflicts spiritual harm on those who are established in a rigorous way of life, not meriting a great effort but extreme caution, since those who have chosen to live according to God should not be wounded by anything damaging.

(5) But what's the harm in this? The distinguished calling lies open to all, both to men and to women. The philosophical way of life has its own particular comportment, which is best accomplished through an unmixed and withdrawn mode of life; its nature is entirely unmingled and unconfounded, since neither women among men nor men among women are very eager to be on guard against indecency. (6) But the exigencies of road travel always break down precision in these matters and lead to indifference concerning observances, for it is impracticable for a woman to travel on such a path unless she has a guardian. Because of her physical weakness, she must be lifted up onto her mount and likewise lifted off it and must be kept from falling off over rough ter-

---

[1] "Calling" is *politeia,* used to refer to ascetic life.

rain. And whatever we may suppose, whether she has an old familiar friend taking care or a hired hand offering his service, in each case the act does not escape reproach, for it is not by laying down next to a stranger or even next to a familiar friend that she preserves the law of chastity! (7) And since the inns and lodgings and the cities of the eastern regions are so fearless and indifferent to evil, how will she be able to keep her eyes from stinging as she passes through the smoke? Whenever the ears are defiled, won't her eyes be defiled, won't her heart be defiled, receiving the sights and the sounds of the unseemly? How can she remain passionless when she travels through these impassioned places?

(8) And what more will that person have who has been in those places, as if even until today the Lord was passing in bodily form in those places, though keeping away from us, or the Holy Spirit was hanging around in Jerusalem, but unable to come up to us? (9) Really, if it is possible for the presence of God to be shown through appearances, someone might rather think that God lived among the Cappadocian people, rather than in those foreign places. As many shrines as there are here in these places, through which the Lord's name is glorified, someone could scarcely count as many shrines throughout the whole world! (10) But then, if there were more grace in those places around Jerusalem, sin wouldn't frequent those who live there; yet now there is no type of sin that isn't tried out among them, even fornications and adulteries and thefts and idolatries and poisonings and jealousies and murders! And evil resides in that place to such an extent that no where is there such a state of readiness for murder as in those places: in the manner of wild animals blood kin attack each other for the sake of heartless advantage. Since these things happen there, what is the proof that there is more grace in those places?

(11) But I know the objection of many people to what I have just said. They say, "Why haven't you made this rule for yourself? For if there were no advantage to the one residing with God in being there, for what reason did you vainly undertake this very journey?" (12) So let them hear my defense for these things. On account of this burden in which I have

been appointed to live my life by the one who arranges our lives, there came from the holy synod an assignment to be present in these places to set straight the churches of Arabia. Since Arabia borders those places around Jerusalem, I was constrained also to make inquiries with the leaders of the holy churches in Jerusalem, since their affairs were in a state of disarray, and to serve as a mediator. (13) Since the most pious emperor had also furnished us with convenient travel through use of the public road system, we did not have to suffer the same burdens that we have observed of others. Our chariot was, for us, like a church and a monastery, since all of us passed the whole journey singing psalms together and fasting together for the Lord. (14) So our own case shouldn't be troublesome for anyone, and our advice should be especially persuasive, since we have glimpsed these matters about which we give advice with our own two eyes. (15) For *we* confessed that Christ who appeared is truly God even before being present at that place, and afterward our faith was not diminished nor afterward was our faith increased, but his incarnation both through a virgin and in Bethlehem we already knew about; likewise we understood his resurrection from the dead even before seeing the tomb, and his ascent into heaven we confessed to be true even apart from the view of the Mount of Olives. We received only this sort of benefit from our voyage: the considered opinion that *our* places are much holier than those abroad.

(16) Whoever of you "fear the Lord, praise him" (Ps 22:23) wherever you are. For a change of scenery will not bring you closer to God, but wherever you may be, God will come to you if he finds the sort of habitation in your soul in which the Lord can dwell within you and walk around in. (17) But if you have an "inner human" (Rom 7:22) filled with evil thoughts, even if you are on Golgotha, even if you are on the Mount of Olives, even in the tomb of the Resurrection, you are as far from receiving Christ within you as those who haven't even confessed him to begin with!

(18) Therefore, beloved, advise your brothers to flee from their bodies to the Lord, not from Cappadocia to Palestine. And if someone should suggest

that the Lord's own words command his disciples not to separate themselves from Jerusalem (cf. Acts 1:4), let him think about what he has said. Inasmuch as the grace of the Holy Spirit and its distribution were not spread all around for the apostles, the Lord ordered them to remain in the same place until they were imbued with power from above (cf. Luke 24:49). (19) So if what applied from the beginning remained in effect until now, with the Holy Spirit in the form of fire

assigning each one his or her own gifts, then everyone would have to be in the place where the distribution of gifts occurred. But if "the wind[2] blows where it wishes" (John 3:8), even the believers here share the gift according to the proportion of their faith, and not according to their vacation in Jerusalem.

---

[2] "Wind" can also mean "Spirit" (*pneuma*).

44. Victricius of Rouen: In Praise of the Saints

Shrines containing relics (literally, "leftovers" or "remains") of holy men and women came to dot the landscape of the Christian Mediterranean in the fourth and fifth centuries, to the delight of many Christians who cherished this physical connection to sacred power and to the horror of others who found the practice of venerating human remains no better than pagan idolatry. This was not a case of a debate between intellectuals and "simple" Christians; rather, contradictory values embedded in the very fabric of Christian belief—the importance of the body and of the soul or spirit—came to a head at all levels of Christian culture.

The treatise presented here, written by a late fourth-century bishop of Rouen (in modern France) named Victricius, demonstrates that defenses of the veneration of relics could draw on images both mundane and sublime. The treatise, *In Praise of the Saints,* is addressed (in part) to Ambrose of Milan (see Text 8) and combines common descriptions of saintly veneration with more abstract philosophical language. Victricius praises the holiness and benevolence of the saints: how can it be wrong to honor those who so perfectly imitated Christ or to seek favors (particularly healing) from the ones God favored above all others? He further provides a dense argument about natures and substances (reminiscent of the difficult theological language of Trinitarian controversy) to explain how parceled human remains might possess sacred power derived from God. The intersection of abstract philosophical discourse and intensely material Christian piety represents a fruitful tension of Christian worship that would continue to encourage both religious development and religious division.

(1) We too, dearest brethren, belong to the mercy of God and the omnipotence of the Savior: the increase of spiritual goods, even in our time, tells us so. We have seen no executioner, we are ignorant of the sword unsheathed, yet we make more altars for divine powers. Today there is no bloodstained enemy, yet we are enriched by the passion of the saints. No

torturer now has oppressed us, yet we carry the trophies of the martyrs. In this time there is no outpouring of blood, no persecutor pursues us, yet we are filled with the joy of triumphs. So we must immerse ourselves in tears and release our great joy in lavish weeping. See, a very great part of the heavenly host deigns to visit our city, so that we are now to live

From Clark, Gillian. "Victricius of Rouen, Praising the Saints." *Journal of Early Christian Studies* 7.3 (1999): 376–399. © The Johns Hopkins University Press. Reprinted with permission of The Johns Hopkins University Press.

among throngs of saints and renowned celestial powers. It is no slight mitigation of sins to have with you those you may brief, to have with you those you may mollify. I myself assess by my present joy how much I had lost until now. Please forgive my impatience: excessive happiness cannot weigh words. I grieve, and in a way, in human terms, I am deeply saddened that these dwellers in our hearts have come so late; had they come before, they would have found fewer faults. So, dearest ones, let this be our first petition to the saints, that they should excuse our sins with the pious compassion of an advocate, not search them out in the spirit of a judge.

For my own late arrival, holy and venerable martyrs, there is an explanation that will, I think, earn pardon from you. It was to carry out your commands that I went to Britain and stayed there. My fellow priests, holy bishops, called me there to make peace. As your soldier, I could not refuse. Obedience to commands is not lack of respect. I knew that you are everywhere by the merit of your virtue; heavenly brilliance is not cheated out of any place on earth. So you ought to pardon me for coming almost too late to meet you, only at the fortieth milestone. I was serving you in Britain, and, though I was separated from you by the ocean that surrounds it, it was on your business that I was detained. That delay made my desire for you painful, but did not neglect my service to you. But I ascribe it all to your majesty, for "you are the body of Christ," and it is "God the Spirit" who "dwells in you" (1 Cor 12:27, 3:16). Because of you, I was absent; because of you I have returned. It remains, then, for me to set out my explanation. You promote the Lord's peace, and you chose me as (so to speak) interpreter of his decision.

I carried out in Britain this salutary command from the Lord Jesus and from you, if not as I ought, at least so far as I could. I instilled in the wise the love of peace. I read to the teachable, I instructed the ignorant, I constrained the unwilling, insisting, as the Apostle says, in season and out of season; I reached their souls with teaching and cajolery. But where speech and human frailty put me to the test, I entreated the protection of your spirit. I did what people at sea do at the height of a storm: they call not on the skill of the helmsman, but on the mercy of the majesty above. Jesus, who is in you, has the power to level the waves and check the winds, as earthly skill cannot. But, indeed, I should not now be concerned with those who have fallen away from the bond of slackened discipline. I have the presence of your majesties: may the authority of your power complete what the officer of religion offers as excuse.

(2) Blessed Ambrose, with what reverence shall I now embrace you? With what love, Theodulus, shall I kiss you? With what inner arms, Eustachius, shall I clasp you to my senses? With what honor from a renewed mind, Catio, with what wonder shall I receive you? Indeed, I do not know; I do not know what to repay for such great deserts. There is only one thing that can answer your good deeds: you must ask the holy apostles and martyrs for what we owe, so that you should not lack those you have wished to be with us. Beloved brother Aelianus, I thank your devotion and your waiting, too, but the apostles and martyrs have already paid in full the wage for your effort and duty: they have been with you a long time. Give them, then, give. Why do you delay? Hold out to me the temples of the saints. It is action, not speech, that we want. If the hem of the Savior's garment cured when lightly touched (cf. Luke 8:42–48), it is beyond doubt that the dwelling places of martyrdoms will cure when we take them in our arms. Moreover, that effort feels no weariness. We have carried our apostles and martyrs before now in faith. The saints come a second time to the city of Rouen: long ago they entered our heart, now they frequent the church of the city. See, all ages pour out to serve you, each one strives to surpass the other in zeal for religion. Thus the priests and deacons and every minister known to you by daily service come to meet you. The devotion of those you know is the more welcome, for it is not just beginning to be loved, but acquiring an increase of love.

(3) Moreover, known and veteran soldiers fear the Lord more. Additional years of service are an increment of fear. There is more alarm in the man who has something he might lose by an offense. Such, then, is the soldier who comes to meet you, tested over time in duty to you, purged of vices, proved by hard work

and watchfulness. Such he is, I say, who hastens to serve you, who turns his effort into longing, to whom the word "fortune" is unknown, who measures this life not by its present brevity, but by the happiness of eternity. His cast of mind is such that he thinks himself enriched by a massive loan whenever his hands are laden with the relics of the saints.

Here clusters a throng of monks refined by fasting. Here the resonant joy of innocent children sounds forth. Here the chorus of devout and untouched virgins carries the sign of the cross. Here the multitude of celibates and widows gathers, entirely worthy of such a duty. The life of these women is the more splendid, the more harsh their lot is in human terms. It is a hard fight to resist a pleasure that you know; if you do not know, the very nature of unknowing defends you. If you do know, the very knowledge of desire assaults you. This one's fire has been extinguished by the chill of her husband's death, and a melancholy tomb enfolds all her longing. A husband still living keeps this one's love, yet she is seduced by the promise of eternity. The palm of virtue is the same, though the condition differs. This woman, though her marriage continues, condemns intercourse with revulsion and shame; this one has committed it to the dead. Nor is this zeal for religion unmerited, for where there is no thought of pleasures, there is the home of chastity. A good conscience gladly shows respect to the saints, for this brings nothing that rumor can hurt or the silent injury of thought can damage. The display of modesty and abstinence shows the devotion of a servant.

Here no one's cloak emits a blaze of purple,[1] nor are waves of rustling silk curled by a skillful walk; no pearl, no ring of gold, is known. Human concerns are despised where divine concerns are taken into account, as the Apostle teaches: "I reckoned all these as rubbish, so that I might profit by Christ" (Phil 3:8). These women advance resplendent, radiant with the intoxication of chastity. They advance decked with divine gifts as ornaments. Their breasts are filled with the riches of psalms. There is no night of vigils in which this jewel does not gleam. There is no place of worship in which this decoration does not shine. The throng of the chaste is the joy of the saints. The multitude of widows and celibates is an invitation to the powers. Hence the mingled tears and joy of the old pour forth, hence the prayers of mothers; these joys pervade even the souls of little children. Hence, in short, is the one feeling of the entire people toward your majesty.

(4) Have mercy, then, have mercy. You know what it is you pardon. We confess God the Father, we confess God the Son, we confess God the Holy Spirit. We confess that the three are one. I said one because as the Son is of one Father, so the Father is in the Son, and as the Holy Spirit is of the Father and the Son, so the Father and the Son are in the Holy Spirit. There is one godhead, one substance, because there is one principle and one perpetuity, both before everything and [the one] through whom everything is; true God of true God, because as one is of another, so one is in another, living from living, perfect from perfect, light of light and light in light. Thus the godhead of this Trinity is from one and perdures in one. The Father is Father, the Son is Son, the Spirit is Spirit. Three in names, three in one principle, three in one perfection, three in one godhead, three in one light, three in one virtue, three in one activity, three in one substance, three in one perpetuity, because just as there are three from one, so there is oneness in three. Thus we confess because thus we believe in the indivisible Trinity, prior to which nothing can be touched or even conceived by the mind, through which exist "all things visible and invisible, whether Thrones or Dominations or Princes or Powers. All things are through him, and without him nothing was made" (Col 1:16). Who, coming down from on high for the salvation of the human race, was incarnate of the virgin Mary and put on humanity, suffered, was crucified, was buried. On the third day he rose from the dead, ascended into heaven, sits at the right hand of God the Father, from whence he shall come to judge the living and the dead. And [we believe] in the Holy Spirit, because [Christ] himself confirmed this mystery to the apostles, saying, "When I ascend to my Father and your Father, I shall ask the Father and he

---

[1] A reference to Vergil, *Aeneid* 4.262.

will give you another advocate, to be with you forever, the Spirit of truth, whom this world cannot accept because it does not see him or know him. But you know him because he remains with you and is with you" (John 14:16–17). And in another passage, "When they set you before the powers of this world, do not be anxious about what you should say. In that hour the words you speak will be given to you. The Spirit of your Father speaks in you" (Matt 10:19–20).

In this unity we confess the lights of your venerable martyrdoms. We read in the gospel that "you are the light of the world" (Matt 5:14). This we proclaim in danger and in happiness. May this confession benefit sinners, for, as the Lord says in the gospel, he who asks has received (cf. Matt 7:7–8). For when the thief hanging on the cross asked that he should remember him, the Savior said, "Truly I say to you, today you shall be with me in Paradise" (Luke 23:42–43). Let no one shake off our faults; let us ask pardon.

(5) Come then, beloved brethren, let us pour out for the sacred relics the words of psalms steeped in honey and milk. Let sobriety drunk on vigils and fasting beg for the cleansing of sins. Let us draw the saints' favor toward us in the fervor of their arrival. Their dwellings are on high, but let us invoke them as guests. Sometimes it is advantageous to hide what you know. They know their own secret. Those who guard the mysteries and do not search out secrets obtain more easily what they ask. You, too, holy and inviolate virgins, chant, chant (cf. Ps 47:6), and in your choirs dance on the paths that lead to heaven. Those who rejoice in the everlasting springtime of paradise, in brilliant light, not darkened by any cloud, those, I say, you must wear out with your dancing, tire with your leaping. Lest anyone should be charged with going astray, the mercy of the Savior has given us other leaders.

(6) What else is a martyr, beloved ones, but an imitator of Christ, a tamer of rabid pleasure, a trampler on ambition ambitious for death, a despiser of riches, a represser of lust, a persecutor of intemperance? Anger never snatched the scepter of wisdom from him, nor did greed claim it back. The Savior ascends by these steps of virtue to the place from which he

had descended, as the Apostle says, "He who descends is the same who ascends above all the heavens" (Eph 4:10). Up these steps [Christ] carried with him those he predestined, saying "Father, I want those you have given me to be with me where I am" (John 17:24). Wisdom, justice, courage, self-control are the way to heaven. The Savior revealed it, saying, "I am the way and the truth" (John 14:6). The trader in heavenly pearls and in eternity walked upon it (cf. Matt 13:45–46). The prophets point it out to Christian travelers. The apostles used it. Cold never freezes it; heat never burns it. In the psalms it is affirmed: "the sun shall not burn you by day, nor the moon by night" (Ps 121:6). So let us pray, beloved ones, let us pray that if the heap of our sins prevents us from ascending, we may at least warm the footsteps of those who ascend with our meager kisses. They are to be venerated; they are the saints, who brought death to death, as we read, "He who believes in me, though he dies, lives" (John 11:25).

O how "precious in the sight of God is the death of his saints" (Ps 116:15), those on whom a menacing persecutor confers more! The torturer shuddered, [the saint] laughed as he was put to the question; the executioner trembled, and he, on the point of death, helped the right hand of the trembling man. The wild beast refused and the martyr thrown to it incited it, not because nature had lost the bodily penalty, but because the Savior, presiding over this great contest, was offering victory, brandishing the palm of immortality. But even though this is so, your bodies still endured the contest with you, in that suffering of the limbs. Then let us, prostrate on the ground and drenching the earth with our tears, cry with one voice that you who always possess the consecrated relics should purify our bodies. You will not despise our offering, venerable ones. The dwelling is worthy to be home to so many victors.

You will find here John the Baptist, he, I say, who stood bloodstained in the common arena, but ascended crowned to heaven, he whom the Lord himself names as greatest "among those born of women" (Matt 11:11). Here you will find Andrew, here Thomas, here Gervasius, here Protasius, here Agricola, here Euphemia, who once, her soul made masculine, did not, though a virgin, pale before the executioner. Here, in fact, is so great a multitude of the citizens of heaven, that on the arrival of your majesty, we should have had to find another place, had you not been joined by your secret and by the unity of power.

These commands are yours: love is not a rival, is not puffed up, does not seek its own (cf. 1 Cor 13:4–5). So I have no qualm that you may be insulted by a place which, by human standard, is too poor. People think these places are much too confined. Divinity rejects rank and is not bounded by place or time. There is no subjection in unity. It is no wonder if there is no difference of earthly substance among you, for whom everything is in common in the light of the spirit. But the glory of your powers will be the greater if you defend the struggling and protect those who confront enemies. Let weapons shield whom they will; your battle line, your standards shall guard us. There is no enemy if you grant pardon for sinners. Let the reins of our lives be held in your hands. Remit our faults, and no wars shall disturb us. But why should I, the poor man Victricius, your devotee, be anxious about the quality of a place? You have come from yourselves to yourselves. Here you will find those you left ministering at the altars of the Lord Jesus Christ. John the Baptist waits for you with arms outstretched. Thomas, Andrew, Luke, and all the heavenly multitude call you to their embrace with equal longing. It is no new host who will receive you: these are they with whom you are soldiers in heaven. But there will be special thanksgiving if those who are joined in spiritual light are joined in relics.

(7) Scripture, indeed, conveys to us that there is one mass of corporeality. Could anyone be found who is so stupid by nature or so lacking in reason as to deny that woman originated from the side of man? From this something further arises: we must understand that the origin of flesh is flesh and that flesh was its own nature, so that if you consider attentively and look for the genus (so to speak) of the genus, you will find that Adam, from a species, was made a genus. It is impossible that he should not be a genus, since it was from his matter and formation that the offspring of the human body developed, diffused among all. So, most holy brothers, we must first know this: peo-

ple differ from each other not in nature, but in time and place and action and thought. Diversity is alien to unity; unity is widely diffused without loss to itself. Now if the eyes of reason have clearly seen that there is one body of all human beings, it follows that we should believe, by a similar argument, that for those who live in Christ and the church there is one substance of flesh and blood and spirit, by the gift of adoption. The beginning of the new law is the cleansing of past faults. And the Savior, though he was surety for the earlier covenant, is nevertheless present as "surety for a better covenant" (Heb 7:22). So there must be one virtue in those in whom there is the one perfection of the sacraments. For the Apostle says, "You are the body and limbs of Christ, and the spirit of God dwells in you" (1 Cor 3:16). So when, taught by Scripture, we are assured that we may be joined to the Spirit by the divine sacrament of baptism, and on the same principle we learn that even our bodies may be fixed to the members of the Son by the bond of a constant confession and that, through grace, nothing is lost to unity, what doubt is there that our apostles and martyrs have earned perfect and absolute concord? For Christ is the Spirit of God and God the Son, Christ who, by equality of power, refuted the idea of injurious subjection, who by the venerable triumph of his members left no room for death, who rejected the name of singularity, who experienced neither end nor beginning in any part of himself. And the apostles and saints ascended to the throne of the Redeemer, both by the ordinance of the spiritual mystery and by the sacrifice of the body as victim and by the payment of the blood and sacrifice of the passion, as Christ himself says in the Gospel: "When the Son of Man is seated on his throne of glory, you, too, shall sit on twelve seats of judgment, judging the twelve tribes of the sons of Israel" (Matt 19:28). And again: "When you have remitted someone's debts, they shall be remitted; when you have bound someone, he shall be considered bound" (Matt 18:18). The consequence is that they are entirely with the Savior in his entirety. For those who have nothing that differs in their profession [of faith] have everything in common in the truth of godhead. By righteousness they are made companions of the Savior, by wisdom his rivals, by the use of limbs concorporeal, by blood consanguineous, by the sacrifice of the victim sharers in the eternity of the cross. For it is written: "I ascend to my Father and to your Father" (John 20:17).

If, then, there is a father, there are common sons; if the sons are in common, the inheritance is in common; if the inheritance is in common, eternity is in common. Now the saints are granted immortality through their victory. It follows that the authority of their wills should not be divided, but one. This is what the Lord himself asked of the Father: "Father, consecrate them in the truth. Your word is truth. As you sent me into the world, I have sent them into the world, and for their sake I consecrate myself, so that they, too, may be consecrated in truth. I pray not only for these, but for those also who through their words will believe in me. May they all be one as you are, Father, in me and I in you; may they also be in us, so that the world may believe it was you who sent me and I who send them. I have given them the glory you gave to me, that they may be one as we are one. I am in them and you in me, that they may be perfected in one, so that the world may know that you sent me and that you loved them as you loved me" (John 17:17–23). For whoever raises the standard of the holy confession seizes from worthy givers the power that brings salvation.

(8) Beloved, there is one immortality that is everlasting, without the conception of fragility, and another that is granted by bounty. Now we cannot deny that immortality was granted to the apostles and martyrs. But we also assume that apart from acquired divinity, there is nothing that separates the Trinity from the offering of the saints because it was the very truth of the Trinity that produced them. For we must confess the nature of God to be complete and perfect. Otherwise, injustice would be done, if we were to deny it, for the Lord says: "He who has denied me and what I have said in the presence of men, I shall deny him in the presence of my Father and his angels" (Matt 10:33). Moreover, completeness can take in nothing further. Now blood, after martyrdom, is on fire with the reward of divinity. So let the injustice of distinction depart, since the bond of glory is the same. "I go," he says, "to my Father and to your Father" (John 20:17). You see, then, most loving ones, that the Father and the Son have, by the property of their nature, what the saints have by the unity of the gift they have received. God is diffused far and wide and lends out his light without loss to himself. Everywhere he is wholly awareness, wholly sight, whole in spirit, whole in himself. It cannot be, then, that he who is perfect in the whole is not perfect in the apostles.

Perhaps, at this point, someone will cry out in protest: "Is the martyr, then, the same as the highest power and the absolute and ineffable substance of godhead?" I say he is the same by gift, not by property; by adoption, not by nature; and that this happens so that when the great day comes, he who received imperial power will not seem to have acquired it, nor he who gave to have suffered loss. A good, merciful judge gives advance notice of what is prescribed. See, the righteous show us the path of truth, as if they carried before us the light of their relics. They teach reverence, faith, wisdom, righteousness, courage, concord, self-control, chastity, while in our besieged bodies they punish that which is opposed to these and remove the stains of vice. But they have this mercy and this concern for teaching, these riches of relics and fiery rays of light in themselves, even when they have begun to weigh our faults. The good king judges without favor. Pure truth is found where the judge has no inclination to one party. And we shall be heard by those very benefactions we now use. So let all the goodness of the saints, now dispersed, be collected as it were into one pile, so that they may hold the judge's scepter without favor and without injustice in the appeal. Sins are darkness; innocence is light. So the prison of darkness must be visible when that which comes from the sun's light has begun to return from itself to itself. The benefactions have been made: [the sun] fills all the places of the earth and every corner of our homes and gives light, and yet his abundance does not withdraw from him. He pours out his gift and receives it, he possesses all that he earlier bestowed, he gives and is found to be the owner of what has been given.

(9) Just so, dearest ones, before the day of judgment, the radiance of the righteous pours into all

basilicas, all churches, the hearts of all the faithful, to return, of course, to itself when it takes on the role of the judge. If anyone thinks this is a base comparison, let him accept that it is because of majesty, not because of error, that we set corruptible things against divine, small against great. First principles cannot be defined because they have no genus. The substance of deity, resting on itself, retains the status of its own likeness to itself. There is no quantity or quality to which the Trinity may be equated. The heavenly principle is taught, not compared; conveyed, not elaborated. So the example of the sun taught us about divinity, but was not involved in the unity. It is already clear to everyone that God made out of nothing that which did not exist, and this often draws out the poison of the dialecticians.

For if God, the author of all things, put together this spiritual vessel and members out of nothing, why could he not convert an animate body, formed (so to speak) by the leaven of blood, into the substance of his light? But, in this great celebration, we have filled a book with a riot of questions. And rightly so, for the search for truth is the delight of the inquirer. Thus God, thus the Savior, is acknowledged, thus we find the triumph that is held out by the arms of salvation, thus eternal splendor is acquired by bodies. We know from the heavenly utterance that angels have the spirit of fiery majesty, for we read, "He who has made his angels spirits and his servants burning fire" (Ps 104:4). So, if there is blood in the body, that very blood is mixed with supernal fire. No difficulty remains to prevent our concluding that the blessed have one and the same concord with the universality. So, dearest ones, we must cleanse that suspicion from our souls and eliminate it, lest anyone, misled by vulgar error, should not think that the truth of the whole corporeal passion is present in fragments of the righteous and in this apostolic consecration.

We proclaim with all our faith and authority that there is nothing in relics that is not complete. Where the healing power is intact, the limbs are intact. We say that flesh is held together by the glue of blood, and we affirm that the spirit also, wet with the moisture of blood, has taken on the fiery heat of the Word. This being so, it is most certain that our apostles and

martyrs have come to us with their powers intact. We are taught that this is so by the benefactions even now present to us. For as we recognize the right to move them, with their good will, we understand this: they do not inflict loss upon themselves by their own dissemination, but being endowed with unity, they distribute benefactions. The flame sheds its light and bestows it, yet does not suffer the expenditure of its bounty. Thus the saints are generous without loss, full without addition; thus they have come to us without the weariness of travel. In relics, then, there is a reminder of perfection, not the injustice of division. Whatever is formed from an unequal conception and is not bathed in the water of the first source must be transitory. Sun and stars, earth, and all the other names of vanities are corruptible because they do not have a spiritual origin. But the suffering of the saints is imitation of Christ, and Christ is God. So division is not to be intruded into completeness, but the truth of completeness is to be worshiped in that very division that is before our eyes.

(10) Why, then, do we call them "relics"? Because words are images and signs of things. Before our eyes are blood and clay. We impress on them the name of "relics" because we cannot do otherwise with (so to speak) the seal of living language. But now, by uttering the whole in the part, we open the eyes of the heart, not the barriers of our bodily sight. Things are not servants of words; words are servants of things. So let the ambushes of language be removed, and let thing war with thing, reason with reason. Every part, every species as it is called, must take upon itself the force and the definition of its genus. For when I have said that an animal is an animate substance, a substance that has sensation, I have, at the same time, spoken of humans and cattle and given the definition of other living creatures (for there are humans who do not accept what is God's). But if that which has weight in the [many] species also counts in the definition of the genus, how is it possible that the plenitude of flesh should not be in relics, when the spiritual principle is the same? Thus we demonstrate that the whole can be in the part. So we can no longer complain of smallness, for when we said that, as in the genus, nothing of sacred bodies

perishes, we certainly reckoned that what is divine cannot be diminished because it is wholly present in the whole. And wherever it is anything, it is whole. Now we learn from Scripture that the body is made eternal by the effect of the spirit. The conclusion, then, is that where plenitude is perceived, nothing more should be wanted.

For the sake of instruction, let us keep to the easy and familiar example. We speak of the brilliance of fire and the color of fire, but they are the same by nature's command; only a verbal distinction divides the one from the other. Light brings forth radiance, yet there is no distinction between light and radiance. A human being, *qua* human, belongs to one association with all humans by their common birth. Bronze, gold, and other kinds of metal, though they are snatched here and there by the crooked talons of avarice, still have the quality of the undivided substance. It is clear, then, that species refers to nature. So it is clear that there is perfection of limbs in relics because in them, there is association in spiritual consecration. As the heavenly one is, so the heavenly ones are. If we said that relics were divided from the spirit, we would be right to look for all the connection and solidity of body parts. But when we realize that the substance is united, it follows that we are searching for the whole in the whole. Looking for a greater power is an offense against unity. This confusion is of the eyes; the vision of reason is clearer. We see small relics and a little blood. But truth perceives that these tiny things are brighter than the sun, for the Lord says in the gospel: "My saints shall shine like the sun in the kingdom of the Father" (Matt 13:43). And then the sun shall shine fuller and brighter than now.

(11) Moreover, their healing power is no less in the parts than in the entirety. Do they offer medicine to the wretched differently in the East, at Constantinople, at Antioch, at Thessalonica, at Naissus, at Rome, in Italy? Do they purify ailing bodies differently? John the Evangelist cures at Ephesus and many other places besides; we are told that he did not leave Christ's breast even before his sanctification and that same healing power is here with us. Proculus and Agricola cure at Bononia, and here, too, we observe their majesty. Antonius cures at Placentia. Saturninus and Troianus cure in Macedonia. Nazarius cures at Milan. Mucius, Alexander, Datysus, Chindeus pour out the favor of health with generous virtue. Ragota, Leonida, Anastasia, Anatoclia cure, as the apostle Paul says "to perfect man, to the measure of the age of the fullness of Christ," by one and the same spirit "who does all in all" (Eph 4:13, 1 Cor 12:6). I ask, do these saints I have named heal in one way among us, in another among others? No: if anything of the saints is anywhere, they defend, cleanse, and protect their worshipers with equal piety. Worship should be offered, not majesty rejected. Even if the full weight of power were not in relics, still no sane person would take anything away from such status. It is not knowledge that helps us, but fear, for we are warned: "the fear of God expels sin, for he who is without fear will never be justified" (Sir 1:27–28 [Vulg]). Countless [arguments] present themselves, but we are hunting for the streams of pure water. I am not tied in the tangle of hypothetical and categorical syllogisms; the empty sophisms of philosophers do not deceive me. Truth herself reveals her face, and faith spurns arguments. Crime seeks a hiding place, innocence a public place. So I point with my hand to what is sought; I touch fragments; I affirm that in these relics is perfect grace and perfect virtue. If this were the place for the matter to be explained by the clash of words, I would say that it is the same in genus and species and number. The faithless malice of the doubter questions this—or perhaps not the doubter, but the one who does not love. Indeed, when I grasp the whole matter by faith, I think superfluous questions should be dismissed for now, but they require sight, not investigation! See, the torturer of unclean and polluted spirits is at work, yet he who tortures is not visible. There are no chains, yet the one who suffers is bound. Heavenly anger has a rack made from air. There is no claw, yet those who confess admit many charges. No wound appears, yet the gnashing of teeth is heard. There is no interrogation by the judge, yet there follows the promise of the one who withdraws.

No one, evidently, can be so devoid of intelligence as to say that plenitude lacks something, when he sees that the examination lacks nothing. It is God, beyond doubt, God who is the executioner and judge of the invisible. Imperfect nature is unable to wound spirit. Only he who heals what is within can judge it. Only he who treads them beneath his feet gives orders to the elements. Only he who is intact in the parts and wholly in the whole grasps the scepter of the Trinity. The highest awareness does not need anything added. Now the apostles and saints not only do not seek additions, but actually distribute the benefits of health and salvation. So there is one awareness, one spirit, one intermingling of these with truth. He who cures, lives; he who lives is in the relics. Now the apostles and martyrs heal and wash clean, so they are bound to the relics by the bond of all eternity. The cloud of death obscures every division. We have made more than enough declaration that the saints do not know the losses of a part. It remains, then, for us to understand that it is a mercy, not a problem to investigate, that the righteous give themselves to all believers.

He who loves, believes. He who believes examines the faith of disputant and priest, not their words. So if anyone finds my speech distasteful, at least my zeal will not displease, for he will see that I have written a book by simple faith, not by words; by worship, not by arguments; by reverence, not by curiosity. The lover of truth is he who has brought reverence; the hater of truth he who has started an investigation.

(12) So, most loving ones, while the crowd of saints is newly arrived, let us bow down and bring forth sighs from the inmost veins of our bodies. Our advocates are here: let us set out in prayer the story of our faults. The judges are on our side and can mitigate the sentence; to them it was said: "You shall sit upon twelve seats of judgment, you shall judge the twelve tribes of the sons of Israel" (Matt 19:28). They are always judges because always apostles. But the duty of faith, rather than enthusiasm for speaking, has carried me too far. Unrestrained thanksgiving cannot be silent. It is a loss to happiness if there is no one to hear. If I could have been silent in so great a crowd of people rejoicing, I should have incurred a charge of sadness: the apostles and martyrs are coming; it is not proper for the bishop to be silent. The altars are being erected: let the people take their lead from the joy of their priest. Who, I ask, is so stupid,

who so profane, who so ignorant of law and religion, as not to feel this joy?

If one of the princes of this world were visiting our city now, every open space would at once be bright with garlands; matrons would fill the rooftops; the gates would pour forth a surge of people; every age, divided in its enthusiasm, would sing of glory and warlike deeds, would admire the brilliance of the military cloak and the Tyrian purple, would marvel at the treasure of the Red Sea and the frozen tears of monsters—and, indeed, these things are to be marveled at if you see them, despised if you think about them, for, after all, we call them stones. These, I say, would keep people agape. But, blessed ones, when it is the triumph of the martyrs and procession of the powers that reaches our houses, why should not we be overcome with joy?

It is not eloquence that is needed here, but the pure simplicity of happiness. There is no lack of things for us to admire: in place of the royal cloak, here is the garment of eternal light. The togas of the saints have absorbed this purple. Here are diadems adorned with the varied lights of the jewels of wisdom, intellect, knowledge, truth, good counsel, courage, endurance, self-control, justice, good sense, patience, chastity. These virtues are expressed and inscribed each in its own stone. Here the Savior-craftsman has adorned the crowns of the martyrs with spiritual jewels. Let us set the sails of our souls toward these gems. There is nothing fragile in them, nothing that diminishes the greater, nothing that experiences loss. They bloom in beauty more and more; even the blood shows that they are presented as signs of eternity, the blood that is still the sign of the fire of the Holy Spirit in the very bodies and relics of the limbs. We rejoice, dearest ones, whenever we see darkness dispersed by light. Why do we not rush to rejoice with yet more exuberance when we see that the salvific radiance of eternal lights has been brought to us? The day seems to me to have taken on the gladness of brighter clarity. And rightly so; as I have said, the martyrs are seven times brighter than the sun.

But now, most loving ones, what we need is prayer, not peroration. Prayer, I say, so that we may repel all assaults of the devil, who secretly slips into our hearts. Strengthen your worshipers, then, O saints, strengthen your worshipers, and establish our hearts on the cornerstone. The enemy is dangerous and strong. He tries every approach, every entrance. But there is nothing to fear: great is the multitude of saints that marches against him. Since such a number of soldiers and kings has come to us from the camp of heaven, let us seize the weapons of justice and wisdom, protect ourselves with the shield of faith, defend our breasts not with scale armor, but with the plating of self-control and modesty. Let us always brandish in our right hands the weapons of faith and endurance. Soon we shall strike a blow if some enemy has attacked. These, these are the weapons carried long since by the apostles. Armed with these, they broke the necks of intemperance, lust, greed, ambition, anger, and pride. So the mercy of the Savior has denied us nothing: not weapons, not guards. We must, then, take care, again and again, that the sloth of vices should not invade us as if we were dozing, that an incredulity hostile to faith should not creep in, that anger should not carry us away or greed torment us or ambition toss us. Our martyrs will willingly associate with us if we bring a pure conscience to their service. If anyone thinks this is hard and inescapable soldiering, let him not throw away his spear before the trumpet sounds, and let not the chill of death invade him before the battle. Let no one desert the Savior's standards. He has given the example; he sends help. To fight together with such fellow soldiers and with Christ in command is certain victory. Then, indeed, the helmet of priesthood will shine on my head if your love has seen me in the battle line. To fight with you watching, with you following, is an incitement to fame.

Unshaken faith and spiritual constancy is a secure post, a well-defended harbor of salvation. A good life is worthless unless you know for whom you live. The whirlwind will snatch the frivolous, disbelieving mind into the deep. It is faith that raised the saints to heaven, faith that unlocked the tombs of the dead, faith that turned flames to dew and sent a saving chill into fireballs, faith that solidified the waters of the restless waves beneath the footsteps of the walkers, faith that showed the martyrs consecrated following

the example of the Lord's death, faith that armed the souls of the confessors in the contest of suffering, faith that feeds in humility on sparse, belated, even dry foodstuffs; faith that guards virginity, widowhood, and continence in modest integrity; faith that removes bodily desire and instills love of the rule of heaven; faith that joins us to the Lord in immortality by his death on the cross. It is faith that, by hatred of this world, shows the Lord those who are hated like him; faith that comforts confessors in prisons, when they are shut up in the foul horror of darkness and, while they lie restless in dirt and rags and are pierced by the very potsherds that are their beds, cannot take even a brief rest when free in sleep. While thus they are lacerated every day by every kind of torment, while they are oppressed by manifold tortures, their virtue advances to the crown. It is faith that, in these many buffetings, shows God beloved unity and repays Christ by dying for him. Just as the head of the body died for the members, so the members die for the head, so that just as the head lives, the members may be made alive with the head. The blessed Paul confirms this: "if we die with Christ," he says, "we live with Christ; if we endure, we reign with him" (2 Tim 2:11–12).

It remains, most loving ones, for the confession of our sins to follow. Not that the divine powers do not know the hidden recesses of our souls, but a confession that has not been extorted elicits with ease the mercy of the judge. Let there be no day, dearest brothers, when we do not linger over these stories. This martyr was not afraid under torture; this one hurried to anticipate the delays of the executioner; this one greedily drank in the flames; this one was cut to pieces, but stood intact; this one said he was fortunate because it was his lot to be crucified; this one, in the hands of the executioners, told rivers to draw back, lest he should be delayed in his haste. This one grieved for her father's tears as a daughter, but despised them as a martyr; this one, eager for death, provoked a lion to anger against her; this one, while her child went hungry, offered full breasts to the wild beasts; this virgin submitted to the executioner a neck adorned with the necklace of eternity. There are thousands of examples of virtue, dearest brothers, recorded in the holy pages. But we have selected a few from the many, rather for exhortation than for instruction. A few suffice for the faithful; many are no help to the unfaithful.

The longing of the saints is not to be deferred. Why do we delay? Let the court stand open for the divine martyrs; let the relics be joined, the favors also joined; let the first fruits of the resurrection come together as one. Meanwhile, let our confession slip in. The pardoning of crimes is rejoicing for the powers. Rightly, dearest brothers, did I, a zealous builder, seize a place for the basilica. The arrival of the saints excuses my eagerness. They themselves, by the hidden means of my longing, ordered a court to be prepared for them. That is how it is, it is indeed. We have laid the foundations and extended the walls, and today we learn for whom the commitment of our work was growing. So all delays are subject to reproof. Nothing slow and lazy delights me. It is a pleasure to roll great stones with the hands and carry them on the shoulders. Let the earth drink my sweat; I wish it could drink my blood, shed in the name of the Savior!

Meantime, let the earth, about to receive altars, drink sweat. If our apostles and martyrs see us, the faithful, engaged in this labor, they will invite others.

45. Lucianus: On the Discovery of Saint Stephen

Many fourth- and fifth-century texts recount the "invention" (from the Latin *inventio,* "discovery") of the long-lost remains of Christian saints. Perhaps the most famous of these inventions was the discovery of the True Cross by Constantine's mother, Helena (one of the earliest versions of which is record by Ambrose; see Text 8). While inventions of relics occurred throughout the empire, the holy land was particularly rich with the remains of martyrs, apostles, prophets, and patriarchs. The discovery of the bones of Saint Stephen, the Protomartyr (see Acts 7), occurred in 415. The bones, once unearthed, were distributed to bishops across the Mediterranean. Augustine recounts the miracles they effected in a chapter of the *City of God* (22.8). Their arrival on the small Spanish island of Minorca occasioned an upheaval in the local relations between Jews and Christians (see Text 13). They even played a role in the political maneuvers of the imperial court in Constantinople.

The narrative of the relics' discovery became a template for most late antique and early medieval "inventions": the vision of the saint, the intervention of signs and portents, the role of the bishop, the wonder-working power of the relics, and their eventual distribution all became hallmarks of the relic invention. The *Revelation of Saint Stephen,* presented here, depicts ancient Jews (particularly Gamaliel) in collusion with fifth-century Christians in the ongoing "Lord's war against the Jews," another motif frequently adapted by later tales of relic discovery. This text is prefaced by a letter from the priest Avitus, who convinced the *inventor,* Lucianus, to write the Greek account from which Avitus then produced a Latin translation. A second, longer Latin translation was also made at the time, and that longer version is reproduced here.

From "*Revelatio Sancti Stephani* (BHL 7850.6)." S. Vanderlinden. *Revue des Études Byzantines,* 4, (1946): 178–217. (Translated by Andrew S. Jacobs.)

LETTER OF AVITUS

To the very blessed and always very beloved in the Lord, Pope Balconius, and to all the clergy and the people of the church of Braga, from Avitus, priest in the eternal salvation of the Lord.

I desire and plead for you to remember me; so even I, as much as I am able, have not ceased to remember you among the saints, sympathizing with your tribulations through my own suffering; on account of your separation from your homeland I have shed unceasing tears in the holy places, so that either the Lord will restore freedom to you whom he wishes to encourage, or he will ascribe greatness to those to whom he has promised strength. So I, too, most blessed brothers (I speak with the witness of our Lord Jesus Christ), often have wished to come to you, so that with you I might suffer ill or enjoy good times, but my desire has been impeded, for the enemy has already spread out throughout all of Spain. Indeed, I was afraid I might leave the holy places and perhaps not reach you, somehow being intercepted I might pay the price for unreasonable audacity. Then merciful God deigned to grant his indulgent grace to my wish and your reward: first that the African bishops sent the most beloved son and my fellow priest Orosius to these parts, whose love and consolation has rendered all of you present here; then that, in these very days he himself has answered your incredible desire: holy and sainted, truly the crown of our glory in Christ Jesus, the first martyr Stephen deigned to reveal himself and to show himself by signs and the clearest of subsequent miracles. This one have I taken care to send forth worthily to Your Charity (with the opportunity given by God who regulates such matters), so that he himself, present as an advocate and patron for the requests of those beseeching him, might be of assistance—he who, when he suffered, even still deigned to pray for his enemies. Accordingly, most blessed and beloved Brothers, being forever mindful of you and seeing how fitting were the arrangements regulated by God, I have been attentive concerning the priest who was made worthy to have the discovery of the body revealed to him in

some part. I have not delayed to lay out for you what has been desired so eagerly and obtained in secret. On this account I have sent to you, through my holy son and fellow priest Orosius, relics of the body of blessed Stephen, the first martyr, that is, the dust of the flesh and the nerves and, which is more faithfully and certainly to be believed in, solid bones made manifest in their sanctity with new colorings and slathered with many scents. So there may be no doubt, I have also sent to you the very letter and description, copied out in my own writing, of that holy priest to whom this revelation was made, which, since I inquired and sought after to ensure a fuller understanding of the truth, I dictated first in his own Greek language and later translated into Latin. Blessed and holy brothers, I implore you to believe faithfully that these events transpired in truth. I am quite certain, since even so that blessed martyr deigned to speak forth and expose himself for the salvation of a world in danger, with the aid of such a patron on the spot, if you cherish such a token with due zeal, you will live from this time on in safety and calm.

The grace of our Lord Jesus Christ and the Holy Spirit be with you, most beloved to me in the Lord.

THE REVELATION OF SAINT STEPHEN

(1) To holy and venerable lord Bishop Hymneius, from the most humble and unfit Lucianus, priest of the town of Caphargamala in the Jerusalem territory, perpetual salvation in Christ Jesus. I have laid out the revelation that I was judged worthy to have shown to me so that I might unfold it to Your Holiness, not from boasting but for the fortifying of the audience.

(2) Three times in a row was it shown to me as I was resting in the basilica of the baptistery on my cot. As the sixth day was beginning, around the third hour of the night, while I kept watch, it was as if I had been put into a trance: I saw an old man, tall in stature, dignified of expression, with an abundant beard, in shining garments, girded in a cloak in which the upper part was interwoven with golden crosses (and

in his hand he held a golden wand), shod in boots gilded on the surface, walking around and facing me in silence.

And when I saw this, doubting I said to myself: "Who do you think this is? Does he come from God's side or the adversary's?" For I was not unmindful of the Apostle's words when he said: "for even Satan transfigures himself into an angel of light" (2 Cor 11:14). So when I saw him walking around, I began to think to myself, "If this person is from God, he will call my name three times in succession, but if he addresses me only once, I shall not answer him." Without hesitation, he stopped his walking and came toward me. While the wand in his hand pulsed, he called out my name three times: "Lucianus, Lucianus, Lucianus!"

I answered him: "Who are you, lord?"

He said to me: "Rise, go, and say to John the Bishop of Jerusalem: 'How long shall we be shut in? How long will you not disclose us? Especially in your time we should be revealed. Disclose us quickly so that through us God may disclose to the human race the gate of his mercy. Indeed, the time draws near when this world will nearly perish from the multitude of the iniquities that it performs daily.'" He also said: "Not only am I concerned for my own sake, but also on behalf of those who are with me (for they are much more worthy to have honors heaped on them), since the place in which we lie has been thoroughly neglected."

(3) So when I heard this, I said to him: "Tell me, lord, who are you? Who is with you?"

He said to me: "I am Gamaliel, who reared Paul, who himself afterward was made an apostle. Moreover, lying with me is Lord Stephen, who was stoned by the Jews of Jerusalem; day and night he lay there in the gates of the city that lead out to Cedar, by the order of the impious priests, so that he would be devoured by wild beasts and birds. But even, so no dogs or birds dared to touch him.

"Moreover I, Gamaliel, when I knew the sanctity of the man and his faith and devotion, hoping that I might have a part with him in the resurrection, I sent for religious and faithful men and summoned them to me; when they came, and I said to them: 'I beg you, according to your devotion and faith, fearing nothing, heed my advice, and gather the body of blessed Stephen and bear him off to my holding (which I called by my own name, Caphargamala) and deposit him in my new tomb and make the customary rites for forty days in that holding, which is at the twenty-second marker. And whatever ritual expenses must be paid out, I shall make good on them from my own pocket.'

"Now the second one who lies with him is Nicodemus, my nephew, who came by night to the Lord Savior so that he might know the words of truth and be reborn from water and the Holy Spirit (cf. John 3:5). When he heard the Lord's words, he was baptized by the holy apostles Peter and John. On account of this baptism, the princes of the priests became angry and plotted to murder him, but on account of my honor and the law of consanguinity, they did not. But nevertheless, after afflicting him with many wounds, they let him half-dead, and they anathematized him and publicly exiled him from the city, stripping him of all his property. So I had this one gathered up, too, and I led him to my holding, instructing my steward that he should have whatever he needed. When he perished a little later, he slept in the Lord. I had him entombed at blessed Stephen's feet under the title of confessor.

"But the third one who lies with me is my son Abibas, who with me believed equally in Christ's teachings and with me equally followed into baptism by the abovementioned apostles, when he was about twenty years old. He had full knowledge of the law, being chaste in body and knowing no woman's stain, but always devoting himself to God's temple with my disciple Paul. He passed on to God stainless. Next to him were placed those about whom I spoke before, with whom I also lie.

"Now my wife Ethena and firstborn son Selemias who did not know to believe in Christ withdrew from us and were buried in his maternal holding, called the holding of Capharselemia, for they were considered unworthy of our company. So that you might believe, when you begin to dig you will find the place of my wife and son empty" (and so we found it just as he said).

Now I, most humble, questioned him: "Where shall we find you, lord?"

He said to me: "You will find us in my holding, which now in Syriac is called Delagabria or Debatalia, which means *Holding of God's men* or *of warriors.*" And when he had said these things, he vanished before my eyes.

(4) Now after this speech I arose, and prostrate in prayer, I begged the Lord's mercy: "Lord Jesus Christ, if this revelation or vision is of your will, ensure that a second and third time it be made manifest to me so that, firmly assured, I might announce the revelation of your servants." And I began from that day to fast and abstain from everything except bread; I ate no salt in the food that I did consume, nor did I drink water, as we are accustomed to do during the Forty Days.

Then again the next, sixth, day, holy Gamaliel came to me in the same outfit as before. He came in the very same hour of the night to me, when I was not too sleepy. He said to me, "Why do you delay, dearest one, and why do you not arise and report to Bishop John? Do you not see how much drought and suffering there is throughout the world? Yet you act negligently. Rise, therefore, and go and tell him to disclose us and make a place of prayer, and through our intercession the Lord will have mercy on his people."

So I said to him: "I was not delaying, my lord, but I begged the Lord: 'Lord Jesus Christ, if this revelation comes from you, let it appear to me a second and third time.' And now, lord, behold you have come a second time in succession, and you have delighted me; if therefore you come a third time, I will be full of exaltation."

When he heard this, he gestured with his hand, saying: "I don't know, I don't know, I don't know." When he had said this, he said to me: "Listen, priest."

I answered him: "Speak, lord, for I am listening."

He said to me: "Since you doubted in your mind, thinking, 'If I should happen to find the place, do you think I would find everything set in a single place? If this should happen, how would I be able to distinguish the individuals' remains?' This is what you were thinking to yourself."

I couldn't deny this and said: "It is true, lord, so was I turning over in my mind. You know all, and nothing escapes you."

He said to me: "We are not, as you think, set in a single place, but each one of us has his own place. So consider what I am telling you and pay attention."

Looking out, I saw him extending his hands to the sky and praying. And immediately from there, he set out four baskets, three golden and one of silver, full of roses. But one of them was full of crocuses, and one of the three baskets overflowed with red roses, the color of blood, which he set to my right. The other two were full of roses as white as lilies, but they were roses. And the fourth basket had crocuses whose odor wafted in a most lovely manner.

He placed them before my gaze, and he said: "Do you see these baskets?"

I said to him: "Indeed, Lord."

He said to me: "These are the coffins in which we lay, and these roses are our remains; even as you see this basket holding the most beautiful roses set on your right side, so, when you begin to open up the place, you will find the gate of the tomb, and entering in you will come upon a coffin on the right: this is holy Stephen's. Have no doubt: for he alone of us merited to be crowned with martyrdom. So he is set in the eastern part. But that coffin that is to the north, that is the place of the neophyte, that is, Nicodemus.

"Yet another coffin is set slightly higher, for myself and my son, since we were also neophytes."

I said to him: "I beg you, my lord, why is one basket silver?"

He said to me: "Since my son was chaste and left this world without stain, on this account he appeared in the likeness of most ornate silver. Don't you see the crocus inside it that gives off the sweetest odor?" And when he had said these things, once more he vanished before my eyes.

(5) Since I was stirred up, I gave thanks to almighty God, and I performed the customary fasts until the third revelation. So in the third week, on the same day and hour, the abovementioned man came, menacing and muttering, and he said to me:

"Why do you delay until now? Why don't you go and tell John, the bishop, what has been said and shown to you? What excuse do you have before God? What kindness do you expect for this contempt on the day of judgment? Can't you see how much drought and suffering there is throughout the world? And yet you act negligently. Don't you know how many holy men there are better than you throughout the desert, whom we passed over because we wished to be made known through you? Even so, we wished you to be the priest, in this city rather than another, so that we might be made manifest through you."

Although I trembled within at his words, I said: "I was not negligent, my lord, but I was waiting for your third appearance. But now, indeed, shall I go forth tomorrow, ready to say all those things that you have commanded me."

As he stood indignantly opposite me, I saw myself as if in another trance arriving in Jerusalem. It was as if I stood under the gaze of John, the bishop, telling him the entire vision.

From him I seemed to hear: "If these things are as you say, dearest one, and the Lord has revealed these things to you in our time, it is fitting for me to collect from the holding that greatest plow ox that is fit for both carriage and for plow and to leave to you the holding with everything else."

To him I said: "My lord, what use is the holding if I don't have that ox through which the holding may be measured and maintained?"

The bishop said to me: "If it please, dearest one, for our city is served by wagons and we are short one ox for the greatest carriage, which you say is hidden in your holding. So it is fitting that it be in this more famous city, rather than in some tiny holding. Can't you make do with the two remaining smaller oxen and the one calf and the use of the greater ox for tending the land with your wagon?"

(6) When I heard this in the trance (that is, outside my own mind), right away rejoicing, I blessed the Lord and went forth to the city to holy John, the bishop. And although I recounted all that I had seen, I kept silent about the vision of the ox, waiting to see what I would hear from him. For I understood that holy Stephen himself was that great ox and that those carriages about which he spoke were the holy churches and that Zion, the first church itself, was the greater carriage. Since the holy bishop had me seek out the remains of holy Stephen, I did not wish to tell the bishop about the vision of the ox.

When John, the bishop, heard these things, he cried out in joy and he said: "Blessed be the Lord God, Son of the living God! If these things are as you say, dearest one, just as you saw, and God has revealed them to you, it is fitting for me to transfer from there blessed Stephen, the first martyr and archdeacon of Christ, who first waged the Lord's war against the Jews and, while set on the earth, saw God standing in heaven and appeared just like an angel in the company of humans." When he said this, holy John sent me away. When I arrived at the estate, I sent heralds for all the town's inhabitants to gather at dawn so they might dig in the heap.

(7) But that very night, holy Gamaliel himself appeared with a certain monk called Migetius, an innocent and simple man, in the same likeness with which he had appeared to me, and he said to him:

"Go, say to Lucianus the priest: 'In vain do you labor in that heap, since we aren't there, but we were placed here when they were lamenting us according to the ancient custom, on which account the heap was made there as witness to the lament. But look for us in another part, in the place that is called in Syriac Debatalia, which means in Greek Andragathon (or, as we might say, 'of good men')."

When we gathered together at dawn for the hymns, I found that monk preaching to all the brothers. Then when the hymns had been said, I began to speak: "Let us go to that mound, and let us dig in it." Then some of them said to me: "First listen to what the monk Migetius has to say."

When the monk Migetius had been summoned, I asked him what the matter was. He told me of all the signs that I had seen of Gamaliel and how he had seen opposite in the southern field a site and a tomb in a somewhat neglected and ruinous state, where he saw three golden biers laid out, and one of them was higher than the others, in which two were lying, one old man and the other a youth, and in the other two biers there were individuals.

And the one in the higher bier answered and said: "Go and tell Lucianus, the priest, that we are the masters of this place. If you wish to find the great righteous one, he is laid out in the eastern zone." And hearing these things from the monk, I glorified the Lord, since another witness had been discovered for the revelation. Moreover, all these things, as I saw, so they came to pass, and everything appeared to be consonant.

(8) So right away I made my announcement to the blessed bishop. He sent to his fellow bishops. When they had met together, they came to the site. When they gave the command to dig, and the greatest part of the earth had been removed, we found a stone in which was carved *Celiel, Nasaom, Gamaliel, Abibas:* Hebrew words, although carved in Greek letters. But the meaning of the names is thus: Celiel means Stephen [crown], Nasaom is Nicodemus [the people conquers], and Abibas was the son of Gamaliel.

Moreover, when we investigated beneath, we found holy Stephen's place in the eastern part, just as I had heard. And right away the earth was moved away, and such sweetness and fragrant scent came from there that no one could recall such a sensation: we thought we had been set down in the delight of paradise.

Now a great crowd of people was with us, among whom many were sick with various illnesses. And in that very hour, straightaway seventy-three souls were cured by the sweetness of the scent. Demons fled from some, while blood clots were healed in others; some were freed from tumors and boils, others healed of ulcers, still others of three- and four-day fevers; fever left some, epilepsy others; some were cured of headaches and migraines; more than a few were freed from the suffering of blocked intestines. And people experienced many other cures, which it would take too long to list.

Then at that time came Bishops John of Jerusalem and Eutonius of Sebaste and Eleutherius of Jericho; all these came with their own clergy. So with psalms and hymns, they bore off the relics of blessed Stephen to the holy Zion church, where the archdeacon had even been ordained, leaving for us some small bits from the saint's limbs, really a great amount of remains with the dust where all his flesh had wasted away.

From these therefore I have sent remains to Your Blessedness. When you receive them, pray for my puniness that I may be found worthy in the gaze of the Lord, assisted by the merits of blessed Stephen. Also be mindful of our humility and cherish it as if present, in reigning Christ Jesus our Lord who lives and reigns with the Father and the Holy Spirit forever and ever.

CHAPTER 11

Saints' Lives

The classical biography (*bios*) of "great men" and the miraculous narratives of the lives of Jesus and his apostles (both canonical and noncanonical Gospels and Acts) merged with the rising tide of asceticism (see Chapter 9) to crystallize into a new Christian literary form in Late Antiquity: the saint's life, or hagiography. Like classical *bioi,* the saint's life recounted the character and virtues of an extraordinary and exemplary figure. Like the Gospels and Acts, the saint's life embedded that figure's extraordinary example in the miraculous stream of sacred history and redemption. The stars of this literary pastiche were those holy men and women who chose to live apart from this world, to embrace the renunciatory life of angels and so approach divine perfection.

Although Eusebius's *Life of Constantine* (see Text 4) is arguably an early effort to meld the *bios* with the symbolic vocabulary of sacred history, Athanasius's *Life of Antony* (see Text 46) is usually recognized as the first saint's life, in which one person's renunciation becomes a pattern of redemption for all Christians. Subsequent hagiographies mimic the *Life of Antony*'s structure: the call to renunciation; the obstacles (both human and demonic) to Christian perfection; the miracles and virtues of the saint; and, often, an account of the saint's death. The saint's life was, above all, a model for imitation, either for other ascetics who might emulate the rigors of the saint or for the lay Christian who might adopt the saint's virtues in more general ways.

The saint's life served to encode other important Christian issues as well. Antony, as portrayed by Athanasius, is a vigorous opponent of Athanasius's own theological enemies, the Arians and the Meletians; Theodoret's Syrian monks, for all their occasional ascetic extremity, are constantly loyal to the institutions of the church, particularly their bishop; and the wonder-working monks of the *History of the Monks of Egypt* perhaps prove their Christian superiority to a world that held them under suspicion of heresy. The ambiguous role of gender and sexuality in the economy of salvation might find engaging expression in the life of a saint such as Pelagia, who went from scandalous actress/prostitute to walled-up, cross-dressing monk. This blend of holy exemplar, authorial motives, and cultural exploration would continue to flourish after Late Antiquity, when medieval and Byzantine Christians produced hagiographies on such figures as the Virgin Mary.

Often hagiography is viewed as Christian popular fiction: imaginative, at times clever, often excessive, but with little relation to the figures or settings it professes to describe. The actual existence of some subjects of hagiography remains doubtful, and creative license abounds in even the most historically grounded hagiography. Few doubt the existence of Antony, but there is less certainty as to his resemblance to Athanasius's "Antony." Nonetheless, saints' lives are historically valuable on other grounds. Their incidental details, while perhaps invented, are nonetheless "realistic"; for instance, the financial details of the lives of noble women who renounced public life, such as Melania the Elder or Melania the Younger, are often plumbed by economic historians. In addition, the crafting of a persuasive narrative of imitation tells us something about the moods and currents of Christian society in the day, the ideas and images that everyday Christians heard read aloud in church or in private readings that conveyed new ideals of Christian perfection and salvation.

FOR FURTHER READING

Brown, Peter. *The Cult of the Saints: Its Rise and Function in Latin Christianity.* Chicago: University of Chicago Press, 1981.

Coon, Lydia. *Sacred Fictions: Holy Women and Hagiography in Late Antiquity.* Philadelphia: University of Pennsylvania Press, 1997.

Delehaye, Hippolyte. *The Legends of the Saints,* trans. Donald Attwater. New York: Fordham University Press, 1962 [1955].

Frank, Georgia. *The Memory of the Eyes: Pilgrims to Living Saints in Late Antiquity.* Berkeley: University of California Press, 2000.

Harvey, Susan Ashbrook, and Brock, Sebastian, eds. *Holy Women of the Syrian Orient,* 2nd ed. Berkeley: University of California Press, 1998.

Howard-Johnston, James, and Hayward, Paul Antony, eds. *The Cult of Saints in Late Antiquity and the Middle Ages: Essays on the Contribution of Peter Brown.* Oxford, England: Oxford University Press, 1999.

Ward, Benedicta. *Harlots of the Desert: A Study of Repentence in Early Monastic Sources.* Kalamazoo, Mich.: Cistercian Publications, 1987.

The Texts

46. Athanasius: Life of Antony

Athanasius spent much of his turbulent episcopacy in exile, having drawn the anger of various theological and political opponents (see the introduction to Text 26). It was probably during the last of his exiles from Alexandria (around 356) that he composed what would become the gold standard for all future Christian saints' lives: the *Life of Antony*. (It should be noted that some scholars question the Athanasian authorship of the *Life,* but nonetheless attribute it to Alexandrian circles closely related to Athanasius.) In the *Life of Antony,* we meet an illiterate villager who embraces a life of renunciation and dedication to God, moving throughout his life farther and farther into the desert and achieving increasing closeness to God. Athanasius recounts Antony's temptations (food, money, sex), his struggles with the devil and demons, his performance of miracles (as a simple conduit for God), his confounding of (pagan) philosophers and heretics, and his moral instruction. Although Antony is praised as a model of ascetic renunciation and monastic withdrawal (see Chapter 9), Athanasius's *Life of Antony* presents him as a model for all Christians: guided in all things by the Word of God; obedient in all matters to the wisdom of the bishops; resistant at all times to the wiles of the devil, pagans, and heretics. Antony was, for Athanasius, not just the perfect ascetic, but the perfect human.

The *Life of Antony* was an immediate "best-seller" throughout the Mediterranean (translated twice before the end of the century into Latin and soon after into other languages). The story of inspiration, renunciation, struggle, and triumph provided a model for subsequent hagiography, locating the ultimate model for Christian imitation in the sanctified, miraculous person of the holy man or woman. We should, however, note the degree to which the *Life of Antony,* as well as hagiography later modeled on it, reflects the concerns of its author more than those of its subject. The Antony of the *Life* is simple and uneducated, whereas Antony's own *Letters* (see Text 40) portray a sophisticated theologian and thinker. Included here are the opening and closing chapters of the *Life.*

(1) Antony was an Egyptian by birth, and his parents were well born and possessed considerable wealth. Since they were Christians, he was raised in a Christian manner. As a child, he lived with his parents and was familiar with nothing other than them and their house. When he grew to become a boy and became older, he did not put up with learning letters because he wanted to be removed even from the companionship of children. It was his complete desire, as it is written, to live in his house as an unformed person

From *Medieval Hagiography,* trans. David Brakke, ed. Thomas Head. New York: Garland Press, 2000. Used with permission of David Brakke.

(see Gen 25:27). He would go to church with his parents. As a boy, he was not lazy, nor did he become rude as he got older. Rather, he was obedient to his parents, and by paying attention to the readings (see 1 Tim 4:13), he preserved in himself what was beneficial in them. Although as a boy he lived in moderate wealth, he did not trouble his parents for diverse and expensive foods, nor did he seek such pleasures. He was happy merely with whatever he found and asked for nothing more.

(2) After the death of his parents, he was left alone with one small sister; he was about eighteen or twenty, and it was his responsibility to care for the house and his sister. Not six months after his parents' death, he was going to church as usual, and he was thinking to himself and considering all this: how the apostles abandoned everything and followed the Savior (see Matt 4:20; 19:27), how the people in Acts [of the Apostles] sold their possessions and brought the proceeds and laid them at the feet of the apostles for distribution to the needy (see Acts 4:35–37), and how such a great hope was stored up for these people in heaven (see Col 1:5). Considering these things, he entered the church, and it happened that just then the Gospel was being read, and he heard the Lord saying to the rich man, *If you wish to be perfect, go, sell all your possessions, and give the proceeds to the poor, and come, follow me, and you will have treasure in heaven* (Matt 19:21). And Antony, as if the remembrance of the saints had been placed in him by God and as if the readings had been made on his account, left the church immediately and gave to the villagers the possessions he had received from his ancestors—three hundred *arourae* of fertile and very beautiful land—so that they would no longer trouble him and his sister. He sold all their other movable possessions, collecting a sizable sum of money, and gave it to the poor, although he kept a little for his sister's sake.

(3) But when he again entered the church and heard in the Gospel the Lord saying, *Do not worry about tomorrow* (Matt 6:34), he could not stay: he went out and gave even that [little money remaining] to the common people. When he had delivered his sister to known and faithful virgins in order to be brought up for virginity, he at last devoted himself to the discipline outside the house, attending to himself and guiding himself with patience. For there were not yet so many monasteries in Egypt, and no monk knew the great desert; rather, each of those who wanted to attend to himself practiced the discipline alone, not far from his own village. Now, at this time there was an old man in the neighboring village who had practiced the solitary life from his youth; when Antony saw him, he imitated him in virtue (see Gal 4:18). At first he, too, began by remaining in the places around the village; then if he heard of some zealous one somewhere, like the wise bee, he went and sought that person, and he did not return to his own place until he had seen the man and had received from him, so to speak, travel supplies for the road to virtue.

And so, spending time there at first, he strengthened his intention never to return to the things of his parents or to remember his relatives, but he directed all his desire and all his zeal toward the effort required by the discipline. Therefore, he worked with his hands, since he had heard, "Let not the idle one eat" (see 2 Thess 3:10), and he spent some of the money on bread and some for the needy. He prayed continuously, since he knew that it is necessary to pray in secret without ceasing (see Matt 6:6; 1 Thess 5:17). For, indeed, he so devoted himself to the reading that nothing of what is written fell from him to the ground (see 1 Sam 3:19), but he retained everything, so that his memory replaced books for him.

(4) Conducting himself in this way, then, Antony was loved by everyone. He sincerely submitted to the zealous ones whom he visited, and he learned thoroughly the advantage in zeal and discipline that each one possessed in comparison to himself. He contemplated the graciousness of one and the devotion to prayers of another; he observed one's lack of anger and another's love of people; he attended to the one who kept vigils and the other who loved to study; he admired one for his perseverance and another for his fasting and sleeping on the ground; he watched closely the gentle nature of one and the patience of another; but in all he noticed piety toward Christ and love for one another. And when he had been filled in

this way, he returned to his own place of discipline, and then he gathered into himself the virtues of each and strove to display them all in himself. Indeed, he was not contentious with those of his own age, except only that he should not appear to be second to them in the better things. And he did this in such a way that he did not hurt anyone's feelings; rather, they rejoiced in him. And so when the people of the village and the lovers of virtue with whom he associated saw that he was this kind of person, they all called him "Beloved of God"; some welcomed him as a son, others as a brother.

(5) But the devil, who hates and envies the good, could not bear to see such resolution in a young man, but set out to do against Antony the kinds of things he usually does. First he tried to dissuade him from the discipline by suggesting the memory of possessions, the care of his sister, the intimacy of family, love of money, love of glory, the varied pleasure of food, and the other indulgences of life—and finally the difficulty of virtue and the great effort that it requires. He introduced the weakness of the body and the long duration of time. In short, he raised up a dust cloud of thoughts in Antony's mind, desiring thereby to separate him from his upright intention.

But the enemy saw that he himself was weak in the face of Antony's resolve and saw instead that he was defeated by the other's stubbornness, overthrown by his faith, and falling due to Antony's constant prayers. Then he took confidence in the weapons of the belly's navel (see Job 40:16) and, boasting in these—for they are his primary means of trapping the young—he advanced against the youth, troubling him at night and harassing him by day so that those who watched could sense the struggle that was going on between the two. The one would suggest dirty thoughts, and the other would turn them back with prayers; the one would titillate, and the other, as if seeming to blush, would fortify his body with faith and fasts. And the miserable devil dared at night to dress up like a woman and imitate one in every way merely to deceive Antony. But Antony, by thinking about Christ and the excellence one ought to possess because of him and by considering the soul's rational faculty, extinguished the ember of the other's deception.

Once again the enemy suggested the ease of pleasure. But Antony, like someone fittingly angry or grieved, thought about the threat of fire and the torment of the worm, and by setting these thoughts against [those of the enemy], he passed through these things unharmed. All this was a source of shame for the enemy, for he who had considered himself to be like God (see Isa 14:14; Ezek 28:2) was now being mocked by a youth, and he who boasted over flesh and blood was being overthrown by a human being who wore flesh. For working with Antony was the Lord, the one who for our sake took flesh and gave to the body the victory over the devil, so that each of those who truly struggle says, *Not I, but the grace of God that is with me* (1 Cor 15:10).

(6) At last, when the dragon could not defeat Antony in this way but instead saw himself thrust out of his heart, he gnashed his teeth, as it is written (see Ps 35:16; 37:12; 112:10). As if he were beside himself, he finally appeared to Antony in his form just as he is in his mind, as a black boy. And as though he had fallen down, he no longer attacked Antony with thoughts—for the crafty one had been tossed down—but finally he used a human voice and said, "Many people I have deceived, and most I have defeated, but now coming against you and your efforts as I have against others, I have been weakened." Antony asked, "Who are you who say such things to me?" Immediately he answered with a pitiful voice, "It is I who am fornication's lover. It is I who have been entrusted with its ambushes and its titillations against the youth, and I am called the spirit of fornication. How many persons who desired to be prudent I have deceived! How many persons who professed to be so I have persuaded to change by titillating them! It is I on whose account even the prophet blames those who have fallen, saying, *You have been deceived by the spirit of fornication* (Hos 4:12). For it was through me that they were tripped up. It is I who so often troubled you and who as often was overthrown by you." But Antony gave thanks to the Lord and took courage in him, and he said to him, "You are very despicable, then, for you are black in your mind and as weak as a boy. From now on, I will have no anxiety about you, *for the Lord is my helper, and I will*

look down on my enemies (Ps 118:7)." When he heard this, the black one immediately fled, cowering before these words and afraid even to approach the man.

(7) This was Antony's first struggle against the devil, or rather this was the achievement in Antony of the Savior, *who condemned sin in the flesh so that the righteousness of the Law might be fulfilled in us, who walk not according to the flesh, but according to the spirit* (Rom 8:3–4). But Antony did not, because the demon had fallen, now become negligent and take no thought of himself, nor did the enemy, because he had been defeated, stop lying in ambush. For the enemy went around again like a lion, looking for some opportunity against him (see 1 Pet 5:8). But Antony, since he had learned from the Scriptures that the wiles of the enemy are numerous (see Eph 6:11), practiced the discipline intensely, figuring that even if the enemy had been unable to deceive his heart through bodily pleasure, he would attempt to trap him by another method. For the demon is a lover of sin.

Therefore, Antony more and more punished his body and enslaved it (1 Cor 9:27), so that even though he had triumphed in some ways, he would not be overcome in others; he resolved, then, to accustom himself to more severe training measures. Many people were amazed, but he himself endured the labor with ease, for his soul's intention, which had lasted for a long time, created in him a good habit, so that when he received even slight encouragement from others, he would show great enthusiasm for the task. He would keep vigil to such an extent that often he spent the entire night without sleep, and when he did this not once but many times, people were amazed. He ate once a day after sunset, but there were times when he went two days and often four days without eating. His food was bread and salt; his drink, only water. Indeed, it is superfluous even to speak about meat and wine, for nothing of the sort was ever found among the other zealous ones. For sleeping he was content with a rush mat, but mostly he lay upon the bare ground. He would not anoint himself with oil, saying that young men ought to pursue the discipline with zeal and should not seek what would pamper the body, rather that they should accustom the body to

labors and consider the Apostle's statement, *Whenever I am weak, then I am strong* (2 Cor 12:10). For at that time, he used to say that the soul's intellect grows strong when the body's pleasures are made weak.

He had this truly wonderful thought: that one should not measure progress in virtue or withdrawal made for this purpose by the length of time, but by the desire and intention. Therefore, he himself did not keep track of the time that had gone by; rather, every day, as if he were just starting the discipline, he would make his effort toward advancement greater, constantly saying to himself Paul's statement, *forgetting what lies behind and straining forward to what lies ahead* (Phil 3:13), and remembering also the voice of the prophet Elijah, saying, "The Lord lives, before whom I stand today" (see 1 Kings 17:1; 18: 15). He observed that in saying "today," he was not measuring the time that had gone by, but, as if he were always making a new start, he was zealous every day to show himself to God to be such that one should appear to God: pure in heart and ready to obey his will and nothing else. He would say to himself, "The ascetic ought always to observe his own life in the conduct of the great Elijah as if in a mirror."

(8) Having constrained himself in this way, Antony departed to the tombs, which happened to lie far outside the village. He commanded one of his acquaintances to bring him bread every several days, and he himself entered one of the tombs; when the other had shut the door, he remained inside by himself. Then, when the enemy could not bear this but was afraid that in a short time Antony would fill the desert with the discipline, he came one night with a crowd of demons and so cut Antony with wounds that he lay on the ground speechless from the tortures. For he used to maintain that the pains were so severe that he would say that blows inflicted by human beings could not have inflicted such torture. But by God's Providence—for the Lord does not neglect those who hope in him—his acquaintance came the next day to bring him the bread. When he opened the door and saw Antony lying on the ground as if dead, he lifted him up, carried him to the village church, and laid him on the ground. Many of his relatives and the vil-

lagers sat around Antony as if beside a corpse. But around midnight, Antony came to himself and got up; when he saw everyone asleep and only his acquaintance keeping watch, he motioned with his head for him to approach and then asked him to pick him up again and carry him to the tombs without waking anybody.

(9) And so he was carried back by the man, and, as usual, the door was shut, and he was once again inside by himself. He was unable to stand because of the blows from the demons, and so he prayed lying down. After the prayer, he said with a loud voice, "Here I am: Antony! I do not flee from your blows. For even if you do more, nothing shall separate me from the love of Christ" (see Rom 8:35–39). Then he sang, *"Though an army encamp against me, my heart shall not fear"* (Ps 27:3). This is what the ascetic thought and said.

But the enemy, who hates the good, was amazed that he dared to return after such blows. He called together his dogs and burst out, "See that we have not stopped this one with the spirit of fornication or with blows; rather, he bravely comes against us. Let us attack him in some other way." It is easy for the devil to change forms for his evil purposes, and so at night they raised such a tumult that it seemed as though that entire place was being shaken by an earthquake. The demons, as if they had shattered the four walls of the dwelling, seemed to enter through them, transformed into the appearance of beasts and serpents. And the place was immediately filled with the appearances of lions, bears, leopards, bulls, snakes, asps, scorpions, and wolves, and each of them was moving according to his own form. The lion was roaring, wishing to attack; the bull seemed to butt with his horns; the serpent writhed but did not approach; and the wolf rushed forward but was restrained. Altogether the ragings of their apparitions and the sounds of their voices were completely terrifying. Antony, whipped and tortured by them, felt even more severe bodily pain, but his soul was not trembling, and he remained vigilant. He groaned because of his body's pain, but he was sober in his thinking, and as if to mock them, he said, "If you had had the power, it would have been enough for one of you to come alone. But since the Lord has made you weak, you are trying to frighten me by your number. But it is a proof of your weakness that you imitate the shapes of irrational beings." And again he took courage and said, "If you are able and have received authority against me, don't delay, but attack! But if you cannot, why are you harassing me in vain? For faith in our Lord is our seal and wall for safety." And so after many attempts, they gnashed their teeth against him because they were making fools of themselves, rather than of him.

(10) Meanwhile the Lord had not forgotten Antony's struggle, but came to him in assistance. Thus, Antony looked up and saw the roof as if it were being opened (see Acts 7:55–56) and a certain ray of light coming down to him. The demons suddenly vanished, his body's pain immediately stopped, and the building was once again intact. When Antony perceived the assistance, got his breath back, and was relieved of his pains, he asked the vision that appeared to him, "Where were you? Why didn't you appear at the beginning and make my pains stop?" And a voice came to him, "Antony, I was here, but I waited to see your struggle. Because you endured and were not beaten, I will always be your help, and I will make you famous everywhere." When he heard this, he got up and prayed, and he became so strong that he felt that he had more strength in his body than he had had before. At this time he was around thirty-five years old.

(11) The next day Antony went out even more enthusiastic about the piety, and when he came to that old man [whom he had imitated earlier], he asked him to live with him in the desert. But when this man declined due to his age and because there was not yet such a custom, immediately he himself set out for the mountain. Yet again the enemy, when he saw his zeal and wanted to impede it, cast in his way an apparition of a large silver disk. But Antony recognized the trick performed by the hater of good; he stood and said to the disk because he saw the devil in it: "How did a disk end up in the desert? This path is not well trod, nor is there any trace of people having traveled through here. If it had fallen, it would have been missed thanks to its size; rather, the one who lost it

would have turned back, searched, and found it since the place is a desert. This is the devil's work. You will not impede my intention in this way, devil! Indeed, let this go with you into destruction" (see Acts 8:20). When Antony had said this, it vanished like smoke from before a fire (see Ps 68:2).

(12) Next, as he went along, he again saw this time not an apparition, but real gold scattered in the path. He himself has not said nor do we know whether it was the enemy who showed this to him or whether it was some better power who was training the athlete and showing the devil that he truly did not care about money at all, but what appeared really was gold. Antony marveled at the amount, but as if stepping over fire, he passed by it so as not to turn back; rather, he ran so fast that the place became hidden and forgotten.

Having intensified his resolve more and more, he hurried to the mountain. On the other side of the river, he found a deserted fort, abandoned for so long that it was full of serpents; he situated himself there and lived in it. The reptiles, as if someone were chasing them, immediately withdrew, but he barricaded the door, and since he had stored up enough bread for six months—the people of the Thebaid do this, and their bread often stays fresh for a year—and since he had a water supply inside, he descended as if into a shrine, and he remained alone inside the monastic retreat, neither going out himself nor seeing anyone who came. And so in this way he devoted himself to the discipline for a long time, receiving only bread let down from above the house twice each year.

(13) Those of his acquaintances who came, since he would not allow them to enter, often used to spend days and nights outside, and they would hear what sounded like crowds making a commotion, clamoring, raising up pitiful voices, and crying out, "Leave our places! What have you to do with the desert? You cannot endure our attack!" At first those outside thought that there were certain people fighting with him and that these people had gone in to him by ladders. But when they stooped and peeped through a hole and saw no one, then they reckoned that they were demons; they became frightened and called for Antony. He heard them, although he did not give a

thought to the demons; coming near to the door, he exhorted the people to withdraw and not to be afraid, for he said, "In this way the demons create apparitions against the cowards. Therefore, seal yourselves [with the sign of the cross] and depart with courage and let these [demons] make fools of themselves." And so they went away fortified with the sign of the cross, but he stayed behind and was in no way harmed by the demons, nor did he grow weary of fighting them. Indeed, the assistance of the visions that came to his intellect and the weakness of the enemies gave him much rest from his labors and made his intention even greater. For his acquaintances would always come, expecting to find him dead, but instead would hear him singing, *"Let God rise up, and let his enemies be scattered; and let those who hate him flee before him. As smoke disappears, let them disappear; as wax melts before fire, let the wicked perish before God"* (Ps 68:1–2). And again: *"All nations surrounded me; in the name of the Lord I repelled them"* (Ps 118:10).

(14) For nearly twenty years, he continued to discipline himself in this way, not going out himself and being seen by others only rarely. After this, when many eagerly desired to imitate his discipline and others of his acquaintances came and were pulling down and wrenching out the door by force, Antony emerged, as if from some shrine, initiated into the mysteries and filled with God. Now for the first time he appeared outside the fort to those who had come to him. And they, when they saw him, were amazed to see that his body had its same condition; it was neither fat as if from lack of exercise nor withered as if from fasting and fighting demons, but it was such as they had known it before his withdrawal. The disposition of his soul was pure again, for it was neither contracted from distress nor dissipated from pleasure nor constrained by levity or dejection. Indeed, when he saw the crowd, he was not disturbed, nor did he rejoice to be greeted by so many people. Rather, he was wholly balanced, as if he were being navigated by the Word and existing in his natural state.

Therefore, through Antony the Lord healed many of the suffering bodies of those present, and others he cleansed of demons. He gave Antony grace in speaking, and thus he comforted many who were grieved and reconciled into friendship others who were quarreling, exhorting everyone to prefer nothing in the world to the love for Christ. While he discussed and recalled the good things to come and the love for humanity that has come to us from God, *who did not withhold his own son, but gave him up for all of us* (Rom 8:32), he persuaded many to choose the solitary life. And so at last there came to be monasteries even in the mountains, and the desert was made a city of monks, who left their homes and enrolled in the heavenly commonwealth (see Phil 3:20; Heb 12:23).

(15) When it was necessary for him to cross the canal of Arsinoë—he needed to visit the brothers—the canal was full of crocodiles. Simply by praying, he entered it, he and all those with him, and they crossed it safely. When he returned to his monastic retreat, he resumed the same holy and vigorous labors. By his constant discourses, he increased the zeal of those who were already monks, and most of the rest he moved to a love for the discipline. Soon, thanks to the drawing power of his speech, there came to be many monasteries, and he directed them all like a father. . . .

(83) Such was Antony's life. We should not doubt that such marvels happened through a human being. For it is the promise of the Savior, who said, *If you have faith the size of a mustard seed, you will say to this mountain, "Move from there," and it will move, and nothing will be impossible for you* (Matt 17:20). And again: *Very truly, I tell you, if you ask anything of the Father in my name, it will be given to you. Ask and you will receive* (John 16:23–24). And it is he who says to the disciples and to all who have faith in him: *Cure the sick; cast out demons. You received without payment; give without payment* (Matt 10:8).

(84) It was not by giving commands that Antony healed, but by praying and saying the name of Christ, so that it was clear to everyone that it was not Antony who was doing this, but the Lord, who was, through Antony, expressing his love for humanity and healing those who suffered. Only this belonged to Antony: the prayer and the discipline, on account of which he sat on the mountain.

Antony rejoiced in the contemplation of divine matters, but he grieved that he was troubled by so many visitors and drawn to the outer mountain. For even all the judges demanded that he come down from the mountain because they could not come there on account of the accused persons who followed them around. Nevertheless, they would demand that he come so that they might at least see him. But when he turned aside and refused to make such journeys to them, they persisted and even sent to him accused persons in the custody of soldiers so that he might come down on account of them. When Antony saw these persons lamenting, he was affected by this pressure and came to the outer mountain. Once again his effort was not without profit, for his arrival resulted in benefit and advantage for many. He benefited the judges by advising them to put justice before everything else, to fear God, and to know that by the measure with which they judge they shall be judged (see Matt 7:2). Still, he loved the time he spent on the mountain above everything else.

(85) Once he was subjected to this kind of pressure by those who had need of him, and the military commander asked him through many messengers to come down. After Antony had come and had spoken briefly about what pertains to salvation and about those persons in need, he hastened to return. When the one who was called the duke asked him to stay, he said that he could not stay long with them and convinced him with this charming analogy: "Just as fish that stay too long on dry land die, so, too, monks who stay with you and spend time among you slack off. Therefore, we must hurry back to the mountain, just as a fish must to the sea, so that we do not, by lingering, forget the interior matters." When the commander heard this and many other things from him, he marveled and said, "Truly this man is a slave of God (see Matt 27:54; Mark 15:39). For how could an uneducated man have an intellect of such quality and magnitude unless he is loved by God?"

(86) A certain military commander named Balacius was brutally persecuting us Christians because of his zeal for the hateful Arians. Since he was so savage that he beat virgins and stripped and flogged

monks, Antony sent to him and wrote a letter that said: "I see wrath coming upon you! Stop persecuting Christians or the wrath will seize you! Indeed, already it is about to come!" But Balacius laughed, threw the letter to the ground, and spat on it; then he insulted those who had brought it and commanded them to tell Antony this: "Since you are concerned about the monks, I am going to come after you, too, right away!" And five days had not gone by before the wrath seized him. For Balacius and Nestorius, the prefect of Egypt, went out to the first stopping place beyond Alexandria, called Chaireu, and both were riding horses. The horses belonged to Balacius and were the gentlest of all those that he had trained. But before they got to the place, the horses began to play with each other, as they do, and suddenly the gentler one, which Nestorius was riding, seized Balacius by biting him and attacked him. And it mangled his thigh with its teeth so badly that he was immediately carried back into the city, and in three days he died. Everyone marveled that what Antony had predicted had come to pass so quickly.

(87) In this way, then, he warned the cruel, and he so exhorted those who came to him that they immediately forgot their lawsuits and blessed those who withdrew from this life. He so defended those who were being wronged that one would think it was he and not other people who was suffering. Moreover, he was of such benefit to everyone that many soldiers and persons who had lots of possessions renounced the burdens of life and at last became monks. Truly, it was as if a physician had been given by God to Egypt. For who came to him grieving and did not return rejoicing? Who came to him mourning for their dead and did not immediately cast off grief? Who came angry and was not converted to friendship? What poor and weary person came and did not, after hearing and seeing him, despise wealth and become consoled in his poverty? What neglectful monk came to him and did not become even stronger? What young man who came to the mountain and saw Antony did not immediately find the pleasures to be dried up and begin to love self-control? Who came to him tempted by demons and did not find rest? Who

came to him troubled by thoughts and did not become calm in his mind?

(88) For this, indeed, was the great thing about Antony's discipline: that, as I said before, he had the gift of discerning spirits (see 1 Cor 12:10), he recognized their movements and toward what end each of them focused its intention and zeal for attack. Not only was he himself not mocked by them, but he also taught those who were troubled by thoughts from them how they could turn back their attacks, explaining the tricks and weaknesses of the spirits that were working against them. Thus, each person, as if he had been oiled up for battle by Antony, departed ready to take on the plans of the devil and his demons. How many girls who had suitors ready to marry them, just by seeing Antony from afar, remained virgins for Christ! People would come to him even from foreign lands: they, too, with all the others, received benefit and returned, as if sent off by a father. No doubt when he died, they all, like orphans deprived of a father (see John 14:18), consoled themselves only with his memory, preserving both his admonitions and his exhortations.

(89) It is worthwhile for me to recall, and for you to hear as you would like, what the end of his life was like, for this, too, is worthy of emulation. As was his custom, he was visiting the monks of the outer mountain, and when he had learned in advance about his end from Providence, he said to his brothers, "This is the last visit to you that I shall make, and I shall be surprised if we see each other again in this life. At last it is time for me to depart, for I am nearly 105 years old." When they heard this, they wept and embraced and kissed the old man. But he, as if he were sailing from a foreign city to his own, discoursed joyfully and exhorted them not to be negligent in the labors or to grow weary in the discipline, but to live as if they were dying daily (see 1 Cor 15:31). And as he had said before, he told them to guard zealously their soul from impure thoughts and to have a rivalry with the saints, not to approach the Melitian schismatics—for you know their wicked and impure intention—nor to have any fellowship with the Arians, for their impiety is *plain to everyone* (2 Tim 3:9). "Even if you should

376 | SAINTS' LIVES

see the government officials acting as their patrons, do not be disturbed, for it shall cease, and their appearance is mortal and of short duration. Therefore, keep yourselves pure of these things and preserve the tradition of the fathers and especially the pious faith in our Lord Jesus Christ, which you have learned from the Scriptures and of which I have often reminded you."

(90) But when the brothers were pressing him to stay with them and to die there, he would not for many reasons, as he indicated by keeping silent, but especially for this reason. The Egyptians like to honor with funeral rites and to wrap in fine linens the bodies of the zealous ones who have died, and especially those of the holy martyrs, but they do not bury them under the ground; rather, they place them on stretchers and keep them inside among themselves, supposing that in this way they honor those who have departed. But Antony often demanded that the bishops command the people concerning this, and he shamed the laity and chastised the women, saying that it was neither lawful nor pious to do this. For the tombs of the patriarchs and prophets are preserved until today, and the body of the Lord himself was placed in a tomb, and a stone was placed there and hid it until he arose on the third day. And by saying these things, he showed that that person transgresses who does not after death bury the bodies of the departed, even if they happen to be holy. For what is greater or holier than the Lord's body? And so many people, when they heard this, thereupon buried their dead under the ground and gave thanks to the Lord that they had been taught so well.

(91) But since Antony knew this and was afraid that they would do the same thing to his body, he left quickly after he said farewell to the monks on the outer mountain. And after he had arrived at the inner mountain, where he was accustomed to remain, he became sick a few months later. When he had called those who were with him—there were two who stayed there, practicing the discipline for fifteen years and attending to him on account of his old age—he said to them, "As for me, as it is written, I am going the way of the fathers (see Josh 23:14; 1 Kings 2:2), for I see that I am called by the Lord. As

for you, be watchful and do not ruin your discipline, which has lasted so long, but as if you were starting now, be zealous to preserve your intention. You know the scheming demons; you know how fierce they are, but how weak they are in power. Therefore, do not be afraid of them; rather, always breathe Christ and have faith in him. Live as if you were dying every day (see 1 Cor 15:31) by paying attention to yourselves and remembering the exhortations that you heard from me. Have no fellowship with the schismatics and not at all with the heretical Arians, for you know how I myself turned away from them because of their hostility to Christ and their heterodox policy. Rather, be zealous to attach yourselves chiefly to Christ and next to the saints, so that after death they may receive you as familiar friends into the eternal tents (see Luke 16:9). You, too, consider these things and reflect upon them.

"If you care about me and remember me like a father, do not permit anyone to take my body into Egypt lest they deposit it in houses, for this is why I entered the mountain and came here. You know also how I rebuked those who do this and commanded them to stop this custom. Therefore, bury my body yourselves and hide it under the ground. Closely guard what I am saying, so that no one will know the place except you alone. For I myself at the resurrection of the dead will receive my body back from the Savior incorruptible. But divide my clothes, and to Athanasius the bishop give the first sheepskin and the garment on which I lay, which he himself gave to me new and which has grown old with me. And to Serapion the bishop give the other sheepskin, and you yourselves keep the hair garment. And finally, farewell, children! For Antony departs and is with you no more."

(92) When he had said these things and they had kissed him, he lifted up his feet, and as if he saw friends coming to him and was glad because of them—for he appeared to lie there with a cheerful face—he expired and was himself gathered to his fathers (see Gen 49:33). And then they, as he had commanded them, buried, wrapped, and hid his body under the ground, and no one knows, even until now, where he is hidden except these two alone. But each

of those who received the sheepskin of the blessed Antony and the garment he wore guards it as a great possession, for just seeing them is like gazing at Antony, and wearing them is like bearing his admonitions with joy.

(93) This was the end of Antony's life in the body, and the preceding has described the beginning of the discipline. Even if this account has been brief in comparison to his virtue, nevertheless consider from it for yourselves how great was this man of God, Antony: from his youth to such a great age he kept the same enthusiasm for the discipline; he neither was lessened by extravagance in food on account of old age, nor did he, because of his body's weakness, change his way of dressing or wash even his feet in water. Yet he remained completely healthy in every way. For even his eyes were unharmed and healthy: he could see clearly (see Deut 34:7). He had not lost even one of his teeth, but they had become worn down to the gums because of the old man's great age. He remained healthy in both his feet and hands, and while everyone else was making use of varied foods, baths, and different kinds of clothing, still it was he who appeared more cheerful and more ready for exertion.

It is proof of his virtue and of his soul's friendship with God that he is proclaimed everywhere, that he is the object of everyone's amazement, and that even those who have not seen him long for him. For Antony has become famous not through writings or through external wisdom or on account of any skill, but solely because of his piety. That this was a gift of God no one will deny. For how did news about a man who settled and was hidden in a mountain make it to Spain and Gaul, how to Rome and Africa, unless it was the God who makes his own people known everywhere who promised this also to Antony at the beginning? For even if they work in secret, even if they want to be ignored, still the Lord reveals them like lamps to all people, so that in this way those who hear might know that the commandments can be performed successfully and so receive zeal for the path to virtue.

(94) Therefore, read this to the remaining brothers, so that they might learn what sort of life the monks ought to lead and they might be persuaded that our Lord and Savior Jesus Christ glorifies those who glorify him (see 1 Sam 2:30). He not only leads into the kingdom of heaven those who serve him to the end, but even in this place, those who hide themselves and are eager to withdraw, he makes famous and proclaimed everywhere because of their virtue and for the benefit of others. And if there is need, read this even to the pagans, so that even in this way they might recognize not only that our Lord Jesus Christ is God and Son of God, but in addition that the Christians, those who serve him truly and believe in him piously, not only prove that the demons, whom the Greeks themselves consider gods, are not gods, but also tread on them and chase them away as deceivers and corrupters of humankind, in Christ Jesus our Lord, to whom be the glory for ever and ever. Amen.

47. Theodoret: The Religious History

Theodoret (393–ca. 466) was bishop of the small city of Cyrrhus, in northeastern Syria, for more than forty years. Born and raised in comfortable circumstances in Antioch, as bishop, Theodoret became a staunch opponent of what he perceived to be the Christological and allegorical excesses of the patriarchs of Alexandria (see Chapters 7 and 12). He wrote numerous exegetical and theological treatises, a continuation of Eusebius's *Church History,* and an apologetic treatise against "Greek maladies" (i.e., paganism). He was also a staunch patron and spokesperson for the various monks and holy persons who dotted the landscape of an-

From *A History of the Monks of Syria,* trans. R. M. Price. Kalamazoo, Mich.: Cistercian Publications, 1985. Used with permission.

cient Syria. Some time in the 440s, he wrote a set of brief biographies of thirty of those holy people, called *Religious History* or *Ascetic Life*. His purpose, as he said many times, was to provide models of imitation for Christians seeking a life of dedication to God. The narrative elements are, by this time, stock features of ascetic hagiography: inspiration (often by Scripture), renunciation, temptation, miracles, and inspiration of others. There is also an emphasis on the eyewitness testimony of the author: Theodoret has seen much of what he reports.

Syrian Christianity is often thought to have been especially prone to ascetic rigor from its origins, and it seems that Christian renunciation there occasionally took unusual forms (see the famous account of Symeon Stylites, the first of many "pillar saints"). Nonetheless, Theodoret takes care to frame his hagiographies in almost strangely classicizing terms, avoiding all specifically Christian terms (including, even, "bishop"). The asceticism of his heroes is "philosophy," monasteries are "wrestling schools," and monks and ascetics are "athletes." Theodoret also makes a concerted effort to include women in his account, to demonstrate that the Godly life is not restricted by gender. The inclusiveness of his hagiography probably also reflects an inclusive ideal of imitation: ascetics and laypeople, men and women, can all strive to imitate the virtues of the Syrian saints.

PROLOGUE

(1) How fine it is to behold the contests of excellent men, the athletes of virtue, and to draw benefit with the eyes; when witnessed, the objects of our praise appear enviable and become desirable and impel the beholder to attain them. No middling profit, however, derives from the mere narration of such achievements, communicated by those who know of them to the hearing of those who do not. Some say that sight is more trustworthy than hearing; however, we also believe hearing when it judges what is said from the truthfulness of the speakers. Just as the tongue and palate have been entrusted with decision over sweet and sour and other qualities of this kind and deliver their verdict accordingly, so, too, hearing has been empowered to discriminate between utterances and knows how to distinguish those that bring some profit from harmful ones.

(2) If the memory of profitable narratives remained inviolate and the injury of oblivion did not, like some spreading mist, render it extinct, it would of course be superfluous and redundant to record such actions, since the benefit from them would most easily make its way to posterity. But since time injures bodies by inflicting old age and death and injures achievements by causing oblivion and blunting

memory, surely no one could reasonably be indignant with us for trying to write down the way of life of the men who have loved God; just as those who have been entrusted with treating bodies prepare medicines in order to fight the disease and aid the patients, so the welcome labor of such composition becomes like some preventive medicine, a device against oblivion and an aid to memory. When poets and historians record acts of bravery in war, when tragedians make conspicuous in tragedy misfortunes that had rightly been hidden away and leave their memory written up, when certain others expend their words on comedy and laughter, how would it not be absurd if we let be consigned to oblivion men who, in a mortal and passible body, have displayed impassibility and emulated the bodiless beings? What penalty would we not justly pay for letting be dimmed the memory of these contests worthy of admiration? If they, in emulation of the consummate philosophy of the holy men of old, did not engrave their memory in bronze letters, but receiving the impress of all their virtue have made themselves, as it were, living images and statues of them, what pardon could we reasonably receive if we do not honor their celebrated lives in writing?

(3) Especially when the athletes and pancratiasts who compete in the Olympic games are honored with

images, and even the victorious charioteers appearing in the horse races receive this same honor. And not only these but also men who are womanish and effeminate, so that it is ambiguous whether they are men or women, are painted on panels by those who love to gaze on them, in emulous zeal to extend their memory as long as possible, although this memory causes not profit but injury to their souls; nevertheless, they who love either these or those, even to their own detriment, honor them in portraiture; since death despoils the nature that is mortal by mixing colors and placing their appearance on panels, they contrive that their memory will last much longer than their lives. But we are recording a life that teaches philosophy and has emulated the way of life in heaven; we do not portray their bodily features, nor do we display for those in ignorance representations of them, but we sketch the forms of invisible souls and display unseen wars and secret struggles.

(4) For such, too, is the armor that Paul, the general and champion of their host, has put upon them: "Take up," he says, "the panoply of God, so that you may be able to withstand in the evil day and having done all to stand" (Eph 6:13), and again, "Stand therefore having girded your loins with truth and having put on the breastplate of righteousness and having shod your feet with the preparation of the Gospel of peace, above all taking the shield of faith with which you will be able to quench all the flaming darts of the evil one, and receive the helmet of salvation and the sword of the Spirit that is the speech of God" (Eph 6:14–17); it was after putting this panoply upon them that he led them into combat. For such, too, is the nature of the enemy: bodiless, invisible, encroaching unperceived, plotting secretly, setting ambush and attacking suddenly. This same general taught this when he said, "Not ours is the wrestling against flesh and blood, but against the principalities, against the powers, against the world rulers of the darkness of this age, against the the spiritual beings of evil in the heavenly places" (Eph 6:12). Nevertheless, though having such adversaries, the company of these saints or, rather, each one of them, surrounded by enemies of such number and such a nature (for they do not assail them together but attack now one,

now another), have won so radiant a crown of victory as to rout their adversaries, pursue them forcibly, and erect a trophy with nothing standing in the way.

(5) It is not their nature that afforded them victory—for it is mortal and full of innumerable passions—but their resolve, attracting divine grace. As fervent lovers of the beauty of God, choosing to do and suffer all things gladly on behalf of the Beloved, they bore nobly the revolt of the passions and were steadfast in shaking off the showers of the devil's darts. Repressing the body and subduing it, to use the apostolic phrase (cf. 1 Cor 9:27), they soothed the inflammation of the irascible part and compelled the madness of the desires to be at rest. So by fasting and sleeping on the ground, they lulled the passions and put a stop to their restiveness; they compelled the body to make a treaty with the soul and put an end to their innate war.

(6) So, after arbitrating peace between them, they expelled the whole array of their adversaries, for they are not able to make war when they lack the thoughts that betray the interior and are deprived of the cooperation of the human limbs, since the devil uses our own limbs as weapons against us, for if the eyes are not enticed nor the hearing bewitched nor touch titillated nor the mind receptive of evil intentions, the zeal of those plotting harm is in vain. For just as a city built on a height, walled round with a strong circuit and surrounded on all sides by a deep moat, would not be taken by an enemy unless one of those within played traitor and slipped open some postern, so, too, it is impossible for the demons making war from outside to overcome a soul surrounded by divine grace, unless the compliance of some thought opens some postern in our senses and receives the enemy within it. The men we are extolling had been taught this plainly by divine Scripture. Hearing God saying through the prophet that "death has come up through the windows" (Jer 9:21), they barred up the senses with God's laws as if with bolts and bars and entrusted their keys to the mind. The tongue did not open the lips except at the command of the mind, nor was the pupil allowed to peep out from the eyelids without permission; the hearing, though unable to wall up the entrance with eyelids or lips, rejected

words that were senseless and admitted only those that the mind took pleasure in; so they taught the sense of smell not to hanker after fragrant odors, since by nature they produce flaccidity and limpness. So, too, they expelled the satiety of the belly and taught it to accept what satisfied, not pleasure, but need, and indeed just so much as could prevent death from hunger. So, too, they deposed the sweet tyranny of sleep, and freeing the eyelids from slavery to it, taught them to be masters not slaves and to accept its services not when it assailed, but when they themselves invited it to assist nature briefly. So therefore, taking thought for the guard of walls and gates and bestowing harmony on the thoughts within, they laughed at the antagonists assailing from without, who, because of the protection of divine grace, were unable to force a way in, since they found no traitor who chose to admit the foe. Although the enemies have an invisible nature, they could not master a visible body subject to the necessities of nature, for its charioteer and musician and helmsman, by holding the reins, well induced the horses to run in proper order; by striking the strings of the senses in rhythm, made them produce sound that was perfectly harmonious; and by moving the rudder skilfully, put an end to the blows of the billows and the blast of the winds.

(7) Therefore these who have followed the path of life through innumerable labors and broken the body in with sweat and toil, who have not experienced the passion of laughter but spent all their lives in mourning and tears, who have deemed fasting Sybaritic nourishment, laborious vigil a most pleasant sleep, the hard resistance of the ground a soft couch, a life of prayer and psalmody a pleasure measureless and insatiable, these who have attained every form of virtue—who would not rightly admire them? Rather, who could extol them as they merit? I, too, am well aware that no words can attain to their virtue. Nevertheless, the attempt must be made; it would not be right if men who became perfect lovers of true philosophy should for this very reason fail to receive even modest praise.

(8) We shall not write a single eulogy for all together, for different graces were given them from God; the blessed Paul taught this when he said, "To

one through the Spirit is given a word of wisdom, to another a word of knowledge according to the same Spirit, to another gifts of healing in the same Spirit, to another workings of powers, to another prophecy, to another varieties of tongues, to another the interpretation of tongues" (1 Cor 12:8–10), and to indicate the source of all these he added, "All these are worked by one and the same Spirit, apportioning individually to each one as he wills" (1 Cor 12:11). Since, therefore, they have received different gifts, we shall rightly compose the narrative of each one individually. We shall not work through the whole course of their actions, since a whole life would not be enough for such writing. Instead, we shall narrate a selection from the life and actions of each and display through this selection the character of the whole life and then proceed to another.

(9) We shall not try to transmit to history the way of life of all the saints who have been prominent everywhere, for neither do we know those who have been prominent everywhere, nor is it possible for them all to be written down by one man. So I shall record the lives of those alone who have appeared like stars in the East and reached the ends of the world with their rays. The account will proceed in narrative form, not following the rules of panegyric, but forming a plain tale of some few facts.

(10) I ask those who will read this *Religious History* or *Ascetic Life*—let one call the composition as one chooses—not to disbelieve what is said if they hear something beyond their own power nor to measure the virtue of these men by themselves, but to recognize clearly that God is wont to measure the gifts of the all-holy Spirit by the resolve of the pious and gives greater gifts to those with more perfect resolve. Let me say this to those who have not been initiated into divine truths with real accuracy, for the initiates of the sanctuary of the Spirit know the munificence of the Spirit and what miracles he works in men through the agency of men, drawing the faithless to a knowledge of God by the mighty working of prodigies. Quite obviously, he who will disbelieve what we are about to tell does not believe either in the truth of what took place through Moses, Joshua, Elijah, and Elisha and considers a myth the working of miracles

that took place through the sacred Apostles. But if truth bears witness on behalf of those men, let him believe these stories also to be free of falsehood, for the grace that worked in those men is the same that through these men performed what it has performed. Grace is ever flowing: it elects the worthy and through them as through springs pours forth the streams of beneficence.

(11) Of some of what I shall tell I was myself the eyewitness; whatever I have not seen I have heard of from those who have seen these men, those who as lovers of virtue were counted worthy to see them and be taught by them. Trustworthy as writers of the Gospel teaching are not only Matthew and John, the great and first Evangelists, the eyewitnesses of the Master's miracles, but also Luke and Mark, whom "the first eyewitnesses and ministers of the Word" (Luke 1:2) instructed accurately in not only what the Lord suffered and did, but also what he taught continually. Despite the fact that he had not been an eyewitness, the blessed Luke at the beginning of his work says that his narration concerns facts about which there is full assurance. And we, hearing that he was not an eyewitness of these very narratives, but received this teaching from others, pay equal attention to him and Mark as to Matthew and John, for each of the two is trustworthy in his narration because he was taught by those who had seen. For this very reason, we, too, shall tell of some things as eyewitnesses and of others trusting the narration of eyewitnesses, men who have emulated their lives. I have expended rather many words on this point in my wish to carry conviction that I shall be narrating the truth; so starting from there, I shall begin my narrative.

CHAPTER 26: SYMEON STYLITES

(1) The famous Symeon, the great wonder of the world, is known of by all the subjects of the Roman empire and has also been heard of by the Persians, the Medes, the Ethiopians, and the rapid spread of his fame as far as the nomadic Scythians has taught his love of labor and his philosophy. I myself, though having all men, so to speak, as witnesses of his con-

tests that beggar description, am afraid that the narrative may seem to posterity to be a myth totally devoid of truth. For the facts surpass human nature, and men are wont to use nature to measure what is said; if anything is said that lies beyond the limits of nature, the account is judged to be false by those uninitiated into divine things. But since earth and sea are full of pious souls educated in divine things and instructed in the grace of the all-holy Spirit, who will not disbelieve what is said but have complete faith in it, I shall make my narration with eagerness and confidence. I shall begin from the point at which he received his call from on high.

(2) There is a village lying on the border between our region and Cilicia; they call it Sisa. Originating from this village, he was taught by his parents first to shepherd animals, so that in this respect, too, he might be comparable to those great men the patriarch Jacob, the chaste Joseph, the lawgiver Moses, the king and prophet David, the prophet Micah, and the inspired men of their kind (cf. Gen 30:29–43, 37:2; Exod 3:1; 1 Sam 16:11). Once when there was much snow and the sheep were compelled to stay indoors, he took advantage of the respite to go with his parents to the house of God. I heard his sacred tongue recount the following: he told how he heard the Gospel utterance that declares blessed those who weep and mourn, calls wretched those who laugh, terms enviable those who possess a pure soul, and all the other blessings conjoined with them (cf. Luke 6:20–26). He then asked one of those present what one should do to obtain each of these. He suggested the solitary life and pointed to that consummate philosophy.

(3) Therefore, having received the seeds of the divine word and stored them well in the deep furrows of his soul, he hastened—he said—to a nearby shrine of the holy martyrs. In it he bent his knees and forehead to the ground and besought the One who wishes to save all men to lead him to the perfect path of piety. After he had spent a long time in this way, a sweet sleep came upon him, and he had the following dream: "I seemed," he said, "to be digging foundations, and then to hear someone standing by say that I had to make the trench deeper. After adding to its depth as he told me, I again tried to take a rest, but

once more he ordered me to dig and not relax my efforts. After charging me a third and a fourth time to do this, he finally said the depth was sufficient and told me to build effortlessly from now on, since the effort had abated and the building would be effortless." This prediction is confirmed by the event, for the facts surpass nature.

(4) Getting up from there, he repaired to the dwelling of some neighboring ascetics. After spending two years with them and falling in love with more perfect virtue, he repaired to that village of Teleda that we mentioned above, where the great and godly men Ammianus and Eusebius had pitched their ascetic wrestling school. The inspired Symeon, however, did not enter this one, but another that had sprung from it; Eusebônas and Abibion, having enjoyed sufficiently the teaching of the great Eusebius, had built this retreat of philosophy. Having shared throughout life the same convictions and the same habits and displayed, as it were, one soul in two bodies, they made many love this life as they did. When they departed from life with glory, the wonderful Heliodorus succeeded to the office of superior over the community. He lived for sixty-five years and spent sixty-two years immured within, for it was after three years of rearing by his parents that he entered this flock, without ever beholding the occurrences of life. He claimed not even to know the shape of pigs or cocks or the other animals of this kind. I, too, had often the benefit of seeing him; I admired his simplicity of character and was especially amazed at his purity of soul.

(5) After coming to him, this all-round contestant in piety spent ten years contending. He had eighty fellow contestants and outshot all of them; while the others took food every other day, he would last the whole week without nourishment. His superiors bore this ill and constantly quarreled with it, calling the thing lack of discipline, but they did not persuade him by their words, nor could they curb his zeal. I heard the very man who is now superior of this flock recount how on one occasion Symeon took a cord made from palms—it was extremely rough even to touch with the hands—and girded it round his waist, not wearing it on the outside but making it touch the skin itself. He tied it so tightly as to lacerate in a circle the whole part it went round. When he had continued in this manner for more than ten days and the now-severe wound was letting fall drops of blood, someone who saw him asked what was the cause of the blood. When he replied that he had nothing wrong with him, his fellow contestant forcibly inserted his hand, discovered the cause and disclosed it to the superior. Immediately reproaching and exhorting and inveighing against the cruelty of the thing, he undid the belt, with difficulty, but not even so could he persuade him to give the wound any treatment. Seeing him do other things of the kind as well, they ordered him to depart from this wrestling school, lest he should be a cause of harm to those with a weaker bodily constitution who might try to emulate what was beyond their powers.

(6) He therefore departed and made his way to the more deserted parts of the mountain. Finding a cistern that was waterless and not too deep, he lowered himself into it and offered hymnody to God. When five days had passed, the superiors of the wrestling school had a change of heart and sent out two men, charging them to look for him and bring him back. So after walking round the mountain, they asked some men tending animals there if they had seen someone of such a complexion and dress. When the shepherds pointed out the cistern, they at once called out several times, and bringing a rope, drew him out with great labor—for ascent is not as easy as descent.

(7) After staying with them for a short time, he came to the village of Telanissus, which lies under the hilltop where he now stands; finding a tiny cottage in it, he spent three years as a recluse. In his eagerness to be always increasing his wealth of virtue, he longed to fast forty days without food, like the men of God Moses and Elijah (cf. Exod 24:18; 1 Kings 19:8). He urged the wonderful Bassus, who at the time used to make visitations of many villages as supervisor of the village priests, to leave nothing inside and seal the door with mud. When the other pointed out the difficulty of the thing and urged him not to think suicide a virtue, since it is the first and greatest of crimes, he replied: "But you then, father, leave me ten rolls and a jar of water, and if I see my

body needs nourishment, I shall partake of them." It was done as he bade. The provisions were left, and the door was sealed with mud. At the end of the forty days, Bassus, this wonderful person and man of God, came and removed the mud; on going in through the door, he found the complete number of rolls, he found the jar full of water, but Symeon stretched out without breath, unable either to speak or to move. Asking for a sponge to wet and rinse his mouth, he brought him the symbols of the divine mysteries, and so strengthened by these, he raised himself and took a little food—lettuce, chicory, and similar plants, which he chewed in small pieces and so passed into the stomach.

(8) Overwhelmed with admiration, the great Bassus repaired to his own flock to recount this great miracle, for he had more than two hundred disciples, whom he ordered to possess neither mounts nor mules nor to accept offerings of money nor to go outside the gate whether to buy something necessary or see some friend, but to live indoors and receive the food sent by divine grace. This rule his disciples have preserved to this day. They have not, as they become more numerous, transgressed the injunctions that were given them.

(9) But I shall return to the great Symeon. From that time until today—twenty-eight years have passed—he spends the forty days without food. Time and practice have allayed most of the effort. For it was his custom during the first days to chant hymns to God standing, then, when because of the fasting his body no longer had the strength to bear the standing, thereafter to perform the divine liturgy seated, and during the final days actually to lie down—for as his strength was gradually exhausted and extinguished, he was compelled to lie half-dead. But when he took his stand on the pillar, he was not willing to come down, but contrived his standing posture differently; it was by attaching a beam to the pillar and then tying himself to the beam with cords that he lasted the forty days. Subsequently, enjoying henceforward still more grace from above, he has not needed even this support, but stands throughout the forty days, not taking food but strengthened by zeal and divine grace.

(10) After spending three years, as I said, in this cottage, he repaired to that celebrated hilltop, where he ordered a circular enclosure to be made. After procuring an iron chain of twenty cubits, nailing one end to a great rock and fixing the other to his right foot, so that not even if he wished could he go outside these limits, he lived all the time inside, thinking of heaven and compelling himself to contemplate what lies above the heavens—for the iron chain did not hinder the flight of his thought. But when the wonderful Meletius, who had at that time been appointed to supervise the territory of the city of Antioch and was a wise man of brilliant intelligence and gifted with shrewdness, told him that the iron was superfluous, since the will was sufficient to impose on the body the bonds of reasoning, he yielded and accepted the advice with compliance: And bidding a smith be called, he told him to sever the chain. When a piece of leather, which had been tied to his leg to prevent the iron injuring his body, had to be torn apart (for it had been sown together), people saw, they said, more than twenty large bugs lurking in it, and the wonderful Meletius said he had seen this. I myself have mentioned it in order to show from this example as well the endurance of the man: for though he could easily have squeezed the leather with his hand and killed them all, he steadfastly put up with their painful bites, welcoming in small things training for greater contests.

(11) As his fame circulated everywhere, everyone hastened to him, not only the people of the neighborhood but also people many days' journey distant, some bringing the paralyzed in body, others requesting health for the sick, others asking to become fathers, and they begged to receive from him what they could not receive from nature. On receiving it and obtaining their requests, they returned with joy, and by proclaiming the benefits they had gained, they sent out many times more, asking for the same things. So with everyone arriving from every side and every road resembling a river, one can behold a sea of men standing together in that place, receiving rivers from every side. Not only do the inhabitants of our part of the world flock together, but also Ishmaelites, Persians, Armenians subject to them, Iberi-

ans, Homerites, and men even more distant than these, and there came many inhabitants of the extreme West: Spaniards, Britons, and the Gauls who live between them. Of Italy it is superfluous to speak. It is said that the man became so celebrated in the great city of Rome that at the entrance of all the workshops men have set up small representations of him, to provide thereby some protection and safety for themselves.

(12) Since the visitors were beyond counting and they all tried to touch him and reap some blessing from his garments of skins, while he at first thought the excess of honor absurd and later could not abide the wearisomeness of it, he devised the standing on a pillar, ordering the cutting of a pillar first of six cubits, then of twelve, afterward of twenty-two and now of thirty-six—for he yearns to fly up to heaven and to be separated from this life on earth. I myself do not think that this standing has occurred without the dispensation of God, and because of this, I ask fault finders to curb their tongue and not to let it be carried away at random, but to consider how often the Master has contrived such things for the benefit of the more easygoing. He ordered Isaiah to walk naked and barefoot (Isa 20:2); Jeremiah to put a loincloth on his waist and by this means address prophecy to the unbelieving (Jer 13:1) and on another occasion to put a wooden collar on his neck and later an iron one (Jer 27:2, 28:13); Hosea to take a harlot to wife and again to love a woman immoral and adulterous (Hos 1:2, 3:1); Ezekiel to lie on his right side for forty days and on his left for one hundred and fifty and again to dig through a wall and slip out in flight, making himself a representation of captivity, and on another occasion to sharpen a sword to a point, shave his head with it, divide the hair into four and assign some for this purpose and some for that (Ezek 4:4–6, 12:4–5, 5:1–4)—not to list everything. The Ruler of the universe ordered each of these things to be done in order to attract, by the singularity of the spectacle, those who would not heed words and could not bear hearing prophecy and make them listen to the oracles. For who would not have been astounded at seeing a man of God walking naked? Who would not have wanted to learn the cause of the occurrence? Who would not

have asked how the prophet could bear to live with a harlot? Therefore, just as the God of the universe ordered each of these actions out of consideration for the benefit of those inured to ease, so, too, he has ordained this new and singular sight in order by its strangeness to draw all men to look and to make the proffered exhortation persuasive to those who come—for the novelty of the sight is a trustworthy pledge of the teaching, and the man who comes to look departs instructed in divine things. Just as those who have obtained kingship over men alter periodically the images on their coins, at one time striking representations of lions, at another of stars and angels, and at another try to make the gold piece more valuable by the strangeness of the type, so the universal Sovereign of all things, by attaching to piety like coin types these new and various modes of life, stirs to eulogy the tongues not only of those nurtured in the faith, but also of those afflicted by lack of faith.

(13) Words do not testify that these things have this character, but the facts themselves proclaim it, for the Ishmaelites, who were enslaved in their many tens of thousands to the darkness of impiety, have been illuminated by his standing on the pillar. For this dazzling lamp, as if placed on a lamp stand, has sent out rays in all directions, like the sun. It is possible, as I have said, to see Iberians and Armenians and Persians arriving to receive the benefit of divine baptism. The Ishmaelites, arriving in companies, two or three hundred at the same time, sometimes even a thousand, disown with shouts their ancestral imposture, and smashing in front of this great luminary the idols they had venerated and renouncing the orgies of Aphrodite—it was this demon whose worship they had adopted originally—they receive the benefit of the divine mysteries, accepting laws from this sacred tongue and bidding farewell to their ancestral customs, as they disown the eating of wild asses and camels.

(14) I myself was an eyewitness of this, and I have heard them disowning their ancestral impiety and assenting to the teaching of the Gospel. And I once underwent great danger: he told them to come up and receive from me the priestly blessing, saying they would reap the greatest profit therefrom. But they

rushed up in a somewhat barbarous manner, and some pulled at me from in front, some from behind, others from the sides, while those farther back trod on the others and stretched out their hands, and some pulled at my beard and others grabbed at my clothing. I would have been suffocated by their too ardent approach if he had not used a shout to disperse them. Such is the benefit that the pillar mocked by lovers of mockery has poured forth; such is the ray of divine knowledge that it has made descend into the minds of barbarians.

(15) I know another case of such behavior by these men. One tribe begged the man of God to utter a prayer and blessing for their chieftain; but another tribe that was present objected to this, saying that the blessing ought to be uttered not for him but for their own leader, since the former was extremely unjust while the latter was a stranger to injustice. A long dispute and barbarian quarrel ensued, and finally they went for each other. I myself exhorted them with many words to stay calm, since the man of God had power sufficient to give a blessing to both the one and the other, but these said that that man should not get it, while those tried to deprive the other of it. By threatening them from above and calling them dogs, he with difficulty extinguished the dispute. I have told this out of a wish to display the faith in their understanding, for they would not have raged against each other if they did not believe the blessing of the inspired man to possess the greatest power.

(16) On another occasion I witnessed the occurrence of a celebrated miracle. Someone came in—he, too, was a tribal chieftain of Saracens—and begged the godly person to assist a man who on the road had become paralyzed in the limbs of his body; he said he had undergone the attack at Callinicum—it is a very great fort. When he had been brought right to the center, Symeon bade him disown the impiety of his ancestors. When he gladly consented and performed the order, he asked him if he believed in the Father and the only-begotten Son and the Holy Spirit. When the other professed his faith, he said: "Since you believe in these names, stand up!" When he stood up, he ordered him to carry the tribal chieftain on his shoulders right to his tent, and he was of great bodily size.

He at once picked him up and went on his way, while those present stirred their tongues to sing hymns to God.

(17) He gave this order in imitation of the Master, who told the paralytic to carry his bed (Matt 9:6). But let no one call the imitation usurpation, for his is the utterance, "He who believes in me will himself do the works that I do, and greater than these will he do" (John 14:12). Of this promise we have seen the fulfillment, for while the Lord's shadow nowhere performed a miracle, the shadow of the great Peter canceled death, drove out diseases, and put demons to flight (cf. Acts 5:15). But it is the Master who through his servants performed these miracles, too, and now likewise it is by the use of his name that the godly Symeon performs his innumerable miracles.

(18) I have been not only an eyewitness of his miracles, but also a hearer of his predictions of the future. The drought that occurred, the great crop failure of that year, and the simultaneous famine and plague that followed, he foretold two years beforehand, saying that he had seen a rod threatening humankind and indicating the scourging it would cause. On another occasion he revealed beforehand an attack of what is called the grasshopper, and that it would not cause serious harm, for the mercy of God would follow hard on the punishment. When thirty days had passed, a countless swarm so swooped down as to intercept the rays of the sun and create shade, and this we all saw distinctly. But it harmed only the fodder of the irrational animals, while causing no injury to the food of human beings. Also to me, when under attack from someone, he disclosed the death of my enemy fifteen days in advance, and from experience I learned the truth of his prediction.

(19) Although I know very many other occurrences of this kind, I shall omit them, to avoid length in the account—and the preceding are sufficient to show the spiritual perception of his mind. His reputation is also great with the king of the Persians. As the envoys who came to see Symeon related, he wished to inquire carefully about the man's way of life and the nature of his miracles, and his spouse is said to have asked for oil honored by his blessing and to have received it as a very great gift. All the king's

courtiers, struck by his reputation, and despite hearing from the Magians many calumnies against him, wished to inquire precisely, and on being informed, called him a man of God. The rest of the crowd, going up to the muleteers, servants, and soldiers, offered them money, begging to receive a share in the blessing attached to the oil.

(20) The queen of the Ishmaelites, being sterile and longing for children, first sent some of her highest officials to beg that she become a mother, and then when she obtained her request and gave birth as she had wished, took the prince she had borne and hastened to the godly old man. Since women are not allowed access, she sent the baby to him together with a request to receive blessing from him. "Yours," she said, "is this sheaf, for I brought, with tears, the seed of prayer, but it was you who made the seed a sheaf, drawing down through prayer the rain of divine grace." But how long shall I strive to measure the depth of the Atlantic Ocean? For just as the latter cannot be measured by men, so the daily deeds of this man transcend narration.

(21) More than all this I myself admire his endurance. Night and day he is standing within view of all, for having removed the doors and demolished a sizable part of the enclosing wall, he is exposed to all as a new and extraordinary spectacle—now standing for a long time, and now bending down repeatedly and offering worship to God. Many of those standing by count the number of these acts of worship. Once one of those with me counted 1,244, before slackening and giving up count. In bending down, he always makes his forehead touch his toes—for his stomach's receiving food once a week, and little of it, enables his back to bend easily.

(22) As a result of his standing, it is said that a malignant ulcer has developed in his left foot and that a great deal of puss oozes from it continually. Nevertheless, none of these afflictions has overcome his philosophy, but he bears them all nobly, both the voluntary and the involuntary, overcoming both the former and the latter by his zeal. He was once obliged to show this wound to someone; I shall recount the cause. Someone arrived from Rabaena, a worthy man, honored with being a deacon of Christ. On

reaching the hilltop, he said, "Tell me, by the truth that has converted the human race to itself, are you a man or a bodiless being?" When those present showed annoyance at the question, Symeon told them all to keep silence and said to him, "Why on earth have you posed this question?" He replied, "I hear everyone repeating that you neither eat nor lie down, both of which are proper to men—for no one with a human nature could live without food and sleep." At this Symeon ordered a ladder to be placed against the pillar and told him to ascend and first examine his hands and then to place his hand inside his cloak of skins and look at not only his feet but also his severe ulcer. After seeing and marveling at the excess of the wound and learning from him that he does take food, he came down from there, and coming to me recounted everything.

(23) During the public festivals, he displays another form of endurance: after the setting of the sun until it comes again to the eastern horizon; stretching out his hands to heaven he stands all night, neither beguiled by sleep nor overcome by exertion.

(24) Despite such labors and the mass of his achievements and the quantity of his miracles, he is as modest in spirit as if he were the last of all men in worth. In addition to his modest spirit, he is extremely approachable, sweet and charming, and makes answer to everyone who addresses him, whether he be artisan, beggar, or peasant. And he has received from the munificent Master the gift also of teaching. Making exhortation two times each day, he floods the ears of his hearers, as he speaks most gracefully and offers the lessons of the divine Spirit, bidding them look up to heaven and take flight, depart from the earth, imagine the expected kingdom, fear the threat of hell, despise earthly things, and await what is to come.

(25) He can be seen judging and delivering verdicts that are right and just. These and similar activities he performs after the ninth hour—for the whole night and the day till the ninth hour he spends praying. But after the ninth hour, he first offers divine instruction to those present, and then, after receiving each man's request and working some cures, he resolves the strife of those in dispute. At sunset he begins his converse from then on with God.

(26) Although engaged in these activities and performing them all, he does not neglect care of the holy churches—now fighting pagan impiety, now defeating the insolence of the Jews, at other times scattering the bands of the heretics, sometimes sending instructions on these matters to the emperor, sometimes rousing the governors to divine zeal, at others time charging the very shepherds of the churches to take still greater care of their flocks.

(27) I have proceeded through all this trying from a drop to indicate the rain and using my forefinger to give readers of the account a taste of the sweetness of the honey. The facts celebrated by all are many times more numerous than these, but I did not promise to record everything, but to show by a few instances the character of the life of each one. Others, doubtless, will record far more than these, and if he lives on, he will perhaps add greater miracles. I myself desire and beg God that, helped by his own prayers, he may persevere in these good labors, since he is a universal decoration and ornament of piety, and that my own life may be brought into harmony and rightly directed in accordance with the Gospel way of life.

CHAPTER 29: MARANA AND CYRA

(1) After recording the way of life of the heroic men, I think it useful to treat also of women who have contended no less if not more, for they are worthy of still greater praise, when, despite having a weaker nature, they display the same zeal as the men and free their sex from its ancestral disgrace.

(2) At this point I shall treat of Marana and Cyra, who have defeated all the others in the contests of endurance. Their fatherland was Beroea, their stock the glory of their fatherland, and their upbringing appropriate for their stock. But despising all these, they acquired a small place in front of the town, and entering within it, walled up the door with clay and stones. For their maidservants who were eager to share this life with them, they built a small dwelling outside this enclosure, and in this they told them to live. Through a small window they keep a watch on what they are doing and repeatedly rouse them to prayer

and inflame them with divine love. They themselves, with neither house nor hut, embrace the open-air life.

(3) In place of a door, a small window has been constructed for them, through which they take in the food they need and talk with the women who come to see them. For this intercourse the season of Pentecost has been laid down; during the rest of the time, they embrace the quiet life. And it is Marana alone who talks to visitors; no one has ever heard the other one speak.

(4) They wear iron and carry such a weight that Cyra, with her weaker body, is bent down to the ground and is quite unable to straighten her body. They wear mantles so big as to trail along behind and literally cover their feet and in front to fall down right to the belt, literally hiding at the same time face, neck, chest, and hands.

(5) I have often been inside the door in order to see them, for out of respect for the episcopal office, they have bidden me dig through the door. And so I have seen that weight of iron that even a well-built man could not carry. After long entreaty I succeeded in getting it off them for the nonce, but after our departure, they again put it on their limbs—round the neck the collar, round the waist the belt, and on hands and feet the chains assigned to them.

(6) In this mode of life they have completed not merely five or ten or fifteen years, but forty-two, and despite having contended for so long a time, they love their exertion as if they had only just entered on the contests. For contemplating the beauty of the Bridegroom, they bear the labor of the course with ease and facility and press on to reach the goal of the contests, where they see the Beloved standing and pointing to the crown of victory. Because of this, in suffering the assaults of rain and snow and sun, they feel neither pain nor distress but from apparent afflictions reap joy of heart.

(7) Emulating the fast of the inspired Moses (cf. Exod 24:18), they have three times spent the same length of time without food, for it was at the end of forty days that they took a little nourishment. Three times also have they emulated the abstinence from eating of the godly Daniel, completing three weeks and only then supplying nourishment to the body (cf.

Dan 10:2–3). On one occasion, out of a desire to behold the sacred places of the saving sufferings of Christ, they hastened to Aelia,[1] enjoying no nutriment on the way. It was after reaching that city and accomplishing their worship that they took nourishment and then returning back, completed the journey without food—and there are not less than twenty stages. Conceiving a desire to behold as well the shrine of the triumphant Thecla in Isauria, in order from all sources to kindle the firebrand of their love for God, they journeyed both there and back without food—to such a degree has divine yearning driven them to frenzy, so much has divine love for the Bridegroom driven them mad. Since by such a way of life they have adorned the female sex, becoming as models for other women, they will be crowned by the Master with the wreaths of victory. I myself, having displayed the benefit therefrom and culled their blessing, shall pass on to another account.

CHAPTER 30: DOMNINA

(1) Emulating the life of the inspired Maron,[2] whom we recalled above, the wonderful Domnina set up a small hut in the garden of her mother's house; her hut is made of millet stalks. Passing the whole day there, she wets with incessant tears not only her cheeks but also her garments of hair, for such is the clothing with which she covers her body. Going at cockcrow to the divine shrine nearby, she offers hymnody to the Master of the universe, together with the rest, both men and women. This she does not only at the beginning of the day but also at its close, thinking the place consecrated to God to be more venerable than every other spot and teaching others so. Judging it, for this reason, worthy of every attention, she has persuaded her mother and brothers to spend their fortune on it.

(2) As food she has lentils soaked in water, and she endures all this labor with a body reduced to a skeleton and half-dead—for her skin is very thin and covers her thin bones as if with a film, while her fat and flesh have been worn away by labors. Though exposed to all who wish to see her, both men and women, she neither sees a face nor shows her face to another, but is literally covered up by her cloak and bent down onto her knees, while she speaks extremely softly and indistinctly, always making her remarks with tears. She has often taken my hand, and after placing it on her eyes, released it so soaked that my very hand dripped tears. What discourse could give due praise to a woman who with such wealth of philosophy weeps and wails and sighs like those living in extreme poverty? For it is fervent love for God that begets these tears, firing the mind to divine contemplation, stinging it with pricks and urging it on to migrate from here.

(3) Though spending in this way both the day and the night, nor does she neglect the other forms of virtue, but ministers, as far as she can, to the heroic contestants, both those we have mentioned and those we have omitted. She also ministers to those who come to see her, bidding them stay with the shepherd of the village and sending them all they need herself, for the property of her mother and brothers is available for her to spend, since it reaps a blessing through her. To myself, too, when I arrived at this place—it is to the south of our region—she sent rolls, fruit, and soaked lentils.

(4) But how long can I expatiate in my eagerness to relate all her virtue, when I ought to bring into the open the life of the other women who have imitated both her and those we recalled above? For there are many others, of whom some have embraced the solitary life and others have preferred life with many companions—in such a way that communities of two hundred and fifty or more or less share the same life, putting up with the same food, choosing to sleep on rush mats alone, assigning their hands to card wool, and conscreating their tongues with hymns.

(5) Myriad and defeating enumeration are the philosophic retreats of this kind not only in our region but throughout the East; full of them are Palestine, Egypt, Asia, Pontus, and all Europe. From the time when Christ the Master honored virginity by being born of a virgin, nature has sprouted meadows of virginity and offered these fragrant and unfading flowers to the Creator, not separating virtue into male and fe-

---

[1] That is, Jerusalem.

[2] Maron's deeds are recounted in Chapter 16 of the *Religious History;* he lived outdoors in a tent.

male nor dividing philosophy into two categories. For the difference is one of bodies not of souls: "in Christ Jesus," according to the divine Apostle, "there is neither male nor female" (Gal 3:28). And a single faith has been given to men and women: "there is one Lord, one faith, one baptism, one God and Father of all, who is above all and through all and in us all" (Eph 4:5–6). And it is one kingdom of heaven that the Umpire has set before the victors, fixing this common prize for the contests.

(6) As I have said, numerous are the pious wrestling schools of men and women not only among us but also in all Syria, Palestine, Cilicia, and Mesopotamia. In Egypt, it is said, some retreats have five thousand men each, who work and in between sing hymns to the Master, not only providing themselves with the necessary food out of their labor, but also supplying guests who come and are needy.

(7) But to recount everything is impossible not only for me but for all writers. Even if it were possible, I consider it superfluous and an ambition without gain; for those who wish to cull some profit, what has been said is sufficient to provide what they desire. We have recalled different lives and added accounts of women to those of men, for this reason: that men old and young and, women too, may have models of philosophy and that each person, as he receives the impress of his favorite life, may have as a rule and regulator of his own life the one presented in our account. Just as painters look at their model when imitating eyes, nose, mouth, cheeks, ears, forehead, the very hairs of the head and beard, and, in addition, the sitting and standing postures and the very expression of the eyes, whether genial or forbidding, so it is fitting that each of the readers of this work choose to imitate a particular life and order their own life in accordance with the one they choose. Just as joiners straighten their planks with a measuring cord and remove what is excessive to the point where, applying the rule, they see the plank is equal, so, too, one who wishes to emulate a particular life must apply it to himself in place of a rule and cut off the excesses of vice, while supplying what is lacking in virtue. It is for this reason that we have undertaken the labor of composition, offering to those who wish it a means of benefit. I ask my future readers, as they luxuriate effortlessly in the labors of others, to repay my labors with prayer.

(8) I also beg those whose lives I have written down not to leave me tarrying at a distance from their spiritual choir, but to draw me up, who am lying below; lead me up to the summit of virtue; and join me to their own choir, so that I may not only praise the wealth of others, but also myself have some cause to give praise—by deed, word, and thought glorifying the Savior of the universe, with whom to the Father be the glory together with the Holy Spirit, now and always and forever and ever. Amen.

48. History of the Monks of Egypt

Some time in the 380s, a group of monks traveled from the Mount of Olives, outside Jerusalem, to visit the famous monastic settlements of Lower (northern) Egypt. After their return, some time before 400, one of them wrote an account of their journey that circulated as the anonymous *History of the Monks of Egypt.* This account was translated into Latin by the head of the Jerusalem monastery, Rufinus, and circulated widely throughout the Mediterranean. Much like the *Life of Antony* before it, the *History of the Monks of Egypt* depicted the deserts of Egypt as a magical landscape, the terrain of demon fighting, wonder working, and ascetic superheroes. Focusing particularly on the monastic settlements of Nitria and Scetis, the *History of the Monks of Egypt* portrays Egyptian monasticism as a sacred chain of monas-

From *The Lives of the Desert Fathers,* trans. Norman Russell. Kalamazoo, Mich.: Cistercian Studies, 1981. Used with permission.

tic *virtuosi,* stretching from Amoun (who reportedly preceded Antony into the desert) down to the contemporary monks whom intrepid seekers might visit in person. Here we have a hagiography of place as well as of person: the extraordinary tales included in this text highlight the special holiness to be obtained in the wilderness of Egypt.

It is likely that the *History of the Monks of Egypt* did more than simply disseminate images of human perfection for popular consumption. Hagiography of this sort might also have served as a form of propaganda among competing Christian groups. Like a later text, the fifth-century *Lausiac History* of Palladius of Helenopolis, the *History of the Monks of Egypt* emerged in the midst of theological and political struggles that were rumbling through the churches of the eastern Mediterranean. In the 390s, soon after the monks' journey and perhaps around the time of the text's composition and circulation, Bishop Theophilus of Alexandria forced the expulsion of several monks from the deserts of Lower Egypt. Theophilus claimed to be purging the desert of heretics who followed the errant teachings of the third-century Christian Origen. This "Origenist controversy" eventually spread outside Egypt: John Chrysostom, bishop of Constantinople, was deposed for Origenist sympathies; John, bishop of Jerusalem, was also implicated; monks, priests, and lay Christians of elevated social status from Italy to Palestine, including Rufinus's own monastery, were divided along partisan lines.

Many of the heroes praised for emulation in the *History of the Monks of Egypt* were precisely those theological partisans of the desert who were being tarred with the brush of heresy by Theophilus. By including controversial figures, such as Evagrius of Pontus, Ammonius, and the so-called Tall Brothers (in the section "On the Monks of Nitria"), alongside universally revered holy figures, such as John of Lycopolis, the Jerusalem monks who circulated these biographies could, in fact, promote their ascetic, and perhaps theological, heroes in a persuasive format. The saints' lives might function not only to provide model of imitation for all Christians, but to recuperate the reputation of one party's besieged heroes.

PROLOGUE

(1) Blessed be God "who desires all men to be saved and to come to the knowledge of the truth" (1 Tim 2:4). For he brought us to Egypt and showed us great and wonderful things that are worthy of being remembered and recorded. He granted to us who desire to be saved both the foundation and the knowledge of salvation. He provided us not only with a model of the good life but also with an exposition sufficient to arouse the soul to devotion. He gave us a noble testimony to the way of virtue.

(2) I myself am not worthy to undertake such an exposition because it is not appropriate for humble men to treat of great themes. Their powers are not equal to the task of explaining the truth in a fitting manner, particularly when they presume to commit themselves to writing and give inadequate expression to difficult matters. Since we are of no account, it is too presumptuous and dangerous for us to proceed at once to write on this most sublime theme. Nevertheless, the pious community that lives on the holy Mount of Olives has asked me repeatedly to write them an account of the practices of the Egyptian monks that I have witnessed, their fervent love and great ascetic discipline.

I have therefore trusted in their prayers and presumed to apply myself to the composition of this narrative so that I, too, should derive some profit from the edifying lives of these monks through the imitation of their way of life, their complete withdrawal from the world, and their stillness, which they achieve through the patient practice of virtue and retain to the end of their lives. (3) For I have truly seen the treasure of God hidden in human vessels. I did not wish to keep this to myself and conceal something that would benefit many. On the contrary, I have contributed my profit to the common fund, for I consider that this transaction, the sharing of what I have gained with the brethren, will be to my advantage because then they will pray for my salvation.

(4) I shall therefore begin this work with the coming of our Savior Jesus Christ and with the assertion that it is by his teaching that the Egyptian monks regulate their lives. (5) For in Egypt I saw many fathers living the angelic life as they advanced steadily in the imitation of our divine Savior. I saw new prophets who have attained a Godlike state of fulfilment by their inspired and wonderful and virtuous way of life. For they are true servants of God. They do not busy themselves with any earthly matter or take account of anything that belongs to this transient world. But while dwelling on earth in this manner, they live as true citizens of heaven. (6) Some of them do not even know that another world exists on earth or that evil is found in cities. For them the almighty Lord's saying, "Much peace have those who love your law" (Ps 119:165), is a reality. Many of them are astonished when they hear what goes on in the world, for they have attained a complete forgetfulness of earthly affairs.

(7) One can see them scattered in the desert waiting for Christ like loyal sons watching for their father or like an army expecting its emperor or like a sober household looking forward to the arrival of its master and liberator. For with them there is no solicitude, no anxiety for food and clothing. There is only the expectation of the coming of Christ in the singing of hymns. (8) Consequently, when one of them lacks something necessary, he does not go to a town or a village or to a brother or friend or relation or to parents or children or family to procure what he needs, for his will alone is sufficient. When he raises his hands to God in supplication and utters words of thanksgiving with his lips, all these things are provided for him in a miraculous way.

(9) Why should we speak at length about their faith in Christ, seeing that it can even move mountains? For many of them have stopped the flow of rivers and crossed the Nile dry shod. They have slain wild beasts. They have performed cures, miracles, and acts of power like those that the holy prophets and apostles worked. The Savior performs miracles through them in the same way. Indeed, it is clear to all who dwell there that through them, the world is kept in being and that through them, too, human life is preserved and honored by God.

(10) I also saw another vast company of monks of all ages living in the desert and in the countryside. Their number is past counting. There are so many of them that an earthly emperor could not assemble so large an army. For there is no town or village in Egypt and the Thebaid that is not surrounded by hermitages as if by walls. And the people depend on the prayers of these monks as if on God himself. Some of them live in desert caves, others in more remote places. (11) All of them everywhere by trying to outdo each other demonstrate their wonderful ascetic discipline. Those in the remotest places make strenuous efforts for fear anyone else should surpass them in ascetic practices. Those living near towns or villages make equal efforts, though evil troubles them on every side, in case they should be considered inferior to their remoter brethren.

(12) Accordingly, since I have derived much benefit from these monks, I have undertaken this work to provide a paradigm and a testimony for the perfect and to edify and benefit those who are only beginners in the ascetic life. (13) Therefore, if God wills, I shall begin this account with a description of the way of life of the holy and great fathers and show that even in these times the Savior performs through them what he performed through the prophets and apostles. For the same Lord now and always works all things in all men (cf. Heb 13:8; 1 Cor 12:6).

1. ON JOHN OF LYCOPOLIS

(1) In the territory of Lyco in the Thebaid, we visited the great and blessed John, a truly holy and virtuous man. From what he did it was obvious to everyone that he possessed the gift of clairvoyance. To the most pious Emperor Theodosius, he not only pre-

dicted everything that God was going to bring about in the world, but also indicated the outcome, foretelling the rebellion of the tyrants against him and their subsequent swift destruction and also the annihilation of the barbarians who had burst into the empire.

(2) A similar story is told of a general who went to see him to inquire whether he would overcome the Ethiopians, who at that time had fallen on Syene—which stands on the frontier of the Thebaid—and had devastated the surrounding country. John said to him, "If you march against them, you will take them by surprise and defeat them and subdue them, and you will find favor with the emperors." And that is what actually happened, the event proving as John had predicted. He also said, "The most Christian Emperor Theodosius will die a natural death."

(3) The fact that this father really did have an extraordinary gift or clairvoyance was corroborated for us by the fathers who lived near him, whose way of life is held in high esteem by all the people of that region. Whatever they said about the man was not in the least embellished to enhance his reputation, but on the contrary tended to be understated.

(4) For example, a tribune went to see him and begged him to allow his wife to visit him, too. She desired very much to see him because she was about to go upstream to Syene and wanted the father to intercede for her and send her on her way with a blessing. The father, however, who was about ninety years old and had not seen a woman throughout the forty years that he had already spent in the cave, neither going out himself nor allowing a woman to come into his sight, refused to see the tribune's wife. (5) As a matter of fact, not even male visitors ever entered into his cave. He merely gave his blessing through the window and in this way greeted those who came and spoke with each of them about his personal affairs.

(6) The tribune, however, persisted in pressing him to send for his wife—for the father lived on the desert escarpment about five miles from the city. But John would not agree. He said that such a visit was out of the question and sent the man away crestfallen. Despite this, his wife did not stop pestering him every

day, swearing on oath that under no circumstances would she set out on the journey without seeing the prophet. (7) The woman's oath was reported to the blessed John by her husband. Perceiving her faith, he said to the tribune, "I shall appear to her tonight in a dream, and then she must not still be determined to see my face in the flesh" (cf. Col 2:1). The man told his wife what the father had said. (8) And, indeed, while she slept the woman saw the prophet coming toward her. He said to her, " 'Woman, what have I to do with you?' (John 2:4). Why have you desired to see my face? Am I a prophet, or do I stand in the ranks of the just? I am a sinful man and of like passions with you (cf. Acts 14:15). Nevertheless I have prayed for you and for your husband's household, that you may walk in peace according to your faith." With these words, he disappeared.

(9) When the woman woke up, she repeated to her husband what the prophet had said and described his appearance. Then she sent a message of thanks to him by her husband. When he saw him again, the blessed John anticipated his news, saying to him, "See, I have fulfilled your request. When I saw her, I gave her confidence no longer to desire to see me but to go on her journey in peace."

(10) The wife of another high-ranking officer was expecting a baby. While her husband was away, on the very day when he was speaking with Father John, she gave birth, and losing consciousness, hovered on the brink of death. The saint announced this to her husband, saying, " 'If you knew the gift of God' (John 4:10), namely, that a son has been born to you today, you would glorify God. His mother, however, has come very near to losing her life. When you go home, you will find the child seven days old, and you will name him John. Bring him up in the knowledge of God, and when he has reached his seventh year, send him to the monks in the desert."

(11) These are the wonders that he performed before strangers who came to see him. As regards his own fellow citizens, who frequently came to him for their needs, he foreknew and revealed things hidden in the future; he told each man what he had done in secret, and he predicted the rise and fall of the Nile and the annual yield of the crops. In the same way, he

used to foretell when some divine threat was going to come upon them and exposed those who were to blame for it.

(12) The blessed John himself did not perform cures publicly. More often he gave oil to the afflicted and healed them in that way. For example, the wife of a senator who had lost her sight through developing cataracts on her corneas asked her husband to take her to the saint. When he told her that the saint had never spoken with a woman, she begged only that he should be told about her and offer a prayer for her. This he did and moreover sent her some oil. She bathed her eyes in the oil only three times, and on the third day regained her sight and publicly thanked God.

(13) But what need is there to speak of any of the works of this saint other than those that we perceived with our own eyes? We were seven brothers, all of us foreign, who went up to see him. When he had embraced us and welcomed each of us with a bright smiling countenance, we asked him at once, before anything else, to say a prayer for us. For this is the custom of the Egyptian fathers. (14) He, however, asked whether anyone in our party was a cleric. When we all replied that none of us was, he looked at us all in turn and knew who was secretly in orders. And, indeed, one of us had been raised to the diaconate, though only one of the brethren was aware of this, and he had told him not to tell anyone for the sake of humility and because in comparison with such saints, he scarcely considered himself to be worthy of the name of Christian, let alone the rank of deacon. Then pointing to him, the saint declared, "This one is a deacon." (15) But as the brother continued to deny it and tried to remain concealed, the saint reached out through the window, took his hand and kissed it, and admonished him, saying, "Do not spurn the grace of God, my child, and do not lie by denying the gift of Christ. For a lie is something alien, regardless of whether its matter is grave or light. And even if one lies with the intention of attaining some good, it is nevertheless not praiseworthy, for the Savior said that a lie 'comes of evil' (Matt 5:37; John 8:44)." The brother, having been proved wrong, remained silent and accepted his mild rebuke.

(16) We then prayed, and when we had finished praying, one of our number, who had already been suffering from a fever for three days, asked to be healed. The father said to him that for the present this affliction was to his advantage and had come to him because of the weakness of his faith. However, he gave him some oil and told him to rub himself with it. When he did this, he brought up through his mouth all that was in his stomach and, delivered of the fever, walked to the guest cell without any assistance.

(17) One could see the saint already in his ninetieth year with his body so completely worn out by his *askesis* that even his beard no longer grew on his face. For he ate nothing apart from fruit, and after sunset at that, in spite of his advanced age, having formerly lived a life of great ascetic discipline. And he never ate bread or anything that needed to be cooked.

(18) When he invited us to sit down, we thanked God for our meeting with him. He for his part, after welcoming us like his own dear children after a long absence, addressed us with a smiling face in the following words: "Where are you from, my children? Which country have you traveled from to visit a poor man?" (19) We told him where we were from, adding, "We have come to you from Jerusalem for the good of our souls so that what we have heard with our ears we might perceive with our eyes—for the ears are naturally less reliable than the eyes—and because very often forgetfulness follows what we hear, whereas the memory of what we have seen is not easily erased but remains imprinted on our minds like a picture."

(20) The blessed John replied, "And what remarkable thing did you expect to find, my dearest children, that you have undertaken such a long journey with so much labor in your desire to visit some poor simple men who possess nothing worth seeing or admiring? Those who are worthy of admiration and praise are everywhere: the apostles and prophets of God, who are read in the churches. They are the ones you must imitate. (21) I marvel at your zeal," he said, "how taking no account of so many dangers you have come to us to be edified, while we from laziness do not even wish to come out of our cave.

(22) "Well now," he said, "even though your undertaking deserves praise, do not imagine that you

have done enough, that you have achieved something good, but imitate the virtues that our fathers are practicing. And if you have attained them all, which is rare, do not on that account trust in yourselves. For some who have been confident in this way and have approached the very summit of the virtues have, in the end, fallen from their position of eminence. (23) On the contrary, be sure that your prayers are going well, that the purity of your understanding has not been sullied, that your mind does not suffer distractions when it appears before God in prayer, lest any untoward thought insinuate itself into your mind and turn it toward something else, lest any recollection of indecent images disturb your understanding. (24) Be sure that you have renounced the world according to God's truth, that you have not come 'to spy out our liberty' (Gal 2:4), that you are not hunting out our virtues for the sake of vainglory, so that like men displaying their talents, you may appear to others to be imitators of our works. (25) Be sure that no passion disturbs you or honor and glory and human praise, or the simulation of priestly virtue and self-love, or the thought that you are righteous, or boasting about righteousness, or the memory of any of your relatives when you pray, or the recollection of some happy experience or of any other emotion, or even the remembrance of the world itself as a whole. Otherwise the entire undertaking becomes pointless when, in conversing with the Lord, one is seduced by opposing thoughts.

(26) "Everyone who has not renounced the world fully and completely but chases after its attractions suffers from this spiritual instability. His preoccupations, being bodily and earthly, distract his mind through the many enterprises in which he is engaged. And then, absorbed in his struggle against the passions, he cannot see God. However, one should not try to explore this knowledge in any great depth, for fear that one should be granted some small part of it and being unworthy of such a gift should think that one has apprehended the whole and so fall away utterly to perdition. (27) On the contrary, it is necessary that one should always approach God in a moderate and devout manner, making spiritual progress according to one's capacity and within the bounds permitted to men. The will, then, of those who seek God must be free from all other concerns. For Scripture says, 'Be still and know that I am God' (Ps 46:10). (28) Therefore, he who has been granted a partial knowledge of God—for it is not possible for the whole of such knowledge to be received by anyone— also attains to the knowledge of all other things. He sees mysteries, for God shows him them; he foresees what belongs to the future; he contemplates revelations like the saints did; he performs mighty works; he becomes a friend of God and obtains from God everything he asks."

(29) The saint taught us much else about *askesis,* including the following: "One should await death as a transition to a happy life and not look ahead to the feebleness of the body. And one should not fill the belly even with ordinary things—for a man," he said, "who is satiated suffers the same temptations as those who live in luxury—but try through *askesis* to free the appetites from passion. And let no one seek his ease and convenience but let him be strong now and suffer affliction that he may inherit the breadth of the kingdom of Christ. (30) For Scripture says, 'We must through much tribulation enter into the kingdom' (Acts 14:22); 'Because strait is the gate and narrow is the way that leads to life, and few there be that find it' (Matt 7:14); and, 'Wide is the gate and broad is the way that leads to destruction, and many there be which go through it' (Matt 7:13). Why should we be fainthearted," he said, "in this life, seeing that a little later we shall go to eternal rest?" (31) And again: "One should not be puffed up about one's own achievements but always be humble and flee to the farthest parts of the desert if one realizes that one is becoming proud. For living near villages has often harmed even the perfect. That is why David after a similar experience, sings, 'Lo, I flee far off and have taken up my abode in the desert; I wait for God who delivers me from faintheartedness and tempest' (cf. Ps 55:7, 8). Many of our own brethren have experienced something similar and through arrogance have failed to reach their goal.

(32) "For example, there was a monk," he said, "who lived in a cave in the nearer desert and had given proof of the strongest ascetic discipline. He obtained

his daily bread by the work of his own hands. But because he persevered with his prayers and made progress in the virtues, he came eventually to trust in himself, placing his reliance on his good way of life. (33) Then the Tempter asked for him, as he did with Job, and in the evening presented him the image of a beautiful woman lost in the desert. Finding the door open, she darted into the cave, and throwing herself at the man's knees, begged him to give her shelter since darkness had overtaken her. He took pity on her, which he should not have done, and received her as a guest in his cave. Moreover, he asked her about her journey. She told him how she had lost her way and sowed in him words of flattery and deceit. She kept on talking to him for some time and somehow gently enticed him to fall in love with her. The conversation became much freer, and there was laughter and hilarity. (34) With so much talking, she led him astray. Then she began to touch his hand and beard and neck. And finally she made the ascetic her prisoner. As for him, his mind seethed with evil thoughts as he calculated that the matter was already within his grasp and that he had the opportunity and the freedom to fulfill his pleasure. He then consented inwardly and, in the end, tried to unite himself with her sexually. He was frantic by now, like an excited stallion eager to mount a mare. (35) But suddenly she gave a loud cry and vanished from his clutches, slipping away like a shadow. And the air resounded with a great peal of laughter. It was the demons who had led him astray with their deception, rebuking him and calling out with a loud voice, '"Whosoever exalts himself shall be abased" (Luke 14:11; 18:14). You once exalted yourself to the heavens, but now you have been humiliated and brought down to the depths.'

(36) "In the morning he got up, dragging behind him the miserable experience of the night. He spent the whole day in lamentation, and then, despairing of his own salvation, which is something he should not have done, he went back to the world. For this is what the evil one generally does: when he overcomes someone, he makes him lose his judgment, that afterward he should no longer be able to raise himself up.

"Therefore, my children, it is not in our interest to have our dwellings near inhabited places or to associate with women. For meetings of this kind give rise to an unexpungeable memory, which we draw from what we have seen and from what we have heard in conversation. And we must not despair of our salvation and bring ourselves to a state of despondency. For even now many of those who have despaired have not been deprived of the love of God, who is always merciful.

(37) "For example," he said, "there was another young man in the city who had done many evil deeds and had sinned gravely. At God's bidding, this youth was struck by compunction for his many sins. He made straight for the cemetery, where he bitterly lamented his former life, throwing himself down on his face and not daring to make a sound or to pronounce the name of God or to entreat him, for he considered himself unworthy even of life itself. While still living, he incarcerated himself among the tombs, and renouncing his own life, did nothing but lie underground and groan from the depths of his heart.

(38) "After a week had gone by, some of the demons that had earlier done such great harm to his life appeared to him in the night, calling out and saying, 'Where is that abominable fellow? Now that he has really satiated himself with his debaucheries, he has, at an inopportune time for us, suddenly turned chaste and good, and when he is no longer able to do so wishes to be a Christian and a clean liver. But what good does he expect to attain, laden as he is with our vices? (39) Will you not get up and leave this place at once? Will you not go back with us to your old haunts? Whores and tavern keepers are waiting for you. Will you not come and indulge your desires, since every other hope has been extinguished for you? Judgment will inevitably come upon you quickly if you destroy yourself in this way. Why do you hasten toward your punishment, you wretched man? Why do you strive so hard to make your condemnation come quickly?' And there was much else that they said, for instance: 'You belong to us; you are bound to us; you have practiced every kind of lawlessness; you have become subject to us all, and do you dare to escape? Have you no answer? Do you not agree? Will you not come away with us?' (40) But he simply went on groaning, neither listening to them nor answering them a single word, al-

though the demons stayed with him for a considerable time. Since they gained nothing by repeating the same things over and over again, the wicked demons seized hold of him and tortured his whole body savagely. And having lacerated him and tormented him cruelly, they went away leaving him half dead.

(41) "When he recovered consciousness, he continued to lie where they had left him, as motionless as before, and began groaning again. In the meantime, his relations had been searching for him. When they found him and learned from him the cause of his terrible physical state, they thought it best to take him home. (42) But although they tried to force him many times, he strongly resisted them. Again the following night the demons put him to the same tortures, but even worse than before. And again in the same way his own people tried to persuade him to move to another place. But he said that it was better to die rather than live a life polluted by such defilements.

(43) "On the third night the demons came very near to killing the man altogether. They fell on him mercilessly with tortures and maltreated him to his last breath. When they saw that he would not surrender, they withdrew, leaving him, however, senseless. As they departed, they cried out, saying, 'You have won; you have won; you have won.' And nothing frightening ever happened to him again. On the contrary, he dwelt in the tomb as a pure man without any defilement for as long as he lived, practicing the virtue of purity. In this way, he was not only held in honor by God, but also gave such striking proof of the power to work miracles that he excited admiration in many and stimulated zeal in them for good works. (44) As a result of this, a great number of those who had utterly despaired of themselves pursued good practices and lived a virtuous life. They realized in their own lives the text of Scripture that says, 'Whosoever humbles himself shall be exalted' (cf. Luke 14:11; 18:14). And so, my children, first of all let us discipline ourselves to attain humility, since this is the essential foundation of all virtues. At the same time, the remoter desert is also profitable to us for the practice of *askesis*.

(45) "For example, there was another monk who had settled in the farther desert and had practiced the

virtues for many years. Now it happened that in his old age he was tested by the assault of demons. For this ascetic was particularly devoted to stillness. Spending his days as he did in prayer and hymnody and much contemplation, he saw clear visions of a divine nature, sometimes while fully awake, and sometimes while asleep. (46) He had almost succeeded in laying hold of the traces of the incorporeal life (cf. 1 Tim 6:12). For he did not cultivate the soil; he did not worry about what he had to eat; he did not seek to satisfy his bodily needs with plants, not even with grass; and he did not go hunting for birds or any other animals. Instead, from the day when he abandoned the world for the desert, he was filled with confidence in God and took no thought how his body should find nourishment. On the contrary, oblivious to everything, he voluntarily kept himself in the presence of God by a perfect desire and awaited his departure from the world. He was nourished, for the most part, with the delight of what is hoped for and not seen (cf. Heb 11:1). And neither was his body exhausted by the long duration of this regime, nor did his soul lose heart. On the contrary, he maintained this good state of life in a sober manner.

(47) "However, since God held him in honor, at a prescribed time every two or three days he made a loaf appear on the table, a real loaf that could be eaten. And so whenever the monk felt the pangs of hunger and went into the cave, he found food. After prostrating and eating well, he used to go back to his hymns, persevering patiently with prayer and contemplation. He grew spiritually every day, adding to his present virtue and future hope and always advancing toward something better. But he came to be almost certain that the better portion was indeed his, as if he already had it in his grasp. And once this had happened, it only needed a little to make him fall as a result of the temptation that was to come to him afterward. (48) Why do we not say that he narrowly avoided falling? Because when he came to this presumption, he began without realizing it to think that he was superior to most men and that he had attained something greater than others, and having arrived at this opinion, he began to trust in himself. (49) Before long, there was born in him first of all some small in-

dolence, so small as not to seem to be indolence at all. Then there developed a more serious negligence. Then it became just perceptible. For he became more reluctant to rise from sleep and sing hymns. The work of prayer now became more sluggish. The singing of psalms was not so prolonged. The soul," said John, "wished to rest. The mind turned its gaze earthward. Thoughts became subject to distractions. And perhaps, in the secret recesses of his heart, he began to plan some wickedness.

"The habits, however, that the ascetic had acquired in the past, the momentum, as it were, of his initial effort, still restrained him in some way and for the moment kept him safe. (50) One day, coming in toward the evening after his customary prayers, he found the bread on the table that God had provided for him and refreshed himself. But from this point onward, he did not shake off those reductions of the time he gave to prayer, nor did he think that these oversights harmed his zeal. On the contrary, he supposed it a trivial matter to be only just short of failing in his obligations. (51) As a result of this, a powerful sensual desire seized him and diverted him by evil thoughts toward the world. However, for the moment, he checked himself until the following day and turned to his customary *askesis*. Then having prayed and sung hymns, he went into the cave and found the bread lying there, now not so white or well prepared but looking rather gray. He was surprised and a little dismayed; nevertheless, he partook and was refreshed.

(52) "The third night came, and the evil returned three times more fiercely than before. His mind fell upon the thoughts with even greater alacrity, while his memory composed an image like that of a woman actually present and lying with him. He had the whole scene in front of his eyes as if all along he was actually performing the act. However, on the third day, he came out again to do his work and to pray and sing hymns, but he could no longer keep his thoughts pure. On the contrary, he felt unsettled and turned about restlessly, glancing this way and that. For the memory of his reflections interrupted his good work. (53) In the evening, he went back in, feeling the need to eat some bread. He found the loaf on the table, but

it looked as if it had been gnawed by mice or dogs; all that remained was a part of the outer crust. He then groaned and wept, but not as much as he should have done, not as much as was needed to check the evil. And since he had not eaten as much as he wanted, he was unable to sleep. (54) The thoughts then returned in throngs, enveloping him on all sides and battling against his understanding, and quickly taking him prisoner, they dragged him back to the world. Then getting up, he set off for the inhabited region, traveling by night through the desert.

"When dawn broke, the settled region was still far away, but he toiled on, suffering from the burning heat of the sun. He began to look around him, scanning the horizon on all sides to see if a monastery would appear where he could go and refresh himself. (55) As it happened, a monastery did appear. Some pious and faithful brethren received him, and treating him like their true father, washed his face and his feet. Then, after saying a prayer, they prepared a table and invited him with love to partake of whatever they had. When he had eaten his fill, the brethren asked him to speak a word of salvation to them and tell them by what means they could be saved from the snare of the devil (cf. 1 Tim 3:7), and how they should overcome shameful thoughts. (56) He, like a father admonishing his children, encouraged them to persevere with their labors, because in a little while they would depart and enjoy ample rest. And telling them many other things about the ascetic life, he edified them greatly.

"When he had finished his admonition, he reflected silently for a moment that although he had counseled others, he had remained without counsel himself. (57) Then his own failure struck his conscience, and he set off into the desert again at a run, bewailing himself and saying, 'Unless the Lord had been my help, my soul had almost dwelt in hell' (Ps 94:17); and, 'I was almost in all evil' (Prov 5:14); and, 'They had almost consumed me upon earth' (Ps 119:87). We may apply to his case the text that says, 'A brother helped by a brother is like a strong city and like an impregnable wall' (cf. Prov 18:19). (58) From that time he spent the rest of his life in sorrow, bereft of the meal that came from God and gaining his bread by his labor. He shut himself in the cave, and spreading sackcloth and ashes under him, did not rise up from the ground or cease lamenting until he heard the voice of an angel saying to him in a dream, 'God has accepted your repentance and has had mercy on you. In the future, take care that you are not deceived. The brethren to whom you gave spiritual counsel will come to console you, and they will bring you gifts. Welcome them, eat with them, and always give thanks to God.'

(59) "I have narrated these things to you, my children, that whether you consider yourselves to be among the little ones or the great ones, you may make humility your chief aim in the ascetic life—for this is the first commandment of the Savior, who says, 'Blessed are the poor in spirit, for theirs is the kingdom of heaven' (Matt 5:3)—and that you may not be deceived by the demons, who raise up images before you. (60) No, if someone should come to you, whether brother or friend or sister or wife or father or teacher or mother or child or servant, first stretch out your hands in prayer, and if it is a phantasm, it will flee from you. If either demons or men seek to deceive you by flattery and praise, do not believe them and do not become conceited. (61) As for me, the demons have often tried to deceive me in this way in the hours of darkness and have not allowed me either to pray or to rest raising up images before me throughout the night. And in the morning they have mocked me, falling at my feet and saying, 'Forgive us, Abba, for having troubled you all night.' But I said to them, "'Depart from me, all you workers of iniquity" (Ps 6:8; Matt 7:23), for you shall not tempt a servant of God' (cf. Matt 4:7).

(62) "And so you, too, my children, should cultivate stillness and ceaselessly train yourselves for contemplation, that when you pray to God, you may do so with a pure mind. For an ascetic is good if he is constantly training himself in the world, if he shows brotherly love and practices hospitality and charity, if he gives alms and is generous to visitors, if he helps the sick and does not give offense to anyone. (63) He is good, he is exceedingly good, for he is a man who puts the commandments into practice and does them. But he is occupied with earthly things. Better and

greater than he is the contemplative, who has risen from active works to the spiritual sphere and has left it to others to be anxious about earthly things. Since he has not only denied himself but even become forgetful of himself, he is concerned with the things of heaven. He stands unimpeded in the presence of God, without any anxiety holding him back. For such a man spends his life with God; he is occupied with God and praises him with ceaseless hymnody."

(64) The blessed John narrated these things to us and much else besides, conversing with us for three days until the ninth hour and healing our souls. Then he gave us gifts and told us to go in peace, uttering a prophecy that "Today the victory proclamation of the pious Emperor Theodosius has arrived in Alexandria announcing the destruction of the tyrant Eugenius" and that "The emperor will die a natural death." These things truly happened as he said.

(65) We then went to see a number of other fathers, and while we were with them, some brothers came to tell us that the blessed John had died in a wonderful manner. He gave orders that for three days no one would be allowed to visit him, and then, bending his knees in prayer, he died and departed for God, to whom be glory for all eternity. Amen.

20. ON DIOSCORUS

(1) We visited another priest in the Thebaid called Dioscorus, the father of a hundred monks. He used to say to those who were intending to approach the grace of God, "Take care that no one who has pondered on the image of a woman during the night dare to approach the sacred Mysteries, in case any of you has had a dream while entertaining such an image.

(2) "For seminal emissions do take place unconsciously without the stimulus of imagined forms, occurring not from deliberate choice but involuntarily. They arise naturally and flow forth from an excess of matter. They are therefore not to be classed as sinful. But imaginings are the result of deliberate choice and are a sign of an evil disposition.

(3) "Now a monk," he said, " must even transcend the law of nature and must certainly not fall into the

slightest pollution of the flesh. On the contrary, he must mortify the flesh and not allow an excess of seminal fluid to accumulate. We should therefore try to keep the fluid depleted by the prolongation of fasting. Otherwise, it arouses our sensual appetites.

(4) "A monk must have nothing whatever to do with the sensual appetites. Otherwise how would he differ from men living in the world? We often see laymen abstaining from pleasures for the sake of their health or for some other rational motive. How much more should the monk take care of the health of his soul and his mind and his spirit."

ON THE MONKS OF NITRIA

(5) We also put in at Nitria, where we saw many great anchorites. Some of them were natives of that region, others were foreigners. They excelled each other in the virtues and engaged in rivalry over their ascetic practices, giving proof of all the virtues and struggling to surpass each other in their manner of life. (6) Some applied themselves to contemplation, others to the active life. When a group of them saw us approaching from a distance through the desert, some came to meet us with water, others washed our feet, and others laundered our clothes. Some of them invited us to a meal, others to learn about the virtues, and others to contemplation and the knowledge of God. Whatever ability each one had, he hastened to use it for our benefit. Indeed, how can one relate all their virtues, since one is totally unable to do them justice?

(7) They inhabit a desert place and have their cells some distance from each other, so that no one should be recognized from afar by another or be seen easily or hear another's voice. On the contrary, they live in profound silence, each monk isolated on his own. They come together in the churches only on Saturdays and Sundays and meet one another. Many of them who die in their cells are often not found for four days because they do not see each other except at the *Synaxis*. (8) Some of them, living as they do so far apart from each other, travel three or four miles to the *Synaxis*. They have so much love for each other

and for other monks, too, that when, as often happens, many come desiring to attain salvation by joining them, each one hastens to give them his own hermitage as a temporary cell.

(9) I also visited one of the fathers there called Ammonius, who possessed beautifully constructed cells with a courtyard, a well, and other necessary things. Once a brother came to him, eager to attain salvation. He asked Ammonius to assign him a cell to live in, whereupon the father at once went out, ordering the brother not to leave the cells until he should find him suitable accommodation. And leaving him all he had, together with the cells themselves, he immured himself in a small cell some distance away.

(10) If there were many who came to him wishing to be saved, he called together the whole community, and giving bricks to one and water to another, completed the new cells in a single day. (11) Those who intended to live in the cells were invited to the church for a feast. And while they were still enjoying themselves, each brother filled his cloak or his basket with loaves or other suitable things from his own cell and brought them to the new ones, so that no one should know which gifts had been brought by which brother. When those who were to live in the cells returned to them in the evening, they were surprised to find everything that they needed.

(12) We saw there a father called Didymus, a man of advanced years with a charming countenance. He used to kill scorpions, horned vipers, and asps with his bare feet. Nobody else dared do this. Many others who thought they could do the same were killed by the creatures as soon as they touched them.

(13) We also saw another father of monks called Cronides, who had reached a tremendous age. He was a hundred and ten years old, having been one of Antony's original companions. He delivered many admonitions and spiritual discourses to us, but such was the humility that he had guarded right into old age that he considered himself a nonentity.

(14) We also saw three brothers who were very fine men. Because of their virtuous way of life, they were under compulsion to become bishops. Their great piety, however, drove them to cut off their ears. This was a very daring thing that they did—although

their motive was good—so that no one should bother them in the future.

(15) We also visited Evagrius, a wise and learned man who was skilled in the discernment of thoughts, an ability he had acquired by experience. He often went down to Alexandria and refuted the pagan philosophers in disputations. (16) This father exhorted the brothers who were with us not to satiate themselves with water. "For the demons," he said, "frequently light on well-watered places." He taught us much else about *askesis,* strengthening our souls.

(17) Many of them ate neither bread nor fruit but only endives. Some of them never slept at night, but either sitting or standing persevered in prayer until morning.

21. ON MACARIUS

(1) Many of the fathers who lived there told us about the life of Macarius, the disciple of Antony, who had only just died. Like Antony, he had performed so many miracles and cures and works of power that one could not possibly describe them all. However, we shall record a few of his achievements, relating them briefly.

(2) Once he saw some choice palm leaves lying beside Father Antony, with which the great man was working, and asked him for a bundle of them. Antony said to him, "It is written, 'you shall not covet your neighbor's goods' (cf. Exod 20:17). And as soon as he said this, all the leaves immediately shriveled up as if they had been parched by fire. On seeing this, Antony said to Macarius, "See, my spirit has come to rest on you, and you will now be the heir to my virtues."

(3) Some time after this, the devil found Macarius in the desert physically exhausted and said to him, "Look, you have received the grace of Antony. Why not use this privilege and ask God for food and strength for your journey?" Macarius replied, "'The Lord is my strength and my song' (Ps 118:14). As for you, you shall not tempt the servant of God." (4) The devil then conjured up a mirage for him, a baggage camel lost in the desert and laden with all kinds of useful provisions. When she saw Macarius, she came

and couched in front of him. But realizing that this was a phantasm, which indeed it was, he began to pray. And immediately the camel was swallowed up into the ground.

(5) Another time after much fasting and prayer, he asked God to show him the paradise that Jannes and Jambres had planted in the desert in their desire to make a copy of the true paradise (cf. Exod 7:11–12; 1 Tim 3:8). (6) When he had wandered through the desert for three weeks, and not having eaten during this time was already fainting, an angel set him near the place. There were demons everywhere guarding the entrances of the paradise and not allowing him to enter. The garden was very large, covering an enormous area.

(7) After he had prayed, he made a bold effort and succeeded in entering. Inside the garden he found two holy men. They had entered by the same means themselves and had already spent a considerable time there. When they had said a prayer, they embraced each other, overjoyed at the meeting. Then they washed his feet and set before him some of the fruit of paradise. He partook and gave thanks to God, marveling at the size of the fruit and its varied colours. And they said to each other, "How good it would be if all the monks were here." (8) "In the middle of the paradise," he said, "there were three large springs that welled up from the depths and watered the garden and its huge trees, which were very productive and bore every kind of fruit that exists under the heavens."

(9) When he had stayed with them for seven days, Macarius asked if he could go back to the settled region and bring the monks with him. But those holy men said to him that he could not do this. For the desert was a vast trackless waste, and there were many demons in every part of it who made monks lose their way and destroyed them, so that many others who had often wished to come had perished. (10) But Macarius could not bear to remain here any longer and said, "I must bring them here that they might enjoy this delight." He set off in haste for the settled region, carrying some of the fruit as proof. And taking with him a large bundle of palm branches, he planted them as markers in the desert so that he should not lose his way

when he came back. (11) Then he slept for a while in the desert, and when he woke up he found that all the palm branches had been gathered up by the demons and placed by his head. Then getting up, he said to them, "If it is the will of God, you cannot prevent us from entering into the garden."

(12) When he arrived at the settled region, he kept showing the fruit to the monks to persuade them to come away to the paradise. Many fathers gathered round him and said to him, "Could it not be that this paradise has come into being for the destruction of our souls? For if we were to enjoy it in this life, we should have received our portion of good things while still on earth. What reward would we have afterward when we come into the presence of God? For what kind of virtue shall we be recompensed?" And they persuaded Macarius not to return.

(13) Another time he was sent some fresh grapes. He desired to eat them, but showing self-control, he sent them to a certain brother who was ill and who was himself fond of grapes. When the brother received them, he was delighted, but wishing to conceal his self-mastery, he sent them to another brother, pretending that he had no appetite for any food. When the next brother received the grapes, he did the same, in turn, although he too had a great desire to eat them.

(14) When at length the grapes had been passed round a large number of the brethren without any of them deciding to eat them, the last one to receive them sent them again to Macarius, thinking that he was giving him a rich gift. Macarius recognized them and after inquiring closely into what had happened, marveled, giving thanks to the Lord for such self-control among the brethren. And in the end not even he partook of the grapes.

(15) Another time, they say, Macarius was praying in his cave in the desert. There happened to be another cave nearby that was the den of a hyena. While he was at prayer, the hyena suddenly appeared and began to lick his feet. And taking him gently by the hem of his tunic, she drew him toward her own cave. He followed her saying, "I wonder what this animal wants to do?" (16) When she had led him to her own cave, she went in and brought out to him her own

cubs, which had been born blind. He prayed over them and returned them to the hyena with their sight healed. She, in turn, by way of a thank offering, brought the man the huge skin of a large ram and laid it at his feet. He smiled at her as if at a kind and sensitive person, and taking the skin, spread it under him. This skin is still in the possession of one of the brothers.

(17) They also tell the following story of him. A certain evildoer had, by magic arts, transformed a girl who had consecrated her virginity into a mare. Her parents brought her to him and begged him, if he would be so kind, to change her back into a woman by his prayers. Accordingly, he shut her up on her own for seven days, her parents staying nearby, while he occupied himself with prayer in another cell. On the seventh day, he went in with her parents and rubbed her all over with oil. Then he bent his knees and prayed with them, and when they got up they found her transformed back into a young girl.

22. ON AMOUN

(1) Before Macarius, there was a Nitrian monk called Amoun, whose soul Antony saw borne up to heaven. He was the first of the monks to settle in Nitria. He was of noble birth and had rich parents, who forced him to marry against his will. When they had compelled him to do this, he persuaded the girl in the bridal chamber that they should both preserve their virginity in secret. (2) A few days later he departed for Nitria, while she for her part exhorted all her servants to adopt the celibate life and, indeed, converted her house into a monastery.

(3) Now when he was living as a solitary in Nitria, a child suffering from rabies was brought to him, bound with a chain, for a rabid dog had bitten him and given him the disease. His suffering was so unbearable that his whole body was convulsed by it. (4) When Amoun saw the child's parents coming to entreat him, he said, "Why are you troubling me, my friends, seeking something that is beyond my merits, when the remedy lies in your own hands? Give back to the widow the ox that you have killed surrepti-

tiously, and your child will be restored to you in good health." Their crime having thus been exposed, they happily did what they had been told, and when the father prayed, the child instantly recovered.

(5) Another time some people came to visit him. To test their inward dispositions, the saint said to them, "Bring me a storage jar that I may have an ample supply of water for the reception of visitors." They promised to bring him a jar, but when they came to the village, one of them changed his mind and said to the other, "I am not going to kill my camel; she would die if I loaded a storage jar onto her." (6) The other, when he heard this, yoked his asses together and with much labor transported the jar. Before he could speak Amoun said, "What has happened that your companion's camel has died, while you have made your way here?" When the man returned, he found that the camel had been devoured by wolves.

(7) The saint did many other miracles in the sight of all. Once some monks were sent to him by Antony to fetch him, for Antony was in the farther desert. When they were on their way back, they came to a branch of the Nile. The brothers suddenly saw Amoun transported to the opposite bank, but they themselves crossed over by swimming. (8) When they came to where Antony was, he spoke first to Amoun, saying, "God has revealed to me many things concerning you, and he has manifested your departure from this life. I therefore felt compelled to summon you to me that we might enjoy each other's company and intercede for each other." (9) Then he set him at a spot some distance away and ordered him not to leave it until he departed this life. When he died, completely alone, Antony saw his soul borne up to heaven by angels.

23. ON MACARIUS OF ALEXANDRIA

(1) They say that there was another Macarius who was the first to build a hermitage in Scetis. This place is a wasteland lying at a distance of a day's and a night's journey from Nitria through the desert. It is a very perilous journey for travelers. For if one makes even a small error, one can get lost in the desert and find one's life in danger. All the monks there have at-

tained perfection. Indeed, no one beset with imperfections could stay in that place, since it is rugged and inhospitable, lacking all the necessities of life.

(2) Now this Macarius whom I have mentioned, who was a native of the capital city, one day met with the great Macarius. Since they both had to cross the Nile, it so happened that they boarded a very large ferry that two tribunes had also boarded with much commotion. They had a chariot covered entirely in bronze and horses with gold bridles and a military escort and servants appareled in collars and gold cinctures. (3) When the tribunes saw the monks sitting in the corner dressed in old rags, they blessed their simplicity of life. One of these tribunes said to them, "Blessed (*makarioi*) are you who have mocked the world." (4) Macarius of Alexandria said to him, "We have mocked the world, but the world mocks you. You should know that you have said this not of your own accord but by prophetic inspiration. For we are both called Macarius." The tribune, moved to compunction by this remark, went home and took off his uniform, and after a generous distribution of alms chose to live as a monk.

24. ON PAUL

(1) There was a disciple of Antony called Paul, who was surnamed "the Simple." He caught his wife in the very act of adultery, and without saying a word to anyone set off into the desert to find Antony. And falling at his knees, he begged him to let him live with him because he wished to be saved. Antony said to him, "You can be saved if you have obedience; whatever I tell you, that is what you will do." Paul replied, "I shall do everything you command." (2) To test his inward disposition Antony said to him, "Stand on this spot and pray while I go in and fetch some work for you to do." He went into the cave and watched Paul through the window. The latter remained motionless on that spot the whole week, roasting in the sun.

(3) At the end of the week, he came out and said to him, "Come and have something to eat." When he had prepared the table and set out the food, he said, "Sit down and do not eat until the evening; simply

keep watch over the dishes." (4) When it was evening and Paul had still not eaten, Antony said to him, "Get up and pray and then lie down and sleep." Leaving the table, Paul did as he was told. At midnight Antony woke him up for prayer and prolonged the prayers until the ninth hour of the day. He then set the table and again ordered him to eat. (5) As Paul was about to take his third morsel of bread, Antony commanded him to get up without touching any water, and sent him out to wander in the desert, saying to him, "Come back after three days."

(6) After he had returned, some brothers came to visit Antony. Paul watched the father to see what tasks he would set him. Antony said to him, "Serve the brethren in silence and do not taste anything until the brethren have resumed their journey." (7) When they had stayed a full three weeks without Paul's having eaten anything, the brethren asked him why he kept silent. When he did not reply, Antony said to him, "Why are you silent? Speak to the brothers." And he spoke to them.

(8) Another time, when he had brought Antony a jar of honey, the father said, "Break the jar and pour out the honey." He did so. Then he said to him, "Gather up the honey again with a spoon without collecting any dirt with it." (9) And again, he ordered him to draw water the whole day. He taught him to weave baskets, and some days later ordered him to undo them all. He unstitched his cloak and ordered him to sew it up again. Again he unstitched it, and again Paul sewed it up. (10) And the disciple acquired such absolute obedience that God gave him the grace to drive out demons. Indeed, those demons that Antony was unable to exorcise he sent to Paul, who drove them out instantly.

25. ON PIAMMONAS

(1) There is another desert in Egypt close to the sea but very harsh and cruel, where many great anchorites live. It is near Diolcopolis.

(2) We saw a priest there called Piammonas, a holy and very humble man who frequently saw visions. Once when he was celebrating the Eucharist, he saw an angel standing to the right of the altar. The angel was noting the brethren who came up for Communion and writing down their names in a book. As for those who were not present at the *Synaxis,* he saw their names erased. And, in fact, thirteen days later these died.

(3) The demons often tormented this father and made him so weak that he could not stand at the altar or offer the sacrifice. But an angel came, and taking him by the hand, filled him at once with strength and set him at the altar in good health. When the brethren saw the marks of the tortures, they were amazed.

26. ON JOHN

We also visited another John in Diolcos, who was the father of hermitages. He, too, was endowed with much grace. He looked like Abraham and had a beard like Aaron's. He had performed many miracles and cures and was especially successful at healing people afflicted with paralysis and gout.

EPILOGUE

(1) We also saw many other monks and fathers throughout Egypt who performed many signs and wonders. Because of their great number, we have not mentioned them all. Instead, we have selected a few to represent the many. What should one say about the Upper Thebaid in the district of Syene, where even more wonderful men are to be found and an infinite number of monks? One would not believe their ascetic practices, which surpass human capabilities. (2) To this day they raise the dead and walk on the water just like Peter. And all that the Savior did through the saints, he does in our own times through these monks.

(3) However, as we would have been in the greatest danger if we had gone up beyond Lyco, because of attacks by brigands, we did not dare to visit these saints. As a matter of fact, it was not without danger or hardship that we visited those fathers whom we have mentioned. Nor was it without considerable effort that we saw what is reported in this work. On the contrary, we suffered much on our journey and came

very near to losing our lives before we were counted worthy to see these things. Indeed, we came face to face with death seven times, and "the eighth time no evil touched us" (cf. Job 5:19).

(4) The first time we almost fainted with hunger and thirst after spending five days and five nights walking through the desert.

(5) The second time we blundered into some marshy ground full of thorns and prickles, and our feet were so lacerated that the pain became unbearable and we almost perished.

(6) The third time we sank into a swamp right up to our waists, "and there was no deliverer" (Judg 18:28), and we called out in the words of David, "Save me O God, for the waters are come in unto my soul. I sink in deep mire, where there is no standing. Deliver me out of the mire, and let me not sink" (Ps 69:1, 2, 14).

(7) The fourth time a mass of water encircled us because of the rising of the Nile, and for three days we waded through the water, almost sinking under the surface in the potholes. Whenever this happened, we cried out, saying, "Let not the water flood overflow me, neither let the deep swallow me up, and let not the pit shut her mouth upon me" (Ps 69:15).

(8) The fifth time we ran into robbers as we were making our way along the shore to Diolcos. They pursued us so hard in their desire to capture us that there was scarcely any breath left in our nostrils; indeed, they chased us for about ten miles.

(9) The sixth time we were in a boat on the Nile when it capsized and we were nearly drowned.

(10) The seventh time we were on Lake Mareotis, where papyrus comes from, when we ran aground on a small desert island. We remained in the open for three days and three nights with rain and a heavy hailstorm beating down on us. For it was the season of Epiphany.

(11) As for the eighth time, the story is superfluous but nevertheless profitable. On our way to Nitria, we passed by a certain place where there was a hollow in the land full of water. A number of crocodiles had been stranded there when the floodwaters receded from the surrounding countryside.

(12) There were three great crocodiles stretched out on the edge of the pool, and we went up to look at the beasts, thinking that they were dead.

(13) Suddenly they lunged at us. We called on Christ with a loud voice, crying, "Christ, help!" The beasts, as if turned aside by some angel, darted into the water. We set off for Nitria at a run without stopping, meditating on the words of Job, where he says, "He shall deliver you seven times from tribulations, and in the eighth time no evil shall touch you" (cf. Job 5:19).

(14) We therefore give thanks to the Lord for delivering us from such great dangers and for showing us such wonderful sights. To him be glory for all eternity. Amen.

---

49. The Life of Pelagia

The holy life of the "repentant harlot" proved to be one of the most enduring and popular forms of hagiography from antiquity through the Middle Ages. There could be no more compelling sign of the power of Christianity, it was believed, than the conversion of the impure woman to ascetic virtue. The *Life of Pelagia* (the longer, Syriac version of which is reproduced here) was an extremely popular version of such a narrative. In many ways, the narrative of Pelagia follows the same basic structure as other hagiographies: inspiration (here by the eloquence of a saintly bishop), renunciation (including repentance for past sins), mira-

From *Holy Women of the Syrian Orient,* trans. and ed. Sebastian Brock and Susan Ashbrook Harvey. Berkeley: University of California Press, 1998. Used with permission.

cles, and inspiration of others. The particularities of this *Life* are also noteworthy, such as the thorny problem of how to dispose of Pelagia's ill-gotten wealth (the solution devised by the bishops is a well-thought-out compromise). Pelagia's conversion also entails an extraordinary renunciation of her own gender, so that she transforms herself into the eunuch-monk Pelagios; no longer male nor female, she becomes a truly genderless model of Christian piety (legends of "cross-dressing" saints were also very popular in Late Antiquity and the Middle Ages).

Extraordinary hagiographies, such as the *Life of Pelagia,* demonstrate that "imitation" of the saint portrayed in a *Life* was often meant to be abstract and suggestive. It is doubtful that female readers of the *Life of Pelagia* would actually be encouraged to cut their hair, put on men's clothes, and wall themselves up in a cave for the rest of their lives (in fact, such transvestism was condemned by local church councils). Likewise, Bishop Nonnos's claim in the beginning of the *Life,* that the assembled priests and bishops should imitate a prostitute's desire to please her customer shows that the ethics of imitation, central to the whole enterprise of hagiography, was perhaps intended to be taken in a more metaphorical manner.

(1) Greetings from the sinful deacon Jacob to the spiritual believers in our Lord.

I wanted to write to you, my holy fathers and brethren, about the conversion of the prostitute Pelagia, in the hopes that you might find great benefit in hearing and learning of it and accordingly give praise to our merciful Lord God who does not wish anyone to perish, but rather that all sinners should be saved and return to the knowledge of truth.

(2) The beginning of this account is as follows: the bishop of Antioch, the capital of Syria, was obliged to summon his fellow bishops because of some pressing church business that concerned them. In accordance with his summons, eight bishops assembled in the city. It is not necessary for me to record their names, with the exception of one: this was the holy bishop Nonnos, whose deacon I, the sinner Jacob, am in his own town. This glorious man excelled and was most perfect in his whole way of life; his religious upbringing was in Egypt, for he was from a famous well-populated monastery called "of Tabennesi," situated in the Thebaid.[1]

Because of his chaste and perfect way of life, this glorious man was held worthy of the rank of bishop through the will of God who chose him. (3) This holy

bishop Nonnos, then, came to Antioch along with seven fellow bishops, and I, the miserable Jacob, his deacon, accompanied him.

When we had paid our respects to the archbishop of Antioch, he told us to lodge at the hostel of the shrine where the bones of the glorious martyr Julian are preserved. Accordingly we and the other bishops lodged there. Now it so happened there was a delay for some reason, and on one particular day all the bishops left their cells and met together, sitting by the outer gate of the shrine of the glorious martyr Julian, and they were conversing among themselves on various topics; (4) then they begged the holy Nonnos, my bishop, to speak the word of God with them as they sat, so as to benefit them with his wise teaching, for they knew that he used to speak in the Holy Spirit and that he uplifted everyone who heard him with his divine teaching.

This God-loving and holy bishop Nonnos therefore spoke before his companions in an excellent way, and they, full of wonder at his teaching, rejoiced at his words. At that moment, as they were sitting—and I, his deacon Jacob, was near them, standing out of respect for him—all of a sudden a rich prostitute, the leader of the troupe of actors, happened to pass by us. It is her story that I, the wretched Jacob, have endeavored to write down and tell for the benefit of all those who are desirous of the truth and who love God.

---

[1] That is, the monastery of Pachomius; see Text 38.

This prostitute then appeared before our eyes, sitting prominently on a riding donkey adorned with little bells and caparisoned; in front of her was a great throng of her servants, and she herself was decked out with gold ornaments, pearls, and all sorts of precious stones, resplendent in luxurious and expensive clothes. On her hands and feet she wore armbands, silks, and anklets decorated with all sorts of pearls, while around her neck were necklaces and strings of pendants and pearls. Her beauty stunned those who beheld her, captivating them in their desire for her. (5) Young boys and girls accompanied her in haughty fashion, holding her lascivious feet; they, too, were adorned with golden girdles and had jewelry strung round their necks. Some ran in front of her, while others escorted her with great pomp. Thus it was that her beauty and finery lured everyone who saw her to stare at her and at her appearance.

As this prostitute passed in front of us, the scent of perfumes and the reek of her cosmetics hit everyone in the vicinity. (6) The bishops as they sat there were amazed at her and her clothes, as well as the splendor of her cortege and the fact that she went by with her head uncovered, with a scarf thrown round her shoulders in a shameless fashion, as though she were a man; indeed, in her haughty impudence her garb was not very different from a man's, apart from her makeup and the fact that her skin was as dazzling as snow. To put it briefly, her appearance incited everyone who set eyes on her to fall in love with her.

When the holy bishops saw her, they averted their eyes from her, as though she was some sinful object. (7) The holy bishop Nonnos, however, observed her carefully in his mind, filled with wonder. Once she had passed in front of them, he turned away his face, placed his head between his knees, and wept with great feeling, so much so that his lap was filled with tears.

Lamenting greatly for her, the holy bishop Nonnos sighed and said to his fellow bishops, "To be honest, fathers, did not the beauty of this prostitute who passed in front of us astonish you?" They kept silent and did not answer a word. (8) But the holy Nonnos went on sighing bitterly, striking his chest, deeply moved and weeping so much that even his clothes—

a hair shirt—got soaked with his tears. (He always wore a hair shirt next to his skin, hiding it with a soft woollen garment on top, so that it could not be seen; he spent his entire life in a harsh regime of strict asceticism.)

Having wept a great deal, he said to his fellow bishops, "I beg you, my brothers, tell me, did you lust in your minds after the beauty of that prostitute who passed in front of us? And did you suffer for her? I myself was greatly astonished at her beauty, and I suffered because of her ornaments, which were a baited snare for all who beheld her, a stumbling block leading to perdition. In my weakness I beseech and supplicate God to turn her to a life of truth and to let her stand chastely before the awful throne of his majesty.

"Up to the present she has been a snare and a stumbling block for mankind; she has lived her life in the world in the vain pursuit of adorning herself, causing harm to many. (9) I imagine she must have spent many hours in her boudoir putting on her eye black, making herself up, and dressing in her finery; she will have looked at her face in the mirror with the greatest attention, making sure there is not the slightest speck of dirt on it or anything that might not please those who behold her. And all this in order to lead astray and lure her lovers after her—lovers today, but gone tomorrow.

(10) "In this prostitute we should reprove ourselves: we believe that we have a bridal chamber in heaven that will not pass away, in a place that will last forever and ever, and we have a fiancé who will neither die nor become corrupted; we have in heaven an inheritance to which the entire world cannot be compared; a happiness whose joy and felicity cannot be described is ours; ours, too, is the fragrance that never fades away: 'eye has not seen, nor ear heard, nor has the mind of man imagined what God has prepared for those who love him'" (1 Cor 2:9). What more need I say: we have vast promises in the supernal heights stored up with our hidden Lord who cannot be seen. It is he we should please, but we fail to do so; it is for him that we should adorn our bodies and souls, but we totally fail to do so. We should take pains over ourselves in order to scrub away the dirt of

sins, to become clean from evil stains, but we have paid no attention to our souls in the attempt to adorn them with good habits so that Christ may desire to dwell in us. What a reproach to us, seeing that we have not taken pains to make ourselves pleasing to God nearly as much as this prostitute we saw passing in front of us has taken pains to please men—in order to captivate them, leading them into perdition by her wanton beauty.

"Truly, my brothers, I am in a state of great amazement and wonder at my own soul and at her: we should have been trying to please our Lord in all things with even greater effort than she has expended on her embellishment and adornment. And maybe we should even go and become the pupils of this lascivious woman."

(11) When the God-loving bishop Nonnos had uttered these words, his fellow bishops sighed with emotion at his wise words, so filled with feeling. Full of grief and compunction, they got up and went off to the places where they were staying.

The holy bishop Nonnos took me, his deacon Jacob, and we went off to where we were lodging. Once we had climbed up, he threw himself onto the ground (on which a sackcloth lay spread out) and, beating his hand against his face, said as he wept, "Lord God, have mercy on me a sinner: I am not worthy to stand before you seeing that I have never tried to embellish my soul for your presence. What that prostitute accomplished in a single day in beautifying herself surpasses everything I have ever achieved during all the years of my life. How can I have the face to look upon you, my God? I do not know what words to use in the attempt to justify myself in your presence, Lord. What excuse have I before you, seeing that all my hidden secrets are laid open before you? No, alas for me the sinner who, as I enter the threshold of your sacred temple and appear before your glorious altar, have failed to offer the beauty in my soul that you want.

(12) "Instead, having failed to adorn myself as you would like, I stand before you who are so full of awe and are so mighty, despicably unworthy. You have allowed me to be a servant who shares in your mystery: I beseech you, Lord, do not remove me

from your heavenly altar; let not the beautification of this prostitute bring about my condemnation in front of the fearful tribunal of your mighty and exalted throne. For she, a creature of dust and ashes, has employed the utmost zeal in trying to please Satan, (13) whereas I have neglected pleasing you the living and immortal one, seeing that I have given myself over to laxity. Indeed, through my neglect I have stripped off the fine robe of your holy commandments. That prostitute has given her promise to please lascivious men, and she has kept it by adorning herself like this, whereas I made a promise to you the compassionate God, undertaking a solemn pact to please you, but I have proved false to you, and here I am stripped of all the spiritual adornments on earth and in heaven. Consequently I have no hope of salvation resulting from my deeds; instead my wretched soul looks to your mercy, Lord, and to your hope, for it is only through the multitude of your mercies that I can hope to live. I, a sinner, Lord, beseech you, be pleased to choose me for your divine glory, for it is you who have adorned me in your heavenly beauty that does not pass away. I beg you, too, to call this lost woman, so that she, too, may be found when you seek her: she has not neglected anything devised by sinful men in her ceaseless hunting after the lost. Change her in accordance with your will, Lord, as you consented to change the water into delicious wine that brings joy (cf. John 2)."

This is what the God-loving Nonnos said, groaning as he wept and confessed to God. He spent the whole of that day in prayer, fasting and praying. It was a Saturday, (14) and the next day was Sunday, the holy day. After we had said the night office, the holy Nonnos called to me, his deacon Jacob, and said, "My son, I saw a vision this night, and I am much perturbed when I ponder on it. In any case, let God do whatever is beneficial, as he likes. What I saw in my dream just now was this: it was as though I was standing beside the horns of the altar, and all of a sudden a black dove, befouled with mud, flew above me. I was unable to endure the disgusting stench of the mud on this dove that I saw, but it fluttered above me until the prayer of the catechumens was ended. Then, as the deacon proclaimed, 'Depart, catechumens,' in my dream I saw the dove fly off at once, and it disappeared from my sight. (15) After the prayer of the faithful, when the oblation had been offered, and once the service had finished and I had left the sanctuary, I again saw the dove flying toward me, still befouled with a lot of mud, just as before. I stretched out my hands and grasped it, whereupon I immediately threw it into a basin of water that happened to be in the courtyard of the church. Once I had thrown the bird in, I saw in my dream that it left behind all its mud, washed off in the water, and the foul stench disappeared. I further saw the dove emerge from the water and fly off at once into the heights above until it had vanished from sight and was no longer visible. This is the dream I saw, my son, and I have been pondering much about it. I think that its explanation will come about in truth, if God wills."

(16) This is what the holy bishop Nonnos told me, his deacon Jacob. He got up and took me with him to the great church, along with the seven other bishops who were with us. We approached together to greet the archbishop of the city of Antioch on the holy day of Sunday.

When it was time for the priests to enter the *thronos* of the church as was customary, the archbishop asked the eight bishops to come into the *naos* of the church for the holy office. Accordingly they went in and sat down on the *bema,* each sitting in his appropriate place in accordance with the honor of his see. After the completion of the office and once the Scriptures and holy Gospel had been read, it was time for the homily, which follows the lections from the holy Scriptures. Everyone was waiting expectantly to see and hear who would give the homily. The archbishop decided to send the holy Gospel in the hands of his archdeacon to be given to the holy bishop Nonnos, with the permission that he should preach.

(17) Thereupon the holy bishop Nonnos stood up and, opening his mouth, began to speak the word of God in glorious fashion. Fervent in the Holy Spirit, he gave his homily, not using ornate and pompous words employing human skill (for he had no secular education), but rather, being filled with the gift of the Holy Spirit, he uttered weighty and perfect words. He brought out clearly the meaning of the Gospel text, using wise words as he taught, with the result that the entire people were moved to contrition in their emotion as they listened. Now the subject of his sermon was the judgment in store for the wicked and the good hope stored up for the righteous. The whole congregation was reduced to weeping at his words, and the floor of the church became soaked with tears.

(18) Through the merciful providence of God, an excellent plan entered the head of the prostitute we have been talking about: her thoughts unsettled her so much that, against her custom, she came to church that day. She had joined the other women and gone into the church, where she had diverted her attention to the holy Scriptures, and she had even stayed on to listen to the homily.

As she heard the homily and the teaching of the God-loving bishop Nonnos, she was greatly moved, and her conscience was pricked: tears poured down as she sobbed, and amid heavy sighs she recalled all her sins. She was groaning so much over her life as a prostitute that the congregation became aware of her emotion. Everyone recognized her as the city's famous playgirl, for as she groaned out aloud, people were telling each other, "It really is the sinful woman, and she's been converted by the teaching of the God-loving and holy bishop Nonnos. She, who had never paid the slightest attention to her sins, has all of a sudden come to penitence; she who never used to come to church, all of a sudden has had her mind turned to religion and to prayer as a result of the divine words she has heard from the mouth of the holy bishop Nonnos."

When she had wept a great deal, moved to compunction and ensnared for life by the holy Nonnos's sermon, it was then time for the oblation to be offered. She left at the start of the holy Mysteries with the catechumens and (19) called two of her household servants, telling them, "Wait here till church is finished, and when the disciple of Christ, the holy bishop Nonnos, whose sermon we have heard, comes out, make careful inquiries and find out where he is staying so that you can tell me."

Once the oblation had been offered and church was ended, we left to go to our lodgings, but the servants of the prostitute followed us as they had been instructed until they had found out where we were staying; then they returned at once to inform their mistress. She was extremely pleased to learn this, and she was praying that she might be allowed to see the holy and God-loving Nonnos and listen to his teaching. Her former haughtiness had been completely removed from her mind, and she was now full of compunction, shaking as she pondered the punishment that she had heard was due to sinners in the next world at the hand of God's justice. She was greatly afraid in her mind and sobbed with tears before God.

(20) Stirred by contrition, Pelagia wrote down on a wax tablet a passionate and moving message with a plea concerning her salvation. This she sent to the holy bishop Nonnos by the hands of her servants. It read as follows: "To the holy bishop Nonnos, from the sinful woman Pelagia who is a disciple of Satan, many greetings. I supplicate your saintly feet, my lord, for I have now heard something about the God whom you love with all your heart: how he bent down his majesty toward us and descended from heaven to earth—and this was not for the sake of the righteous, but in order to save sinners in his mercy. This is what I gather the Christians say, that he, upon whom the cherubim and seraphim dare not look in heaven, has sat down and eaten and drunk with tax collectors and sinners (cf. Matt 9:10–12), out of his love, during the time he appeared on earth and went around among us in human body, (21) as you yourself know, holy sir, even though you did not see him with the physical eye. He spoke with the Samaritan woman at the water well; with the Canaanite woman who cried out after him; with the woman who was smitten with illness, whom he healed; with Mary and Martha whose brother he raised (cf. John 4; Matt 15:22–28; Luke 13:11–12; John 11). He did all this, as I have heard from Christians, and now, my lord, if you are the disciple of this God who has done all this, do not reject me or turn me away when I ask to appear before you and to see you in person, in case there is a possibility that I might be saved at your hands. You might thus take some pride in me the sinner if I were to become a disciple of your health-giving instruction."

(22) The holy bishop Nonnos wrote the following reply to the prostitute: "God is well aware of what you are; he knows and sifts out your will, your intention, and your thoughts. This, however, is what I have to say to you: do not try to tempt me who am both insignificant and weak, for I am a sinful person and one who has never been righteous. If you want to see me, do so with the seven holy bishops: I cannot see you alone, lest the simple, who lack understanding, stumble and be offended."

(23) Receiving this message, the prostitute got up at once and hurried to the shrine of the glorious martyr Julian. When she reached the shrine, she sent a note to us to inform us of her arrival. Now, previous to her arrival, the holy and God-loving bishop Nonnos had called his fellow bishops and made them sit with him. He then bade her approach for an audience with them. (24) As she drew near and saw them, she prostrated herself before them all together and ended by throwing herself down on the ground, clasping the feet of the holy Nonnos in a state of great emotion. She started to weep and groan, and the holy man's feet got soaked with the prostitute's tears. Without noticing what was happening, she wiped onto herself the dirt from his feet. As she groveled before him, she was throwing dust from the ground onto her head, beseeching him amid loud groans, and saying, "I beg you, have pity on me a sinner. I am a prostitute, a disgusting stone upon which many people have tripped up and gone to perdition. I am Satan's evil snare: he set me and through me he has caught many people for destruction. I am a ravenous vulture, and many chicks of the heavenly Eagle have been caught by me. I am a sly she wolf, and by my crafty wiles I have destroyed innocent lambs and sheep. I am a deep ditch of mire in which many have befouled themselves and got filthy: they had been clean, but I corrupted them. Have mercy on me, O pure and holy sir, I beg you; be like your leader Christ, who never averted his face from sinners, but instead out of his graciousness had compassion on them. Pour over me your kindness, imitating him, otherwise I shall perish and die in my sins. I am a destructive moth, and I have gnawed into many bodies that had previously been unscathed. Make me into a Christian this very day—for I am a sea of sins. Take me, sir, and make me holy by means of your pure instruction—for I am

an abyss of evils. Take from me my sins and wickednesses today, and through your prayers cast them away from me in the cleansing bath of your God's baptism. Stand up, I beg you, my lord, and invoke over me the name of the holy Trinity; baptize me for the remission of my sins. Stand up, my lord, and strip off from me the dirty clothing of prostitution; clothe me with pure garments, the beautiful dress for the novel banquet to which I have come."

(25) When they saw the prostitute's emotion and faith, the bishops and all the priests, as well as everyone else who happened to be present, wept plentiful tears. Only with difficulty did the holy bishop Nonnos persuade her to get up from his feet; when she had done so, he addressed her: "My daughter, the canons of the church require that one should not baptize a prostitute without her having some sponsors, otherwise she may continue in her old ways."

(26) On hearing these words, the prostitute at once threw herself down onto the ground again and clasped hold of the holy and God-loving Nonnos's feet. As she wept and groaned, she spoke as follows: "You will have to answer for me to God if you do not baptize me now: God will require my soul at your hands, and he will inscribe all the bad things I have done against your name if you refuse to baptize me now; you will share in the wickedness of my ways. No, you must baptize me at once, and so make me a stranger to my evil deeds. You will become a stranger to your holy altar and deny your God if you don't make me a bride of Christ this very day, giving me rebirth by saving baptism and offering me up to your God—who will himself be a sponsor for me to you today. For I will not return to the ditch of mire from which you shall raise me to eternal life. My lord, have no fear of me; get up and receive me a sinner, just as your Lord received sinners."

(27) The bishops and everyone with them gave praise to God when they saw how the mind of this sinful prostitute was set on fire and was burning with the love of God.

Now the holy bishop Nonnos summoned me, his deacon Jacob, and, giving me instructions, sent me off into the city to inform the archbishop of all that had taken place, in order that he might give permission to act in whatever way he wished with the prostitute. He also gave me strict orders, saying, "Let the archbishop send back with you one of the deaconesses if he gives you permission for us to baptize the prostitute."

(28) So I, the wretched Jacob, went off to the archbishop and told him everything that the God-loving Nonnos, my bishop, had bidden me to say. I informed him about the prostitute's conversion, and I described to him her emotion and her promise. I repeated everything, not omitting a word.

The archbishop was absolutely delighted, and he said to me, "Return to our brother, the holy bishop Nonnos, the blessed father and wise teacher, and tell him that I am most pleased with the message he has sent me and that I had actually had it in my mind that this great and wonderful event might be in store for you, waiting to be fulfilled at your hands. For I know that you are like God's own mouth; for it was he who said, 'If you bring out something valuable from what is base, you shall be like my own mouth (Jer 15:19).' For the rest, be assured that I am very happy that you should carry out to the end what you have already commenced upon: it will please Christ, and it will edify the entire church, as well as bring salvation to the life of this prostitute. Baptize her, then, on the confession of her own mouth. So, we have now heard of the matter, and we are in agreement with your wise handling of it that will prove full of joy. It is right that you should baptize, just as you have converted her: simply let the lascivious woman become chaste, let the sinner be justified, and let our God be praised."

He then sent for the deaconess Romana from her house (she was the head deaconess). He told her to go with me and obey the holy bishop Nonnos and do whatever he told her.

(29) So I and the deaconess Romana returned to our holy father Nonnos to find the prostitute still sprawling on the ground, weeping at his feet. Then the deaconess Romana approached and begged her to get up, saying, "Rise up, my sister, collect yourself together. Recover your strength in preparation to receive what Grace has summoned you for. Get up, sister, and let us pray over you to remove all the power of the Adversary from you."

Only with difficulty was she persuaded to get up, but she still went on crying. Then the holy bishop Nonnos gave us instructions to get everything requisite ready for holy baptism. He addressed the prostitute and said, "Open your mouth and acknowledge God; renounce your sins before him."

Weeping, the prostitute said, "If I examine myself thoroughly, I cannot find a single good deed that I have done. I know that my sins are heavier and more numerous than all the grains of sand on the seashore, and all the sea's water is not sufficient to wash away my wicked and evil deeds. But I believe that God is merciful and will not look upon the multitude of my sins—just as he did not look upon the sin of that sinful woman in the Gospels or that of the Canaanite woman or the one from Samaria (Luke 7; John 4; Matt 15): he did not shut his door in their faces but had pity and compassion upon them; he held them to be worthy of healing in their bodies and of forgiveness of their sins. I, too, have acknowledged and do acknowledge that I am wicked and bad, whereas my God is compassionate and merciful. And I beg you, my lord, a true priest and forgiving father who gives spiritual rebirth, be merciful to me; take me and wash me with fire and the Spirit."

(30) Thereupon the holy Nonnos said to her, "Give me your name so that I can offer it up to God." The prostitute replied, "My actual parents called me Pelagia, but the entire city of Antioch, where I was born, called me Marganito[2] because of the quantities of jewelry I wore and prided myself on. You see, up to now I have been Satan's well-decked shop front and home."

The holy Nonnos went on, "From birth your name was Pelagia?" "Yes, my lord," she replied. Having learned her name, the bishop said the exorcism over her, marked her, and sealed her with the oil of anointing as she made the renunciation, saying, "I renounce you, Satan, and all your might." She went on to cry out, "I acknowledge you, Christ, and your Father and your living and holy Spirit. I acknowledge your church and your baptism; I acknowledge your king-

dom on high and the heavenly powers; I acknowledge your holy altar on earth and your fearful mysteries in heaven and your illustrious and pure priests who minister before you. I renounce the falsehood I have wrought and the prostitute's profession I have been following up to now."

Then after this confession, the holy Nonnos baptized Pelagia, and her spiritual mother, Romana the deaconess, received her from the baptismal waters. She received the body and blood of Christ from the hands of the illustrious and holy Mar Nonnos.

The occasion brought great joy to God and his angels in heaven and on earth to the entire church and its priests. Once Pelagia had been perfected as the bride of Christ, the deaconess Romana took her up to our lodgings after the bishops themselves had gone up there.

(31) The holy Nonnos said to me, his deacon Jacob, "We should rejoice today, my son, and exult with the holy angels of God who today rejoice at the finding of Pelagia, Christ's lamb. Today, my son, let us eat our food with oil and let us drink some wine because of the new birth and mighty salvation of this glorious bride of Christ, Pelagia."

I got everything ready as he had instructed, and while we were eating, full of joy, all of a sudden Satan appeared to us, furious, in the form of a scowling man with tangled long sleeves and his hands on his head; he wailed out loudly, saying (32) "Fie on you, foolish old man who eats his own white hairs: the thirty thousand Arabs, whom you snatched from me, baptized, and donated to your God should suffice for you. Weren't you satisfied with my city Heliopolis—Baalbek—where you converted a large number of women who worshipped and honored me? And now you've gone and captured from me this seductive lady and baptized her, removing her from my service and offering her to your God? Weren't you satisfied with the pagans you enticed away from me, converting them and donating them to your God? But now you have gone and cut off all my hopes today. Fie on you, ill-fated and luckless old man: I cannot endure your crafty tricks; cursed be the day that had the misfortune to see you born. The river full of tears you poured out has swept away the oaths and prom-

---

[2] That is, "pearl."

ises that large numbers of people had made with me. You have shattered my hopes today. What have I to do with you, you grave robber who has despoiled me as though I were a tomb, wickedly removing this woman alive from me, where she had been like a corpse confined by me in her error."

Such were Satan's words when he appeared to us and to all the bishops with us. Everyone present, including Pelagia and the deaconess Romana, who both had their eyes fixed on that Satan, heard him shouting and reviling the holy Nonnos. (33) Then Satan left the holy man and turned to address Pelagia; groaning, as though he was someone in tears, he cried out to her, "Is this my due, Pelagia? Didn't you belong to me, and I to you up to just now? How can you do this to me: you've made me a laughingstock to this old white head and to everyone who hears that you have jilted me. Wasn't it I who taught you how to make yourself up and become an object of lust for many? Didn't I bring you crowds of lovers to satisfy your prostitute's profession? Didn't I subject both the rich and the noble to you, so that they brought you expensive presents as a result of their lust-ridden passion? Why have you turned against me and tricked me like this? Why have you done this to me and jilted me, just because of a few misleading words from this ill-starred old man? All his life he has been annoying me with his tricks all over the place: he's like a nasty thorn to me wherever he goes. I'll bring about some calamity if you don't renounce him and acknowledge me—just as in the past you used to do what I wanted."

Then the holy Nonnos said to Pelagia, Christ's bride, "Rebuke this Satan, my daughter, rebuke him and don't be afraid of him, for he is weak and helpless before the Holy Spirit whom you have put on today."

Pelagia immediately crossed herself, plucked up courage, and rebuked the Satan who had turned up. In this way she quickly put him to flight, and he vanished from our sight.

(34) Two days later he came along quietly and manifested himself to Pelagia as she was asleep beside her spiritual mother, the deaconess Romana. Satan quietly awoke Pelagia and said to her gently,

"Marganito, what wrong have I done you that you've turned against me? Didn't I deck you out with gold and pearls, piling up riches upon you? I beg you, tell me why have you deluded me and played me false? Please let me explain, and don't jilt me, otherwise everyone will laugh at me because of you."

(35) Pelagia, however, bravely crossed herself and blew at Satan, whereupon he disappeared. She had shouted at him as follows: "May our Lord Jesus Christ Son of the living God rebuke you. It was he who seized me from you and made me a bride for his heavenly marriage chamber."

Then she woke up Romana the deaconess and said, "Mother, pray for me, because that wicked man came and troubled me." "Don't be disturbed by him, my beloved daughter," she replied, "for from now on he is afraid of you and will run away from your very shadow."

Thereupon the two of them, mother and daughter, signed themselves with the cross, rebuked Satan in the name of Christ, and he vanished and was not seen by them again.

(36) The following day the holy Pelagia, like an eagle whose youthfulness had been renewed, having been weaned away from evil deeds, aroused her mind and summoned the head of her household who was in charge of all her belongings. She told him to go to her house, make an inventory of all she possessed—her gold, silver, and quantities of jewelry, together with her expensive wardrobe. He was to bring the list to her because ever since this glorious lady had heard the words of the holy bishop Nonnos and had been converted, making a start on a life of penitence, she had not returned to her house at all or crossed its threshold; instead she had remained with us in penitence in the shrine of Christ until the completion of her baptism.

Her steward went off to her house as she had instructed and brought back an inventory listing all her wealth, not hiding anything. (37) Thereupon the glorious Pelagia sent by the deaconess Romana a request that the holy bishop Nonnos should come and pay her a visit. On his arrival at the place where she was staying, Pelagia asked him earnestly to accept her entire fortune. She handed over to him all that she desired with the words, "My lord, here is the wealth that Satan has bestowed upon me as a result of the sin of prostitution. From now on, my lord, it is entrusted to your care: do with it whatever you want. As far as I am concerned, from today on Christ's riches that were granted to me at your hands are sufficient for me; I have grown rich many times over through them."

(38) Then she summoned all her servants and maids, freed them in accordance with the law, and gave each one of them an appropriate present. Whereupon she dismissed them, saying, "Up to now you have been my servants, living a life of sin and licentiousness, enslaved to sinful servitude to prostitution. Now I have freed you from this slavery of wickedness; it is up to you for your own part to free your souls from the slavery of sin. Henceforth you shall no longer work for me, and you will no longer have the reputation of belonging to a prostitute."

She then dismissed them, and they bade her farewell and left, astonished by the change that they beheld in their mistress Pelagia. (39) On receiving Pelagia's entire fortune, the holy Nonnos sent for the steward of the great church at Antioch, and in Pelagia's presence he handed over to him all that had belonged to her, telling him, "I adjure you by the exalted Trinity, let nothing out of all these belongings enter the church of God or be given to any of the bishops; let none of it enter the house of any of the clergy, or even your own house: do not let anything be defiled by it, whether through your agency or through the agency of anyone else; for even though it might seem desirable and good, considering that there is so much of it, nevertheless this wealth has been amassed as the result of the sin of prostitution. So do not take any delight in these belongings. If this bride of Christ has renounced and rejected it as being nothing, for the sake of the spiritual possessions she has discovered, how much more should we consider it filthy; we must not exchange it for the heavenly riches stored up for us, which are pure, undefiled, and glorious. Take care, then, my son, in view of what I have bidden you under oath; if you transgress this oath, God's curse shall enter your house and you will be accounted as one of those who cried, 'Crucify him, cru-

cify him' (John 19:6). No, you must use it only to provide for the orphans and widows, for the poor, the needy, and the destitute, so that they can live off it. In this way, just as it was amassed in a wicked and wrong manner, so it shall now be administered in an upright and just fashion. What was sin's wealth shall henceforth be righteousness' treasury."

Accordingly he received this trust from the holy man as though it was from God's own apostle. The steward took it all and administered it, exactly following the instructions given by the saintly bishop Nonnos in the presence of the holy Pelagia; he did not go against or alter his orders in anything.

Everyone was astonished at all that Christ's bride, Pelagia, had done, how she had benefited many through this action of hers. All her licentious acquaintances, however, were extremely put out, and they were reduced to tears on seeing her abrupt new way of life. She kept herself away from her old friends, and they all felt puzzled and asked, "How is it that a famous prostitute can become a woman of renowned chastity overnight?" But many were uplifted by her example.

When Pelagia's fellow prostitutes and neighbors saw what she had done, they were themselves moved to compunction and started weeping over themselves. Many of them turned to chastity and abandoned their life of prostitution, going off to receive instruction about Christ; these came to the chaste Pelagia, and she exhorted and urged them to do what she had done. Numerous prostitutes listened to her advice and were converted by the chaste bride of Christ.

Many people thought highly of Pelagia for what she had done, and because of her, our Lord was glorified by everyone.

(40) The handmaid of God kept herself apart from eating or drinking anything from her own house for the seven days following her baptism. During this time, she did not use anything of her own; instead Romana the deaconess provided food and everything she required from her own pocket; in her faith and her love, like a fond mother, she considered Pelagia to be her own beloved daughter and so looked after her. Now Pelagia had sworn not to touch anything ever

again that had been bought out of the wealth she had amassed through sin. She kept to her oath and did not eat or drink anything derived from what had formerly been hers. She even refused to receive anything from her house, and she never again entered it. Nor did she ever again take anything that had belonged to her to give away, telling everyone, "Far be it from me that I should live off the wages of prostitution any longer or think anything of them." Instead she held her fortune to be worse than blood and fouler than the smelly mud of the streets.

(41) When the bridal days following Pelagia's baptism were at an end and the blessed eighth day, Sunday, had arrived, it was time for her to take off her holy baptismal robes, in accordance with the canon of the church, and to put on ordinary everyday clothes. So, when Sunday was over, she got up during the night on which Monday dawned and went in to the holy bishop Nonnos; she prostrated herself before him and received his blessing, whereupon he gave her permission to take off her holy baptismal garments. But the holy Pelagia earnestly besought the priest of Christ that she might receive her clothing from some of his, rather than put on something else. The holy bishop Nonnos acceded to Pelagia's request and gave her some of his own clothing—a hair shirt and a woolen mantle. Straightaway she took off her baptismal robes and put on his clothes. Then she knelt down at his feet and received his blessing, having revealed to him all her plans.

That night she left dressed as a man and secretly went off without our being aware of it. She was no longer to be seen in the city. Now the holy bishop Nonnos, who knew her secret, did not tell anyone what had happened—not even me, Jacob, who served as his deacon.

When morning came, there was great consternation, for Pelagia was nowhere to be found: she was not with us, nor anywhere else in the entire city. (42) Stricken with grief, the deaconess Romana was in tears and kept inquiring after her all over the place. The holy bishop Nonnos, however, rejoiced greatly for only he knew of Pelagia's departure. He told the deaconess Romana, "Do not be despondent or weep for your daughter Pelagia. Rather, rejoice greatly

over this, for she has chosen the good portion, just as did Mary, Lazarus's sister (cf. Luke 10:42)."

All this took place in the great city of Antioch. (43) A few days later the archbishop of Antioch dismissed all the foreign bishops who were there, and we and everyone else went back to our respective towns.

Three years later I, the deacon Jacob, felt the urge to go and pray in Jerusalem, the city of our Lord; I wanted to venerate his cross and receive a blessing from the site of his resurrection. I approached the holy Nonnos, my bishop, and sought his permission. He allowed me to go, giving me the following instructions: "When you reach the holy place of Jerusalem, remember me there in your prayer—in all those sacred sites that our Lord visited. And afterward be sure to make inquiries there about a certain monk Pelagios, a eunuch; when you have ascertained he is there, go and see him, for there is much that you can benefit from him. For truly he is a true and faithful servant of God, a monk who is perfect in his service."

Now he was speaking to me about Pelagia, the handmaid of God, but I did not grasp the meaning of his allusion, and he did not want to reveal the matter to me openly. So he sent me off with his blessing, and I set out in peace.

(44) Eventually I arrived at the holy place, Jerusalem; I prayed and received a blessing from the tomb of our Lord and from all the places where he traveled, performing his glorious actions. The next day I, Jacob, went out to ask where the monk Pelagios lived. After a great deal of inquiry, I learned that he dwelt on the Mount of Olives, where our Lord used to pray with his disciples. Accordingly I went up to the Mount of Olives and kept on asking until I discovered his cell. He was very well known in the area and held in high honor.

As I approached his cell, I saw it had no door to it; on close examination, I espied a small window in the wall in front of me. I knocked, and Pelagia, the handmaid of God, opened it. She was dressed in the habit of a venerable man. (45) She came up and greeted me with great humility, clasping my hands and kissing them from within. She was overjoyed at my arrival, for the moment she saw me she recognized me. She was inside, and I outside, and I failed to recognize her because she had lost those good looks I used to know; her astounding beauty had all faded away, her laughing and bright face that I had known had become ugly, her pretty eyes had become hollow and cavernous as the result of much fasting and the keeping of vigils. The joints of her holy bones, all fleshless, were visible beneath her skin through emaciation brought on by ascetic practices. Indeed, the whole complexion of her body was coarse and dark like sackcloth as the result of her strenuous penance.

The whole of Jerusalem used to call her "the eunuch," and no one suspected anything else about her, nor did I notice anything about her that resembled the manner of a woman. I received a blessing from her as if from a male eunuch who was a renowned monk, a perfect and righteous disciple of Christ.

(46) The holy Pelagia opened her mouth and spoke to me like a man. She said, "I think I have seen you somewhere, my brother, unless it was someone who looked just like you. By your life, do not conceal the truth from me, are you not the deacon of the holy bishop Nonnos who belongs to the archdiocese of Antioch? He was trained in Egypt."

I replied, "Yes, my lord, I am indeed the disciple of that servant of God, your admirer."

"Does he still live in the body?" she asked.

"Yes, he is still alive," I replied, "and he told me to make careful inquiry about your excellent life and to come to see you and greet you who are so full of virtues." She then went on and said, "Blessed is our Lord who has preserved his life up to today. May he pray for me henceforth, for I know him to be an apostle of our Lord. And do you, too, my brother, pray for me and greet the holy bishop Nonnos and all his companions."

This is all that the blessed Pelagia said to me. Since she was dressed as a man, I did not recognize her. She then closed her window at once and went into her cell, without uttering a further word to me.

When she had gone in and I was still standing there full of wonder, she began to sing the office of the Third Hour. (47) I joined at once in prayer just by her lavra. I gave thanks and departed, moved by the virtuous way of life of this man of God—not realizing she was a woman, and unaware that she was Pelagia, our daughter in Christ.

I, Jacob, spent every day wandering around to see the holy monasteries; I received blessing from them and heard how they would relate stories of the virtuous deeds of the monk Pelagios who lived the life of a recluse on the Mount of Olives, performing miracles. (48) I was filled with amazement at him. Then along came some other people who announced that the monk Pelagios, the recluse on the Mount of Olives, had fallen asleep. As I heard this I rejoiced greatly, giving thanks to our Lord who had held me worthy to receive a blessing from him.

(49) Then the monasteries around Jerusalem and those of Jericho and Transjordan and of the town of Nikopolis all gathered on the Mount of Olives, a huge crowd of monks, to see the burial of Pelagios, the recluse. Quantities of other people, men and women from the whole of Jerusalem, went up to join the funeral procession for the holy Pelagia who was known as a righteous man. The bishop and entire clergy of Jerusalem, together with the honorable abbots, approached and opened up the holy Pelagia's cell; they took out her body, laid it on a bier, whereupon the bishop and all the local holy men came close to anoint it decently with fragrant unguent. As they did so, they saw she was a woman. They gasped with astonishment in their hearts, then, raising their voices, they cried out to God, saying, "Praise to you, Lord; how many hidden saints you have on earth—and not just men, but women as well!"

(50) They wanted to hide this astonishing fact from the people but were unable to do so. This was to fulfill what is written in the holy Gospel: "There is nothing hidden that shall not be revealed, and nothing concealed that shall not be made known" (Matt 10:26). This wonder immediately became known to the entire people.

The whole crowd of men and women, carrying innumerable tapers and torches, then began to process for the blessed Pelagia, as for a righteous woman. They carried and escorted her holy body in true faith, and in this way they buried her amid great honor and much splendor, giving praise to God. The Gospel words "Let your light shine before men that they may see your good works and praise your Father who is in heaven" (Matt 5:16) were fulfilled with reference to her.

(51) I, Jacob, sinner and deacon, have written down for you who love God these glorious deeds that concern a woman who previously had been a prostitute, but who later became a "perfect vessel." This is the panegyric we have received concerning her who was formerly an outcast, but who subsequently was chosen. Let us pray that our Lord will grant us mercy, along with her, at the judgment when the righteous receive reward and sinners, censure.

From all men and women who have repented or who shall repent, and from sinful me who saw and wrote this life, praise, thanksgiving, and honor be raised up to Father, Son, and Holy Spirit, now and always and to eternal ages, amen.

CHAPTER 12

The Christian Bible

By the fourth century, certain assumptions about the Christian Bible were widespread: the division of the Bible into Old and New Testaments; the historical, symbolic, and theological continuity of these two Testaments; the sanctity of the Bible as the "Word of God"; and the need to subject both Testaments to some form of interpretation to arrive at this sacred, integral meaning. Agreement on these points, however, did not preclude continued debate and controversy over how best to approach the Bible to preserve its integrity, sanctity, and significance. While some interpreters were content to establish simple correspondences among the Old Testament, New Testament, and Christian doctrine (e.g., Red Sea = Jordan River = baptism), others sought more spiritual modes of interpretation that brought the Bible into alignment with Greek philosophy and mysticism. One Christian's guidebook to practice and belief was another Christian's esoteric window into divine mysteries.

Julian the Apostate's edict against Christians teaching the Greek and Roman "classics" (see Text 6) prompted Christians to begin emphasizing the cultural significance of the Bible, as well. Educated Christians were determined to demonstrate that the Bible was the Christian classic par excellence. Some Christians attempted to use the Bible as a source for new "classics," rewriting biblical narratives as heroic sagas in the style of Homer or high drama in the style of Euripides. More common was the concerted attempt to apply the methods of rhetorical and philosophical interpretation of texts that were taught in the urban centers of the Roman Empire directly to the biblical texts. Some of the great biblical preachers of this period—such as John Chrysostom, Gregory of Nyssa, and Augustine of Hippo Regius—had received rigorous training in the interpretation of classical texts that they ingeniously applied to the Bible in order to uncover its spiritual messages.

Increasingly sophisticated methods of interpretation led to increased attention to the text of the Bible. Greek-speaking Christians could access the New Testament and the time-honored Septuagint translation of the Old Testament in their original Greek. Nevertheless, in an age of premodern book production, texts had to be copied by hand, leading to numerous accidental and deliberate alterations of the biblical text. The situation was even more confused among non-Greek speakers, such as in the Latin West or Syriac East, where translations were often piecemeal and unreliable. Jerome's solution, to produce a brand-new translation of the entire Bible from its original languages (the genesis of the medieval Vulgate Bible), was only satisfying to a few educated supporters; most Christians preferred to rely on God's providence in matters of scriptural translation and transmission.

Issues of textual criticism, interpretive perspective, and spiritual meaning all propelled the Bible to a new centrality in Christian life. The Bible became the coherent (although infinitely reinterpretable) measure by which to understand the universe. Emperors took on the mantle of biblical kings; holy men and women were compared to prophets; and stories of ancient Israelite punishment and redemption could make sense not only of Christian salvation, but of the many vagaries of life. By the Middle Ages, the Bible was "the Book," a source of images, symbols, narratives, and truths that could structure all of society and culture.

FOR FURTHER READING

Clark, Elizabeth A. *Reading Renunciation: Asceticism and Scripture in Early Christianity.* Princeton, N.J.: Princeton University Press, 1999.

Dawson, David. *Allegorical Readers and Cultural Revision in Ancient Alexandria.* Berkeley: University of California Press, 1992.

Ferguson, Everett, ed. *The Bible in the Early Church.* New York: Garland Press, 1993.

Froehlich, Karlfried, ed. *Biblical Interpretation in the Early Church.* Philadelphia: Fortress Press, 1984.

Metzger, Bruce. *The Canon of the New Testament: Its Origin, Development, and Significance.* Oxford, England: Clarendon Press, 1997 [1987].

Simonetti, Manlio. *Biblical Interpretation in the Early Church: An Historical Introduction to Patristic Exegesis,* trans. John A. Hughes, eds. Anders Bergquist and Markus Bockmuehl. Edinburgh: T & T Clark, 1994 [1981].

Young, Frances M. *Biblical Exegesis and the Formation of Christian Culture.* Cambridge, England: Cambridge University Press, 1997.

Canon and Apocrypha: The Texts

The formation of a standardized list of recognized books of Christian Scripture—a canon (from the Greek for "standard," the same term used for official church rulings)—was a gradual and contentious process in Late Antiquity. Even the notion that such a standard list should exist was probably not common until the second century, as various Christian groups debated the value of the Hebrew Bible and the written records of the sayings and acts of Jesus and the apostles. Marcion, in the second century, argued that the whole Jewish Bible should be jettisoned and that Christians should consult only those portions of the New Testament (several letters of Paul and a modified Gospel of Luke) that did not rely on connections to the Old Testament at all (a position rejected by mainstream Christians). In the third century, the integrity of Scripture and its containment within a canon took on theological as well as practical importance as Christians contemplated the unity and mystery of God's Word. Intertwined with the definition of canon was the delimitation of books of apocrypha (literally "secret" or "hidden" books), books that claimed scriptural status (often by attribution to an apostle or disciple of Jesus) but that were deemed illegitimate. Indeed, canon may be said to have come into existence as a byproduct of the exclusion of apocryphal books.

As imperial Christianity pressed for unity and uniformity, the unity of canon was thought to reflect the unity of the entire church. The distinction between canon and apocrypha was increasingly portrayed as the opposition between orthodoxy and heresy. Tertullian, in the second century, had condemned the Eastern priest who had authored the *Acts of Paul and Thecla,* but conceded that he had had good intentions. Athanasius, almost 200 years later, had no doubts that apocryphal acts, gospels, and letters were all produced as deliberate forgeries by the most vicious of heretics to destroy Christian truth. Heretics were the devil's army, and they wielded apocrypha in their battle.

Despite the push for uniformity and canonicity, we know that many Christians who were otherwise doctrinally and ritually orthodox derived religious satisfaction from literature that was deemed apocryphal and heretical by bishops like Athanasius. Not just "fringe" groups, such as the Manicheans and Melitians, read apocrypha. Egeria, the fourth-century pilgrim, enjoyed reading from the *Acts of Thecla* while visiting Thecla's shrine in Asia Minor (see Text 42). Other Christians, such as Priscillian, the fourth-century Spanish bishop whose treatise "On Faith and Apocrypha" is included here, saw the distinction between canon and apocrypha not as the dividing line between absolute orthodoxy and heresy, but as an intellectual division within orthodox Christianity. Canon and apocrypha were not just labels applied to "good" and "bad" Scripture; they were categories by which Christian communities came to understand their own relationship to God's Word.

50. Eusebius: Church History

In the second book of his *Church History,* Eusebius of Caesarea describes the life and works of the apostles and companions of Jesus. As a digression, he describes which New Testament books are "recognized" as truly attributed to the apostles and their companions. On the basis of historically determined criteria of authorship, he also categorizes popularly read books as "disputed" (among which number many books others included in their canon), "spurious," and even "beyond the pale." Eusebius's view of the canon as a function of historical reliability also explains his concern to harmonize the various gospel accounts so that they will produce a single, seamless historical narrative of Jesus' life. Following Eusebius, authorship remained an important component of canon formation through Late Antiquity and the Middle Ages. Texts securely ascribed to their authors could be taken as divinely sanctioned, while those falsely attributed to apostles or disciples were, conversely, the devious product of heretics seeking to fool the Christian faithful.

THE ORDER OF THE GOSPELS

(24) Now let me indicate the unquestioned writings of this apostle (John). Obviously, his gospel, recognized as it is by all the churches in the world, must first be acknowledged. That the early fathers had good reason to assign it the fourth place after the other three can easily be seen. Those inspired and wonderful men, Christ's apostles, had completely purified their lives and cultivated every spiritual virtue, but their speech was that of every day. The divine wonder-working power bestowed on them by the Savior filled them with confidence, and having neither the ability nor the desire to present the teachings of the Master with rhetorical subtlety or literary skill, they relied only on demonstrating the divine Spirit working with them and on the miraculous power of Christ fully operative in them (cf. 1 Cor 2:4). Thus they proclaimed the knowledge of the Kingdom of Heaven through the whole world, giving very little thought to the business of writing books. The reason for this practice was the ever-present help of a greater, superhuman ministry. We may instance Paul,

who, though he surpassed all others in the marshaling of his arguments and in the abundance of his ideas, committed to writing nothing but his very short epistles; and yet he had countless unutterable things to say, for he had reached the vision of the third heaven, he had been caught up to the divine paradise itself, and had been privileged to hear there unspeakable words (2 Cor 12:2–4).

Similar experiences were enjoyed by the rest of our Savior's pupils—the twelve apostles, the seventy disciples, and countless others besides. Yet of them all, Matthew and John alone have left us memoirs of the Lord's doings, and there is a firm tradition that they took to writing of necessity. Matthew had begun by preaching to Hebrews, and when he made up his mind to go to others, too, he committed his own gospel to writing in his native tongue, so that for those with whom he was no longer present the gap left by his departure was filled by what he wrote. And when Mark and Luke had now published their gospels, John, we are told, who hitherto had relied entirely on the spoken word, finally took to writing for the following reason. The three gospels already

Pp. 86–88 from *The History of the Church from Christ to Constantine* by Eusebius, translated by G. A. Williamson, revised and edited with a new introduction by Andrew Louth (Penguin, 1965). Copyright © G. A. Williamson, 1965. Revisions © Andrew Louth, 1989. Used with permission.

written were in general circulation, and copies had come into John's hands. He welcomed them, we are told, and confirmed their accuracy, but remarked that the narrative only lacked the story of what Christ had done first of all at the beginning of his mission.

This tradition is undoubtedly true. Anyone can see that the three evangelists have recorded the doings of the Savior for only one year, following the consignment of John the Baptist to prison, and that they indicated this very fact at the beginning of their narrative. After the forty days' fast and the temptation that followed, Matthew shows clearly the period covered by his narrative when he says: "Hearing that John had been arrested, he withdrew from Judaea into Galilee" (Matt 4:12). In the same way, Mark says: "After the arrest of John, Jesus went into Galilee" (Mark 1:14). Luke, too, before beginning the acts of Jesus, makes a similar observation, saying that Herod added one more to his other crimes by shutting up John in jail (Luke 3:19–20).

We are told, then, that for this reason the apostle John was urged to record in his gospel the period that the earlier evangelists had passed over in silence and the things done during that period by the Savior, i.e., all that happened before the Baptist's imprisonment; that this is indicated, first by his words "Thus did Jesus begin his miracles" (John 2:11), and later by his mentioning the Baptist in the middle of his account of Jesus' doings, as then still baptizing at Aenon near Salim; and that he makes this plainer when he adds "for John had not yet been thrown into jail" (John 3:23–24).

Thus John in his gospel narrative records what Christ did when the Baptist had not yet been thrown into jail, while the other three evangelists describe what happened after the Baptist's consignment to prison. Once this is grasped, there no longer appears to be a discrepancy between the gospels because John deals with the early stages of Christ's career, and the others cover the last period of his story, and it seems natural that as the genealogy of our Savior as a man had already been set out by Matthew and Luke, John should pass it over in silence and begin with the proclamation of his divinity, since the Holy Spirit had reserved this for him, as the greatest of the four.

This is all that I propose to say about the composition of John's gospel: the origin of Mark's has already been explained. Luke's work begins with a preface in which the author himself explains the reason for its composition. Many others had somewhat hastily undertaken to compile an account of things of which he himself was fully assured (Luke 1:1), so, feeling it his duty to free us from doubts as to our attitude to the others, he furnished in his own gospel an authentic account of the events of which, thanks to his association and intercourse with Paul and his conversations with the other apostles, he had learned the undoubted truth (Luke 1:3–4). This is how I see the matter: at a more appropriate moment I shall endeavor to show, by quoting early writers, what others have said about it. Of John's writings, besides the gospel, the first of the epistles had been accepted as unquestionably his by scholars both of the present and of a much earlier period; the other two are disputed. As to the Revelation, the views of most people to this day are evenly divided. At the appropriate moment, the evidence of early writers shall clear up this matter, too.

WRITINGS ACCEPTED AS SACRED AND THOSE NOT ACCEPTED

(25) It will be well, at this point, to classify the New Testament writings already referred to. We must, of course, put first the holy quartet of the gospels, followed by the Acts of the Apostles. The next place in the list goes to Paul's epistles, and after them we must recognize the epistle called 1 John; likewise 1 Peter. To these may be added, if it is thought proper, the Revelation of John, the arguments about which I shall set out when the time comes. These are classed as recognized books. Those that are disputed, yet familiar to most, include the epistles known as James, Jude, and 2 Peter and those called 2 and 3 John, the work either of the evangelist or of someone else with the same name.

Among spurious books must be placed the "Acts" of Paul, the "Shepherd," and the "Revelation of Peter," also the alleged "Epistle of Barnabas" and the

"Teachings of the Apostles," together with the Revelation of John, if this seems the right place for it; as I said before, some reject it, others include it among the recognized books. Moreover, some have found a place in the list for the "Gospel of Hebrews," a book that has a special appeal for those Hebrews who have accepted Christ. These would all be classed with the disputed books, but I have been obliged to list the latter separately, distinguishing those writings that, according to the tradition of the Church, are true, genuine, and recognized from those in a different category, not canonical but disputed, yet familiar to most churchmen; for we must not confuse these with the writings published by heretics under the name of the apostles, as containing either Gospels of Peter, Thomas, Matthias, and several others besides these or Acts of Andrew, John, and other apostles. To none of these has any churchman of any generation ever seen fit to refer in his writings. Again, nothing could be further from apostolic usage than the type of phraseology employed, while the ideas and implications of their contents are so irreconcilable with true orthodoxy that they stand revealed as the forgeries of heretics. It follows that so far from being classed even among spurious books, they must be thrown out as impious and beyond the pale.

51. Athanasius: Easter Letter 39

Athanasius (see the introduction to Text 26) took the occasion of his annual letter to the churches of Egypt in which he set the official date for Easter to explore the question of canon and apocrypha. This letter, dating from 367, is notable as our earliest surviving list of New Testament books that contains the same twenty-seven books as the current canon (although not in the same order). This list of Old Testament books agrees with the canon of the Hebrew Bible. In addition, Athanasius lists several books that the Catholic and Orthodox churches would later recognize as deuterocanonical (the Protestant Apocrypha), as well as popular Christian texts, such as the *Shepherd* of Hermas and the *Didache* (the Teaching of the Apostles). He distinguishes these latter books, which may be usefully read by Christians, from those that he says are in the official canon. For Athanasius, every book read as Scripture beyond these two lists is apocrypha, the devious and deliberate "invention of heretics" (he singles out the schismatic Melitian group for condemnation). For him, the concept of canon is driven by his understanding of the disparate scriptural books as a single, coherent Bible, the Word of God that conveys Christian teaching in a perfect, complete form. To seek beyond that coherent perfection must therefore signal heretical disagreement with God's Word.

[*The beginning of the text is lost.*] . . . although alive, he came to those who are dead, and although God, he came to human beings. In this way those who sought him found him, and he was made manifest to those who did not question him. So, too, he became a light for the blind when he opened their eyes, and he became a staff for the lame when he healed them and they walked. Once and for all he became a teacher for everyone in everything.

For the teaching of the worship of God is not from human beings; rather, it is the Lord who reveals his Father to those whom he wishes, since it is he who knows him (Matt 11:27). And first he did this to the Apostles; one of them, Paul, writes to the Galatians:

From Brakke, David. *Athanasius and Asceticism*, pp. 326–332. © 1998. David Brakke. Reprinted by permission of The Johns Hopkins University Press.

"I am informing you, brothers and sisters, about the gospel that was proclaimed through me, that it is not of human origin, nor did I receive it from any human being, nor was I taught it; rather, it is according to a revelation of Jesus Christ" (Gal 1:11–12). Moreover, writing to those in Ephesus, he said, "If you have heard about the working of the grace of God that has been given to me for you, how in a revelation I was informed about the mystery, just as I wrote to you earlier in a little bit as you are able, you desire to understand my teaching in the mystery of Christ, which was not revealed to the generations of the children of humanity as it has now been revealed to his prophets and holy apostles" (Eph 3:2–5).

Not they alone, brothers and sisters, are the ones to whom the Lord has become a teacher by revealing the mystery to them; rather, he is a teacher to us all. [For] Paul rejoices with his disciples that they have been taught about the gospel in this way. He prays in behalf of those in Ephesus that "the God of our Lord Jesus Christ, the Father of glory, might give to you a spirit of wisdom and revelation in his knowledge" (Eph 1:17). The Apostle knows that we all share in this prayer that he made for them (the Ephesians) and not only at that former time. When the Lord reveals knowledge to human beings, it is he who commands forever, he who teaches humanity about knowledge, according to the word of the Psalmist (cf. Ps 18:35; 94:10). It is he whom his disciples asked to teach them how to pray, and he who taught daily in the temple, as Luke said (Luke 11:1, 19:47). It is he whom his disciples asked, "Teacher, when will these things happen, and what is the sign that all these things are going to be fulfilled?" (Matt 24:3). When his disciples asked him, "Where do you want us to prepare to eat the Passover?" he answered, saying to them, "Behold, when you enter this city, a man will meet you carrying a jar. Follow him into the house that he enters and say to the master of the house, 'It is the Teacher who says to you, Where is my guest room where I will eat the Passover with my disciples?'" (Luke 22:9–11).

Well, indeed, he spoke like this, for the name of Wisdom is fitting for him because it is he alone who is the true Teacher. For who is to be trusted to teach human beings about the Father, except he who exists always in his bosom? (John 1:18). Thus, who can convince those whom he teaches about "things that eye has not seen nor ear heard nor have arisen upon the human heart" (1 Cor 2:9), except he who alone is acquainted with the Father and has established for us the way to enter the kingdom of heaven? Therefore, he charged his disciples, just as Matthew said, "Let none of you be called 'Rabbi,' for your Teacher is one and you are all brothers and sisters. And do not call for yourselves 'Father' on earth, for your Father in heaven is one. And do not be called 'Teacher,' for your Teacher, Christ, is one. And the great one among you will be your servant" (Matt 23:8–11).

It is not fitting, brothers and sisters, that we should listen to the holy words carelessly. Therefore, why does the Apostle in one place call himself "teacher of the gentiles in faith and truth" (1 Tim 2:7), and in other places say about the Lord, "It is he who has made some apostles, others prophets, and some preachers, others pastors and teachers" (Eph 4:11)? And James commands, saying, "Let not many be teachers, my brothers and sister; you know that we will receive a more severe judgment than you all" (Jas 3:1). He did not say this as if there were no teachers, but as if there were some, although it was not necessary that there be teachers. While these people are speaking like this, it is written in the gospel that the Lord commanded that we not be called "Rabbi" and that no one be called "Teacher" except the Lord alone.

While I was examining these (passages), a thought occurred to me that requires your scrutiny. What I thought is this: The task of the teacher is to teach, and that of the disciple to learn. But even if these people teach, they are still called "disciples," for it is not they who are the originators of what they proclaim; rather, they are at the service of the words of the true Teacher. For our Lord and God Jesus Christ, wanting to inform us of this, said (to) his disciples, "What I say to you in the darkness, receive in the light, and what you hear with your ears, proclaim upon the rooftops" (Matt 10:27). For the words that the disciples proclaim do not belong to them; rather, they heard them from the Savior. Therefore, even if it is Paul who is teaching, it is nevertheless Christ who is speaking in him. And even if he says that the Lord has appointed teachers in the churches (1 Cor 12:28), he (the Lord) nevertheless first teaches them and then sends them out.

For the nature of everyone who is of the created order is to be taught, but our Lord and Craftsman (demiurge) is by nature a teacher. For he was not taught by another person how to be a teacher, but all human beings, even if they are called "Teacher," were nevertheless disciples first. Moreover, every (human being) is instructed because the Savior supplies them with the knowledge of the Spirit, so that they might be students of God. But our Lord and Savior Jesus Christ, being the Word of the Father, was not instructed by anyone.

Rightly he alone is the Teacher, as I have said, so that the Jews were astonished when they heard him and said, "How does he know the Scriptures without being taught?" (John 7:15). Therefore, when he was teaching in the synagogue and healing the sick, the Jews persecuted him. Therefore, "from their feet to their head they do not lack wounds or bruises" (Isa 1:6); rather, such punishment came upon them as a great madness. For "they have not understood," as it is written, "nor have they learned wisdom; rather, they walk in darkness" (Ps 82:5). And, following them, those from the heresies who have caught up to them, namely the wretched Melitians, by denying him, have walked in waterless places and have abandoned the spring of life (cf. Luke 11:24). Therefore, even if they talk about the Passover hypocritically for the sake of the glory of human beings, their gathering is a bread of mourning, for they take counsel evilly against the truth, so that whoever sees such a gathering speaks the word that is written as suited to them: "Why have the nations become arrogant, and why have the peoples worried about vain things?" (Ps 2:1). For the Jews gather together like Pontius Pilate, and the Arians and the Melitians like Herod, not to celebrate the feast, but to blaspheme the Lord, saying, "What is truth?" (John 18:38) And also: "Take him away! Crucify him! Release to us Barabbas!" (Luke 23:18). For it is just like the request for Barabbas to say that the Son of God is a creature and that there was a time when he was not.

As for them, it is no surprise that they have remained dead in their unbelief by being bound by their evil thoughts, just as the Egyptians were bound by their own axles (Exod 14:25).

But for our part, let us now keep the feast according to the tradition of our ancestors, since we have the Holy Scriptures, which are sufficient to instruct us perfectly. When we read them carefully with a good conscience, we will be "like the tree that grows upon places of flowing water, which brings forth its fruit in its season and whose leaves do not wither" (Ps 1:3). But inasmuch as we have mentioned that the heretics are dead but we have the divine Scriptures for salvation, and we are afraid that, as Paul wrote to the Corinthians (2 Cor 11:3), a few of the simple folk might be led astray from sincerity and purity through human deceit and might then begin to read other books, the so-called apocrypha, deceived by their having the same names as the genuine books, I exhort you to bear with me if, to remind you, I write about things that you already know, on account of the Church's need and advantage.

As I begin to mention these things, in order to commend my undertaking, I will employ the example of Luke the evangelist and say myself: "Inasmuch as certain people have attempted" (Luke 1:1) to set in order for themselves the so-called apocryphal books and to mix these with the divinely inspired Scripture, about which we are convinced it is just as those who were eyewitnesses from the beginning and assistants of the Word handed down to our ancestors, it seemed good to me, since I have been urged by genuine brothers and sisters and instructed from the beginning, to set forth in order the canonized and transmitted writings, those believed to be divine books, so that those who have been deceived might condemn the persons who led them astray, and those who have remained pure might rejoice to be reminded (of these things).

There are, then, belonging to the Old Testament in number a total of twenty-two, for, as I have heard, it has been handed down that this is the number of the letters in the Hebrew alphabet. In order and by name they are as follows: first Genesis; then Exodus; then Leviticus; and after this, Numbers; and finally,

Deuteronomy. After these is Joshua, the son of Nun; and Judges; and after this, Ruth; and again, next four books of Kings, the first and second of these being reckoned as one book, and the third and fourth likewise being one.[1] After these are First and Second Chronicles, likewise reckoned as one book; then First and Second Esdras, likewise as one.[2] After these is the Book of Psalms; and then Proverbs; then Ecclesiastes and the Song of Songs. After these is Job; and finally the Prophets, the twelve being reckoned as one book; then Isaiah, Jeremiah and with it, Baruch; Lamentations and the Letter; and after it, Ezekiel and Daniel. To this point are the books of the Old Testament.

Again, one should not hesitate to name the books of the New Testament. For these are the four Gospels: Matthew, Mark, Luke, and John; then after these, Acts of the Apostles and seven letters, called catholic, by the apostles, namely: one by James; two by Peter; then three by John; and after these, one by Jude. After these there are fourteen letters by Paul, written in this order: first to the Romans; then two to the Corinthians; and after these, to the Galatians; and next to the Ephesians; then to the Philippians and to the Colossians; and after these, two to the Thessalonians; and that to the Hebrews; and in addition, two to Timothy, one to Titus, and finally that to Philemon. And besides, the Revelation of John.

These are the springs of salvation, so that someone who thirsts may be satisfied by the words they contain. In these books alone the teaching of piety is proclaimed. Let no one add to or subtract from them (cf. Deut 12:32). Concerning them the Lord put the Sadducees to shame when he said, "You err because you do not know the Scriptures or their meaning" (Matt 22:29), and he reproved the Jews, "Search the Scriptures, for it is they that testify to me" (John 5:39).

But for the sake of greater accuracy, I add this, writing from necessity. There are other books, in addition to these, which have not been canonized, but have been appointed by the ancestors to be read to those who newly join us and want to be instructed in the word of piety: the Wisdom of Solomon, the Wisdom of Sirach, Esther, Judith, Tobit, the book called Teaching of the Apostles, and the Shepherd.

Nevertheless, the former books are canonized, the latter are (only) read, and there is no mention of the apocryphal books. Rather (the category of apocrypha) is an invention of heretics, who write these books whenever they want and then grant and bestow on them dates, so that, by publishing them as if they were ancient, they might have a pretext for deceiving the simple folk. Great is the hard-heartedness of those who do this and do not fear the word that is written: "You shall not add to the word that I command you, nor shall you subtract from it" (Deut 12:32). Who has made the simple folk believe that those books belong to Enoch even though no Scriptures existed before Moses? On what basis will they say there is an apocryphal book of Isaiah? He preaches openly on the high mountain and says, "These words are not hidden or in a dark land" (Isa 45:19). How could Moses have an apocryphal book? He is the one who published Deuteronomy with heaven and earth as witnesses (Deut 4:26, 30:19). No, this can be nothing except "itchy ears" (2 Tim 4:3), trading in piety, and the pleasing of women. Paul spoke about such people beforehand when he wrote to his disciple: "A time will come when they will not keep to the salvific teaching, but according to their own desire they will produce teachers for themselves, when their ear will itch, and they will turn their ears away from the truth and go after myths" (2 Tim 4:3–4). For truly the apocryphal books are filled with myths, and it is a vain thing to pay attention to them because their voices are empty and polluted. For they are the beginning of discord, and strife is the goal of people who do not seek what is beneficial for the Church, but who desire to receive compliments from those whom they lead astray, so that, by publishing new discourses, they will be considered great people.

Therefore, it is fitting for us to decline such books. For even if a useful word is found in them, it is still not good to trust them. For this is a work of the wickedness of those who have conceived of mixing one or two inspired texts so that, through such de-

---

[1] In modern Bibles, these four books are divided into 1-2 Samuel and 1-2 Kings.

[2] In modern Bibles, Ezra and Nehemiah.

ception, they might somehow cover up the the evil teachings that they have clearly created. Therefore, it is even more fitting for us to reject such books, and let us command ourselves not to proclaim anything in them or to speak anything in them with those who want to be instructed, even if there is a good word in them, as I have said. For what do the spiritual Scriptures lack that we should seek after these empty voices of unknown people? It is appropriate for us to cite the text that is written about them: "Is there no balm in Gilead or physician there?" (Jer 8:22) and again "Of what profit to you is the road to Egypt so that you drink the troubled water from Gehon?" and again "Of what profit to you is the way to Assyria that you drink the water from their rivers?" (Jer 2:18).

Therefore, if we seek the faith, it is possible for us to discover it through them (the Scriptures), that is, we believe in Father and the Son and the Holy Spirit. Or on the subject of his humanity, John cried out, "The Word became flesh and lived among us" (John 1:14). And on the subject of the resurrection, the Lord put to shame the Sadducees, saying, "Have you not read what is said to you by God, saying, 'I am the God of Abraham, the God of Isaac, the God of Jacob'? He is not the God of the dead, but of the living" (Matt 22:31–32). On the subject of the coming judgment, it is written, "We shall all stand . . ." (Rom 14:10) [*The text is missing here.*] . . . among human beings? Who among those who have no hope could at all think that the Word would become flesh (cf. Eph 2:12; 1 Thess 4:13; John 1:14)? Have the things in God's heart arisen upon the heart of human beings (1 Cor 2:19)? When has anyone known his heart (Rom 11:34; 1 Cor 2:16)?

[. . .] and "these are the things that he proclaimed" or "as he said" or "Isaiah charges and says" and "as David says" and also "Moses says beforehand" and again "the Scripture says that Elijah was." Even if it says "as it is written," it does not make clear where the text is written or who proclaimed it. Rather, we are the ones who read and learn where it is written in the (Hebrew) Scriptures. And this text, "What eye has not seen . . ." (1 Cor 2:9), we do not find written in the Scripture as it is. But if it is extant in the apocryphal books as the heretics says,

then those who invented these books have secretly stolen from the words of Paul and written it at a later time.

Therefore, inasmuch as it is clear that the testimony from the apocryphal books is superfluous because it is unfounded—for the Scripture is perfect in every way—let the teacher teach from the words of the Scripture, and let him place before those who desire to learn those things that are appropriate to their age. In the case of those who begin to study as catechumens, it is not right to proclaim the obscure texts in the Scripture, since they are mysteries, but instead to place before them the teaching that they need: what will teach them how to hate sin and to abandon idol worship as an abomination. The wisdom . . . [*The text is missing here.*] . . . in the Scriptures. I am satisfied that this will remind you, so that, when you take for yourselves the saints as patterns and administer well the words of the Holy Scriptures, you will hear sometime, "Well done, good and faithful servant! Since you are trustworthy in small things, I will place you over great things" (Matt 25:21, 23).

For I have not written these things as if I were teaching, for I have not attained such a rank. Rather, because I heard that the heretics, particularly the wretched Melitians, were boasting about the books that they call "apocryphal," I thus have informed you of everything that I heard from my father (Bishop Alexander of Alexandria), as if I were with you and you with me in a single house, i.e., the Church of the living God, the pillar and strength of truth. When we gather in a single place, let us purify it (the Church) of every defilement, of double-heartedness, of fighting and childish arrogance. Let us be satisfied with only the Scripture inspired by God to instruct us. Its books we have set forth in the words above: which they are and how many their number. For in this way we now celebrate the feast as is fitting, not with old leaven or with evil or wicked leaven, but with pure and true leaven (1 Cor 5:8).

We will begin the holy Lent on the 25th of the month of Mechir (19 February), and the great week of the saving Passover on the last of the month of Phamenoth (26 March). And we will finish the holy fast on the 5th of the month of Pharmuthi (31 March). And next we will celebrate the seven weeks of the holy Pentecost, remembering the poor and sharing with one another and with the needy, in accordance with the word of Esdra (Neh 8:10). Once and for all we do everything, glorifying God, in accordance with the command of Paul in Christ Jesus our Lord, through whom be glory and power with the Holy Spirit for ever and ever. Amen.

Greet one another with a holy kiss. All the brothers and sister with me greet you.

I inform you of this as well: that when the blessed Lampon, bishop of Darnei, fell asleep, [. . .] was appointed . . . [*The remainder of the text is lost.*]

52. Priscillian: On Faith and Apocrypha

Priscillian (d. ca. 386) was a popular preacher and ascetic leader in Spain, who, shortly after being ordained bishop of Avila, was accused of heresy by his fellow bishops and executed on charges of sorcery by the imperial court. His name was associated with Manicheism and Gnosticism by writers, such as Jerome (see Text 27). During his brief and turbulent ecclesiastical career, Priscillian wrote a series of theological and exegetical treatises that were discovered in the nineteenth century and that have shed new light on a universally condemned "heretic" of the late fourth century. Among these treatises was a text *On Faith and Apocrypha,* in which Priscillian defended his ecclesiastical use of noncanonical texts as sources of Christian teaching and faith.

The portrait of a self-consciously orthodox Christian who acknowledged the authority of the church and confessed a theologically correct creed defending the use of apocryphal writings significantly challenges the view of Eusebius and Athanasius that apocrypha were produced by heretics to pervert scriptural truth. Priscillian's defense of his reading of apocrypha is, by turns, serious and mocking and is ultimately grounded in a strong sense of theological, ascetical, and intellectual elitism.

THE ACCUSATION

". . . would be condemned, since novelty of intellect is the mother of contention, erudition is the author of scandal, the fuel of schism, nourishment of heresy, form of mortal sin. Indeed, everything that seems to have been said or done, by God or by the apostles such that it might be approved, concerning this it has been written: 'Yes is yes, no is no' (Matt 5:37). Moreover, that which has been newly discovered by intellects and trickeries is here exposed by the witness of divine virtue, which says: 'That which surpasses this is from the Evil one' (Matt 5:37)."

THE CANON POINTS TO APOCRYPHA

Let us see, therefore, if the apostles of Jesus Christ, master of our conduct and life, did not read from outside the canon. Judas the apostle, himself the Lord's twin—he who believed more in Christ God after the remarkable passion, when it is recounted that he was tested; he who both saw and touched the vestigial marks of the chains and the glories of the divine cross—he proclaimed: "Concerning these things Enoch prophesied in the seventh [generation] from Adam, saying, 'Behold the Lord is coming with thousands of saints to make judgment and to convince

From *Priscilliani Quae Supersunt,* ed. G. Schepss. Vienna: F. Tempsky, 1889. (Translated by Andrew S. Jacobs.)

everyone . . . also concerning all of the harsh things that sinners have said against him'" (Jude 14–15). Who is this Enoch whom the apostle Jude enlists in the witness of prophecy? And who would prophesy concerning God, with nothing but this prophecy to refer to, rather than (if these things are said truly) condemn himself according to the canonical ordering? Or perhaps Enoch was not considered to be the prophet whom Paul in his letter written to the Hebrews testified that he had "borne witness before his translation" (Heb 11:5) or that one in the beginning of Genesis (when still the form of the world and the nature of the crude age, retaining the sin of the deceived human, did not believe in the conversion toward God after sin) whom God preferred to translate among his own rather than let him die? If it is not disputed, but is believed among the apostles, that he is a prophet, then why is it called a matter of consideration rather than commotion, counsel rather than temerity, faith rather than falsehood that, when an opinion is offered to avenge grudges and a prophet who preaches God is condemned?

Are we dealing in trivial matters? Are we casting bones and dice?[1] Do we trot out trifling plays on a stage so that, while we follow humans of this age, we condemn the words of the apostles? By what peaceful compromise is there grace for people who wish to believe, yet do not hold to apostolic words?

Now perhaps someone follows these lines of reasoning: although indeed a single testimony might suffice to confirm the faith of saints in God, nevertheless he may say that it is not to be believed of one, but that "two and three witnesses secure more completely the reason of the word" (Deut 19:15; Matt 18:16). Let our inquisitor turn to anything at all of this sort, seeking diligently, poring over the Scriptures to see whether or not we speak truly.

This is Tobit's testimony, the saint of the life to come, laying out rules for his son, pronouncing what things he should guard: "We are the sons of prophets: Noah was a prophet, and Abraham, and Isaac, and Jacob, and all of our ancestors who prophesied from the beginning of the age" (Tob 4:12). When do we read from the book of the prophet Noah in the canon? Who reads the Book of Abraham among the prophets of the established canon? Who ever taught that Isaac prophesied? Who has heard the prophecy of Jacob set in the canon? If he reads of them in Tobit and values the witness of canonical prophecy, then is it given to him as a testimony of valuable virtue, or is it assigned to others as an opportunity for just condemnation? In these matters let each one have a little patience if we prefer to be condemned with the prophets of God, rather than condemn those things that are religious along with those who make imprudent assumptions.

Who, indeed, would not fear the accuser of Noah, dispenser of divine judgment? Concerning him the apostle says: "Righteous Noah did he preserve, that herald of justice, when he brought down the destruction of the world upon the impious" (2 Pet 2:5). Who would not seek the "bosom of" the prophet "Abraham" (cf. Luke 16:22, 23) as a testimony of serenity? Who would not wish to be considered the seed of Isaac (cf. Gal 4)? Who would not love Jacob, called by God "a God to Pharaoh"?[2] And who would not tremble at rejecting the memory of the saints, since it is written: "Truly I say to you that whoever placed a stumbling block before the smallest of those who has believed in my name, it is better for that one to be tied to a millstone and cast into the depths of the sea" (Matt 18:6)? If this is said concerning the littlest ones, I would like to know what is pronounced concerning those who are first in faith!

Moreover, in all these books there is no fear— if some things have been inserted by miserable heretics—in deleting and in agreeing to reject that which is not found in the prophets and Gospels. Indeed, for that saint of God himself, a lie is not embraced by the truth, nor are sacrilegious and hateful things set before saints; it is better to "lift out the tares from the harvests" (cf. Matt 13:29), rather than have the hope of a good harvest destroyed on account of

---

[1] "Bones and dice" may be a reference to Cicero's condemnation of such practices in *On Divination*.

[2] Priscillian seems to be referring to Exod 7:1, although here the subject is Moses, not Jacob.

tares. This is why the devil inserted his own words into the holy words, in order that (without a careful harvester) the harvest should perish with the tares and the good be made to fall with the worse. The same judgment binds the one who has joined the worst to the good as the one who has destroyed the good with the bad.

So in the Gospel according to Luke, God testified: "Let them investigate the blood of all the prophets, which has been shed since the creation of the world, from the blood of Abel until the blood of Zechariah who was cut down between the altar and the temple" (Luke 11:50–51), and Elijah says in Kings: "They have thrown down your altars and killed your prophets, and I alone am remaining and they seek after my life" (1 Kings 19:10). Who is this prophet Abel, from whom the prophets' blood first flowed, whose beginning ended in Zechariah? Who are these intermediary prophets who appear to have been killed? If indeed everything that is said is sought in the books of the canon, and to read beyond that is to sin, we read of no one killed among those who are established as prophets in the canon. If nothing is to be assumed or maintained beyond the authority of the canon, we cannot simply believe in stories and, by agreement, retain an account of events not in the text. Maybe someone will jump up and say that Isaiah was dismembered;[3] if he is among those who condemn my practice, let him shut his mouth or, offering forth the story of how this happened, let him say that he also believes in painters and poets! For already they casually allow the fancies of philosophers to be mentioned, doubtless so that they might find a witness of this matter of the blood of the prophets slaughtered since the creation of the world. If the evangelist saying these things correctly came forward to testify, saying, "Search the Scriptures" (John 5:39), indeed he drew me forward to read what he read.

Moreover, I cannot say that which I am compelled to speak, that my following the apostle was not the learnedness of faith but, rather, the trap of one de-

ceived. For once again, the text is brought forth from the Gospel according to Matthew: "Rising then Joseph received the boy and his mother by night, and he went into Egypt and was there until the death of Herod, so that which was said by the Lord through the prophet was accomplished: 'out of Egypt I called my son'" (Matt 2:14–15). Who is *this* prophet, whom we do not read in the canon, whose faithful prophecy the Lord fulfilled like the guarantor of a promised obligation? Certainly, no tremendous amount of toil is required to believe that God would prepare the future road of the divine path with the witnesses of prophecy, from which God would not then wish to deviate, so that we might admit that he did, in fact, speak through the one who prophesied.

THE IMPORTANCE OF THE CREED

Certainly a book cannot be condemned whose witness fulfills the faith of canonical speech. Nor is it possible to pick and choose, as if selecting among delicacies at a banquet! Nor is it a question of clever reasoning, whereby someone has assumed that which follows: while they claim to see the dialectical work of intellects, they have made sects through persuasion. The Scripture of God is a solid matter, a true matter not to be chosen by a person but transmitted to that person by God, of whom if "the first fruits are holy, so also is the whole matter holy" (Rom 11:16). Here is the source of heresies: when each individual serves his own intellect, rather than God, and is not disposed to follow the creed but, rather, to argue over the creed, even though, if they knew faith, they would hold to nothing outside the creed. The creed is the seal of the true matter, and to pick apart the creed is to prefer to argue over the creed, rather than to believe in it.

The creed is the work of the Lord, in the name of the Father, Son, and Holy Spirit, faith in one God, from whom Christ God is the Son of God, savior born in the flesh, suffering, who rose up on account of love of humanity, who, handing over the creed to his apostles, taught what he was and would be, showing in himself and in his creed that the Son is the name of

---

[3] According to the popular *Martyrdom of Isaiah* to which Priscillian refers, Isaiah was sawn in half by Manasseh, son of Hezekiah of Judah.

the Father and the Father is that of the Son, lest the error of the Binionites should prevail.[4] For he showed to the apostles who inquired that he was everything that has a name (cf. Eph 1:21); he wished to be believed in as One and indivisible, as the prophet says: "This is our God, no other is to be compared to him who showed the way of discipline and gave it to Jacob his son and to Israel his beloved; afterward he appeared on the earth and associated with humans, the Lord God is his name" (Bar 3:35–37, Amos 5:8).

"A CLOUD OF WITNESSES"

But now lest we be said to be drawn by love of faith to have acted otherwise than we have suggested (certainly from an overwhelming refutation against diverse heresies, one passage may lie vulnerable), so on this account we especially wish this work to be accepted, that we might triumph over that faithless lie by a cloud of witnesses (cf. Heb 12:1). So now let us return to the matter: whether we are to be found credible in the matter of which we are accused; indeed, we may rightly be seen to be arguing about leftovers.

So even Paul says that God said: "More blessed is it to give than to receive" (Acts 20:35), and we do not read of God speaking thus in the canon. Also Daniel testifies that God has spoken, saying, "Since wickedness came forth from Babylon from elders who were supposed to rule the people" (Sus 5). Even though we should believe that these things were said and written, in the words of an evangelist and in the declamation of apostles and divine speech, yet look! The time has come: while the debate over superfluous matters is being carried out, stupidity is introduced among the faithful! We cannot say that God has not said what the apostle said he has said or that the prophet made no prophecy about which the Scripture testifies. Since we correctly believe these things on faith, we do not see these texts in the canon, and, therefore,

if everything outside the canon is to be condemned, either the testimony of the condemned is received or else there is no authority in these things written in the Scriptures.

So, too, the prophet Ezekiel says: "Thus says the Lord to Gog: 'You are the one of whom I spoke in the ancient days through the hands of my servants the prophets'" (Ezek 38:14, 17). I believe he said that (and I am not playing false), so I must either affirm that the prophet has invented what God had said or that God lied: for who might that prophet *be* through whom God said this? I do not see him in the canon; although we have faith in these words, we haven't found the author of this text in the canon.

So also in Chronicles we do not find Nathan, the prophet; Ahijah, the Selonite; the visions of Iddo; the words of Jehu, son of Hanani, for the faith but, rather, the authority of what they recount, when Scripture says: "and the rest of the deeds of Jehosaphat from the first to the most recent, behold, are written in the Deeds of Jehu, son of Hanani, who recorded them in the Book of the Kings of Israel" (2 Chr 20:34), and we do not read these texts in the canonical books, but we show them to be held apart from the canon. So also it says there: "and the rest of the deeds of Solomon from the first to the most recent, behold, they are written in the words of Nathan, the Prophet, and the words of Ahijah, the Selonite, and in the visions of Iddo, which he saw concerning Jereboam, son of Nebat" (2 Chr 9:29); and again there: "and the remaining deeds of Rehoboam from first to most recent, are they not written in the words of Shemaiah, the prophet, and Iddo, the Seer, and all his deeds?" (2 Chr 12:15); and again there: "and the remaining deeds of Abijah and his acts and words are written in the book of the prophet Iddo" (2 Chr 13:22); and again there: "and the remaining deeds of Amaziah from first to most recent, are they not written in the Book of the Days of the Kings of Judah and Israel?" (2 Chr 25:26); again there: "are these things not written in the Book of the Days of the Kings of Judah?" (2 Chr 26:26); again there: "and the remaining deeds of Manasseh and his prayer, which he prayed to the Lord in the name of the God of Israel, behold, they are written in the acts of his speeches, in the deeds of the seers" (2 Chr 33:18–19). Who there-

---

[4] "Binionites" seems to be a coinage of Priscillian, perhaps referring to creeds that draw too much of a distinction between the Father and the Son. Priscillian's particular phrase "Christ God," by contrast, emphasizes their unity.

fore would patiently receive such a torrent? Here, on the one hand, as unlearnedness urges insanity and rage drives ignorance to say nothing unless it be Catholic, are you not saying: "damned what *I* do not know, damned what *I* do not read, damned what I do not seek through the zeal of my sluggish leisure!" When, on the other hand, divinity urges eloquence, it says "Search out the Scriptures" (John 5:39), particularly showing this: though their blood is sought as a testimony of revenge, their words will not be denied.

Necessarily set amid these matters, we want you to be confident that we spoke before out of certainty. I have the witness of God, I have that of the apostles, I have that of the prophets; if I seek out that which characterizes the Christian person, if (I seek) that which characterizes the ecclesiastical disposition, if (I seek) that which characterizes God Christ, I find those who preach God, I find those who prophesy. It is not fear, it is faith, because we have cherished that which is better and have rejected that which is worse. Diligence has kept certain books outside the body of the canon, preserving them for the labor of reading and for the confirmation of those texts that we read inside the canon. Indeed, it is through these certain books that the greater part of heretical senses has waged war against the Catholic, thereby showing that they prefer to falsify, rather than to hold true. Yet it is by preserving one or other of such books that we might uphold that justly apostolic opinion that "every spirit that denies Jesus is not from God, and every spirit who confesses Jesus Christ from God" (cf. 1 John 4:3, 2); so is it written: "no one indeed says in the Holy Spirit 'Jesus is cursed,' and no one says unless they are in the Holy Spirit 'Jesus is Lord' " (1 Cor 12:3).

Citing once more from the ancient monuments of books: When the devil was jealous of the witness (*testimonium*) of the Scriptures, it was not enough that Jerusalem was captured, that the altar of the Lord polluted, and that the Temple had been destroyed, but since it was easy for humans to reconstruct with their hands that which had been originally built by their hands, the Ark of the Covenant (*arca testimonii*) was burned, since the devil knew that human nature plagued by the world might easily lose faith if it did not have the testimonies of the Scriptures for the

preaching of the divine name. But the nature of the divine mystery shines brighter than that of the devil; because of this, in order that God might be able to demonstrate this fact to humanity, he desired that Ezra be preserved, who rewrote those items that had been burned (4 Ezra 14). Now if we truly believe that these were burned, so, too, we believe they were rewritten. Although it may be read in the canon that the covenant was burned, it is not read in the canon that it was rewritten by Ezra; nevertheless, since after the covenant was burned, it could not have been restored unless it was written down, we correctly give faith to that book that claims Ezra as its author: even if it is not established in the canon, it should be retained as a record of the restored divine covenant with veneration appropriate to such matters. There also we read it written that the Holy Spirit penetrated the heart of the elect person from the beginning of the age, guiding the actions of humans and their affairs; so, because the form of the text was hardly retained by human memory, it reconstructed all those acts that we read about and that seem to have been rewritten from human memory, recapitulated in an orderly form while he wrote, "speaking by day and not silent by night" (4 Ezra 14:43). At this it seems right to say: Yes! That's it!

THE CHRISTIAN INTELLECT SEEKS GOD EVERYWHERE

So then, I ask, are we guilty for having read a few bits of this material? We would be more criminal if we did not read all the things that were prophesied concerning God! I have no doubt what will be said by one of those who cherish malicious subterfuge more than faith: "Seek nothing more! It suffices for you to read what is written in the canon!" Against the words of that one, whose natural human intellect easily seeks leisure, rather than toil, I would stand up, if the witness of the evangelist Luke were not pressing down upon me in the Acts of the Apostles, saying: "Equally inquisitive, they consulted the Scriptures to see if it were so" (cf. Acts 17:11), about what Paul had said to them. Their understanding is what I desire: I recognize that the witness of prophecy has been transmitted in the canon. Although it would indeed be a crime not to have believed the apostolic speeches, nevertheless it is no damnable guilt to shore up support for the affirmation of the faith of Scriptures, and there is no reproof of the devil in this that might render us unfit. Divine speech could not (since everything it had said belonged to it) speak a text about another when speaking about itself, but only report about itself; saying therefore that "it is written" necessarily offers a responsible basis for our reading. Nor did it set aside its own prophesied glory, nor its grace that was prophesied as the due of future generations. Concerning both these things "I am under obligation" (Rom 1:14): so I may read about the one who prophesied for divine commemoration, and I may believe in God.

Who indeed would not take delight in the fact that Christ was prophesied before the ages, not just by a few, but by all? And who would appraise divine greatness so cheaply—both that God was born by such an incredible miracle, having a virginal mother in the service of the divine word for conception and birth, and that he suffered in the dwelling place of a body—that he would think that the mysteries of the divine sense did not cry out in every land and in all people, as it is written: "every tongue will confess that the Lord Jesus is in the glory of God the Father" (Phil 2:11)?

And so whoever would deny these things, I know for certain that he will receive the wage of that Pharisee, who, at the coming of the Lord, when the whole crowd cried out with the apostles joining in: "Hosanna, Hosanna in the heavens, blessed is he who comes in the name of the Lord," said they ought to be stopped (Luke 19:37–79). Even though doubtless they could not be silent at the coming glory of the Lord. But let the one of that stripe see what the Lord said: "Even if they keep silent, the stones will shout out" (Luke 19:40). So let him understand that if the hardness of naturally dead stones is animated into the use of human speech to give witness to God, how is the tongue of the saints closed off, which is pressed to confession both by its very nature and by divine grace? If indeed the gentile souls, hindered by the

forms of idols and divine mummeries, speak of the flying movement of birds and the paths of feathers driven by winds as omens for the foreknowledge of future events, as well as the veins of entrails throbbing with the life force of earthly spirits, while they give faith to demons, (and) they affirm that the innards of animals that are about to die at any moment foretell the future, and they beseech the dead about life, saying to the stone "rise up" and to the tree "keep watch" (Hab 2:19), thus zeal is called sacrilege from this, wisdom is named ignorance for those who do not know that by these actions, they "sacrifice not to God but to a demon" (1 Cor 10:20). If in such actions there is any glory for that one, how can we reject the divine prophecies of the saints and, when we are obedient to our own wills, how can we look askance at those who have prophesied God and still retain the apostolic precepts that say: "do not extinguish the spirit, do not reject the prophecies" (1 Thess 5:19, 20)?

PRISCILLIAN'S FAITH ACTS AS HIS GUIDE

And thus, since "where there is freedom there is Christ" (2 Cor 3:17), allow me to proclaim alone before all that "I, too, have the spirit of the Lord" (1 Cor 7:40); let the devil's jealousy cease! The Lord was proclaimed by all, Christ was prophesied by all, by Adam, Seth, Noah, Abraham, Isaac, Jacob, and by all the others "who have prophesied from the beginning of the world" (Tob 4:13). And I dare to say that the devil is jealous: every human knew that God was coming in the flesh, and I shall not even speak of those whom, in the disposition of his generation, God established in the gospel that they would surpass the faith of divine nature and the collection of the canon. For just as the penalty is greater for those who know and deny, so, too, complete glory means not only to believe in one's heart, but also not to deny glory "in the confession of the mouth" (Rom 10:10), as David says: "I believed and because of this I spoke" (Ps 116:10). On this point also the apostle Peter[5] (aware of the reason for the lim-

---

[5] Priscillian means, of course, Paul, not Peter.

ited number of the books in the canon and still relaxing the freedom to read those things written concerning Christ), when he sent a letter to the Colossians, said: "When this letter is read among you, have it also read in the church of the Laodiceans; also you should read that which was sent to the Laodiceans" (Col 4:16). Now is it a fact that the apostle was condemned among you, he who allowed his followers to read a letter that was not in the canon? Do you care more about yourselves than about Christ, and so you bend your wills to extend even an unjust judgment in the matters decided before you?

Indeed, for all of us who believe in Christ God, the fullness of faith is the day of the Lord, and the law of the apostolic life is the form of the command (since if "faith comes from hearing, hearing moreover is established through faith" [Rom 10:17]), but is the hope of future things established for us if the things that used to be taught as written or said about Christ and preserved in memory, not ever rejected by the apostles but read [by them], are now not only rejected by us but condemned as sacrilege, although it is written in the Gospel: "whosoever has done a miracle in my name, he cannot speak ill of me" (Mark 9:39)?

On that count, furthermore, I do not refuse, nor do I reject those things that should not be communicated to ignorant ears, lest—since many things have been falsified by heretics—as they seek a divine work under the famous names of prophets, in the words of the saints, they rush into the pit of heretical falsehood, for they do not maintain the discipline of apostolic speech to its fullest. But not on account of the villainy of the worst men should the prophecy of saints be condemned. For all heresies have persuasively made the perverse bases of their miserable sects through the interpretation of all the Scriptures, and all of them affirm that they believe that Christ is God and that they are Christians. So divine Scripture is not to be condemned, or the faith of Christ repudiated, or the name of Christian refused, just because they wish to push their own sacrileges, and so they dare to usurp the fellowship of the Catholic name. If indeed we wish to condemn everything they read, we would also have to condemn those books that are set in the canon! So it is better to condemn deadly interpretation and sacrilegious behavior, rather than divine Scripture, since it is written: "to you it is given to know the mystery of the kingdom of God; to others, however, I shall speak in parables, so that seeing they may not see and hearing they may not hear" (Mark 4:11–12). To me, certainly, a servant of the Lord contemplating these matters, remains this one idea, that "who does not love Christ, let him be anathema. *Maranatha*" (1 Cor 16:22).

53. Augustine: On Christian Doctrine

As a young man, Augustine had been disappointed with the literary quality of the Bible, deeming it vulgar and crude in comparison with the Latin classics he studied and taught. As a bishop, preaching the word of God from the Scriptures, Augustine endeavored to demonstrate how the Bible could function as the foundation of a Christian culture, a system of signs and meanings that gave the world a definitively Christian shape. The result of this quest was his treatise *On Christian Doctrine,* which he began as a newly ordained bishop in 396 but did not complete until 426, a few years before his death.

On Christian Doctrine raises theoretical and practical questions of reading, centered on biblical interpretation. In this excerpt from the second book, Augustine emphasizes the im-

From *The Works of Saint Augustine: A Translation for the 21st Century,* Part I, Volume 11: *Teaching Christianity,* trans. Edmund Hill, O.P. Hyde Park, N.Y.: New City Press, 1996. Used with permission.

portance of the text itself. Augustine provides a list of Old and New Testament books that matches the later, medieval canon. His stance on apocrypha is mild (he was less sanguine in other, antiheretical writings): apocrypha are dangerous only in proportion to the mental fragility of their readers. As a Latin-speaking Christian of the fourth and fifth centuries (Augustine complained notoriously in his *Confessions* about his inability to learn Greek), Augustine faced the additional problem of textual transmission and translation, of choosing from among myriad Latin versions. He was uncomfortable with the solution proposed by his elder contemporary, Jerome, who attempted to produce an entirely new translation from the original Hebrew and Greek. Instead, Augustine constructs a notion of textual tradition, guided by past experts, the hand of God, and the watchful eye of the learned interpreter.

(8) But let us turn our attention back to that third stage,[1] about which we had undertaken to set out and discuss whatever the Lord might suggest. So then, the really accomplished investigators of the divine Scriptures will be those who have begun by reading them all and becoming familiar with them at least by reading, if not yet by understanding them all—just those, that is, that are called canonical because the others are best left to be read by people who are well instructed in the truths of faith, or else they may so enthrall the feebler spirits that they delude them with dangerous falsehoods and fancies to the prejudice of sound understanding. But for the canonical Scriptures, they should follow the authority of the majority of the Catholic churches, among which, of course, are those that have the privilege of being apostolic sees and have received letters from the apostles.

They will hold, therefore, to this standard with the canonical Scriptures, that they will put those accepted by all the Catholic churches before those that some do not accept; among these that are not accepted by all, they will prefer those accepted by most of them, and by the greater ones among them, to those that fewer churches and ones of lesser authority regard as canonical. Should they, however, discover that different ones are held to be canonical by the majority of churches from those so regarded by the greater churches—though this would be very un-

likely—I consider that both should be regarded as having equal authority.

But the whole canon of the Scriptures, which we are saying is to be the subject of our consideration, consists of the following books: The five of Moses, that is, Genesis, Exodus, Leviticus, Numbers, Deuteronomy, and one book of Joshua, son of Nun, one of Judges, one little book that is called Ruth, which seems rather to belong to the beginning of the Kings; then the four of Kings and the two of the Chronicles, which do not follow on, but run parallel beside them. This is all history, which contains the sequence of times and the order of events. There are other historical books, which are not connected to each other or to this order and sequence, such as Job and Tobit and Esther and Judith, and the two books of the Maccabees, and the two of Ezra, which do seem more to follow the order of that history which ended with Kings or Chronicles.

Next the prophets, among whom are David's one book of psalms and three books of Solomon: Proverbs, the Song of Songs, and Ecclesiastes. The fact is, those two books, one of which is entitled Wisdom and the other Ecclesiasticus, are said to be Solomon's only from a certain resemblance to the others because it is the constant tradition that Jesus son of Sirach wrote them, but since they have been thought worthy of being accorded canonical authority, they are to be counted among the prophetic books. The rest are the books of those who are properly called prophets, each single book of the twelve prophets, which joined together, since they have never been separated, are treated as one book; the

---

[1] Augustine has just enumerated six stages by which a Christian comes to scriptural meaning: fear, piety, knowledge, courage, counsel, and understanding.

names of the prophets being these: Hosea, Joel, Amos, Obadiah, Jonah, Micah, Nahum, Habakkuk, Zephaniah, Haggai, Zechariah, Malachi; next, the four prophets, each with his greater volume, Isaiah, Jeremiah, Daniel, Ezekiel. To these forty-four books is confined the authority of the Old Testament.

But in the New Testament, there are the four books of the gospel, according to Matthew, according to Mark, according to Luke, according to John; the fourteen letters of the apostle Paul, to the Romans, to the Corinthians two, to the Galatians, to the Ephesians, to the Philippians, to the Thessalonians two, to the Colossians, to Timothy two, to Titus, to Philemon, to the Hebrews; two letters of Peter, three of John, one of Jude, and one of James; the one book of the Acts of the Apostles, and the one book of the Apocalypse of John.

(9) What those who fear God and have a docile piety are looking for in all these books is the will of God. The first step in this laborious search, as I have said, is to know these books, and even if not yet so as to understand them, all the same by reading them to commit them to memory or, at least, not to be totally unfamiliar with them. Next, those things that are put clearly in them, whether precepts about how to live or rules about what to believe, are to be studied with the utmost care and diligence; the greater your intellectual capacity, the more of these you will find. The fact is, after all, that in the passages that are put plainly in Scripture is to be found everything that touches upon faith and good morals, that is to say hope and charity, which we dealt with in the previous book.

Only then, however, after acquiring some familiarity with the actual style of the divine Scriptures, should one proceed to try to open up and unravel their obscurities, in such a way that instances from the plainer passages are used to cast light on the more obscure utterances, and the testimony of some undoubted judgments is used to remove uncertainties from those that are more doubtful. In this matter, what is of the greatest value is a good memory; if this is wanting, these instructions cannot be of any great assistance.

(10) Now there are two reasons why texts are not understood: if they are veiled in signs that are either unknown or ambiguous. Signs, for their part, can be either proper or metaphorical. They are said to be proper when they are introduced to signify the things they were originally intended for, as when we say "ox" to signify the animal that everyone who shares the Latin language with us calls by this name. They are metaphorical when the very things that we signify with their proper words are made use of to signify something else, as when we say "ox," and by this syllable understand the animal that is usually so called, but again by that animal understand the evangelist, whom Scripture itself signified, according to the apostle's interpretation of *You shall not muzzle the ox that threshes the corn* (1 Cor 9:9; Deut 25:4).

(11) The best remedy for ignorance of proper signs is the knowledge of languages, and in addition to the Latin language, the people whom I have now undertaken to advise have need of the two other languages of the divine Scriptures, namely, Hebrew and Greek, so that they can have recourse to the earlier versions whenever doubt about the meaning of a text is raised by the infinite variety of Latin translations. Although we also often find Hebrew words untranslated in the books of the Bible, like Amen and Alleluia and Raca (cf. Matt 5:22) and Hosanna, and any others there may be. Of these some, though they could have been translated, have been traditionally kept as they are because of their more sacred associations, like Amen and Alleluia; while of others it is said that they could not be translated, like the other two I mentioned. There are some words, after all, in particular languages that defy translation into any other language. And this is above all the case with exclamations, which are words indicating some emotion of the spirit, rather than any part of a connected sentence. These two, in fact, are generally considered to be such words; they tell us that Raca is a word expressing ill-natured contempt, while Hosanna expresses joy.

But it is not because of these few words, which can be very easily noted and asked about, that knowledge of these languages is necessary, but because of the variety of the translations, as has been said. Those who translated the Scriptures from Hebrew into Greek can be counted; this is certainly not true of

Latin translators. The fact is that whenever in the early days of the faith a Greek codex came into anybody's hands, and he felt that he had the slightest familiarity with each language, he rushed in with a translation.

(12) In fact, this state of affairs has been more of a help than a hindrance to the understanding of the Scriptures, provided only that readers are not casual and careless. The examination of several versions has often been able to throw light on obscurer passages, as with that text of the prophet Isaiah (58:7), where one translation has, *And do not despise the household of your seed,* and another has, *And do not despise your own flesh.* Each corroborates the other; that is, each can be explained by the other, because, on the one hand, flesh could be taken in the proper sense, so that the reader could suppose he was being warned not to despise his own body, while on the other, the household of one's seed could be understood metaphorically as Christians, born spiritually from the same seed of the word as ourselves.

But now, putting the minds of the translators together, we hit upon the more probable meaning that we are being commanded, according to the literal sense, not to despise our blood relations, because when you connect the household of your seed with your flesh, it is your blood relations that immediately occur to you. I am sure that that is what the apostle meant when he said, *If I may by any means provoke my own flesh to jealousy, in order to save some of them* (Rom 11:14); that is, that by being jealous of those who had believed, they themselves might come to believe as well. By his flesh, clearly, he meant the Jews, because of their blood relationship.

Again, there is that text of the same prophet Isaiah, *Unless you believe, you shall not understand,* which another translator rendered, *Unless you believe, you shall not endure* (Isa 7:9). Which of these two, though, followed the original words one cannot tell, unless one reads copies of the original language. But all the same, for those who are shrewd readers, something important is being suggested by each version. It is difficult, after all, for translators to differ so much from each other, that they do not come close to some extent. So then, understanding refers to ever-lasting sight, while faith in temporal things as in a kind of cradle is, so to say, nourishing little ones on milk, now, however, *we are walking by faith and not by sight* (2 Cor 5:7), but unless we walk by faith, we shall never be able to reach the sight that does not pass away but endures, when with our understanding purified we cleave to Truth. And that is why one translator says, *Unless you believe, you shall not endure,* while the other has, *Unless you believe, you shall not understand.*

And translators are often misled by ambiguities in the original language, when they are insufficiently familiar with the context, and translate the meaning of a word that is clearly far from the author's mind. Thus some versions have, *Their feet are sharp to shed blood; oxys,* you see, in Greek can mean both "sharp" and "swift." So the one who got the author's meaning was the one who translated, *Their feet are swift to shed blood* (Rom 3:15), while the other went wrong by following in the wrong direction a sign that points two ways. And in such cases we have to do, not with obscurity, but with falsehood; so here another condition has to be met, the requirement being to correct, rather than simply to understand, copies of such versions. Here, too, is another instance: because the Greek *moschos* means "calf," some translators failed to understand that *moscheumata* means "seedlings," and so they translated it as "calflings." This mistake has indeed infected so many copies that you can scarcely find one with the other reading. And yet the meaning is as plain as can be because the next words make it quite clear; after all, *Bastard seedlings will not strike deep roots* (Wis 4:3) makes better sense than *calflings,* which walk on the ground with four feet and do not strike roots. The rest of the context in this place also confirms this translation.

(13) But the proper meaning of a passage, which several translators attempt to express, each according to his capacity and judgment, can be definitely ascertained only from an examination of it in the language they are translating from, and translators frequently deviate from the author's meaning if they are not particularly learned. So one should either aim at a knowledge of those languages from which the Scriptures have come to their Latin versions or else get

hold of translations that have been the most strictly literal, word for word, renderings of the original, not because they are sufficient in themselves, but because they can help one to control the freedom, or even the mistakes, of those translators who have preferred to follow the meanings, rather than the words, of the authors. It is often the case, after all, that not only single words but also whole phrases are transposed that simply cannot go into correct Latin usage if one wishes to stick to the standards of the old classical authors who spoke the languages. Sometimes this in no way prevents one from understanding a passage, but still it does offend those who find greater pleasure in the substance of the things said, if a certain propriety is preserved in the signs by which they are conveyed.

What are called solecisms, after all, are simply cases where words are put together without observing the rules followed by our predecessors, whose manner of writing and speaking was not without authority. I mean, whether you say in Latin *inter homines* or *inter hominibus,* or *between you and me or between you and I,*[2] makes no difference to our ability to get the meaning. Again, what else is a barbarism but the spelling or pronunciation of a word in a way that was not accepted by received authors of the past? I mean, whether you pronounce *ignoscere* with a long or short e in the third syllable or *forgive* to rhyme with "hive" or "sieve,"[2] is of little concern to those who are begging God to forgive their sins, however they may manage to pronounce that word. What else, then, is correctness of speech but the observation of a manner that is foreign to one, which has been established by the authority of past speakers?

But for all that, people are the more readily offended by such instances the less sense they have, and they show less sense the more they wish to be thought learned or well educated, not by knowledge of things that build up, but by knowledge of signs, which it is very hard to avoid being puffed up by,

since even knowledge of the substance of things can give us swollen heads and stiff necks, unless we submit them to the Lord's yoke. After all, is one in the least prevented from understanding this passage because it is written as follows: *What is the land in which these people reside upon it, whether it is good or bad, and what are the cities in which they dwell in them* (Num 13:19)? I consider this is just a form of expression derived from a foreign language, rather than any hint of some deeper meaning. There is also that mistake we cannot now remove from the mouths of our psalm-singing congregations, *But on him my sanctification* floriet (*shall flourish*) (Ps 132:18), which in no way detracts from the sense; still, the better educated listener would prefer it to be corrected, and *florebit* substituted for *floriet,* and the only thing that stops such a correction being made is the habit the singers have got into. So these things can even be easily shrugged aside if you are not fussy about avoiding little errors that do not get in the way of a proper understanding.

But as for this that the apostle says, *The folly of God is wiser than men, and the weakness of God is stronger than men* (1 Cor 1:25), if someone had wished to preserve the Greek idiom, and instead of saying, *Quod stultum est Dei sapientius est hominibus, et quod infirmum est Dei fortius est hominibus,* had said *Quod stultum est Dei sapientius est hominum, et quod infirmum est Dei fortius est hominum,* a sharp-eyed reader might have got the right sense, but the less quick-witted might either not have understood at all or else have even got a back-to-front meaning out of it because such an expression is not only bad Latin, it is also ambiguous, so that it could be taken to mean that the folly of men and the weakness of men seems to be wiser or stronger than the folly or weakness of God, though even the correct *sapientius hominibus* is not without the possibilities of ambiguity because only the whole sentence can tell us whether *hominibus* is in the dative or the ablative case; so it would be better to say, *Sapientius est quam homines* and *fortius est quam homines.*

(14) But we shall talk about ambiguous signs later on; for the time being, we are dealing with unknown ones, of which there are two sorts, as far as words are

---

[2] These English examples were inserted by the translator for clarity and are roughly parallel to Augustine's examples of solecism and barbarism.

concerned, because it is either an unknown word or an unknown expression that causes a reader to get stuck. If these come from foreign languages, their meaning can either be sought from people who speak those languages, or the languages can be learned, if you have the leisure or the knack, or several translations can be compared. But if it is some words or expressions of our own language that we are ignorant of, we can get to know them through the habit of reading or listening. None, certainly, are to be more carefully committed to memory than those words and expressions that we do not know; so that when we meet someone more learned whom we can ask about them, or when what goes before or what follows in such a reading can show what their force is, and what is signified by what we do not know, then with the aid of memory we can easily notice and learn.

Though such, as a matter of fact, is the power of habit even for learning, that people who have been as it were reared and brought up on the Scriptures are more surprised at other nonscriptural forms of expression and think they are less proper Latin than the ones they have learned in the scriptures, which are not found in authors of classical Latin. Here, too, the examination and discussion of a variety of versions that can be compared are of the greatest help—provided only that they are not full of mistakes. The first thing, in fact, to which those who wish to know the divine Scriptures should devote their careful attention and their skill is the correction of their copies, so that the uncorrected ones give way to the corrected ones, when they derive, that is, from one and the same type of translation.

(15) Among the versions themselves, however, the *Itala* is to be preferred to the rest because it sticks more closely to the actual words, while at the same time has a clear perception of the meaning. And for correcting any Latin versions at all, Greek ones should be employed, among which, as regards the Old Testament, that of the Seventy Translators has the greatest authority. These are said, throughout all the more learned churches, to have been so directed by the Holy Spirit in their translations that while being so many, they had but a single mouth. If, as the story goes, and many by no means unreliable authors declare, they were all kept apart from each other in separate rooms, and when they had finished their translations nothing was to be found in any of their copies that was not there in exactly the same words and the same order as in all the others, who could possibly put any other version on a level with such an authority, let alone prefer one to it? If, on the other hand, they collaborated in order to speak with one voice by the common consideration and judgment of them all, even in that case no single individual, however well qualified, may decently aspire to correct what was agreed to among so many venerable and learned scholars.

For this reason, even if things are found in Hebrew codices that differ from what the Seventy have put, in my judgment they should give way to what divine providence has achieved through these men, and that is that the books which the Jewish people were unwilling to share with others, whether out of a religious sense or out of envy, were made available by the Lord, using the royal authority of Ptolemy, to the nations that were going to believe. And so it can well be the case that these translated the Hebrew in such a way as the Holy Spirit, who was guiding them and gave them all one mouth, judged would be most suitable for the gentiles. But still, as I said above, comparing their text with that of translators who stuck more closely to the words of the original is often useful for explaining the meaning.

So then, Latin volumes of the Old Testament, as I had started to say, should be corrected where necessary according to the authority of the Greek ones, and particularly of the Seventy who are held to have translated in unanimous agreement. But as for the books of the New Testament, if there are any hesitations about the text because of the variety of Latin translations, nobody doubts that one should bow to the authority of the Greek texts, and of those especially that are to be found in the more learned and careful churches.

Biblical Interpretation: The Texts

Over the course of the fourth and fifth centuries, the Bible was subjected to increasingly creative and ingenious modes of interpretation, often based on classical methods of textual interpretation. The practice of writing commentaries—detailed, often verse-by-verse expositions of biblical books—probably originated by the end of the second century and became a veritable literary industry by the fourth century. Although much of this interpretive material is dense with arcane philosophical, literary, and linguistic expertise, we should not too quickly dismiss it as the erudite ramblings of a tiny elite. Many of the same well-educated Christians who produced lengthy commentaries (such as Origen, Ambrose of Milan, Gregory of Nyssa, and Augustine of Hippo Regius) also preached sermons in their churches every week, drawing on the same exegetical resources.

Theological controversies and the rise of the ascetic and monastic movements often influenced late ancient biblical interpretation. As Jerome's letter to Eustochium (see Text 37) shows, many monks used the Scriptures as a sort of ascetic guidebook, full of examples and rules for pursuing a life of moral exertion. Biblical interpretation was also central in debates over heresy and orthodoxy, as theological combatants launched verse after verse as proof of their respective positions (there were usually more than enough proof-texts for both sides of any debate). A paradox also informs late ancient biblical interpretation: on the one hand, interpreters viewed the Bible as a single, coherent message that could never contradict itself; on the other hand, they believed that the Bible was the Word of God, whose divine mysteries could never be fully appreciated or circumscribed.

The task of deriving human meaning from this divine complexity often involved reading Scriptures "spiritually," that is, as possessing meaning that transcended the literal text. Christians in the second and third centuries had already perfected this practice when dealing with the troubling legal sections of the Old Testament, retaining these sacred books without submitting themselves to Jewish Law. The third-century Christian philosopher Origen was a master of spiritual interpretation, who employed the literary mode of allegory, by which the text literally "says something else," to discover in the mundane epics, dramas, and love songs of the Bible a sublime story of the soul's origins in and eventual return to unity with God. Allegory had been practiced for centuries by Greek philosophers who were troubled by the unseemly carrying on of divine figures in Homer's *Iliad* and *Odyssey* and employed by Jewish philosophers, such as the first-century Philo of Alexandria, to derive deeper, Platonic meaning from the Jewish Scriptures. Origen's spiritual reading of the Christian Bible was an ingenious adaptation of his literary forebears.

Although Origen had many admirers who pursued allegorical interpretation in the fourth century, some Christians abhorred what they perceived to be his rhetorical excesses. They accused allegorists of rejecting sacred history in favor of ephemeral (and, they hinted, heretical) philosophical notions. Even though these anti-allegorists favored a more historicized form of interpretation, they did not reject spiritual interpretation altogether. Debates over biblical interpretation often encompassed larger debates over the nature of Christian society, culture, and community. Although the Bible became the center of conceptions of Christian culture in Late Antiquity, the richness and creativity of its interpreters ensured that Christian culture, like the Bible, would always remain highly varied and multifaceted.

54. Tyconius: Book of Rules

Tyconius was a member of the Donatist church of North Africa (see Chapter 7) in the late fourth century. He achieved prominence in the second half of the century as an expert in scriptural interpretation; in addition to the *Book of Rules,* excerpted here, he wrote an influential commentary on the book of Revelation. Although censured by the Donatist bishop of Carthage (possibly for his views on the mixed nature of the Church contained in the *Rules*), it is unlikely that he ever joined the Catholic church. Nevertheless, the Catholic bishop Augustine used Tyconius's guide to biblical interpretation to craft his own theories of sacred reading and meaning.

In Tyconius's *Rules* we see a concerted effort to harness the multiplicity of the Bible to produce a singular scriptural message. Toward this end, Tyconius proposes seven rules (or guides) to biblical interpretation and suggests that the Bible might speak simultaneously or in series about any of these rules. He was particularly concerned to explain seemingly contradictory statements about law and salvation, which might detract from a harmonious reading of the Old and New Testaments. In Tyconius, we see a conception of the Bible as an arcane, but not impenetrable, guide to Christian truth; with the proper "keys," the windows and doors of the divine message could be opened to let their "light" shine on the Christian reader.

PROLOGUE

I thought it necessary before anything else that occurred to me to write a brief book of rules providing something like keys and windows to the secrets of the law. For there are certain mystical rules that govern the depth of the entire law and hide the treasures of truth from the sight of some people. If the logic of these rules is accepted without prejudice as we set it down here, every closed door will be opened and light will be shed on every obscurity. Guided, as it were, by these rules in paths of light, a person walking through the immense forest of prophecy may well be defended from error.

These rules are as follows:

1. Of the Lord and His Body
2. Of the Lord's Bipartite Body
3. Of Promises and the Law
4. Of Species and Genus

Reprinted from *Biblical Interpretation in the Early Church,* translated and edited by Karlfried Froehlich, copyright © 1984 Fortress Press. Used by permission of Augsburg Fortress.

1. OF THE LORD AND HIS BODY

(1) Reason alone discerns whether Scripture is speaking of the Lord or his Body, that is, the church. It suggests the appropriate referent by convincing argument or by the sheer power of the truth that forces itself on the reader. In other instances, Scripture seems to speak of one person only, but the fact that this person functions in different ways indicates a double meaning. Thus, Isaiah says: "He bears our sins and suffers pain for us; he was wounded for our offenses, and God abandoned him for our sins"; and so on (Isa 53:4–5). This is a passage that the confession of the whole church applies to the Lord. But Isaiah continues, speaking of the same one: "And God wants to cleanse him from the stroke and to relieve his soul from pain, to let him see the light and to fashion him in wisdom" (Isa 53:10–11). Does God want to let him see the light whom he abandoned for our sins and fashion him in wisdom who is already the light and the wisdom of God? Does this continuation not rather apply to his Body? This example shows that one can discern by reason alone the point at which the text makes the transition from the head to the body.

(2) Daniel calls the Lord "the stone hewn from the mountain" that struck the body of the kingdoms of this world and "ground it to dust." But when "the stone became a mountain and filled the whole earth," he is speaking of the Lord's Body (Dan 2:34–35). The Lord does not fill the world only by his power but not by the fullness of his Body, as some maintain. Such a statement is an insult to the kingdom of God and the invincible inheritance of Christ. It is painful for me even to mention it. Indeed, some claim that the mountain filling the earth is the fact that the Christian may now present his offering everywhere, while formerly sacrifice was allowed only on Mount Zion. If this were the case, it would be unnecessary to say that the stone grew into a mountain and began to fill the

world by its growth. For our Lord Christ "had this glory before the world was made" (John 17:5), and since in him God's Son became man, he received "all power in heaven and on earth" (Phil. 2:11), not gradually like the stone, but all at once. The stone, however, became a large mountain by a process of growth and, in growing, covered the whole earth. If Christ filled the whole earth just by his power and not by his Body, there would be no point in comparing him to a stone, for power is something intangible, but a stone is a tangible body. Moreover, that growth occurs in the body and not in the head is demonstrated not only by reason, but is also confirmed by apostolic authority. "We grow up in all things," says the apostle, "into him who is the head, Christ, from whom the whole body, fashioned and knit together through every joint of the system in the measure of each and every part, derives its increase to the building up of itself" (Eph 4:15–16). And also: "(Such a one) is not united to the head from whom the whole body, supplied and built up with joints and ligaments, attains a growth that is from God" (Col 2:19). What grows, therefore, is not the head. The head is the same from the very beginning. Instead, the body grows from the head.

(3) But let us return to our theme. The following passage concerns the Lord and his Body, but the correct referent must be discerned by reason: "To his angels he has given command about you, that they guard you in all your ways. Upon their hands they shall bear you up lest you dash your foot against a stone. You shall tread upon the asp and the viper; you shall trample down the lion and the dragon. Because he hopes in me, I will deliver him; I will protect him, for he knows my name. He will call upon me, and I will answer him; I am with him in distress. I will deliver him and glorify him. I will make full for him the length of days and will show him my salvation" [Ps 91:11–16]. Tell me, did God show his salvation to the one whom he commanded angels to serve? Did he not rather show it to his Body?

Another instance: "Like a bridegroom he crowned me with a mitre; like a bride he adorned me with adornment" (Isa 61:10). The text speaks of one body of two sexes, the groom's and the bride's. Reason discerns what applies to the Lord and what applies to the church. The same Lord says in the Book of Revelation: "I am the bridegroom and the bride" (Rev 22:17), and also: "They went out to meet the bridegroom and the bride" (Matt 25:1). Once more, Isaiah makes clear which part reason must attribute to the head and which to the body: "Thus says the Lord to the Christ, my Lord, whose right hand I grasped so that nations might listen to him" (Isa 45:1). This statement is followed by another that applies to the Body only: "And I will give you hidden treasures, invisible treasures I will open up for you that you may know that I am the Lord, the God of Israel, who calls you by your name for the sake of Jacob, my son, and of Israel, my chosen one" (Isa 45:3). Having made covenants with the fathers in order that he might be known, God opens invisible treasures to the Body of Christ, treasures that "eye has not seen or ear heard, nor have they entered into the heart of man" (1 Cor 2:9). "Of man"–this, of course, is said of a hardened man who is not in the Body of Christ. To the church "God revealed them through his Spirit" (1 Cor 2:10). Nevertheless, the use of reason sometimes helps to perceive these treasures more easily even though this perception occurs through the grace of God as well.

(4) In other cases, such reasoning is less successful because the text can be applied correctly to both, either the Lord or his Body. In such instances, the proper meaning can be perceived only by an even greater grace from God. Thus, we read in the gospel: "From now on you will see the Son of Man sitting at the right hand of the power and coming on the clouds of heaven" (Matt 24:64). But Scripture states elsewhere that he will be seen coming on the clouds of heaven only on the last day: "All the nations of the earth will mourn, and then they will see the Son of Man coming on the clouds of heaven" (Matt 24:30). Indeed, two things must happen: first, the advent of the Body, that is, the church, which is continually coming in one and the same invisible glory; then the advent of the head, that is, the Lord, in manifest glory. If the text had read: "Now you will see him coming," it would refer only to the advent of the Body; if it had read: "You will see him coming," it

would refer only to the advent of the head. But it actually reads: "From now on you will see him coming," for he comes continually in his Body, through a birth and through the glory of sufferings like his. Since those who are reborn are made members of Christ, and these members constitute the Body, it is Christ himself who is coming. Birth means coming as when Scripture says: "He enlightens every man who comes into this world" (John 1:9) or "One generation passes and another comes" (Eccl 1:4) or "As you have heard that Antichrist is coming" (1 John 2:18). And concerning this latter body: "For if he who comes preaches another Jesus" (2 Cor 11:4). Therefore, when the Lord was asked for a sign of his coming, he began to speak of that coming which can be imitated in signs and wonders by the opposing body. "Take heed," he said, "that no one leads you astray, for many will come in my name" (Matt 24:4–5), that is, in the name of my Body. At the last coming of the Lord, however, that is, at the advent of the final consummation and open manifestation of his coming in its entirety, there will be no deceiver, as some people think. But this matter will be more fully discussed in its proper place later.

(5) Therefore, our wish to apply the mention of one person to the whole Body, to interpret, for example, the Son of Man as the church, implies no absurdity. After all, the church, that is, the children of God gathered into one Body, is called "son of God," or "one man," or even "God," as in the words of the apostle: "above all that is called God or that is worshiped" (2 Thess 2:4). Here, "that is called God" means the church, and "that is worshiped" means the highest God. The apostle continues: "so that he takes his seat in the temple of God pretending to be God" (2 Thess 2:5), that is, to be the church. It is like saying: "He takes his seat in the temple of God pretending to be the temple of God" or "He takes his seat in God pretending to be God." The apostle wants to veil this understanding by using synonyms. Daniel says the following about a king of the end time: "In God will his place be glorified" (cf. Dan 11:38), that is, made famous. This king will secretly establish something like a church in the place of the church, in the

holy place; an "abomination of devastation" (Matt 24:15) in God, that is, in the church.

(6) The Lord himself calls the whole people "bride" and "sister" (Song 5:1). The apostle calls it a "holy virgin" but terms the opposing body "the man of sin" (2 Cor 11:2; 2 Thess 2:3). David calls the whole church "the anointed": "He showed mercy to his anointed, David and his seed forever" (Ps 18:50), and the apostle Paul calls the Body of Christ "Christ" when he says: "For just as the body is one but has many members, and all the members of the body, though many, are one body, so also is Christ" (1 Cor 12:12), that is, Christ's Body, which is the church. And also: "I rejoice in the sufferings I bear for your sake and complete what is lacking from the afflictions of Christ" (Col 1:24), that is, of the church. There was certainly nothing lacking from the sufferings of Christ; rather, "it is enough for the disciple to be like his master" (Matt 10:25). Thus, we will take the coming of Christ to mean what each passage suggests. Likewise, we recognize that in the Book of Exodus all sons of God are one son, and all firstborn of Egypt are one firstborn, for God says: "So you shall say to Pharaoh: Thus says the Lord, Israel is my firstborn son. Hence I tell you: Let my people go that it may serve me. But you refuse to let it go. Therefore, behold I kill your firstborn son" (Exod 4:22–23). Also, David calls the vineyard of the Lord one son when he says: "Turn again, O God of hosts! Look down from heaven and see; visit your vineyard and perfect what your right hand has planted, what you have confirmed as a son for yourself" (Ps 80:14–15).

(7) The apostle gives the name "Son of God" to one who is merely mingled with the Son of God: "Paul, a servant of Jesus Christ, called to be an apostle, set apart for the gospel of God that he promised beforehand through his prophets in the holy Scriptures, the gospel concerning his Son who was born to him of the seed of David according to the flesh, who was the predestined Son of God in power according to the spirit of holiness by the resurrection from the dead of our Lord Jesus Christ" (Rom 1:1–4). If the text simply read: "the gospel concerning his Son, by the resurrection from the dead," it would refer to one son only. But it reads: "the gospel concerning his Son, by the resurrection from the dead of our Lord Jesus Christ." The phrase, "who was made Son of God by the resurrection of Christ," is explained more fully by the preceding words: "concerning his Son who was born to him of the seed of David according to the flesh, who was the predestined Son of God." For our Lord, being himself God and coequal with the Father, is not "the predestined Son of God," gaining his sonship through his birth. Rather, he is the one to whom God said at his baptism, as Luke tells us: "You are my Son, today I have begotten you" (cf. Luke 3:22). The one "born of the seed of David" is mingled with the "principal spirit" (Ps 51:12) and was made "Son of God by the resurrection of our Lord Jesus Christ," which means, when in Christ the seed of David rises up. He is not that other one of whom David said: "Thus says the Lord to my Lord" (Ps 110:1). The two were made one flesh. "The word was made flesh" (John 1:14), and the flesh was made God, for "we are born not of blood but of God" (John 1:13). The apostle writes: "The two shall become one flesh. This is a great mystery; I mean it in reference to Christ and the Church" (Eph 5:31–32). God promised Abraham one seed; as many as would be mingled with Christ, there would be one person in Christ as the apostle himself says: "You are all one (*unus*) in Christ Jesus. But if you are one in Christ Jesus, you are Abraham's seed and heirs according to the promise" (Gal 3:28–29). Now there is a difference between "you are one" (*unum*) and "you are one person" (*unus*). When one person is mingled with another in (an act of) will, they are one, as the Lord says: "I and the Father are one (*unum*)" (John 10:30). When they are also mingled in body, however, and are joined into one flesh, the two are one person (*unus*).

(8) In its head, therefore, the Body is the Son of God, and in his Body God is the Son of Man who comes daily through a birth and "grows into God's holy temple" (Eph 2:21). Now the temple itself is bipartite. Its second part, though built of large stones, suffers destruction; in it, "not one stone will be left upon the other" (Matt 24:2). We must beware of its

continual coming until the church departs from its midst.

2. OF THE LORD'S BIPARTITE BODY

(1) The rule about the bipartite body of the Lord is of the utmost necessity. We must investigate it all the more carefully and must keep it constantly before our eyes when reading Scripture. Now just as reason alone perceives the transition from the head to the body, as I pointed out above, so it is with the transitions from one part of the body to another, from right to left or from left to right, as the title of our present chapter indicates.

(2) When the Lord says to one body: "Invisible treasures I will open up for you that you may know that I am the Lord, and I will adopt you," and then continues: "But you did not recognize me, that I am God and there is no God beside me, and you did not know me" (Isa 45:3–4), do the two statements, though they are addressed to one body, actually refer to the same entity: "Invisible treasures I will open up for you that you may recognize that I am God, for the sake of my servant Jacob," and: "But you did not recognize me"? Did Jacob not receive what God had promised? Do the two verbs even refer to the same action: "You did not recognize me," and "You did not know me"? "You did not know" can only be said to someone who now does know, but "you did not recognize" is addressed to someone who, though he should have recognized (God) and seems to belong to the same body, "draws near to God with his lips only, while his heart is far from him" (Isa 29:13). To such a person God can say: "But you did not recognize me."

(3) Here is another instance: "I will lead the blind on a journey they do not know; they shall walk in paths they do not know, and I will turn darkness into light for them and will make the crooked straight. What I have said, I will do for them, and I will not forsake them. But they turned back" (Isa 42:16–17). Did the very ones of whom he said, "I will not forsake them," all turn back? Was it not just part of them?

(4) Again, the Lord says to Jacob: "Fear not, for I am with you; from the East I will bring back your seed, and from the West I will gather you. I will say to the North: Bring back! and to the South: Do not withhold! Bring back my sons from a distant land and my daughters from the ends of the earth, everyone over whom my name has been pronounced! For in my glory I created (this seed), formed and made him, but I brought forth a blind people; their eyes are blind, and their ears are deaf" (Isa 43:5–8). Are the very people whom he created for his glory also blind and deaf?

Or: "Your forefathers and their princes did evil to me; your princes defiled my sanctuary so that I left Jacob to perish and Israel to be cursed. Now, hear me, my son Jacob; Israel whom I have chosen!" (Isa 43:27–44:1). God makes it clear that he "left to perish and to be cursed" only the Jacob and the Israel whom he had *not* chosen.

(5) Or: "I formed you as my son; you are mine, O Israel, do not forget me! For behold, I have taken away your iniquities like a cloud and your sins like a storm cloud. Return to me, and I will redeem you!" (Isa 44:21–22). Does he say "return to me" to the same person whose sins he took away, to the one whom he assures: "you are mine," and whom he reminds not to forget him? Are anyone's sins taken away before he returns?

Or: "I know that you will surely be rejected. For the sake of my name I will show you my excellence and will cause my magnificence to rise over you" (Isa 48:8–9). Is he showing his excellence and displaying his magnificence to the reprobate?

(6) Or: "Not an elder, or an angel, but the Lord himself saved them because he loved them and forgave them; he himself redeemed them and adopted them and exalted them throughout all the days of this age. But they were rebellious and grieved his holy spirit" (Isa 63:9–10). When were those "whom he exalted throughout all the days of this age" rebellious? When did they "grieve his holy spirit"?

(7) Consider another instance in which God openly promises to one body both enduring strength and destruction. First, he says: "Jerusalem is a rich city, tents that will not be moved; the pegs of your

tent will never be pulled up, nor will its ropes be severed"; but then he continues: "Your ropes are severed because the mast of your ship was not strong; your sails hang idly, and the ship will not raise anchor until it is left to perish" (Isa 33:20, 23).

(8) Again, that the Body of Christ is bipartite is shown in this brief sentence: "I am dark and beautiful" (Song 1:5). I cannot think for a moment that the church "without spot or wrinkle" (Eph 5:27), whom the Lord "cleansed for himself by his blood" (Titus 2:14), should be dark anywhere except on her left side by which "the name of God is blasphemed among the Gentiles" (Rom 2:24). Otherwise she is entirely beautiful, as the author himself says later: "You are all beautiful, my most beloved, and there is no blemish in you" (Song 4:7). Our text gives an explanation of why she is both dark and beautiful: "like the tent of Kedar, like the leather tent of Solomon" (Song 1:5). It shows us two tents, the king's and the slave's; yet both are Abraham's offspring, for Kedar is the son of Ishmael. Elsewhere, the church bemoans her long sojourn with this same Kedar, that is, with the slave from Abraham: "Woe is me that my wandering has been made long; I have dwelt amid the tents of Kedar, my soul has wandered much. I kept peace with those who hate peace; when I spoke to them, they made war on me" (Ps 120:5–7). Nevertheless, we cannot say that the tent of Kedar is outside the church. Our text speaks of the tent of Kedar and of Solomon, and therefore it says both: "I am dark" and "I am beautiful." But the church herself is not dark because of those who belong outside.

(9) In the same mysterious fashion, the Lord mentions seven angels in the Book of Revelation, pointing to a sevenfold church (Rev 1:20–3:22); sometimes its members are saints and keepers of the commandments, sometimes they are guilty of numerous sins and need to repent. In the Gospel, he attributes various kinds of merit to one body of stewards, saying first: "Blessed is that servant whom his master, when he comes, shall find so doing," but continuing about the same person: "but when that wicked servant . . ." and adding: "The Lord will divide him in two parts" (Matt 24:48, 51). I ask, will the Lord divide or cut him up as a whole? Note the

final statement: "He will give him a part"—not the whole!—"with the hypocrites" (Matt 24:51). Thus, in the one person, the text points to a (bipartite) body.

(10) Therefore, all the statements throughout Scripture in which God announces that Israel will perish deservedly or that his inheritance will be cursed must be understood in terms of this mystery. The apostle makes ample use of this mode of expression, especially in Romans; statements about a whole body must be understood to apply to a part only: "What does God say to Israel? All the day long I stretched out my hands to a contradictory people" (Rom 10:21). In order to make it clear that he is speaking of a part only, he continues: "I say then, has God rejected his inheritance? By no means! For I also am an Israelite of the seed of Abraham, of the tribe of Benjamin. God has not rejected his people whom he foreknew" (Rom 11:1–2). And having set forth the correct understanding of this statement, he uses the same mode of expression to show us that the one body is both good and evil: "As regards the gospel, they are enemies for your sake, but as regards election, they are beloved for the sake of the fathers" (Rom 11:28). Are the beloved the same as the enemies? Can both terms apply to Caiaphas? Thus, the Lord testifies in all of Scripture that the one body of Abraham's seed is growing and flourishing, but also perishing in all (its various parts).

3. OF PROMISES AND THE LAW

(1) Divine authority tells us that no one has ever been able to achieve justification by works of the law. The same authority asserts in the strongest terms that there have always been people who kept the law and were justified.

It is written: "Whatever the law says, it is speaking to those who are under the law, so that every mouth may be stopped and the whole world may become subject to God. For by the law no flesh shall be justified in his sight" (Rom 3:19–20), and: "Sin shall have no dominion over you, since you are not under the law" (Rom 6:14), and: "We also believe in Christ, that we may be justified by faith and not by the works of the law, for by the works of the law no flesh will be justified" [Gal 3:16]; and: "For if a law had been given that could bestow life, righteousness would certainly be by the law. But Scripture confined all things under sin, that by the faith of Jesus Christ the promise might be given to those who believe" (Gal 3:21–23). Now someone might say: From Christ's time onward, the law does not justify; it did, however, justify in its own time. But this argument is contradicted by the authority of the apostle Peter who, when his colleagues were trying to force the gentiles under the yoke of the law, said: "Why do you test the Lord by trying to impose on the neck of the disciples a yoke that neither our fathers nor we have been able to bear?" (Acts 15:10). The apostle Paul states: "While we were in the flesh, the sinful passions that come through the law were at work in our members to bear fruit for death" (Rom 7:5). Yet, contrary to this, the same apostle also writes: "As regards the righteousness of the law, (I was) leading a blameless life" (Phil 3:6). And if the authority of such a great apostle were lacking, how could one criticize the testimony of the Lord who said (of Nathanael): "Behold, a true Israelite in whom there is no guile" (John 1:47)? And even if the Lord had not seen fit to furnish this testimony, who would be so impious, so inflated by senseless pride, as to assert that Moses, the prophets, and all the saints (of old) did not fulfill the law or were not justified? Scripture itself says of Zechariah and his wife: "They were both righteous in God's sight, walking in all his commandments and justifications blameless" (Luke 1:6), and our Lord did not come "to call the righteous, but sinners" (Matt 9:13).

(2) But how could a law justify from sin when it was given for the purpose of multiplying sin as it is written: "The law came in, so that sin might be multiplied" (Rom 5:20). There is one thing we must know and keep in mind: To this very day, the seed of Abraham has never been entirely cut off from Isaac; I am speaking not of the carnal, but of the spiritual seed of Abraham that does not come from the law but from promise. The other seed is indeed carnal; it comes from the law, "from Mount Sinai which is Hagar, bearing children for slavery" (Gal 4:24); "the son of the slave woman was born carnally, the son of

the free woman by virtue of the promise" (Gal 4:23). The apostle even states that there is no seed of Abraham but the one that comes from faith: "So you see that those who are from faith are the children of Abraham" (Gal 3:7), and: "But you, brethren, like Isaac, are children of the promise" (Gal 4:28).

(3) Thus, the seed of Abraham comes not from the law but from the promise and has remained uninterrupted from Isaac on. But if it is a fact that Abraham's seed existed before the law and is that seed that comes from faith, then it is also a fact that it never came from the law. It cannot come both from the law and from faith, for law and faith are quite different. The law is not a law of faith but of works, as Scripture says: "The law does not rest on faith; rather, he who does these things shall live by them" (Gal 3:12). Therefore, Abraham always had children by faith, but never by the law. "For not through the law but through the righteousness of faith was the promise given to Abraham or his seed, that he should be heir of the world. For if they are heirs who are heirs through the law, faith is made empty and the promise void, for the law works wrath" (Rom 4:13–15). Therefore, if faith and the promise to Abraham cannot be abolished at all, the promise has been in force continuously from its inception. Even the giving of the law did not hinder children being born to Abraham by faith according to the promise. The apostle states that the law, given 430 years later, neither impeded nor annulled the promise (Gal 3:17). "For if (the inheritance) is from the law, it is no longer from the promise. But God gave it to Abraham by promise" (Gal 3:18); and later: "Is then the law contrary to the promise? By no means!" (Gal 3:21). We see that the law does not touch the promise. Rather than impinging upon one another, each of the two preserves its own order. For just as the law never hindered faith, so faith never destroyed the law. We read: "Do we therefore through faith destroy the law? By no means! Rather we establish the law" (Rom 3:31), that is, we strengthen it, for the two strengthen each other.

(4) Thus, children of Abraham do not come from the law but from faith through the promise. But in taking seriously the denial of their justification by the works of the law, we must ask how they were justi-

fied once they were placed under the law and were observing it. We must ask further why, after the promise of faith that cannot be annulled, the law was given at all, a law not based on faith, a law whose works do not justify anyone. For "all who rely on the works of the law are under a curse, since it is written: Cursed is everyone who does not abide by all things written in the book of the law to do them" (Gal 3:10). The apostle anticipates this question. While asserting uncompromisingly that there have always been children of Abraham by God's grace through faith, not through the law of deeds, he makes this objection to himself: "Why then the law of deeds?" (Gal 3:19). That is to say: If there are children by virtue of faith, why was the law of deeds given, when the promise was sufficient to produce children of Abraham and to nourish them in faith, since "he who is righteous lives by faith"? Even before posing the question, "why then the law of deeds?", he stated that those who cannot be justified by virtue of the law will live in that other manner: "By the law no one is justified before God, but he who is righteous lives by faith" (Gal 3:11). He points out that the prophet said "He who is righteous lives by faith," precisely because it should be made clear how those unable to fulfill the law might live.

(5) The meaning of the phrase, "he who is righteous lives by faith," is less clear. For a righteous person, placed under the law, can live only if he performs the works of the law, indeed all its works, otherwise he would be cursed. God gave the law. He said: "You shall not covet." But immediately "sin, finding an opportunity, wrought every kind of covetousness by means of the commandment" (Rom 7:7–8), for "the sinful passions that come through the law" (Rom 7:5) are inevitably at work in the members of anyone under the law. The law was given "so that sin might abound" (Rom 5:20) because "the power of sin is the law" (1 Cor 15:56). Now anyone sold under sin does not do the good that he wants, but the very evil he does not want. According to his inner self, he consents to the law, but is overpowered by another law in his members (Rom 7:14–23). Dragged along captive, he can never be freed except by grace alone, through faith. But there is one kind of weapon that can check the violence of sin; failure to heed it is a great crime of faithlessness; to seek and identify it, on the other hand, is the sign of a marvelous faith. A mind realizing that humans cannot possibly fulfill the law that stands ready to take revenge, and yet failing to understand that there is a life-giving remedy, is nothing less than perverse and blasphemous. It simply is not possible that a good God, knowing that the law cannot be fulfilled, should provide no other access to life and close off all roads to life for human beings whom he created for life. Faith cannot bear or admit this thought; instead, when it is beset by the weakness of the flesh and the power of sin, it gives God the glory. Knowing that the Lord is good and just and that he does not close the depths of his mercy against the works of his hands, faith realizes that there *is* a way to life and sees a remedy enabling us to fulfill the law. In the words "you shall not covet," God did not reveal how this might be done successfully. He simply said sternly and tersely: "You shall not covet," leaving the rest to be discovered by faith. If he had commanded that we ask him for the result, he would have destroyed both the law and faith. For why would God even give the law if he had already promised to fulfill the law in each and every person? And what would he leave to faith, if his promise of assistance already preceded it? God gave the law as an agent of death for the good of faith; those who love life should see life by faith, and the righteous should live by faith, believing that they cannot do the work of the law by virtue of their own strength but only by virtue of God's gift. The law cannot be fulfilled by the flesh; it punishes everything that is left undone.

(6) How, then, can a human being hope to fulfill the law and escape death except by God's rich mercy, which only faith can discover? "The flesh does not submit to the law of God, indeed it cannot, for those who are in the flesh cannot please God. But you are not in the flesh, you are in the spirit, if indeed the Spirit of God dwells in you. But if anyone does not have the Spirit of Christ, he does not belong to him" (Rom 8:7–9). Paul makes the point that the Spirit of God and of Christ is the same. He points out also that the one who has the Spirit of God is not in the flesh.

But if God's Spirit and Christ's Spirit are one and the same, then the prophets and saints who had God's Spirit also had the Spirit of Christ. Since they had the Spirit of God, they were not in the flesh. Since they were not in the flesh, they fulfilled the law, for the flesh is at enmity with God and does not submit to his law. Therefore, anyone who flees to God receives God's Spirit, and once the Spirit is received, the flesh is put to death. Once the flesh is put to death, one can fulfill the law as a spiritual person, freed from the law, for "the law is not laid down for the righteous" (1 Tim 1:9), and: "If you are led by God's Spirit, you are not under the law" (Gal 5: 18).

(7) It is therefore quite clear that our forefathers, who had God's Spirit, were not under the law. As long as one is in the flesh, that is, without God's Spirit, the law is in command. But by surrendering to grace, one dies to the law; now the Spirit fulfills the law in one's person while the flesh, unable to submit to the law of God, is dead. What went on before is still going on now. The commandment prohibiting covetousness has not ceased to be valid because we are no longer under the law, nor has it been made more severe. But we seek refuge through faith in the revealed grace; being taught by the Lord to ask for our doing of the law as a gift of his mercy, we pray: "Your will be done," and "deliver us from evil" (Matt 6:10, 13). The fathers acted by this same faith, though it was the fear of death that compelled them to seek a grace not yet revealed; through the agency of the law, they saw death threatening them with its sword drawn.

(8) The law was given "until the time when the seed to whom the promise was made would come" (Gal 3:19) and proclaim the good news of faith. Before this time, however, it was the law that drove people toward faith, for faith as the search for God's grace cannot be expressed without the law because sin would have no power. But once the law was given, "the passions that come through the law were at work in our members" (Rom 7:5), forcing us into sin and driving us necessarily toward faith, which would cry out for God's grace to help us endure. We were kept in prison, while the law threatened death and surrounded us with an insurmountable wall wherever we turned. Grace was the one and only door in this wall. Faith was the guard in charge of this door, so that no one could escape from the prison unless faith opened the door. Failure to knock at this door meant dying within the walls of the law. We suffered under the law as under a tutor who drove us to be eager for faith and thus drove us to Christ. The apostle says that the law was given that it should confine us by its custody toward the faith that was to be revealed as faith in Christ, who is "the end of the law" (Rom 10:4); he is the one by whom all who have sought the grace of God by faith have found their life: "Before faith came, we were kept under the law, confined unto that faith which was to be revealed. Thus, the law was our tutor in Christ that we might be justified by faith" (Gal 3:23–24).

(9) I said that the law demonstrated the need for faith. But someone might object: If the law was given to benefit faith, why did its giving not coincide with the beginning of Abraham's seed, if it was constantly present? Indeed, it was there all the time. Faith was continuously present, giving birth to the children of Abraham, and so was the law, in the ability to discern good and evil. But once the promise of children had been given to Abraham and his seed according to the flesh was growing in numbers, his seed from faith had to grow also. Now this expansion could not occur without the help of an expanded law, so that an ever greater multitude would be led almost by necessity to a faith not yet revealed, as I pointed out above. Thus, it was an act of God's providence for the increase and guidance of the seed of Abraham, that the severity and fear of the law drove many to faith and strengthened the seed until faith was revealed. "The law came in, so that sin might be multiplied. But where sin was multiplied, grace abounded yet more" (Rom 5:20). Paul did not say: "grace was given," but: "grace abounded yet more." For through Christ it had been given from the beginning to those who sought refuge from the vexations and the domination of the law. Grace was already abundant through the expansion of the law, but it abounded yet more when it was revealed to all flesh in Christ. He came to "restore things in heaven and things on earth" (Eph 1:10) and announced faith as the "good tidings to those nearby

and those far off" (Eph 2:17), that is, both to the sinners of Israel and to the gentiles. Those Israelites who were righteous by virtue of faith had already been called to the same faith. For the Spirit, the faith, and the grace given by Christ have always been the same. By his coming, Christ bestowed the fullness of these gifts upon the whole race, having removed the veil of the law. The difference between their earlier and their later bestowal was one of degree, not of kind. By other means there never was a seed of Abraham.

(10) Justification apart from these gifts did not make anyone a child of Abraham. A man cannot be called a son of Abraham if he is justified by virtue of the law, not by virtue of faith like Abraham. Indeed, the apostle teaches that the church passed from one image of grace and spirit into the very same, when he writes: "But we all with unveiled faces, reflecting as in a mirror the glory of God, are being changed into the same image from glory to glory" (2 Cor 3:18). He implies that there was glory even before the Lord's passion and denies that such glory could be extracted, that is, expressed, brought forth, or effected from the law. Thus, glory was obviously coming from faith. "Where then is the boasting?" he asks. "It is excluded. By what law? By the law of works? No, but by the law of faith" (Rom 3:27). "For what does scripture say? Abraham believed God, and it was reckoned to him as righteousness" (Rom 4:3). We have passed into glory from the same glory, which did not come from the law. Had it been based on works, it would have been glory, but not glory given to God (cf. Rom 4:2).

(11) To repeat: It is impossible to have any glory without the grace of God. There is only one glory, and it has always been of one kind. No human being has ever triumphed for whom God has not won the victory. This is not so under the law; there, the one who fulfills it is the victor. But under faith, it is God who renders our adversary powerless, so that "he who glories should glory in the Lord" (1 Cor 1:31). For since the victory is not ours, it is not achieved by works but by faith, and there is nothing of ourselves in which to glory. We have nothing that we have not received (cf. 1 Cor 4:7). If we exist, we have our existence from God, so that the greatness of power may

be God's and not ours. All our work is faith, and it is as great as God working with us. Solomon glories in the knowledge that continence does not come from a human source but is a gift of God: "Knowing that I could not be continent unless God granted it—and this itself is wisdom, to know whose gift it is—I went to the Lord and besought him" (Wisd 8:21). We must accept the judgment of Solomon that all the justified exist by the grace of God, not by virtue of works. They know that the doing of the law in which they can glory must be requested from God. The apostle, however, clarifies why no flesh should glory before God; the wicked, of course, because they do not know God, and the righteous because they are not their own work but God's. He writes: "God chose what is useless and discarded, even things that are not, to bring to nothing things that are, so that no flesh might glory before God. From him you are in Christ Jesus, who has become for us the wisdom from God, our righteousness, holiness, and redemption; therefore, as it is written: Let him who glories, glory in the Lord" (1 Cor 1:28–31); and: "By grace you have been saved through faith, and this is not your doing, it is the gift of God; not because of works, lest anyone should boast. For we are his handiwork, created in Christ" (Eph 2:8–10).

(12) Therefore, no flesh can ever be justified by virtue of the law, that is, by works, so that any righteous person may have his glory from God. There is another reason why no one should boast before God. God works with his own in such a way that there is always something for him to forgive; for "no one is free from defilement, though his life were only one day long" (Job 14:4–5). David pleads: "Enter not into judgment with your servant, for before you no man living is justified" (Ps 143:2). And Solomon prays at the dedication of the Temple: "For there is no one who does not sin" (1 Kings 8:46). Also: "Against you alone have I sinned" (Ps 51:4), and: "Who can boast to have a pure heart, or who can boast to be clean from sin?" (Prov 20:9). To speak of a pure heart, that is, of freedom from evil thoughts, is not enough; it must be added that no one should boast to be clean from sin! Every victory is granted by God's sheer mercy, not by virtue of works, as it is written: "He

crowns you with mercy and compassion" (Ps 103:4). The mother of the (Maccabean) martyrs said to her son: "In that mercy, may I receive you again with your brothers" (2 Macc 7:29). The righteous perfect the will of God through their prayer and effort by which they strive and desire to serve God.

(13) The law leaves no room for good and better; if it could justify, all the righteous would have shared one merit because it demands equal observance of all its precepts. If one did less, the curse would become effective. But if the righteous showed unequal merit, each person receiving as much of the merciful God's grace as his faith told him he had been given, they were transformed "from glory into glory, as through the Spirit of the Lord" (2 Cor 3:18), that is, from one state into more of the same state. After Christ, the gift of faith was the same in kind as the Holy Spirit, since every prophet and righteous one always lived by the same Spirit. They could not live otherwise but by the Spirit of faith. For all who were under the law were killed because "the letter kills, but the Spirit makes alive" (2 Cor 3:6). And yet the Lord said of the same Spirit: "If I do not go away, he will not come" (John 16:7), though he had already given this very Spirit to his apostles. The apostle expresses the fact that the same Spirit was with the ancient generations in these words: "Because we have the same Spirit of faith, as it is written: I believed, and so I spoke" (2 Cor 4:13). He implies that the one who said, "I believed, and so I spoke," had this same Spirit of faith, and he confirms it by adding: "We, too, believe, and so we also speak." By saying "we, too," he makes clear that the ancient generations believed through the same Spirit of faith. Thus it is obvious that the righteous have always had their gifts not by virtue of the law but through the Spirit of faith.

(14) Whatever comes through the Lord is a whole whose every part is from the same author. Think of a young boy. He has nothing less than a man, but he is not yet a man; full bodily stature comes to him by the growth not of new members but of the ones that are already there. Still, the person who has reached perfection is the same one who was a small boy. In the full and proper sense, the Holy Spirit "was not yet" before the Lord's passion (John 7:39). But he existed

in those who had faith through him being present so that, sealed by him, the victor and perfector of all things, they might reach perfection. Clearly the righteous people whom Christ met already possessed the Holy Spirit—men and women like Simeon and Nathanael; Zechariah and Elizabeth; and the widow Anna, the daughter of Phanuel.

(15) Therefore, the promise is independent of the law, and since it is something so different, the two cannot be mixed, for any condition weakens the promise. At this point I am forced to say things that I cannot hear without the burn of deep pain. Some people who are ignorant about the firmness of the promise and about the transgression brought on by the law maintain that God promised Abraham all the nations, but did so without prejudice to their free will—under the condition that they would keep the law. Now it may be useful for their own salvation to expose the dangers that the inexperience of certain people breeds. But if our topic is the omnipotent God, we must exercise restraint in what we say so that we do not mention what ought to be passed over in silence and allow unworthy things to be heard from our lips. I speak, therefore, with some trembling and leave to each side the consideration of its own dangers.

(16) God obviously knew beforehand whether those whom he promised to Abraham would exist of their own free will or not. There are two options: Either they would; in this case, the question is settled. Or they would not; in this case, the God who gave the promise did not keep his word. If it was God's decision to give the promised (nations) if and when they were willing, God certainly would have said so in order to prevent games from being played on his servant Abraham, who believed that "what God has promised, he is able also to do" (Rom 4:21). God's promise does not allow any condition; else the promise would not be firm, nor would faith retain its integrity. For how could God's promise or Abraham's faith remain stable if that which was promised and believed depended upon the choice of the promised ones? God would have been promising something that was not his, and Abraham would have believed incautiously. How, then, was it possible that the promise turned into nothing less than an obligation

very soon, when God said: "In you all the nations of the earth shall be blessed because you have listened to my voice and have not withheld your own beloved son from me" (Gen 22:18, 16)? Now some people find it easy to taunt Abraham's merit with the calumny of free choice on the basis of these texts; so God confirmed his debt to Abraham once more after Abraham's death, promising his son what he was going to do on Abraham's account. These are his words: "I will be with you and will bless you, for to you and your seed I will give this land, and I will fulfill the oath that I swore to your father Abraham. I will multiply your seed like the stars of heaven and will give all the nations of the earth to you and your seed because your father Abraham listened to my voice" (Gen 26:3–5). Thus the debt to Abraham was confirmed, for Abraham could not lose after his death through someone's free choice what he had merited while he was alive.

(17) But the nations were not willing to believe. What could Abraham do being owed this debt? How was he to collect the debt owed to his faith and trial? He was certain of it, since God was his debtor. If God had said to him: "I will give what I promised and deliver on my oath if the nations are willing," Abraham would not have believed but taken a chance. If there must be a condition, it can apply to the laborer only but not to the wages. The laborer may or may not be willing to accept payment, but this does not go for the wages. All the nations were given to Abraham as wages of faith. God said: "Your wages are great" (Gen 15:1). God did not make his promise on the condition that they would exist, nor did he make it because they were going to exist. If it was God's good pleasure to save all nations, it was not on account of Abraham's faith at all; they were God's possession not only before Abraham's faith, but before the foundation of the world. Rather, God sought a faithful person to whom he wished to give that from which would come what he had determined would exist anyway. Thus, Abraham did not merit the existence of those future nations, whom God had elected and foreknown to become conformed to the image of his Son (Rom 8:29), as such; rather, he merited their existence *through him*. Scripture testifies in Genesis

that God promised all nations to Abraham on the basis of his foreknowledge: "Surely Abraham shall and will become a great and numerous nation, and all the nations of the earth shall be blessed in him." For God "knew that Abraham charged his sons and his household after him, and they were going to observe the ways of the Lord, exercising righteousness and judgment, so that the Lord might bring upon Abraham all that he had told him" (Gen 18:18–19).

(18) But we also encounter conditions, for instance: "If you listen to me and are willing" (Isa 1:19). Where is God's foreknowledge, where is his firm promise in such conditions? The apostle said that the promise was given by virtue of faith, not of the law, precisely in order that it might stand firm. "The law," he said, "works wrath, for where there is no law, neither is there transgression. Therefore, the promise was by virtue of faith, that it might be firm for all the seed according to grace" (Rom 4:15–16). "That the promise might be firm" is correct, for with a condition attached to it the promise would not be firm. It is rather foolish and arrogant to believe that something addressed to the bipartite body applies to the whole body. God could not say, "*if* you hear me," to those who he knew would hear, when he had known even before he made them that they would remain in the image of God; he could not say this to the very seed that was promised. The condition, that is, the law, was given for the impious and sinners only (cf. 1 Tim 1:9), so that they might either flee to grace or receive punishment more justly if they robbed grace of its effect. Why should the law apply to the righteous for whom it was not made, who fulfill the law without the law because God is gracious, who serve God freely and live according to the image of God and Christ? They are good by their own volition. The person under the law may not be an open murderer for fear of death, but he is not merciful; he does not bear the image of God. He does not like the law, but he fears its revenge. He cannot fulfill what he thinks he ought to do if he does it out of necessity, rather than by his own decision. He has no choice but to fall back on his own will, which means that he will receive the sure reward of the one who has not fused his soul with the will of God. What God wills is not

to his liking. In fact, someone who is good only out of necessity has an evil will. The law curbs the deed, not the will. Someone who would embrace evil if there were no penalty for it is not in tune with God. Complaining that one cannot do one's own will is not equivalent to doing God's will. The fear of being cruel does not make one merciful; such a person is under the law, is a slave. He does not detest stealing but only fears punishment. But he must do his stealing persuaded and convinced because he is a carnal being under the power of sin and does not have the Spirit of God. On the other hand, he who loves what is good bears the image of God and lives by faith in the Lord; in him the heir is no longer the son of the slave woman, receiving the law in fear. Rather, like Isaac, he is the son of the free woman, the one who "has not received a spirit of slavery so as to be again in fear, but a spirit of adoption as sons crying Abba, Father" (Rom 8:15). He who loves God is not fearful like a slave. It is written: "There is no fear in love, but perfect love casts out fear because fear brings punishment; he who fears is not consummated in love" (1 John 4:18). Servile fear is coupled with hatred of discipline, but a son's fear goes together with the honor of the father.

(19) To live in fear because of the law is one thing, but to honor God out of veneration for his awesome majesty is another. People who do the latter resemble their Father who is in heaven; reminded by him and taught, they love the good and hate evil. They do not shun evil out of fear; they do not do good out of necessity. They are without a law; they are free; they are the promised ones. "If you hear me" is not addressed to them. Those to whom it is may choose not to hear. Can the phrase apply to one of whom God foreknew before the world began that he would hear? True, even the righteous "whom God foreknew" (Rom 8:20) live under this law. They also are addressed by these words, "if you hear me," but for a different reason; not because they may choose not to hear, but so that they may always be solicitous for their salvation, since they do not know their end. Indeed, no one is certain of belonging to the number of the foreknown; even the apostle is concerned "lest I myself be rejected" (1 Cor 9:27). For the righteous, therefore, that

law does not work wrath, but it exercises their faith. It is by faith that they must constantly seek God's grace while they are laboring, so that what God foresaw in them might be perfected, and they might be destined for life by their own free choice. In any other sense, it is impossible that the one who God foresaw, promised, and even swore would hear, should not hear.

(20) In the Gospel the Lord explains to which part the law properly applies even though it is given to the one body. He says to the apostles: "If you know these things, blessed are you if you do them. I do not speak of you all; I know whom I have chosen" (John 13:17–18). What admirable brevity! He points out the one body, and at the same time divides it. If he had said: "I do not speak of you" or "I do not speak of all," he would not point out the one body. But by saying, "I do not speak of you all," he makes it clear that even though he is not speaking of them all, he is speaking nonetheless of them. It is as if someone said: "I am not speaking of your whole person." Two bodies are mingled as if they were one, and the one body is praised or rebuked in common. This is like God's words addressed to Moses in Exodus, after some Israelites had gone out to collect manna against the Sabbath prohibition: "How long do you refuse to obey my law?" (Exod 16:28); in fact, Moses himself had always obeyed.

(21) But what shall we say of a law that seems openly opposed to the promise? In Isaiah, we read: "If you had hearkened to me, O Israel, your number would be like the sand of the sea" (Isa 48:18–19). Here, Israel is rebuked for not having become like the sand through its own fault. The inference must be that if it will always fail to hearken, it will always remain small in number. Now where is the firmness of the promises? The problem is our wish to understand before we believe; we want to subjugate faith to reason. If we firmly believe that things come to pass entirely as God has sworn, then faith will give a reason that reason would find faithless to question. We will then understand that there is more firmness to the promise than infirmity, as we tend to think. For the statement, "if you had hearkened to me, O Israel," is a reminder of God's righteousness and a confirmation of his

promises; no one should dare to think that not by their free choice but by God's disposition some are destined for death and others for life. God said to the generation then living: "If you had hearkened to me," in order to leave no doubt after the giving of the promise that they would be like sand; he did foresee others who would listen. When anything was said about this matter before the time of our Lord Jesus Christ, the seed of Abraham was not yet like the sand of the sea. This is easy to prove. First, because God promised this large number in Christ only: "Not to seeds, referring to many, but referring to one: 'and to your seed,' which is Christ" (Gal 3:16). Second, because he promised all nations, and this promise could not be fulfilled before Christ. If the number of the children of Israel really was like the sand of the sea even before the Lord's coming, it included the false brethren who are not children of Abraham; for not all who are from Abraham are children of Abraham, and not all who are from Israel are Israel. When the apostle "wished to be accursed" for the sake of Israel, "who possessed the adoption as sons and the covenants" (Rom 9:3–4), he made it very clear that he did not mean those (false) children of Abraham; rather, because of his love for them out of fleshly necessity, he deplored the fact that they did not belong to that number; he did not imply that God's promise had failed: "It is not as though the word of God had failed. For not all who are descended from Israel are Israel, neither are they all children because they are the seed of Abraham; but in Isaac shall your seed be named. This means that it is not the children of the flesh who are the children of God, but the children of the promise are reckoned as the seed" (Rom 9:6–8).

(22) In the multitude of ancient Israel, therefore, the only seed of Abraham were those who, like Isaac, were children of faith and of promise. Paul gives a further example: "Though the number of the children of Israel be as the sand of the sea, only a remnant shall be saved" (Rom 9:27), that is, a small part. And: "If the Lord of hosts had not left us a seed, we would be like Sodom" (Rom 9:29). This remnant was the seed of Abraham, so that not all of Judea would be like Sodom. Again, Paul claims that God never abandoned his inheritance; rather, the situation has always

been what it was at the time of the Lord's coming, when only part of Israel was saved; he writes: "What is the answer? 'I have kept for myself seven thousand men who have not bowed their knees to Baal.' Even so now, a remnant has been saved, according to the election of grace" (Rom 11:4–5). By saying, "even so now, at the present time," he points out that it had always been this way in Israel: a remnant, that is, a small number, was saved.

(23) If, however, neither faith nor reason make a persuasive case, there are still the words addressed to him who was promised: "If you had hearkened to me, O Israel, your number would be like the sand of the sea" (Isa 48:18–19). The same Jacob who had been chosen even before he was born was later rejected through his own free choice, as Hosea says: "The judgment of the Lord is upon Judah that he will punish Jacob for his conduct and repay him for his pursuits. For in the womb he cheated his brother, and by his labors he stood up to God and stood up to the angel and became powerful" (Hos 12:2–4). Now if it is true that God's beloved reached fullness in Jacob, then the one who "by his labors stood up to God" and the "cheater" are not one and the same, but two in one body. What we have here is a figure of the twofold seed of Abraham, that is, of the two peoples struggling in the one womb of Mother Church. One of them is beloved according to the election by God's foreknowledge, the other wicked by the election of his own will. Jacob and Esau exist in one body from one seed. The clear fact that two were generated demonstrates that there are two peoples.

(24) Lest someone think, however, that the separation of the two peoples is so clear, it was arranged for both to exist in one body, in Jacob, who was called both "beloved" and "cheater of his brother." Therefore, the two express the quantity, not the quality, of the separation. One further point is made: The two who are separated will be present in one before there is a division. Isaac said: "Your brother came with cunning and took your blessing" (Gen 27:35). Now this may be a mystical expression by which (the author) briefly hints at the two in one body. But is it not contrary to reason that the cunning one should receive the blessing meant for his neighbor, when even

Scripture says: "He who does not swear to his neighbor with cunning will receive a blessing from the Lord" (Ps 24:4–5)? In fact, Jacob, that is, the church, never came and took the blessing without the accompaniment of cunning, that is, of false brethren. But even if innocence and cunning come to take the blessing together, this does not mean that they are blessed together, for only "he who can take it, takes" (Matt 19:12). One seed only, because of the quality of its soil, grows up.

(25) If the text does not say: "In the womb he cheated Esau," but: (he cheated) "his brother," this does not contradict the fact that he cheated a wicked brother. Esau is the symbol and the designation for the wicked everywhere, while Jacob stands for both because the bad part pretends to be Jacob; thus the two appear under one name. But the good part cannot pretend to be Esau. Therefore, the latter is the name for wicked people only, while the former is bipartite. Moreover, by his free choice Jacob does not include all the good seed, nor Esau all the bad; but both kinds come from both of them. Abraham's seed was twofold; this is the point. One of his sons was born of a slave woman figuratively in order to show that slaves, too, would come from Abraham. This son went away with his mother. But after he was gone, the one who received the law "on Mount Sinai, which is Hagar, bringing forth children for slavery" (Gal 4:24), was found even in the seed of the other, coming from the free woman, from Israel. There, in the same people, children of the promise like Isaac, saints, and believers were generated in large numbers from the free woman. Thus, even when the figurative Ishmael and Esau were separated from the believers, still the whole (process) resulted in one people later on. From the beginning both covenants, that of Hagar and that of Isaac, lay hidden and still lie hidden in it, even though for a time one appeared under the name of the other, because the old covenant did not stop generating when the new one was revealed. Scripture does not say: "Hagar who bore children in her old age," but "which is Hagar, bearing children for slavery."

(26) Both, however, must "grow together until the harvest" (Matt 13:30). In the past, the new covenant revealed in Christ lay hidden under the proclamation of the old covenant—(the new covenant of) grace that would generate children of the promise, like Isaac, from the free woman. In the same way, now that the new covenant prevails, there is no lack of children of slavery born of Hagar, as Christ's appearance as judge will reveal. The apostle confirms this picture: The struggle of the brothers continues even now, the same struggle that went on between them in the past: "You brethren, like Isaac, are children of the promise. But just as at that time he who was born according to the flesh persecuted the spiritual one, so it is now also," and he adds the necessary conclusion: "What does scripture say? Cast out the slave woman and her son, for the son of the slave woman shall not be heir with the son of the free woman" (Gal 4:28–29). The wording here is not without significance: "Just as he persecuted, so it is now also." "He persecuted" is the apostle's interpretation. For Scripture says: "Ishmael was playing with Isaac" (Gen 21:9). The false brethren who were preaching circumcision to the Galatians did not attack them openly. Did they not rather attack playfully, that is, without the signs of open persecution? Paul calls the "playing" Ishmael a persecutor. He does the same with those who are striving to separate the children of God from Christ and to make them children of their mother Hagar by appealing as if to the common welfare, namely, the discipline of the law.

(27) The only reason the children of the devil slip in "to spy upon our liberty" (Gal 2:4), pretend to be brothers, and play in our paradise like children of God is their desire to glory in the suppression of the freedom of the children of God. "They incur the judgment, whoever they are" (Gal 5:10), they persecute every saint, they kill the prophets (cf. Matt 23:37), they "always resist the Holy Spirit" (Acts 7:51). As "enemies of the cross of Christ" (Phil 3:18), "denying Christ in the flesh" (1 John 4:3) while hating his members, they are "the body of sin, the son of perdition" revealing the "mystery of iniquity" (2 Thess 2:3, 7). They are the ones whose coming is "according to the working of Satan with all power and signs and false miracles" (2 Thess 2:9), "spiritual

forces of wickedness on high" (Eph 6:12). Christ the Lord, whom they persecute in the flesh, will "slay them with the breath of his mouth and will destroy them by the manifestation of his coming" (2 Thess 2:8). For now is the time in which these things should be set out openly, not in riddles, the time when that departure which is the revelation of the man of sin is imminent, the time when Lot leaves Sodom.

55. Diodore of Tarsus: Commentary on Psalms

Diodore, bishop of Tarsus from 378 to 390, was a teacher of John Chrysostom (see Texts 15 and 30) and a theological opponent of Apollinaris of Laodicea (see the introduction to "Christological Controversy" in Chapter 7). Highly educated in rhetoric and philosophy, Diodore also established among his pupils and followers an abiding mistrust of the exegetical "excesses" (as he saw them) of the allegorical interpretation of Origen. Diodore rejected allegory as the fanciful tool of the Greeks (i.e., pagans) and instead proposed "higher contemplation" (*theōria*) as the goal of Christian biblical interpretation. As Diodore explains in these excerpts from his *Commentary on Psalms,* the difference between allegory and *theōria* lay in the affirmation of a text's historical significance: allegory, he claimed, denied the historical truth of the biblical text. Allegorists, therefore, were ready to accuse the Bible—the Word of God—of, at best, misrepresentation and, at worst, deceit. While it is true that Origen, on rare occasion, proposed that certain biblical narratives were "impossible" and therefore indicative of a higher truth, a certain amount of indignant exaggeration fuels Diodore's distinction between allegory and *theōria.*

Based primarily on the polemic of Diodore and his students, scholars used to imagine a long-standing rivalry between two interpretive "schools" dating back to the third century: the sober, historical Antiochenes versus the wild-eyed, allegorizing Alexandrians. It is more likely that, in Diodore's writings, we are witnessing not the culmination but the beginning of a particular interpretive stance that is at once theoretically specific but also ecclesiastically divisive. Particularly when placed in the context of the theological rivalries between Constantinople (many of whose bishops were trained in Antioch) and Alexandria in the fourth and fifth centuries (see Chapters 7 and 8), the aggressive biblical interpretation of Diodore suggests how the Bible functioned not only as a guidebook for Christian life, but also as a rallying point for Christian division.

PROLOGUE

According to the blessed Paul, "all Scripture is inspired by God and profitable for teaching, for reproof, for correction, for training in righteousness" (2 Tim 3:16). Indeed, Scripture teaches what is useful, exposes what is sinful, corrects what is deficient, and thus it completes the perfect human being, for Paul adds: "that the man of God may be complete, equipped for every good work" (2 Tim 3:17). Certainly, one would not be mistaken in concluding that all this praise of holy Scripture is also applicable to the book of holy psalms. This book teaches righteousness in a gentle and suitable manner to those who are willing to learn; it reproves kindly and without harshness those who are too presumptuous; it corrects whatever regrettable mistakes we make unwittingly or even deliberately.

This understanding, however, does not impress itself upon us in the same way when we are just chanting the psalms as when we find ourselves in those very same situations that suggest to us our need for the psalms. Of course, those who need only the psalms of thanksgiving because life has been exceedingly kind to them are very fortunate. But we are human, and it is impossible for us not to experience difficulties and encounter the forces of necessity rising both from without and from within ourselves. Thus, when our souls find in the psalms the most ready formulation of the concerns they wish to bring before God, they recognize them as a wonderfully appropriate remedy. For the Holy Spirit anticipated all kinds of human situations, setting forth through the most blessed David the proper words for our sufferings through which the afflicted may find healing. Thus, whatever we treat lightly when merely chanting the psalms and grasp only superficially at first, we come to understand and own when we encounter the forces of necessity and affliction. In an almost natural fashion, the very wound in us attracts the proper remedy, and the remedy adapts itself in turn, expressing the corresponding sentiment.

Therefore, I thought it might be proper for me to offer a concise exposition of the subjects of this very necessary part of Scripture, I mean the psalms, as I myself have received it: an exposition of the arguments as they fit the psalms individually and an explanation of their plain text. In this way, the brothers should find no occasion to be carried away by the words when they chant or to have their minds occupied with other things because they do not understand the meaning. Rather, grasping the logical coherence of the words, they should be able to "sing intelligently" as it is written (Ps 44:8), from the depth of their mind, not from shallow sentiments or just with the tip of their tongues.

Now the subject matter of the psalter in general is divided into two categories: ethical and doctrinal. In addition, the ethical category has the following subdivisions: Some of the psalms correct the moral behavior of the individual, others of the Jewish people only, still others of all human beings in general. Our detailed commentary will specify to which group each psalm belongs. It also will point out two subcategories within the doctrinal subject matter. Some psalms argue against the idea that all beings are self-moved, others against the claim that not all beings are subject to divine providence. Now the advocate of the opinion that they are self-moved automatically assumes that they are not subject to divine providence either. But the skeptic who denies that they are subject to divine providence does not necessarily imply that they are also self-moved. He may, in fact, confess a creator of the universe under whatever name he gives him, but he will either strip him of providence altogether or restrict his providence to celestial phenomena. Against such opinions, the psalms present their proofs that all being has one and the same God and creator, that his providence extends even to the smallest things, and that nothing that owes him its existence escapes his continuing providence. It is not true that God was concerned only about his power to create small and insignificant things but cared little about exercising providence over his weakest creatures or that, because of the absolute preeminence of his own worth, he relinquished his concern for things whose creator he did not disdain to be. In following our detailed commentary, the reader will certainly recognize this category of psalms.

Still another subject appears in the psalms: the Babylonian captivity. Here again we have a subdivision or, rather, several subdivisions. Some of these psalms seem to be spoken by people facing deportation, others by people already in captivity, others by people hoping to return, still others by people who have returned. There are also other psalms describing past events in which, for the benefit of later generations, the prophet recalls what happened in Egypt and in the desert. There are even Maccabean psalms, some spoken in the person of specific individuals, such as Onias and leaders like him; others in the collective person of all Israelites enduring the sufferings of that time. There are still other psalms that fit Jeremiah and Ezekiel specifically. Even these, however, belong to the predictive genre. For some of them reveal misfortunes that were going to come upon the nation on account of its numerous sins; some announce the incredible wonders that were to follow upon such misfortunes. There is a great variety in their composition corresponding to the variety of those future events, for the Holy Spirit was providing a remedy in advance for those who suffered.

But we do not want to bore our readers who wish to get to the detailed commentary on individual psalms by keeping them busy with this great variety of subjects. Therefore, let us stop here and move on to the texts themselves. We only want to remind the brothers of one more preliminary point, though they know it already: The entire prophetic genre is subject to the threefold division into future, present, and past. For even Moses' account of the events concerning Adam and of the very early times from the beginning on is prophecy. By the same token, the disclosure of hidden things in the present is equally prophetic; an example is Peter's knowledge of the theft of Ananias and Sapphira (Acts 5:1–11). Most prominent, however, is the prophecy predicting future events, sometimes many generations in advance. Thus, the prophets predicted the coming of Christ, and the apostles the acceptance of the Christian faith by the gentiles and its rejection by the Jews.

Let us begin now, following the order of items in the Book of Psalms itself, not the order of events that they reflect. For the psalms are not arranged in chronological order but in the order of their discovery. Numerous psalms will provide evidence of this, most strikingly a comparison of the inscription of Psalm 3, "A Psalm of David when he fled from the face of his son Absalom," with the inscription of Psalm 143, "A song against Goliath." Who does not know that the Goliath episode occurred much earlier than the events concerning Absalom? The psalms suffered much displacement because the book was accidentally lost during the Babylonian captivity. Afterward, about the time of Ezra, it was rediscovered, though not the whole book at once but piecemeal— one, two, or perhaps three psalms at a time. These were then reassembled in the order in which they were found, not as they were arranged originally. Hence, even the inscriptions are mostly incorrect; more often than not, the collectors tried to guess the context of the psalms they found but did not treat them according to a scholarly method.

Nevertheless, with the help of God, we shall attempt an explanation even of these errors as far as this is possible. We will not shrink from the truth but will expound it according to the historical substance (*historia*) and the plain literal sense (*lexis*). At the same time, we will not disparage anagogy and the higher *theōria*. For history is not opposed to *theōria*. On the contrary, it proves to be the foundation and the basis of the higher senses. One thing is to be watched, however: *theōria* must never be understood as doing away with the underlying sense; it would then be no longer *theōria* but allegory. For wherever anything else is said apart from the foundational sense, we have not *theōria* but allegory. Even the apostle did not discard history at any point, although he could introduce *theōria* and call it allegory (cf. Gal 4:28). He was not ignorant of the term but was teaching us that if the term "allegory" is judged by its conceptual content, it must be taken in the sense of *theōria,* not violating in any way the nature of the historical substance. But those who pretend to "improve" Scripture and who are wise in their own conceit have introduced allegory because they are careless about the historical substance, or they simply abuse it. They follow not the apostle's intention but their own vain imagination, forcing the reader to take one thing for another. Thus they read "demon" for abyss, "devil" for dragon, and so on. I stop here so that I will not be compelled to talk foolishly myself in order to refute foolishness.

While repudiating this (kind of interpretation) once and for all, we are not prevented from "theorizing" responsibly and from lifting the conceptual content into higher anagogy. We may compare, for example, Cain and Abel to the Jewish synagogue and the church; we may attempt to show that like Cain's sacrifice the Jewish synagogue was rejected, while the offerings of the church are being well received as was Abel's offering at that time; we may interpret the unblemished sacrificial lamb required by the law as the Lord. This method neither sets aside history nor repudiates *theōria.* Rather, as a realistic, middle-of-the-road approach that takes into account both history and *theōria,* it frees us, on the one hand, from a Hellenism that says one thing for another and introduces foreign subject matter; on the other hand, it does not yield to Judaism and choke us by forcing us to treat the literal reading of the text as the only one worthy of attention and honor, while not allowing the exploration of a higher sense beyond the letter also. In summary, this is what the person approaching the interpretation of the divine psalms ought to know.

ON PSALM 118 [LXX]

In any approach to holy Scripture, the literal reading of the text reveals some truths while the discovery of other truths requires the application of *theōria.* Now, given the vast difference between *historia* and *theōria,* allegory and figuration (*tropologia*) or parable (*parabolē*), the interpreter must classify and determine each figurative expression with care and precision so that the reader can see what is history and what is *theōria* and draw his conclusions accordingly.

Above all, one must keep in mind one point that I have stated very clearly in my prologue to the psalter: Holy Scripture knows the term "allegory" but not its application. Even the blessed Paul uses the term: "This is said by way of allegory, for they are two covenants" (Gal 4:25). But his use of the word and his application is different from that of the Greeks.

The Greeks speak of allegory when something is understood in one way but said in another. Since one or two examples must be mentioned for the sake of clarity, let me give an example. The Greeks say that Zeus, changing himself into a bull, seized Europa and carried her across the sea to foreign places. This story is not understood as it reads but is taken to mean that Europa was carried across the sea having boarded a ship with a bull as figurehead. A real bull could not possibly swim such a distance across the ocean. This is allegory. Or another example: Zeus called Hera his sister and his wife. The plain text implies that Zeus

had intercourse with his sister Hera so that the same person was both his wife and his sister. This is what the letter suggests; but the Greeks allegorize it to mean that when ether, a fiery element, mingles with air, it produces a certain mixture that influences events on earth. Now, since air adjoins ether, the text calls these elements brother and sister because of their vicinity, but husband and wife because of their mixture. Of such kind are the allegories of the Greeks. The above examples should suffice lest, with all this allegory, I as an interpreter fall into foolishness myself as I mentioned earlier.

Holy Scripture does not speak of allegory in this way. In what way, then, does it speak? Let me explain briefly. Scripture does not repudiate in any way the underlying prior history but "theorizes," that is, it develops a higher vision (*theōria*) of other but similar events in addition, without abrogating history. As a test case, let us consider the very text of the apostle quoted above. This will be the most effective demonstration of our affirmation that the apostle means this *theōria* when he speaks of allegory. Based on the historical account of Isaac and Ishmael and their mothers, I mean Sarah and Hagar, Paul develops the higher *theōria* in the following way: He understands Hagar as Mount Sinai but Isaac's mother as the free Jerusalem, the future mother of all believers. The fact that the apostle "theorizes" in this way does not mean that he repudiates the historical account. For who could persuade him to say that the story of Hagar and Sarah was untrue? With the historical account as his firm foundation, he develops his *theōria* on top of it; he understands the underlying facts as events on a higher level. It is this developed *theōria* that the apostle calls allegory. As we said, he is aware of the term "allegory" but does not at all accept its application. I have expressed this conviction in my prologue to the psalter already, but for the sake of clarity it bears repetition here.

Figuration (*tropologia*) is present when, in describing an event, the prophet turns words with an obvious meaning into an expanded illustration of what he is saying. The figurative expression is then clarified by the continuation of the text. For instance, David says of the people: "You (God) removed a vine from

Egypt" (Ps 80:8); then, having identified the people with the vine and leaving no doubt by adding, "you drove away the nations and transplanted it," he continues describing the people as if he were speaking of a vine. He mentions that the vine grew and unfolded its shoots (Ps 80:9–10), he asks: "Why have you broken down its hedge so that all who pass by on their way pick its fruits?" (Ps 80:12) and then adds: "A wild boar from the thicket has laid it waste" (Ps 80:13). Now it is quite clear that this is a covert allusion to Antiochus Epiphanes who brought great harm upon the Maccabees, yet at the same time the prophet continues his figure; speaking of the people as a vine, he calls Antiochus a wild boar who tramples down the vine. Isaiah also uses this figure of the people, calling them a vineyard and saying: "My friend had a vineyard on the hillside on fertile ground. I surrounded it with a wall and fenced it in," and so on (Isa 5:1–2). At the very end, clarifying the figurative character of the account, or rather of his prophecy, he adds: "For the vineyard of the Lord of hosts is the house of Israel, and the man of Judah is his beloved plantation. I waited for him to execute judgment, but he acted lawlessly; instead of righteousness there was an outcry" (Isa 5:7). This is figuration (*tropologia*).

A parabolic expression (*parabolē*) is easy to recognize when it follows upon an introductory "like" or "as." To give some examples: "Like water I am poured out and all my bones are scattered" (Ps 22:14) or "I have become to them like a dead abomination" (Ps 37:2 [LXX]). There are many instances that follow this pattern. Often, however, Scripture speaks parabolically even without this introduction. It says, for instance: "You have made my arm a brazen bow" (Ps 18:34) instead of "like a brazen bow" or "And when Abraham looked up with his eyes, he saw three men" (Gen 18:2) instead of "something resembling three men." In these cases, Scripture formulates parables by way of ellipsis, omitting the word "like." Frequently, Scripture also calls a narrative or a teaching "parable," for instance, when we read: "I will open my mouth in a parable, I will utter problems from the beginning" (Ps 78:2). Here the author's teaching or, at least, the narrative is called a parable. Actually, the parable itself may sometimes be called a "prob-

lem." Thus, it is even possible to speak of a problem as an "enigma": Samson proposed such a "problem" to the Philistines, or rather to the Palestinians—the Philistines are in fact the Palestinians—by saying: "Out of the eater came forth food, and out of the strong one came forth sweetness" (Judg 14:14). He would have defeated the Palestinians had he not been betrayed, being unable to resist his lust for women, so that his sophisticated problem ended up being foolishness. This is the language of parable and problem, sometimes introduced by "like" or "as," sometimes not.

One would probably classify much of the material in the books of Moses as enigmas (*ainigmata*), rather than allegories. When the author writes: "The serpent said to the woman"; "the woman said to the serpent"; "God said to the serpent," we have enigmas. Not that there was no serpent; indeed, there was a serpent, but the devil acted through it. Moses speaks of the serpent as the visible animal but under this cover hints at the devil in a hidden way. If this was allegory, only the word "serpent" should be there as we explained earlier. The truth is that there was both a reality and an enigma. The reality was the serpent, but since a serpent is by nature irrational and yet was speaking, it is obvious that it spoke empowered by the devil. (Christ), who has the authority to reveal mysteries and enigmas, points this out in the gospels when he says of the devil: "He was a murderer from the beginning and has not stood in the truth . . . , for he is a liar and the father of it" (John 8:44). This phrase, "and the father of it," is very apt, for the devil was the first one to lie as well as the one who begot lying. Therefore Christ adds, "and the father of it," instead of saying, "the lie in person." Now the Lord was able to clarify enigmas; the prophets and apostles could only report realities. Therefore, both Moses and the Apostle Paul said "serpent." The latter puts it this way: "I fear lest, as the serpent seduced Eve by its guile, so your minds may be corrupted" (2 Cor 11:3); here he also hints at the devil by mentioning the serpent. The serpent is not a rational animal for him but points enigmatically to the devil acting through it. Scheming is not the action of an irrational animal but of a rational being. Our brief remarks here must suffice on the topic of these figurative expressions. We have mentioned only a few points among many, leaving room for industrious scholars to make further points on the basis of similar examples.

In contrast, history (*historia*) is the pure account of an actual event of the past. It is authentic if it is not interwoven with the speaker's reflections, extraneous episodes, characterizations, or fictitious speeches as is, for example, the story of Job. A plain, clear, and concise historical account does not weary the reader with reflections of the author and long characterizations.

Let this be enough on this mode of expression. But since, by the grace of God, I intend to interpret the 118th psalm, I had to discuss in detail the above-mentioned modes of expression, since this psalm contains many of them. Therefore, I had to give my readers a clear statement about them in the preface already in order to alert them to the fact that some parts of the psalms are meant to be taken literally while others are figurative expressions, parables, or enigmas. What is emphatically not present is allegory. Of course, some interpreters have fancied that it is. They brush aside any historical understanding, introduce foolish fables of their own making in place of the text, and burden their readers' ears, leaving their minds devoid of pious thoughts. If they said that being an utterance of God, this psalm accompanies generations of human beings, conforming itself to events both actual and on a higher plane, their interpretation would be quite correct. I am attempting to say something like this: In predicting future events, the prophets adapted their words both to the time in which they were speaking and to later times. Their words sounded hyperbolic in their contemporary setting but were entirely fitting and consistent at the time when the prophecies were fulfilled. For the sake of clarity, there is nothing wrong with stressing this point more than once.

Historically, Psalm 30 was spoken by Hezekiah at the occasion of his deliverance from an illness and from the threat of war with the Assyrians (2 Kings 19–20). These are his words after he was delivered from those ills: "I will extol you, O Lord, for you have protected me and have not let my foes rejoice over me. O Lord, my God, I cried to you and you have healed me. O Lord, you have brought up my soul from Hades, you have rescued me from those who go down to the pit" (Ps 30:1–3). Now these words did fit Hezekiah when he was delivered from his ills, but they also fit all human beings when they obtain the promised resurrection. For at that moment it will be timely for everyone to say to God what Hezekiah said: "I will extol you, O Lord, for you have protected me and have not let my foes rejoice over me." In Hezekiah's case, the foes were the Assyrians and those who rejoiced over his illness; the primary foes of all human beings are physical sufferings, death itself, and the devil, the whole range of experiences connected with mortality. Again, when the psalm continues: "O Lord, my God, I cried to you and you have healed me; Lord, you have brought up my soul from Hades," Hezekiah seems to have used hyperbole to describe his own situation; he was not actually rescued from Hades but from circumstances comparable to Hades on account of his very serious illness. But what sounded hyperbolical at that time, "you have brought up my soul from Hades," will fit his situation much more precisely when he rises from the dead. The same applies to the following verse: "You have rescued me from those who go down to the pit." It is quite clear that by the pit the author means death, but when he first uttered these words, they were used hyperbolically. When he actually rises from the dead, the former hyperbole will come true; the events themselves will have moved in the direction of the formerly hyperbolic expression. One will find more or less all utterances of the saints to be of this kind when one observes how they are made to fit the events of their own time but are also adapted to the events of the future. For this is the grace of the Spirit who gives eternal and imperishable gifts to human beings; I am speaking of the divine words that are capable of being adapted to every moment in time, down to the final perfection of human beings.

In the same way, Psalm 85 was pronounced in the person of those Israelites who had returned from Babylon. It says: "Lord, you were favorable to your land, you have brought back the captivity of Jacob; you forgave your people their iniquity," and so on (Ps

85:1–2). These words were certainly fitting at the time of Israel's return, but they will be even more suitable at the resurrection when, freed from our mortality, we shall be liberated from all sins even more truly. Now if one understands Psalm 118 in this way, namely, as fitting (the circumstances) of those who first uttered it, as well as those who come after them, one is entirely correct. But this is not a case of allegory; rather, it is a statement adaptable to many situations according to the grace of him who gives it power. This great, rich, and beautiful psalm was pronounced in the person of the saints in Babylon who were longing to return to Jerusalem on account of the divine laws and the holy mysteries celebrated there and who were emboldened to make such petitions by their pious lives. A man caught up in sin cannot pray for all his wishes except perhaps for deliverance from his ills; his conscience does not allow him to pray for greater gifts because it means sufficient grace for him if he is set free from his present ills. Therefore, the prayer of great and more saintly people is supported by lives accompanied by virtue. It is their virtues that allow them to make their request boldly.

Now, if this is the subject of the psalm and someone says that Psalm 118 fits all saints everywhere and that one should always pray to God for the general resurrection, as the exiles in Babylon prayed for their return to Jerusalem, this is no violation of propriety. Being so rich and lavish, the psalm adapted itself readily to the exiles in Babylon for their request and prayer, but it adapts itself even more precisely to those who fervently long for the general resurrection. Now the understanding of such a *theōria* must be left to those endowed with a fuller charism. For the purpose of our exposition, let us concentrate on the historical prayer of the saints, the prayer about Jerusalem. But if anyone should doubt that there were saints in that captivity, he is totally mistaken. Yes, there were many saints; some of them were famous, others turned to the Lord humble and unknown, suffering no harm by being unknown to the world. Paul says about them: "Many went about in skins of sheep and goats, destitute, afflicted, ill treated," and adds: "of whom the world was not worthy" (Heb 11:37–38). He has added this clause so that no one may wonder why they were not known. There was no harm in being unknown, but the world proved unworthy of knowing such saints. There were, however, famous people also—I mean in Babylon—outstanding in piety and virtue, men such as Daniel and the three youths; Ezekiel; Zerubbabel; Jesus, son of Jozadak; Ezra; and others like them. But this psalm is on the lips of all saints in captivity or on the way home. They all teach us that it is the practice of virtue and piety above all that has the strength and power to render our prayers effective before God. Thus, David the prophet begins the psalm with these words: "Blessed are those who are blameless in their way," and so on (Ps 118:1 [LXX]).

56. Gregory of Nyssa: Homily on the Song of Songs

Gregory of Nyssa (see introduction to Text 43) was a prominent ecclesiastical leader, ascetic adviser, and Christian philosopher. Heavily influenced by the writings of Origen, Gregory believed that the Bible transmitted a mystical message about humanity's potential union with God. Narratives like the Exodus (which Gregory explored in his *Life of Moses*) were not just (or even primarily) historical narratives of ancient Jews; they were spiritual guides to divine union through virtue and contemplation. Gregory, like Origen, proposed that the Bible con-

From *Biblical Interpretation,* ed. and trans. Joseph W. Trigg. Wilmington, Del.: Michael Glazier, 1988. Used with permission of Joseph W. Trigg

tained deliberate impossibilities and contradictions implanted by God (through the biblical authors) to spur Christians to a higher understanding. (It was this suggestion of scriptural impossibility that Diodore [see Text 55] and his followers found offensive.) The Word of God in textual form was an infinite mystery that invited its more enlightened human readers to transcend literary limitations.

Gregory's interpretation of the racy Song of Songs, which he originally delivered as sermons and later edited around 390, put this theory of deeper spiritual meaning to the test. More than a century earlier, Origen had spiritually interpreted the Song of Song as a guide to union between Christ and the Church, or the soul and God. Gregory, relying on Origen's precedent, pushes this allegorical interpretation even further by reading an erotic text as a guide to ascetic virtue (his commentary is dedicated to Olympias, a famous ascetic noblewoman of Constantinople). Here, in the prologue, Gregory gives a classic defense of Christian spiritual interpretation.

Greetings in the Lord to Olympias, most worthy of reverence, from Gregory the bishop of Nyssa.

I have approved your zeal concerning the Song of Songs, with which you have instructed me in person and by letters, as appropriate to your reverent life and pure soul, so that by the appropriate insight there may be manifested the philosophy hidden in the words, cleansed of the obvious meaning of the text as it stands in simple sense of the words. Therefore I have eagerly accepted your concern about this, not as if it could be useful to you in terms of morals (I am persuaded that the eye of your soul is pure from any perception sullied by passion and that it is able to look without embarrassment toward simple grace through these divine words), but so that those more fleshly than you are might have guidance toward the spiritual and immaterial condition of the soul toward which this book leads through its hidden wisdom.

Because it seems to some churchmen that the letter of sacred Scripture is always to be adhered to, and they do not admit that anything at all useful to us in it is said by means of riddles and deeper meanings, I first consider it necessary to respond to those who accuse us of these things and to show that we are not out of line in searching out in every way possible what is useful in the divinely inspired scripture (see 2 Tim 3:16). Even if the letter, as it is called, should be somewhat useful to the reader (since it readily yields the meaning one is concerned with), if something is spoken that is concealed in deeper meaning and rid-

dles, it is idle in its usefulness to us as far as the immediate sense is concerned. For this reason, the Logos educating us through Proverbs guides us to ponder such words, so as to understand whether what is said is spoken as "a proverb," as "a figure," as a "word of the wise," or as "riddles" (see Prov 1:6).

We shall not quibble over which term—"insight (*theōria*) through elevation," "figurative interpretation," "allegory," or whatever else one chooses to call it—as long as that term is joined to useful concepts. The great Apostle himself, saying that "the law is spiritual" (Rom 7:14), included in the word "law" even the historical narratives, for all divinely inspired Scripture is law to those reading it, educating not only through manifest words of command but through historical narratives to knowledge of mysteries and to pure behavior those who attend to it carefully. Paul used it in his interpretation as it seemed best to him, looking toward what was useful. He did not bother about what term he used to describe this form of interpretation. But now he says that the phrase changes, as he is about to translate the history into demonstration of the dispensation of the two covenants. When he mentions the two children of Abraham, those born to him from bondage and from freedom, he calls the insight concerning them "allegory" (see Gal 4:24). Again, narrating something from history, he says: "These things happened to them in a typical way, but they were written down for our exhortation" (1 Cor 10:11). Again, when he said:

"You shall not muzzle an ox when it is treading out the grain," he added "Is it for oxen that God is concerned? Does he not speak entirely for our sake?" (see 1 Cor 9:9–10). In some places the dimmer perception, and the understanding which is in part, he calls a "mirror" and a "riddle" (see 1 Cor 13:12). Again, the transition from corporeal things to those that are intellectual he calls "turning to the Lord" and "lifting the veil" (see 2 Cor 3:16).

Nonetheless, in all these diverse ways and terms for the insight according to the intellect, he guides us to one form of teaching: we must not stay altogether at the concrete reality because the immediate sense of things said often harms us when it comes to a virtuous manner of life, but we must remove ourselves to the immaterial and intellectual insight, so that those senses that are a little more corporeal might be translated into intellect and thought, having shaken out the dust that settles on account of the more corporeal appearance of what is said. Therefore he said, "the letter kills, but the spirit gives life" (2 Cor 3:6), since often if we were to stand in the mere concrete realities of the history, it would offer us no patterns at all of the good life. How is hearing that Hosea the prophet begot children by a prostitute (Hos 1:2) useful for virtue, or that Isaiah went into the prophetess (Isa 8:3), unless someone should move beyond the letter of what is said? Or how do the narratives about David contribute to a virtuous life, when adultery and murder in the same case have coincided in one pollution? But if some reason should be found, which would show that what was arranged through these things was guiltless, then his words would be demonstrated to be all the more true that "the letter kills" (for it contains in itself the patterns of wicked behavior), "but the spirit gives life" (2 Cor 3:6), for it transforms the superficial and blameworthy sense into more divine meanings.

We know, moreover, that the divine Word himself, who is worshiped above all creation (see Ps 19:1–7, Deut 32:43, Heb 1:6), when in the likeness of man and in the form of flesh (see Phil 2:7), transmitted divine mysteries, so revealing to us the concepts of the law—that the two men whose testimony is true are actually himself and the Father (see John 8:17–18

and Deut 19:15), and that the brazen serpent that was lifted up, which served the people as a remedy for death-dealing bites, is to be understood as the dispensation that has come about for us through the cross (see John 3:14 and Num 21:8). And training the shrewdness of his holy disciples themselves through revealed and hidden words, in parables, in similitudes, in dark sayings, and in apothegms that are brought forward through riddles, concerning which, taking them aside, he provided the interpretations, resolving the obscurity for them (see Matt 13:34–36). There were occasions when, if those who were speaking did not comprehend the meaning, he reproached their slowness and lack of wit. When he told them to avoid the leaven of the Pharisees, they abjectly looked in their pouches, in which they had not provided for themselves rations of bread; he then corrected those who did not understand, explaining that teaching was what was intended by the leaven (see Matt 16:6–2). Again, when the disciples were preparing a meal for him, he answered them with the words "I have food to eat of which you do not know," while they understood him to be referring to corporeal food that had somehow been brought to him in another way, but he interpreted his own word, that the appropriate food for him was to fulfill the Savior's will (see John 4:31–34).

In this manner, we can gather together many such instances from phrases in the gospels in which one thing is understood in the immediate sense of the words, but the meaning of the words has another purpose. Examples are the water promised to those who thirst, which wells up in streams for those who believe (see John 7:37–38 and 4:13–14); the bread that came down from heaven (see John 6:53); the temple destroyed and raised up in three days (John 2:19); the way (John 14:5); the door (John 10:9); the stone rejected by the builders, which had become the head of the corner (see Ps 118:22 and Luke 17:34); the two lying in one bed, the mill, the women grinding, the one taken, and the one left (Matt 24:41); the body and the eagles (Matt 24:28); and the fig tree that had become tender and put forth shoots (Matt 24:32). In all these cases and others like them, it is incumbent on us to search the Scriptures (see John 5:39) and to pay careful attention to the reading and to track it down in every way, if we can somehow find a meaning more lofty than the immediate sense of the words guiding our thoughts to things more divine and incorporeal.

For this reason, the fruit from the tree that it was forbidden to eat we do not believe to have been a fig, as some have held, or any other product of a fruit-bearing tree (see Gen 2:16–17). If the fig were to cause death, not every food would now be permitted, but we have learned this is so from the voice of the Lord, who made this pronouncement: "there is nothing outside a man that by going into him can defile him" (Mark 7:15), but in this law we must seek a different meaning, worthy of the majesty of the Lawgiver. And if we hear that Paradise was the work of God's planting (see Gen 2:8–9), and if the tree of life was planted in the midst of Paradise, we should seek from that which is revealed to learn the hidden mysteries concerning those things of the Father in the farmer and gardener and how it is possible that there are two trees in the midst of Paradise, one of salvation and one of destruction. That which is exactly in the middle, as within the circumference of a circle, can only be at one point. If, however, there should be another center set in another place alongside the center, it is necessary that the whole circle be moved with the center, so that the first spot is no longer the center. Since there was one Paradise, why does the word say in a peculiar way that another of the trees could be seen and that both the one and the other were in the midst? Does not the Bible contradict the notion that one of the trees was death bearing when it says that all God's works were very good (see Gen 1:31)? In these things, if someone does not have some insight into the truth through philosophy, what is said will seem to be inconsistent or mythical to those who are inattentive.

It would take a long time to collect all the instances from the prophets, as when Micah says that in the last days a mountain will be manifest on the peaks of the mountains (Micah 4:1), in such a way referring symbolically to the mystery of piety, which is shown destroying adverse powers; or when it says that a rod shall rise up and a flower from the root, the sublime Isaiah thus signifying the revelation of the Lord through the flesh (Isa 11:1); or the curdled mountain in the great David (whatever sense it may seem to have literally) (Ps 67:16 [LXX]); or the ten thousandfold chariot (Ps 67:18 [LXX]); or the assembly of bulls let loose upon the young calves of the peoples (Ps 67:31 [LXX]); or Lebanon with its cedars skipping in the likeness of a calf (Ps 29:6); or the foot dipped in blood and tongues of dogs (Ps 67:24 [LXX]). It is possible to collect thousands more citations from the rest of the prophets, to show the necessity of an insight into the sense of the words. If such an interpretation is rejected, as some prefer, the result seems similar to me to what would happen if someone were to serve unprocessed grain as food at a meal for men, not grinding the ears, not winnowing the chaff from the grains, not thrashing the wheat on a threshing floor, nor preparing bread in the usual manner for use as food. Just as unprocessed grain is food for beasts, so someone might say that the divinely inspired words unprocessed by winnowing insight are food for the irrational, rather than for the rational. This is true not only of the Old Testament, but of much of the gospel teaching: the winnowing fan purifying the threshing floor, the chaff blown away by the wind, the grain that remains at the feet of him who threshes, the unquenchable fire, the good granary, the trees that bear bad fruit, the threat of the axe fearfully foreshadowing destruction to the tree, the stones transformed into human nature (see Matt 3: 9–12).

This book dedicated to your understanding, I have written as an explanation to those who exhort us to seek no meaning in the divine sayings beyond the immediate sense of the letter. If Origen had investigated this book laboriously, and we have been eager to devote ourselves to writing, let no one accuse us, citing the words of the divine Apostle, who said: "each shall receive his wages according to his labor" (1 Cor 3:8). This book, moreover, I did not compose for display, but because many of the things said in the churches, some with whom I associate have noted because of their love of learning. Some of the things I received from them maintained their signification consistently, but others were added by me, of which the addition was necessary. I have constructed them in the form of homilies, introducing successively the letter and the insight of the sayings, in so far as I have had leisure for this activity during the days of fasting. For in these we have anxiously looked to the exposition so as to enable the people to hear it. If God, who dis-penses of our life, should grant me the time of life and the peaceful tranquility, perhaps I shall pursue my interest in the rest of the book, for now my exposition and insight have proceeded only through half the book. The grace of our Lord Jesus Christ be with all of us forever and ever. Amen.

CHAPTER 13

Christian Art and Architecture

Christianity identity, of course, was not just articulated through texts. Christianity also left its mark on Late Antiquity through its material presence in the Roman Empire. Before the conversion of Constantine, Christian art and architecture were modest and unimposing. Churches were usually private dwellings converted for ritual use, such as the famous house-church in the city of Dura Europos that was destroyed, along with the rest of this Eastern border city, in 256. Earliest Christian art, when it can even be recognized, typically drew on the same biblical subjects as those of Jews and employed a standard palette of Greco-Roman stock images. Christ "the Good Shepherd" was not noticeably different from Hermes "the Good Shepherd" or, simply, "a shepherd." Moses reading the Ten Commandments looked much like any depiction of a Roman official reading a proclamation. We need not attribute this aesthetic indistinctiveness to the failure of Christian creativity or a rustic lack of artistic sophistication. Christianity before Constantine was not a public religion, but rather one constrained by its social circumstances to more private material expressions.

The conversion of Constantine put a new public face on Christianity. Constantine built enormous public structures to house Christian religious services. These buildings took their form and name, *basilica* (i.e., "royal house"), from other public government buildings. Eusebius notes in his *Life of Constantine* (see Text 4): "[Constantine] instructed those who governed the Eastern provinces by generous and lavish grants to make the buildings out of the ordinary, huge, and rich." Christian churches were now the object of imperial and aristocratic patronage, and personal reputations were enriched by monumental donations. The urban landscape was utterly transformed by the architectural presence of Christians, as by St. Peter's in Rome and the Church of Holy Wisdom (Hagia Sophia) in Constantinople. The interiors of churches were splendid, vast halls in which the Word of God was augmented by pictorial representations, painted on the walls or embedded mosaic tiles (see the images presented in this chapter). Symbols, such as the cross and the Chi-Rho (the first two letters of "Christ"), as well as images from the Old and New Testaments, were now displayed prominently in the public square. This artistic and architectural presence captured and elaborated non-Christian aesthetics, while employing a new range of symbols and idioms that were particular to the theological and scriptural sensibilities of Christian communities. The particular theological and cultural ideals of Christianity, however, might also test and reorient late antique aesthetics. The profound paradoxes and intersections of materiality and spirituality that were articulated in doctrines of the incarnation and resurrection (see Chapter 7) and embodied in practices of asceticism and pilgrimage (see Chapters 9 and 10) also influenced the way that Christians viewed art.

This Christian architectural and artistic aethestics also imbued the literature of the age. A common form of literary expression in Late Antiquity, the *ekphrasis*, combined the rhetorical expertise of the educated elite with theories of vision, aethetics, and artistry to produce long, narrative descriptions of art. These *ekphrases* can often give us a precious sense not only of what art looked like, but of how art was *seen*. Included here is an architectural and artistic *ekphrasis* by the Italian nobleman turned ascetic and bishop Paulinus of Nola. Following this textual foray into art and architecture are included a selection of images of Christian art, architecture, and crafts from the fourth through sixth centuries, to give a sense of how Christian aesthetics, both monumental and personal, transformed the material world of Late Antiquity.

FOR FURTHER READING

Beckwith, John. *Early Christian and Byzantine Art.* London: Penguin Books, 1970.

Elsner, Jaś. *Imperial Rome and Christian Triumph: The Art of the Roman Empire,* A.D. *100–450.* Oxford History of Art. Oxford, England: Oxford University Press, 1998.

Finney, Paul Corby, ed. *Art, Archaeology, and Architecture of Early Christianity.* New York: Garland Press, 1993.

———. *The Invisible God: Early Christians on Art.* New York: Oxford University Press, 1994.

Grabar, André. *The Beginnings of Christian Art, 200–395,* trans. Stuart Gilbert and James Emmons. London: Thames and Hudson, 1967.

Jensen, Robin. *Understanding Early Christian Art.* London: Routledge, 2000.

Lowden, John. *Early Christian and Byzantine Art.* London: Phaidon, 1997.

Mathews, Thomas F. *The Clash of Gods: A Reinterpretation of Early Christian Art.* Princeton, N.J.: Princeton University Press, 1993.

The Texts

57. Paulinus of Nola: Song on Felix's Church

Meropius Pontius Paulinus (ca. 352–431) was born into an aristocratic family in Aquitaine, but renounced his promising career in politics to pursue a life of ascetic devotion. In 395 he settled in the Italian countryside and became bishop of Nola. He continued to correspond with a prominent network of ecclesiastical and secular luminaries, including professor-turned-aristocrat Ausonius, Augustine of Hippo Regius (see Texts 11, 14, 29, and 53), Sulpicius Severus (see Text 12), and Jerome (see Texts 27 and 37). Paulinus has left us some of the most erudite letters and poems of the period.

Paulinus used his nobility and influence to promote the shrine of Nola's patron saint, Felix. He expanded the shrine with a new basilica, adjoining courtyards, inscriptions to the martyr-saint, and painted representations of biblical scenes. At the renovated shrine, Paulinus delivered festival poems on the anniversary of Felix's martyrdom (collectively called the *Natalica*). Here is the tenth *Natalicum,* translated into prose; it was written, and presumably performed, in early 404. In the poem, Paulinus describes the architectural and artistic glory on display at the renovated shrine. This poem is thus provided as an example of the late ancient literary form called *ekphrasis:* a detailed description of artistic work. Paulinus employs *ekphrasis* here not only to promote his saint's shrine, but also to draw theological parallels between architectural and artistic renovation and the renewal of human souls that could be accomplished within the Christian fold. This overlay of aesthetics, ascetic longing, and classical poetry brings together many of the theological, cultural, and material strands that weave through late ancient Christianity.

As we perform our longstanding practice, a new element is introduced, for the usual festival is enhanced by the completion of a novel vow. These buildings newly risen in Felix's house provide a theme for redoubling my song and amplify the birthday of our kindly patron. As you see, they have shot up, built high all round, and glitter with matching beauty. On this side a courtyard is open to view with extended cloisters forming a wide circle round it, an open area enclosed by the covered structure, so that the stars are open to view and the courtyard is available for strolling. On the other side are the churches, companions because their walls adjoin. Side by side they are outspread on extensive sites, yet their vying roofs are joined by interlocked beams. Their beauty is different but equal, with the adornment of marble and paintings, paneled ceilings and columns; amid this decoration small recesses provide pleasing variation.

These recesses are set in the side of the cloisters where one portico covers a narrow unbroken stretch,

From *The Poems of Saint Paulinus of Nola,* trans. P. G. Walsh. Mawhah, N.J.: Paulist Press, 1975. Used with permission.

and three entrances close to each other provide admission to them, three gates in a continuous lattice. The middle one is adorned with the holy names and portraits of martyrs, who though of different sexes, are crowned with equal glory. The two extending on the right and left are adorned each with a twofold inscription and depiction of faith. One is covered by the holy achievements of saintly men—the trial of Job by ulcers and of Tobias through his eyes (cf. Job 2:7; Tob 2:11). The other gate is occupied by the lesser sex in the portrayal of renowned Judith and also the powerful queen Esther.

The inner court smiles with varied embellishment—overhead, cheerful with roof and facade bright under the open sky, and below, wreathed with snow-white columns. In the open area of it a shining fountain wells up, enclosed by a protective structure of bronze with latticework around it. The other basins equipped with miniature fountains stand beneath the open sky. They have been installed with pleasing variation, the workmanship being different but the nature of the material the same. From these different mouths the same stream flows out, into basins large enough to contain it.

This open courtyard adjoins all three basilicas and provides entry to all by different routes from the one starting point. So, too, with its spacious central paving, it welcomes in its single embrace the separate exits from the three churches. However, its succession of bright basins, planned and built in five rows, crowds the courtyard with an accumulation of marble and makes it confined to walk in though marvelous to look at. But there is plenty of space for walking in the surrounding colonnades, and when one is tired, one can lean on the latticework between the columns and from there view the plashing basins, eye the soaked turf without treading on it (thus keeping the feet dry), and admire the fountains as in agreeable competition they spurt forth with tranquil murmur. It is not merely in the winter season that this amenity is there to provide pleasure, for the roof's shade is no less pleasant in the heat than is its sunny warmth in the cold season and its shelter when it rains.

On the other side is an open outer court likewise surrounded by porticoes, less embellished but more spacious. This forecourt extends in front of the holy shrines and is visible from afar. With its cells constructed as a second story, the sight of its wall presents the appearance of a fortress, for the converging beams interconnect the buildings. This open space is suitable for gatherings, and there is plenty of room to walk about.

I shall now quickly tell of the sign that our revered Felix recently made manifest to us on this spot. In the middle of the open space facing the threshold of our honored church, there stood two huts, made of wood. They were inconveniently placed and were eyesores; they annoyingly ruined the whole beauty of the buildings, for their grisly appearance interposed itself and blotted out the view. When the basilica lay open, the entrance was darkened because one of these little huts excluded the light, so that the door was open to no effect, being in fact closed. When we sought to pull down the huts, the people lodging in them mocked us and swore to put their lives at possible risk before they could be forced out of their dwellings. Such threats seemed to carry little weight, but I must confess that the situation was hateful to me, for even victory was repugnant if it meant a brawl.

Then one night, when people were asleep in initial enjoyment of early repose, in a corner of one of these huts a spark flew from the deserted hearth and suddenly ignited the layer of hay on which it lighted. Then it spread through the hut, gaining strength from the dry fuel feeding it, and from this light tinder it raised a huge flame. It glided easily on and burst up through the rotten timbers of the old roof. It sent boisterous flames issuing in great whirling motions, filled the air with a hot cloud, and blotted out the stars with black smoke. Then, too, the angry fire made a fearful din, ringing out with a crackling all the louder because the timber was thin. The whole vicinity inhabited by the countryfolk of the village, and even farms quite a long way from it, were so afflicted by the heat, the inhabitants so dazzled by the fearful light, the roofs far and near so besprinkled by the fiery shower of flying sparks, that we were suddenly aroused by the wails of grief on every side. When we saw the buildings wreathed in monstrous light and beheld everything around us shining as brightly as if it were day, we believed that the whole complex of buildings was being harried and burned by the flames, that the very palaces of the saints were ablaze in that great fire, and that the glow emanated from all the roofs combined. For the flames were filling even distant areas with scattered fire and roasting the countryside with excessive heat, so that each individual feared the flames as if they were all encroaching on his own house. All felt the heat around them, and the air they breathed was polluted by the foul smell.

In our fear at the proximity of the danger to our own buildings, we put no trust in our own powers, for where in our weakness could we obtain the strength and resource sufficient to quench that massive fire once the flames waxed hotter from the tinder feeding them, burst suddenly out of that tiny hut, and sprayed all the roofs simultaneously with threatening fire? So relying on faith and suppliant prayer alone, we ran to the threshold of my Felix close by, and from there to the neighboring church, making similar prayers and demanding a remedy from the power of the apostles' ashes as we pressed our lips on the altar that covered the relics. When I left to return to my lodging, I took out that piece of wood, small in itself but a huge aid to salvation, which was obtained for me from a fragment of the eternal cross. I held it in my hand and carried it all the way to the confronting flames. I kept it as a shield before my breast, to protect myself and to ward off and drive back the enemy by a thrust of the boss.

You must believe and impute nothing to me, but render thanks to Christ and offer to the Almighty the praise that is his due. For our salvation resides in the cross and the name of Christ. So also in this crisis, our faith, relying on the cross, proved beneficial; the fire experienced our Salvation. No word or hand of mine deterred that fire, but the power of the cross, which compelled the flames to die down on the spot where they had flared up, as though they were walled in within set limits. So the fire went out, its roaring died, and the tempest that blew up from ashes returned to ashes. How great is the power of the cross! To make nature unnatural, the fire that devours all wood was burned by the wood of the cross! At that time many hands had sought to conquer that fire by

pouring gallons of water on it from numerous vessels. But though they exhausted the wells and poured on it a virtual rainstorm, the fire had greater power and defeated all the water, so that those who poured it on grew tired. But we put out the fire with wood; the flames that water could not quench were defeated by a tiny splinter.

Later on, when our fears had vanished and the toilsome day had brought back the light for which we longed, we went out to inspect what had happened in the night and to survey the traces of the fire with eyes untroubled, though smoke from it still billowed over a wide area. We assumed that we would see extensive damage to the buildings when we recalled the great fire and the panic it had caused, but once we had seen the actuality, our premonitions quickly vanished. We saw that nothing was burned except what had deserved to be consumed, for the only casualty of the fire was one of the two cottages that we would have demolished in any case, even if the fire had not. In fact, Felix in his kindness was thinking of us and doing us a favor. He made this fire usefully anticipate our toil, and he shortened our building operations in a further way. The flames had left there the cottage that was the mate of the burned one, but his intention was not to allow even this to remain as a similar barrier blocking the double doors of the church. The fire was intended to punish the rustic owner in a second way, by preserving one dwelling for him to demolish personally subsequently. Only days previously he had put more value on his huts than on the sacred dwellings, but first he was punished when the fire deprived him of one, and then he began to lay waste the other mean dwelling with his own hand. With swift destructive rage, he made his loss complete as he wept for his beloved dwellings that he loved superfluously. When he saw the burned and the demolished houses side by side, he gazed in wonder at the parallel mounds surviving from dissimilar modes of destruction, rubble and ashes side by side manifesting the twin colors of their fallen remains. And thus realizing that we had gained the victory without a dispute, the wretched man had only himself to blame for losing the lasting goodwill of deferring to us and for gaining the lasting shame of his punishment.

So now the obstacle is removed, and the view of the facade is open, and we can happily stroll in the precincts in both mind and speech. We can hasten into the holy churches and admire the sacred representations that recall the men of old. In the three areas inside the courtyard, we can read the two Testaments and understand in the proper light the arrangement by which the new Law is painted on the old building and the old Law on the new one. The new theme in an old setting and the ancient theme in a new setting are decorations equally useful to us, for thus we can have both new life and the wisdom of age. Old in our seriousness yet babes in our simplicity, we can derive balance of mind from the two ages and unite these different stages of life in our characters.

Somewhat farther within the larger church, a room has been built into the outer wall, almost as a kind of offspring. Its star-spangled dome makes it beautiful, and it winds in and out with three parallel recesses. The source of devotion at its center lends it brilliance, and in a remarkable way it both transforms the whole and is itself transformed. Today a twin renovation embellishes it, for the bishop there wields two gifts of Christ. He consecrates that revered shrine for a double purpose, associating the holy sacrament of the Eucharist with the font that purifies. In this way the Victim transforms the shrine and grace renews the font; the font renewed renews humanity and bestows the gift it receives, or rather it begins to pass on to humans by God's use the new life that it loses by use. When once the font has been used for causing new life, it ceases to be new, but since it will be used perennially to bestow this gift, it will never cease to bring new life to the old man.

Observe here, in the twin basilicas of Felix with their walls renewed, this gift of the Lord, this manifestation by which through Christ's gift the old man dies and the new man is born in the same person. The old is now seen to emerge as new. Previously it had stood on unsightly pillars in a crude line, but now it is transformed and rests on the columns that have been erected. These give it more space and light, so that it has cast off its grime and become young again. In fact, these buildings afford to the eyes bright pleasure that is redoubled because the restored building

vies with the new one in matching brilliance. The ages of the structures differ, but their appearance merges, for the workmanship of past and present craftsmen is in harmony. The same embellishment adorns the similar facades of both buildings, so that the ancient foundation accords with the new. The eyes detect no difference, for old and new sites gleam with identical elegance. The grimy blackness is covered over, and the paintings have restored the gleam of youth to the ancient building by the application of various colors. This is how the different ages of the buildings merge. A new look gleams on the outside of the walls, while the antiquity is hidden, enclosed within. The old age is concealed and daubed with the face of youth, so that advanced years have blossomed afresh with youthful appearance. They are simultaneously old and new—neither equally new nor equally old. They are the same yet not the same as they depict the shape of future and present blessings. For it is salutary for us even now to wipe off the filth of our former life and to become renewed in devotion of mind, to follow Christ, and to prepare ourselves for the kingdom.

So will it be on the day when people are permitted to rise again with life renewed. Among those who rise, precedence will be given to the group whose flesh is covered with a shining garment. They will change their slaves' appearance for the likeness of the Lord; soon to reign with God, through similarity to Christ but by his gift, they will obtain a distinction resembling his.

The renewed appearance of the church also warns us to shed our former appearance and to wear a new one, to erase our past deeds and to direct our changed hearts to the future that lies with God; to draw an apposite oblivion over our former preoccupations and to introduce into our minds zeal for the kingdom of heaven; to be dead toward human things and the ways of the world in spirit before the death of the flesh and not to be freed from the chains of the body before being loosed from those of sin. Therefore, let us renew ourselves in mind and hasten to prise away from our bodies the filthy activities of our earthly forms, so that, having sloughed off our external apparel, having shaken off this grime, we may shine and may cleanse the clothing that is our body and soul.

Let us avoid not merely committing sin but even thinking of it, as we would hold our noses to avoid the infectious emanation and the foul stench from a rotting corpse. Solomon warns us that sin is to be feared and loathed like the appearance of a snake, and says it is armed with lion's teeth (Sir 21:2–3). He speaks the truth, for sins with bestial maw savagely devour the soul conquered by the sick pleasure of the body and appropriated after defeat by the serpent for his meal. That serpent devours "the peoples of the Ethiopians" (cf. Ps 74:14), not those roasted by the sun, but those whom sin has darkened and guilt has made black as night. Such are the Ethiopians that the serpent devours, and among them the condemned Satan finds food to eat. God used the single word "earth" to describe both the sinner and serpent's food, and so the man who devours sins (cf. Prov 19:28) is devoured by the dragon.

It is time to change our ways, to rise from sleep, and at last to remain awake for God (cf. Rom 13:11) and, on the other hand, to remain asleep to those activities in which the mind dead to Christ remains awake. If God's teaching does not give us understanding from the light of the Word, let us at least obtain a model for life from these buildings. Let the stone and timber teach us dullards, so that by faith we may achieve the kind of building we have completed here with our hands. The mental achievement and the manual labor are not identical, but from these different sources a like pattern of work is derived. Observe my demonstration that these dissimilar types of activity are in harmony by their similar form.

The sites of the new buildings can be recalled by many, for it is not long since that all now standing were begun. The works we sweated over for two years have been completed in the third, through the prayers of the saints and Christ's aid. Part of the building area was a small garden, part a heap of rubble, which was removed by the combined efforts of our diligent people, who also dug out the paltry vegetable herbs and the thorns to leave the cleared site bare, its surface spick and span. Now its extensive

paving gleams, its area adorned with marble blocks, and it has forgotten its former appearance. How splendidly it has changed its face! The adornment of marble has followed the application of manure. The ground bears Parian marble basins after cheap cabbages, its waters shining out where previously filth shone.

How, then, can this structure furnish for me a pattern by which I can cultivate, build, and renew myself inwardly and make myself a lodging for Christ? It is clear how we are to explain my earth, the rubble within me, and the source of the thorns sprouting in my land. My earth is my heart, the rubble the sins of that debased heart. Slothful pleasure, polluted love, stained lust are the rubble of the soul; so, too, troubled care for the body, devouring envy, greedy hunger, oppressive anger, unsubstantial hope, aspirations spendthrift with personal possessions and thirsty for those of others—all these are thorns for the soul because they are ever pricking ambivalent souls with their pointless goads and making them smart continually with the fear of wretched failure and the wretched zeal for possessions. In this fashion they are poor amid their wealth, thirsting like the fabled Tantalus amid water. They do not possess what they seem to possess, for they are afraid to enjoy the wealth they have gained, and they bequeath all they have saved, and so they waste the days of their lives in laying up resources for their sustenance.

So we must dig out these thorns, this rubble from our overgrown minds. We must tear out from our hearts this initial root of all our sins from which a barren tree shoots forth. That tree must be excised at the roots by the Lord's ax and must fall so that it may never bud in our fields. Once this root has withered after all that nourished it has been cut away from us, all the wickedness will fall away, all the sin will die, all evils will fall with the fall of the mother tree, for when the tree dies, its fruit will perish with it.

Then, when the garden is well cleared, the house will be built, and the materials of God's structure, founded on living soil, will rise gloriously to heaven. Christ himself will set up columns in us and dismantle the old pillars that impeded the path within our souls. So the King will clear an area within our minds for strolling in, just as Wisdom used to stroll with healing presence and holy words in the five colonnades of Solomon, healing bodies by his touch and hearts by his teaching (cf. John 5:2).

Therefore, let us not continue old amid new buildings, so that Christ who dwells in human hearts may return to find our hearts renewed. For when old and new are forced together, the rent becomes worse, and it is good to put new wine in new bottles (cf. Matt 9:16–17). Let our earlier lives die so that our future lives may not die. Let us leave the world of our own accord because if we do not flee it voluntarily, we will have to forgo it under compulsion. Let us die so that we may not die. Let us supplant death-bringing life with life-bringing death. Let our earthly form die and our heavenly form replace it. Let Adam be transformed into Christ. Let us change ourselves here so that we may be changed also in heaven. He who persists in remaining inwardly unchanged now will likewise experience no change forever.

The Images

58. Christian Art in Late Antiquity

1. Remains of a statue of Constantine (Rome; marble, ca. 315–330). These pieces of marble are the remains of a monumental statue of the Emperor Constantine dating from after 315 C.E. The statue, which stood 9 meters high (the head pictured here is 2.6 meters), loomed in a massive new public structure in the city of Rome, the Basilica Nova. Construction of the basilica was begun under Maxentius, the rival emperor defeated by Constantine in 312. The installation of this monumental statue marked the triumphant presence of the new emperor in the ancient capital of the empire.

2. Arch of Constantine (Rome; marble, ca. 312–315). This is another triumphant memorial of Constantine's defeat of Maxentius and his imperial rule from the city of Rome. Erected soon after Constantine's triumph in 312, the arch incorporates *spolia,* artistic elements taken from imperial, monumental structures of the second and third centuries. This incorporation and rearticulation captures some of the aesthetic sense of Late Antiquity, stressing at once tradition and continuity, as well as self-promotion and progress. Like much of Constantine's legacy—apart from his church construction—the Arch of Constantine is ambiguous concerning the emperor's purported conversion to Christianity: the inscription refers only to the "inspiration of the divinity" that assisted the emperor.

3. Missorium [serving dish], detail (Spain; silver, 388). This commemorative silver dish was cast for the *decennalia* (tenth anniversary) of the imperial ascension of Theodosius I. This detail from the center of the dish (which weighs more than 30 pounds and is more than two feet in diameter) depicts Theodosius himself in grand, sacred splendor: dressed in his imperial robes and passing on an official document, the emperor sits in an abstract architectural space in perfect serenity. The sanctifying halo imbues his political triumph with an explicit sense of God's protection and favor (see Text 8).

4. Santa Sabina, interior (Rome; ca. 430–450). Following the patronage of Constantine, public Christian structures adopted the open hall architecture of other public, Roman buildings (basilicas). The result, visible in this Roman church, was a vast interior space in which to enact the dramas of Christian liturgy and preaching. Probably only the presiding clergy (bishop or priest) would have had a chair; the worshipers would have stood or (for particularly long church vigils) perhaps sat on the floor. Like the Arch of Constantine (Image 2), this fifth-century church used *spolia,* that is, stonework (bricks and columns) taken from second-century Roman buildings. Church construction was costly for even the most generous of benefactors.

5. Orthodox baptistery, interior (Ravenna; ca. 458). Free-standing baptisteries built adjacent to churches were common at a time when many Christians waited until adulthood to be baptized. They also gave wealthy donors (emperors and nobles) additional opportunities to express their largesse and provided dramatic spaces in which to participate in Christian liturgies. Like many baptisteries and small church structures of this period, both the architecture and the baptismal font are octagonal. The eight sides may have symbolic significance (the resurrection of Christ supposedly took place on the eighth day of the week), or the eight-sided structure may have been a simplified form of a circular plan, which was a much more difficult engineering feat. The scale and intricacy of this baptistery give a sense of the very public and elaborate role that Christian initiation came to play in the period of Late Antiquity.

6. Orthodox baptistery, interior ceiling (Ravenna; mosaic, ca. 458). This ceiling mosaic depicting the baptism of Christ by John the Baptist was directly above the baptismal font in the Ravenna baptistery (Image 5). When baptizands stepped into the font and looked up, they would see this image of Christ being baptized. The figure to Jesus' left is labeled *Jordan*—that is, a personification of the Jordan River. It was traditional in non-Christian art to figure rivers as old men (river gods), a practice that has been adopted wholesale into this representation of Christ's baptism. When the Germanic rulers began their own building projects in the late fifth and early sixth centuries, they mimicked the architecture and decor of this ("Orthodox") baptistery, including their own version of this image of Christ and John the Baptist.

7. Mausoleum of Galla Placida, interior mosaic (Ravenna; ca. 450). This cross-shaped chapel is often attributed to the patronage of Galla Placidia, the daughter of Theodosius I; later tradition even claimed that she was buried here. This lunette (i.e., "half-moon") mosaic is an archway above a sarcophagus. It features a saint (perhaps Saint Laurence) who is facing a burning grill (the legendary method of Laurence's martyrdom). The mosaic showcases the spectacular array of colors and techniques that were used even in small-scale mosaic projects. Opposite Laurence stands a bookcase containing four codices (bound volumes) labeled Matthew, Mark, Luke, and John. Early Christians preferred to use the *codex* instead of the more common scroll (*volumen*) format for the production of biblical books.

8. Jesus and the Samaritan Woman at the Well (Via Latina, Rome; fresco, mid-fourth century). Contrary to popular, romantic imagination, the chambers carved out of soft rock beneath the city of Rome (the catacombs) were not the clandestine meeting places of early Christians fleeing persecution. They were burial sites used by non-Christians as well as Christians. Even so, some of our earliest unambiguously Christian art is found in the decorated walls of the catacombs. Pre-Constantinian catacomb painting often employed "pagan" images (a hero fighting a lion, a shepherd saving his sheep) to express Christian identity.

Post-Constantinian Christian catacomb painting, such as the scriptural depictions found in the mid-fourth century Via Latina catacombs, continued to finesse Christian artistic expression in registers that were meaningful to imperial aesthetics. Here, Christ speaking to the Samaritan woman (see John 4:6–29) is figured as a respectable, clean-shaven Roman man in a toga, serenely addressing an eastern provincial woman with magisterial gestures. The Christian viewer gains a sense at once of the saving activity of Christ (appropriate for a burial site) and the dovetailing of Christian salvation and Roman imperialism.

9. The Binding of Isaac (Via Latina, Rome; fresco, ca. 320). This representation of Abraham's near-sacrifice of Isaac (see Gen 22:1–19) likewise portrays the heroes of the Bible in serene and dignified postures worthy of Roman noblemen. Once again, the power of God's promise of salvation is figured through a scriptural scene: not only God's testing of Abraham, the forefather of "Christian faith," but also the typological melding of the (near) sacrifice of Isaac with the ultimate redemptive sacrifice of Christ. The course of the narrative (Abraham's offering, God's intervention, even the slave waiting at the foot of the hill) is compressed into a single, complex image. This sort of abstract Roman aesthetics combines here with Roman artistic naturalism (the surprising detail given to the depiction of Abraham's slave and donkey).

10. Tombstone of Severus (Rome; marble, fourth century). This stone cover for a *loculus* (a shelf carved into the side of a cave or catacomb for interment) marked the grave of a Christian named Severus (or, as it is spelled here, *Seberus*). Severus was apparently an artisan or publican (depending on the significance of the barrel, which presumably indicates his profession). Even though he did not have enough money to afford an elaborate sarcophagus (see Image 11), he (or his family) was able to purchase a high-quality piece of stone with a selection of specific images, including his own name. In the center is a ribboned wreath inside of which is a "Chi-Rho" (the first two Greek letters of "Christ"), flanked by an omega and an alpha (see Rev 1:8, 21:6, 22:13), common Christian symbols in the fourth century. It is possible that Severus (or his family) ordered a premade "Chi-Rho/alpha-omega" stone and paid extra to have a personal name and professional marker engraved alongside it.

11. Sarcophagus of Junius Bassus (Rome; marble, 359). More elaborate forms of Christian burial art were available to the growing number of Christian upper-class elites, such as Junius Bassus, who served as prefect of the city of Rome. This sarcophagus, a masterpiece of Roman Christian art, contains a running inscription, across the uppermost band, that emphasizes Bassus's high rank and Christian status. The registers depict a series of biblical scenes that emphasize worldly and divine suffering and salvation: on top, Abraham's offering of Isaac, the arrest of Peter, Christ ruling in glory, the arrest of Christ, and his trial before Pontius Pilate; on

the bottom, the suffering of Job, the Fall of Adam and Eve, the entry of Christ into Jerusalem, Daniel in the lion's den, and the arrest of Paul. This elaborate and expensive work of Christian burial art shows how quickly Roman elitism and Christian aesthetics came together in the city of Rome.

12. Sarcophagus of Junius Bassus, detail (Rome; marble, 359). This detail, from the bottom register of biblical images, gives a sense of the intricacy, delicacy, and impact of the sequence of scriptural motifs inscribed into Bassus's tomb. A significant moment in the history of humanity and salvation has been frozen, as Adam and Eve turn away from the Tree of Knowledge of Good and Evil in shame, covering up their nakedness. The serpent, coiled around the tree, reminds the viewer of the dangerous intersection of temptation and evil. The totality of salvation history depicted on the sarcophagus both highlights and ameliorates the catastrophe of the Fall.

13. Vienna Genesis (Constantinople?; purple-dyed parchment, sixth century). Christian attention to sacred Scripture was not limited to debates over canon and interpretive method. The Bible was also an object of spiritual and aesthetic devotion. This leaf from the so-called Vienna Genesis (now located in a library in Austria; although it originated in an Eastern, urban setting, scholars still debate exactly where) contains a text of the Bible, supplemented with detailed illustrations of appropriate scenes. Here is the bottom of a page narrating the visit of Abraham's servant to find a wife for Isaac (Genesis 24). The depiction collapses the progressive narrative into a single image, as Rebecca (Isaac's future wife, in a modest head covering) leaves the city, goes to the spring (personified by a half-naked woman; see Image 6), and waters the servant's camels. The luxuriousness of this biblical manuscript attests not only to the wealth and privilege of some upper-class Christians, but to the ways in which their financial and artistic expenditures came to center increasingly on their religious devotion.

14. Santa Pudenziana, mosaic (Rome; ca. 390). This former public bathhouse was converted into a small church toward the end of the fourth century and given a stunning mosaic depiction of Jesus (probably post-Resurrection) instructing his apostles before an architecturally detailed backdrop of Jerusalem. Although the mosaic has been truncated and restored over the centuries, it serves as a fitting aesthetic encapsulation of how Christians came to view their religious and cultural identities in the fourth and fifth centuries. The delicate glasswork of this mosaic portrays an imperial Christ, enthroned on gold and gems, holding a book, the enormity of which is reflected in the four beasts (each representing a Gospel writer) hovering in the cloudy Jerusalem skies. Christian time collapses as the Roman viewer gazes upon charged moments of the past (the first-century apostles) and the future (stormy clouds over the holy city hinting, perhaps, at an apocalyptic end time). Christian space collapses as well, as the center and periphery of the Roman Empire (Rome and Jerusalem) come together in the majestic, imperial gaze of Jesus. Religion and politics, image and word, spirit and matter intersect here in the apse of a Christian house of worship.

CHAPTER 14

Christianity Outside the Roman Empire

Throughout the fourth and fifth centuries, Roman Christians came increasingly to view their religious identity as conterminous with their political and cultural identities: to be Roman was, more and more, to be Christian, and vice versa. During the same period, however, Christianity was spreading beyond the political boundaries of the Roman Empire. Some Christians deliberately set out to convert their non-Roman neighbors. The two most famous examples are Ulfilas, the fourth-century Cappadocian who transmitted an Arian form of Chrisianity to the Goths and other Germanic tribes, and Patrick, the fifth-century British bishop who preached Christianity in Ireland. More often it seems that Christianity spread throughout the Western and Eastern borderlands of the Roman Empire much as it had centuries before as a fledgling movement within the empire: through social and commercial networks. The borders of the Roman Empire were porous, allowing for frequent trade and travel (see Egeria's account of travel in Mesopotamia in Text 42). It is likely that Christians traveling the everyday routes of commerce through northern Europe, Mesopotamia, and Africa transmitted religious convictions along with Roman glass and wine.

By the fourth century, Christianity was well established in the border lands: Germans, Arabs, Armenians, Axumites (northern Ethiopians), and Georgians all had small Christian communities. The vibrant Christian communities in Syria made religious inroads into the Persian Empire. As Christianity gained a foothold, especially in the East, these new religious communities found themselves facing many of the same challenges that Christians in the second and third centuries had faced within the Roman Empire. A powerful new dynasty, the Sassanians, came to power in Persia in the third century, and the official religion of this new dynasty was Zoroastrianism (also called Mazdeism). The Zoroastrian priests, the *magi* (mages), maintained close ties with the Sassanian King of Kings, and by the fourth century, under Shapur II, religious persecution had begun against non-Zoroastrian Persians. The mages accused Persian Christians of being sympathetic to the Roman Empire and incited systematic persecutions beginning in the fourth century. Much as they had in Rome during the Great Persecution, religious and political affiliations appeared entirely inextricable to the

Persian rulers. When Shapur wrested control of Nisibis from the Romans after Julian's botched invasion in 363, the entire Christian population of the city migrated West across the border (see Text 7). Likewise, imperial support in the Roman Empire for untenable theological positions drove Nestorians and Monophysites in the sixth century back across that border, to contend with Persian "paganism," rather than Roman heresy. Intervals of war and détente between Rome and Persia continued into the seventh century, when war finally exhausted both sides and left them vulnerable to the new force rising in the East, Islam. In the meantime, border territories in both empires (Syria, Arabia, Armenia, and Georgia) suffered the onslaught of religiopolitical aggression.

Included here are texts recounting the circumstances and consequences of the spread of Christianity, especially in the East. Sozomen, the fifth-century Roman historian, describes the process of Christianization in almost hagiographic terms that would become common in the East and the West, as Christian captives convert a royal family, and a "top-down" conversion of an entire kingdom ensues. Sozomen also signals Roman awareness of and solidarity with Christians persecuted in the Persian Empire. Internal accounts of Persian persecution, written in Syriac, share the sense of paradoxical physical suffering and spiritual triumph that are already familiar from earlier, Roman martyr-texts, infused further with a particular Syriac asceticism. Finally, a Georgian story of a royal martyr poignantly describes the ways in which loyalties fractured along familial, religious, and political fault lines.

FOR FURTHER READING

Brock, S. P. "Christians in the Sasanian Empire: A Case of Divided Loyalties." In *Religion and National Identity,* ed. S. Mews. Oxford: Blackwell, 1982.

Fowden, Elizabeth Key. *The Barbarian Plain: Saint Sergius Between Rome and Iran.* Berkeley: University of California Press, 1999.

Harvey, Susan Ashbrook. *Asceticism and Society in Crisis: John of Ephesus and the "Lives of the Eastern Saints."* Berkeley: University of California Press, 1990.

Lang, David. *The Georgians.* New York: Praeger, 1966.

Mgaloblishvili, Tamila, ed. *Ancient Christianity in the Caucasus.* Richmond, England: Curzon, 1998.

Munro-Hay, Stuart H. C. *Aksum: An African Civilization of Late Antiquity.* Edinburgh: Edinburgh University Press, 1991.

Thomson, R. W. *Studies in Armenian Literature and Christianity.* London: Variorum, 1994.

The Texts

59. Sozomen: Church History

The historian Sozomen (Salminius Hermias Sozomenus; d. ca. 450) was raised in a Christian household in southern Palestine, where he received a thorough classical education. As a young man, he moved to Constantinople to pursue a career in civil service (perhaps in law) and decided to write a history of the Christian church that would continue Eusebius's *Church History* (see Text 50) from 325 down to his present day. Sozomen used many sources, including an older contemporary named Socrates, but also included his own store of anecdotes from the Eastern provinces. His history is particularly valuable for its chapters on the spread of Christianity beyond the bounds of the Roman Empire, among the German tribes, the Iberians (present-day Georgia), the Armenians, the Persians, and the Axumites (northern Ethiopians; Sozomen calls them "Indians" because their kingdom was on the Indian Ocean).

Given our dearth of sources from these times and places, Sozomen's second- (or third- or fourth-) hand reports give us some of our best information on the contexts in which Christianity became insitutionally established in these border provinces of Europe, Asia, and Africa and the particular challenges Christians faced there. The accounts are at once exotic, yet familiar: amid the flurry of Aramaic and Persian names (Greekified by Sozomen) in the chapters on the perseuctions of Shapur II, a Roman Christian reader would find familiar tales of ascetic virtue and heroic martyrdom (based, probably, on Persian accounts; see Text 60). The distant kingdom of Axum was wild and uncivilized, a place where philosophers sought outlandish wisdom and Roman citizens were attacked straight off the boat. Yet, at the end of the tale, the Axumites have a bishop ordained by the archorthodox bishop Athanasius of Alexandria. Insofar as they saw the exotic and strange, the readers of this text were typical Romans; insofar as they saw religious connections beyond the limits of the Roman Empire, the readers were being shown a more transcendent Christian identity.

THE WESTERN BARBARIANS AND THE CAPTIVE PRIESTS

6 (1) While the church was expanding through the whole Roman world in this way, religion advanced throughout the barbarians themselves. For already tribes on both sides of the Rhine had been Christianized, the Celts and those Gauls who lived at the ends of the Ocean, and the Goths, and a great many bordering peoples who were at that time on both banks of the Danube river. As they had long ago taken part in faith in Christ, they had adopted a more cultivated and reasonable aspect. (2) For nearly all the barbarians, a motive arose for them to honor Christian

From *Histoire ecclésiastique: Sozomène*, ed. J. Bidez. Paris: Editions du Cerf, 1983. (Translated by Andrew S. Jacobs.)

teachings at the time when they were doing battle against the Romans and against other tribes, under the reign of Gallienus and the emperors who came after him. For at that time, an unspeakable throng of disorderly peoples crossed over out of Thrace and into Asia, and other barbarians pillaged elsewhere and did the same to the habitations of the Romans; many of Christ's priests were taken prisoner and lived among them. (3) Since they cured the sick on the spot and purified demoniacs, calling only upon Christ and invoking the Son of God, and besides this they pursued the philosophical life through blameless conduct and defeated blame through virtues, the barbarians, amazed at these men for their way of life and miraculous deeds, considered it prudent and that they also would have the favorable God if they imitated these men who seemed better and served the Almighty like they did. So they offered themselves to these men as guides of correct behavior, and they were taught and they were baptized, and subsequently they formed a church.

THE IBERIANS AND THE PRISONER

7 (1) It is said that, in the same reign, the Iberians came to know Christ. This great and very warlike barbarian people inhabits the interior of Armenia, toward the north. A Christian woman who had been taken prisoner prepared them to look down upon their ancestral religion; indeed, she was very faithful and exceedingly pious, and she did not compromise her customary conduct, even among foreigners.[1] It happened that she found fasting quite useful, and night and day she prayed and blessed God. The barbarians inquired why she would persist in this; when she answered quite simply that it was necessary to pay reverence to Christ, the Son of God, both the name of the one being worshipped and the manner of

worship seemed strange to them. (2) When a young boy there happened to become dreadfully sick, his mother carried him to each house and displayed him. For this is a custom among the Iberians, so that, if some healer of the sick were found, relief from suffering would be easily procured for the afflicted. (3) Since he was in no way cured, the boy was also carried to the prisoner. She said: "I have no knowledge or experience with drugs or salves (*christōn*) or poultices, but I believe that Christ (*christon*), whom I revere, the true and great God, will become the savior of your boy, dear woman." Immediately, when she prayed on his behalf, she delivered him from the sickness that was expected to have been his demise.

(4) Not much later, in the same manner, she also saved the wife of the ruler of this people, who was about to be destroyed by an incurable ailment, and she instructed her in the knowledge of Christ, explaining that he is the dispenser of health and life and sovereignty and Lord of all things. Through the experience of what had happened to her, this woman believed that the prisoner's words were true. She honored the religion of the Christians, and she held the prisoner in great esteem. (5) Now the king, marveling at the speed and wonder of the faith and of the healing, learned the cause from his wife and commanded that the prisoner be repaid with gifts. The queen said: "But these count little for her, even if they are held in great esteem. The only thing she holds dear is the service of her own God. So if we want to be gracious to her and if we are eager to go on safely and happily, well then, we should revere him, too, since he is a powerful God and a Savior who (should he so wish) causes kings to remain where they are but, then again, is capable of quite easily rendering the great small or exalting the lowly, saving those who are fearful." (6) Although his wife seemed to make many good points, the leader of Iberia was dubious and not at all persuaded, being suspicious of this new matter and respectful of his ancestral religion. Not long after, he went into the woods to go hunting with his retinue. Then suddenly a very dense mist and a thick gloom, pouring around them from everywhere, hid the sky and the sun; a deep night and great darkness seized the woods. Each one, fearing

---

[1] Sozomen's account of the conversion of Iberia (Georgia) is also found in the accounts of the earlier historians Rufinus and Socrates. The unnamed slave woman was later venerated as Saint Nino, the founder of Georgian Christianity.

for himself, scattered from the others. (7) The king, wandering by himself (just as people do when they are at a loss in fearsome situations) thought about Christ. He determined in his mind to consider him a God and to pay reverence to him henceforth if he should escape the present evil. Even as he was considering these things, immediately the mist dissolved, and the gloom changed into clear air, and as a ray burst down into the forest, he was saved from there. (8) And as he was sharing the event with his wife, he summoned the prisoner, and he commanded that she teach him what manner was fitting for the worship of Christ. When she had explained to him (to the extent a woman can) what it is right to say and do, he gathered together his subjects and publicly announced the divine activities that had happened to him and to his wife. Although he was not yet initiated, he imparted the matters of doctrine to those under his rule. So they persuaded the entire people to pay reverence to Christ; he taught the men, and the queen, with the prisoner, taught the women.

(9) Quickly, by a common covenant of the whole people, they prepared to construct a church in the most lavish manner. When they had erected the enclosure of the temple in a circle, after positioning devices they raised up the columns and fixed them onto their bases. They say that once the first and second columns were set correctly, it became troublesome to raise up the third; not by the skill of artisans could they make it straight, nor could they accomplish it by brute force, even though many of them were pulling. (10) When evening fell, the prisoner spent the night there alone, beseeching God that the straightening of the columns should become easy; meanwhile all the others withdrew angrily, especially the king. For the column, erected halfway, remained at an oblique angle, and since it was stuck in the ground, it was immovable from beneath the bottom. But through this miracle and through those miracles that came before, she was going to make the Iberians more steadfast in divine matters. (11) Now when they came to the church around dawn (what a marvelous occurrence, like a dream!) the column, which, the night before, was immovable, appeared straight, lifted up by a small distance from its own base. While all of them were as-

tounded and confessing together that Christ was the only true God, and as they all looked on, it gently floated under its own power, as if by some art, and attached itself to its base. After this, the others were easily set straight, and eagerly the Iberians accomplished the rest of the work. (12) Once the church had been constructed with zeal, on the advice of the prisoner they sent delegates to Constantine, emperor of Rome, bearing an alliance and treaties, requesting in return for these that priests be dispatched to their people. As the delegates related fully what had happened among them and how the whole people revered Christ with much diligence, the Roman emperor delighted in the delegation, and he sent back the delegates, who did everything according to their plan. So it was that the Iberians came to know Christ, and even now they revere him diligently.

THE ARMENIANS AND THE PERSIANS

8 (1) I heard that the Armenians were Christianized even earlier. For they say that Tiridates, the leader of this people at that time,[2] following some miraculous sign from God that occurred concerning his household, became a Christian and at the same time also ordained in a single proclamation that all those under his rule must worship as he did.

(2) Immediately afterward, the doctrine swept across the border tribes and increased greatly. And, I suppose, Christianization among the Persians had its start when those who, on the occasion of dealings with the Osroenes and the Armenians, as is likely, had extended contact with the holy men there and experienced their virtue.

SHAPUR, THE PERSIAN, AND CHRISTIAN MARTYRS

9 (1) When, in time, they became very numerous and began to form churches, and they had both priests

---

[2] Tiridates III of Armenia supposedly converted in 301, giving Armenia claim to be the oldest Christian nation.

and deacons, this immoderately annoyed the mages,[3] those who administered Persian religion as if they were some sort of priestly tribe, according to family tradition. It also annoyed the Jews, who, in some way, are naturally incited to jealousy toward Christian teaching. They made accusations to Shapur, who was king at that time, against Symeon, archbishop of Seleucia and Ctesiphon (imperial cities of the Persians), claiming that he was an ally of the Roman emperor and was revealing Persian intelligence to him. (2) Persuaded by these accusations, Shapur first of all afflicted the Christians with immoderate taxes, since he knew that a great number of them practiced the discipline of poverty, and he entrusted the tax collection to hardened men, with the result that forced by a lack of sustenance and the inflexibility of the tax collectors, they abandoned their own religion, for this had been his goal. After this he ordered that the priests and the ministers of God be executed by sword, that the churches be razed to the ground, that their valuables become public property, and that Symeon be brought up on charges of treason to the Persian Empire and its native religion. (3) Then the mages, and the Jews along with them, zealously demolished the houses of prayer.

Once Symeon was captured and bound in chains, he was brought to the king; there, indeed, he held forth as a good and brave man. For when Shapur ordered that he be taken out and tortured, he was not afraid, nor did he prostrate himself. (4) Extremely irritated at this, Shapur inquired: "Why aren't you prostrating yourself *now?* You've done it before!"

Symeon said: "Because before I was not led in chains to betray the true God, and, as I was in no way making myself conspicuous, I fulfilled the customary duties concerning the sovereignty. But now it is not right to do this, for I come contending for a prize on behalf of piety and our doctrine." (5) When he said such things, the king ordered him to prostrate himself before the sun, and he promised that, if he obeyed, he would give him many gifts and hold him in honor;

but he threatened that if he disobeyed, he would destroy him and the entire Christian tribe. He was neither impressing Symeon with his threats nor softening him with his promises; instead Symeon bravely remained strong in his conviction never to prostrate himself before the sun or to appear as a traitor to his own religion. Shapur commanded that he remain in chains for a while, reasoning that surely he could change his mind.

(6) Seeing him being led off in chains, a certain old eunuch named Ousthazades, Shapur's personal tutor and head of the royal household, rose up and prostrated himself before him (for he happened to be sitting before the palace gates). But Symeon censured him with disdain and, enraged, he cried out and, turning, passed by him. For he was a Christian who, not long before, had been forced to prostrate himself before the sun. (7) Straightaway the eunuch, with tears of lamentation, took off the bright clothing that he was wearing, and wrapping himself in black mourning clothes, he sat down outside the king's house, weeping and moaning: "Woe is me," he said, "how should I expect anything for me from the God whom I denied? This is why my old, dear friend, Symeon, without imparting one word, has just now turned away from me and rushed off." Then Shapur learned of these things; summoning him, he inquired as to the cause of his grief and whether it concerned some misfortune about his household. (8) In reply, Ousthazades said: "O King, I have had no bad luck concerning this household here. Would that instead of what has happened to me I might have encountered all manner of misfortunes, and I would be at ease. But I mourn now because I live and ought to have died long ago and because I see the sun, which I appeared to adore by prostration, not by my own mind but in order to gratify you. So on both counts, it is right that I should die: for having become a traitor to Christ and for having deceived you." After he said these things, he swore by the Creator of heaven and earth that he would no longer change his mind.

(9) Now Shapur, struck with amazement by the eunuch's alteration, was even more savagely angry at the Christians, as if they had accomplished such things through sorcery. So that he might spare the old

---

[3] The mages were the priestly class of Zoroastrianism, the official religion of Sassanid Persia.

man, seeming partly mild and partly harsh, he attempted by every force to persuade him to change his mind. (10) Since he accomplished nothing (for Ousthazades remained firm that he would never become so simpleminded as to worship in place of the God who created all things those things that were created by him), then, moved by anger, he ordered that his head be cut off by the sword. As he was being led off to this with the executioners, he asked them to wait a little bit, so he could explain this to the king. (11) Calling one of the most faithful eunuchs, he commanded him to say this to Shapur: "The goodwill I had from childhood until the present, O King, concerning your household, serving both your father and you with fitting enthusiasm, it seems to me has no need of witnesses before you, as you are well familiar with these things. In return for all the things that I have yet been gracious enough to do for you, grant me this compensation: that I not appear to those unfamiliar with me to suffer this punishment as one faithless to the kingdom or otherwise as one apprehended as a criminal. (12) And so this will be clear, let a herald signal this, crying out to all that Ousthazades suffers the plight of having his head cut off in no way indicted for anything having to do with royal matters, but for being a Christian and for not being persuaded by the king to deny his own God." (13) And the eunuch announced these things.

Shapur, according to Ousthazades's request, ordered the herald to cry this out. For he supposed that the others would readily cease becoming Christians if they kept in mind how he would spare no Christian and even put to death an old personal attendant who was full of goodwill. But Ousthazades was eager to have the cause of his punishment publicly announced, figuring that, when he circumspectly prostrated himself before the sun, he instilled fear in many Christians; but now, if they learned that he had been done away with for his religion, many would imitate his own bravery.

10 (1) So Ousthazades, in a most glorious manner, left behind this life. When Symeon learned of it in prison, he made prayers of thanksgiving to God for him. On the next day (it happened on the sixth day of the week that fell before the Feast of the Resurrec-

tion, which annually marks the commemoration of the Savior's passion) the king condemned Symeon also to be done away by the sword. Having been led out from the prison to the palace once more, very nobly he debated with Shapur concerning doctrine and would not suffer to prostrate himself before the king or the sun. (2) On that same day likewise the order went out that he was to be executed and with him one hundred others who were in prison; Symeon was to have his throat cut last, after observing the deaths of all the others. Some of them were bishops, others priests, and still others were various orders of clergy. (3) As all of them were led to death, the great archimage accompanied them and asked them if they wished to live, to practice religion alongside the king, and to worship the sun. No one chose life with these stipulations. They were led into the place where they would soon be put to death, and the executioners got to work toiling at slashing the martyrs' throats. (4) Symeon, meanwhile, as he stood by those being put to death, exhorted them to have courage, and he lectured about death and about resurrection and about piety. Relying on the sacred Scriptures, he showed that dying in this way was truly life, but that to betray God through fear was assuredly death. For not long after, even if no one killed them, they would die a natural death, since this was the inescapable end to everything that was born. But what comes after, which is eternal, will not occur in the same way to all humans, since, as if on some scale, they will give a precise account of their lives on earth. And unending life would remain the compensation of those who did well while their opposite number would sustain their corrections eternally. Better than all these in good deeds and most blessed by God were those who chose to die. (5) Symeon discussed such matters in the manner of a schoolhouse lesson, proclaiming how it was necessary to enter into the contests; and so, each one in understanding entered wholeheartedly into his slaughter. When the executioner had completed the hundred, he finally killed Symeon himself, along with Abedechalaas and Anninas. Both of them were two old priests of the church under him; they had been apprehended along with him and were in prison with him.

POUSIKES, CHIEF OF SHAPUR'S ARTISANS

11 (1) At that time Pousikes, who was head of all the king's artisans, standing there and seeing Anninas trembling as he prepared himself for the slaughter, said: "For a moment, old man, close your eyes and take courage, for straightaway you will see the light of Christ." After he said this, he was apprehended and brought to the king. (2) He confessed that he also was a Christian; since he disputed in a manner of open speech with the king concerning doctrine and the martyrs, the king ordered that as one who spoke in an inappropriately frank manner, he should die in a strange and most savage manner. The executioners, rooting around through the tendon of his neck, thus pulled out his tongue. Moreover, from the accusations of certain persons, his daughter, a sacred virgin, was also apprehended and put to death at that time.

(3) The following year, on the same day when, on the one hand, the commemoration of Christ's passion was celebrated and, on the other, they waited for the feast of the resurrection of the dead, a most savage command of Shapur sprung up throughout all of Persia, sentencing to death all those who confessed that they were Christian. At that time it is said that a crowd of Christians too great to be counted died by the sword. (4) Some of the mages, in the cities and the countryside, carefully hunted down those who had escaped; others informed against themselves, with no one leading them, lest, by their silence, they might seem to be denying Christ. While all the Christians were being killed unsparingly, many also among them were executed in the royal houses, such as Azades, the eunuch, who was especially beloved by the king. (5) When Shapur heard that he had died, he became filled with the deepest grief, and he put a stop to this public slaughter; he ordered that only the leaders of the religion should be put to death.

TARBOULA, SISTER OF SYMEON

12 (1) At this time, when the queen had fallen sick, Bishop Symeon's sister was apprehended, whose name was Tarboula, a sacred virgin, with a servant woman who shared the same way of life, and a sister who had renounced marriage after her husband's death and who was likewise led off. Their apprehension came about through the accusation of the Jews, who charged that, with poisons, they had plotted against the queen in order to vent their wrath on account of Symeon's death. (2) Now the queen—in the way it is customary for the sick to listen to horrible things—accepted that the accusation was true, especially since she was often among the Jews, for she was of their mind and lived her life Jewishly, and she supposed that they didn't lie and were of goodwill toward her. The mages, when they took custody of Tarboula and the other women, sentenced them to death. They were cut into pieces with a saw and impaled. In order to ward off her sickness, they had the queen pass in between the pieces. (3) It is said that this Tarboula was pretty and had a very beautiful form and that some of the mages lusted after her and had sent secret messages to her in the hopes of having sex with her, promising as payment, if she agreed, salvation for her and her companions; refusing to listen to such licentiousness, she mocked them and reproached their intemperance, much more eager to choose death than to betray her virginity.

(4) When, as was mentioned before, Shapur's command came forth to spare the others and to apprehend only the priests and the teachers of doctrine, the mages and the archimages went around throughout the land of Persia with care, doing evil against the bishops and priests, especially in the country of Adiabene, for this region of Persia was almost entirely Christianized.

AKEPSIMAS AND HIS COMPANIONS

13 (1) Around this time also Akepsimas the bishop was taken in and many of the clergy under him. After thinking it over, they were satisfied with the catch of the leader, and they released the others, having deprived them of their possessions. (2) A certain priest, James, willingly followed Akepsimas, and having made the request of the mages, was bound along with him. And as Akepsimas was an old man, he eagerly acted as his servant and, as much as he was able, he alleviated his misfortunes and tended to his wounds. Not long after their apprehension, the mages tortured him with painfully cruel lashes, to force him to prostrate himself before the sun. Since he did not yield, they held him again in chains. (3) At that time also Aeithalas and James, the priests, along with Azadanes and Abdiesous, the deacons, were living in the prison on account of their doctrine, having been most harshly scourged by the mages. After some time passed, the great archimage held a meeting with the king concerning them. And since he was empowered to punish them as he wished, unless they should prostrate themselves to the sun, he had Shapur's order displayed to those in prison. (4) When they replied openly that they would never freely appear as traitors of Christ or prostrate themselves before the sun, he tortured them unsparingly. Now Akepsimas, remaining brave, met his end in confessions of doctrine. Some of the hostages from Armenia among the Persians secretly took away his remains and buried them. (5) But others, although they had been scourged no less, miraculously lived. And, since they did not change their opinion, they were again placed in chains. With them was also Aeithalas, who was stretched during his beating and drawn by so much force that his arms were torn out from his shoulders. He had to walk around with his hands hanging off him, as if they were dead; others had to bring his food up to his mouth.

(6) Under this reign, an incalculable number of priests and deacons and monks and sacred virgins and those who served the church in other capacities and those who settled doctrinal matters left this life through martyrdom. Bishops whose names I have learned: Barbasumes, Paul, Gaddiabes, Sabinus, Mareas, Mokimos, John, Hormizdas, Boulidas, Papas and James, Romas, Maares, Agas, Bochres, Abdas, Abdiesous, John and Abraham, Abdelas, Shapur, Isaac, along with Dausas, who was taken prisoner by the Persians at a place called Zabdaion and who died for the sake of the doctrine at the same time as the chorepiscopus Mareabes and with around 250 clergy under him, who were apprehended with him and imprisoned by the Persians.

MILES THE BISHOP; SHAPUR AND 16,000 MARTYRS

14 (1) About this time Miles was also martyred. This man had first served in the Persian army, but after leaving behind the military, he was eager to lead an apostolic way of life. It is said that having been ordained as bishop of a Persian city, he suffered many diverse things and endured blows and was stretched on the rack. Since he persuaded no one to become a Christian, taking it poorly he cursed the city and withdrew. (2) Not long after, when the first citizens there committed crimes against the king, an army brought in with 300 elephants, trampled the city and, like farmers tilling arable land, spread their seed. (3) Miles, carrying a single pouch in which he kept the sacred book of the Gospels, went into Jerusalem to pray, and from there into Egypt to gaze upon the monks there. We have heard reports that this man became the creator of divine and miraculous work, as the Syrian people bear witness, who have recorded his acts and life. (4) It is enough for me, I suppose, meanwhile to recount these things about him and about the martyrs in Persia under the rule of Shapur. For someone could scarcely enumerate all the things that happened to them: who they were and from where and how they achieved martyrdom and what sorts of punishments they endured. For there are all manner of such things among the Persians, who take special pride in cruelty. (5) Insofar as I can summarize, it is said that of the martyrs at that time reported by name, men and women, there were 16,000. But the crowd of martyrs beyond this is too great to count, and for this reason it appears troublesome to enumerate their names for the Persians and the Syrians and for those who live in Edessa, who take great care in this matter.

CONSTANTINE'S LETTER TO SHAPUR

15 (1) When Constantine, emperor of Rome, learned that the Christians in Persia were being attacked, he was distressed and very angry. Although he was eager to be of assistance to them, he did not know

what to do so that they also might live safely. It happened around this time that ambassadors came to him from the king of Persia. Consenting to their requests, he sent them back, having done as they desired. (2) Considering this to be an opportune occasion to endorse the Persian Christians to Shapur, he wrote to him, confessing that he would have a great and eternally inscribed kindness toward him if he should become humane concerning those under him who respected Christian doctrine.[4] Since even in their manner of worship, he said, there is nothing objectionable, if they are satisfied with prayers alone, unstained by blood, for the supplication of God. For gushing blood is not congenial to him, but he delights only in a soul purified for virtue and incited to piety, such that we must praise those who have faith in this way. (3) Then he promised that through a good opinion concerning this doctrine, he would have God as his own propitious guardian, using as positive proofs what had occurred with Valerian and himself. As for himself, through his faith in Christ, finding an ally at the turning point in God's favor, he ruled the entire Roman world, from the ocean to the West, and he succeeded in many wars, fighting against foreigners and against those who were tyrants at the time. And he had no need of slaughtered animals or any oracles, but it was enough for him to achieve victory through the symbol of the cross going in front of his own armies and prayer purified of blood and filth. (4) As for Valerian, because he did no evil toward the churches, he accomplished his rule successfully. But when he considered enacting a persecution against the Christians, the impulse of divine anger set him under the Persians, and taken prisoner among them, he finished his life pitiably.[5] (5) Writing such things to Shapur, Constantine tried to persuade him to think well of this religion, for he possessed a great solicitude for Christians everywhere, Romans and foreigners. . . .

COASTAL INDIANS RECEIVE CHRISTIANITY FROM SLAVES

24 (1) At about this time, as we have heard, the coastal Indians,[6] who remained unacquainted with the preaching of Bartholomew,[7] partook of the doctrine from Frumentius, who was a bishop and became their guide of the holy teachings. So we might know that what happened in a miraculous fashion among the Indians was not of human doing, as it might seem to those who tell tall tales, it is necessary also to narrate the cause of Frumentius's ordination: here's what happened.

(2) To investigate unknown cities and places holds a high value among the most famous Greek philosophers. For this reason, Plato, Socrates' companion, dwelled among the Egyptians in order to learn their ways, and he also sailed to Sicily in order to see the craters there in which fire perpetually boils up on its own as if surging up from a spring and, often, pouring out in the manner of a river, gushes and feeds upon the neighboring land, such that, even now, many fields appear to have been scorched and receive neither sowing nor the planting of trees, just as they report concerning the land of the Sodomites. (3) Empedocles also investigated these same craters; he was an illustrious man who philosophized among the Greeks and who systematically treated his knowledge in heroic verses. In doubt about the upsurge of the fire or deeming it better to die in this fashion or (the most likely reason) not even knowing himself at that time why he found for himself this particular way of leaving his life, he jumped into the fire and killed himself. (4) And so, moreover, also Democritos of Cos investigated a great many cities, environments, countries, and peoples. He says about himself somewhere that he spent eighty years abroad. Beyond these, many more of the

---

[4] Sozomen's chronology is confused: Constantine wrote to Shapur before the outbreak of Persian persecutions.

[5] Valerian was captured and executed by Shapur I in the third century.

[6] A geographically confusing term for the Kingdom of Axum (Ethiopia). This story was also told by Rufinus of Aquileia in the fourth century, who supposedly heard it from Edesios.

[7] Bartholomew was the apostle traditionally considered to have evangelized the interior of Ethiopia.

Greek sages, ancient and more recent, were eager for this. (5) In imitation of them, a certain philosopher named Meropios, from Phoenician Tyre, went to India. Two youths followed him, Frumentius and Edesios, both members of his family. He taught them literature and liberal arts. Once they had investigated everything possible in India, they were on their return trip, on a ship bound for Egypt. It happened that because they needed water or some other services, the ship came into some cove, where the Indians of that place overran them and killed everyone, even Meropios, for it so happened that, at that time, they had dissolved their treaties with the Romans. (6) Taking pity on the boys for their youth, they took them captive and led them off to their own king. This one appointed the younger man his wine steward, and Frumentius his head of household and chargé d'affaires, for he recognized that he was sensible and most competent at administration. After a long time, they had shown themselves to be useful and trustworthy; as he was dying, leaving behind a child and a wife, the king repaid their good will with freedom and permitted them to live wherever they wished. (7) Now they were eager to return to their own relatives in Tyre, but, because the king's son was still quite young, his mother asked them both to stay for a little while and take charge of the kingdom until the child became a man. They respectfully took account of the queen's supplications and administered the kingdom and the realm of the Indians. (8) Now Frumentius, perhaps impelled by divine apparitions or spontaneously moved by God, inquired whether there were any Christians among the Indians or Romans among the seafaring merchants. Carefully seeking them out,

he summoned them before him. Embracing them warmly and showing them kindness, he had them assemble for prayer and form churches following the Roman custom, and he exhorted them in all things to pay reverence to God, after constructing houses of prayer. (9) Now when the king's son reached adolescence, they declined his requests and those of his mother (who could not bear to be separated from these men), and they persuaded them and they were released as friends. Then they came into Roman-controlled country. Edesios went back to Tyre to see his relatives, where soon after he was deemed worthy of the priesthood. Frumentius, delaying for a while his trip to Phoenicia, went down to Alexandria, for he didn't think it was seemly to place his zeal for divine matters second to home and family. (10) Upon meeting with Athanasius, who was head of the Alexandrian church, he recounted what had occurred among the Indians and how they needed a bishop to take care of the Christians there. Assembling the local bishops, Athanasius took counsel with them concerning this matter. Then he ordained Frumentius bishop of India, reasoning that he was most suitable for and capable of increasing the religion, for he had been the first to reveal the name of Christians among them and he prepared the seeds of sharing the doctrine. (11) So Frumentius returned again to India and, it is said, pursued his episcopacy so famously that he was praised by all who were acquainted with him, no less than they admire the apostles, since God had shown him also to be most renowned, effecting many miraculous healings and signs and wonders through him. So, indeed, this was the beginning of the episcopacy among the Indians.

60. Acts of the Persian Martyrs

Based on eyewitness accounts, but edited over time, these martyr tales are set during the persecution of Persian Christians by the Sassanian ruler Shapur II in the mid-fourth century (see Text 59). These martyr stories were written and circulated in Syriac, the language of the Christian East; many of the names given Greek form by Sozomen are rendered here in forms closer to the original: Guhshtazad instead of Ouasthazades, Posi instead of Pousikes, Tarbo instead of Tarboula. The emphasis on asceticism in these martyr accounts is also distinctly Syriac: many of martyrs are "covenanters," members of the *b'nay qyama,* the Syriac order of monastic lay Christians (see Text 41). The virtues of renunciation so central to Syriac Christianity are given a particular depth here, since all these stories end in the ultimate renunciation, death in martyrdom. For all the Syriac particularities of these stories, however, there is also a profound connection to Greek and Latin Christian identity: when compared with the martyrdom of Felix (see Text 1) or the more famous martyrdoms of the second and third centuries, these Persian martyrdoms resonate with many of the same situations and issues. They attempt to make sense of a religious conviction at odds with the political order, and they struggle to understand how the pursuit of a morally superior life (as they view it) can be the cause of such violence, bloodshed, and moral degeneration. Ultimately, like the Christians of the Roman Empire centuries earlier, the Persian Christians of the fourth through sixth centuries viewed strength and virtue in the pain and ignominy of suffering and death.

THE MARTYRDOM OF MARTHA, DAUGHTER OF POSI, WHO WAS A DAUGHTER OF THE COVENANT

Now the glorious Posi also had a daughter called Martha, who was a "daughter of the covenant." She, too, was accused, and at the third hour on the Sunday of the great feast of the Resurrection she was arrested. They brought the blessed Martha, daughter of the glorious Posi, into the presence of the chief Mobed, who then went in to inform the king about her. The king bade him to go out and interrogate her, saying, "If she abandons her religion and renounces Christianity, well and good; if not, she should be married off. If, however, she fails to follow either of these courses, she should be handed over to be put to death."

So the chief Mobed went out and started to interrogate the glorious Martha as follows: "What are you?" To which the blessed Martha replied derisively, "I am a woman, as you can see." Those who happened to be there in the presence of the chief Mobed blushed and bent down their heads when they heard the wise Martha's reply to his question. The Mobed's face became green with anger and shame, but he controlled his feelings and said, "Reply to my question." To which the wise Martha said, "I did reply to the question I was asked."

The Mobed then said, "What did I ask you, and what reply did you give?" Martha said, "Your honor asked 'what are you?' and I replied, 'I am a woman as you can see.'"

"I asked you what is your religion," said the Mobed. The glorious Martha replied, "I am a Christian, as my clothing shows." The Mobed went on, "Tell me the truth, are you the daughter of that crazy Posi who went out of his mind and opposed the king, with the result that he was put to an evil death?" To

From *Holy Women of the Syrian Orient,* trans. and ed. Sebastian Brock and Susan Ashbrook Harvey. Berkeley: University of California Press, 1998. Used with permission.

this the blessed girl replied, "Humanly speaking, I am his daughter, but also by faith I am the daughter of the Posi who is wise in his God and sane in the firm stand he took on behalf of the King of kings, the King of truth, the Posi who yesterday acquired everlasting life by means of his dying for his God. If only God would hold me worthy to be a true daughter of this blessed Posi, who is now with the saints in light and eternal rest, while I am still among sinners in this world of sorrows."

The Mobed then said, "Listen to me, and I will advise you what is your best course: the king of kings is merciful, and he does not desire anyone's death, but in his goodness he wishes all his friends to become fellow religionists of his and so be honored by him. So it was in the case of your father: because the king liked him, he honored him and gave him advancement; but your father acted foolishly and said things that were quite out of place, whereupon the king of kings urged him not to be stubborn, but to no effect. This was the reason why he was put to death. And now in your case, do not act stubbornly as your father did, but do the will of Shapur, king of kings and lord of all regions. As a result you will be greatly honored, and whatever you ask for your own comfort will be granted by the king."

The glorious Martha replied, "May king Shapur live, may his graciousness never leave him, may his compassion continue; may his graciousness be preserved by his children and his compassion redound to himself and on the people who deserve it. May the life that he loves be accorded to all his brethren and friends, but let all who imitate my father meet the evil death you said my father died. As for me, a wretched handmaid, the dregs of the handmaids of God and of the king, why should any transient honor come to me? I have decided to become the object of abuse like my father for the sake of my father's God, and I will die like him because of my faith in God."

The Mobed said, "I am aware of the hardness of heart you Christians have—a people guilty of death. Furthermore, no obedient offspring is likely to come from a rebellious man like Posi. Nevertheless, simply so that I shall not be held guilty before God of not having done my best to warn you, I am taking all this

trouble over you in order to bring you over to the religion of the excellent gods who care for the world."

The holy Martha replied, "You have said your part, and I have said mine—unless you are quite blind and are paying no attention to the true state of affairs that I have described. Otherwise you have both heard and seen which exhortation is profitable and which harmful; which leads to the kingdom of heaven, which leads to the fire of Gehenna, which provides life, and which engenders death."

The Mobed went on: "Listen to me and don't be stubborn and obstinate, following your own perverted wishes in everything. Instead, seeing that you are set on not giving up your religion, act as you like, but do this one thing only, and you shall live and not die: you are a young girl, and a very pretty one—find a husband and get married, have sons and daughters, and don't hold on to the disgusting pretext of the 'covenant.'"

The wise virgin Martha replied, "If a virgin is betrothed to a man, does the natural law order that someone else should come along, attack her fiancé, and snatch away this girl who has already been betrothed? Or does it say that such a virgin should give herself up to marry a man who is not her fiancé?"

"No," answered the Mobed.

The betrothed of Christ, Martha, then said, "So how can your authority order me to marry a man to whom I am not betrothed when I am already betrothed to someone else?"

To which the Mobed said, "Are you really betrothed, then?" And the blessed Martha replied, "I am in truth betrothed." "To whom?" asked the Mobed. "Is not your honor aware of him?" said the glorious Martha. "Where is he?" asked the Mobed. Wise in our Lord, she replied, "He has set out on a long journey on business, but he is close by and is on the point of coming back." "What is his name?" inquired the Mobed. "Jesus," replied the blessed Martha.

Still not understanding, the Mobed went on, "What country has he gone to? In which city is he now?" The splendid Martha replied, "He has gone off to heaven, and he is now in Jerusalem on high."

At this point the Mobed realized that she was speaking of our Lord Jesus Christ, whereupon he said, "Didn't I say at the very beginning that this was a stubborn people, not open to persuasion? I will spatter you from head to toe with blood, and then your fiancé can come along to find you turned into dust and rubbish: let him marry you then."

The courageous Martha replied, "He will indeed come in glory, riding on the chariot of the clouds, accompanied by the angels and powers of heaven, and all that is appropriate for his wedding feast; he will shake from the dust the bodies of all those who are betrothed to him, wash them in the dew of heaven, anoint them with the oil of gladness, and clothe them in the garment of righteousness, which consists of glorious light; he will place on their fingers rings as the surety of his grace, while on their heads he will put a crown of splendor, that is to say, unfading glory. He will allow them to sit on his chariot—the glorious cloud—and will raise them up into the air, bringing them into the heavenly bridal chamber that has been set up in a place not made by hands, but built in Jerusalem, the free city on high."

When the chief Mobed heard this, he left her in his palace and went in to inform the king of everything. The king then gave orders for the impudent girl and daughter of an impudent father to be taken outside the city and immolated on the very spot where her father had been killed.

So they led the chaste virgin Martha off on the Sunday of the great feast of Christ's resurrection, at midday. As they were getting ready the place where she was to be put to death, she fell down on her face and, as she knelt before God facing east, she said, "I thank you, Jesus Christ, my Lord, my King and my Betrothed, for preserving my virginity sealed up with the imprint of the seal ring of your promise, and for preserving my faith in the glorious Trinity—the faith in which I was born, in which my parents brought me up, and in which I was baptized. For this confession, for which my father Posi was also crowned, I give you thanks, O Lamb of God who takes away the sin of the world, for whose sake the bishops, our shepherds, have been sacrificed, as have the head pastors; the priests; and, along with them, the members of the holy covenant, and slaughtered, too, have been the

sheep—Guhshtazad and Posi my father. And now it is the turn of me, the young lamb who has been fattened up on the pastures of your promises and by the springs of your declarations: here I am being sacrificed before you. At your hands, Jesus, the true High Priest, may I be offered up as a pure, holy, and acceptable offering before the glorious Trinity of the hidden Being, in whose name you taught us to be instructed and baptized. Visit, Lord, your persecuted people; preserve them in true faith in the midst of their enemies, and may they be found to be like pure gold in the furnace of persecution that has been erected against your people; may they be strengthened in the worship of your majesty, fearlessly worshipping and confessing Father, Son, and Holy Spirit, now and always and for eternal ages, amen."

The moment she had finished her prayer, while no one was near at hand, she rushed off and stretched herself on the ground above the pit they had dug for her. When the officer approached to tie her up, she said, "Do not tie me up, for I am gladly accepting immolation for the sake of my Lord." When she saw the knife being brandished by the officer, she laughed and said, "Now I can say, not like Isaac, 'Here is the fire and the wood, but where is the lamb for the burnt offering?' (Gen 22:7) but rather I can say, 'Here is the lamb and the knife, but where is the wood and the fire?' But I *do* have wood and fire, for the wood is the cross of Jesus my Lord, and I *do* have fire, too—the fire that Christ left on earth, just as he said, 'I came to cast fire on earth; I only wish it had already caught alight!' (Luke 12:49)."

The thousands of spectators who stood by were astounded at the chaste girl's courage, and everyone gave praise to the God who encourages those who fear him in this way.

The officer then approached and slaughtered her like a lamb, while she entrusted her soul to Christ. Guards stayed by her corpse, and it remained there for two days, but on the night of Tuesday, thanks to a bribe handed over to the guards, it was taken away. By this time many had been slain for the sake of Christ. The blessed girl's brother, who had earlier buried his father, provided the money and took off the corpse; he then embalmed the body and laid it beside her father's.

The blessed Martha was crowned on the Sunday of the great feast of the Resurrection.

The blessed woman who had helped prepare them for burial used to keep their memorial each year in her home, close by where the priests and clergy lived. This she did all her life, and after her death her house passed to her brother's son. He, too, diligently kept their memorial, following that blessed woman's custom. When this nephew died, he left behind him two sons, and sometime after his death they had a quarrel over the saint's bones: one of them wanted to divide them up between himself and his brother because the house of the blessed woman had fallen to his share. The matter came to the knowledge of Sawmay, bishop of Karka, of blessed memory, and he persuaded the two of them to let him take away the bones, whereupon he presented them to the people of the church of Karka, to serve as a fair memento, and to be a valued treasure in the church of Christ. This was done by the holy bishop Sawmay in the eighth year of king Barharan, son of Yazdgard, eighty-nine years after their crowning.

This was what happened to Posi and his daughter.

THE MARTYRDOM OF TARBO, HER SISTER, AND HER SERVANT

At this time it so happened that the queen fell ill. Since she was favorably inclined to the enemies of the cross, the Jews, they told her, making their customary false accusation: "The sisters of Simeon have put spells on you because their brother has been put to death." Once this reached the queen's ears, Tarbo, a "daughter of the covenant," was arrested, together with her married sister, who was living in continence, and her servant, who was also a "daughter of the covenant" and who had been instructed by Tarbo in the excellent teaching of Christ.

They brought the women to the queen's residence for interrogation. The head Mobed and two officers were sent for so that they could adjudicate their case.

When the women were introduced into their presence, these men saw the valiant and holy Tarbo's beautiful looks and her fine appearance, excelling that of all other women. Straightaway all three of them conceived the same filthy thought and disgusting intentions concerning her, though none of them revealed anything to the others. They proceeded to speak harshly to the women, saying, "You deserve to die, seeing that you have brought these evil effects upon the person of the queen, the mistress of the entire Orient."

The holy Tarbo replied, "What false charges are you bringing against us, charges that are quite out of keeping with our way of life? What wrong have we done you that you falsely accuse us of something quite alien to the truth for which we stand? Are you thirsting after our blood? If so, what prevents you from drinking it? Are you aiming at our death? Your hands are already befouled by killing us Christians every day: we may be put to death, but we will not renounce our religion. It is written down for us that we should serve one God alone, and not consider alongside him any likeness in heaven or on earth. Furthermore, the following is written down for us: 'If a sorcerer should be found, he is to die at the hands of this people' (Lev 20:27). How, then, could we perform sorcery? Sorcery is in the same category as the denial of God; in both cases the sentence is death."

Those evil judges sat there listening to her in silence, enjoying the occasion—that is, in their own bitter way, stunned as they were by her astonishing beauty and exceptional wisdom. Each one of them said to himself in the vain hope conjured up by his evil thoughts concerning her, "I'll rescue her from death so that she can be my wife."

The Mobed then spoke to the women: "In your anger over your brother being put to death, you have gone so far as to transgress your own law, performing sorcery on the queen, despite the fact that you are not allowed to do this, as you yourself have said."

The glorious Tarbo spoke: "What bad or hateful thing has been done to my brother Simeon so that as a result we should risk losing our salvation at God's hands? For even though you may have killed him out of hatred and jealousy, he is nevertheless alive in the Kingdom on high—the Kingdom that will make your kingdom down here on earth pass away and that will dissolve your position of authority and render useless this honor of yours that does not last."

After this they sent the three women off to prison, to be detained there. The next day the Mobed sent a message to Tarbo, saying, "I will intercede with the king and I will save the three of you from death—on the condition you become my wife." On hearing this the glorious woman was greatly shaken, replying, "Shut your mouth, you wicked man and enemy of God; don't ever again utter anything so disgusting. Your filthy words make no impression on ears that are pure, and your foul proposition does not have any effect on my mind, which is chaste and holy: for I am the betrothed of Christ. In his name I am preserving my virginity, and upon my hope in him I am hanging my sure conviction. I entrust my life to him, since he is able to deliver me from your impure hands and from your evil intentions concerning me. I am not afraid of death or alarmed at the thought of being killed, seeing that you are marking out a path for me whereby I shall travel to behold my beloved and dearest brother Simeon, the bishop. In this way I shall receive consolation for all my pains and sufferings, as I follow in his footsteps."

The two officials likewise sent messages to her on the same lines, each concealing the matter from the other. With indignation and great anger, she gave them an adamant refusal.

The three of them then decided together on a stratagem that would bear bitter fruit. Bringing totally false testimony, they gave a wicked verdict, saying that they were indeed witches. The king then sent word to the effect that if they worshipped the sun, they need not be put to death, on the grounds that they might really not know how to cast spells. When the women heard this, they cried out, "We will not exchange our God for something created by him; we will not worship the created sun in place of our Creator, nor will we abandon our Savior Jesus just because of your threats."

The mages immediately started making an uproar: "These women should perish from beneath the face of the heavens; they have cast spells on the queen, and she has fallen ill." Permission was then given to the mages to employ on the women whatever means of execution they liked. Now they said that their bodies should be cut in two and that the queen should pass between the two halves, after which she would be healed.

Once again, as the women were being taken out for execution, the Mobed sent a message to the glorious Tarbo to the effect that if she listened to his proposal, neither she nor her companions would be put to death. The chaste woman, however, cried out with a loud voice, reviling him: "Foul and perverted man, why do you crazily rave after something that is neither proper nor permissible? I shall die a heroic death, for thus shall I obtain true life; I will not live in an ignominious way and then eventually die."

They took the three holy women outside the city and drove into the ground two stakes for each woman, and they stretched them out, attaching them by their hands and feet, like lambs about to be shorn. Thereupon they sawed their bodies in halves, cut them up into six portions, placing them in six baskets, which they suspended on six forked pieces of wood; these they thrust into the ground, three on each side of the road. These were shaped like half crosses, carrying half a body each. Hung upon them were fruits that blind those who pluck them, and they bore produce that is bitter to those who pick it.

This was a bitter spectacle that spoke for itself, girt with suffering—a grievous sight, carrying with it groans and lamentation. If anyone cannot weep, let him come here and bathe himself in tears; if anyone's eyes are dry, let him come here and wash himself in weeping as he recalls the groans uttered by the pure and chaste bodies of those holy women. In their lifetime they were modestly dressed while in their own rooms, but in their death they were naked by the roadside. These are women who did not betray their freedom for a life of shame, whose chaste nature was handed over to be abused. How silent and quiet is Justice, who is normally not lenient or forgiving when she exacts the penalty. How daring and bold is Pride, which, once shattered, does not normally recover! These were merciless men, deprived of any pity or compassion; they resembled ravening wolves that tear out living flesh. The men who cut in half and strung up these women are cannibals who eat people alive; as it is written, "They swallowed us up alive" (Ps 124:3). Who got any joy out of this lugubrious spectacle? Who took any pleasure in this awesome sight? Who could look on with dry eyes? Who could steel himself to turn round and look upon them? If any such person exists, his nature is not the same as our nature, and he cannot belong to the race of Adam.

They conveyed the queen along that road and made her get out in between the bodies. The entire entourage came out after her, for it was the time when the king was moving up to his summer residence.

The glorious women were crowned on the fifth of the lunar month Iyyar.

THE MARTYRDOM OF THEKLA, A DAUGHTER OF THE COVENANT, AND OF FOUR OTHER DAUGHTERS OF THE COVENANT WITH HER

At this time an impious man named Pawle, nominally a priest in the village of Bekhashaz, was accused before Narsai Tahmshabur. Narsai Tahmshabur was told, "He is very rich and has a lot of property"; so straightaway he sent some men to surround his house and arrest him. They ransacked the house and took away a great deal of money that they found there. Because of him, they also arrested along with him the "daughters of the covenant" of his village, whose names are Thekla, Mary, Martha, and Emmi. These were all brought bound, together with Pawle, to the village of Hazza and taken into the presence of the accursed Tahmshabur. He told Pawle, "If you do the king's will, by worshipping the sun and eating blood, I will return to you everything that has been confiscated from you." Whereupon this impious son of Gehenna, hungering after his riches and yearning for his money (which would result in his burning in Gehenna), did everything he was told to do.

When Tahmshabur realized that he no longer had any pretext for putting him to death, he thought up the following plan: he would tell him to kill the "daughters of the covenant," in which case he might feel ashamed, and this would provide an excuse for putting him to death. Thus he would be able to confiscate the belongings that had been seized from Pawle's house.

Tahmshabur at once ordered the women to be brought into his presence and told them menacingly, "Do the king's will, worship the sun, and get married. If you do this, you will avoid beating, and you will save yourself from the sentence of death by the sword, which has been decreed for you. If you fail to obey, I will carry out my orders, and no one will be able to deliver you from my hands."

The holy women cried out in a loud voice, "You proud and insolent man, don't try to frighten or beguile us with these deceiving words; no, put into effect what you have been ordered to do without any further delay; far be it from us to turn away from our God and our Creator to take advantage of anything that you have urged us to do."

Tahmshabur gave orders that they be taken out of the place where he was sitting, and he had each one of them thrashed with a hundred strokes of the rod, while they confessed with a loud voice, saying, "We will not exchange God for the sun; we will not become foolish and senseless like you who have abandoned the Creator and worshipped instead what he has created."

Their sentence of death was immediately given, and the impious Pawle was told, "If you kill these 'daughters of the covenant,' you can have back all that has been taken from you." Satan, who had entered and breathed upon Judas Iscariot, likewise entered him and won him over by enticing and seducing him with the thought of gold and silver. In this way he destroyed his own soul as a result of his greed, just like the traitor. In the end he, too, met his lot and, like his mate, inherited the throttling noose. Maybe he, too, like Judas, burst asunder and his entrails popped out (cf. Acts 1:18): perhaps the thief left him this inheritance, too? The one killed Jesus, the other killed Christ who was in the virgins. For those who have been baptized in Christ have put on Christ. What will be the judgment and punishment for these two men? What will be the heavier, which the more bitter? Is the one more fearsome, or the other more severe? Justice will mete out punishment to them in boundless measure, since they committed a crime that is beyond measure or restraint.

Lured by his possessions (which he did not manage to keep) and trusting in the wicked Tahmshabur's enticements, the grasping Pawle hardened his heart and put on a brazen face, took the sword, and had the audacity to lift it against the holy women. In unison they cried out, "O base shepherd, are you beginning with your own sheep, slaughtering the lambs of your own flock? In your greed have you turned into a wolf, destroying the lambs in your own sheepfold? Is this the holy and saving Bread that we used to receive at your hands? Is this the life-giving Blood that you offered our mouths? But now the sword in your hands is indeed our salvation and deliverance: we go now to Jesus, our true possession and eternal inheritance. As for the possessions and inheritance you love so much, you will not even get the benefit of them. We shall reach the place of judgment before you, and with us will come accusation of you; it will not stay behind, but God's judgment will overtake you at once. As for the money for whose sake you are killing us, you will not stay alive to enjoy it. You are committing a sin, but for the sake of what are you doing so? We are about to die, but for whose sake are we doing so? Woe, however, to the man at whose hand we die. Approach at once, grasping man; let the consummation of your sins find their limit in us, let the beginning of the harsh punishment due to you be called forth in us. Get on with it quickly, shameless man, save us from having to behold you when you burst asunder throttled by the rope, when your hands and legs flay each other as you are strung up and are dying a cruel death."

The audacious man, doomed to destruction, raised up the sword (which sent him to Gehenna) and struck the five of them in turn, thus dispatching them, taking off their heads as though he was skillful and well practiced as an executioner. Did not the impious man's arm get tired, seeing that he was not experienced at beheading people? Did not his sword get blunt, seeing that it was not in the hands of a professional warrior? Had he just been waiting with his fangs sharpened in expectation for just such an opportunity? Did

not the traitor's hand tremble as he raised the sword and brought it down? Maybe it was the love of his money that gave him strength; perhaps he was fortified by his lust for gold. Was not the shameless man afraid, seeing that he was not accustomed to grasping a sword? Was not the vicious man terrified, seeing that he had never tasted human blood? In his brazenness, was he not ashamed of the people who stared at him at the time as if he was someone utterly accursed? Nevertheless, Satan, who not so long ago had manifested murder upon earth by means of Cain, quickly trained him and made him used to such things. "You are children," Scripture says, "of him who was from the beginning a murderer" (John 8:44).

The holy women met a brave death; valiantly did these chaste ladies depart this life to become a sweet savor before their Lord who has doubly rewarded them for their excellent course with glory that surpasses the suffering they underwent.

The glorious women were crowned on the sixth of the lunar month Ḥaziran.

Had this mindless man never read or heard the Gospel words about the rich man whose lands produced large crops, and how, when he said, "My soul, eat, drink, and enjoy yourself," he was told, "Senseless man, this night your soul will be required of you; what will happen to all your preparations?" (Luke 12:19–20). The same thing happened to Pawle: imagining that they would restore to him his ill-gotten gains (for whose sake he eventually died), his life was in fact taken that very night, the reason being that the judge was afraid lest, in his impudence, Pawle would complain to the king and get back what had been taken from him; he accordingly sent some men who were in collusion with him to the prison, where they threw a rope round his neck and hanged him. His death was kept secret.

How similar were the deaths of these two grasping men. Maybe Judas was not as bad as Pawle, for Judas actually repented and then hanged himself, whereas Pawle never felt any shame and was hanged by others. Because his eyes satisfied themselves with the innocent blood he shed, no sentence or punishment that might come upon him was too small or short as his due reward.

61. The Passion of Saint Shushanik

According to Christian historians (see Sozomen's description in Text 59), Iberia (Georgia) converted to Christianity because of the pious example of a slave girl and the enthusiastic conversion of the king early in the fourth century. By the end of the fourth century, Iberia was under the political control of Persia to the east, and the small kingdom was caught up in Persia's religious and political controversies. Politics, religion, and family drama vividly intersect in "The Passion of Saint Shushanik," the oldest extant piece of Georgian literature, written in the late fifth century by Shushanik's personal Christian priest. Shushanik was the Christian daughter of an Armenian general, married to a prominent Georgian who had also been raised as a Christian. When Shushanik's husband renounced Christianity and became a Zoroastrian (Mazdean) to gain favor with the Persian king—this is, at least, how his conversion is portrayed by the author—a struggle ensued between Shushanik and her husband. According to this account, she was beaten, tortured, and imprisoned for years until her death of disease and neglect. The religious violence of this tale is familiar from other Christian martyr texts. The brutality of Shushanik's life, however, is at once excruciatingly personal and also momentously political, as her family drama becomes a microcosm of the religious and political conflicts crashing down on the Christian minority of the Persian Empire.

It was in the eighth year of the reign of the king of Persia that Varsken the Pitiakhsh, son of Arshusha, traveled to the royal court. Formerly he, too, was a Christian, born of Christian father and mother. And his wife was the daughter of Vardan, generalissimo of the Armenians, bearing the name of Varden, or Rose, after her father, and the pet name of Shushanik, or Susanna, and she lived in the fear of God from her childhood days. Because of the unrighteousness of her husband, she prayed perpetually in her heart and besought all to pray God to convert him from his deluded ways, so that he might become wise in Christ.

But who could describe the wickedness of that abandoned and thrice-wretched Varsken? For when he appeared before the king of the Persians, it was not to receive honor by rendering service to the monarch, but to deliver himself up body and soul by denying the True God. So he bowed down to the fire, utterly cutting himself off from Christ. And this miserable man sought to win favor in the eyes of the king of the Persians by asking him for a wife, adding, "The lawful wife and children I already have, these I will likewise convert to your faith, just like myself." (In making this pledge, however, he had reckoned without Shushanik.) Then the king rejoiced and gave him his own daughter to be his bride.

Soon after the Pitiakhsh took leave of the king. And as he was approaching the borders of Georgia, the land of Hereti, it occurred to him to have the noblemen and his sons and retainers informed that they were to meet him, so that in their company he might enter the country like a snake. He therefore dispatched one of his servants on a post-horse. When the servant had arrived at the township that is called Tsurtav, he came in and appeared before Shushanik, our queen, and inquired after her well-being. But the blessed Shushanik said with prophetic insight, "If he is alive in soul, you are both alive, both he and you. If you are both dead in your spirit, that inquiry of yours needs to be addressed to yourself." But the man dared not answer her. St. Shushanik, however, insisted and questioned him urgently, until the man told

From *Lives and Legends of the Georgian Saints*, 2nd ed., pp. 45–56, trans. David Lang. Crestwood, N.Y.: St. Vladimir's Seminary Press, 1976. Used by permission of St. Vladimir's Seminary Press.

her the truth, saying, "Varsken has renounced the True God."

When the blessed Shushanik heard this, she fell upon the ground and beat her head on the floor and said with bitter tears, "Pitiable indeed has become the unfortunate Varsken! He has forsaken the True God and embraced the religion of fire and united himself to the godless." And she arose and left her palace and went into the church, filled with the fear of the Lord. With her she took her three sons and one daughter and brought them before the altar and prayed. And when the evening service was over, she found a small cottage near the church and went into it, filled with grief, and leaned against the wall in a corner and wept bitterly.

Now the bishop attached to the Pitiakhsh's household, whose name was Aphots, was not at hand, having gone to the house of a certain holy man to consult him about some question. And I, too, the confessor of Queen Shushanik, was with the bishop. Suddenly a deacon came to us from home and told us all that had occurred: the arrival of the Pitiakhsh and the conduct of the queen. We were filled with sorrow and wept abundantly, being weighed down by the consciousness of our sins.

But I got up early and went to the village where the blessed Shushanik was. And when I saw her afflicted with sorrow, I also wept with her.

While we were conversing, a certain Persian arrived and came in before the blessed Shushanik and said in lachrymose tones, "How so? A peaceful household has become miserable, and joy has turned to grief!" But he had actually come on a secret errand from Varsken and said this as a ruse to ensnare the blessed one.

But the saint recognized his cunning intention and became all the more firm in her resolve.

Three days after, Varsken, the Pitiakhsh, came. And the Persian spoke to him privately and said, "I gather that your wife has left you. I would advise you, however, not to speak harsh words to her. After all, women are always liable to be unreasonable."

The next day, the Pitiakhsh summoned us priests as soon as he had got up, and we went to him. He received us agreeably and said to us, "Be at your ease

and do not shrink away from me." In reply we said to him, "You have brought damnation on yourself and on us also!" Then he began to speak and said, "How could my wife allow herself to do such a thing to me? Now go and tell her that she has degraded my person and sprinkled ashes upon my bed and forsaken her rightful place and gone elsewhere."

To this St. Shushanik replied, "It is not I who either exalted your person or degraded it. Your father raised up sepulchers for the martyrs and built churches, and you have ruined the deeds of your father and destroyed his good works. Your father invited saints into his house, but you invite devils. He confessed and believed in the God of heaven and earth, but you have renounced the True God and bowed down before the fire. Just as you have despised your Creator, so I pour contempt upon you. Even if you inflict many tortures on me, I will have no part in your doings."

We reported all this to the Pitiakhsh, as a result of which he became angry and bellowed with rage. Then the Pitiakhsh commissioned Jojik, his brother, and Jojik's wife, his sister-in-law, and the bishop attached to his household, and told them to speak to her in the following terms: "Get up and come to your rightful place and give up these notions of yours! If not, I shall drag you back by force."

So they came and entered in before the queen and spoke many reassuring words to her. Then St. Shushanik said to them, "O wise men! Do not think I was nothing but a wife to him. I had imagined that I could convert him to my faith, so that he would acknowledge the True God. And do you now try to force me to act thus? Let this never happen to me! You, Jojik, are no longer my brother-in-law, nor am I your sister-in-law, nor is your wife my sister, since you are on his side and take part in his doings."

And as they were pressing and urging her excessively, the saintly and blessed Shushanik arose to go. Taking her copy of the Gospels with her, she said with tears, "O Lord God, you know that I am resolved in heart to meet my death." When she had spoken these words, she went with them and carried her Gospel with her, as well as the holy books of the Martyrs.

When she came into the palace, she took up her residence not in her apartments, but in a small chamber. And St. Shushanik raised her hands to heaven and said, "O Lord God! Not one merciful man, neither priest nor layman, has been found among this people, but they have all handed me over to die at the hands of Varsken, that enemy of God."

Two days later that wolf came into the palace and said to his retainers, "Today, I and Jojik and his wife are dining together. Do not allow anyone to come in to us." And when it was evening, they called Jojik's wife and decided to bring the holy Shushanik to dine with them, too. When they had wearied her with their insistence, they obliged her to accompany them to the palace, but she had no appetite for anything. Jojik's wife, however, offered her wine in a glass and tried to make her drink a little of it. St. Shushanik said to her angrily, "Whenever has it been the custom for men and women to dine together?" And stretching out her arm, she flung the glass in her face, and the wine was spilled.

Then Varsken began to utter foul-mouthed insults and kicked her with his foot. Picking up a poker, he crashed it on her head and split it open and injured one of her eyes. And he struck her face unmercifully with his fist and dragged her to and fro by her hair, bellowing like a wild beast and roaring like a madman.

Jojik, his brother, rose to protect her and came to grips with him and struck him. After her veil had been torn from her head, Jojik dragged her from Varsken's hands, like a lamb from the claws of a wolf. St. Shushanik lay like a corpse upon the ground, while Varsken abused her kinsfolk and called her the defiler of his home. And he commanded her to be bound and chains to be attached to her feet.

When he had calmed down a little from his outburst of rage, the Persian came to him and urgently begged him to free St. Shushanik from her chains. After insistent pleading, he ordered her to be unchained and taken to a cell and carefully guarded. She was to have one servant, and nobody else would be allowed to visit her, neither man nor woman.

When it was dawn, he asked her servant, "How are her wounds?" He said to him, "They are past healing." Then he himself went in and looked at her and was greatly astonished at the size of her swelling. And he directed the servant not to let anyone come and see her. He himself went out hunting.

But I got up and went and said to the guard, "Just let me in by myself to have a look at her wounds." But he said to me, "What if he finds out and kills me?" I said to him, "Miserable man, did she not bring you up and educate you? If he kills you for her sake, what have you to regret?" Then he let me in secretly.

When I went in, I saw her face all slashed and swollen, and I raised my voice and wept. But St. Shushanik said to me, "Do not weep for me, since this night has been for me the beginning of joy." And I said to St. Shushanik, "Let me wash the blood from your face and the dust that has fallen into your eyes and apply ointment and medicine, so that, please God, you may be cured." But St. Shushanik said to me, "Do not say that, Father, for this blood is for the cleansing of my sins." But I gently forced her to take some food, which had been sent by Bishop Samuel and John, who secretly watched over her and saw to her welfare. St. Shushanik said to me, "Father, I cannot taste anything, because my jaws and several of my teeth are broken." Then I brought a little wine and bread and dipped it in, and she tasted a little. And I made haste to go out. Then St. Shushanik said to me, "Father, shall I send him back this jewelry of his? Even if he does not require it, I shall have no more use for it in this life." But I said, "Do not hurry, let it remain in your keeping."

While we were discussing this, a boy came in and said, "Is Jacob here?" And I said, "What do you want?" He said, "The Pitiakhsh is calling for you." And I was surprised and wondered why he called for me now, so hurried to go. He said to me, "Do you know, Priest, that I am leaving to fight against the Huns? I have no intention of leaving my jewelry with her, now that she is not my wife. Someone else will have to be found to wear it. Go and bring whatever there is of it."

So I went and told this to St. Shushanik. She was very glad and thanked God and handed everything over to me, and I delivered it all to the Pitiakhsh. He received it from me, inspected it, and found everything complete and again said, "At some later time, someone will be found to adorn herself with it."

And when Lent was come, the blessed Shushanik came and found a small cell near the church and took up her abode in it.

On Monday in Easter week, the Pitiakhsh returned from fighting against the Huns. The devil animated his heart, and he arose and went to the church and said to Bishop Aphots, "Give me my wife! Why are you keeping her away from me?" And he began to curse and utter violent maledictions against God. But a priest said to him, "Lord, why are you behaving like this and uttering such evil words and cursing the bishop and speaking with anger against the saintly Shushanik?" But he struck the priest in the back with his staff, so that he dared not say anything more.

So St. Shushanik was dragged out by force through the mud and over the thorns from the church to the palace, just as if they were dragging a corpse along. And he ordered her to be tied up and beaten and reviled her saying, "Now you see that your Church is no help to you, nor those Christian supporters of yours, nor that God of theirs!" Three hundred blows they struck her with a stick, without any moan or complaint passing her lips. After this St. Shushanik said to the impious Varsken, "Unhappy man, you have had no pity on yourself and cut yourself off from God, so how can you have pity on me?"

When he saw the blood flowing abundantly from her tender flesh, he ordered a chain to be fastened round her neck and commanded a chamberlain to take St. Shushanik to the castle and imprison her in a dark dungeon to die.

A certain deacon belonging to the bishop's staff stood near St. Shushanik when she was being taken from the palace and tried to encourage her to stand fast, when the Pitiakhsh cast his eye on him. He only managed to say, "Sta . . . ," and then was silent and hastily took to his heels and ran away.

Then they took her out. St. Shushanik was led barefoot, with her hair disordered, like some woman of the common folk. Nor did anyone dare to cover her head because the Pitiakhsh followed on horseback behind her, cursing her with much foul language. With the saint was a great mob of women and men, countless in number, following behind her, and they raised their voices and wept and tore their cheeks and shed tears of pity for St. Shushanik. But St. Shushanik looked upon the crowd and said to them, "Weep not, my brothers, my sisters, and my children, but remember me in your prayers now that I am taking leave of you from this world. For you will not see me leave the castle alive."

When the Pitiakhsh saw the mob and the lamentation of men and women, old and young, he charged at them on his horse and forced them all to run away. When they reached the castle bridge, the Pitiakhsh said to St. Shushanik, "This is all the walking you will ever do, for you will not come out alive until the time comes for four bearers to carry you out." When they had entered the castle, they found a small dark hut to the north of it, and there they locked up the saint. They left her with the chain still fastened round her neck, and this the impious Varsken stamped with his seal. Then he left the castle.

On the third Sunday, he summoned a jailer and asked him, "Is that miserable woman still alive?" He replied, "Lord! She appears nearer to death than to life. She is likely to die from hunger alone, since she will eat nothing." To which he answered, "Never mind, leave her alone, let her die."

Then the Pitiakhsh went off to Chor. Jojik, his brother, was not present when these things were done to St. Shushanik. When Jojik arrived, he hastened after the Pitiakhsh, caught up with him on the borders of Hereti, and implored him to have her released from her fetters. After he had greatly importuned Varsken, he ordered her to be unchained. When Jojik returned, he removed the chain from her neck.

But St. Shushanik was not released from her shackles until her death. For she remained six years in the castle and blossomed forth with her religious observances, ever fasting, keeping vigil, and watching, in unwearying adoration and assiduous reading of holy books. The entire castle was made radiant and beautiful by the lyre of her spirit.

From now on, her works became renowned throughout all Georgia. Men and women used to come for the fulfillment of their vows. Whatever they had need of was bestowed on them through the holy prayer of the blessed Shushanik, namely, a child to the childless, healing to the sick, and to the blind, restoration of sight.

They told St. Shushanik, "Your children have been converted to Mazdeism." Then with many tears she began to worship God and beat her head upon the ground and groaned, saying, "I give thanks to you, O Lord God of mine, for they were not mine, but gifts from you! As you wish, your will be done, O Lord. Save me from the schemes of the Evil One."

Then the Pitiakhsh sent messengers and said, "Either do my will and return to the palace, or if you will not come home, I will send you under guard to Chor or to the Persian court."

St. Shushanik, however, answered, "Wretched and stupid man! If you send me to Chor or to the Persian court, who knows if some good may not come to me and this evil be averted?"

The Pitiakhsh pondered over these words that she had uttered, "Who knows if some good may not come to me?" which he took to mean, "Perhaps one of the princes there might take her to wife." From then onward, he sent no one to her.

Later, however, the Pitiakhsh deputed her own foster brother to bring her back to the palace. When he said to her, "Listen to me and come back to the palace and do not leave your home desolate," then St. Shushanik replied, "Tell that godless man this: You have killed me, and you declared that I should never come out of this castle on my feet alive! And now, if you can raise the dead, first raise your mother who is buried at Urdi. For if you cannot raise her up, neither can you bring me out of here, unless you drag me by force."

When she had passed six years in this prison, excessive weariness from her feats of courage and devotion brought sickness upon her. Furthermore, that place was incredibly infested with fleas and lice. In the summertime, the heat of the sun burns like fire, the winds are torrid, and the waters are infected. The inhabitants of this region are themselves afflicted with various diseases, being swollen with dropsy, yellow with jaundice, pockmarked, withered up, mangy, pimply, bloated of face and brief of life, and nobody attains old age in that district.

When the seventh year had begun, the holy and thrice-blessed Shushanik was afflicted with an ulcer of the flesh. As a result of her tireless acts of piety, her feet became swollen, and pustules broke out on various parts of her body. The ulcers were very large and infested with worms. One of these she held out in her hand and showed it to me and gave thanks to God, saying, "Father, do not let the sight of this upset you. There (i.e., in Hell) the worm is greater and never dies." When I saw this worm, I was afflicted with inexpressible distress and wept greatly. But she retorted sharply, "Father, why are you sorrowful? Rather than being eaten by those immortal worms, it is better to be consumed here in this life by mortal ones!"

When Jojik heard that the blessed queen St. Shushanik was near to death, he went out and brought with him his wife and children and his servants and retainers and came to the castle to see the saintly Shushanik, the martyr. Then she blessed Jojik and his wife and children and his servants and retainers and all the members of his household and bade them walk in the ways of God. And she took leave of them and sent them away in peace.

After Jojik there came Archbishop Samuel and his friend Bishop John, who had encouraged her and taken part in her good works. Likewise there came the grandees and noble ladies, the gentry and common folk of the land of Georgia. Their eyes were filled with tears as they said farewell to her, and they offered up praise to God for her glorious works and then they left the castle and departed.

Then came the day when she was to be called away. And she summoned the bishop attached to her household, Aphots, and thanked him for his kindness, which equaled that of a father and a foster parent. She called for me, sinner and wretch that I am, and committed to us the relics of her bones, commanding us to bury them in that place from which she was first dragged forth. And she said, "Though I am but a worker of the eleventh hour in the vineyard (cf. Matt 20:1–16), if I have any merit, you shall all be blessed for ever and ever."

Then she gave thanks to God, saying, "Blessed is our Lord God, for on him I will lay myself down and sleep in peace." And she entrusted her soul to the Lord, who receives all mankind in his mercy.

The beginning of the torments of St. Shushanik was in the month of January, on the eighth day, being a Wednesday. Her second beating took place on Monday in Easter Week. And her death was in the month of October, on the seventeenth day, being the festival of the blessed saints and martyrs Cosmas and Damian, and it was a Thursday. This anniversary we set apart for the commemoration of St. Shushanik and for the praising of God the Father, Son and Holy Ghost, to whom belong glory forever and ever, Amen.